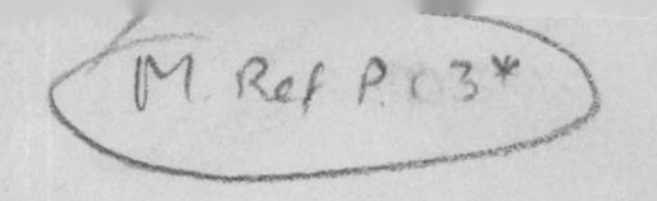
M. Ref P. 03*

D0364553

INSTITUTE of HISTORICAL RESEARCH

London

Corrections and Additions to the Dictionary of National Biography

Cumulated from the Bulletin of the Institute of Historical Research

University of London

Covering the years 1923-1963

G. K. HALL & CO., 70 LINCOLN STREET, BOSTON, MASSACHUSETTS

1966

The "Corrections and Additions" comprising this volume are derived solely from the *Bulletin of the Institute of Historical Research* and are reproduced with the consent of the Institute of Historical Research and of The Clarendon Press.

This publication is printed on Permalife paper, developed by W. J. Barrow under a grant from the Council on Library Resources.

PREFACE

This is a cumulation, in alphabetical order, of the "Corrections and Additions" to the *Dictionary of National Biography* which have appeared in the *Bulletin* of the Institute of Historical Research, University of London, from Volume I (1923) to the end of Volume XXXVI (1963). The factual information supplied in this form may be regarded as an essential supplement to any set of the *Dictionary.*

Volume and page references are to the 1908-9 reissue of the *Dictionary,* because that is the version possessed by the Institute. Where a correction falls in the lower half of the page, the lines are counted from the last line of text, ignoring footnotes.

Occasionally, and especially when the correction may be a matter of opinion, or when the author was not working at the Institute, the contribution is signed. The names or initials following certain corrections are those of the contributors. Corrections by the staff of the *Bulletin* are in square brackets.

Contributors were as follows: W. B. G. Allsebrook; C. P. Bagg; E. S. de Beer; H. Hale Bellot; S. T. Bindoff; T. A. M. Bishop; C. S. B. Buckland; W. Bulloch; J. P. T. Bury; J. F. Chance; W. H. Coates; H. A. Cronne; Godfrey Davies; M. R. Dobie; R. Dudley Edwards; Miss Eunice Falhope; Sir Charles Firth; Arthur J. Hawkes; R. M. Hewitt; Miss Dora Howard; C. Roy Hudleston; John A. Inglis; G. F. James; J. L. Kirby; W. T. Mellows; Dudley Mills; A. T. Milne; T. W. Moody; Miss Natalie Narishkine; J. E. Neale; R. A. Newhall; J. A. Nixon; J. B. Oldham; George Parker; W. G. Perrin; E. Perroy; A. F. Pollard; H. G. Pollard; Mrs. Frances Rose-Troup; G. O. Sayles; G. Seaver; J. J. Sutherland Shaw; A. E. Stamp; C. Sturge; P. G. Ward; A. S. White; Mrs. N. Whittall.

Several corrections were derived from the articles by Professor A. F. Pollard on "Fifteenth-century clerks of parliament" and "Queen Elizabeth's under-clerks and their Commons' Journals" in the *Bulletin,* XV, 137-61 and XVII, 1-12.

Most of the corrections relating to persons described in the *Dictionary* as Fellows of the Royal Society were contributed by Dr. W. Bulloch; the references to *The Record of the Royal Society* are to the third edition, 1912.

The additions to the lives of officers who fought in the Civil War and initialled G. D. were supplied by Godfrey Davies, mainly from lists originally compiled by Sir Charles Firth.

Articles marked * were Sir Charles Firth's corrections of, or additions to, articles of other contributors.

Corrections relating to persons connected with University College, London, were supplied by Professor H. Hale Bellot.

Abbot, John (*fl.* 1623), i. 21*a*, l. 9. For 'received his education at Sidney Sussex College, Cambridge, graduating B.A. in 1606–7, M.A. in 1610, and B.D. in 1617', read 'he matriculated at Balliol College, Oxford, 16 Nov. 1604 and was made B.A. on 20 April 1608 (*Registers of the English College at Valladolid, 1589–1862* (Cath. Rec. Soc. xxx, 1930), p. 105).'

To list of authorities add: 'Biographical studies 1534–1829. Materials towards a biographical dictionary of Catholic history in the British Isles from the breach with Rome to Catholic Emancipation, ed. A. F. Allison & D. M. Rogers (1951), vol. i, no. 1, pp. 22–33, no. 4, pp. 245–50.'

Adair, Sir Robert. i. 73*b*, ll. 14–7. For 'From 1831 to 1835 . . . Dutch troops' read 'On 3 Aug. 1831 he was appointed ambassador on a special mission to the newly crowned king of the Belgians, and immediately on his arrival at Brussels was called upon to negotiate an armistice between the Dutch and Belgian armies engaged in the so-called Ten Days' Campaign. He remained at Brussels until July 1835' (credential, P.R.O., F.O. 95/100, and dispatches, F.O. 10/6, 7).

Adam of Buckfield. 3*b*, n. 5. After '289).' add 'Undated references appear in *Cartulary of Oseney*, iv. 14, v. 334.'

Adams, Andrew Leith. i. 94*a*, l. 1. For '(*d.* 1882)' read '(1827–1882)' (Information from family papers).

Adams, William. i. 108*b*, l. 22. For 'sent to conclude' read 'who concluded'

Ibid. l. 25. After 'signed' insert 'in London'

Add to list of authorities: Hertslet's Commercial Treaties, ii. 386–91.

Agnew, Sir Andrew. i. 177*b*, l. 6. After 'Malplaquet.' insert 'On 9 Dec. 1709 he was promoted captain in Lord Strathnaver's regiment of foot (Dalton, *English Army Lists*, vi. 217).'

Ibid. ll. 7–8. After 'Utrecht' insert ', when his regiment was disbanded,'; delete 'of the Scots Greys'

Ibid. l. 21. After 'becoming' insert 'major, 16 Jan. 1737 and'; for 'in 1740' read '2 Nov. 1739 (*ibid.* 315)'

Ibid. l. 18 from foot. After 'marines' insert '15 Aug. 1746 (*ibid.* vi. 315)'

Ainslie, Sir Robert (1730?–1812). i. 189*b*, ll. 1–2. For 'in November . . . 1792' read 'on 2 October. He was recalled in September 1793, but remained at Constantinople until 22 June 1794 (D. B. Horn, *British Diplomatic Representatives*, p. 155; P.R.O., F.O. lxxviii. 15, Ainslie's account of expenses).'

Airey, Sir George. i. 201*b*, l. 5 from foot. For '71st' read '91st (*Army List*, 1780, p. 168)'

Ibid. l. 3 from foot. For ', when' read '; on 2 Jan. 1782 (*ibid.* 1782, p. 119)'

Ibid. 202*a*, ll. 9–8 from foot. For 'in that year' read 'on 4 June 1811'; for '4 June 1811' read '19 July 1821 (*ibid.* 1822, p. 9)'

Aislabie, John. i. 204*a*, ll. 9–10. For 'In 1712 he was appointed' read 'From 4 Oct. 1710 to 9 Apr. 1714 he was (Patent roll, 9 Anne, pt. ii, 22; 13 Anne, pt. i, 12):'

Albini (Brito), William de. i. 233*b*, ll. 28–30. After 'Brito' insert ', senior.' For 'son and heir' read 'the husband of Cecily de Belvoir, grand-daughter'; for 'lord of Belvoir' read 'whose mother obtained Belvoir in or before 1129'

Ibid. l. 16 from foot. After '1135.' insert 'He was succeeded at Belvoir by his son, William (Brito, junior).'

Add to list of authorities: *Rutland MSS.*, Hist. MSS. Comm., iv. 105–7.

Alcock, John. i. 236*a*, l. 28. After 'Salisbury.' insert 'In 1470 he was sent on a mission to Spain to treat with the king of Castille (*Foedera*, xi. 653).'

Ibid. ll. 17–11 from foot. For 'During the intervening . . . on record' read 'When Thomas Rotheram [q.v.] accompanied Edward IV on his expedition to France, Apr.–Sept. 1475, Alcock acted as chancellor in England, receiving 100*l.* for his services (C. L. Scofield, *Edward the Fourth*, ii. 125–6).'

Aldrich, Henry (1647–1710). i. 251*a*, l. 19. For 'was born. . .' to l. 30 'was bestowed upon Aldrich' substitute 'was the son of Henry and Judith Aldrich of Westminster, where he was born, and baptized 22 January 1647. His father was a Londoner who died in 1683 (Wood, *Life and Times*, ed. A. Clark, (1894), iii. 39). He was enrolled at Westminster School in 1656 under Busby, and was king's scholar in 1658 (*Record of Old Westminsters*, ed. G. F. R. Barker and A. H. Stenning (1928), i. 10). He became student of Christ Church in 1662, B.A. 1666 and M.A. 1669. In 1675 he was tutor to Charles' son, the duke of Southampton (*Letters of Humphrey Prideaux to John Ellis* (Camden Society, 1875), p. 48). Dr. John Fell recommended Aldrich as tutor to the duke of Ormonde's grandson, James Butler; in 1679 the appointment was made, but Aldrich found the care of the young student no sinecure (Hist. MSS. Comm., *Ormonde Papers*, new ser., v. 11–13, 46). He is said to have been rector of Wem, in Shropshire, but no confirmation has been found (*List of the Queen's Scholars at St. Peter's College, Westminster*, ed. J. Welch (1852), p. 155). He was installed Canon of Christ Church 15 February 1682; the following March he received his B.D. and D.D. (Wood, *Life and Times*, iii. 4–6). He showed his gratitude to the ecclesiastical commission by promptly preaching a sermon against Samuel Johnson's *Julian the Apostate* (*ibid.*, iii. 19). In 1687 he wrote from Oxford a *Reply to Two Discourses*, thus joining the controversy over the Anglican attitude to transubstantiation occasioned by Obadiah Walker's publishing the manuscript "concerning the adoration of our blessed Saviour in the Eucharist" written by Abraham Woodhead before his death in 1678. In 1686, 29 December, he helped to install the Roman Catholic John Massey as Dean of Christ Church under James II (*ibid.*, iii. 201), but when Massey fled at the time of the Revolution, the vacant deanery was bestowed upon Aldrich'.

Ibid., after l. 32 insert 'The "sov'reign pow'r" he exercised at Christ Church and his influence over its musical members are celebrated by Thomas Tickell in *Oxford, A Poem*, ll. 255 ff.'.

Ibid., after l. 40 insert 'His interest in science is attested by attendance at meetings arranged by Robert Plot and others "to talk of Chymicall matters" (*Wood*, iii. 75–6) and by his membership in the new Philosophical Society of Oxford (*ibid.*, iii. 78).'

Ibid., l. 43. For 'He was . . .' to l. 44 '. . .1692' substitute 'He himself was not idle: the list of the works he edited is in Watt, *Bibliotheca Britannica*, and in the *British Museum Catalogue*. He was vice-chancellor from 1692 to 1695'.

Ibid., 251*b*, l. 7 through l. 13. Read 'He was also entrusted, together with Sprat, with the publication of Clarendon's *History of the Rebellion*, and was accused by Oldmixon in *Clarendon and Whitlock Compar'd* (1727, Preface)—after his death—of interpolating and altering them. The accusation was resented by Atterbury in *The Late Bishop of Rochester's Vindication* (1731), and appears to have been entirely groundless'.

Ibid., l. 37. After 'his pipe' insert 'As told in Sir John Hawkins' *General History of the Science and Practice of Music*, (1776), v. note on p. 11.'

Ibid., insert before last paragraph 'Two letters he wrote to Robert Harley in Anne's reign suggest more than a mere acquaintance with the politician (Hist. MSS. Comm., *Portland*, iv. 113). His memory was long cherished by Swift and his correspondents. Lord Castle-Durrow in 1736 recalls how the Dean "smoked many a pipe, and drank many a quart with me" (Swift, *Correspondence*, ed. F. E. Ball, v. 399; cf v. 164). His portrait by Kneller is in Christ Church Hall, and another is in Bodley. A marble bust was donated by his pupil John Hammond; it was once over the Chapter House door, is now at the Library entrance (Poole, *Catalogue of Portraits in . . . the University . . . of Oxford*, (1926), iii. 40–43).'

Alexander Neckam of St. Albans. 14*b*, l. 5 from foot. After '222–5.' add 'Some of his ideas have been recently discussed by B. Landry in *Revue des Cours et Conférences*, xli (1940). 562–72.'

Alfred Ernest Albert, duke of Edinburgh and duke of Saxe-Coburg and Gotha (1844–1900). xxii. 34*b*, l. 13. For 'The queen was not averse . . . refused', read 'But the protocol of 3 Feb. 1830, by which the princes of the reigning families in Great Britain, France and Russia were excluded from the Greek throne, was at first considered by the British government as an insurmountable obstacle. When subsequently Russia seemed to be of the opinion that that protocol did not exclude the nephew of the Tsar, the duke of Leuchtenberg, Palmerston suggested the acceptance of the Greek throne by Prince Alfred. (Palmerston to Russell, letters of 16 and 17 Nov., 1862. P.R.O., G.D. 22/14). The queen, however, being from the outset strongly averse to the idea, the crown was refused. (*Letters of Queen Victoria*, 2nd ser., i. 48.)'

Allen, Bennet (fl. 1761–1782). i. 302*b*. Article largely superseded by two articles in *The Maryland Historical Magazine*, xxxviii (1943), 299–322; xxxix (1944), 49–72.

Allen, John (1476–1534). i. 305*a*, 8 ll. from foot. After 'at Cambridge, where' add 'he entered Gonville Hall as a pensioner in 1491, graduated B.A. in 1494–5 and became a probationer of Peterhouse in 1495, being admitted full fellow in 1496. He appears to have retained his fellowship until 1503–4, which is the last year in which he received a *pensio* (*Eng. Hist. Rev.* xliii. 159).'

Allestree, Richard (1619–1681). i. 324*a*, l. 33. For 'In the following year' to l. 38 'studies' substitute 'He took up arms for the King when Sir John Byron arrived at Oxford on 28 August 1642, but stayed behind when the royalist leader departed on 10 September (Anthony Wood, *Life and Times*, (ed. Andrew Clark), i. 56–67).'

Ibid., l. 40. For 'Say' read 'Saye and Sele'.

Ibid., l. 5 from foot. Add 'Wood, on the contrary, states that the plate of Christ Church and of Dr. Fell was carried off, but on this point Fell's authority is superior (Preface to *Forty Sermons*).'

Ibid., l. 3 from foot. For 'Kineton Field' substitute 'Edgehill on 23 October'.

Ibid., 324*b*, l. 11. After 'arms' add 'and fought to the end of the first civil war' (Fell's Preface).

Ibid., l. 13 from foot. After 'a royalist gentleman of fortune' add '; he was approved to officiate as chaplain 12 July 1656 (*Cal. State Papers, Dom.*)'

Ibid., l. 10 from foot. After 'king' insert 'In 1659 he carried letters from Sir Edward Nicholas to John Mordaunt (*Letter-book of John Viscount Mordaunt, 1658–1660*, ed. Mary Coate, (Camden Society, 1945), p. 16).'

Ibid., l. 5 from foot. For 'he was arrested at Dover, brought to London, and' substitute 'Having left Brussels by the 18th of January, he was arrested at Dover, on information received from Sir William Lockhart (Hyde's letter of 20 February, 1660, in Barwick's *Life*, (ed. 1724), appendix 25, p. 502); he had, however, already safely delivered his letters. As "Richard Allison" he was ordered to be sent with other prisoners to London (21 January); on 3 February, the Lieutenant of the Tower was instructed to keep him in custody on suspicion of treason, although an order of the Council to set him at liberty was dated 1 February, 1660 (Mordaunt's *Letter-book*, pp. 178–9, and *Cal. State Papers, Dom., passim*).'

Ibid., 325*a*, l. 2. After 'release' insert 'For particulars of his connection with the business of selecting bishops to preserve the succession of the Church of England, see Barwick's *Life* p. 235 ff'.

Ibid., l. 17. For 'in December' substitute 'on 22 December (*Cal. State Papers, Dom.*).'

Ibid., l. 19. After 'divinity' add 'He was granted the canonry at Christ Church, annexed to the professorship, the following 10 February (*Ibid.*)'.

Ibid., l. 20 from foot. Insert 'He was always an admirer, supporter, and friend of Dean John Fell; their names are frequently linked on college affairs. On 8 January 1664 a play was "encouraged" by Fell at Christ Church. The undergraduates were the actors. "The deane gave them a supper; Dr. Allestree gave each of them a booke of 7s price" (Wood, *Life and Times*, ii. 2). In 1666, Mr. Arthur Brett, preaching at Christ Church, said, "now wee have orators [Dr. Smith] that can speake, governors [Fell] that can rule, professors [Allestree] that can read and moderat" (*Ibid.*, ii. 93). Wood describes him as a "leane man with a red face," "the red herring," as a waggish scholar called him in 1664 (*Ibid.*, ii. 26). In a note added to Wood by Andrew Allam, Allestree is called "the very learn'd, most loyal, honest, good man, and incomparably throly accomplish'd Divine" (*Ibid.*, ii. 514)'.

Ibid., 325*b*, l. 19. For 'It has by some been . . .' through l. 23, substitute 'The authorship of *The Whole Duty of Man* was much in dispute from the time of its first publication (1659). Bishop Atterbury referred to its complete anonymity thus: "the Author took not more care to do good to the world than he did to conceal the doer of it." The various contemporary opinions of the authorship are given in detail in Nichols, *Literary Anecdotes*, (1812), ii. 597–604. Bishop Burnet, in his work *Of the Pastoral Care*, (1692), highly recommends *The Whole Duty of Man* (p. 163). If Allestree is the author of this devotional work, he therefore also wrote the other works listed in the folio edition, 1704: *Private Devotions, Causes of* *the Decay of Christian Piety, Gentleman's Calling, Ladies Calling, Government of the Tongue, Art of Contentment, Lively Oracles Given to Us.* The preface indignantly denies he is the author of a number of other tracts claimed to be by him'.

325*b*. To list of authorities at end, after 'Fell's Preface to the Forty Sermons, 1684' add 'This is the sole authority for Allestree's parentage and early life'.

Allestree, Richard. i. 325*b*, last three lines of article. Add : 'He was apparently son of William Allestree, recorder and M.P. for Derby in the Long parliament until his election was declared void in 1641. Richard was town clerk of Derby and M.P. from 1660 till his death in 1664/5 (*Return of M.P.'s*, i. 487, 513, 521), when he was succeeded by Anchitell Grey [q.v.].'

Allin, Sir Thomas (1612–1685). i. 332*a*, ll. 12–29. For 'whose name . . .; and' substitute 'was the son of Robert Allin (d. 1613) of Lowestoft, and his wife Alice. He married Rebecca Whiting in 1635. At least as early as 1644 he became a Royalist privateer. In 1648 and 1649 he cruised at sea, taking several prizes. Prince Rupert's *Further Instructions for Cap. Thomas Allen* 8 Jan. 1649 n.s. deal with the disposal of captured goods. They were printed by order of the Parliament 5 June 1649 with an introduction calling them the "Pirats Grammar." Allin was captured in 1649 by Edward Popham; escaping he joined the Royalist fleet in the Mediterranean where he was accused of failure to support his consorts against Blake. He took refuge in Jersey; there he may have been captured on the surrender of the Islands to the Parliamentarians. He was imprisoned in England in 1653 and two years later (Allin's *Journals*, I. xi–xiii)'.

Ibid., l. 30. After 'restoration,' add 'he'.

Ibid., ll. 31–32. For 'one of the first ships . . . Duke of York' substitute 'a fourth rate. (*Cat. of the Naval Manuscripts in the Pepysian Library.* Navy Records Soc. 1903, I, 272–3). Exchanging into Plymouth, he conveyed the earl of Winchelsea to Constantinople as ambassador, and after various adventures and efforts to conclude a treaty with the Algerine pirates, arrived back in September 1661 (*Journals*, II, ix–x)'.

Ibid., ll. 36–38. Put period after 'Lawson', delete 'and with . . . fleet', and insert 'A warrant from James, duke of York, authorizing him to appoint officers to vacancies, and dated 8 August 1664, is printed in *Memoirs of the English Affairs . . . 1660–1673*, (1729), pp. 98–99. He concluded in October 1664 a treaty of peace with the city of Algiers, the terms being the same as those obtained by Lawson, 23 April 1662. (Reprinted in Somers' *Tracts*, 1812, vii). His instructions seem to have authorized him to seize Dutch men-of-war or the Smyrna fleet (*Cal. State Papers Dom.*, William Coventry to Bennet, 15 Nov. 1664). Whether these instructions were later enlarged or not matters little, in view of the declaration that letters of reprisal would be granted against subjects of the States General, 16 December 1664'.

Ibid. 332*b*, l. 18. After 'coast.' insert 'He was wounded in several places in an encounter with De Ruyter on 26 July (*Journals*, i. 279')'.

Ibid., At end of paragraph 1, insert 'For an account of the capture, see *Ibid.*, 291–2'.

Ibid., l. 22 from foot. After 'commerce' insert 'His instructions dated 29 June 1669 and signed by James are given at length in *Memoirs of the English Affairs*, pp. 162–171. Additional instructions dated 29 June, 6 July, 13 July, 25 July and 29 August are printed *Ibid.*, 171–8. All these are reprinted in the Appendix to volume ii of the *Journals*'.

Ibid., l. 17 from foot. Place a period after 'third Dutch war' delete 'till 1678, when,' insert 'In 1678'.

Ibid. 333*a*. To the authorities add '*The Journals of Sir Thomas Allin, 1660–1678*, ed. R. C. Anderson, (Navy Records Society, 1939–1940), 2 vols.; A. W. Tedder, *The Navy of the Restoration*'.

Altham, Sir James. i. 348*b*, last line. For 'Richard Stapers, Esq.' read 'Richard Staper (or Staperr), whom he married about 1598 (Hist. MSS. Comm., *Salisbury MSS.* xi. 468).'

Ames, William (1576–1633). i. 356*a*, l. 15 from foot. For 'Dr. Burgess' read 'Dr. John Burgess [q.v.]'.

Ames, William (*d.* 1662). Transpose to follow **Ames, William** (1576–1633).

Amherst, William Pitt, Earl Amherst of Arracan. i. 360*a*, l. 21. After 'affairs' read 'He was appointed envoy extraordinary and minister plenipotentiary to Sicily in Feb. 1809, residing at Palermo from 19 Apr. 1809 to 1 May 1811, when he came away on leave, his recall being dated 4 June following (*Brit. Dipl. Repr., 1789–1852*, Camden 3rd series, l. 131).'

Amos, Andrew. i. 366*a*, last line. For '1829' read '1828.' 366*b*, l. 1. For '1837' read '1834.' See *The Times*, 12 Nov. 1828, 2*c.*; *University of London, Report and Appendix, February* 1834, p. 6; *ibid.* 1835, p. 4.

Amos, Sheldon. Suppl. 44*a*, l. 33. For '1879' read '1878' (*University College, London. Report of the Council . . . at the Annual General Meeting . . . 26th February* 1879, p. 14).

Andrews, John. i. 408*a*, l. 25. After '1655' insert '8. "A subpaena [*sic*] from the High Imperial Court of Heauen to be serued vpon all men," etc. (1623), would appear to be also his work' (*Times Lit. Suppl.*, 31 July 1930, p. 628, col. 4).

Annand, William. i. 420*a*, ll. 15–16. For 'a few years afterwards . . . the Tron Church' read 'in 1672 to the charge of the Tron Church and in 1675 to the High Kirk parish (Scott's *Fasti*, 1866, II. Pt. I, 55), both.'

Anne (1456–1485). i. 424*b*, l. 21. For 'there seems to be no precise record of the date of the event,' read 'they were married on 12 July 1472' (*Complete Peerage*, iii. 439). l. 26. For '1476' read '1473' (*Ib.*, p. 440)'.

Anne (1665–1714), **Queen.** i. 441*b*, l. 8. After 'Mary and Anne' insert 'attained maturity; two other children, Edgar, Duke of Cambridge, and Catherine, also,' and after 'church of Rome' add 'Both the younger children died during the same year' (B.M. *Add. MS.* 36916, ff. 224, 234).

Ibid., l. 25 from bottom. Delete 'and when about five years of age . . . benefit of her health' and read 'and in July 1668 was sent over to France for the benefit of her health (*Cal. State Papers, Dom.*, 1667–1668, p. 476). She was accompanied by Charles Scarburgh, M.D. [*q.v.*] (B.M. *Add. MS.* 36916, f. 106), who appears to have been in England again in August 1669, when he was knighted. Anne remained in France until 1670, being for part if not all of the time under the care of Henrietta Anne, Duchess of Orleans [*q.v.*]. After the latter's death she returned to England, arriving at Rye 23 July 1670 (*Cal. State Papers, Dom.*, 1670, pp. 301, 343).'

Annesley, Arthur, First Earl of Anglesey. (1614–1686). i. 473*b*. To the bibliography add Diary (1675–1684) in B.M. *Add. MS.* 18730. R. M. H.

Apsley, Sir Allen (1616–1683). i. 523*b*, l. 20 from foot. For '6 Sept.' read '5 Sept.' (Joseph Foster, *Alumni Oxonienses*, i. 29). *Ibid.*, l. 13 from foot. For 'afterwards went . . .' read 'entered Trinity College, Oxford, in 1631.' *Ibid.*, p. 524*a*, ll. 2–4. Substitute 'From numerous references in the *Calendar State Papers, Domestic*, it is clear the disputes continued well into the reign of Charles II.' *Ibid.*, l. 8. After 'knighthood' add 'apparently in 1646' (W. A. Shaw, *Knights of England*, ii. 221). *Ibid.*, l. 11. After 'behalf' add 'and tried to seize his brother-in-law Colonel Hutchinson in Leicestershire' (Lucy Hutchinson, *Memoirs of Colonel Hutchinson*, ed. C. H. Firth (1906) p. 97). *Ibid.*, ll. 12–13. After 'where . . . Exeter' substitute 'his regiment first reinforced the garrison at Winchester in 1643 and then formed part of Charles's army which forced Essex to surrender in Cornwall' (*Bellum. Civile. Hopton's Narratives (1642–4)* ed. Charles E. H. Chadwyck Healey, p. 64; Richard Symonds, *Marches of the Royal Army*, ed. C. E. Long, p. 160). 'After serving as Sir John Berkeley's lieutenant governor at Exeter' (*Memoirs of Sir John Berkley* in Francis, Baron Maseres, *Select Tracts*, I, 356, 363). *Ibid.* For ll. 22 to end of paragraph substitute 'The articles of surrender' (R. W. Cotton, *Barnstaple . . . during the Civil War*, [1889] pp. 512–5; *Calendar of State Papers, Domestic, 1645–7*, pp. 409–10) 'provided that his fine for delinquency should not exceed two years' value of his real estate. Actually he and his brother James were discharged on Oct. 21, 1646 from delinquency on payment of £438, 8s' (*ibid.*, p. 448; *Calendar of the Committee for Compounding*, p. 1295). 'From the vexatious charges against him for destruction of private property during the siege of Barnstaple, so graphically described by his sister, Mrs. Hutchinson, he was finally relieved by an order of the Council of State on August 29, 1654' (*Calendar, 1654*, p. 338). 'In 1647 he was sent by Cromwell and other army leaders with letters, a cipher, and instructions to meet Sir John Berkeley, coming to England to take part in the negotiations between Charles I and the army. Apsley accompanied Berkeley to London but took no part in the negotiations' (Berkeley's *Memoirs*, pp. 356–8). For ll. 3 from the bottom to 'Holland' substitute 'There seems no evidence that he left England during the Commonwealth or Protectorate, but inasmuch as he refers, June 1660, to an office granted to him by the King at the Hague, he probably was one of the cavaliers who went thither in 1660' (*Calandar State Papers, Domestic, 1660*, pp. 76–7). *Ibid.*, p. 524*a*, last line. Omit 'It was' add 'served in the west of England and at sea' (see his letter to Sir Edward Hyde, 20 Dec. 1645, repr. in Cotton's *Barnstaple*, pp. 443–4). 'At the restoration, he claimed to have served Charles I and Charles II throughout the wars, and to have been captured in Scotland, brought prisoner to London, and condemned to death' (*Calendar State Papers, Domestic, 1660–61*, p. 443). 'No substantiation of this claim has been found, but he was'. *Ibid.*, p. 524*b*, l. 10. For 'In June' read 'By a patent dated 12 July'. *Ibid.*, l. 12. After 'perquisites' add '(The date is given in a new grant to Sir Allen and his son Peter of 20 Sept. 1671. *Calendar State Papers, Domestic*, p. 492). *Ibid.*, l. 16. After 'hands,' add 'Apsley was present with James, duke of York, at the sea battle of 3 June, 1665, and wrote a very good account of it to his wife (Hist. MSS. Comm., *Bathurst MSS.* (1923), pp. 2–3).' *Ibid.* For 'shortly afterwards' substitute, 'In 1666 or before'. *Ibid.*, l. 21. After 'keeping' add '(*Calendar State Papers, Domestic*, 11 May 1666 cf. *ibid.*, 23 Feb. 1665 for a grant to Apsley of £2000 for secret service for the duke).' *Ibid.*, l. 24. After 'Dutch' add '(Charles Dalton, *English Army Lists*, I, 82)'. *Ibid.*, l. 22 from bottom. After 'rulers' add 'The reduction by a half is recorded in the *Calendar of State Papers* under 16 March 1668. He and his son surrendered the mastership of the hawks in 1675' (*ibid.*, 30 April). *Ibid.*, l. 7 from bottom. For 'But . . .' substitute 'He supplied Joseph Williamson with a copy of the letter of repentance which John Hutchinson had sent to the Commons in 1660 and which was in Lucy Hutchinson's handwriting in order that Williamson could compare it with other papers in his possession. Apsley suggested that Hutchinson be informed that the letter would be produced and so lessen his reputation if he did not abstain from political action' (*Calendar State Papers, Domestic, 14 Jan. 1664*); the letter in question is printed by Firth in his edition of Hutchinson's *Life*, pp. 446–8). *Ibid.*, p. 525*a*, l. 2. Add 'When the duke of York hurriedly returned from Brussels on the news of the King's illness, Sep. 1679, he stayed at Apsley's house on the way to Windsor, thereby showing his confidence in Sir Allen. (J. S. Clarke, *Life of James II* (1816), i. 566). *Ibid.*, l. 31. Add 'Among the Clarendon papers preserved in the Bodleian Library are letters from Apsley to Sir Edward Hyde, the first dated in 1645, which is printed in Cotton, *Barnstaple*, pp. 440–1, and the rest in 1657. They contain little news but are full of amusing gossip, and the literary references show him to have been well-read in the classics, and to have been interested in the books then being published, including Muffet's work on insects'.

To the authorities add: 'A. B. Bathurst, *History of the Apsley and Bathurst Families*, pr. pr. 1903'.

Archer, Sir Symon. i. 545*a*, l. 16. For 'M.P. 1640' read 'M.P. for Tamworth in the Short Parliament, 1640.'

Archer, Thomas (*d.* 1743). i. 545*b*. This article should be re-written as follows :

Archer, Thomas (*c.* 1668–1743), architect, was a younger son of Thomas Archer of Umberslade, Tamworth, M.P. for Warwick in 1659 and for Warwickshire in 1660, and son of Sir Symon Archer [q.v.] ; his mother was Ann, daughter of Richard Leigh, a London merchant. He entered Trinity College, Oxford, matriculating in 1686 ; after three years at the university he spent four years in foreign travel. About 1705 he was appointed groom-porter, an office which he retained until death (for it, see *Notes and Queries*, clxxvii. 445) ; and in 1715 he was appointed comptroller of the customs at Newcastle, a small office which he also retained until death. He built St. Philip's church, Birmingham, between 1711 and 1715 ; and St. John's, Westminster, between 1721 and 1728 (the building as completed diverges from the original design ; there have been later alterations, and it has been much damaged recently) ; a design for St. Paul's, Deptford, is also by him, and he probably built the church (1712–1730) and its vicarage (since destroyed). He built Roehampton House about 1710–1712 for Thomas Cary, and a garden pavilion at Wrest Park, Beds. (both buildings still exist, the former apparently altered from the original design, apart from modern extensions); and also the colonnades at Cliefden, Bucks (now destroyed). He appears to have rebuilt his family's house at Umberslade; and other buildings are attributed to him. In 1715 he bought an estate at Hale, Hants., where he built himself a house, still existing, and rebuilt the church. In style his buildings resemble those of Vanbrugh and Hawksmoor; no information is available about his training. He died in 1743 and is buried at Hale; he married twice, but left no issue. He is said to have left £100,000 to a nephew.

[Archer pedigree in Burke, Extinct Peerage; epitaph, etc., in Times Literary Supplement, 1941, p. 528 (published by Mrs. A. Esdaile); V.C.H., Hants., iv. 562, 578–9; Gent. Mag., xiii. 275; Colin Campbell, Vitruvius Britannicus, vol. i, figs. 10, 11, 31, 33, 80, 81; vol. ii, figs. 70–4; Architectural Publishing Society's Dictionary of Architecture, art. Archer; Wren Society, vii. 215–6; xvii. 13–4 (and plates); Sir John Vanbrugh, Complete works, ed. Dobrée and Webb, 1928, vol. iv, p. xxxix.]

Arden, Richard Pepper, Baron Alvanley. i. 546*b*, l. 13 from foot. For '1745' read '1744'.

Ibid. l. 12 from foot. For 'in 1745' read 'on 20 May 1744' (G. E. C., *Complete Peerage*, i. 118).

Ibid. 547*b*, l.11 from foot. For 'vol. lix' read 'vol. lxix'.

Argall, Sir Samuel. i. 550*b*. See also Alexander Brown's *Genesis of the United States*, 1890.

Armstrong, Sir Thomas (1624?–1684). i. 572*a*, l. 19 from foot. For '1624?' read '1633'.

Ibid., l. 13 from foot. For 'about 1624' read '27 December 1633. His mother was Anna Anderson (*Nieuw Nederlandsch Biografisch Woordenboek*, 1911, *sub* Armstrong, Sir Thomas)'. For 572*a*, ll. 13 from foot to 573*a*, 1 l. from foot, read 'The father was made quartermaster general of horse in Ireland at 10s. a day in 1640, and served as a captain of horse under Ormonde, by whom he was knighted before March 1643 (*Calendar of State Papers, Ireland, 1633–47*; Hist. MSS. Comm., *Ormonde Papers*, , also New Series i and iii; W. A. Shaw, *Knights*). He was granted estates at Corbellis, co. Dublin in 1643, and became M.P. for Dublin in 1647. He surrendered Trim in 1650 (R. Bagwell, *Ireland under the Stuarts*, ii. 225) and, according to his own account, he was granted permission to go to Holland, but bad weather forced his ship to the Isle of Man where he made the articles for Lady Derby's surrender, and obtained leave to settle anywhere in the Commonwealth. He was expected to take part in an insurrection in England in 1654–1655 (*Calendar Clarendon State Papers*, ii. 387, 440; Eva Scott, *Travels of the King*, pp. 75–6), and this may explain why in April, 1655, he was brought from Shrewsbury to London and committed by Cromwell to the Gatehouse. He was a prisoner there, in Jersey, and elsewhere, until 15 June 1659, when the Long Parliament ordered his release on security for good behaviour (*Commons' Journals*). He signed the "Declaration of the Nobility and Gentry that adhered to the late King" in April, 1660 (Kennet, *Register*, i. 120–1). His loyalty was rewarded at the Restoration by a grant of a monopoly to make farthings for Ireland (*Calendar of State Papers, Ireland, 1660–1662*, 5 November 1660) and by reappointment as quartermaster general of horse (*ibid*, 1 April 1662). He died 19 November 1662, and "has left few officers behind him who are his betters" (Ormonde to Charles II, *ibid.*, 27 November 1662).

Little is certainly known about the son before the Restoration except that he married one Katharine, and then became, according to Oldmixon (*History of England under the Stuarts*, p. 687), Clarendon's nephew by marriage (Marriage settlement dated 10 February 1656/7. *Calendar of Treasury Books, 1681–1685*, p. 1391). He served the royalist cause by taking the King a considerable sum of money entrusted to him by the earl of Oxford, and may have suffered a year's imprisonment on his return (Burnet, *Own Time*, i. 580). Burnet (*ibid*, i. 579) relates that Charles II asserted at the time of the Rye House Plot that Armstrong, when he visited him in exile, confessed that Cromwell had employed him to assassinate the king. Inasmuch as Armstrong, in the paper he left behind on the scaffold, merely denied that he had ever been a Cromwellian spy, it is probable that Burnet got hold of a wrong version of the King's allegations.

Certainly it is difficult to believe that after the Restoration Charles would have employed to guard his person a would-be assassin.

Armstrong was commissioned as captain-lieutenant of Oxford's Horse Guards in 1661, major of the King's own troop of Horse Guards in 1673, lieutenant-colonel of the Queen's regiment of horse in 1678 and of the King's own troop of Horse Guards in 1679 (C. Dalton, *Army Lists*, i. 4, 155, 201, 252). Because he was styled a captain 23 October 1667, and Sir Thomas on 7 September 1668 (*Calendar State Papers Domestic*), he must have been knighted between these dates. In 1670 he brought from Paris the news of Madame's death and witnessed the King's first grief at the loss of a beloved sister (Julia Cartwright, *Madame*, pp. 358–9). About this time he became the inseparable companion of the duke of Monmouth. He served with the duke in the French army in 1672, was wounded in his company fighting on the Dutch side in 1678, and accompanied him in his brief campaign against the Scottish covenanters in 1679 (Elizabeth D'Oyley, *James Duke of Monmouth*, pp. 74, 81, 89, 122; Reresby's *Diary*, ed. Andrew Browning, pp. 184–5). He seems to have shared the debauchery of Monmouth's entourage, gambling beyond his means and killing a Mr. Scroope in the duke of York's playhouse on 28 August 1675, though he did not start the affray (*Hatton Correspondence*, ed. E. M. Thompson, i. 121; Echard's accusation, *History of England*, iii. 675–6, that he murdered Scroope is too strong). He was twice elected M.P. for Stafford in 1679 and again in 1681 (Josiah C. Wedgwood, *Staffordshire Parliamentary History*, ii. 139–40). About September 1679, he was banished from the court as Monmouth's great favourite, but it is said he was allowed to sell his commission in the Horse Guards (*Calendar State Papers Domestic, 1679–1680*, pp. 240, 243, 272). Until 1683 he and Lord Grey of Werk were Monmouth's right-hand men. His precise share in the plans for an insurrection is obscure, but there is no valid reason to doubt his complicity in the schemes for which William, Lord Russell, Algernon Sidney and others were executed. Whether he took part in the Rye House Plot is more questionable, though Monmouth and he are said to have gathered adherents in the City on the day in October 1682, when Charles II was to have been killed on his return from Newmarket (Ferguson's account in James Ferguson, *Robert Ferguson the Plotter*, p. 82), and though he is alleged to have spied out the position at Whitehall and reported that the guards were remiss and "the thing [? assassination or seizure of Charles II] very feasible." (See Burnet's criticism of this evidence, *Own Time*, i. 578).

When in June 1683 Keeling and others revealed the plots, Armstrong's arrest was ordered, but he escaped with Grey to Cleves (Ford, Lord Grey, *Secret History*, p. 66). In his absence the grand jury of the City found a true bill of high treason against him in July, and in Michaelmas term sentence of outlawry was pronounced (*Impartial Account of all the material circumstances relating to Sir Thomas Armstrong, 1684*). He was seized at Leyden, brought to England, and lodged in Newgate, 11 June 1684. He was immediately brought before Jeffreys, now lord chief justice, who denied him a trial on the ground that he was a condemned outlaw. Armstrong's plea that he was entitled to a trial because he had surrendered within a year and a day of outlawry was overruled because he had not voluntarily given himself up. His condemnation was reversed on a writ of error on 15 November 1694, but it is by no means clear that Jeffreys misinterpreted the law, although he applied it with his usual harshness.'

Ibid. 573*b*, l. 4. For 'Huggons' read 'Higgons.'

Add at end of paragraph. 'In the paper he had written: "I have lived and now die . . . a true and sincere Protestant . . . and in the Communion of the Church of England; and I heartily wish I had more strictly lived up to the religion which I believed" (*Proceedings against Sir Thomas Armstrong*, 1684). Several contemporary tracts and a ballad, "The Bully Whig," all revile his private life: one related that he read *The Whole Duty of Man* on his way to the gallows (*Impartial Account of the behaviour of Sir Thomas Armstrong*, 1684). The severe strictures Sprat (*True Account*, ed. Edmund Goldsmid, 1886, pp. 29–30) passed on his character seem to have been substantially true. He left a widow, whom he had scandalously neglected, and three daughters, of whom Jane (Matthews) attended her father's trial and pleaded for his life.'

In bibliographical note omit *Clarendon Hist.* and add 'For the crucial period of Armstrong's life, 1679–1684, all lives of his associates as Monmouth, Russell, Ferguson, and all accounts of the plots are relevant.'

Arnald, Richard. i. 575*a*, l. 20. For 'degree' read 'degrees'; after 'M.A.' insert 'in 1721, and B.D. in 1728 (Venn, *Alumni Cantab.*, pt. 1, i. 41).'

Arnold, Samuel James. i. 585*a*, l. 19. After 'Society' insert 'but his name does not appear in the society's "Record."'

Ascham, Roger. i. 630*b*, l. 23 from foot. For '1771' read '1761'

Ashe, Simeon (d. 1662). i. 640*b*, ll. 13–14. For 'nonconformist divine, was educated' substitute 'Presbyterian minister, was admitted sizar, April 1613'.

Ibid., ll. 15–16. For 'He began his ministration in Staffordshire,' read 'He was ordained (Peterborough) deacon and priest, October 1619 (J. and J. A. Venn, *Alumni Cantabrigienses*, Pt. I, Vol. i). He was vicar of Rugeley, Staffordshire, in 1627,'

Ibid., l. 19. After 'ceremonies.' insert Edmund Calamy, *An Account of the Ministers . . . Ejected*, 1713, p. 2)'.

Ibid., l. 24. For 'chaplain' read 'one of the chaplains'.

Ibid., l. 25. For 'joined with' read 'published for'

Ibid., l. 27. Omit 'in writing'. After 'entitled' insert '"A Particular Relation . . . of the Earl of Manchester's Army" and collaborated with him in'.

Ibid., l. 30. After 'North' add 'covering –10 July 1644'.

Ibid., ll. 30–31. For 'another pamphlet' read 'two other pamphlets'.

Ibid., l 32. After 'entitled' insert '"A Continuation of True Intelligence" (10–27 July), and'.

Ibid., ll. 35–36. For 'in both cases was to indicate the conduct of his patron' substitute may have been to vindicate his patron, but actually he wrote valuable accounts of the campaigns in which he took part, although vague in details of the fighting. The tribute Robert Baillie pays to Ashe's "known integrity" seems well deserved (*Letters and Journals*, 1841, II. 209).'

Ibid., l. 19 from foot. After 'Cornhill lecturers.' add 'His prominence secured him an appointment as one of the "triers" of the elders of the fifth classis, established in London 20 October 1645, 26 September 1646, and 29 August 1648 (*Acts and Ordinances of the Interregnum*, ed. C. H. Firth and R. S. Rait, 1911).'

Ibid., l. 16 from foot. After 'Cromwellians' substitute a period for the semicolon. Insert 'When the two factions into which the Scottish kirk became divided in the 1650's appealed to Cromwell for support, the Resolutioners enlisted the services of Ashe and other eminent English Presbyterians. He rebuked Samuel Rutherford, a leader of the Protesters, in a letter of 19 Jan. 1657 (*Register of the Consultations of the Ministers of Edinburgh*, ed. W. Stephen, (Scottish History Soc. 1921), i. 288–90). He was in consultation with Monk early in 1660 (*Ibid.* (1930), ii. xxx).'

Ibid. For l. 3 from foot to 641*a* l. 11 read 'Ashe published at least seventeen tracts or sermons, of which the only one to attain a third edition was "The Living Loves," a funeral tribute to Jeremiah Whitaker. His other funeral sermon, "Gray Hayres Crowned with Grace," for Thomas Gataker, reached a second edition. All the tracts he wrote are to be found in the British Museum, except "Real Thankfulnesse" 1645. A good bibliographical note is to be found in A. G. Matthews, *Calamy Revised*, 1934.'

Ashley, Robert. i. 644*a*, l. 14. For '*Add. MS.* No. 2105' read '*Sloane MS.* 2131.'

Ashmole, Elias. i. 645*a*, ll. 10–13. Ashmole's second wife was Mary, daughter of Sir William Forster, of Aldermaston, Berks. Information about her first three husbands is given in 'The Genealogist,' new ser., xxix (1913). 86–7. Her third husband was a distant relation of Ashmole's first wife. Ashmole is said to have obtained by the marriage £600 a year or more (*Cal. Committee for Advance of Money*, p. 1231).

Ashmole, Elias. i. 646*a*, 7 ll. from foot. Add: 'It has again been reprinted, from the MS. original, Bodl. MS. Ashmole 1136: "The Diary and Will of Elias Ashmole, edited and extended from the original manuscripts by R. T. Gunther," Oxford, 1927 (Old Ashmolean Reprints, no. 2). This edition has an appendix of letters to and from Ashmole, and notes giving references to other MSS. in the Bodleian. "Surrey Arch. Collections," ii. contains abstracts of deeds relating to his house at Lambeth.'

Ashton, Thomas. i. 652*a*, ll. 23–19 from foot. For 'where he graduated B.A. . . . into orders' read 'was elected a fellow of St. John's, Cambridge, in 1524.'

Ibid. 652*b*, ll. 3–4. For 'Soon . . . same year' read 'About the year 1571.'

Add to list of authorities : J. B. Oldham's Headmasters of Shrewsbury School, 1552–1798, pp. 3–5.

Astley, Sir Jacob (1579–1652). i. 677*a*, l. 8. After 'Norfolk.' insert '(F. Blomefield, *History of the County of Norfolk*, (1808), ix. 420)'.

Ibid., ll. 18–28. After 'In 1638 . . . Scotch invasion.' insert 'He was knighted 17 July 1624. On 3 December 1638 he was made governor for life of the fort of Plymouth and of St. Nicholas' Isle. On the 8th of that month, because of the activities of the Covenanters in the North, and apprehension of a Scotch invasion, Charles issued a declaration for mustering the forces, placing his "trusty and well beloved Sir Jacob Astley" in charge of the counties of Leicester, Stafford, Derby, Rutland, Lincoln, Nottingham, Northumberland, the West Riding of Yorkshire, the towns of Hull, Carlisle, and Newcastle. On January 6 the counties of Chester and Lancaster were added to his authority (Many references in *Cal. State Papers Dom.*). During December and January he was busy bringing munitions and equipment from Rotterdam, and travelling through the counties, inspecting levies and making recommendations. He found the weapons in very poor condition, and not "any armourers that know how to make or mend arms." He urged the fortification of Hull, and a tax on merchants not living there who made use of that excellent harbour. His plans for fortifying Holy Island, Berwick, Carlisle, Newcastle, and other strategic places were well received by the King and the Council of War.'

Ibid., l. 32. After 'he pleased.' insert '(*Cal. State Papers Dom.* 11 Jan. 1638/9)'.

Ibid. 677*b*, ll. 11–16. For 'In 1164 . . . upon it.' insert 'Charles, in an attempt to coerce Parliament, in June 1641 approved of a petition drawn up by a few officers, proposing to back the king against Parliament with force. He initialed it "C. R." and then it was taken to the Army for signatures. Astley would have nothing to do with it (Gardiner, *History of England*, ix. 398–400)'.

Ibid., l. 17. After 'it' insert '(Clarendon, *History of the Rebellion*, V. 4, 169)'.

Ibid., l. 23. Add '(Clarendon, iv. 14)'.

Ibid., ll. 28–29. For 'commendations . . . case' substitute 'character is brief but highly eulogistic and'.

Ibid., l. 30. Add '(Clarendon, viii. 32)'.

Ibid., ll. 32–36. For 'He was among . . . Gloucester' substitute 'At the battle of Edgehill (23 Oct. 1642) he was major general of the army under the earl of Lindsey. Sir Philip Warwick (*Memoirs of the Reign of Charles I*, (1791), p. 229) recounts: "Before the charge he made a most excellent, pious, short and soldierly prayer: for he lifted up his eyes and hands to heaven, saying 'O Lord! Thou knowest how busy I must be this day: if I forget Thee, do not Thou forget me.' " He was wounded during the battle (Clarendon, vi. 94). He was the first governor of Oxford (Nov. 1642) appointed by Charles (F. J. Varley, *Siege of Oxford*, 1932). Fully recovered from his wounds, he was major general of the foot at the siege of Gloucester (September 1643), and retained this position in Charles' army until after the battle of Naseby.'

Ibid., l. 37. For 'that city' read 'Gloucester'.

Ibid., l. 21 from foot. After 'Arundel' add '(Clarendon, viii. 5)'.

Ibid., l. 17 from foot. After 'Essex' add '(Clarendon, viii. 45–6)'.

Ibid., l. 8 from foot. For 'His . . . 1644' substitute '(Clarendon, ix. 37, 39). He was made Baron Astley of Reading, 4 November 1644 (W. H. Black, *Docquets of Letters Patent*, p. 230).'

Ibid., l. 3 from foot. For 'and his charge was' substitute 'and August 1654 the governship of Worcester was'.

678*a* ll. 2–10. For 'From Oxford . . . (21 March 1646)' substitute 'On his march with two thousand horse and foot from Worcester to Oxford to meet the king's party of fifteen hundred, he was intercepted by Sir Thomas Brereton and Colonel Morgan at Stow-on-the-Wold, 21 March 1646, defeated and captured (Clarendon, x. 31).'

Ibid., l. 18. After 'experience.' insert '(For an account of this battle, see J. W. Willis Bund, *Civil War in Worcestershire* (1905), p. 175).'

Ibid., l. 24. For 'An ordinance' read 'An order of Parliament'.

Ibid., l. 25. After 'delinquency' insert '(*Cal. of Committee for Compounding*, pp. 1202–3).'

Ibid., l. 15 from foot. For 'One son . . . Bristol' substitute 'The eldest son, Isaac, was knighted at Oxford 23 Feb. 1643, and inherited the barony. Astley's only daughter, Elizabeth, married her cousin Sir Edward Astley, and their son Sir Jacob, 1st Bart., was, until his death in 1729, knight of the shire for the county of Norfolk. Bernard, Sir Jacob's younger son, received with his father for life the office of captain of the fort of Plymouth, 3 Dec. 1638. He was wounded at the siege of Bristol, 26 July 1643 (Clarendon, vii. 133), and knighted 18 June 1644. At the battle of Newbury he fought with his father at Shaw House. He headed a sally from Bristol, when the New Model Army besieged it, 26 August 1645, was wounded, captured, and within a few days died of his wounds. (Sprigge, *Anglia Rediviva*, (1647), p. 91).'

Aston, Sir Arthur (d. 1649). i. 680*b*, l. 10 from foot. After 'flourished' insert 'A list of officers slain at the retreat from the Isle of Rhé, 29 October, 1627, includes the name of Sir Arthur Aston (*Cal. S. P. Dom.* 1625–49, p. 232).'

Ibid., l. 9 from bottom. For 'he' substitute 'his son Arthur'.

Ibid. 681*a*. At end of paragraph 2 insert 'Among the Harleian manuscripts (2149, 28–32) are papers testifying to his continental military service, summarized in G. Ormerod, *History of . . . Chester*, (1819), ii. 46–47.'

Ibid., After l. 17 from foot add 'He was called colonel in a dispatch of 6 May from the earl of Northumberland; on 28 June he was recommended as successor to Colonel Goring. On 11 August, the earl of Northumberland declared if Aston's quarrel with Sir John Marley was not concluded before his arrival, he would be Aston's second. From 5 to 11 August he received the pay of a sergeant major general. In August he defended to the lord-lieutenant of Ireland, and also to the king, the conduct of Viscount Conway in not pursuing the war more vigorously (*Cal. S. P. Dom.* 1640, 122, 354, 573, 579, 646).'

Ibid. 681*b*, l. 11 After 'to him' insert 'This story is found in Dodd's *Church History* (1742), iii. 57–58, and is unlikely. No Catholic would have offered his services to the Parliamentary army, and, in any case, at this time Sir Thomas Fairfax was not a general.'

Ibid., l. 12. After 'dragoons' correct from 'with . . . army' to read 'with which regiment he dispersed the musketeers on the Parliamentary right wing, and prepared the way for Wilmot's charge (Clarendon's *History of the Rebellion*, ed. W. D. Macray, vi. 85).'

Ibid., add at end of paragraph 2: 'He was appointed governor of Reading 2 December 1642, and on 10 February 1643 was commissioned sergeant major general of all the horse forces. (Information taken from a compilation made by William Henry Black of the letters patent and other instruments passed under the Great Seal of King Charles I at Oxford 1642–46, from the originals in the Ashmolean Museum. Printed, not published, 1837, pp. 4–5, 97).'

Ibid., l. 35. After 'afterwards' insert '22 April 1643'.

Ibid., l. 38. From 'an accident' to 'the siege' substitute 'an accident which to a certain extent incapacitated him for the rest of the siege.'

Ibid., l. 15 from foot. After 'dread' insert 'He was probably quite willing to allow the blame of the inevitable surrender to fall on the shoulders of another. The spirit in which he approached his work is shown by the letter of 12 April 1643 to Rupert in which he says "I am grown weary of my life with perpetual trouble and vexation" (E. Warburton, *Memoirs of Prince Rupert*, (1849), ii. 175).'

Ibid., l. 10 from foot. After 'Oxford' insert 'The articles of surrender are given in Rushworth's *Historical Collections*, Part iii, vol. ii. (1691), 266.'

Ibid., l. 4 from foot. After 'in the west' insert 'Aston commanded the horse at the siege of Gloucester (Aston to Rupert, 7 Aug. 1643. Warburton's *Memoirs*, ii, 276–77)'. After 'In the following month' insert '23 August 1643'.

Ibid. 682*a*, l. 2. After 'Pennyman' insert 'He was commissioned to maintain a regiment of foot, 11 September 1643 (Black, *Letters Patent*, p. 73). On 22 December, 1643, he was wounded in a scuffle (Frederick J. Varley, *The Siege of Oxford*, (1932), p. 7)'.

Ibid., l. 4. After 'university' insert '(*ibid*, p. 72)'.

Ibid., end of paragraph 1, insert 'He was most reluctant to give up his office, complaining of the conduct of his successor-to-be, Col. Henry Gage. However, Charles expressed every confidence in Gage, knighted him November 1st, and gave him the office on Christmas day. The new governor was killed 11 January 1644, while on a foray with Rupert (Clarendon, *History of the Rebellion*, (1849), iii. 457; Varley, *Siege of Oxford*, p. 74).'

Ibid., paragraph 2. For the first seven lines substitute 'Where Aston spent the next four years is uncertain. He may have lived in retirement with his wife's family in Ireland, where he is said to have been in 1646 (*ibid.* p. 72), or he may have resided at his estate of Cattenhall in Cheshire. The first definite news is that he was captured at Warrington on 29 May 1648 with a body of Royalists Colonel John Booth was assembling, apparently in anticipation of the Scots' invasion (*Letters and Papers of Thomas Mytton*, ed. Stanley Leighton for the Powysland Club, (1875), p. 166) Whether he escaped or was released is unknown.'

Ibid., l. 32. From 'Being left . . .' through l. 11 '. . . Tredagh' substitute 'He was governor of Drogheda in August 1649, when he wrote a series of letters to the lord lieutenant-general of Ireland, Ormonde, complaining of the conduct of Lady Aston's relatives, headed by Lady Wilmot, in plotting to betray the city to Cromwell. Throughout the month he presented the situation of the garrison, urging haste in bringing new men, arms and food. These dispatches are printed in full in *A Contemporary History of Affairs in Ireland from 1641 to 1652*, ed. John T. Gilbert, (Dublin, 1880), ii, pt. ii. pp. 232–76.'

Ibid., l. 34. For 'three times' substitute 'twice (Gardiner, *Commonwealth and Protectorate*, i. 130–31)'.

Ibid. 682*a*. Between paragraphs 2 and 3, insert this paragraph: 'He married Elinor, daughter of Sir Samuel Beganel (G. E. C. *Complete Peerage*, ed. Vicary Gibbs, v. 609, note c). A son, a royalist captain, is said to have been slain in November 1645 during a skirmish between Bridgnorth and Kidderminster (Hist. MSS. Comm., *Portland*, i. (1891), 306). A daughter, Elizabeth, wife of Mr. Thompson, may be the woman who, Gage complained, invited him to mass at her home in Oxford in 1643. His estate was compounded. His son and heir, Samuel, was allowed for himself and sisters one-fifth of his father's estate, 3 June 1651. His widow also begged discharge of Cattenhall from sequestration (*Comm. for Compounding*, no. 2450)'.

Aubrey, John. i. 716*a*, l. 21 from foot. For 'May' read 'January (BULLETIN, xv. 83)'

Audley or **Audeley, James de** (1316?–86), i. 722*b*, ll. 20–23. For a discussion on the squires of James Audley implying a revision of this sentence, see H. J. Hewitt, *The Black Prince's Expedition of* 1355–7, (Manchester Univ. Press, 1958), App. A, p. 193.

Austin, John (1790–1859). i. 738*a*, ll. 28–9. For 'he resigned his chair in 1832. The year before' [etc.] read: 'he ceased to lecture after June 1833, although he retained his chair until January 1835. In 1831 he published' [etc.]. See London University [now University College], Minutes of the Sessions of the Council, ii. 460, 464–5, 467; *University of London, Report and Appendix, February* 1834, p. 6; *ibid.* 1835, p. 4. For many details of his character and domestic life see also J. A. Ross, *Three Generations of Englishwomen*, 1st ed., 2 vols., 1888; new, revised, and enlarged edition, 1 vol., 1893. For his appointment as lecturer at the Inner Temple see *Report of the Commissioners appointed to inquire into the Arrangements in the Inns of Court and Inns of Chancery, for promoting the Study of the Law and Jurisprudence; together with Appendices.* Parl. Pp. [1998], H. of C. 1854–5, *i.e.* xviii. 357, 550.

***Axtell, Daniel.** i. 748*b*. The account of his military career is vague and inaccurate. Axtell was a captain in Hewson's regiment of foot in the New Model Army in 1645, major in 1646, and made lieut.-col. 27 March 1648. In the campaign of 1648 he fought in Kent, was at the siege of Deal and Walmer Castles, but not at Colchester (Rushworth, vii. 1240). Axtell was employed to present a message from the Army to the House of Commons on 6 Dec. 1648, and assisted Col. Pride in 'purging' the House. As his regiment guarded Westminster Hall during the king's trial, and his colonel sat in the court as one of the judges, Axtell was prominent in the proceedings. He accompanied Cromwell to Ireland, was made by him governor first of Ross, afterwards of Kilkenny, and was promoted to the command of a regiment about May 1650. On 25 Oct. 1650 he defeated the Marquis of Clanricard at Meleek (*Old Parliamentary History*, xix. 439; Borlase, p. 314; Gilbert, *Aphorismical Discovery*, iii. 184, 224). He also distinguished himself by his severity to the Irish, which he defended later by the text 'Give her blood to drink, for she is worthy' (*State Trials*, v. 1288; *cf.* Clarendon, *Rebellion*, ed. 1849, vii. 235). In 1651 Ireton suspended him from his command for not keeping a promise of quarter (Ludlow, ed. 1894, i. 263). Soon after, on his voyage to England, Axtell with two other colonels was captured by a privateer from Scilly, and threatened with death in retaliation for his cruelties, but Blake's capture of the islands rescued him (*ibid.*, i. 265; *Mercurius Politicus*, p. 686). In 1652 he was again in command at Kilkenny (Whitelocke, iii. 309, 395, 405).

Axtell's regiment was disbanded in August 1653, but he was employed in some inferior command till 1656 (Thurloe, iii. 710, 715). Being an Anabaptist he disapproved of the establishment of the Protectorate and intrigued against Henry Cromwell, but did not openly oppose him, and in November 1656 resigned his commission (Thurloe, ii. 163; v. 670). In July 1658 he returned to England and apparently thought of taking service in Flanders or Jamaica (*ibid.*, vii. 306). The republican reaction of 1659 brought him back into the Irish army as colonel of the regiment of foot late Fleetwood's (*Cal. S. P., Dom.*, 1659–60, p. 12). Ludlow chose him to command the thousand foot sent to England at the time of Sir George Booth's rising (Ludlow, ii. 110, 112; *Portland MSS.*, i. 684). He signed a couple of the letters in which Lambert's supporters endeavoured to persuade Monck to acquiesce in the expulsion of the Long Parliament (*Clarke Papers*, iv. 68, 146).

Ayloffe, John. i. 756*a* and *ante*, ii. 93–4. A second poem entitled 'Marvell's Ghost' is printed in 'Poems on Affairs of State,' iv. (1707), 318. It belongs to 1689 and is, of course, not by Ayloffe.

A poem entitled 'A Litany,' 1681, attributed to Ayloffe, is printed in 'Poems on Affairs of State,' iii. (1698), 71. A corrupt text, without the attribution, is given ibid., iii. (1704), 208.

E. S. de Beer.

Ayloffe, John. i. 756*a*. The article requires revision as follows:—He was the author of *Marvell's Ghost*, which Grosart describes as 'one of the most drastic and powerful satires against the Stuarts,' and is perhaps to be identified with the John Ayloffe executed in 1685 for his share in the Rye House Plot. The earliest account of Ayloffe as a writer appears to be in G. Jacob's *Historical Account . . . of the English Poets*, 1720, i. 3. Jacob states that 'Captain John Ayloffe' was educated at Trinity College, Cambridge, and of his poems mentions only *Marvell's Ghost* by name. But Jacob was confusing John Ayloffe with William Ayloffe; no John Ayloffe is mentioned in Ball and Venn's *Admissions to Trinity College, Cambridge.* Jacob describes him as 'Captain Ayloffe,' John Nichols, in his *Select Collection of Poems*, 1780, iii. 186–9, repeats Jacob's notice, and prints a poem, *On the Cambridge Commencement*; but the political allusions in this make it unlikely that it is by the author of *Marvell's Ghost*, while there is reason to believe that it may be by William Ayloffe. Two poems of an amatory nature attributed to Captain Ayloffe appear among the odd poems in *Miscellaneous Works written by His Grace, George, Late Duke of Buckingham*, 1704, pt. i. pp. 79–81 (and elsewhere), and are probably also by William Ayloffe.

Jacob, when noticing Ayloffe as a satirist, does not suggest that he had any political career. It is probable, however, that the writer and the politician are the same person.

The politician was a kinsman of the Hattons (*Hatton Correspondence*, Camden Soc., i. 118) and, according to Macaulay (*History of England*, 1858, i. 526), of the Hydes (Edward Hyde, Earl of Clarendon's first wife was an Ayliffe; the name is written both ways). He may be the John Ayliffe, son of John Ayliffe of Foxley, Wilts., who matriculated from St. Edmund Hall, Oxford, 19 July 1662, and who was a member of the Inner Temple in 1664 (J. Foster, *Alumni Oxonienses*, 1500–1714, i. 47). Charles Hatton describes Ayloffe's throwing a sabot, bearing a satirical inscription, under the Speaker's chair at the opening of Parliament, probably 20 October 1673 (*Hatton Corr.* i. 118). Ayloffe appears to have given, or tried to give, some information to the Commons concerning the Popish Plot (A. Grey, *Debates*, vi. 170). He was certainly a member of the Green Ribbon Club and apparently very active (G. R. Sitwell, *The First Whig*).

For his part in the Rye House Plot Ayloffe was indicted for high treason; according to Lord Howard of Escrick he had volunteered to kill the Duke of York, but had been withheld by Shaftesbury (*A True Account . . . of the Horrid Conspiracy against the late King*, 3rd ed. 1686, part ii. p. 107). Ayloffe fled, and was outlawed. He was captured while taking part in the Earl of Argyle's expedition to Scotland, and attempted to commit suicide; this failed, and he was brought to London. As he already stood attainted of high treason there was no need for a trial; on 27 October 1685 he was sentenced to be executed on 30 October; on 29 October it was decided that the execution should take place 'over against the Temple Gate, in Fleet Street.' He apparently died with composure. Macaulay says that he was brought before the Council, but refused to betray his companions, and repeats the story that the king said, 'You had better be frank with me, Mr. Ayloffe. You know that it is in my power to pardon you.' Whereupon Ayloffe replied, 'It may be in your power, but it is not in your nature' (Macaulay, *History of England*, 1858, i. 568).

[Authorities quoted above; also *Cal. State Papers Dom.* 1680–1681, p. 165, etc.; *Hist. MSS. Comm.* 4th Report, App. p. 235*a*; and the authorities referred to by Macaulay. For the proceedings relating to Ayloffe's execution, etc., see *An Account of the Proceedings against John Ayloff and Richard Nelthorp Esquires at the King's Bench-Bar, on the 27th of October, 1685* (pp. 4. Licensed R. Lestrange, 30 October 1685); *The Tryals of Thomas Walcot, William Hone, William Lord Russell*, etc. 12, 13, 14 July 1683 (West's evidence referring to Ayloff is on p. 15); *The Free and Voluntary Confession and Narrative of James Holloway* (April 1684, p. 3*b*). See also J. E. Jackson, 'The Ayliffes of Grittenham' in *Wilts Arch. and Nat. Hist. Magazine*, xxi. 194–211. *Marvell's Ghost* appears to have been first printed in *A Third Collection of the Newest and Most Ingenious Poems, Satyrs, Songs, etc.*, 1689, and is always assigned to John Ayloffe].

Ayloffe, **Sir Joseph.** i. 756*b*, ll. 14–17. For 'On 10 Feb. 1731–2 . . . Royal Society,' read 'On 27 May 1731 he was elected a fellow of the Royal Society and on 10 Feb. 1731–2 a fellow of the Society of Antiquaries' (*Record of Royal Soc.*, p. 335).

Ayscue, Sir George. i. 770*a*. This article needs revision. See Sir Charles Firth in *The Mariner's Mirror*, xii. 253–54.

Ayscue, Sir George. i. 771*b*, ll. 28–36. For 'It may be doubted . . . has been preserved' read 'According to Pepys's Register of Sea Officers, Ayscue served on the *Triumph* in 1668 and on the *St. Andrew* in 1671/2 (*Cat. Pepysian MSS.*, I. 320, Navy Record Soc., Pub. xxvi.). In the third Dutch war, commencing in the latter year, Ayscue was appointed Vice-Admiral of the Red (*ibid.* p. 313), but died before 6 April 1672, and was succeeded by Sir Edward Spragge [*q.v.*] (*Cal. State Papers, Dom.*, 1671–1672, pp. 291, 609).'

Baber, Sir John. i. 779*b*. See *Notes and Queries*, 12th Ser., xii. 516, for names, etc., of his wives.

Baber, Sir John. i. 780*a*, ll. 3, 4. For ‘the Grateful Nonconformist (1665)’ read ‘R. Wild, The Grateful Non-conformist (1665), printed with his other poems.’

Bacon, Nathaniel (1593–[illegible]). [illegible]*b*, l. 23. After ‘Nathaniel Bacon’ insert ‘having graduated in arts at Christ’s, Cambridge, in 1610 (*Mariner’s Mirror*, xiii. 341).’

Bacon, Richard Mackenzie. i. 844*a*, 21–20 ll. from foot. For ‘born at Norwich in or about 1775’ read ‘born in St. Peter Mancroft parish, Norwich, on 1 May 1776 (*Daylight*, Norwich, No. 1393, 25 July 1903, p. 11).’

Ibid. 7 ll. from foot. For ‘30 Nov.’ read ‘3 Dec.’ A copy of the newspaper is in the central public library, Norwich, which also contains photographs of two painted portraits of Bacon.

G. A. S.

Badiley, Richard. i, 861*a*, l. 20. After ‘11 Aug. 1657’ insert: ‘but Salvetti, the resident of the grand duke of Tuscany, says he died on the same day as Blake, viz. 7 Aug. Salvetti’s letter is quoted in T. A. Spalding’s *Life of Richard Badiley*, 1899, p. 1 (Sir Charles Firth in *The Mariner’s Mirror*, xii. 254).’

Bagot, Sir Charles. First Supplement, i. 99*a*, ll. 50–56. For ‘Bagot incurred . . . health’ read: ‘Contrary, however, to the generally accepted opinion, Bagot’s experiment did not meet with censure from Lord Stanley, the colonial minister. It is true that Stanley deplored that the French had been recognised as a party, and that he considered that the executive council had gone beyond constitutional custom in advising Bagot to send for La Fontaine and Baldwin (Stanley to Bagot, 16 October 1842, Bagot Correspondence, M. 165, Canadian Archives). On the other hand, after a special meeting of the cabinet he wrote: “her majesty’s government are prepared to acquiesce in the line of policy which you have taken and to advise the queen to sanction and confirm it. It will be my duty . . . to give to your administration a cordial support and to the measures which it may bring forward the most favourable consideration . . . her majesty cheerfully assents in the composition of your executive council to that which appears to be the general wish of the colony” (Same to Same, 2 November 1842, *ibid.*, G. 115). “We do not disapprove your policy, we are prepared to support it and defend you for having pursued it” (Same to Same, 3 November 1842, *ibid.*, M. 165). The strain, however, soon began to tell on Bagot’s weakly constitution, and within a short time he requested his recall.’ W. P. M. Kennedy.

Baker, Philip. i. 934*b*, l. 22. For ‘He was living in 1601 . . . England’ read ‘According to the entry in the parish register of St. Margaret Moses he was buried on 12 Aug. 1590. (Harl. Soc. *Registers*, xlii. 70; cf. *Notes and Queries*, cli. 314.)’

Balchen, Sir John. i. 946*a*, l. 18 from foot. After ‘Surrey’ insert ‘The paybook of H.M.S. Dragon shows that Balchen was 2nd lieutenant from 15 March 1693 to 28 March 1693, then 1st lieutenant till discharged on 9 Jan. 1696–7, on preferment. The list books show him in 1697 as 3rd lieutenant of H.M.S. Cambridge, the flagship of Admiral Nevill’ (*Mariner’s Mirror*, xvi. 296).

Ibid. 948*a*, l. 6. After ‘Greenwich’ insert ‘Another portrait is in the town hall, Godalming.’

Ibid. l. 9. After ‘1745’ insert ‘His daughter, Frances, married Vice-Admiral Temple West [q.v.]’ (*Mariner’s Mirror*, xvi. 296).

Balfour, Sir William. i. 979*a*. At the beginning read: ‘son of Colonel Henry Balfour, a Scottish officer in the Dutch army, and of Christian Cant, was probably born about 1579, as his father was killed in 1580. William Balfour entered the Dutch service in 1604 as a captain in Buccleuch’s regiment. In recommending (15 April 1605) a petition made by him for a debt due from the Dutch government to his father, James I described him as a knight and “notre serviteur domestique.”’ The debt was satisfied by a pension granted in 1615 (Ferguson, *Papers Illustrating the History of the Scots Brigade in the Service of Holland*, i. 43, 69, 199, 251–5). Mr. Ferguson’s introduction and notes give a good life of Henry Balfour.

Ibid., l. 19. Insert: ‘In 1622 he was taken prisoner by the Spaniards at Emmerich, but ransomed (Dalton, *Life of Sir E. Cecil*, ii. 7).’ In 1627 he took part in the expedition to the Isle of Rhé, etc.

Ibid., l. 32. After 'employed in England' add the following references: (Rushworth's *Collections* i. 474, 612; *Court and Times of Charles I*, i. 321; Gardiner, *History of England*, vi. 224). These engagements obliged Balfour to resign his commission in the Dutch service, though Charles I made great efforts to persuade the States to permit his prolonged absence (Ferguson, i. 369–70). As Lieutenant of the Tower, Balfour is said to have saved the life of the Earl of Loudoun in 1640, when Charles I ordered his execution for his part in the appeal of the Covenanting leaders to the King of France (Birch, *Enquiry into the Transactions of the Earl of Glamorgan*, ed. 1756, pp. 370–376; Scot's *Staggering State of Scottish Statesmen*, ed. Roger, p. 51; Gardiner, *History of England*, ix. 97). His expenses as Lieutenant of the Tower are set forth in a petition in Dec. 1641 (*Hist. MSS. Comm.*, 10th Report, vi. 86).

979*b*, l. 32. The story of Balfour's escape in 1644 is told in detail in Sir Edward Walker's *Historical Discourses*, ed. 1705, pp. 70–73, 80. His letter announcing it to General Middleton, written on a piece of yellow silk, is preserved by his descendants and is printed in the report on the papers of Mr. R. P. Balfour of Townley (*Hist. MSS. Comm.*, 10th Report, vi. 255).

The evidence as to the date of Sir William's death seems to me rather unsatisfactory, and the particulars as to his children as given in the pedigree rather vague (Ferguson, i. 377).

He had three sons, William, Alexander, and Charles. Major William contracted in 1646 to raise 600 foot and a troop of horse for service in Ulster (*Cal. State Papers, Ireland*, 1633–47, pp. 506, 519, 528). He was probably the Major Balfour killed near Derry in April 1649 (Gilbert, *Contemporary History of Affairs in Ireland*, ii. 440). Another son was killed in September 1642 in a skirmish near Yeovil (*Bellum Civile*, ed. C. E. Chadwyck Healey, Somerset Record Society, 1902, p. 15). His second daughter married about 1658 the Earl of Murray (Baillie, *Letters*, ed. Laing, iii. 366). Susanna, youngest daughter of Sir William, married Hugh, first Lord Hamilton of Glenawly (Chester, *Westminster Registers*, p. 265). The Balfours of Townley Hall trace their descent from Charles, the third son of Sir William.

Balfour, Sir William. i. 979*b*, ll. 12, 11 from foot and above, iii. 186. For 'Sir William Balfour's will was proved in 1660' read 'Balfour was buried in St. Margaret's, Westminster, on 28 July 1660 (A. M. Burke, *Memorials of St. Margaret's*, p. 661).' E. S. de B.

Balfour, William, i. 980*a*, l. 1. For '1785' read '1784'. l. 2 after 'lieutenant-colonel' add 'was born at Edinburgh on 16 July 1784. He was appointed ensign in the Hon. George Hanger's recruiting corps on 31 August 1798, in the 40th regiment on 25 July 1799 and was promoted lieutenant on 8 August 1799'. l. 4. After 'He' add 'was promoted captain on 22 September 1802'. l. 7. After 'Copenhagen' add 'became a regimental major on 4 February 1808'. l. 10. After '1813–14' add 'being present at the battles of Nivelle, Nive, Orthes and Toulouse. He received the gold medal in command of his regiment at Nivelle'. l. 14. After 'Mauritius' add 'He married in 1810, at Dublin, Charlotte Stanley Clarke (died 22 August 1825 at Launceston, Tasmania) by whom he had five sons and three daughters'.
Authorities: P.R.O., War Office, Returns of Officers' Services, W.O. 25/801; R.H.R. Smythies, *Histor. Records of the 40th Regt.*, p. 518.

Banister, or Banester, John (1540–1610). i. 1038*b*–1039*a*. A volume of 'Anatomical Tables (with Figures)' by Master John Banister in the collection of Hunterian manuscripts contains a portrait on which is written 'Iohannes Banister Aetatis sui Anno 48 Anno Domini 1581.' If the age and date are correct, Banister must have been born in 1533 (Young and Aitken, *Catalogue of the Manuscripts in the Library of the Hunterian Museum in the University of Glasgow*, 1908, pp. 290–1). W. R. C.

Banks, Sir Joseph. i. 1052*a*, 10 ll. from bottom. For 'are preserved . . . in Cromwell Road' read 'were removed by their legal owner and dispersed by auction, April 1886. (Sir Joseph Banks' *Journal*, ed. Hooker, 1896, p. x). Transcripts of Banks' correspondence (17 volumes, 1766–1819), fully indexed under writers, are preserved in the British Museum (Natural History Museum). (*Times Lit. Supp.* 25 August, 1921, p. 548).'

Bard, Henry, Viscount Bellamont. i. 1095. For a more accurate chronology, see G. E. C., *Complete Peerage*, art. 'Bellomont.'

•**Bard, Henry, Viscount Bellamont.** i. 1095. Nicolao Manucci, Bard's fellow-traveller, gives an account of their journey to India. Mr. William Turner, the editor of Manucci's *Steria di Mogor* (Indian Text Series, 4 vols. 1907), gives a long note on Bard (vol. i. pp. 72–83), showing that he was born about 1615, was admitted a scholar of King's College, Cambridge, 23 Aug. 1632, and a Fellow 24 Aug. 1635; and that he reached India and died at Hodál, near Agra, on 20 June 1656. There are in the note many other corrections, and particulars about his family and descendants.

Bard, Henry, Viscount Bellamont. *Ante*, iv. 123. For 'William Turner' read 'William Irvine.' Sir W. Foster's 'The English Factories in India' 1651–1654 and 1655–1660 (1915 and 1921) contain references to Bard's embassies to Persia and India.

Barkstead, John. i. 1136*b*, l. 23. After 'bodkins' insert 'He was probably the son of Michael Barkstead, goldsmith, of London, by his wife Anne, daughter of John Downing, a skinner. His grandfather had been settled at Lichfield and his great-grandfather had come from Germany. His brother Michael was also a goldsmith (pedigree printed in *Miscellanea Genealogica et Heraldica*, 5th ser., ii. 218).'

E. S. de B.

Barkstead, Sir John, regicide (*d.* 1662). i. 1136*b*, l. 28. He was governor of Reading from 1 July 1644 to 9 January 1646–7 (*Commons Journals*, vi. 471). The dates given in the article are reappointments. In 1647, on the breach between the army and Parliament, Barkstead was made colonel of the regiment of foot previously commanded by Colonel Richard Fortescue, who had taken the side of the Parliament. In April and May 1648 he suppressed royalist riots in London, marched under Fairfax against the Kentish royalists, took an active part in the siege of Colchester (*Clarke Papers*, ii. 4, 12; Rushworth, pt. iv. vol. ii. 1052, 1149, 1168, 1179, 1250, 1268; *Old Parliamentary History*, xvii. 93, 140).

Ibid., l. 48. After Barkstead's regiment was permanently stationed in London it was used as a training corps and a reserve in emergencies. A thousand men were drawn from it in 1651 to form a regiment for Colonel Cobbett, and sent to reinforce the army in Scotland. The deficit was made up by fresh enlistments and it was raised to 1200 or even 2000 men (*Milton State Papers*, p. 7; *Thurloe Papers*, iv. 57; *Mercurius Politicus*, 2–9 April 1657).

1137*a*, l. 6. Barkstead was Major-General of Middlesex in 1656–7 and distinguished himself by the severity with which he maintained order. He stopped bear-baiting, wrestling in Moorfields, races on Lambeth Marsh, suppressed vagrancy, made royalists give bonds for good behaviour, and kept foreign visitors under rigid control (*Clarke Papers*, iii. 64; Carte, *Original Letters*, ii. 91, 94; *Mercurius Politicus*, 1656–7, *passim*). His regulations for the government of the Tower are printed in *Mercurius Politicus* for March 1657, pp. 7637, 7655.

Ibid., l. 21. The charge against Barkstead in Richard Cromwell's Parliament related to the illegal arrest and imprisonment of John Portman, a Fifth Monarchy man (Burton's *Diary*, iii. 306, 448, 494). One of the results was that the restored Long Parliament on 10 June 1659 appointed Colonel Thomas Fitch to be Lieutenant of the Tower in place of Barkstead, whose military career thus came to an end (*Commons' Journals*, vii. 679, 685).

Ibid., l. 29. On the arrest and execution of Barkstead, see Pepys, *Diary*, ed. Wheatley, ii. 202, 205, 221.

Barkstead, Sir John. i. 1136*b*, l. 33. After '(Tanner MSS. vol. lx. f. 512)' add 'He succeeded to the command of Richard Fortescue's regiment of foot in 1647' (P.R.O., Commonwealth Exch. Papers, 46, iii.).

G. D.

Barnes, Richard. (1532–1587). i. 1172*a*, l. 38. For '4 January 1567' read 'March 1566–7' (*Notes and Queries*, cxlvii. 124). l. 42. For 'Sandys' read 'Thomas Young' (*ibid.*).

Barney, Joseph. i. 1182*b*, ll. 22–21 from foot. For '1751' read '1763 (P.R.O., war office, ordnance corresp., 44/686, no. 26)'; after 'born' insert 'on 4 March 1753 (*ibid.*)'

Ibid. ll. 17–16 from foot. For 'whilst quite young' read 'on 15 Oct. 1793 (Col. W. D. Jones, *Records of the Royal Military Academy*, p. 51).'

Ibid. l. 14 from foot. After 'years' insert ', retiring on a yearly pension of 160*l.* 16*s.* (P.R.O., war office, ordnance corresp., 44/686, no. 26)'

Baron, Robert (*fl.* **1645), i. 1192*b*.** Add to sources: G. C. Moore Smith, 'Robert Baron, author of *Mirza, a Tragedie*', *N. & Q.*, 11th ser., ix. 1–3, 22–24, 43–44, 61–63, 206.

Barré, Isaac. i. 1195*b*, l. 2. After '1746' insert 'He was promoted lieutenant of the 32nd foot on 1 Oct. 1755 (P.R.O., war office, succession book, 25/209, p. 110).'

Ibid. l. 28 from foot. After 'picture' insert 'He was made captain of the 28th foot on 27 Feb. 1760 (*ibid.*, p. 106).'

Ibid. l. 23 from foot. After 'motion"' insert 'On 29 Jan. 1761 he was made deputy adjutant-general in North America and lieutenant-colonel of foot (P.R.O., war office, commission book, 25/27, p. 25).'

Ibid. l. 22 from foot. After '106th foot' insert 'or Black Musqueteers (*Journal of the Soc. for Army Hist. Research*, xvii. 58)'; before '1761' insert '17 Oct. (P.R.O., war office, succession book, 25/209, p. 196)'

Ibid. l. 10 from foot. For 'Early in 1763' read 'On 14 May 1763 (*ibid.* p. 251)'

Barrow, Isaac (1630–1677). i. 1220*a*, l. 25 from foot. For 'Dr. Dupont' read 'Dr. James Duport [q.v.].'

Ibid. p. 1220*b*, last line. For 'Dr. Williams' read 'Dr. John Wilkins [q.v.].'

Ibid. p. 1221*a*, l. 3. After 'absence abroad' add 'He was one of the Original Fellows of the Royal Society, having been admitted on 29 October 1662 (BULLETIN, xiv (1937). 84).'

Ibid. l. 12. For 'Williams' read 'Wilkins.'

Ibid. p. 1221*b*, ll. 25–35. For 'Dr. Whewell's . . . long in coming' read 'In 1670 Charles appointed Barrow a chaplain in ordinary (P.R.O., L.C. 3/25, p. 76; lists in E. Chamberlayne, *Angliæ Notitia*).'

Ibid. p. 1222*a*, l. 16 from foot. For 'Dupont' read 'Duport.'

Barry, or Barrey, Lodowick (17th cent.), i. 1246*a*, ll. 33–6. For 'or Barrey . . . Lord Barry,' read 'Lording (1580–1629), poet and pirate'.

***Ibid.*, l. 6 from foot to 1246*b*, l. 5. For 'Barry, concerning . . . have been kept' read 'Barry was a younger son of Nicholas Barry, fishmonger, of St. Laurence, Pountney, where he was baptized on 17 April 1580. He became part-owner of a theatre at the Whitefriars, Fleet Street, was imprisoned for debt, and escaped to Ireland. As Lodowicke Barry of Cork he was tried for piracy, but being acquitted, spent some years as a pirate in the Mediterranean. He joined Raleigh's last expedition in 1617, afterwards returning to trade out of London, where he died in 1629.'**

To list of authorities add: C. L'Estrange Ewen, 'Lording Barry, poet and pirate (1938)'.

Bartholomew Anglicus de Glanville. 22*a*, l. 13 from foot. After '168–89)' add ', and J. W. Draper's "Jacques *Seven Ages* and Bartolomaeus Anglicus" (*Modern Language Notes*, liv (1939), 273–6).'

Barton, Edward. i. 1262*b*, ll. 24–5. For 'He succeeded . . . in 1590' read 'On the return of William Harborne [q.v.] to England in 1588 he became agent and was given the rank of ambassador in 1591 (*Cal. State Papers, Venetian*, 1581–1591, p. 536).'

Barton, Edward. i. 1262*b*–1263*a*. This article should be re-written as follows:

Barton, Edward (*c.* 1563–*c.* 1598), second English ambassador to Turkey, after some education at a grammar school, went to the Levant as early as 1582 (I. I. Podea, in *Mélanges d'histoire générale*, vol. ii, Cluj (Klausenburg), 1938, p. 426); he is first mentioned by name in June 1584, when William Harborne [q.v., and BULLETIN, below, p. 160], the English ambassador in Turkey, sent him to Tripoli, Tunis, and Algiers, to establish direct contact with the beglerbeys of the three provinces. Harborne again sent him to Tripoli in 1585 to ensure the release of the ship *Jesus* and her company (Hakluyt, *Principal navigations*, edn. 1903–5, v. 274–5, 316–7). He was by this time Harborne's secretary; and the latter, when applying in 1584 for his recall, proposed that Barton, although rather young for the position, should succeed him with the inferior status of agent; Barton's knowledge of Turkish was an important qualification (*Cal. S.P., For.*, 1584–5, p. 168). He also knew Latin (Podea, p. 426) and presumably Italian and French; and some Greek (*The travels of John Sanderson in the Levant, 1584–1602*, ed. Sir William Foster, Hakluyt Soc., 2nd ser., vol. 67, 1931, p. 126).

When Harborne left Constantinople in August 1588 Barton succeeded him with the rank of agent. Like Harborne he urged the Turks to set out a naval expedition against Spain, a task the more difficult because, until news of the defeat of the Spanish Armada reached Constantinople, he could rely only on his confidence of victory to dispel the general belief among the Turks that England was doomed. No Turkish fleet ever sailed, but early in 1590 and again in autumn 1592 Barton prevented the opening of negotiations between Spain and Turkey for a truce. In this policy he was also forwarding the interests of Henri IV, for whom he acted as agent until Henri IV's own envoy de Brèves had been installed (autumn 1592); Henri III's ambassador, after the latter's assassination, having become a partisan of the League.

The Turkish war against Persia, which the Turks had used as an excuse for their inactivity against Spain, terminated in 1590. Barton wanted them to remain free from other engagements so as to be able to attack Spain; when in the same year war threatened to break out between them and Poland he successfully mediated an agreement (June). Another of his aims was to check the growth of Hapsburg and Roman catholic influence in eastern Europe; accordingly in 1591, when it appeared likely that the Polish throne would become vacant, he used his influence at the Porte on behalf of Sigismund Bathory of Transylvania in opposition to a Hapsburg candidate; and in the same year, in association with the patriarch of Constantinople, procured the voivodeship of Moldavia for Aaron, who promised to defend the protestants there against Jesuit encroachments. He engaged himself financially on Aaron's behalf; when in July 1592 the latter had to leave Moldavia for a time the Venetian ambassador expected that Barton would lose all his influence; apart from his difficulties in Constantinople, he had by his political activities alienated some members of the Levant company, who believed that he was neglecting their interests; he had however been named a member of the company in the patent granted on 7 January 1592. He was probably raised to the rank of ambassador in that year, but the queen's present to the sultan, a requisite for the recognition of his new status, and for the prolongation of the English capitulation, did not arrive until October 1593.

Relations between Turkey and the emperor had become strained in 1591 and Barton and de Brèves in association had encouraged the sultan to take up arms; but in July 1593, as Elizabeth had offered her mediation to the emperor, Barton was instructed to reverse his policy; although the offer of mediation was declined he was obliged to dissociate himself from de Brèves, who however after the abjuration of Henri IV (July 1593) also changed his policy. When Mehmed III succeeded as sultan in January 1595 Barton retained his influence despite Elizabeth's failure to send the present customary on the accession of a new sultan. In 1596, when Mehmed went with his army to Hungary, Barton accompanied him and was thus present at the capture of Erlau (Eger, Agria) and the battle of Keresztes. Not only did he have no share in the fighting, but he took with him, and ultimately despatched to the imperialists' camp, twenty-three members of the former imperial embassy, who had been in prison since 1593; he also sent his interpreter (Bruti) to Prague to offer his mediation; besides further attempts at mediation in 1597 he also tried to reconcile to the Porte Sigismund of Transylvania and the voivodes of Wallachia and Moldavia, all of whom he had formerly befriended, and who had since joined the emperor. These attempts failed; on the other hand his recommendation contributed to the appointment in 1597 of his friend Meletius, patriarch of Alexandria, as patriarch of Constantinople. He died of dysentery in either December 1597 or, more probably, January 1598; he was buried on Halki, one of the Princes' Islands, where his tombstone is still preserved; about three hundred persons attended his funeral from his house to the waterside (Sanderson, pp. 15, 174). According to old readings of his epitaph, which is now partly defaced, he was in his thirty-fifth year. He left a sister Mrs. Mary Lough and a kinsman Robert Barton.

Barton defended his anti-Spanish policy: he thought it 'nothing offensive to God to set one of his enemies against the other, the Infidel against the Idolaters to the end that whilst they were by the ears, God's people might respite, and take strenght' (Podea, *op. cit.*, p. 432, quoting a despatch of Barton's); 'he protested to abhorr from furthering the Turkes designes against any the greatest enemy of his profession and Country, further then to diuert them for the tyme from some malicious attempt' (F. Moryson, *Shakespeare's Europe*, ed. Hughes, pp. 30–1).

Distance from home obliged him to act on his own initiative and he was occasionally reprimanded. He made such use as he could of the influence of the seraglio and of bribery; Turkish guests were frequently made drunk; these courses were common at this time. On one occasion he forged a letter (*Cal. S.P., Venice*, 1592–1603, introd., p. xxxiii *n.*). His household was ill-conducted. In 1594 he was obliged to leave the house called Rapamat (BULLETIN, xix., 130) and to move to the Christian quarter in Pera, where he and his people could give less offence to the Moslems; the removal also made it more difficult to transfer escaped prisoners to Christian ships. The Venetian ambassadors speak of him as a rule very unfavourably; and he alienated the French by offering the protection of the English banner to other foreign traders who were not protected by capitulations of their own, an offer especially acceptable to the Dutch as protestants, but regarded by the French as an infringement of a privilege of long standing. On the other hand Moryson (to whom he showed great kindness) describes him as 'a man of good life and constant in the profession of the reformed religion'; he tried to establish a protestant (Calvinist) church in Constantinople (*Le relazioni degli ambasciatori veneti . . . secolo XVI*, ed. E. Albèri, 3rd ser., iii. 405); Meletius the patriarch was strongly attached to him (S. Purchas, *Hakluytus posthumus*, edn. 1905–7, viii. 483–5; G. Dousa (van der Does), *De itinere suo Constantinopolitano*, 1600, pp. 115–6). John Sanderson and William Biddulph (in Purchas, viii. 259) both testify to the esteem in which he was held; Moryson explains some of the causes of his success: 'He was courteous and affable, of a good stature, corpulent, faire Complexion and a free chearefull Countenance, which last, made him acceptable to the Turkes, as likewise his person . . . but especially his skill in their language made him respected of them, so as I thinck no Christian euer had greater power with any Emperor of Turkye or the officers of his state, and Court, then he had in his tyme.'

[Authorities: Barton's despatches are preserved in the Public Record Office and in the British Museum (Cottonian MSS.). His career until 1593 is admirably treated by I. I. Podea, 'A contribution to the study of Queen Elizabeth's eastern policy (1590–1593),' in Mélanges d'histoire générale, vol. ii, Cluj (Klausenburg), 1938. Diplomatic material in the Calendars of State Papers; Bronnen tot de geschiedenis van den Levantschen handel, ed. K. Heeringa, vol. i. (Rijks geschiedkundige publicatiën, vol. 9); E. Pears, 'The Spanish Armada and the Ottoman Porte,' in Eng. Hist. Rev., viii. (1893), 439–66; documents in H. G. Rosedale, Queen Elizabeth and the Levant Company (text unreliable); Documente privitóre la Istoria Românilor, ed. E. de Hurmuzaki, 1876– , xii. 329, and vol. iii; etc. Further material in Hakluyt; Purchas (especially viii. 304–20, account of the campaign of 1596); Moryson, Shakespeare's Europe, pp. 27–31; Sanderson; Hist. MSS. Comm., especially Salisbury MSS., etc.; G. Dousa (van der Does), De itinere suo Constantinopolitano, 1600, and two letters in Illustrium & clarorum virorum epistolae, ed. S. A. Gabbema, 1669, pp. 343–6. Secondary works include, besides A. C. Wood, A history of the Levant Company, and the histories of the Ottoman empire by Hammer, Zinkeisen, and Jorga, an article on English relation with the Danubian principalities by N. Jorga in Mélanges d'histoire offerts à M. Charles Bémont, 1913. Photographs of Barton's tombstone are given in Ahmet Refik, Türkler ve Kraliçe Elizabet, 1932; all published versions of the epitaph, which is in any case incorrect, are inaccurate; the arms appear to be those of Barton of Smithills, Lancs., or those of Barton of Kent. I am indebted for help and information to Dr. Paul Wittek.]

E. S. DE BEER.

Bastard, John Pollexfen. i. 1307*b*, ll. 19–20. Delete ', as colonel of the East Devonshire militia,'

Ibid. ll. 27–8. For 'to the colonelcy . . . militia' read 'on 1 Aug. 1783 he was appointed lieutenant-colonel of the East Devonshire militia, succeeding to the colonelcy on 8 Nov. 1798 (Col. H. Walrond, *Hist. Records of the 1st Devon Militia*, p. 410; *Militia List*, 1795, p. 58; *ibid.* 1800, p. 84)

Ibid. l. 21 from foot. After 'domestic measures.' insert 'On 22 Aug. 1803, he was appointed colonel-in-chief of the south Devonshire volunteers (*Yeomanry and Volunteers List*, 1804, p. 156).'

Bate, George. i. 1310*a*, 2 ll. from foot. After 'New College, Oxford' insert 'matriculating on 20 February 1623/4, at the age of fifteen' (Foster, *Alumni Oxonienses*, 1500–1714, i. 84).

Ibid. 1310*b*, 2 ll. from end of article. For 'and was buried' etc. read 'he died 19 April 1668 and was buried beside his wife, Elizabeth, at Kingston-on-Thames' (B.M. Add. MS. 36916, f. 93; *Cal. S.P., Dom.*, 1667–8, p. 395; the date was read incorrectly by Munk, *Coll. of Physicians*, i. 228, but is given correctly by E. W. Brayley, *Hist. of Surrey*, iii. 38).

E. S. DE B.

Batten, Sir William. i. 1338–40 and BULLETIN, iv. 183. Batten's resignation on 27 September 1647 was possibly a result of his conduct towards Holles and five of the other fugitive members of parliament. He gives an account of it in 'The True Relation of Capt: Will: Batten: Admirall of the Fleet now at Sea, in the Service of the King, Parliament, and Kingdome. Touching The manner of the transportation of the Six Members,' 1647 (26 August; copy in Bodleian Library; see also Gardiner, *History of the Great Civil War*, iii. 349. For further evidence of Batten's attachment to the Presbyterians at this time see *ibid.*, p. 360).

Batten, Sir William. i. 1338*b*. This article needs revision and expansion. See Sir Charles Firth in *The Mariner's Mirror*, xii. 240–42.

Batty, Robert (d. 1848) i. 1342*b*, l. 22. Delete 'first for' and after 'army' add 'as ensign in the 1st foot guards on 14 January 1813 (*Army List*, 1814, p. 130)'. l. 27. After 'Waterloo' add 'where he was wounded in the thigh by a shell whilst in the square. He was promoted lieutenant and captain on 29 June 1815 (*Army List*, 1816, p. 184) and lieutenant-colonel unattached on 30 Dec. 1828 (*ibid.* 1829, p. 41). He retired on 1 Nov. 1839, (*ibid.* Dec. 1839, p. 78)'. l. 17 from foot. After '1832' add 'He married, 1821, Johanna Maria, eldest daughter of Sir John Barrow, 1st bart. of Ulverstone, Lancs. (Burke's *Peerage, etc.*) He was elected a F.R.S. on 28 Feb. 1822, (A. B. Granville, *The Royal Society*, (1836), p. 244)'. l. 16 from foot. After '1848' add 'aged 59 (*Annual register*, 1848, p. 264)'.

Beale, John. ii. 2*b*, ll. 1–2. For 'the 21st of the same month' read '19 Aug. 1663 (BULLETIN, xv. 92)'

Beaufort, Sir Thomas, Duke of Exeter. ii. 49*b*. See *Notes and Queries*, 13th Ser., i. 286–7, for extracts from Lynn Corporation Records relative to Beaufort in 1423 (cf. *Hist. MSS. Comm.* 11th Report, App. iii. 160).

Beaulieu, Luke de (*d.* 1723) ii. 52, ll. 30–33. Delete '4. "The Infernal Observator, or the Quickening Dead", 8vo, London, 1684 . . . French'. Luke de Boileau or Beaulieu had nothing to do with the *Infernal Observator*: the work is a translation of the second part of Fontenelle's *Nouveaux Dialogues des Morts* (première partie, 1683; seconde partie, 1684), of which the real translator was Alexander Fraser, nephew of the earl of Plymouth (1627?–87). See D. M. Lang, 'Fontenelle and the "Infernal Observator",' *Modern Language Review*, xlv, no. 2 (April, 1950), pp. 222–225.

Bedingfield, Sir Thomas. (1593?–1661). ii. 115*b*. Probably the Thomas Bedingfield, jun., esq., who was returned as member for Dunwich Borough (Suffolk) 18 December, 1620, and also for the parliament of 1625–6 (*Return of Members of Parliament*, i. 453, 471).

Bedloe, William. ii. 116*b*, l. 30. After 'Chepstow' insert '(This date of birth is from the "Life of Captain William Bedloe," 1681. Ashmole's horoscope gives the date as 20 June 1651, Bodleian Library, MS. Ashmole 436, f. 112 v.).'

E. S. DE B.

***Belasyse or Bellasis, John, Baron Belasyse** (*b.* 24 June 1615, *d.* 10 Sept. 1689). ii. 142. The article is past mending. 'A briefe relation of the Life and Memoires of John, Lord Belasyse, written and collected by his secretary, Joshua Moone,' was printed in 1903 in the *Calendar of the MSS. of the Marquess of Ormonde*, New Series, ii. 376–99. It deals mainly with the Civil War. Belasyse was M.P. for Thirsk in both the parliaments of 1640. He raised a regiment of foot and joined the king at Nottingham. He fought at Edgehill, Brentford, the siege of Reading, the storming of Bristol (where he was dangerously wounded), and the first battle of Newbury. Newcastle made him governor of York and commander-in-chief in Yorkshire when he marched against the Scots (February 1644), but he was defeated and taken prisoner on 11 April 1644 by the

Fairfaxes, and confined for ten months in the Tower (*cf.* Rushworth, v. 616). Exchanged, he fought as a volunteer at Naseby, was made commander of the King's horse-guards when the Earl of Lichfield was killed at Rowton, and governor of Newark in place of Sir Richard Willis (October 1645; Walker, *Historical Discourses*, p. 146). He surrendered Newark by the king's orders on 6 May 1646 (Rushworth, vi. 269). Then he went to France, was at the siege of Mardyke with Condé, and thought of entering the service of Venice. Recalled by the king to take part in the second Civil War, for which he returned too late, he was several times arrested and twice imprisoned in the Tower. At the Restoration he was made governor of Hull (1660), and later, colonel of a regiment of foot (January 1673–February 1674). On 4 Jan. 1665 he was appointed governor of Tangier, and was there from April 1665 to April 1666 (Davis, *History of the 2nd Queen's Regiment*, pp. 78–83; E. Routh, *Tangiers*, p. 81; Dalton, *English Army Lists*, i. 13, 134). In October 1678 he (with four other Roman Catholic peers) was arrested on the charge of high treason; it was alleged that he was not merely concerned in the Popish Plot, but designed to be general of the Popish army. On this charge he was confined in the Tower till February 1684, when he was released on bail (*State Trials*, vii. 1235, 1244, 1569; Luttrell, *Diary*, i. 300).

James II made him a privy councillor (17 July 1686), and first lord of the treasury (4 Jan. 1687). He disapproved, however, of the provocative religious policy of James, and feared its results (Ailesbury, *Memoirs*, i. 126, 148). For details as to his marriages etc., see G.E.C., *Complete Peerage*, ed. Gibbs, i. 89.

***Belasyse or Bellasis, Thomas, Earl Fauconberg.** ii. 142. He was the son of Henry Bellasis by his marriage with Grace, daughter of Sir Thomas Barton, and was baptised 16 March 1627–8 (G. E. C., *Complete Peerage*, ed. Gibbs, v. 264). It is probable that he was educated at Trinity College, Cambridge (*Frankland-Russell-Astley MSS.*, p. 51). His father died in 1647. By the death of his grandfather, Thomas Bellasis (created Baron Fauconberg of Yarm, 25 May 1627, and Viscount Fauconberg of Henknowle, 31 Jan. 1643), he succeeded to the titles on 18 April 1653. He married on 3 July 1651 Mildred, daughter of Nicholas, second Viscount Castleton, and she died 8 May 1656.

Fauconberg was not long a widower. On 18 Nov. 1657 he married at Whitehall, Mary Cromwell, third daughter of the Protector. Her dowry, like that of her sister Frances, was £15,000 (*Wombwell MSS.*, p. 115). Probably Sir William Lockhart had a hand in making the match. He wrote to secretary Thurloe, 21 March 1657, characterising Fauconberg as 'a person of extraordinary parts, and hath (appearingly) all those qualities in a high measure, that can fit one for his Highness and Country's service, for both which he owns a particular zeal' (Thurloe, vi. 134). The Protector was disposed to give him opportunities of serving both. Fauconberg was summoned to the Protector's House of Lords (10 Dec. 1657) and was appointed colonel of the regiment of horse lately commanded by Major-Gen. Lambert (*Clarke Papers*, iii. 132). In May 1658 he was sent on a complimentary mission to Louis XIV, and acquitted himself creditably (Thurloe, vii. 151, 158; Guizot, *Cromwell and the English Republic*, ii. 385, 591).

One of the results of Fauconberg's marriage was a friendship with Henry Cromwell, to whom he wrote a series of confidential letters relating the movement in the Army which followed Oliver's death and led finally to the overthrow of Richard. These letters, ten in number, are printed in the *Thurloe Papers* (vol. vii. 365). Fauconberg was all for strong action on the part of the young Protector, but thought that he was hampered by the irresolution of his council, and he warned Henry Cromwell not to leave Ireland. Richard's government fell at the end of April, and Fauconberg was at once deprived of the command of his regiment. He was an object of great suspicion to both the restored Long Parliament and the Army, and on 13 September 1659 he was arrested and sent to the Tower, but released next month on giving bail for £10,000 (*Cal. State Papers, Dom.*, 1659–60, pp. 191, 245). Fauconberg's uncle, Lord Bellasis, had confidently reported his conversion to the king's cause, but he seems to have been too careful to commit himself by any overt action (*Clarendon State Papers*, iii. 500, 506, 528, 544, 609, 676, 698), and Hyde was in doubt as to his real attitude. But he privately sent Charles II a thousand pieces of gold through Dr. Tobias Wickham (*MSS. of Marquess of Ormond*, N.S., ii. 397). In January 1660, when Monck marched into England, Fauconberg joined Fairfax and the Yorkshire gentlemen in occupying York and declaring not merely for the restoration of the old Parliament, but for the election of a new one (*MSS. of Mr. Leyborne-Popham*, p. 147). On 23 April 1660 Monck appointed him colonel of the regiment of horse lately commanded by Sir Arthur Heselrige, and he continued to command a regiment till the Army was disbanded (*Wombwell MSS.*, p. 115; *Clarke MSS.*).

At the Restoration Fauconberg was made Lord-Lieutenant of the North Riding of Yorkshire, and held that post till he was dismissed by James II in 1687. He showed himself active in suppressing plotters and Quakers, and also in raising militia during the Dutch War. In 1665 he had a quarrel with the Duke of Buckingham, who sent him a challenge, but when they met the Duke showed 'more mind to parley than to fight' and contented himself with 'some verbal and superficial satisfaction' (Reresby, *Diary*, pp. 67–9). By the interest of Lord Arlington Fauconberg was appointed ambassador extraordinary to Savoy, Florence and Venice, (2 Jan. 1670), and drew up on his return a report of his observations on the states to which he was sent in the style of one of the relations the Venetian ambassadors were wont to compose (*Wombwell MSS.*, pp. 130–61, 205–26). After his return he was made a privy councillor (17 April 1672) and Captain of the Gentlemen Pensioners (1672–6). For a time he associated himself with the opposition in the House of Lords, but moderately and discreetly (Christie, *Shaftesbury*, ii. 200, 207; Foxcroft, *Life of Halifax*, i. 66). He was one of the members of the new Privy Council established by Charles II (22 April 1679), in pursuance of Sir William Temple's scheme. It seems clear that he voted against the Exclusion Bill. Nevertheless, as he opposed the removal of the Penal Laws against the Catholics, James II removed him from his Lord-Lieutenancy (November 1687). He was restored to it by William III, became a member of that king's Privy Council, and was created by him Earl Fauconberg on 9 April 1689. During the latter part of his life he lived mostly at Sutton House, Chiswick, where he died on 31 Dec. 1700.

Fauconberg's abilities qualified him to play a more considerable part in politics than he did, but from 1682 or earlier he was hampered by the weakness of his eyes, and he declared himself, like Sir William Temple, 'a better gardener than statesman' (*Russell-Astley MSS.*, pp. 49, 62, 89). His widow died 14 March 1712–13 (Le Neve, *Monumenta*, 1717, p. 2). A painting of her by Jansen and a miniature by Cooper are reproduced in Gardiner's *Oliver Cromwell*, 1889, ed. Goupil.

Bell, Sir Charles. ii. 156*a*, ll. 27–9. Omit 'and . . . board.' These words refer to events which happened after Bell's resignation, and then happened to another institution.

Bell, James. (*fl.* 1551–1596). ii. 164*a*, l. 47. After '*Royal*, 17' add 'C. xxix.'

Benet, William. ii. 218*b*, l. 18 from foot. For '(*d.* 1533)' read '(1492?–1533).' *Ibid.*, ll. 11–9 from foot. The statement that Benet was canon of Leighlin does not appear in the authorities for the article and is probably incorrect. He is described as LL.D. in 1523 (*The registers of Thomas Wolsey, bishop of Bath and Wells*, etc. (Somerset Record Society, vol. 55, 1940), p. 76).

Ibid., p. 219*b*, l. 33. To authorities add: Notes and Queries, clxxxv. 166.

Bentham, Jeremy. ii. 274 *b*, ll. 22–21 and 13–12 from foot. For 'Not Paul but Christ' read 'Not Paul but Jesus' (*cf.* p. 280 *a*, l. 21 from foot).

Bentley, Richard (1662–1742). ii. 309*a*, l. 9 from foot. For 'was also' read 'in 1695 was.'

Ibid. l. 8 from foot. For '1695' read 'the latter year' (*Record of Royal Soc.*, p. 320).

Berkeley, John first Baron Berkeley of Stratton. ii. 361*a*, l. 4 from foot. For 'Sir Henry Killigrew' read 'Sir William Killigrew (J. L. Vivian, *Visitations of Cornwall*, pp. 268, 270).'

361*b*, ll. 2–5. There appears to have been only a very distant connexion and no actual relationship between Roe and Berkeley.

Ibid. ll. 8–9. For 'In July . . . year' read 'On 27 July 1639 (W. A. Shaw, *Knights of England*).'

Ibid. l. 12. For 'parliament' read 'the Short parliament.'

Ibid. ll. 21–33. For 'In 1642 . . . before Exeter' read 'In August 1642 he joined Hertford at Sherborne. In September, when Hertford retired to Wales, he accompanied Hopton to Cornwall as commissary-general (Clarendon, ix. 246). He served there with distinction and was one of the four officers commissioned by the king for the joint command of the forces of the six western counties in Hertford's absence (Hopton's narratives, *Bellum Civile*, ed. C. E. Chadwyck Healey, pp. 11, 18, 23 : Somerset Record Society, 1902. See *ante* iii. 192, *s.v.* Hopton). He was present at Stratton on 16 May 1643 and accompanied Hopton to Chard, where Hopton met prince Maurice on 4 June. He took part in the skirmish with Waller at Chewton Mendip on 12 June, and was soon after dispatched to take command of the siege of Exeter (*Bellum Civile*, pp. 33, 43, 49, 50 ; the siege of Exeter had already begun, *Mercurius Aulicus*, 1 June, p. 290).'

Ibid. ll. 28–29. There was no 'pursuit' after Stratton ; and Stamford retreated to Exeter, not Wells.

Ibid. l. 22 from foot. After 'surrender' add '(Good notices of the siege are given in *Mercurius Aulicus*).'

Ibid. ll. 22–16 from foot. For 'In 1644 . . . on 29 March' read 'In November Berkeley brought reinforcements to Hopton, then engaged in relieving Basing House, and stayed with him until about 6 December ; he then went to Oxford, and so to the west (*Bellum Civile*, pp. 67, 69). On 21 July 1644 he was present at the baptism of Henrietta Anne [q.v.] in Exeter Cathedral.' He was not present at Alresford.

Ibid. ll. 16–6 from foot. For Berkeley's superseding Grenville see under Grenville, Sir Richard (1600–58). While reconnoitring Wellington house Grenville was wounded, and Berkeley was persuaded by Capel and Culpeper to take his place for the time being. He captured Wellington house but was unable to prevent the relief of Taunton on 11 May. Grenville's hostility greatly hindered him. He took Grenville's place before Plymouth in June and gave up the command to Sir John Digby in September, his presence being necessary at Exeter (Clarendon, ix. 15, 56, 93 ; Grenville's narrative printed in T. Carte, *Original Letters*, i. 96–109). The date of his commission as colonel-general for the counties of Devon and Cornwall is not clear, but apparently late in May (*Cal. S. P., Dom.* 1644–45, p. 480). Fairfax advanced westward in the autumn and began the siege of Exeter about 21 October. He was forced to remove most of his forces on 8 January 1646, but returned on 27 January. On 9 February he advanced into Cornwall, leaving Sir Hardress Waller to blockade the city. After making his treaty with Hopton he again returned and summoned the city on 31 March. Berkeley surrendered on honourable terms on 9 April (J. Sprigge, *Anglia Rediviva*, 1854, pp. 158–243 ; the terms, pp. 244–9).

Ibid. l. 5 from foot. For 'kinsman' read 'first cousin.'

Ibid. last line to 362*a*, l. 33. For 'Having persuaded . . . to retire to Paris' read 'About June 1647 the queen sent Berkeley to England to negotiate an agreement between the king and the army. At the same time Cromwell, who had perhaps heard of Berkeley's opinion that the independents were more suited than the presbyterians to restore both "king and people to their just and ancient rights" (expressed in conversation with Lambert at the time of the surrender of Exeter), wrote to him, desiring him to act as an intermediary with the queen ; this letter he received on his arrival in England (Berkeley's *Memoirs*, 1699, pp. 6–10). He saw Charles at Reading about the second week in July, and urged him to keep on good terms with the officers of the army. Berkeley evidently understood the situation, but Charles, who was intriguing with the presbyterians, neither confided in him nor followed his advice (*ibid.*, pp. 17, 18). He received no help from John Ashburnham [q.v.], who encouraged Charles in his own views (*ibid.*, p. 32). He was permitted to make some modifications in the "Heads of the Proposals" (*ibid.*, p. 23) and pressed Charles to accept them, but in vain. Charles' conduct, when they were offered to him, rendered any further desire to serve him ineffectual (*ibid.*, pp. 30–35) ; until too late, he could not even be persuaded to write a letter showing any goodwill towards the leaders of the army (*ibid.*, pp. 38–9). After the surrender of London (3 August) nothing further could be done (a full account of these transactions is given by S. R. Gardiner, *Great Civil War*, iii. 317–43).

'Berkeley accompanied the king on his flight from Hampton Court on 11 November; he evidently desired him to leave England (*Memoirs*, pp. 47, 49, 51), but had no influence on his movements. Charles sent Berkeley and Ashburnham forward to Carisbrooke to negotiate with colonel Robert Hammond [q.v.] his coming to the isle of Wight. Berkeley unwisely intimated to Hammond that Charles was in the neighbourhood, but was not satisfied with Hammond's vague engagement about his treatment (*ibid.*, pp. 57, 59; John Ashburnham, *Narrative*, ii. 113, 115). Ashburnham, and not Berkeley, was responsible for bringing Hammond to Titchfield (Ashburnham, ii. 116; Berkeley, p. 62).

'About the end of November Berkeley was sent by Charles to Fairfax and Cromwell, but without success. He returned to Charles, who refused to follow his advice and escape from England until he had come to terms with the Scottish commissioners; but escape then proved impossible (Berkeley, pp. 66–91; Gardiner, iv. 33–35, 48). Berkeley, with Ashburnham and Legge, was dismissed from attending the king on 29 December, after Charles had rejected the four bills; he stayed for a short time in England, but was in France by 29 March 1648 (*Cal. Clarendon State Papers*, i. 417).'

562*a*, l. 13 from foot to 562*b*, l. 15. For 'Meanwhile Berkeley . . . 19 May 1658' read 'By joining Jermyn and the queen Berkeley made a quarrel with his old friend Hyde inevitable. His attitude towards the king's negotiation with the Scots at Breda in 1650 led to differences which were increased by his alternate expressions of contempt for the council and attempts to become a member of it. Eventually Berkeley tried to obtain the mastership of the court of wards, but Hyde advised Charles not to grant it (Clarendon, xiii. 122; the date must be winter 1651; Berkeley was said to have a patent for the office in April 1651, *Nicholas Papers*, i. 233; he alleged a promise of Charles I, *The King's Cabinet Opened*, 1645, p. 3). At the same time Berkeley was courting Anne Douglas, countess of Morton, who had been governess of Henrietta Anne from her birth at Exeter; Hyde was an intimate friend of Lady Morton and, if he did not actually advise her to refuse Berkeley, at any rate showed strong disapproval of his conduct (J. S. Clarke, *Life of James II*, i. 273; Hyde's letters to Lady Morton in *Cal. Clarendon State Papers*, ii.).

'In 1652, in order to gain ground with the duke of York, Berkeley encouraged him in his desire to attend the French campaigns (Clarke, i. 54). Berkeley apparently accompanied James. His position was strengthened by Byron's death and by the entrance into James' service of his nephew Charles Berkeley (later earl of Falmouth; see under BERKELEY, FAMILY OF) and of the younger Henry Jermyn [q.v.]. Berkeley took part in Grenville's charge against Hyde in January 1654. He shared in Jermyn's intrigues and influenced James against Hyde and his friends; Cromwell saw in him the subject for a quarrel between Charles and James (*Thurloe State Papers*, v. 736). When James left France for Bruges in September 1656 he insisted, against his brother's wishes, on bringing Berkeley with him. In January 1657 Charles dismissed Berkeley; James thereupon ran away with him to the United Provinces and the scandal compelled Charles to reinstate him (*Cal. Clarendon State Papers*, iii. 223–7, 237, 307; Clarke, i. 276–93). Berkeley followed James into the Spanish service. On 19 May 1658, at James' request, he was created Baron Berkeley of Stratton. (In general for the above paragraphs see Clarendon's *History*; *Cal. Clarendon State Papers*, ii. and iii.; Clarke's *Life of James II*; and *Nicholas Papers*, i. and ii.).'

363*b*, ll. 13–21. The discrepancies between Berkeley's and Ashburnham's narratives are not of much historical importance. Berkeley is probably more reliable than Ashburnham, and is preferred by Gardiner (*Great Civil War*, iv. 13 *note*, 49 *note*). The writer of the article has not paid proper attention to Berkeley's character, which deteriorated after about 1650, and has overlooked (363*b*, ll. 1–4) the change in Clarendon's attitude towards him in the portions of the 'History' written in 1646–7 and in those written after 1667; in 1646 Hyde had asked Berkeley to furnish materials for the 'History' (*Cal. Clarendon State Papers*, i. 328). Berkeley does not appear to have exaggerated his actions in the 'Memoirs,' and where he censures Ashburnham the latter frequently admits his responsibility for an act.

Ibid. l. 21. After 'narrative,' add 'The "Memoirs" were composed by 1651 ("Sir John Berkeley's relation of that unhappy business of the king's going to the Isle of Wight," Nicholas to Hatton, 2 April 1651, *Nicholas Papers*, i. 233. In June 1657 Colonel Bamfield writes that Berkeley has "recanted a narration, that he had written of the transactions between the late King and the Army, wherein were some undecent reflections," *Thurloe State Papers*, vi. 363). They were read by Clarendon (*History*, x. 134) and closely followed by R. Menteith [q.v.] (*Histoire des troubles de la Grande Bretagne*, 2nd Part, 1661) and independently by Ludlow (*Memoirs*, 1698; see edition by C. H. Firth, 1894, i. 153 *note* 2).'

Ibid. l. 19 from foot. After 'Paris, 1827' add 'They have since been reprinted by Mr. Allan Fea in "Memoirs of the Martyr King," 1905.'

E. S. DE B.

Berkenhout, John. ii. 369*b*, l. 3. For 'where he took his degree of doctor of physic' read 'being entered on the register'

Ibid. l. 5. After '*Students*),' read 'and took the degree of doctor of physic on 25 May following (P. C. Molhuysen, *Bronnen tot de Geschiedenis der Leidsche Universiteit*, vi. 72).'

Ibid. 370*a*, ll. 30–1. For 'revised' read 'fourth'; after 'Admirals' insert 'continuing Campbell's own narrative from 1727 to 1778'

Bernher, Augustine (*fl.* 1554). ii. 393*a*, l. 20. For 'In the reign of Elizabeth he was rector of Sutton (*Memorials*, i. 589), or, according to Tanner, of Southam,' read 'He *may* have been rector of one of the forty parishes of "Sutton"; he *was* rector of Southam, from which place he dated his preface to Latimer's Sermons in 1562.' l. 30. Delete 'He . . . edited Latimer's sermons with a Latin preface addressed to Catherine, duchess of Suffolk, 1572, 1635. and Latimer's Works (Parker Society, i. 311)'. For on 19 April 1566 Bartholomew Greene was instituted to the rectory of Southam 'vacant by the death of Augustine Barnehere' (Dugdale, *Antiq. of Warws.* (ed. 1730), p. 339).

Berry, James. ii. 397*b*. On the formation of the New Model, Berry became a captain in Fairfax's regiment of horse, and in 1647 major to Colonel Philip Twisleton. In June 1651 he was appointed colonel of the regiment of horse lately Sir A. Haselrig's; retained its command throughout the Protectorate, and was confirmed in it by the Long Parliament in June 1659. He was cashiered by Parliament on 12 October 1659, and on 11 Jan. 1660 Major Unton Croke was appointed in his place (*Commons' Journals*, vii. 669, 679, 807; *Clarke Papers*, iv. 93, 210, 216). He survived the Restoration for about thirty years. Charles Fleetwood left by his will, dated 10 Jan. 1690, six pounds 'to my antient friend James Berry' (Waylen, *House of Cromwell*, ed. 1880, p. 69).

The officer who fought at Newton Butler was Lieut.-Col. William Berry (Harris, *Life of William III.* p. 220).

Berry's character is probably best revealed by the letters printed in Thurloe's *State Papers* illustrating his activity as one of Cromwell's major-generals. See 'Cromwell's Major-Generals,' by D. W. Rannie, *E.H.R.* x. 471. He was no orator, and the statement that he was 'chosen president of the council of adjutators' seems incorrect, though he was active in concerting the opposition to the disbanding proposals of Parliament, and on many committees for drawing up papers on behalf of the officers (*Clarke Papers*, i. 45, 151, 415). Berry's activities, first in the movement against Richard Cromwell, and secondly in the movement headed by Lambert against the restored Long Parliament, are both brought out by the *Clarke Papers* (iv. 6, 57, 69, 299).

Bertie, Robert, first Earl of Lindsey. ii. 408*a*, l. 4 from foot. After 'sponsors.' insert 'He was admitted to Corpus Christi College, Cambridge, in 1594 (Venn, *Alumni Cantab.*, i. 143).'

Ibid. last line. Delete '(Oxford).'

Ibid. 408*b*, ll. 4–16. For 'He also displayed . . . in 1601,' read 'He travelled abroad with his tutor in 1598 and 1599, making Orleans his headquarters, and in the summer of 1599, accompanied by his brother Peregrine, made a tour in the west and south of France. He remained abroad continuously until 1601, when he was recalled to England by the death of his father (*Hist. MSS. Comm.*, Ancaster MSS., pp. xxviii–xxix, 341–50). He'

Ibid. ll. 23–4. For 'After his return to England' read 'On the death of the eighteenth Earl of Oxford in 1625' (*ibid.* p. xxx).

Ibid. last line. After 'already' insert 'he had attended the Earl of Nottingham in Spain in 1605, had obtained permission to raise levies for the king of Denmark in 1612, and' (*ibid.* pp. xxix and 353–4).

Beverley, Charles James. ii. 449*a*, ll. 5–6. Delete 'and in May 1821 he was elected . . . Society.'

Ibid. l. 27. After 'home' insert 'In May 1831 he was elected a fellow of the Royal Society' (*Record of Royal Soc.*, p. 391, where the name is mis-spelt 'Beverly').

Bigland, Ralph. ii. 483*b*, l. 12. After '(fol. 1791–2)' add 'The Lincolnshire Collection in the British Museum (Add. MS. 34141, f. 42) is also ascribed to him.'

Bignell, Henry. ii. 483*b*. This article is based entirely on Wood, who states that Bignell went with Sir John Danvers, the Regicide [*q.v.*], to the West Indies 'about 3 or 4 years before the Restoration of King Charles II.' Danvers, however, died at Chelsea in 1655. A singular document purporting to be signed by a Henry Bignell, dated 30 July 1664, is printed in *E. H. R.* xv. 761. Some additional references are given by J. Foster, *Alumni Oxonienses*, 1500–1714, i. 123.

Birch, John (1745?–1815). ii. 526*b*, ll. 26–25 from foot. Delete 'some years'; for 'army' read '2nd troop of horse grenadier guards from 12 Jan. 1770 (P.R.O., war office, succession book, 25/210, p. 27), retiring on 25 Apr. 1779 (*ibid.* 25/211, p. 71)'

Birrell, Augustine (1850–1933), Supp. 1931–40, p. 81*a*, l. 4. The essay on Falstaff attributed to Birrell is by George Heynes Radford, LL.B., M.P. 1906–17 (1851–1917) (*Obiter Dicta*, 1st & 2nd ser. (1910) p. 108, n. 1).

Blacklock, Thomas (1721–1791), ii. 591*a*, l. 19. Omit 'never published'. *Ib.*, l. 20. After 'blind' add 'published in *Poems by the late reverend Dr. Thomas Blacklock* (Edinburgh, 1793)'.

Bladen, Martin, ii. 616*b*. l. 17 from foot. After 'army' add 'as ensign in brigadier-general Thomas Fairfax's regiment, afterwards 5th foot on 12 Dec. 1697 (C. Dalton, *Engl. Army Lists*, iv, p. 175) and on 25 March 1705 he was made captain in Sir Chas. Hotham's newly raised regiment (*ibid.*, v, p. 192)'. ll. 14–13 from foot. Delete 'and rising to the rank of lieutenant-colonel' and add 'On 26 Oct. 1709 he was appointed colonel of a regiment of foot raised in Portugal and on 25 June 1710 he sold the colonelcy retiring from the army (Millan, *Succession of Colonels*, (1742), p. 24)'.

Blake, Robert. ii. 632*b*. This article needs revision and expansion. See Sir Charles Firth in *The Mariner's Mirror*, xii. 244–53.

Blakeney, Sir Edward. ii. 648*a*, l. 7. For 'and entered the army . . . light dragoons' read 'and entered the navy as a volunteer on 17 April 1793, serving as a seaman to 16 August, and afterwards as midshipman to 27 June 1794 (P.R.O., Admiralty Musters, H.M.S. Kingfisher, Ad. 36/13422, 13423; Admiralty Minutes, Admiralty Board, Ad. 3/113, 20 June 1794). He had been appointed a cornet in the 8th light dragoons on 28 Feb. 1794.'

T. S. B.

Blakeney, William, Lord Blakeney. ii. 648*b*, l. 8 from foot. Lord Blakeney was born on 7 Sept. (*Gent. and London Mag.*, xxv. 495), and the year was probably 1671, not 1672. Contemporary obituary notices (see references in *Musgrave's Obituary*, ed. Armytage, i. 193, Harl. Soc. 1899, and *London Chronicle*, No. 743, p. 286, 19–22 Sept. 1761) state that he was 91 years of age, which may be presumed to mean in his ninety-first year.

T. S. B.

Blakeney, William, Lord Blakeney. ii. 649*a*, ll. 4–6. For 'He was permitted . . . Venloo in 1702' read 'He entered the army as an ensign on 14 Sept. 1695 (P.R.O. Index 5437, p. 100). On 9 Feb. 1699 he became adjutant to the Royal Regiment of Ireland and was promoted lieutenant on 1 Aug. 1701 (Dalton, *Eng. Army Lists*, iv. 227), captain on 25 Aug. 1704, and brevet-major on 1 Jan. 1707 (*ibid.* v. 79, 168)'

Ibid. l. 8. Delete 'as adjutant of his regiment,'

Ibid. l. 13. After 'German princes.' insert 'On 9 March 1708 he was appointed lieutenant and captain in the 1st foot guards (*ibid.* vi. 49) and was promoted captain and lieutenant-colonel on 22 Dec. 1712 (P.R.O.,

Index 5437, p. 100).'

Ibid. l. 17. After 'so that' insert ', although he succeeded his uncle, George Blakeney, as lieutenant-colonel of Lord John Kerr's regiment on 3 Apr. 1718 (Dalton, *George the First's Army*, ii. 176),'

Ibid. l. 19. For 'in' read 'on 27 June (P.R.O., Index 5437, p. 100)'

Blakeway, John Brickdale. ii. 651*b*, l. 21. After 'Regeneration.' add 'His unpublished MSS. are in the Bodleian and are described with much detail in Madan's "Summary Catalogue," iv. 636–41 (*Notes and Queries*, clxxvi. 412).'

Blandford, Walter. ii. 663*b*, ll. 2–3. After 'nominated' insert 'clerk of the closet, 7 Feb. 1668, and'; for 'soon afterwards' read 'on 6 Apr. 1669 (*Notes and Queries*, clxxi. 8)'

Bliss, Philip. ii. 684*a*, l. 41. After '22308' insert 'His correspondence for the years 1806–1857, which is chiefly on academical and bibliographical matters, is in the British Museum (Add. MSS. 34567–34582).'

Blomefield, Miles, ii. 690. For additional information see Irvine Gray, 'Footnote to an alchemist', in *The Cambridge Review*, 30 Nov. 1946. He lived in Chelmsford for the last 35 years or so of his life, dying there 29 Nov. 1603. He appeared in a case of suspected witchcraft June 1598 and was churchwarden of Chelmsford parish church, 1582.
To authorities add Chelmsford parish records and Essex Quarter Sessions records in Essex County Record Office.

Bonham, Sir Samuel George. ii. 807*b*, ll. 8–12. For 'In 1851 . . . upon him' read 'On 22 Nov. 1850 Bonham was made K.C.B. as a reward for his services in China, and he was created a baronet on 27 Nov. 1852. He retired from his appointments in China in 1853' (W. A. Shaw, *Knights*, i. 278; Burke, *Peerage* (1890), p. 149).

Bordwine, Joseph. ii. 855*b*, l. 22 from foot. For ', and' read '. On 8 Jan. 1801 he was appointed ensign in the 55th regiment, having previously served in the Canadian volunteers (*London Gazette*, 1801, no. 15,326, p. 38). He was promoted lieutenant in the royal staff corps on 22 Dec. 1803 (*Army List*, 1805, p. 293), and transferred to the 88th regiment on 9 Oct. 1806 (*ibid.* 1807, p. 287). He'

Ibid. l. 16 from foot. After 'Surrey' insert 'in 1811, having been assistant professor since 1809 (Col. H. M. Vibart, *Addiscombe*, pp. 38–9)'

Ibid. l. 2 from foot. After 'He' insert 'retired from Addiscombe on account of ill-health on 4 Feb. 1835 (Vibart, *op. cit.*, p. 127) and'

Borrow, George. ii. 869*a*, l. 1. After 'George' add 'Henry' (W. J. Knapp, *Life of George Borrow*, i. 24).

Ibid. l. 7. For in '1803' read 'on 5 July 1803' (*Ibid.*).

870*a*, l. 20. For 'in August' read 'on 26 July' (*Ibid.* ii. 254).

Ibid. 5 ll. from foot. After 'St. Petersburg, 1835, 8vo' add '3*a*. "The Talisman, from the Russian of Alexander Pushkin, with other Pieces," St. Petersburg, 1835, 8vo (G. A. Stephen, *Borrow House Museum: a brief account of the life of George Borrow . . . with a bibliography*, 1927, p. 21).'

870*b*, l. 13. After '8vo' insert '12. "The Turkish Jester . . . Translated from the Turkish by George Borrow," Ipswich, 1884, 8vo. 13. "The Death of Balder from the Danish of Johannes Ewald (1773), Translated by George Borrow," London, 1889, 8vo.'

Ibid. l. 22. For 'MacAubrey' read 'MacOubrey (W. J. Knapp, *Life of George Borrow*, ii. 218–19).'

G. A. S.

Boswell, Sir Alexander. ii. 892*a*, l. 13 from foot. After 'Julia' insert '(*d.* 1905)' (*Times Lit. Suppl.*, 6 Feb. 1930, p. 85, col. 4).

Boswell, James. ii. 897*b*, ll. 9–6 from foot. For 'Whilst it was . . . revised it throughout' read 'The publication of the "Journal" was due largely to the influence of Malone, who, happening to meet Boswell at this time, succeeded in arousing him from the dissipated stupor into which he had fallen, and revised the entire work' (*Times Lit. Suppl.*, 6 Feb. 1930, p. 86, col. 2).

Ibid. 899*a*, ll. 28–9. For 'His manuscripts . . . immediately destroyed' read 'His literary executors were sir William Forbes [q.v.], Edmund Malone [q.v.], and William Johnstone Temple [q.v.], who were directed to publish at their discretion and for the benefit of his younger children. The baseless story that they destroyed his manuscripts arose from the fact that, after Malone and Forbes had decided (June 1796), in view of the bulk and character of the writings, not to publish until James (the younger son) came of age, the dislike of Alexander (the eldest) to any further revelation of his father's "service" to Johnson prevented any action being taken before the brothers' deaths in 1822, after which the attitude of Alexander became a firm family tradition. The story of the "holocaust," first propagated by Charles Rogers (1825-1890) [q.v.] in his "Boswelliana" (1874), gained additional plausibility from the accidental burning of a few documents, while the originals of the letters used by Boswell in the "Life" probably rotted away in the damp Auchinleck attic between the pages of the copy in which they had returned from the printer. In 1905 the manuscripts came into the possession of James Boswell Talbot, afterwards sixth lord Talbot de Malahide, whose mother was the second daughter of Sir James Boswell, the second and last baronet of Auchinleck. He broke with the family tradition of secrecy, and the manuscripts were eventually acquired by lieut.-colonel Ralph Isham, of Long Island, U.S.A.' (*Times Lit. Suppl.*, 6 Feb. 1930, p. 85).

Boswell, Sir William. ii. 902*a*, ll. 26-5 from foot. For '(*d.* 1649) . . . by the king' read '(*d.* 1650), diplomatist, was educated at Jesus College, Cambridge (B.A., 1604; M.A., 1607; fellow, 1606-29); he was incorporated at Oxford in 1608. He was travelling on the continent early in 1618 (Hist. MSS. Comm., 12th Rep., App. i. [*Cowper MSS.*, i.], p. 96). He was for a time secretary to Sir Edward Herbert, later Lord Herbert of Cherbury [q.v.], ambassador at Paris from May 1619 to April 1624 (Herbert, *Autobiography*, ed. Lee, 2nd ed., p. 106). From April 1622 he was secretary to John Williams, bishop of Lincoln [q.v.], being chiefly engaged in diocesan business. In 1624 he was senior proctor at Cambridge. He was M.P. for Grantham in 1624 and 1625. From March 1627 until 1632 or later he was a clerk of the council extraordinary. In 1628 he accompanied James Hay, earl of Carlisle [q.v.], on his embassy to Lorraine, Savoy, and Venice. In August 1632 he went to the Hague as resident; he was accompanied by his predecessor, Sir Dudley Carleton, who returned to England in November. He was knighted by Lord Vere of Tilbury at Bokstel in Brabant on 25 July 1633 (Shaw, *Book of Knights*, ii. 201).'

Ibid. 902*b*, ll. 9–14. For 'whose leanings . . . his mission.' read 'and obtaining assistance from the prince of Orange for the king (Gardiner, *Great Civil War*, iv. 83). Walter Strickland [q.v.] was sent over by the parliament in 1642 to counteract his and Henrietta Maria's influence.'

Ibid. l. 21. For 'Sir Simon' read 'Sir Simonds' D'Ewes.

Ibid. l. 22. After 'vocabulary' add 'On 21 November 1629 he and Ambrose Randall were appointed joint keepers of the letters and papers at Whitehall (Rymer xix. 111). On 21 Jan. 1631 he, Patrick Young [q.v.], and Inigo Jones [q.v.] were ordered to arrange the king's collection of medals. He was also engaged in cataloguing Sir Robert Cotton's collection, but the work was not completed (*Cal. State Papers, Dom.*, 1631–1633, p. 224). His correspondents included Galileo (*ibid.* 1628–1629, p. 531) and Peiresc.'

Ibid. ll. 26–30. For 'The first . . . Stephen Goffe' read 'The first volume consists largely of papers relating to Laud's attempt to induce the British churches in Holland to conform to the doctrine and ceremonies of the Anglican church.'

Ibid. ll. 27, 26 from foot. For 'in 1649' read 'on 2/12 April 1650 at the Hague (B.M. Add. MS. 37047, f. 92). He married Margaret, daughter of Sir Ralph Bosville of Brabourne, Kent. She died in 1692, aged eighty-eight, leaving benefactions to Sevenoaks and Tonbridge schools and founding two scholarships at Jesus College, Cambridge (Hasted, *Kent*, i. 349–50, 356; ii. 347).'

Ibid. ll. 25–22. For list of authorities read 'B.M. Add. MSS. 6394–5, 37047 (Boswell's letters and papers); Calendars of State Papers, Domestic and Venetian; Calendar of Committee for Compounding, p. 2596; state papers foreign, Holland, etc., in P.R.O.; Rymer's Foedera, xx. 572; Hist. MSS. Comm., 7th Rep., App., pp. 221–2; 12th Rep., App. i., ii. (Cowper MSS. i., ii.); Calendars of Clarendon State Papers, i., ii.; Wood's Athenae Oxon.; Birch's

Court and Times of Charles I, ii. 158; Peiresc's Lettres, ed. de Larroque; Rubens' Correspondence, ed. Rooses and Ruelens.'

E. S. de B.[1]

[1] Some references were kindly supplied by Sir Charles Firth and Mr. J. F. Chance.

Boteler, Nathaniel. ii. 904*b*, l. 18. After 'lxv. 70).' insert 'Born in 1577' (*Times Lit. Suppl.*, 20 March 1930, p. 235, col. 1).

Ibid. l. 21. After 'Isle of Ré' insert 'was a prominent member of the Virginia company and governor of the Bermudas' (*ibid.*).

Bottisham or Bottlesham, William of. ii. 909 *b*, l. 16. After 'bishop of Rochester,' add 'evidently took his name from the village of Bottlesham, also called Bottisham and Bodekesham (W. W. Skeat, *Place-Names of Cambridgeshire*, p. 20: *Dep.-Keeper's Rep.*, xlii. 509). He is also called Boderisham and by foreign writers Boderinensis. He'

Ibid. ll. 20–40. For 'In 1382 . . . the see of Llandaff;' read 'He succeeded Robert Pynke as provincial of the English Friars Preachers between 1366 and 1368 (see *Cal. Pat. Rolls*, 1364–7, p. 278, for the last mention of Pynke in this capacity). Bottisham is first referred to as provincial in 1368 (*Register of Lewis de Charlton*, ed. J. H. Parry, p. 47). As provincial he obtained on 4 May 1370 a royal mandate to reduce to order certain rebellious Oxford Dominican students (*Cal. Pat. Rolls*, 1367–70, p. 425). A month later he was removed from this office (*Acta Capitulorum Generalium O.P.*, ed. Reichert, ii. 416). In 1378 he and other English Dominicans were the objects of an attack made in the general chapter of the order held at Carcassonne. He was deprived of his professorship and removed from his priory of King's Lynn, first to Livardein in Saxony and then to Carlisle; finally he was ordered to go to Rome to have his cause examined. But Urban VI quashed the acts of the Carcassonne chapter; Bottisham was not only reinstated but also appointed papal commissary to see that the decree of reinstatement was enforced (*Archaeol. Journal*, xxxv. 153–4). He was nominated by Urban to the see of Nantes, and sat in the Council of Blackfriars on 22 May 1382, under the style of "Episcopus Nanatensis" (Wilkins, *Concilia*, iii. 158; *Fasciculi Zizan.* (Rolls Series), p. 498). In 1382 he was acting as suffragan to Canterbury (Stubbs, *Reg. Sac.*, p. 144), and in 1383 was translated by Urban VI to the see of Bethlehem (C. Eubel, *Hierarchia*, i. 135). Bottisham was with Urban VI when besieged at Nocera in 1385, and at the end of that year was translated to the see of Llandaff (Wharton, *Anglia Sacra*, i. 379; Eubel, *op. cit.*, i. 292).'

Ibid. l. 21 from foot. For 'in 1389' read '27 Aug. 1389' (Wharton, *op. cit.*, i. 379).

Ibid. l. 5 from foot. After 'compilations,' add 'The following works are attributed to him:—"Disputationes Scholasticae," "Sermones coram Rege," and "Opus quoddam tabulare pro utilitate studentium" (Tanner, *Bibliotheca*, p. 114).'

W. G.

Bourchier, John, second baron Berners. ii. 920*b*, l. 7 from foot. After 'Charles V' insert 'On 25 Oct. 1526 he was succeeded as deputy of Calais by Sir Robert Wingfield [q.v.] (*L.P.* iv. 2518–19, 2546, 2597), and he appears to have spent the greater part of the next five years in England.'

Ibid. 921*a*, l. 1. After 'unpaid' insert 'On 27 March 1531 he was reappointed deputy of Calais and' (*L.P.* v. 166 [48]: in *ib.* v. 156 the reference is wrongly given as '166 [40]').

Bourne, Nehemiah. ii. 939*a*. This article needs revision. See Sir Charles Firth in *The Mariner's Mirror*, xii. 254–56.

Bowack, John. ii. 947*b*, l. 23. After 'library.' insert 'The letter and the poem accompanying it are printed in "Notes and Queries" (clxv. 400–2).'

Bowet, Henry. ii. 971*b*, l. 19. After 'Flanders.' insert 'He had been sent to Rome in 1380 on the king's business and may have helped in obtaining for Spencer a papal bull "Dudum cum filii Belial," empowering him to permit clerks to take up the cross without the consent of their superiors and to dispense with residence (E. Perroy, *L'Angleterre et le Grand Schisme*, p. 176).'

Ibid. l. 24. For 'A few years later' read 'In Jan. 1384 he obtained letters of protection and' (*Diplomatic Correspondence of Richard II*, ed. E. Perroy, Camden 3rd ser., xlviii. 205).

Ibid. l. 31. After 'ii. 124).' insert 'He returned to England and in the spring of 1387 was again sent to the pope' (*ibid.* p. 50).

Ibid. l. 5 from foot. After '(*ib.* viii. 43).' insert 'During his stay in Aquitaine he was engaged in diplomatic negotiations with Aragon on behalf of both Richard II and Lancaster' (*Dipl. Corr.* ed. Perroy, *u.s.* pp. 172, 253–4).

Bowles, Phineas. ii. 976*b*, ll. 9–10. For 'is first mentioned . . . January' read 'was appointed ensign in the Queen Dowager's regiment of foot, 3 Oct. 1688, and on 1 Feb.'; delete 'when'

Ibid. l. 14. For '*Home Off. Mil. Entry Books*, vol. iii.' read 'Dalton, *English Army Lists*, ii. 184'

Ibid. ll. 19–18 from foot. For 'In' read 'On 23 March'; after '8th dragoons' insert 'and on 30 May 1720 he was appointed quartermaster-general and barrack-master-general in Ireland (Dalton, *George the First's Army*, ii. 420)'; for 'in' read 'on 19 Nov.'

Ibid. ll. 15–12 from foot. For 'served long . . . *Entry Books*, vol. viii.' read 'was appointed captain in major-general Thomas Whetham's regiment, 16 March 1710, and on 7 March 1713 became captain and lieut.-colonel in the 3rd regiment of foot guards (Dalton, *English Army Lists*, vi. 60, 62, 234'

Ibid. 977*a*, l. 2. After 'carabineers' insert ', to which regiment he had been transferred in Dec. 1740 (Dalton, *English Army Lists*, vi. 62)'

Boycott, Charles Cunningham, Suppl. 243*b*, ll. 8–11 For 'In 1850 . . . captain' read 'on 15 Feb. 1850 he was appointed ensign in the 39th regiment (*Army List*, March 1850, p. 115) retiring by sale on 17 Dec. 1852 (*ibid.* Jan. 1853, p. 124)'.

Boyle, Charles, fourth Earl of Orrery. ii. 1017*b*, ll. 9–10. For 'As envoy in Flanders he' read 'He was appointed envoy extraordinary in Flanders in Jan. 1711 (*Brit. Dipl. Repr., 1689–1789*, Camden 3rd series, xlvi. 8) and'

Ibid. l. 13. After 'Marston' insert 'He finally left Brussels on 30 June 1713 (*ibid.*).'

Boyle, John. ii. 1019*a*., l. 22 from foot. After '1563.' insert 'He was admitted to Corpus Christi, Cambridge, in 1583, and proceeded B.A. in 1586, M.A. in 1590, B.D. in 1598, and D.D. in 1614 (Venn, *Alumni Cantab.*, pt. 1, i. 196).'

Boyle, John, fifth Earl of Cork. ii. 1020*a*, l. 25. For '1750' read '1746' (*Record of Royal Soc.*, p. 342).

Boyle, Richard, first Earl of Cork. ii. 1023*a*, l. 6. For 'George' read 'Geoffrey.'

Boyle, Richard, first Earl of Cork. ii. 1024 *a*, ll. 22–3. For 'his eldest son was slain on the field' read 'his fourth son, Lewis, Viscount Boyle of Kinalmeaky, was slain on the field' (G.E.C. *Complete Peerage*, iii. 421: note c).

Boyle, Richard. ii. 1024*b*, l. 4. After 'Peacock.' insert 'He entered Corpus Christi, Cambridge, in 1590 and proceeded B.A. in 1594/5 and M.A. in 1598 (Venn, *Alumni Cantab.*, pt. 1, i. 196).'

Add to list of authorities: Masters' Hist. of Corpus Christi Coll., Camb., ed. J. Lamb, p. 239.

Brabazon, Sir William. ii. 1046*b*, ll. 20–14 from foot. Delete 'In the same year he made . . . to the King.' This statement is based upon the forged documents of Robert Ware, printed in 'Harleian Miscellany,' ed. T. Park, v. 595–606 (*see* art. Ware, Sir James, below).

Braddock, Edward. ii. 1061*a*, l. 13. For 'the army' read 'Corpus Christi, Cambridge, as a fellow-commoner in June 1710, but a few months later he abandoned the university for the army (*Masters' Hist. of Corpus Christi Coll., Camb.*, ed. J. Lamb, p. 427) entering'

Braddock, Edward (1695–1755). ii. 1063. For additional authorities, see S. Pargellis 'Braddock's defeat' in *Amer. Hist. Rev.* xli (1936), 253–269; *Military Affairs in North America* 1748–1763, ed. S. Pargellis Amer. Hist. Assoc. (1936).

Bradford, Samuel. ii. 1069*a*, l. 9. After 'the abbey.' add 'A portrait by E. Zeeman is in the hall of Corpus Christi college.'

Bradley, Richard. ii. 1080*a*, l. 17 from foot. For '1720' read '1712' (*Record of Royal Soc*. p. 326).

Bragg, Philip, ii. 1102*a*, ll. 10–11. For 'He appears . . . served' read 'On 25 Aug. 1704 he was appointed captain in (Dalton, *Engl. Army Lists*, v, p. 86)'. ll. 15–16. Delete The English . . . but' and after 'guards' add 'on 6 May 1709 he was appointed Lieutenant colonel in the earl of Ilay's regiment, afterwards 36th foot (*ibid.* vi, p. 139)'. l. 25. After 'George I' add 'He was on half-pay as lieutenant-colonel from 1715 (P.R.O., War Office, Half-pay Lists, 25/2979) until 17 March 1727 when he was appointed captain and lieutenant-colonel in the 3rd footguards Dalton, *op. cit.*, vi, p. 343)'. l. 15 from foot. Add 'In a signed return dated May 1726 he gives his age as 43 and years of service as 27 (P.R.O., War Office, Half-pay Lists, 25/2986)'.

Bramhall, John. ii. 1113*a*, l. 14 from foot. For 'In October . . . England' read 'He was in London on 7 July 1660 and returned to Ireland in October (*Works*, vol. i, p. cii ; *Parliamentary Intelligencer*, 22–9 Oct., p. 696).'

Brereton, Owen Salusbury (1715–1798). ii. 1176*b*, l. 25 from foot. For 'Miss Trelawney' read 'Mary Trelawny,' daughter of Brigadier-General Henry Trelawny of Whitley, Devon, Governor of Plymouth. (Will of Charles Trelawny, 1730).' To the article add 'He married Katherine, daughter of William Whitmore, M.P. of Lower Slaughter, Gloucs., and Apley, Salop. She died 10 May 1800 in Soho Square, London, aged 78. Their issue, five children, all died young. (*Gent. Mag.*, 1798, p. 816; 1800, p. 491: will of Katherine Whitmore.)'

Brereton, Sir William (1604–1661). ii. 1180*a*, ll. 29–33. For 'there is a tradition . . . registers', substitute, 'there is no foundation for the tradition that his body was lost on the journey from Croydon to Cheadle church, Cheshire. His burial at Croydon is recorded in the parish register as having taken place on 29 April 1661.'

Brereton, Sir William (1789–1864), ii. 1180*b*, l. 27. For 'in 1789' read 'at Bath on 29 Dec. 1789'. l. 28 from foot. After 'Matagorda' add 'Where he was wounded' 1181*a*. l. 2. After '1854' add 'a K.H. in 1837, C.B. in 1838'.
Add to list of authorities War Office Library, Officers' Records, Royal Artillery, ii, f. 170.

Briggs, Henry, ii. 1234*a*, l. 26. For 'Norfolk school' read 'Norwich Grammar School'.

Briggs, William. ii. 1237*b*, l. 10 from foot. For 'At thirteen' read 'In 1663 (Venn, *Alumni Cantab.*, pt. 1, i. 218).'

Ibid. l. 9 from foot. After 'Tenison,' insert 'proceeded B.A., 1667 (*ibid.*),'

Brodrick, Alan, viscount Midleton. ii. 1292*a*, ll. 16, 17. For 'In the same year . . . he' read 'In February 1716–7 he had' (*Return of M.P.'s*, ii. 45).

Brooke, Rupert, 1912–21 vol. 66*b*. l. 6. For 'Brooke, Rupert' read 'Brooke, Rupert Chawner'. See *Rugby School Register*, iv. 187.

Brooke, Samuel. ii. 1342*a*, l. 5. After 'died 16 Sept. 1631' insert 'His will (99 St. John) was made 16 Sept. 1631 and proved 20 Sept.'

G. C. M. S.

Brown, John (*d.* 1736). iii. 10*b*, l. 23. For '1722' read '1721' (*Record of Royal Soc.*, p. 329, where the spelling is Browne).

Browne, Sir Richard (*d.* 1669). iii. 54–5. Browne's importance in the royalist movement of 1659 and the complete confidence reposed in him by Charles II are clearly shown by the letters of the King's agents in England (*Clarendon State Papers*, iii. 429, 437, 444, 470, 525, 538, 569, 630, 644, 650). He was credited with the invention of the opprobrious nickname given to the restored Long Parliament. 'If you ask who named it "Rump" know't was so styled in an honest sheet of paper called "The Bloody Rump," written before the trial of our late sovereign of glorious memory : but the word obtained not universal notice till it flew from the mouth of Major-General Browne at a public assembly in the days of Richard Cromwell' (Address to the Reader prefixed to *Rump, or an exact Collection of the choicest Poems and Songs relating to the late Times*, 1662).

On 6 July 1660 Browne was appointed major-general of the forces of the City in the place of Monck (Sharpe, *London and the Kingdom*, ii. 385, 387), and being also Lord Mayor was doubly responsible for the peace of London when Venner's rising took place. (See also Pepys, *Diary*, ed. Wheatley, i. 319–323 ; Kennett Register, 352–8, 361.)

According to Le Neve, Browne's son, the second Sir Richard, 'was after a colonel in King William's army in Flanders and was killed without issue 1693 or thereabouts'

(*Le Neve's Pedigrees of the Knights*, p. 57). It is more likely that the son was the Sir Richard Brown, 'of the English horse guards,' killed in a duel with Captain Billingsley in August 1689 (Luttrell's *Diary*, i. 571; *Hist. MSS. Comm., Report on the MSS. of S. H. Le Fleming*, p. 262; Dalton, *Army Lists*, ii. 2; iii. 19).

Bruce, John (1745–1826). iii. 107*b*. See a paper, with additional information from the East India Company's records, in Sir Wm. Foster's 'John Company,' 1926, pp. 233–45.

Bruce, Robert de (VI). iii. 115*b*, l. 2. For 'the year before his father died' read 'in 1240 (*Cal. Charter Rolls*, 1226–57, p. 252).'

G. O. S.

Bruce, Robert de (VII). iii. 116*a*, last line. For '1253' read '1243 (*Annales de Theokesberia*, p. 129, cited in G. E. C. *Complete Peerage*, ii. 360, *note* c).'

G. O. S.

Brummell, George Bryan. iii. 142*a*, l. 4. For '1790' read '1786 (*Eton Coll. Reg.*, 1753–90, p. 75)'

Add to list of authorities: W. Connely's Beau Brummel at Eton and Oxford (*Notes and Queries*, clxxviii. 185–7).

Buc or Buck, Sir George, iii. 171*a*. After '&c.' in l. 11 insert 'Bodleian MS. Rawl. F. 105 contains the "Preface" and "Eclog" under the title "Δαφνις: or The Polyanthine Ghirland. By George Buc. gent.". This version differs from both printed editions. It is dedicated to Sir John Burroughs a Garter King of Arms. Burroughs became Garter King in 1633'.

Buc or Buck, Sir George. iii. 172*a*, l. 13. 'No copy of "The Baron" is known to exist.' A manuscript volume, very probably a copy of 'The Baron,' is in the possession of Major G. Halswell, of Wylmington Hayes, Honiton, Devon (*Times Lit. Supp.* 1927, p. 193).

Buckingham, James Silk. iii. 202*b*, ll. 1–2. For 'nothing further was done with the scheme' read 'it ran for four weeks only' (J. S. Buckingham, *Argus*, 30 June–26 July 1828).

Bulwer, William Henry Lytton Earle, Baron Dalling and Bulwer. iii. 264*b*, ll. 10–12. For 'On 27 Nov. 1835 . . . at Brussels' read 'He was secretary of legation at Brussels from Nov. 1832 to Sept. 1833 and again from Nov. 1835 to Feb. 1837, resigning the post on both occasions. From Dec. 1835 to Feb. 1836 he was chargé d'affaires during the absence of the envoy' (returns of diplomatic service, P.R.O., F.O. 366/329).

Burchett, Josiah. iii. 291*b*, ll. 15–32. For 'at least three . . . office till 1742' read 'repeatedly to Pepys (Bodl. Libr. Rawl. MSS. A. 179, fos. 16–22; A. 189, fos. 1, 3, 7, 11) begging either a pardon or permission to enter the naval service. Pepys finally relented and on 5 Sept. 1688 Burchett was entered on the pay-book of the Portsmouth, commanded by Capt. St. Loe (P.R.O. Admiralty pay-book, 33/117, no. 99). Relations had become strained between Pepys and the commander-in-chief of the fleet, the earl of Dartmouth, and Burchett was able to make use of his humiliation at Pepys' hands; on 17 Oct. he was entered among Dartmouth's personal retinue on board the flag-ship, the Resolution (*ibid.* 33/116, no. 469). There he met the admiral's secretary, Phineas Bowles, who shortly afterwards entered the service of Admiral Arthur Herbert, afterwards earl of Torrington [q.v.], and who was appointed admiralty secretary 9 Mar. 1689. Burchett left the Resolution 5 Mar., and probably served Bowles at the admiralty as a clerk. Before the end of 1690 he had made the acquaintance of Admiral Edward Russell, afterwards earl of Orford [q.v.], and on 19 Jan. 1691 entered the flag-ship Britannia as the latter's secretary (*ibid.* 33/134, no. 1500), serving in this capacity until the autumn of 1692 (*ibid.* 33/141, no. 600). From 18 July to 28 Aug. 1693 he was acting at the admiralty office during the temporary absence of the secretary (P.R.O., Admiralty out-letters, 2/384, *passim*). On 24 Apr. 1694, when Russell was preparing to sail for the Mediterranean, Burchett resumed his former post under him (P.R.O., Admiralty pay-book, 33/172, no. 1209). At the end of July the admiralty secretaryship fell vacant, and on 26 Sept., together with William Bridgeman, a former clerk of the privy council, Burchett was appointed joint-secretary (Admiralty Library, MS., salary and pension books, ii. 50; Hist. MSS. Comm., 14th *Rep.*, ii. 551). Bridgeman retired in June 1698 (*Cal. S.P. Dom.* 1698, pp. 322,

335) and Burchett remained sole secretary until 20 May 1702, when, after the appointment of Prince George of Denmark [q.v.] as lord high admiral, the latter's private secretary, George Clarke [q.v.], began to transact admiralty business. But whereas there had been no clear distinction or division of duties between Burchett and Bridgeman, on this occasion Burchett definitely ranked as the senior secretary. He continued to attend the admiralty office regularly, while Clarke accompanied the prince on his many absences from London. Clarke received the usual secretarial salary of £800 per annum, but Burchett's seniority was recognized by an additional £200 a year paid by the lord high admiral himself. On Prince George's death in 1708, this extra payment ceased, but in 1717 Burchett successfully petitioned that the increase should be allowed him until the end of the war (P.R.O., Privy council register, 31 July 1717). From Oct. 1705 Burchett was again sole secretary and so remained until 23 April 1741, when Thomas Corbett [q.v.] was appointed as his colleague (*ibid.*), and 14 Oct. 1742, "worn out with age," Burchett successfully petitioned to be superannuated (*ibid.*).'

Ibid. l. 16 from foot. After '1697' add '(French trs. Amsterdam, 1704).'

Ibid. 292*a*, l. 21. After 'conclusive.' add 'For the years 1688–97 the "Memoirs" give the greater detail with regard to dates and statistics; but both works have a valuable preface dealing with administrative problems, in which Burchett's own opinions are partly revealed.'

Ibid. l. 22. After 'Thomasine' add '(*d.* 1713, B.M. Add. MS. 33,512, p. 198)'

Ibid. l. 23. Delete 'and'

Ibid. l. 26. After 'p. 31)' add ', who died 1 Mar. 1740 (*Gent. Mag.*, x. 146). He married (3) on 10 June 1740, Isabella, widow of a Mr. Wood, a Spanish merchant (*ibid.* 316), who survived him and received a pension of £100 per annum (P.R.O., Privy council register, 4 Nov. 1747). Burchett had spent a considerable part of his fortune on pictures, and his collection, consisting of 312 pieces and including many Flemish and Italian masters, was sold by auction 6–9 April 1747 (*Cat. Burchett Collection*, 1747).'

Burdon-Sanderson, Sir John Scott. Second Suppl. i. 268*a*, l. 4. Before 'as' insert 'in 1870' (*University College, London. Proceedings at the Annual General Meeting . . . 22nd February* 1871, pp. 16–17).

Burgess, John. iii. 310*a*, l. 26. For '1563' read '1561?'

Ibid. 310*b*. Delete the second paragraph and read 'Early in 1592 he was appointed town preacher in Ipswich, and its municipal records contain frequent references to his influence. On 14 Aug. 1596 he was sent to London to obtain from the privy council some order to enable Ipswich to extract from the shire part of the ship money levied on the town. On 16 Aug. 1597 the borough council resolved that his salary should be rated upon the inhabitants "and the refusers shall be committed till payment made." On 9 Nov. 1601 it resolved to grant him a patent of his office with 100 marks fee; this appointment was on 22 Jan. 1601/2 confirmed for life, and he was allowed 80 days' absence a year (Nathaniel Bacon, *Annals*, pp. 369, 377, 384, 386, 388, 409). The arrangement was confirmed on 6 May, but on 19 July a successor was appointed, apparently on Burgess's resignation; he was however a benefactor to Ipswich public library in 1613.'

Ibid. 311*b*, ll. 7–9. For 'he does not . . . and' read 'he had promised to remain only one year abroad, and left the garrison at Frankenthal on 17 July 1621 (*Fairfax Corr.*, ed. Johnson, i. p. xliii);'

Ibid. l. 9 from foot. Add '[q.v.]' after 'Thomas Wilcox.'

Ibid. ll. 8–1 from foot. For 'By her he . . . Sloane MS. 250.' read 'A daughter married William Ames (1576–1633) [q.v.] who succeeded him as chaplain to Sir Horace Vere; and a daughter of Burgess's son, a physician (Munk, i. 216), was the second wife of William Hill [q.v.].'

Ibid. 312*a*, l. 12. For 'i. 201' read 'i. 216'.

Burgh, Sir Ulysses Bagenal, second Baron Downes. iii. 327*b*, l. 3 from foot. Delete comma.

Ibid. l. 2 from foot. For 'May 1825, and in March' read 'May 1825. On 18 March'.

Ibid. 328*a*, ll. 4–9. For 'peer, and remained . . . himself with' read 'peer. He remained surveyor general of the ordnance until Wellington's retirement from the government in April 1827 (Haydn, *Dignities*, pp.

259–60). From that time onwards he led.'

Ibid. l. 14. For 'in 1869' read 'on 18 May 1860' (*Times*, 18 May 1860, p. 6*d*).

Burgoyne, John, iii. 340*a*, l. 28. For '13th light dragoons . . . From Preston' read '1st royal dragoons on 23 April 1744, lieutenant 22 Feb. 1745 and captain on 1 July 1745'. l. 21 from foot. For '13th' read '1st'. l. 16 from foot. After 'commission' add 'in October 1751'. l. 12 from foot. For 'seven years' read 'nearly five'. p. 340*b*, l. 13. Delete 'August' and 'lieutenant-'. l. 15. After 'approved' add 'and numbered the 15th and 16th light dragoons', after 'were' add 'subsequently'. l. 17. After 'respectively' add 'Burgoyne's commission as lieutenant-colonel commandant of the 16th being dated 4 August 1759'. p. 341*a*, l. 3. Delete '-commandant'. 342*b*, l. 2. For 'Halford' read 'Hertford'.

Add to list of authorities:—P.R.O., War Office, Commission Registers, 25/21; 25/209. Printed *Army Lists*.

Burney, Charles. iii. 415*b*, l. 34. After 'free school' insert 'from 25 Dec. 1739 until 27 March 1742' (*Notes and Queries*, clviii. 262).

Ibid. l. 40. After 'Blow' insert 'and took part in Handel's first rehearsal of the "Messiah" at Chester' (*ibid.*).

Burrard, Sir Harry. iii. 440*a*, 26 ll. from foot. For '1705 to 1727' read '1705 to 1713 and from 1722 to 1727' (*Return of M.P.'s*, ii. 23, 55).

Bury, Richard de (1281–1345). iii. 477*b*, l. 24. For '1281' read '1287.'

Ibid., ll. 32–33. Delete 'On leaving . . . Durham.'

Ibid., 478*a*, ll. 9–11. For 'Next year . . . treasurer in 1336' read 'Next year he was appointed Lord Treasurer in February and High Chancellor in September.'

Ibid., ll. 16–24. For 'And he was again . . . Scottish king.' read 'And in 1337 he was one of the commissioners appointed to lay before assemblies of magnates at York and Newcastle the details of the king's intention to invade Scotland. On the outbreak of war with France his diplomatic duties abroad came to an end, but in 1340, having been commissioned earlier in the year to treat for peace with Scotland, he was directed, with others, to supervise the defence of the realm against the Scots. After Edward's ineffectual expedition of 1341–2, Richard was once more appointed to negotiate peace with David Bruce.'

Ibid., 478*b*, ll. 12–15. For 'For this end . . . management.' read 'In his *Philobiblon* he expresses his intention of founding a library at an unnamed Hall in Oxford by the donation of his collection of MSS., and he gives rules for its management.'

Ibid., l. 18. After 'Book' insert 'It seems that his wish was never carried out and that on his death his MSS. were sold to pay his debts.'

Ibid., last 2 lines. For 'His rules . . . were founded' read 'The rules for his projected college library may have been founded'.

Ibid., 479*a*, ll. 32–33. For 'At Paris . . . (1500);' read 'At Paris by Badius Ascensius and Jean Petit in collaboration (1500), as *Philobiblion*;'

Ibid., l. 34. For '(1599)' read '(1598 and 1599)'.

Ibid., ll. 34–36. For 'At Leipzig . . . Centuria una;' read 'At Frankfurt (1610 and 1614), in *Philologicarum epistolarum centuria una . . . insuper Richardi de Buri episc. Dunelm. Philobiblion* [sic] . . . *ex bibl. Melchioris Haiminsfeldii Goldasti*, reprinted by Conringius at Leipzig (1674); by J. A. Schmidt at Helmstadt (1703) in the *Nova Accessio* to the 2nd ed. of *De bibliothecis atque archivis virorum clarissimorum libelli et commentationes*;'

Ibid., l. 10 from the end. For '1885' read '1888'.

Ibid. Delete last paragraph.

To authorities add: *Richard d'Aungerville, of Bury. Fragments of his register, and other documents* (Surtees Soc. cxix, 1910); Thomas's introduction to his edition of the *Philobiblon.*

Bury, Richard de (1281–1345). To authorities add: N. Benholm-Young, 'Richard de Bury (1287–1345),' *Royal Hist. Soc. Trans.*, 4th ser., xx (1937), 135–163.

Butler, Samuel (1612–1680). iii. 526–8. Most of this article is superseded by an article, 'The later life of Samuel Butler' (*Review of English Studies*, iii. (1928), 159–66), which also refers to articles on his parentage and education. The only authority for the period *c.* 1630–1660 is Aubrey's 'Brief Lives.' Most of the traditional account of Butler seems to be derived from

' Hudibras ' and the spurious pieces attributed to him (a specimen, p. 527*b*, ll. 4–7) and is untrustworthy. The last volume of Butler's works, ' Satires and miscellaneous poetry and prose,' ed. R. Lamar, appeared in 1928.

Butler, Samuel (1612–1680). iii. 526–8 ; BULLETIN, x. 140. In addition to the article mentioned in BULLETIN, x. 140, see *Times Literary Supplement*, 1940, p. 327.

Butt, Isaac (1813–1879), iii. 545*b*, ll. 38–45. Delete 'he then offered himself as a liberal-conservative . . . defeated by Sir J. M'Kenna'. Insert: 'he then offered himself as a conservative for Youghal. He was opposed by the Hon. J. W. Fortescue, but was elected, and sat from July 1851 to July 1865, when he was defeated by Sir J. M'Kenna. He spoke and voted as a conservative until 1857, but in the general election of that year he declared his support for the government of Lord Palmerston (see his election address in *Freeman's Journal*, 30 March 1857) and from then until he lost his seat he acted as a liberal.'

Cadogan or Martin. 24*a*, n. 7. Add at end ', J. Williams ap Ithel, *Brut y Tywysogion* (Rolls Series), pp. 284–5.'

Ibid. n. 8. Add at end ', Williams ap Ithel, *op. cit.*, p. 324.'

Cadogan, William, first Earl Cadogan. iii. 636*b*, l. 34. For 'the Hague' read 'Antwerp (Dumont, *Corps diplomatique*, viii. pt. 1, 458)'.

Ibid. 637*a*, l. 2. For 'Returning to . . . the Hague' read 'On 17 July he received new credentials and instructions as ambassador, and returning to the Hague in October (P.R.O., F.O. xc. 32).'

Caesar, Sir Julius (1558–1636). iii. 656*b*, 23 ll. from foot. After '21 June' add 'For some years after 1585 he lived in the parish of St. Margaret, Lothbury (*Vestry Min.*, ed. E. Freshfield, 1887, pp. xx, 19, 21).'

Ibid. 657*b*, 20 ll. from foot. After 'by the king at Greenwich' insert 'and in the same year he was still described as "Judge of the Admiraltie" (*Acts of the Privy Council*, xxxii. 496 cited in *Mariner's Mirror*, xiii. 337).'

Cairnes, John Elliot. iii. 669*a*, l. 19. Add 'a post which he held until 1872' (*University College, London. Proceedings at the Annual General Meeting . . . 26th February* 1873, p. 14).

Ibid. l. 21. Add 'During the session 1867–8 T. E. Cliffe Leslie [q.v.] acted as his deputy at University College.'

Calveley, Sir Hugh. iii. 715*b*, ll. 8–10. For 'It is most . . . issueless.' read 'He did, however, marry the infanta Constanza, daughter of Pedro IV of Aragon, but the match was unhappy. Constanza soon left her husband, who had to sue the king of Aragon for the recovery of her dower (*Dipl. Corr. of Rich. II*, ed. E. Perroy, pp. 233–4).'

Cameron, John (*d.* 1446). iii. 745*b*, l. 13 from foot. After 'Concilia Scotiæ, i. lxxii).' insert 'He may possibly be identified with the Johannes de Camera who studied at St. Andrews and was bachelor in 1416 and licentiate in 1419 (Anderson, *Early Records of the University of St. Andrews*, pp. 4, 6).'

J. H. B.

Camocke, George. iii. 757*b*, l. 5 from foot. For 'Three years later he was a' read 'He then entered Jacobite service and took an active part in the preparation for the 1715 invasion (*Stuart MSS.*, Hist. MSS. Comm., i. 371, 372, 382, 428). Despite fears of his possible indiscretion, he was appointed commander of the vessel which was to have taken James Stuart to Scotland (*ibid.* pp. 430, 462, 466). In 1716 he was prepared to transport arms to Scotland (*ibid.* ii. 23), and was maintaining the close connexion with the duke of Ormonde (*ibid.* pp. 219, 364) which he had enjoyed during his previous service in the Irish Sea (*ibid.* i. 481; *Ormonde MSS.*, Hist. MSS. Comm., viii. *passim*). He was also in frequent communication with the duke of Mar (*Stuart MSS.*, iv. 492). In 1717 he was again planning to raise a small squadron to carry further supplies of arms to the Jacobites. By this time he held a commission as'

Add to list of authorities: Byng Papers (Navy Records Soc.), iii. pp. xxi–xxv, 53–63.

Carlile, Christopher. iii. 1008*a*, l. 8 from foot. After 'Cambridge,' read 'whence he graduated B.A., 1538–9 (Venn, *Alumni Cantab.* pt. 1, i. 293*b*), and'

Ibid. l. 7 from foot. After 'fellow' read 'in 1539'

Ibid. After '1541,' read 'in which year he was appointed master of Jesus College Grammar School,'

Ibid. l. 6 from foot. For '1548' read '1547 (C. M. Neale, *Early Honours Lists of Univ. of Cambridge*, pp. 39*n*, 43).'

Ibid. l. 4 from foot. For 'he was' read 'is said to have been (Cooper, *Athenae Cantab.* iii. 76).'

Campbell, Alexander, second Earl of Marchmont. iii. 760*a*, l. 2 from foot. For 'In the same year' read 'In May 1716 (*Brit. Dipl. Repr.*, *1689–1789*, Camden 3rd series, xlvi. 3, 105).'

Campbell, Alexander, second Earl of Marchmont. iii. 760*a*, last 2 ll. For 'In the same year . . . of Copenhagen' read 'In May 1716 he was appointed envoy extraordinary, and in 1720 ambassador extraordinary, to the court of Copenhagen (P.R.O., F.O. xc. 8; and *Diplomatic Instructions* [R. Hist. Soc., Camden 3rd ser. xxxvi.], iii. 45, 60).'

Add to list of authorities: Hist. MSS. Comm., 'Polwarth MSS.,' i–iii.

Campbell, Archibald, ninth Earl of Argyll. iii. 781*b*, l. 36. After '*Scotland*),' insert 'being *receptus in secundam classem* at

St. Leonard's College, St. Andrews, in 1646 (Univ. Munim.).' J. H. B.

Campbell, John, third Earl of Breadalbane. iii. 827*b*, ll. 19–21. For 'in 1718 . . . Denmark' read 'in 1720 he was appointed envoy extraordinary to the court of Denmark, where he remained until March 1729 (P.R.O., F.O. xc. 8; and *Diplomatic Instructions* [R. Hist. Soc., Camden 3rd ser. xxxvi.], iii. 61–88).'

Ibid. ll. 23–4. Delete 'In December . . . to Russia.' There is no evidence to show that Campbell was ambassador to Russia in 1731. The contributor may have been misled by the re-credentials to the king of Denmark, issued to Campbell on 12 Feb. 1731, although he had left that court two years before and did not return. Credentials and instructions were issued to Claudius Rondeau as minister resident at Peterburg, 11 Sept. 1731 (P.R.O., F.O. xc. 57), but no mention of Campbell is made in his dispatches (B.M., Eg. MSS. 2686–7).

Campbell, John, LL.D. (1708–1775). iii. 825*b*, l. 18 from foot. For 'Bevan' read 'Brown' (*Notes and Queries*, 12th ser. xii. 356; Halkett and Laing, ed. 1926–32, vi. 80).

Campion, Thomas. iii. 855–6. This article is superseded by Mr. Percival Vivian's introduction to his edition of Campion's works (Oxford, 1909). To that account (p. xl) should be added the fact that Campion graduated M.D. at Caen on 10 Feb. 1605 (evidently N.S. R. W. Innes Smith, *Students of Medicine at Leyden*, p. xvi).

Caradoc, Sir John Hobart, second Baron Howden. iii. 938*b*, ll. 27–8. For 'returned to Rio de Janeiro' read 'proceeded by way of Monte Video to Rio de Janeiro, where he arrived 7 Aug. 1847' (dispatches in P.R.O., F.O. 13/244).

Carew, George, Baron Carew of Clopton and Earl of Totnes. iii. 962*a*, ll. 1–6. For '. Forty-two . . . lost.' read '(see M. R. James in *Eng. Hist. Rev.*, xlii. 261–7).'

Carey, Robert, first Earl of Monmouth. iii. 984*a*. On his abortive mission to Scotland to explain the execution of Queen Mary, see Tytler's *History of Scotland*, ed. 1843, x. 4.

An edition of his Memoirs, ed. by G. H. Powell, was published in 1905, small 8vo, in the series called 'King's Classics.'

Carleton, George (1559–1628). iii. 999*b*, l. 20 from foot. After 'London' insert '1629, 4to; 4th edn.'; and for '8vo' read '12mo' (Pollard and Redgrave, *Short-Title Catalogue*, p. 101, nos. 4647–8).

Carmichael, John, third Earl of Hyndford. iii. 1040*a*, ll. 18–20. For 'In 1752 he was sent . . . till 1764' read 'From March to Aug. 1752 he was in Vienna on a special mission, chiefly in connexion with the election of a king of the Romans (*Brit. Dipl. Repr., 1689–1789*, Camden 3rd series, xlvi. 38).'

Carne, Sir Edward. iii. 1043*b*, l. 2 from foot. For 'Santa Maria del Populo' read, as in the original edition, 'San Gregorio al Celio.'

Ibid. last line. After 'be read' add '(V. Forcella, *Iscrizioni delle chiese e d'altri edificii di Roma*, ii. 109)'.

Ibid. 1044, ll. 5-6. In list of authorities delete '[N.] Chytræus, Variorum Itinerum Deliciæ, 9,' which is here superseded by Forcella. The wrong alteration was due to a misunderstanding of Chytræus. L. Schrader, 'Monumentorum Italiæ libri iv,' 1592, f. 130, is decisive for the tomb's having been at S. Gregorio already in his time (the first edition of Chytræus is 1594) and there is no suggestion of its ever having been moved. E. S. de B.

Carpenter, William Benjamin. iii. 1075*a*, ll. 20–1. For 'University College, London' read 'London University (now University College).'

Carter, Peter. iii. 1114*b*, ll. 22–20 from foot. For 'and afterwards . . . Sept. 1590' read 'He was appointed headmaster of Whalley grammar school by letters patent on its foundation in 1549 and retained the position, which appears to have become effective only in 1554, until 1571. In 1572 he was appointed master of Bolton grammar school; in 1579 of the common school at Wigan; and by 1588 was master of Preston grammar school. He retained this position until his death in his sixtieth year; and was buried at Preston on 8 September 1590. He married Elitia Radcliffe at Whalley in 1573, probably as his second wife, and left a son Peter.'

Ibid., ll. 15–14 from foot. For '1599,

. . . 1639, 8vo' read '1589, 1611, 1617, and 1639; Cambridge, 1631.'

To authorities add: Venn, Alumni Cantabrigienses; Palatinate of Lancashire Plea Rolls 233, m. 19*d.*; 257, m. 12*d.*; 262, m. 14*d.*; 270, m. 14; S. J. T. Taswell, Whalley church and abbey, pp. 167, 172; Historic Society of Lancashire and Cheshire, vol. lxvii, p. 214; Wigan parish registers; Fishwick, History of Preston, p. 124; Victoria history of the county of Lancaster, ii. 604; Whalley parish register, i. 94.

ARTHUR J. HAWKES.

Carteret, Sir George. iii. 1117–9. A good letter from Carteret on the intrigues of Lord Jermyn with regard to the sale of Jersey is printed in *Nicholas Papers*, i. 258–61. On his colonial activities, see Justin Winsor, *Narrative and Critical History of America*, iii. 421, v. 286, and McCrady, *History of South Carolina under the Proprietary Government* (1897).

Cary, Sir Henry, first Viscount Falkland. iii. 1151*a*, ll. 11–8 from foot. For 'The other two sons . . . catholic church' read 'The other two sons were Patrick [q.v.] and Henry, who became a Benedictine monk under the name of Placid (B. Weldon, *English Benedictine Monks*, app. p. 20).'

Cary, Patrick. iii. 1160*b*, l. 30. For 'a year' read 'three months.'

Ibid. ll. 23–19 from foot. For 'He is said . . . 1887)' read 'He married Susan, daughter of Francis Uvedale, before 1654; by 1655 he was a protestant, living "an unhandsome rambling life" in England and Ireland, and was dead by 1685. The later Viscounts Falkland are descended from his son Edward (*Herald & Genealogist*, iii. 48; *Surrey Arch. Coll.*, iii. 124; *Nicholas Papers*, iii. 99, where however the identification with General Venables's secretary is wrong).'

Ibid. 1161*a*. To list of authorities add: Cal. Clarendon State Papers, vol. ii. (as 'Carey').

Cary, William (1759–1825). iii. 1162*b*, l. 15. Insert 'was the youngest son of George Cary of Warminster, or the neighbourhood. A mural tablet to William and Elizabeth his wife still exists on the wall of the north transept in St. Mary Abbott Church, Kensington. He was . . .'

Add to authorities: Sir H. G. Fordham's John Cary, Engraver, Map, Chart, and Print-seller, and Globe-maker, 1754 to 1835 (1925).

H. G. FORDHAM.

Casteels, Peter. iii. 1180*a*, l. 18. Delete 'and published . . . the profits' (Nichols, *Literary Anecdotes*, i. 387, 407).

Ibid. l. 28. For 'iii.' read 'ii.'

Castell, Edmund. iii. 1181*a*, ll. 21–15 from foot. For 'When worn out . . . in 1685.' read 'From 1636 to 1638 Castell held the living of Hatfield Peverel. In 1647 he appears as rector in the records of the neighbouring parish of Woodham Walters: he held the living until 1670. On 20 Jan. 1663 he was inducted into that of Higham Gobion, but a dispute between rival patrons kept him out until 1664. He held the adjacent cures of Higham and Hexton until his death (*Times Lit. Suppl.*, 1933, p. 751*b*).'

Ibid. l. 15 from foot. After '1685.' insert 'He married on 3 Aug. 1648 Dorothy Fytch of Woodham, who died in March 1651. By her he had one son and one daughter, both of whom died young' (*ibid.*).

Ibid. l. 14 from foot. After 'his' insert 'second'

Ibid. l. 13 from foot. Between 'married' and 'Elizabeth' insert 'also'

Cathcart, Charles, ninth Baron Cathcart. iii. 1194*a*, ll. 19–20. Delete 'The son at an early age . . . foot guards.'

Ibid. ll. 21–2. For 'In 1742 he commanded' read 'On 2 Apr. 1742 (P.R.O., Index 5436, p. 72) he was appointed captain of'; after 'Earl of Stair' insert ', and on 27 May 1745 he became captain and lieutenant-colonel in the 3rd regiment of foot guards (*ibid.* p. 34)'

Ibid. l. 27 from foot. After '1750' insert ', resigning his company in the foot guards on 27 Aug. 1753 (*ibid.* 5438, p. 100),'

Cavendish, Christiana, Countess of Devonshire. iii. 1252*b*, l. 26. For '*d.* 1675' read '1595–1675.'

Ibid., 1253*a*, l. 16. To authorities add: G.E.C.; some letters written by the countess about 1639 are printed in the Maitland Club 'Miscellany', vol. iii, pt. ii (1843), pp. 352–65.

Cavendish, Thomas. iii. 1267*b*, l. 16 from foot. After 'f. 131).' insert 'He matriculated from Corpus Christi, Cambridge, in 1576 (Venn, *Alumni Cantab.*, pt. 1, i. 311).'

Cavendish, William, second Earl of Devonshire. iii. 1273*a*, l. 4 from foot. For 'about 1612' read 'on 10 April 1608 (E. Lodge, *Illustrations of British history*, 2nd ed., 1838, iii. 232–5).'

Cavendish, William, third Earl of Devonshire. iii. 1278*b*, l. 25. After 'Cavendish's wife' add 'in 1639.'

Ibid., 1279*a*. To authorities add: G.E.C.

Cavendish, William, Duke of Newcastle (1592–1676). iii. 1273–8. Since 1887, when this article was published, a considerable amount of new information has come to light. The second volume of the *Report of the Hist. MSS. Comm. on the MSS. of the Duke of Portland*, published in 1893 (13th Report, app. ii.), contained a section devoted to the Cavendish papers (pp. 118–235). It calendared (pp. 134–7) a number of letters from Margaret Lucas to the Marquis of Newcastle, written in 1645, just before their marriage. These were published *in extenso* in 1909 in volume 153 of the issues of the Roxburghe Club by the Duke of Portland.

During his exile Newcastle wrote an elaborate political treatise addressed to Charles II, instructing him how he should act when he became King. One copy of this is in the Bodleian Library (Clarendon MS. 109), and was wrongly attributed to Clarendon himself; the other copy is in the possession of the Duke of Portland, and was printed in 1903 by Mr. S. A. Strong in the *Catalogue of Letters and other Historical Documents exhibited in the Library at Welbeck*, pp. 173–236. The new evidence illustrates Newcastle's interest in literature and science. His intimacy with Hobbes is attested by seven letters from Hobbes, written between 1634 and 1637, discussing scientific and philosophical matters; both, in the philosopher's phrase, were 'in love with knowledge.' Many of the opinions and theories set forth in the treatise addressed by Newcastle to Charles II are derived from Hobbes's *Behemoth* or his *Leviathan*. Ben Jonson's five letters to Newcastle are printed in vol. i. of *Jonson's Works*, ed. by C. H. Herford and Percy Simpson, Oxford, 1925, pp. 210–4. Much new information as to the literary activities and friendships of the Duke is contained in H. T. E. Perry's *The First Duchess of Newcastle and her Husband as figures in Literary History*, Boston, 1918 (Harvard Studies in English, vol. iv.). He points out, following Cokayne's *Complete Peerage*, that Newcastle was baptized on 16 Dec. 1593, at Handsworth, and adds other evidence as to his age (p. 7). He reprints also the twenty-one letters addressed by Margaret Lucas to Newcastle before their marriage.

The edition of the Duchess of Newcastle's Life of her husband, edited by C. H. Firth in 1906, contains matter not in the edition of 1886.

In the list of Newcastle's writings it should be noted that the play called 'The Country Captain' is identical with that printed in 1883 by Mr. A. H. Bullen, in the second volume of his *Old English Plays* (ii. 315), under the title of 'Captain Underwit,' and attributed by him to James Shirley.

The article omits to give an account of the Duke's descendants. By his first wife he had two sons and three daughters who survived infancy. The eldest son, Charles, Viscount Mansfield, died without issue in 1659. The second son, Henry, succeeded to the dukedom in 1676, married Frances Pierrepont, granddaughter of Robert, first Earl of Kingston, and died 26 July 1691. He left four daughters of whom he made the third, Margaret, heiress to his estates; she married in 1690 John Holles, Earl of Clare, created Duke of Newcastle in 1692. Their daughter, Lady Henrietta Cavendish-Holles, married in 1713 Edward Harley, second Earl of Oxford.

Cawthorn, James. iii. 1289*b*, l. 2 from foot. For 'Lord Eardley' read 'sir Sampson Gideon (later lord Eardley).'

Caxton, William. iii. 1292*b*, l. 20. After 'in his native country' add 'The earliest piece of his printing that has survived is an indulgence issued by abbot Sant to Henry Langley and his wife Katherine on 13 December 1476. The use of a different type for seven letters in the indulgence suggests that Caxton was making a new fount of type towards the end of 1476 (*The Times*, 7 Feb. 1928, pp. 15–16).'

1294*b*, 15 ll. from foot. For '1477' read '1476' (*Ibid.*).

Ibid. 10 ll. from foot. For '1479' read '1476' (*Ibid.*).

Cecil, Robert, 1st Earl of Salisbury. The year of his birth is not 'doubtful.' '1563, June 1—Robert Cecil born' is recorded in his father's handwriting (*Hatfield MSS.* v. 69). It is also recorded in a memorial inscription in Westminster Abbey, attributed to Burghley and printed in *Antiquities of St. Peter's*, 1722, and again in Nares's *Life of Burghley* (3 vols. 1828—31), iii. 503. Nares's life is not mentioned in the D.N.B. article on Burghley.

Cecil, William, Lord Burghley. iii. 1316*b*, l. 24. For 'In October 1551' read 'On 11 Oct. 1551 (*Literary Remains of Edward VI*, ii. 352).'

Chamberlayne, Edward (1616–1703). iv. 8*b*, l. 11. For 'Notitiae,' read 'Notitia'. *Ibid.*, ll. 27–33. For 'Hearne tells us . . . all later issues (Hearne, *Collections*, Oxf. Hist. Soc., i. 130), read 'Hearne and Wood tell us that Andrew Allam [q.v.] had contributed largely to one edition (that of 1687, according to Wood, *i.e.* the 16th), and that in subsequent issues his information was inserted by the Chamberlaynes without acknowledgment (Hearne, *Collections, etc.*: Wood, *Athenae Oxonienses*, iv. 174).'

Ibid., ll. 36–8. For 'The twenty-first edition (1708) bears the new title' etc., read 'The twenty-second edition appeared in two forms (1707 & 1708): the second of these bears the new title,' etc.

Ibid., ll. 39–43. For 'John Chamberlayne died . . . in 1723,' read 'The twenty-sixth edition appeared in 1723: John Chamberlayne died in the same year.' For 'fourteen editions' read 'twelve editions.' For 'thirty-sixth' read 'thirty-eighth.'

Chamberlayne, John (1666–1723). iv. 9*b*, l. 11 from foot. For 'five editions' read 'at least five editions.'

Charles II. iv. 89*b*, l. 8 from foot. For 'Early in June' read 'In the middle of July' (*Thurloe State Papers*, ii. 418; *Cal. Clarendon State Papers*, ii. 380, 382, 386). [See also BULLETIN, iii. 64.]

Charles II. iv. 104*b*, ll. 16 from bottom. To end of paragraph add 'Charles first came into the House to attend the debates on 21 March 1669–1670 (*Lords' Journals*, xii. 318).'

Charleton, William (1642–1702), naturalist. [See Courten, William]

Chaucer, Geoffrey. iv. 160*a*, ll. 10–7 from foot. For 'Some time early . . . pension in person' read 'He left England on 1 Dec. and returned on 23 May 1373.'

Ibid. 160*b*, l. 5 from foot. Delete 'It is conceivable Chaucer may have been present at his first lecture on 3 Aug. 1373.'

Ibid. 161*a*, ll. 1–2. Delete 'He returned to England . . . royal satisfaction'

Add to list of authorities: Modern Language Notes, xi. 419–21.

Cheke, Sir John. iv. 180*b*, l. 24. For '1552' read '1551.'

Ibid. l. 25. Delete 'Holland, *Herwologia*, p. 53.'

Cheselden, William. iv. 192*b*, ll. 4–3 from foot. Before 'In' insert 'He was elected a fellow of the Royal Society in 1711 and'; and for 'Royal Society' read 'society'.

Ibid. 193*a*, ll. 1 2. Delete 'and in the same year . . . society'.

Chevalier, John. iv. 214*a*. At end of article add 'The journal has been edited by J. A. Messervy for the Société Jersiaise (9 parts, 1906–14). It contains much important matter in connexion with the royalist fugitives in the Channel Islands, and was used by S. E. Hoskins [q.v.] in his "Charles II in the Channel Islands," 1854.'

E. S. DE B.

Chichele, Henry (1362 ?–1443). iv. 227*a*, l. 20 from foot. For 'July 1405' read 'July 1406'. For chronology of years 1406–8, see *Reg. Chichele*, i (Canterbury and York Society 1943), pp. xxv–xxviii.

Chicheley, Sir John. iv. 231*a*, l. 22. After 'Canterbury' insert 'was the son of Sir Thomas Chicheley [q.v.] by his first wife, Sarah Russell (*Le Neve's Pedigrees of the Knights*, Harleian Society, viii. 1873, p. 234).'

231*b*, l. 1. For 'In 1694' to the end substitute 'He married Isabella, daughter of Sir John Lawson, the admiral [q.v.], and widow of Daniel Norton of Southwick, Hants. Besides John there were five other children by this marriage (Le Neve, *u.s.*).' of Charles II., in James II.'s parliament, and in the Convention parliament; in 1685 he was also returned for Preston, Lancs, but elected to sit for Cambridge

(*Return of Members of Parliament*, i. 552, 553).'

At the end add 'Chicheley married (1) Sarah, daughter of Sir William Russell of Chippenham, Cambridgeshire, by whom he had four children, including Sir John Chicheley [q.v.]; (2) Anne, daughter of Thomas Lord Coventry [q.v.], and widow of Sir William Savile (*d.* Jan. 1643–4). She was buried at Wimpole, 31 July 1662. There were two children by this marriage (Le Neve's *Pedigrees of the Knights*, Harleian Society, viii. 1873, p. 234, and H. C. Foxcroft, *Life of Halifax*, i. 22, where some further notes as to Chicheley's career are given).'

Chicheley, Sir Thomas. iv. 231*b*, 2 ll. from bottom. For 'in 1678, 1679, 1685, and 1689' read 'in the last three parliaments

Chillingworth, William. iv. 256*a*, l. 18. After 'p. 300).' add 'On 30 Nov. 1641 it was alleged in the Commons that he had accused some of the members of treason. He appeared before the House the next day, and on 4 Dec. was committed to the Tower "for scandals and contempts against this howse." He petitioned for his release and was freed 20 Dec. (*Harl. MSS.* 162, fos. 199*b*, 203*b*, 211*b*–212*a*, 256*b*; 164, f. 231*a*; *Commons' Journals*, ii. 327, 329, 332, 350).'

Cholmley, Sir Hugh (1600–1657), royalist. iv. 268–9. He was born 22 July 1600, was married 10 Dec. 1622 (*Memoirs*, pp. 34, 39), and was knighted 19 May 1626 (Shaw, *The Knights of England*, ii. 190).

For his services to the parliament at the end of 1642, see *Hist. MSS. Comm.*, 10th Report, vi. 90, and *Report on the MSS. of the Duke of Portland*, i. 90. During the siege of Scarborough he had a curious epistolary controversy with Sir John Meldrum about the political causes of the war (*MSS. of Lord Braye*, pp. 155–6). Cholmley's narrative of the battle of Marston Moor is printed in *Eng. Hist. Rev.* v. 345; that of the siege of Scarborough in vol. xxxii. p. 568. It cost Cholmley £850 to compound for his estate; £450 was merely the first instalment, *Royalist Composition Papers*, ii. 21 (Yorkshire Archæological Society, Record Series, vol. xviii.). Cholmley's brother, Henry, was knighted 27 Dec. 1641. He it was, not Sir Hugh, who commanded a regiment in Essex's army at Edgehill (Peacock, *Army Lists*, p. 38). Sir Henry remained faithful to the parliamentary cause throughout, though much suspected in 1648; he acted with Fairfax to promote the Restoration in 1660, and died at Tangier about 1668 (*Memoirs*, p. 256).

Richard, another brother, was killed at the siege of Lyme fighting for the King (*Memoirs*, p. 29; Sir E. Walker, *Historical Discourses*, p. 87).

Hugh, the second son of Sir Hugh, ultimately succeeded to the baronetcy, and was the engineer who designed and built the famous Mole at Tangier. His account of the work is printed as an appendix to the *Memoirs* (ed. 1787). See also E. Routh, *Tangier, England's lost Atlantic Outpost* (1912).

Cholmondeley, Hugh, first earl of Cholmondeley. iv. 271*b*, l. 9 from foot. For '1724' read '1725' (*Complete Peerage*, 1913, iii. 202).

Churchill, Arabella (1648–1730), iv. 307*a*, l. 8. For 'Wootton Bassett, Wiltshire', read 'Wootton Glanville, Dorset'. (P. N. Dawe, 'The Dorset Churchills', *Somerset and Dorset N. & Q.*, xxvii (1958), 192.)

Churchill, Charles. iv. 308*b*, l. 5. For 'and' read ','

Ibid. l. 6. After 'buckhounds' read ', and lieutenant of the Tower of London.'

Ibid. ll. 10–13. After 'Nebel' delete ', an achievement . . . London'.

Churchill, Sir John (d. 1685), iv. 314*b*, l. 22 from foot. For 'Bradford, Somersetshire', read 'Bradford Peverell, Dorset'. (P. N. Dawe, 'The Dorset Churchills', *Somerset and Dorset N. & Q.*, xxvii (1958), 192.)

Churchill, John, 1st Duke of Marlborough. *Add* 'He fought two duels with Thomas Otway, the poet, in June 1679, in London.' (*Hist. MSS. Comm.*, 7th Rept., App. p. 473*a*.)

Churchill, Sir Winston (1620?–1688), iv. 342*b*, l. 4. For 'Nunthorn' read 'Minterne'. (P. N. Dawe, 'The Dorset Churchills', *Somerset and Dorset N. & Q.*, xxvii (1958), 192.)

Chute, Chaloner. iv. 348*b*, l. 15. For '(*d.* 1659)' read '(*c.* 1603–1659)'.

Ibid. l. 17. For 'Chaloner Chute' read 'Charles Chute'.

Ibid. ll. 19–21. For 'He was admitted . . . to the bar' read 'He matriculated at Cambridge, as a pensioner of Pembroke college, in 1613 and in the same year was admitted at the Middle Temple; he was apparently called to the bar on 23 May 1623 (Venn, *Alumni Cantab.*; *Middle Temple Records: Minutes*, ii. 572, 682, etc.).'

Ibid. 349*a*, l. 6 from foot. For 'His first wife was' read 'first, in 1627 (his age being given as twenty-four)'

Ibid. l. 5 from foot. After 'Skory' add 'and widow of William Plase (Harleian Soc., *Allegations for marriage licences issued by the bishop of London*, 1611–1828, p. 189)'. To authorities add: Chute pedigree in Harleian Soc., Visitation of London, 1633–5, i. 163.

Clarges, Sir Thomas. iv. 398*a*. This article is so defective as to require re-writing throughout.

Clarges, Sir Thomas (1619?–1695), politician, son of John Clarges, a farrier in the Savoy, by his wife Anne Leaver [see Monck, George, xiii. 608*a*], was probably born about 1619 (Luttrell, *Brief Relation*, iii. 534). During the civil war he served with the king's forces as an apothecary (*Harleian MSS.* 6851, f. 163; 6842, f. 41, etc.; 6804, f. 203, letter from him to Sir Edward Walker [q.v.], no date). On 23 Jan. 1652–3 his sister Anne married George Monck (a letter to Monck in Hist. MSS. Comm., *Buccleuch MSS. at Montagu House*, i. 308, referring to Clarges and Monck's wife, is wrongly dated 8 Nov. 1646; it is addressed to 'General Monck, in Scotland,' and so must be later). On 27 Aug. 1656 Clarges was returned as M.P. for Ross and Cromarty (*Return of M.P.'s*, Index volume, p. xlv). He was from the start a frequent and able speaker in the house and showed some independence (*Thurloe S.P.*, vi. 459; Burton, *Parl. Diary*, ii. 142, 201–2). In 1658 he was the London agent for the army in Scotland, the Council of Scotland, and the Council of Ireland (*Thurloe S.P.*, vii. 492, 563; several letters from him are printed in Thurloe). On the protector's death Richard Cromwell sent Clarges to Monck with dispatches; he brought back Monck's paper of advice to him (*ib.*, vii. 386, 387). In 1658–9 Clarges was member for the Haddington boroughs (*Old Parl. Hist.*, xxi. 261). From Sept. 1659 he was Monck's most important agent in London. He and Lenthall held back Monck's letter of resignation of 3 Sept. for ten days, until Monck changed his mind (Baker, *Chronicle*, cont. E. Phillips, 1674, p. 675; this part of the work was based on material supplied by Clarges: Wood, *Athenae Oxon.*, ed. Bliss, iii. 148). He now acted as the link between Monck and the parliament, keeping Monck fully informed of developments in England and encouraging the parliament in its resistance to the English army leaders. Late in Oct. he was sent by the latter to Monck with their proposals for an agreement. He arrived at Edinburgh on 2 Nov., returned to York where he arranged with Edward Bowles [q.v.] for Fairfax's subsequent action, and then went on to see Rossiter; he was, however, injured by a fall from his horse; he returned to London, arriving there on 15 Nov., but too late to prevent the signing of the agreement between Monck's commissioners and the English army leaders (Baker, pp. 678, 686–8). In London he organised the opposition to the Committee of Safety (Hist. MSS. Comm., *Leyborne-Popham MSS.*, p. 137) until he rejoined Monck at Nottingham on 22 Jan. 1660 (Baker, p. 701). He was appointed commissary general of the musters in Feb. (*C.J.* vii. 828) and clerk of the hanaper in March (*C.J.* vii. 873); he is traceable as commissary general till 1667. (*Cal. S.P.*, Dom., 1667, p. 184). He was returned to the convention for Westminster and Tregony, the latter return being disallowed (*Old Parl. Hist.*, xxii. 212; *C.J.* viii. 13; *Return of M.P.'s*, i. 513 and App. p. xlvi).

As one of Monck's chief political advisers, Clarges helped him to avoid Bordeaux's offers of French mediation (Baker, p. 717; Bordeaux's despatches in Guizot, *Monk*, trans. by Scoble, pp. 203, 232). Monck sent him to Charles II with his answer to Charles's letters of $\frac{4}{14}$ April and the Army's declaration of 2 May (Baker, pp. 727–8, 731; *C. J.* viii. 8). Clarges arrived at Breda on $\frac{8}{18}$ May. Charles knighted him as soon as he had read Monck's communications. Clarges remained with the court until $\frac{7}{17}$ May, when he sailed to England. He was driven by bad weather to land at Aldborough in Suffolk on 21 May, when he at once sent an express to parliament. He rejoined Monck at Rochester (Baker, p. 732; *C.J.* viii. 40).

Clarges is said to have helped to save Milton (MASSON, *Milton*, vi. 185, 187, 189). He was placed on the Irish privy council (*Cal. S.P., Ireland*, 1663–5, p. 49). On 13 March 1665–6 he was returned member for Southwark, and he represented Christchurch in the last three parliaments of Charles II and in James II's parliament. Until 1679 he belonged to the country party. On 21 May 1679 he made a notable speech against the first exclusion bill (Hist. MSS. Comm., *Ormonde MSS. at Kilkenny*, iv. 516; GREY, *Debates*, vii. 313). There are no records of his speeches against the later exclusion bills, but on 22 Nov. 1680 he spoke against the addresses to remove Halifax (*ib.* viii. 42), and his attitude towards exclusion led to his election being contested in 1685 (*Clarendon Corr.*, ed. S. W. Singer, i. 182–3). On 12 Nov. of that year he led the attack on James II's speech from the throne (GREY, viii. 355). In 1688 he was very intimate with Clarendon (*Clarendon Corr.* ii. *passim*). He sat for the university of Oxford in the convention and subsequent parliaments. In Jan. and Feb. 168 8/9 he spoke and voted against the clause declaring the throne vacant, thus approximating to Danby's position (GREY, ix. 15, 55; FEILING, *History of the Tory Party*, p. 497). In his later years he was one of the leading Tories in the lower house, but always remained independent. Towards the end of his life he was a friend of Robert Harley.

He died at his house in Piccadilly on 4 Oct. 1695 (Hist. MSS. Comm., *Portland MSS.*, iii. 568–70; *Topographer and Genealogist*, iii. (1858), 301). From contemporary accounts he was evidently well-to-do. He married Mary, daughter of George Procter of Norwell Woodhouse, Notts., by whom he had a son Walter, born about 1653 and created a baronet on 30 Oct. 1674 (FOSTER, *Alumni Oxon.*).

[Authorites cited].

E. S. DE B.

Clarke, Charles (*d.* 1750). iv. 417*a*, l. 6. After 'Godmanchester.' insert 'A portrait of Clarke in his judge's robes hangs in the hall of Corpus Christi college, Cambridge.'

Clarke, George (1661–1736). iv. 424–5. This article requires revision in the light of Clarke's autobiography printed by the Hist. MSS. Comm., *Leyborne-Popham MSS.*, pp. 259–89. In the following corrections and additions, wherever a statement is without a reference it comes from that work.

424*a*, 3 ll. from foot, to 424*b*, l. 3. For information about Clarke's mother see additions to CLARKE, Sir WILLIAM.

424*b*, l. 5. Clarke was educated at a school kept by a Mr. Gordon in what is now Jermyn Street; he left at the age of ten, thenceforward reading the classical authors with his stepfather until he went to Brasenose College, Oxford, in December 1676; he matriculated 15 Dec. 1675, but did not pay his caution money until the following year (*Brasenose College Registers*, i. 234: Oxford Hist. Soc.). He had previously been entered as a student at the Inner Temple (F. A. Inderwick, *Records of the Inner Temple*, iii. 107).

Ibid. l. 9 seq. He was entered at All Souls on 1 Dec. 1680, in place of one of the Trumbulls, probably Charles [q.v. under TRUMBULL, Sir WILLIAM], who had been deprived of his fellowship. Clarke's retention of his fellowship appears to have been due to his love of Oxford and of his friends there.

Ibid. ll. 19–20. Clarke's office of judge-advocate (425*a*, ll. 11–12) should be mentioned here. He obtained it in succession to Barrow.

Ibid. ll. 20–5, 29–33. Clarke's political attitude in 1685 is not very clear. Anthony Wood disapproved of the choice of Clarke as member for the university (*Life and Times*, iii. 171, where Clarke is described as 'a good fellow'). Clarke had no mind to be 'closeted,' so retired from London to Oxford to avoid James II, and from Oxford to Wales to avoid Obadiah Walker [q.v.]. By judicious travelling he escaped being questioned until parliament was dissolved (July 1687), and so managed to retain his office of judge-advocate. When James II came to Oxford in September 1687 Clarke was present and argued with him about the tenure of lands of All Souls (a second account in Wood, *Life and Times*, iii. 232).

Ibid. l. 33. After 'until it was dissolved' insert 'In November 1688 Clarke followed James as far as Salisbury, as his office required; when the desertion became general he retired to Oxford, only coming to London after the king's first flight. After the declaration of William and Mary as king and queen, Clarke had his commission renewed.

'In 1689 Clarke joined the commissioners

for the regulation of the army, travelling with them as far as Edinburgh, where he saw the surrender of the castle (14 June). In 1690 he went to Ireland with William III, acting as secretary at war there and apparently hoping to succeed William Blathwayt [q.v.] in the same post in England. He was present at the battle of the Boyne, of which he gives an interesting account, and continued with the army until the capture of Limerick (thirteen volumes of his Irish papers are preserved at Trinity College, Dublin : T. K. Abbott, *Catalogue of MSS. in Trinity College, Dublin*, 1900, no. 749 ; some letters from him when in Ireland are printed in Hist. MSS. Comm., *MSS. of A. G. Finch*, ii.). Clarke left Ireland on 5 Dec. 1691. On 3 March 1692 he was given a commission as secretary at war in the king's absence (*Cal. S.P., Dom.*, 1691–92, p. 165); this post he held until William III's death. On Anne's accession he was persuaded to become secretary to prince George of Denmark, recently appointed lord high admiral ; Clarke also assisted Josiah Burchett [q.v.], the secretary to the admiralty.'

Ibid. ll. 33–6. For 'Out of parliament . . . for East Looe' read 'He was elected member of parliament for Winchelsea on 21 May 1702 (prince George was also warden of the Cinque Ports), and for East Looe on 22 May 1705 (in *Return of Members* as "Clerke").'

Ibid. 17 ll. from foot. Clarke gives an interesting account of his dismissal by prince George ; he had sold his place as judge-advocate to Thomas Byde about six months earlier. In the summer of 1706 Clarke travelled in the Netherlands.

425*a*, ll. 1–6. Hearne's story about Clarke and the occasional conformity bill is certainly incorrect as it stands ; he wrote it down on 22 March 1722 (*Collections*, vii. 341 : Oxford Hist. Soc.).

Ibid. ll. 20–25. On 20 Dec. 1710 Clarke was made one of the lords commissioners for the admiralty (Luttrell, vi. 666), and retained that position until 14 Oct. 1714. On 29 May 1711 he was returned to parliament for Launceston in place of Henry Hyde, who had recently succeeded to the title of earl of Rochester. In 1715 Clarke travelled in France. While in Paris he saw Bolingbroke frequently, but just missed meeting his old friend Ormonde (some letters from Clarke to Ormonde are printed in Hist. MSS. Comm., 7th Rep.). Oxford Jacobites at the time of Clarke's first election as member for the university charged him with deliberately avoiding Ormonde (see also Hearne, *Collections*, vi. 98. Hearne describes Clarke as 'what they call an Hanoverian Tory,' vi. 112). He was elected as member for the university of Oxford on 4 Dec. 1717 in place of Sir William Whitlock, and continued to represent the university until his death.

Ibid. l. 15 from foot. The money for the statues is said to have come from Dr. John Radcliffe [q.v.] (Hearne, *Collections*, vii. 14).

Ibid. l. 9 from foot. The design for Christ Church library requires adequate discussion. It is the most important of Clarke's designs and of unusual beauty. It was perhaps directly influenced by the work of the Italian architects of the sixteenth century.

Ibid. l. 7 from foot. After 'Aldrich' insert 'He erected another monument, that of his cousin Elizabeth Cary (died 10 March 1724) in the church of St. Mary the Virgin, Oxford.'

Ibid. l. 3 from foot. After 'and Ben Jonson' add '(for Clarke's interest in the Bodleian see his letter to Edward Harley, earl of Oxford, in Hist. MSS. Comm., *Portland MSS. at Welbeck*, vi. 38).'

425*b*, l. 21. After 'books' add '(for important information concerning them, Clarke's literary interests and his relations with authors, see the note contributed by Mr. C. H. Wilkinson to Andrew Marvell, *Poems and Letters*, ed. H. M. Margoliouth, i. 332–4).'

Ibid. l. 24. After 'Whitehall' add '(for the provenance of the drawings see Jones, Inigo. Other drawings besides those for Whitehall are included in the collection).'

Ibid. l. 27. For the Clarke MSS. see additions to Clarke, Sir William.

Ibid. ll. 19–12 from foot. To list of authorities add : C. E. Mallet, A History of the University of Oxford, iii. Letters are to be found in various volumes of Hist. MSS. Comm.

Note : An adequate list of Clarke's friends would be of value, but lengthy and difficult to make up. It would include admiral George Churchill, James Butler, second duke of Ormonde, Henry Aldrich, Lawrence Hyde, earl of Rochester, Dr. Savage (probably John, 1673–1747), Bernard Gardiner, Richard Hill, Simon Harcourt, first viscount Harcourt, William Bromley [qq.v.]. Mr. C. H. Wilkinson (see above) gives a further list of poets, writers, and politicians with whom Clarke was associated.

E. S. DE B.

Clarke, Sir William. iv. 448*b*, l. 3 from foot, to 449*a*, l. 8. For 'secretary at war . . . (Lysons, *Environs*, iii. 246)' read 'secretary at war, was born in London of unknown parentage. He has been identified with a William Clarke admitted as a student to the Inner Temple in November 1645 (*Students admitted to the Inner Temple*, p. 320) and called to the bar 24 Nov. 1653 (F. A. Inderwick, *Records of the Inner Temple*, ii. 332), but there is no satisfactory ground for the identification; during most of the period Clarke was absent from London.

'When the New Model army was organised in 1645 John Rushworth [q.v.] was appointed secretary to the general and the council of war. Clarke became his assistant, probably on his first appointment, certainly before March 1647 (his name is given in the list of the New Model printed by J. Sprigge, *Anglia Rediviva*, 1647, p. 327. This list notes changes in personnel but is not absolutely reliable).

'In 1650 he took part in Cromwell's invasion of Scotland, and on 19 Oct. the officers of that army recommended him for the post of secretary to the committee of the army (*Clarke Papers*, i. 224–5). This application was unsuccessful, as was another of 19 Aug. 1651 for his appointment as keeper of the Scottish records, recently captured in Stirling castle (H. Cary, *Memorials of the Civil War*, ii. 332). From the autumn of 1651 Clarke was secretary to the army of occupation in Scotland, serving under Deane, Robert Lilburne, and Monck (*Clarke Papers*, iii. *v*, *vi*).

'At the time of the Restoration Clarke adhered to Monck in spite of an attempt on the part of Col. Robert Lilburne [q.v.] to win him over (Edward Phillips, continuation of Baker's *Chronicle*, ed. 1674, p. 684). As a result he was knighted about 1 Jan. 1661 (*Mercurius Publicus*, no. 54, 27 Dec. 1660–3 Jan. 1661, p. 836), and appointed secretary at war on 28 Jan. 1661 (*Cal. S.P., Dom.*, 1660–61, p. 490); in addition he received leases for a term of years of a fourth part of St. John's Wood and of sixty acres of land in Marylebone Park (Hist. MSS. Comm., *Leyborne-Popham MSS.* p. 194; D. Lysons, *Environs of London*, iii. 246).'

Ibid. 449*a*, ll. 26–35. For 'Clarke married . . . judge-martial' read 'About November 1648 Clarke married Dorothy, daughter of Thomas Hilyard of Hampshire and his wife Elizabeth Kympton (for the date of the marriage *Leyborne-Popham MSS.* p. 8; for particulars about the Hilyards *ibid.*, pp. *xi–xiii*); one of her sisters was married to Gilbert Mabbott, the printer and sometime licenser of the press, and another to William Carey, goldsmith of London; there was also a brother, Kympton Hilyard; the three men all corresponded with Clarke. By the marriage there was apparently a child who died young (*Clarke Papers*, ii. p. ix), and George Clarke (1660–1736) [q.v.]. Soon after her husband's death Lady Clarke married Samuel Barrow, M.D. (1625–82), Milton's friend, chief physician to Monck's army in Scotland and, after the Restoration, physician in ordinary to the king and judge-advocate of the army. The marriage was very happy according to George Clarke (*Leyborne-Popham MSS.* p. 260); Barrow is known to have been connected with Clarke in 1660 (*ibid.* p. 211; *Clarke Papers*, iv. 269). His widow died on 27 July 1695 (*Leyborne-Popham MSS.* p. 282); her arms with those of her two husbands are carved on her monument, and are described by D. Lysons, "Environs of London," ii. 371 *n.*'

Ibid. ll. 23–8 from bottom. The note concerning Clarke's papers requires revision as follows:

Clarke formed a valuable collection of military and political papers, of which the greater part was bequeathed by his son George Clarke [q.v.] to Worcester College, Oxford (partial list in H. O. Coxe, *Catalogus Codicum MSS. qui in Collegiis Aulisque Oxoniensibus hodie adservantur*); another part descended to Mr. F. W. Leyborne-Popham of Littlecote, Wilts (the documents forming British Museum Egerton MSS. 2618–21 were once part of the Littlecote collection and were purchased for the Museum in 1884); another part came to light at the sale of some of the MSS. of Sir Thomas Phillipps in 1898 and is now in the National Library of Scotland at Edinburgh (*Clarke Papers*, iv. p. vi). Selections from the collection have been published by Sir Charles Firth as the 'Clarke Papers' (4 vols., 1891–1901, Camden and Royal Historical Societies), and as 'Scotland and the

Commonwealth' and 'Scotland and the Protectorate' (1895, 1899, Scottish Historical Society); and by the Historical MSS. Commission as 'Leyborne-Popham MSS.' (ed. Mrs. S. C. Lomas, 1899; the publication was co-ordinated with that of the 'Clarke Papers'). The letters from Cromwell in Egerton MS. 2620 are included in 'Letters and Speeches of Oliver Cromwell,' by T. Carlyle (ed. Mrs. S. C. Lomas, 1904); a few smaller pieces have appeared elsewhere. Clarke's diary relating to naval affairs (23 April–1 June 1666) is preserved in the British Museum (Add. MS. 14286). Clarke also made a valuable collection of printed pamphlets and broadsides, bequeathed, as were the papers, by his son to Worcester College.

E. S. de B.

Clavel, John (1603–1642). iv. 459*a*, l. 5 from foot. For 'He was apprehended in 1627 . . . death', read 'He was apprehended, convicted and sentenced to death on 30 Jan. 1626 but was reprieved'.

***Ibid.* 459*b*, l. 7. After 'in 1634,' add 'He was probably the author of the play entitled 'The Soddered Citizen' which has been ascribed to Shackerley Marmion. This play was first published in 1936 in the Malone Society Reprints.'**

Cleland, James. iv. 483*b*, ll. 21–18 from foot. For ', and began . . . public works.' read '. He was born in Jan. 1770, was apprenticed to his father, a cabinet-maker, and in 1789 went to London. In 1791 he returned to Glasgow as his father's partner. In Oct. 1803 he became bailie of Glasgow, in Sept. 1804 he was authorised to superintend the building of a new toll-house, and in 1807 his plan for the building of a new grammar school was adopted. On 6 Sept. 1814 he was elected superintendent of public works and superintendent of statute labour to the city of Glasgow, resigning the latter office on 9 May 1818.'

Ibid. l. 14 from foot. After '1831.' insert 'Among his numerous services to the city of Glasgow may be mentioned the adjustment of weights and measures to the legal standards, the erection of St. David's church, the drawing up of the bills of mortality from 1820 to 1834, and the designing of the Candleriggs bazaar. He retired in 1834, and died on 14 Oct. 1840 (*Extracts from the Records of the Burgh of Glasgow*, ix. 378, 422, 601–2; x. 261, 429–31; xi. 18, 198; MacGregor, *History of Glasgow*, pp. 418–9).'

Clephane, John. iv. 493*b*, l. 17 from foot. After '1729' insert ', having previously studied medicine at Leyden and Paris. In 1731 he was in Groningen supervising the studies of Lord Sherard Manners, a younger brother of the duke of Rutland, and during the next six years travelled with his pupil over the greater part of Europe and corresponded regularly with the Rutland family. In 1732 he translated into English "Le tableau du temple des Muses," which was later published in Amsterdam. His connexion with the Rutland family ended in 1739, and in the following year he toured Europe again as the friend and tutor of Lord Mansell. In 1744 he was travelling in the company of the earl of Mountrath. On 22 May 1747 he was appointed one of the physicians to the British hospital at Osterhout.'

Ibid. l. 5 from foot. After 'St. Clair's secretary.' insert 'His brother, James Clephane, was a major in the Scots brigade in Holland (Scot. Hist. Soc. xxxv. 232*n*), later transferred to the 78th regiment, Fraser's Highlanders, and was present at the capture of Louisburg in Sept. 1758.'

Add to list of authorities: W. S. Wallace's Some Notes on Fraser's Highlanders (*Canadian Hist. Rev.*, xviii. 135*n*); C. Innes's Genealogical deduction of the family of Rose of Kilravock (Spalding Club Pub., no. 18), pp. 445–65.

Clerk, William. iv. 500*b*, l. 3. After 'August 1655' insert 'He was buried on 3 Aug. at St. Benet's, Paul's Wharf (*Reg.* iv. 43: Harl. Soc. xli. cited in *Mariner's Mirror*, xiii. 340).'

Clifford, Anne, Countess of Dorset, iv. 513*a*. 'The autobiography . . . was formerly preserved at Skipton Castle, but is no longer there' (1887). It was deposited in the P.R.O. by Lord Hothfield for examination, with other documents relating to her and her father the Earl of Cumberland, by the Hist. MSS. Commission; and an account, with lengthy excerpts from the autobiography, was printed in the Commission's 11th Rep., App. vii. 81–90 (1888).

Clifford, Henry fifth earl of Cumberland (1591–1643). iv. 520*b*, l. 6. The friendship of Clifford and Wentworth did not date from the latter's marriage; Wentworth and Clifford were at school together. (Wentworth Woodhouse Papers, Sheffield.)

Clifton, Richard. iv. 543*b*, l. 11 from foot. For '*d.* 1616' read '1553 ?–1616.'

Ibid. l. 10 from foot. After 'divine' add 'born at Normanton, Derby, eldest son of Thomas Clifton of Normanton by his first wife.'

Ibid. l. 6 from foot. For 'and' read 'He was appointed.'

Ibid. l. 4 from foot. After 'Scrooby' add 'and in September married Ann, daughter of I. Stuffen of Warsop, Notts.'

544*a*, l. 13 from foot. After '1616' add 'aged 63 and was buried in the South-church. His wife had died there on 3 Sept. 1613, aged 58. Their three daughters, born at Babworth, died in infancy; their three sons, also born at Babworth, were Zachary, *b.* 12 May 1589, Timothy, *b.* 29 Sept. 1595, *d.* 7 June 1663 at Amsterdam, and Eleazer, *b.* 1 Nov. 1598, *d.* 18 Jan. 1669 at Amsterdam.'

NOTE.—The above additions are made from a family bible now in the Taylor institution, Oxford.

A. C. M.

Clinton, Sir Henry (1738?–1795), iv. 550*b*, last line. For 'He died at that post on 23 Dec. 1795', read 'From the correspondence of General Charles Rainsford, resident in Gibraltar in 1795 and 1796, it would appear that Clinton never took up his post in Gibraltar (Brit. Mus., Add. MSS. 23660 fo. 128b, 23670, fo. 180b, 23664, fo. 148). According to *The Times*, 26 Dec. 1795, he died in Cornwall.'

Clotworthy, Sir John, first Lord Massereene. iv. 582. Clotworthy took part in the colonisation of Massachusetts and corresponded with Winthrop about it (Winthrop, *History of New England*, i. 206, ed. 1853; *Massachusetts Historical Collections*, 5th Series, i. 203–8).

582*a*, 7 ll. from foot. Read 'Clotworthy's regiment was armed and despatched to Ulster. He served with it himself for about a year; after that it was commanded by his brother, Lieut.-Col. James (Reid, *History of the Presbyterian Church in Ireland*, i. 331, 351–4).' Omit the words 'reprinted by Gilbert.' *A History of the Wars of Ireland from 1641 to 1653 by a British Officer of the regiment of Sir John Clotworthy*, edited by E. H., Dublin, 1873, contains many details about the services of the regiment.

582*b*, l. 7. After 'kingdoms' insert 'one of the lay assessors appointed to represent Parliament in the Westminster Assembly.'

582*b*, l. 13. Add: 'He was an active member of the Committee appointed, on 1 July 1645, to prepare and consider propositions for the relief of Ireland (*Cal. State Papers, Ireland*, 1633–47, p. 405).'

583*a*, l. 7. Add: 'He returned to Ireland about 1655, and in view of his services against the rebels was granted a lease of Lough Neagh on favourable terms by the Protector (*Thurloe Papers*, v. 19, 701, 719). With Lord Deputy Fleetwood and the Irish council he had considerable influence which he successfully exerted for the benefit of the presbyterian ministers of Ulster (Adair's *True Narrative*, pp. 216–220).'

Ibid., l. 23. After 'presbyterians' add the reference '(Adair, pp. 242, 252, 264–7).'

Ibid. At the end add: 'He married Mary, daughter of Roger Jones, Viscount Ranelagh. Their only child, Mary, married Sir John Skeffington, Bart., to whom the title of Massereene descended (Lodge, *Peerage of Ireland*, iii. 63, ed. 1754).'

Ibid. Add to the authorities: '*A True Narrative of the rise and progress of the Presbyterian Church in Ireland*, by Patrick Adair, ed. by W. D. Killen, Belfast, 1866; J. S. Reid, *The History of the Presbyterian Church in Ireland*.'

Clotworthy's portrait was acquired by the National Portrait Gallery in 1925.

Clough, Arthur Hugh. iv. 584*a*, l. 32. After 'appointment' add 'He was elected to the chair of English language and literature at University College, London, in 1850, but resigned in 1852' (*University College, London. Proceedings at the Annual General Meeting . . . 26th February* 1851, p. 6; *ibid., 23rd February* 1853, p. 6).

Cobham, John de, third **Baron Cobham.** iv. 612*a*, l. 55. After 'at Cobham Church' add '(*Antiquaries Journal*, ii. 342).'

Cogan, Thomas (1736–1818), iv. 677*a*, l. 24–31. From the Consistorial records of the English Reform church at Amsterdam it is clear that Cogan was substituting for the Rev. David Longueville, 1st minister of that church, who had obtained leave to go to Great Britain for health reasons. It would appear likely therefore that it was here he met Mr. Gerard Groen, banker, not at the Hague, *ib.* l. 21 from foot.

Cokayne, Sir William. iv. 683*b*, ll. 29–33. For 'In 1612, when the plantation of Ulster was commenced, . . . established' read 'From 30 Jan. 1610 to 27 Aug. 1614 he was governor of the society set up by the City to manage its plantations in Ulster, during which time the new city and county of Londonderry were founded (City Records, Journals 28, ff. 49–49*b*, 29, f. 224*b*).'

T. W. M.

Coke, Thomas William of Holkham, Earl of Leicester. iv. 705*b*, l. 4 from foot. For 'born on 4 May 1752' read 'born on 6 May 1754' (A. M. W. Stirling, *Coke of Norfolk and his Friends*, 1912, p. 46).

Colburn, Henry. iv. 711*a*, l. 22. After 'survived him' add 'and later married John Forster [q.v.].'

Cole, Henry. iv. 723*b*, l. 24 from foot to 724*a*, l. 4. Delete 'Soon afterwards . . . (Cox, *Hist. of Ireland*, i. 308).' This account is based upon the forged documents of Robert Ware, printed in 'Harleian Miscellany,' v. 595–606 (*see* art. Ware, Sir James, below).

Coleman, Edward. iv. 744*a*, ll. 27–21 from foot. A reference to him in A. & J. Churchill, '*A Collection of Voyages and Travels* . . .' vi. 384*a* (1732), is important as identifying, more or less satisfactorily, the conspirator with the Cambridge student and indicates that he was a convert.

E. S. de B.

Colepeper, John, first Baron Colepeper. iv. 752 *a*, l. 16 from foot. For '11 June 1660' read '11 July 1660' (Kennet, *Register*, pp. 203–4).

Coleridge, Sir John Duke, first Baron Coleridge. First Suppl. 469*b*, l. 18 from foot. For '1875' read '1877' (*Record of Royal Soc.*, p. 416).

Coleridge, Samuel Taylor. iv. 768*a*, l. 5 from foot–786*b*, l. 1. For 'In 1811 Josiah Wedgwood . . . unnatural irritation' read 'In 1812 Josiah Wedgwood, owing to financial reverses, withdrew his share of the annuity ; an action, due neither to disapproval nor disappointment, which awakened in Coleridge neither vexation nor complaint' (*Notes and Queries*, clviii. 56).

Ibid. 768*b*, l. 2. After 'Coleridge' insert 'who had transferred his family to Southey.'

Colet, Sir Henry. iv. 777*a*, ll. 14 from bottom. For '21 June' read '21 September.' *Rec. Corp. Lond.*, *Journal* viii. f. 155.

Colet, John. iv. 777*b*, l. 7 from foot. For 'founder' read 'refounder' (*Notes and Queries*, clviii. 257).

Ibid. 780*b*, ll. 22–23. For 'foundation . . . St. Paul's Churchyard' read 're-foundation and endowment of the ancient grammar school of St. Paul's' (*ibid.*).

Colet, John. iv. 778*b*, ll. 9–10. For 'although . . . known' read 'was staying in Rome on 1 Apr. 1493 (letter to Christopher Urswick, *Amer. Hist. Rev.*, xxxix. 696–9).'

Collier, Jeremy. iv. 798*a*, ll. 25–6. For 'For some years . . . of his life' read 'In 1694 Collier published, under the title "Miscellanies," five essays which, with one addition, were re-issued in 1697 as Part I of "Essays upon Moral Subjects." Some had already appeared in separate form.'

Ibid. 798*b*, ll. 28–24 from foot. Delete 'In the course of 1697 . . . in a smaller collection.' and transfer the rest of this paragraph to 798*a*, to follow the preceding correction.

Ibid. 801*b*, ll. 13–12 from foot. For '"Miscellanies in Five Essays," 1694, 8vo (Cole), afterwards in Part I' read '"Miscellanies : in Five Essays," 1694, 8vo (Congregational Libr.), afterwards, with one addition, Part I'

Ibid. l. 11 from foot. After 'Moral Subjects' insert ', 17a. "Miscellanies upon Moral Subjects. The Second Part," 1698, 8vo (Congregational Libr.), afterwards Part II of "Essays on Moral Subjects."'

Ibid. 802*a*, ll. 6–19. For 'has seventeen . . . "Biographia"' read '(see 17a)'

Ibid. l. 19. After 'other editions' insert '3rd, 1698 ;'

Collins, Greenvile. iv. 823*b*, l. 3. For details of Collins' life previous to 1679 and extracts from a journal kept by him see 'Mariner's Mirror,' xiv. 197–219.

Colvin, Sir Sidney (1845–1927), vol. 1922–30, 202*a*, l. 24. For 'He resigned the directorship [of the Fitzwilliam Museum] in 1884' read 'He resigned . . . 12 October 1883 (*The Times*, 12 Oct. 1883, p. 5*f*).'

Combe, Taylor. iv. 886*b*, l. 2. For '1806' read '1807' (*Record of Royal Soc.*, p. 375).

Compton, alias **Carleton, Thomas.** iv. 908*b*, ll. 13–16. Delete 'Having been ordained . . . (Foley, *Records*, vii. 154).' The person ordained in 1622 was not Compton but Thomas Carleton, alias Medcalf, author of a play called 'Fatum Vortigerni' in Lansdowne MS. 723. Compton had been a priest for a year or two in 1622.

Conolly, John. iv. 952*b*, ll. 34–5. Omit 'in the following year.' See *The Times*, 14 July 1827, 2*e*.

l. 36. For 'University College' read 'London University [now University College].'

Conway, Edward. iv. 976*a*, ll. 18–19. For '8 Dec. 1625' read '17 Dec. 1624 (*Cal. S.P., Dom.*, 1623–25, p. 410).' Conway's appointment was known on 27 Nov.; he succeeded Henry Wriothesley, third earl of Southampton [q.v.], in the office (*ibid.* pp. 394, 396).

NOTE: The whole article is inaccurate; a better account, with more reliable dates, is given in G. E. C., 'Complete Peerage,' ed. Vicary Gibbs.

E. S. DE B.

Cook, James (1728–1779). iv. 992*a*, l. 3. After 'village school' insert 'possibly at the expense of Thomas Skittowe, his father's landlord' (*Notes and Queries*, clviii. 100–101).

Cook, James (1728–1779). iv. 994*b*, ll. 21–24. 'Cook's body was partly burnt by the savages, but the most of it was given up a day or two afterwards and duly buried.'

For another account of the disposal of Cook's body see 'Mariner's Mirror,' xiii. 379.

Cook, James. iv. 994*b*, l. 7 from foot. For 'Miss' read 'Elizabeth (*Notes and Queries*, clxxvi. 15)'

Ibid. last line. After 'eldest,' insert 'born 1764 (*ibid.*),'

Ibid. 995*a*, l. 5. After 'Hugh' insert '(1775–1793, *ibid.*)'

Cook, John (*d.* 1660). iv. 995*b*. Read '1608–1660, son of Isaac Cook of Husbands Bosworth, Leicestershire, born there 1608, matriculated 31 Jan. 1622–3, aged 14, from Wadham College, and was admitted to Gray's Inn in 1631 (Foster, *Alumni Oxonienses*; a pedigree of his family is given in the Leicestershire Visitation of 1619).'

The letter to Strafford, referred to, is printed in *Papers relating to Thomas Wentworth*, Camden Miscellany, vol. ix. 1895, p. 14.

996*a*, last line. Add: 'Cook married in 1645, Frances . . . Her petition regarding his lands in Ireland, granted by Charles II to Sir George Lane, is printed in *Cal. State Papers, Ireland*, 1663–5, p. 514. Her daughter, Freelove, married Major John Gunthorpe of Antigua (information from Mr. E. Hampden Cook).'

Cooper, Samuel (1780–1848). iv. 1074*a*, l. 10. For '1831' read '1834.' l. 12. After 'college' add 'from 1831 to 1848.' See London University [now University College], Minutes of the Sessions of the Council, ii. 322, 323–4, 455.

Coote, Richard, First Earl of Bellamont. (1636–1701). iv. 1088*b*, l. 38. He made an attack on Lord Coningsby and Sir Charles Porter on their impeachment in the House of Commons (*D.N.B.* xvi. 172*a*, l. 7). For this action he was dismissed. The Duke of Shrewsbury and the Earl of Sunderland interested themselves in his reinstatement. See *Shrewsbury Correspondence*, p. 40, and Vernon, *Letters of Reign of William III.*, i. 365, 423, 428.

R. M. H.

Cope, Sir Walter. iv. 1093*a*, l. 17 from foot. After 'Discourses' insert 'Faulkner, *Kensington*, pp. 58–67, 139–141.'

Corbett, Thomas. iv. 1132*a*, l. 29. For '*d.*' read '*c.* 1687–'

BULLETIN, xiv. 54*a*, l. 5 from foot. After 'Treasury),' insert 'was a King's Scholar of Westminster School, 1701 (Barker and Stenning, *Record of Old Westminsters*, i. 214), and entered the navy as an ordinary seaman, 23 March 1703/4, on board the Ranelagh, the flagship of Sir George Byng [q.v.] (P.R.O. Admiralty pay-book, 33/236, no. 717), serving during the 1704 operations in the Mediterranean and the capture of Gibraltar. On 14 Dec. 1704 he was appointed admiral's clerk and in this capacity served under Byng on the

Barfleur, 18 Dec. 1704 to 23 Jan. 1704/5 (*ibid.* 33/235, no. 215), on the Ranelagh, 24 Jan. to 9 Apr. (*ibid.* 33/251, no. 814), on the Mary, 10 Apr. to 30 May (*ibid.* 33/247, no. 587), and on the Triumph, from 31 May to 6 Sept. (*ibid.* 33/237, no. 830). In the autumn he was appointed admiral's secretary and acted as judge advocate and deputy treasurer of the fleet. Rejoining Byng on the Royal Anne, 29 Dec. 1705 (*ibid.* 33/249, no. 147), he was present at the relief of Barcelona and the capture of Alicante in 1706 and at the abortive descent on Toulon in the following year. When Byng returned to England in the autumn of 1709, Corbett was transferred to the Royal Sovereign, 6 Dec., and acted as secretary to Admiral Matthew (afterwards Lord) Aylmer [q.v.] until 19 Oct. 1710 (*ibid.* 33/281, no. 85). During the channel operations of 1711 he again accompanied Byng on board the Cumberland (*ibid.* 33/266, no. 685). From Feb. to Aug. 1712 he was at Utrecht, vainly hoping to secure the position of secretary to the earl of Strafford [q.v.], the chief plenipotentiary and the new first lord of the admiralty. His letters to Byng at this period show how completely he had been, and still was, dependent upon the latter's patronage. When Byng returned to the admiralty on the accession of George I, Corbett'

Ibid. l. 3 from foot. For 'and' read In the summer of the same year he accompanied Byng during the channel operations against the Jacobites.'

D.N.B. iv. 1132*a*, l. 31. For ', and' read 'was'

Ibid. ll. 28–25 from foot. For 'was secretary . . . of which he' read 'His younger brother William succeeded him as Byng's secretary during the Baltic operations of 1717 and the Mediterranean campaign of 1718–20, of which latter campaign Thomas'

Ibid. l. 10 from foot. After 'social equal.' insert 'In 1715 Corbett published a translation of Henry Michelet's "Mediterranean Pilot," dedicated to Byng, and in 1731 he supervised the publication of the first edition of the "Regulations and Instructions relating to His Majesty's Service at Sea" (*Mariner's Mirror*, xiv. 165–7). He was secretary of Greenwich Hospital, 1716–36, and was succeeded by his brother William.'

Ibid. l. 9 from foot. For 'till death' read 'until his death, 30 Apr. 1751'

BULLETIN, xiv. 54*b*, l. 7. For 'The' read 'His'

Ibid. l. 10. After 'Admiralty library.' add 'There are portraits of Thomas Corbett by Kneller and of William Corbett by Hudson at the Admiralty.'

Add to list of authorities: Byng Papers, (Navy Records Soc.), iii. pp. xi–xvi, 37–50.

Douglas, Archibald, second Earl of Forfar. v. 1191*b*, l. 16. For '1693' read '1692 (G.E.C. *Complete Peerage*, 2nd. ed., v. 555).'

Ibid. l. 18. For '1693' read '1692.'

Ibid. l. 24. For 'twenty' read 'twenty-one.'

Ibid. l. 25. For '10th.' read '3rd.'

Ibid. l. 18 from foot. After 'extinct' insert 'or possibly dormant (G.E.C. *op. cit.* p. 556).'

Add to list of authorities: *Journal of the Soc. for Army Hist. Research*, xv. 126–43.

Corbett, Thomas. iv. 1132*a*, l. 30. After 'admiralty,' read 'elder son of William Corbett, of the youngest branch'

Ibid. l. 31. After 'Moreton Corbet' read 'and Eleanor, daughter of Col. Jones of Nantoes,'

Ibid. ll. 31–2. For 'apparently a near relation' read 'nephew'

Ibid. l. 34. After 'Treasury),' read 'entered the admiralty office as a clerk, 17 Jan. 1715 and'

Ibid. l. 21 from foot. After 'Burchett [q.v.];' read 'he was appointed joint-secretary in April 1741 (P.R.O., Privy council register) and'

Ibid. l. 9 from foot. After 'death.' insert 'He married, 31 Jan. 1740, Mary Lloyd of Duke St. (*Collectanea Topographica et Genealogica*, iii. 384), and left one daughter, Elizabeth. The collection of transcripts and memoranda concerning all branches of naval administration is now preserved in the Admiralty library.'

Ibid. ll. 4–3 from foot. Delete 'and makes . . . member of it.'

Ibid. 1132*b*, l. 10. Delete 'It seems not improbable that'

Ibid. l. 11. Delete 'that'

Ibid. l. 12. Delete 'that'

Add to list of authorities: A. E. Corbet's The Family of Corbet, ii. 318–20.

Cornhill, William of (d. 1223). iv. 1154*a*, l. 8 from foot. For '*Rot. Lit. Claus.* i. 196*b*' read '*Rot. Lit. Claus.* i. 169*b*'.

Cornwallis, Charles, first Marquis Cornwallis. iv. 1166*a*, l. 16 from foot. For '16 Aug.' read '9 Aug.' (G.E.C., *Complete Peerage*, iii. 457).

Cornwallis, James, fourth Earl Cornwallis. iv. 1167 *a*, l. 27 from foot. For '1769' read '1766' (Foster, *Alumni Oxonienses*, 1715–1886, i. 299).

Cornwallis, Sir William (*d.* 1631 ?). iv. 1169*b*, ll. 1–2. For '(*d.* 1631 ?)' read '(1579 ? –1614)'.

Ibid. l. 4. For 'Farnham' read 'Fincham.'

Ibid. l. 9. Delete 'for Lostwithiel in 1597 and'.

Ibid. l. 10. For 'He appears to have been knighted in 1602' read 'He was knighted at Dublin by Essex on 5 Aug. 1599.'

Ibid. l. 11. For 'He was a friend of Ben Jonson . . . at Highgate on May-day, 1604,' read 'He was a friend of John Donne and wrote a verse epistle to him which is reprinted by Prof. Grierson in "The Poems of John Donne," ii. 171–2 (*Times Lit. Supp.*, 6 Nov. 1930, p. 917, col. 1, 20 Nov. 1930, p. 991, cols. 1–2, and 4 Dec. 1930, p. 1042, cols. 2–3, with references there cited).'

Ibid. l. 18 from foot. For a tentative correction of the list of his works see 'Times Lit. Supp.,' 4 Dec. 1930, p. 1042, cols. 2–3.

Coryate, Thomas. iv. 1186*a*, l. 29. Add 'Wood's account of Coryate's second journey (1612–1617) is derived from *A Voyage to East India*, 1655, pp. 58–77, by Edward Terry [q.v.]. Terry met Coryate in India, and refers to him again at pp. 310, 391.'

E. S. de B.

Cotterell, Sir Charles (1612–1702). iv. 1215*a*, last line. After 'ceremonies' add 'He was knighted on 6 March 1644–5 (R. Symonds, *Diary*, Camden Soc., 1859, p. 162).' 1216*a*, l. 7. After '1661' add 'Cotterell was a friend of Katherine Philips [q.v.]; he published her poems in 1667, after her death, and was the "Poliarchus" of her "Letters of Orinda to Poliarchus," published in 1705 and again in 1709.'

E. S. de B.

Courten, William. iv. 1260*a*, l. 8 from foot. After 'Cromwell Road' add 'Courten had also made a notable collection of coins and medals (R. Thoresby, *Diary*, i. 298–9; Evelyn, *Numismata*, p. 246); Obadiah Walker [q.v.] dedicated to him his book on ancient coins.'

Courtenay, John (1741–1816), iv. 1263*a*–*b*.

Delete: 1263*a*, ll. 1–8, 1263*b*, l. 1, from the beginning to 'ordnance office in 1772'. Substitute:

Courtenay, John (1738–1816), politician, descended from a Devon family settled in Ireland *temp.* Elizabeth I, was the second son of Henry Courtenay (1693–1772), a revenue officer in Ireland, by Mary, daughter of the Rev. —. Major, rector of Tanderaghee. He was born at Carlingford, 22 August 1738, O.S., and educated at Dundalk school, under the care of the Rev. —. Skelton, from whom he received a good grounding in the classics. In 1756 he obtained, by commission dated 9 April, an ensigncy in the 29th Regiment of Foot, in which he served for nine years as ensign and lieutenant, mainly in Ireland and for a brief spell in England. In 1765 he sold his commission, and purchased an appointment as one of the six commissaries of the musters in Ireland. About this time he married and settled down near Dublin. In 1769 he sold his office, in order to pay his debts, and turned to journalism, writing essays for the *Bachelor*, a periodical which supported the castle administration. He soon became a principal contributor and was thus brought to the notice of the lord-lieutenant, Viscount Townshend. When Townshend in 1772 was recalled from Dublin, Courtenay obtained on his recommendation the office of barrack master at Kinsale; accompanied him, at his request, to England; and in 1773, after Townshend had become master general of the ordnance, was appointed his secretary.

Ibid., 1263*b*, l. 15. After 'May 1784' insert 'For the remainder of his parliamentary career he was a steadfast supporter of Fox'. (John Courtenay: Incidental Anecdotes and a Biographical Sketch (London, 1809), pp. 2–42.)

Ibid., 1264*a*, l. 42. After '1808, 8vo.' insert '9. Incidental Anecdotes and a Biographical Sketch, 1809', and renumber the following two publications listed.

Ibid., l. 15 from foot. Delete 'Collins Peerage (Brydges), ii, 575, vi 267'. To list of authorities add, 'John Courtenay: Incidental Anecdotes and a Biographical Sketch (London, 1809)'.

Courtenay, John (1738–1816), iv. 1263*a*–*b* and *ante*, xxvii. 106. For the 'Rev. —. Major' read 'William Major, ex-scholar and M.A., T.C.D., prebendary of Ballymore (formerly Tanderagee), 1704–5 to 1725 (J. B. Leslie, *Armagh clergy and parishes* (Dundalk, 1911), p. 66)'. For the 'Rev. —. Skelton', read 'John Skelton, ex-scholar and B.A., T.C.D., head-master of Dundalk grammar school and curate of Dundalk parish (died 31 Jan. 1767, brother of the Rev. Philip Skelton, *q.v.*) . . . (J. B. Leslie, *op. cit.*, p. 283 and *Supplement* (Dundalk, 1948), p. 105).

Courtenay, Peter. iv. 1264*b*, l. 8. After 'Padua' insert 'On his way to Italy he was enrolled in the University of Cologne, on 3 Nov. 1457, in the faculty of law (Keussen, *Matrikel der Univ. Köln*, i. (Bonn, 1928), no. 275, 30, p. 617).' J. H. B.

Coventry, Thomas, first Baron Coventry. i. 1287*a*, ll. 6–7. After 'a daughter, Elizabeth,' add 'who married Sir John Hare of Stow Bardolph, Norfolk (Blomefield, *History of Norfolk*, 1805, i. 414–6, and references to a "daughter Hare" in Coventry's will at Somerset House).'

Ibid., l. 20. After 'Halifax,' add 'after Savile's death she married Sir Thomas Chicheley [q.v.] (H. C. Foxcroft, *Life of Halifax*, i. 22, 29–30, and authorities there given).'

Coventry, Sir William.

The article gives no account of Coventry's life between 1669 and 1679, when he was one of the most important members of the Country party. (Anchitell Grey's *Debates*; Foxcroft's *Halifax*.)

Coventry, Sir William. iv. 1287*b*, l. 21. For 'born about 1628' read 'baptized at St. Mary's Church, Islington, 4 October 1627 (Parish Registers, St. Mary's Church, Islington).' If he was baptized soon after birth, he would have been about 58 years and 8 months old at his death, instead of the 60 years (or 60th year) mentioned in the statement on his tombstone that he died 'viii calend. Julii (*i.e.* 24 June) An. Dom. 1686 aetatisq. suae lx.'

Ibid., p. 1289*a*, l. 11. For 'Coventry sent to press . . . Burnet's *History of the Reformation*' read 'To Coventry have also been attributed *England's Appeal from the Private Cabal at White-Hall to the Great Council of the Nation, the Lords and Commons in Parliament assembled, by a True Lover of his Country*, printed in 1673; and *A Letter Written to Dr. Burnet, giving an Account of Cardinal Pool's* (*i.e.* Pole's) *Secret Powers*, printed in 1685. But *England's Appeal* was written by Franz Paul von Lisola (A. F. Pribram, *Lisola*, p. 353, n. 1), possibly with some assistance from a Peter du Moulin who is not the Peter du Moulin [q.v.]. Du Moulin was probably responsible for the English translation (*cf.* V. Barbour, *Henry Bennet, Earl of Arlington*, p. 213 n., where du Moulin is held to have written the work without any collaboration from Lisola); it appeared also in French, Dutch, and German, and three more parts appeared in Dutch and German. The *Letter Written to Dr. Burnet* was apparently written by Burnet himself (Clarke and Foxcroft, *Life of Burnet*, p. 532). It corrects some statements in Burnet's *History of the Reformation*.'

Cowley, Abraham. iv. 1307*b*, ll. 2–3. For 'A portrait by Lely was bought by the nation in Peel's collection,' read 'A portrait by Lely was bought by Sir Robert Peel from Strawberry Hill in 1842 and is now in the gallery of Dulwich college (*A descriptive and historical catalogue of the pictures in the gallery . . . at Dulwich*, 1926, p. 267).'

Cowper, William, first earl Cowper. iv. 1316*a*, l. 27. For '9 Nov.' read '14 Dec.' (*Complete Peerage*, 1913, iii. 483).

Crawford, William Sharman (1781–1861), v. 59*a*, l. 34. For '1846' read '1847 (*Londonderry Standard*, 2 July 1847)'.

Crichton, James, surnamed **The Admirable** (1560–1583). The article requires revision in the light of a paper by G. B. Intra, *Una Pagina della Giovinezza del Principe Vincenzo Gonzaga* (Archivio Storico Italiano, Serie Quarta, t. xviii. disp. 5, 1886), and a brochure by D. Crichton, *The Admirable Crichton* (L. Upcott Gill, Bazaar Buildings, Drury Lane, London, 1909). The former confirms the date of death as 3 July, 1582, from letters preserved in the Gonzaga Archives. The latter solves the 'impossibility' of that date by calling attention to evidence of the presence of another James Crichton in Italy who appears to have been a kinsman of the murdered Crichton, and to whom may be attributed the works published in 1584 and 1585. Moreover, a newsletter which from internal evidence seems to be correctly placed in the Domestic Calendar (1581–90, p. 64) under July 1582 refers to 'the young gentleman of Scotland who became so famous in Italy for his disputing' as being 'now lately slain in Mantua.'

Croft, Herbert. v. 106*a*, l. 12. For 'March' read '6 Apr. (*Notes and Queries*, clxxi. 8).'

Croker, Temple Henry. v. 132*b*, l. 14. After 'Huggins' add '(the respective shares of Huggins and Croker are set out in Boswell's "Life" of Johnson, ed. Hill, revised edn. by L. F. Powell, 1934, iv. 473–5).'

L. F. Powell.

Croker, Thomas Crofton. v. 133*b*, l. 33. For 'Grimston Church' read 'Kirby Wharfe Church in Grimston Park (*Notes and Queries*, clxix. 241).'

Cromer, George. v. 144–5. This article should be rewritten as follows :—

Cromer, George, (d. 1543), archbishop of Armagh, was an Englishman by birth. He was a master of arts (*L.P.* i. [ed. 1920], 3617, p. 1530). He was on 19 July 1511 presented to the rectory of Stanford-le-Hope, Essex (Newcourt, *Rep. Londin.* ii. 548), and in the same year was appointed to the parish churches of Guldeford (Chichester diocese) and Murston (*L.P.* i. 3616, p. 1525). In 1512 he was presented by the king to the mastership of Cobham College (Rochester diocese), which he held together with his other benefices (*ibid.* 1221 [47], 3617, p. 1530). On 2 Oct. 1521, John Kite [q.v.] having been translated from Armagh to Carlisle, Cromer was appointed to the vacant archbishopric by papal provision on the king's supplication ; in the provision he is described as a royal chaplain (W. M. Brady, *Episcopal Succession*, i. 216).

Cromer appears as a member of the Irish council in 1528. On 5 July 1532, at the time of the restoration of Gerald Fitzgerald, earl of Kildare [q.v.], to the deputyship, he was appointed lord chancellor in succession to John Allen, archbishop of Dublin [q.v.], an opponent of Kildare (Rymer, vi. ii. 173). He became associated with the Geraldine party, although he opposed the rebellion of Thomas Fitzgerald, Lord Offaly [q.v.] (*State Papers*, Henry VIII, ii. 168 ; Stanyhurst, in Holinshed, ed. 1808, vi. 289–92). But as a result of his association with the Geraldines and after a severe illness he was deprived of the chancellorship in August 1534 (Lascelles, *Liber Munerum Publicorum Hiberniae*, I. ii. 13). Owing to his continued illness, Sir William Skeffington [q.v.], who was ordered to arrest him and examine him on a charge of high treason, presumably arising out of the Geraldine revolt, was unable to have him interrogated before the council (*State Papers*, Henry VIII, ii. 243). Cromer did not take part in the reforming activities of George Browne, archbishop of Dublin, or Edward Staples, bishop of Meath [qq.v. ; and below for Staples]. The record of attendances at the parliament of 1536 is lost, but he was unquestionably absent from that of 1541, when Henry VIII was proclaimed king of Ireland (Sir J. Ware, *Rerum Hibernicarum Annales*, Henry VIII, p. 161 ; *State Papers*, Henry VIII, iii. 305) ; at the same time his name disappears from the lists of signatories of the council's letters. The problem of appointing a successor was already under consideration ; the reversion was granted to George Dowdall [q.v., and below], who succeeded Cromer on the latter's death in March 1543.

There can be no doubt that Cromer accepted the religious changes of Henry VIII. On 23 July 1539 he was suspended by the papal authorities on an accusation of heresy, and the administration of his see was entrusted to Robert Wauchop (Brady, i. 216). The story of his parliamentary opposition to the Reformation legislation can be traced no further back than Robert Ware's life of Archbishop Browne [see art. Ware, Sir James, below]. Two letters concerning Cromer in the Ware MSS. are from the same source (B.M., Sloane MS. 4789, f. 328).

Cromer's register is now in Trinity College, Dublin; it contains no information of importance regarding him.

Cromwell, Ralph, fourth Baron Cromwell (1394?–1456) xxii (supplement), 516*a*, ll. 26–7. For 'chamberlain of the exchequer' read 'king's chamberlain'.

Ibid., ll. 35–6. Delete 'of the exchequer'.

516*b*, l. 18. After 'king' add 'He was granted the reversion of one of the chamberlainships of the receipt of the exchequer in 1442, and held it from 1443 until his death. (*Cal. Pat. Rolls, 1441–6*, p. 158; P.R.O., Exchequer, Issue Rolls, *passim*)'.

Cromwell, Thomas, Earl of Essex. v. 201*b*, ll. 6–4 from foot. Delete 'A year before . . . the realm, and' (G.E.C., *Complete Peerage*, iii. 557).

Ibid. last line. For 'the young man' read 'Gregory Cromwell'

Ibid. 202*a*, l. 4. For 'in 1557' read 'on 4 July 1551' (*ibid.* p. 558).

Crow, Mitford. v. 236*a*, ll. 14–13 from foot. For 'Crow was employed . . . in Catalonia' read 'In May 1705 Crow arrived in Genoa on a special mission "to make propositions for the mutual advantage of trade," though his real object was to watch the Catalan revolt and report naval movements. He was in Barcelona, 2 Nov. 1705 (*Brit. Dipl. Repr., 1689–1789*, Camden 3rd series, xlvi. 73, 128)'

Cumming, Alexander. v. 296*a*, l. 18 from foot. After 'Society' insert 'although his name does not appear in the society's "Record".'

Cunningham, Alexander. v. 307*a*, l. 28 from foot. For '1720' read 'November 1719 (*Brit. Dipl. Repr., 1689–1789*, Camden 3rd series, xlvi. 84)'

Cunningham, Alexander, first Earl of Glencairn. v. 303*a*, l. 29. For '1450' read '1463 (G.E.C., *Complete Peerage*, v. 669)'

Cunningham, Peter (1816–1869). v. 316*b*, l. 13 from foot. At end of article add 'In 1842 Cunningham married Zenobia, daughter of John Martin, the painter [q.v.] (M. L. Pendered, *John Martin*, 1923, p. 259).'

Curwen or Coren, Hugh. v. 351*b*, ll. 30–9 from foot. Delete 'and he occurs . . . 10 Sept. 1559.' This account is based on Robert Ware's 'Hunting of the Romish Fox,' and is without other foundation (*see* art. Ware, Sir James, below).

Dale, Sir Thomas (*d.* 1619). v. 385*b*. See also Alexander Brown's *Genesis of the United States*, 1890.

Dale, Thomas (1797–1870). v. 386*b*, 10 ll. from foot. For '1836 to 1839' read '1835 to 1840' (King's College, London, *Calendar*, 1835–6, p. 4).

Dalrymple, John, second Earl of Stair. v. 422*a*, l. 32. After 'history' add 'Stair was at once raised to the rank of ambassador extraordinary to Louis XV, with new instructions, dated 21 Sept. 1715 (*Diplomatic Instructions* [R. Hist. Soc., Camden 3rd ser.], ii. 97).'

Ibid. 422*b*, ll. 4–6. Delete 'was raised . . . ambassador, and'.

Ibid. 423*a*, l. 26. After 'there' add 'on 31 March he was appointed ambassador extraordinary and plenipotentiary to the United Provinces (P.R.O., F.O. xc. 33).'

Dandridge, Bartholomew. v. 465*a*, l. 17. Add to list of authorities: Notes and Queries, clxv. 219–22, 236–41, 259–61.

Dangerfield, Thomas. v. 467*b*, l. 26. After 'printed).' add 'He obtained the money by borrowing it "und the guise of a decayed Gent. or a Kt y^t had been rob'd on the high way &c" (MS. note by Antony Wood in his copy of *Dangerfield's Memoires*, Bodleian Library, Wood 372/16).'

E. S. DE B.

Davidson, John (1797–1836). v. 578*a*, ll. 7–8. Delete 'Elected a fellow of the Royal Society in 1832.'

Ibid. l. 13. After 'pp. 481–3)' insert 'In June 1835 he was elected a fellow of the Royal Society' (*Record of Royal Soc.*, p. 394).

Davis, David Daniel, M.D. v. 614*b*, l. 2. Insert after 'He was': 'professor of Midwifery and Diseases of Women and Children in London University [University College since 1836] from 1828 to 1841, and.'

Davison or Davidson, William. v. 632–3. This article is almost entirely superseded by an article in Muséum (national) d'histoire naturelle (Paris), 'Nouvelles archives,' 3rd ser., x. 1–38; see further the article there cited in Society of antiquaries of Scotland, 'Proceedings,' vol. x, pt. i, pp. 265–80. Davison's wife's name was Charlotte de Thégny (Soc. de l'hist. du protestantisme francais, *Bulletin*, xiii. 228.)

Davy, John, M.D. (1790–1868). v. 645*b*, l. 9 from foot. For '1834' read '1814' (*Record of Royal Soc.*, p. 379).

Deane, Sir Anthony. v. 701*a*, ll. 17–8. Delete 'He was knighted . . . *Ped.* 127).'

Ibid. l. 23 from foot. After '1686–8.' insert 'He was knighted in the king's bedchamber at Titchfield on 3 July 1675 (*Cal. S. P., Dom.*, 1675–6, pp. 197, 198).'

Ibid. 701*b*, ll. 9–8 from foot. After 'Buckingham).' insert 'His first wife, named Anne, died in child-bed in March 1677 (*Registers of St. Olave, Hart Street, 1563–1700*, Harl. Soc., pp. 82, 216); in 1675 Deane is described as a "brother" of Isaac Dorislaus the younger [q.v., art. Dorislaus] and a connexion by marriage may be implied (*Cal. S. P., Dom.*, 1675–6, p. 198).'

Deane, Richard. v. 704. This article needs revision. See Sir Charles Firth in *The Mariner's Mirror*, xii. 243–44.

De Caus, Cauls, or Caux, Salomon. v. 715*a*, l. 11. For '1576' read '1577?'.

Ibid. l. 13. For 'in 1576' read 'about 1577.'

Ibid. ll. 17–26. For 'he came . . . Elizabeth' read 'he came to Brussels and was in the service of the Archdukes Albert and Isabella from January 1605 to August 1610; his principal work was the laying out of the park attached to the palace (*Revue d'histoire et d'archéologie*, i. 430–44). From Brussels he came to England, where he obtained employment as *ingénieur* to Henry, prince of Wales, who in March 1611 granted him a pension of £100 per annum (Birch, *Life of Henry, Prince of Wales*, p. 466). To Prince Henry de Caus dedicated his 'La Perspective avec la raison des ombres et miroirs,' 1612 (the dedication is dated at Richmond, 1 Oct. 1611).'

Ibid. ll. 10–9 from foot. For 'his experiments . . . were commenced' read 'his treatise on hydraulic machines (part of "Les Raisons des Forces Mouvantes") was begun.'

Ibid. 715*b*, ll. 23–22 from foot. For 'He seems . . . 1626' read 'He was buried in the protestant cemetery of La Trinité in Paris on 28 Feb. 1626, N.S. (Soc. de l'hist. du protestantisme français, *Bulletin*, xii. 279). In 1606 he married at Brussels Esther Picart, by whom he had a son Guillaume, born 1607 (*Revue d'histoire et d'archéologie*, i. 435, 441–2).'

Ibid. ll. 9–7 from foot. For 'He left . . . himself, who' read 'ISAAC DE CAUS (1590 ?–1648) may have been a nephew, he calls himself a native of Dieppe. He'

Ibid. 716*a*, l. 8. After 'engenier' add 'He was buried, like his uncle, at the Trinité in Paris, on 24 Feb. 1648, N.S. (Soc. de l'hist. du protestantisme français, *Bulletin*, xiii. 228).'

Ibid. l. 11. After '(xviii. 193).' add 'A medal by himself is figured in "Revue belge de numismatique," 1879 (pl. xv; see also pp. 279–87).'

Ibid. l. 12. Before 'Walpole's' add 'De Caus's age from the portrait and medal.'

To list of authorities add: 'Further reference in articles on the de Caus in U. Thieme's Allgemeines Lexikon der bildenden Künstler.'

Dee, John. v. 729*a*, ll. 11–9 from foot. Delete 'A portrait of Dee . . . Billingsley's Euclid.' The portrait represents John Day (1522–1584) [q.v.], the printer of the book (R. B. McKerrow, *Printers' and publishers' devices, 1485–1640*, 1913, no. 145).

M. F. WILD.

Defoe, Daniel. v. 734*a*, l. 25 from foot. For 'Four months later, in August' read 'Immediately afterwards, in May (*Eng. Hist. Rev.* xv. 240*n*).'

Defoe, Daniel. v. 737*b*, l. 28. After 'are known' insert 'although there are six copies of the number of 21 July 1715 extant (P.R.O., S.P. Dom. George I, iii. 78).'

Ibid. l. 34. For '24' read '27.'

L. W. H.

Defoe, Daniel. v. 742*a*. *Economical and Social Tracts*, No. 1, the 'Essay upon Projects,' was published in 1697, not 1698.

De Morgan, Augustus. v. 781*a*. For further details about his literary activities see *The Athenæum*, 25 March 1871, p. 370; C. Knight, *Passages of a Working Life during Half a Century* [etc.], 3 vols., 1864–5, ii. 209. For a genealogical tree see A. M. W. Stirling, *William de Morgan and his Wife*, 1922.

Denham, Sir John (1615–1669). v. 799*a*, ll. 21 seq. For a reference to improved translations of the second and fourth books of the Aeneid, and translations of the third, fifth and sixth books, probably the work of Denham but not mentioned in the article, see 'Times Lit. Supp.' 1927, p. 472.

Denne, Samuel. v. 817*b*, l. 16. After '1833, 12mo.' add 'his particular contribution was the history of Rochester priory (*Gentleman's Magazine*, vol. lvii, pt. ii, p. 1052).'

Desaguliers, Thomas. v. 852*a*, l. 23 from foot. For '1763' read '1780' (*Record of Royal Soc.*, p. 361).

***Desborough, John.** v. 853. A good article so far as his family history is concerned, but his political career should be made clearer. At the opening of the war Desborough was quarter-master of Cromwell's troop of horse in Essex's army. In April 1643 he was captain in Cromwell's regiment of horse in Manchester's army. In April 1645 he was major in Fairfax's own regiment of horse in the New Model. He became colonel of the regiment of horse previously Cromwell's after Cromwell went to Ireland. 'Col. Disbrow, governor of Portsmouth, is appointed to command that regiment of horse lately under the command of the Lord Lieutenant of Ireland,' says the newspaper entitled *The Moderate*, under 15 Sept. 1649.

There is a gap between April 1646 and September 1648 in the article. In May 1647 Desborough energetically represented the grievances of his regiment to the parliamentary commissioners (*Clarke Papers*, i. 50, 74, 80, 207), and did not shrink from attacking a troop of another regiment which adhered to the side of the Parliament. This was denounced as 'a barbarous and bloody murder,' and left a slur on his reputation (Rushworth, vii. 741; Maseres, *Select Tracts*, i. 282). In May 1648 he suppressed an attempted rising at Bury St. Edmunds (*Old Parliamentary History*, xvii. 149–58), and later in the year fought in Fairfax's Kentish campaign and at the siege of Colchester.

As commissioner for the admiralty he was in chief charge of the preparations for the West Indian expedition under Penn and Venables, and the latter blames him for its inefficient equipment and insufficient provisioning. He asserts that 'though General Desborough was no victualler, yet it was believed upon very strong presumption that he had a share in the profits of the place' (*Narrative of General Venables*, pp. xxxii, 4). This may be a slander, but it is clear that the preparations for the expedition do him no credit as an administrator.

In March 1655 Desborough was despatched to the West of England to put down the royalist rising under Penruddock, but it was suppressed before he arrived. He was then made major-general of the six western counties, and was very energetic in purging the municipal corporations of royalists, organising the new militia troops, levying taxes on the cavaliers, and other repressive measures (*English Historical Review*, 1889, p. 223; Thurloe, vols. iii., iv.; Gardiner, *Commonwealth and Protectorate*, iii. 288, 340; iv. 51). Not only was he the prototype of the major-generals, he was also the chief champion of military government. He wished to make the institution of the major-generals permanent, and introduced a bill for the purpose which was rejected on 29 Jan. 1657. In his speech Desborough declared that 'it was blows, not fair words, that settled and must settle the peace of England' (*Burton's Diary*, i. 230, 316; *Clarke Papers*, iii. 88). Desborough rather than Fleetwood was the instigator of the military movement which overthrew the Protectorate by obliging Richard Cromwell to dissolve parliament, and its object was to make Richard the tool of the higher officers, not to overthrow him (Baker, 657–661, 669; *Clarke Papers*; Ludlow, ii. 66–73).

Though he concurred in the invitation to the Long Parliament to resume its sittings, he contemned their authority, especially when officers were required to take out new commissions. He 'openly said that he accounted the commission he had already to be as good as any the Parliament could give, and that he would not take another' (Ludlow, ii. 90). Nevertheless he submitted to do so (*Commons' Journals*, vii. 704–6), but he continued to agitate, hoping to become lieutenant-general of all the horse in the three nations, instigated the Derby petition and other mutinous addresses to parliament, and was naturally one of the nine officers whose commissions were annulled by parliament on 12 Oct. 1659. During the brief period of military rule which followed the second expulsion of the Rump (13 Oct.), Desborough's influence reached its highest point. His political views are set forth in a speech made to the Lord Mayor and the Corporation of London on 8 Nov., which begins with a vindication of the Army, and ends by bidding the citizens 'follow after peace, and meddle not with affairs beyond your sphere.' Some say, he confessed 'we shall not have settlement till the old family comes in, which if it should enter into any one of our hearts, we should be like the dog returning to his vomit.' (Three speeches made to the right honourable the Lord Mayor, etc., reprinted in the *Old Parliamentary History*, xxii. pp. 10–17.) Ludlow found him and other officers resolved to oppose to the last the restitution of the expelled parliament, preferring to run the risk of calling a new one, and proposing the establishment of a Select Senate in order to control it (*Memoirs*, ii. 161, 166, 182). The collapse of the military revolt ended his constitution-making. His own regiment forwarded its submission to parliament on 24 Dec., and Desborough himself on 29 Dec. with a letter of submission to the Speaker (printed in *Mercurius Publicus*, 29 Dec.–5 Jan.; *cf.* Whitelocke, iv. 385).

A portrait in the possession of Miss Disbrowe of Walton Hall near Burton-on-Trent is reproduced in Gardiner's *Oliver Cromwell*, 1899 (Goupil series).

As to Samuel his brother, a letter from him to Cromwell dated 18 Jan. 1650–1 announcing his return from New England, and wish for employment, is printed in Nickolls, *Original Letters addressed to O. Cromwell*, p. 54. In Richard Cromwell's parliament he made an excellent speech in defence of the union with Scotland (*Burton's Diary*, iv. 167), and probably the speech attributed to his brother on Scottish politics was really his (*ibid.*, ii. 307).

D'Ewes, Sir Simonds. v. 903*a*, ll. 11–19 from foot. For 'Mr Marsden . . . compiled' read 'John Howard Marsden [q.v.] in 1851 published'

Digby, Sir Kenelm. v. 971*b*, l. 15. At end of list of authorities add: 'Twenty-one letters from Digby to Cavaliere Cassiano del Pozzo were preserved in the library of the duchess of Aosta at Turin in 1875 (G. Lumbroso, "Notizie sulla vita di Cassiano del Pozzo" (extract from "Miscellanea di storia patria," vol. xv), 1875, pp. 21, 23; one of the letters is there printed, pp. 104-5).'

E. S. de B.

Digby, William, fifth Baron Digby. v. 973*a*, l. 26. For '1685' read '1686' (G.E.C., *Complete Peerage*, iv. 354).

Ibid. ll. 31–2. For 'In 1689 he represented Warwickshire' read 'From 1689 to 1698 he represented Warwick Borough' (*Return of M.P.s*, i. 562, 569, 576).

Ibid. l. 35. For 'in December' read 'on 29 Nov.' (G.E.C., *Complete Peerage*, iv. 355).

Dillon, Sir John Talbot (1740?–1805), v. 989*a*. This entry confuses two men: Sir John Talbot Dillon, author of the works ascribed to him in the article, but who died in London in 1806 (*Gent. Mag.* for March 1806), and Sir John Dillon of Lismullen, co. Meath, father of Sir William Henry Dillon (*q.v.*), and who died in Dublin in 1805. See *Dillon's Narrative*, vol. i, 1790–1802 (Navy Record Soc. 1953), Introduction, pp. xiv ff.

Dirom, Alexander. v. 1001*b*, l. 21. For 'Banffshire' read 'Aberdeenshire.' *Ibid.*, 18 ll. from foot. Delete 'An Inquiry into the Corn Laws . . .' It was written by his father (F. Miller, *A Bibliography of the Parish of Annan*, 1925, p. 28).

Diss or Dysse, Walter. v. 1025*a*, l. 13 from foot. For 'before 26 April 1381 . . . i. 620)' read 'at least since 12 Jan. 1375 (*John of Gaunt's Register*, Camden 3rd Ser., xx. 252; *The Times Lit. Suppl.*, 26 May 1932, p. 390).

Dixon, John. v. 1030*a*, l. 19 from foot. After 'Dance.' read 'He lived in Kemps Row, Chelsea, 1771–5 (City of Westminster archives, C. 313–8, 350).'

Ibid. l. 18 from foot. For 'between 1770 and 1775' read 'during this period'

Dixwell, John, regicide. v. 1035*a*, 11 ll. from bottom. After 'During the protectorate he disappeared altogether from public life,' read 'on the fall of Richard Cromwell he was Ludlow's colleague in the negotiations with the Wallingford House party' (Ludlow, *Memoirs*, ed. 1894, ii. 66). When the Rump was recalled to power he became again a member of the Council of State. On 12 October 1659 Parliament made him governor of Dover Castle in place of Colonel Kelsey (*Commons' Journals*, vii. 796).

Ibid., 1035*b*, l. 27. Dixwell's second wife was not named 'Bathsheba,' but 'Bathshua' How, and his will mentions two children only, not three.

In 1900 Mr. Franklin B. Dexter published in the New Haven Colony Historical Society's papers, vol. vi., a small collection of 'Dixwell Papers,' consisting mainly of letters addressed to Dixwell by his niece, Elizabeth Westrowe, between 1676 and 1690, with notes on the history of the Dixwell family, which supplement the account given by Stiles.

Docwra, Sir Henry. v. 1046*b*, l. 6. For '1608' read '1606' (Docwra's *Narrative*, Celtic Society Miscellany, 1849, p. 282).

T. M.

Dodsley, Robert. v. 1076*b*, l. 16. For 'the author printed it' read 'was printed.'

1078*b*, last line. Between 'London' and '1745' insert 'Printed for M. Cooper at the Globe in Pater-Noster-Row' (Birrell and Garnett, *Catalogue*, no. 16, 1927, pp. 32–3).

Donaldson, Thomas Leverton. v. 1119*b*, 23 ll. from foot. Delete 'emeritus.'

Donkin, Sir Rufane Shaw. v. 1125*a*, l. 50. 'the earliest, 21736, f. 127, is a schoolboy note.' This letter is not from R. S. Donkin, but from his father, Colonel R. Donkin, Exeter, 24 August 1785.

Donne, John (1604–62). v. 1139*a*, l. 22 from foot. After 'Padua' add 'he registered there in 1635 (H. F. Brown, *Inglesi e Scozzesi all' Università di Padova*, 1921, p. 149) and was in Rome in Feb. of that year (letter to Denbigh, mentioned in Hist. MSS. Comm., 6th Rep., App. p. 279*b*).'

Ibid. ll. 17–12 from foot. Donne's livings are not clear. In Jan. 1641 he complained that he had been cheated out of the living of Tillingham in Essex by means of a pretended exchange to Ufford (*Cal. Clarendon S.P.* i. 216). There was some trouble about Ufford (*Cal. S.P.*, Dom. 1641–3, p. 526; other documents relating to the presentation in *Cal. S.P.*, Dom., 1639, pp. 33, 204; Richard Tilley was presented 29 Nov. 1641, J. Bridges, *History of Northants.*, ed. 1791, ii. 603). Later, perhaps between 1654 and 1658, Donne made some claims to the living of Hartfield in Sussex (Hist. MSS. Comm., 4th Rep., App. p. 310*a*).

Ibid. l. 9 from foot. After 'sermons' insert '(1649).' Donne's connexion with the Fielding family goes back at least to 1635.

Ibid. l. 3 from foot. After 'committee' add '(from the dedication of "Biathanatas," by his father, 1644). He is known to have been released from restraint in June 1643 (*Cal. S.P.*, Dom., 1625–49, p. 650).'

1139*b*, l. 8. After 'to this house' add 'In 1649 and the following years Donne was engaged in publishing his father's works (see DONNE, JOHN, the elder, and G. Keynes, *Bibliography of the Works of Dr. John Donne*, 1914). In 1650 he proposed going abroad but was kept in England by the gout (*Cal. Clarendon S.P.*, ii. 44). His health was evidently uncertain (*Cal. S.P.*, Dom., 1650, p. 446). He was arrested about July 1651, being in suspected company (*ibid.* 1651, p. 280). Henceforward he appears to have been engaged in literary work.'

Ibid. l. 19. After 'solutions and answers' add 'Donne also wrote a burlesque petition for the removal of Dr. Babre (Sir John Baber, q.v.; ascription by Anthony Wood on his copy in Bodleian Library). His will, also in burlesque style, was published soon after his death, and has been printed in "Notes and Queries" 2nd ser., iv. 175, and elsewhere.'

Ibid. l. 25. After 'indecencies' add 'several of his letters have been preserved; the most important are printed by Thomas Zouch [q.v.] in his edition of Walton's "Lives," 1796. pp. xv, 115, 116.'

Ibid. l. 37. After 'Cathedral library' add 'Besides his father's works, Donne edited in 1660 the "Collection of Letters made by Sr Tobie Mathews" [see MATTHEW, SIR TOBIE] and the "Poems written by the Right Honourable William, Earl of Pembroke," etc. [see HERBERT, WILLIAM, THIRD EARL OF PEMBROKE].'

Dr. Donne is apparently not identical with the John Donne who was secretary to the commissioners sent by the Scots to the English parliament in Feb. 1644. The latter continued in England until 1648 (Hist. MSS. Comm., 13th Rep., App. i. 169, 354, 435. In that year he was acting as the London agent for the Hamilton party (*Hamilton Papers*, p. 179); a packet of intercepted letters shows the nature of his activities (*Designs and Correspondencies of the present Committee of Estates*, printed 16 Aug. 1648).

Apparently the same man accompanied the commissioners of the Scottish clergy to Breda in 1650 (*Brief Historical Relation of the Life of Mr. John Livingstone*, ed. T. Houston, 1848, p. 127). On 1 October 1661 Robert Baillie, writing to Lauderdale, refers to 'your servant, John Don' (*Letters and Journals*, ed. D. Laing, 1842, iii. 481). There was a Scottish notary named John Don living in 1666 (*Register of the Great Seal of Scotland*, 1660–68, pp. 492*a*, 559*b*). The arrest of Dr. Donne in 1648 about the time of the Scottish Donne's greatest prominence is very striking, and the identification with Dr. Donne, though open to question, seems most probable, as he was already suspect before the arrival of the Scottish commissioners.

E. S. DE B.

Douce, Francis. v. 1162*a*, l. 12. Add to list of authorities Bodleian Quarterly Record, vii. 359–82.

Douglas, Archibald, second Earl of Forfar. v. 1191*b*, ll. 16, 18. For '1693' read '1692' (G.E.C., *Complete Peerage*, v. 555).'

Ibid. ll. 25–9. For '10th' read '3rd'; for '1714' read '1715'; for 'sent' read 'appointed'; for 'and' read 'but never took up his duties in Berlin (*Brit. Dipl. Repr., 1689–1789*, Camden 3rd series, xlvi. 105). In 1714'; and delete 'in that year.'

Ibid. l. 22 from foot. After 'He was' insert 'taken prisoner (G.E.C., *loc. cit.*) and'

Ibid. l. 21 from foot. For '3' read '8'

Douglas, Archibald, second Earl of Forfar. v. 1191*b*, ll. 26–9. Delete 'he was sent . . . Prussia, and' and 'in that year'.

Ibid. l. 33. After '3,000*l.*' insert 'He was appointed envoy extraordinary to Prussia in 1715 (credentials dated 14 July) but never took up his post (D. B. Horn, *British Diplomatic Representatives*, p. 105).'

Douglas, Sir Howard. v. 1205*b*, l. 4 from foot. For '1812' read '1816' (*Record of Royal Soc.*, p. 380).

Douglas, James, second Duke of Queensberry, v. 1229*a*, l. 20. For 'sixth' read 'fourth' and add date 'on 31 Dec. 1688. (Millan, *Succession of Colonels*, (1742), p. 2).'

Douglas, William, seventh or eighth Earl of Morton. [Note: G. E. C. and Sir J. B. Paul (*Scots Peerage*, vi. 378) describe this William as the sixth Earl.] v. 1273*b*, l. 22. After '9 Nov. following' add 'Robert married Anne, daughter of Sir Edward Villiers [q.v.] (her name is given incorrectly as Elizabeth in G. E. C. and Paul; it is given correctly in the pedigree in J. Nichols's *Leicestershire*, iii. 198). As Lady Dalkeith (her husband's courtesy-title) she was given charge of the infant Henrietta Anne [q.v.] at Exeter, and carried her over to the queen in France in 1646. She is said to have returned to England in 1651 and to have died in 1654 (J. Cartwright, *Madame*, pp. 3–16; a series of letters to her from Sir Edward Hyde [q.v.] is in the *Calendar of Clarendon State Papers*, vols. i and ii).' E. S. de B.

Dover, Thomas, M.D. v. 1287*a*, l. 12. 'For 1660' read '1662.'

Ibid. l. 14. For 'in Warwickshire about 1660' read 'at Barton-on-the-Heath, Warwickshire, and was baptized on 6 May 1662 (Baptismal register). He was grandson of Capt. Robert Dover [q.v.] and younger brother of John Dover [q.v.] (*Visitation of Warwickshire*, 1682 3, Harl. Soc., pp. 95–6).'

Ibid. ll. 15–6. For 'Where he studied and graduated is unknown, but he' read 'He matriculated from Magdalen Hall, Oxford, 1 Dec. 1680, graduated B.A. in 1684, entered Gonville and Caius, Cambridge, as a pensioner, 4 Nov. 1686, and took his M.B. in 1687 (Venn, *Alumni Cantab.* pt. 1, ii. 59*b*). He'

Ibid. 1287*b*, l. 18. For ', and there died in 1742' read '. Later he returned to Stanway House, Gloucestershire, and was buried in the Tracy vault in Stanway church, 20 Apr. 1742 (Register; *London Mag.*, Apr. 1742, p. 206).'

Dowdall, George. v. 1289*a*, l. 26 to 1289*b*, l. 4. For 'His zeal for the Church of Rome . . . *Church of Ireland*, i. 207–11)' read 'Although a believer in the doctrine of the royal supremacy, Dowdall was not prepared to accept the innovations under Edward VI, which were introduced into Ireland on the authority of the administration, the Irish parliament not being convened to express any opinion. The new lord deputy, Sir Edward Bellingham [q.v.], late in 1548 remonstrated with him for his adherence to the old liturgy, and attempted to prevail on him to aid in spreading the new (P.R.O., State Papers, Ireland, Edw. VI, i. 162). Dowdall, however, would not be moved, but if he failed to keep the pace of the reformers in doctrine, he was not slow to follow up the traces of his rival Wauchop, who had been appointed to Armagh by papal provision on the death of Cromer. Dowdall persuaded the O'Neill to hand over letters received from agents of the French king in the north of Ireland, and to give information as to the activities of the papal primate, all of which he duly sent on to the Dublin authorities (*Cal. State Papers, Ireland*, 1509–73, p. 106; E. P. Shirley, *Original Letters . . . on the Church in Ireland*, no. xv). His anti-papal activities did not satisfy such extremists as George Browne, archbishop of Dublin [q.v.], who made further efforts with Bellingham's successor, Sir Anthony St. Leger [q.v. and below], to compel the primate to conform. St. Leger sympathised more with Dowdall than with Browne and suffered the former to continue his unreformed practices. On the appointment of the new lord deputy, Sir James Croft [q.v.], in May 1551, it was determined that the new liturgy should be made compulsory in all dioceses. Rather than accept such a position, Dowdall sought a voluntary exile, saying "that he wolde neuʳ be bushope wher tholie masse was abolished" (*Cal. State Papers, Ireland*, 1509–73, p. 115; Shirley, no. xxiii).'

Downing, Calybute. v. 1303*b*, 5 ll. from bottom. Requires correction. See below, *s.v.* George Downing.

Downing, George (1623–84). v. 1304–6. This article, written in 1888, is not inaccurate but rather inadequate. Much new evidence as to Downing's career has been published since that date, and a full and detailed biography of him has just appeared, viz. *The Godfather of Downing Street, Sir George Downing*, by John Beresford (1925), 8vo, pp. 318. It contains the only known portrait of Downing, which is in the possession of a member of the Winthrop family, Downing's will, documents relating to his property in what is now Downing Street, etc. The list of authorities in Mr. Beresford's preface entirely supersedes that appended to the article.

As to Downing's career the fact that he was originally chaplain to Okey's regiment is proved by John Winthrop's *History of New England*, ii. 242–3, as well as by Ludlow's *Memoirs* (ed. 1894, ii. 330). A passage in T. Edwards's *Gangraena*, pt. iii. pp. 81–2, mentions a sermon delivered at Hackney, in August 1646, by 'one Master Downing a preacher of the Army, and a young Peters, as he was called.' The comparison with Peters, another New Englander, shows that

George Downing was the man meant. The passage has no reference to Calybute Downing (1606–44) [*q.v.*], and the six lines devoted to it in the bibliography to the article upon him ought to be omitted. Downing was next 'attached in some capacity unknown,' says Mr. Beresford, to Sir Arthur Haselrig, governor of Newcastle, quoting a letter of Downing's, written in March 1648 (p. 49). It is probable that he was chaplain to Haselrig as governor, or to Haselrig's regiment. Newcastle was the observation post from which Scotland was watched, and to collect information about events there was one of the most important duties of the governor. Probably Downing was employed by Haselrig in the business of intelligence, and this would explain his employment by Cromwell as scoutmaster-general during the invasion of Scotland in 1650. One of his functions was to report the progress of the campaign and events in Scotland to authorities in England, viz. to William Rowe, scoutmaster-general there, and to Thomas Scot, who managed the intelligence department of the Council of State. Two letters to Rowe, dated 18 Oct. and 21 Oct. 1650, are printed in Grey's *Impartial Examination of Neal's History of the Puritans*, iv, appendix, pp. 47–53. Two others, dated 9 October 1650 and 22 March 1651, are to be found in the *Old Parliamentary History*, xix. 411, 465. One dated 7 Aug. 1651, relating the march of Charles II into England, was printed as a pamphlet (B.M. Cat. E. 640), another relating the battle of Worcester is printed in Cary's *Memorials of the Civil War* (ii. 357). *Mercurius Politicus* contains an account of the battle of Inverkeithing, signed G. D. (p. 953); there are also an anonymous relation of Dunbar (p. 226), and a number of unsigned letters about the campaigns of 1650–1, which were probably written by him.

Apart from his brief mission to France in 1655, Downing's diplomatic career is entirely connected with Anglo-Dutch relations.

Mr. Beresford elucidates it by copious extracts from Downing's journal in the possession of Mr. G. H. Gurney. Unluckily it only covers the period from January to September 1658; the rest of it has disappeared. A transcript of Mr. Gurney's MS. made for Dawson Turner was number 296 in the Phillipps' MSS. sold in March 1895. Three letters from Downing in *Clarke Papers*, iii. 170, 174, 177, help to fill the gap.

On Downing's pardon and knighthood see Pepys, *Diary*, ed. Wheatley, and the passage from Sir William Lower's *Relation*, quoted by the editor (i. 154). He was knighted 21 May 1660.

The negotiations between England and the Dutch for the next five years have recently been set forth in great detail by Japikse in *De verwikkelingen tusschen de Republiek en England van* 1660–1665 (Leiden, 1900), which contains a number of extracts from Downing's letters. As Downing was allowed to remain at the Hague for full six months after the war began his letters to Arlington are of great value. They were printed in 1919 by Dr. H. T. Colenbrander, in *Bescheiden uit vreemde Archieven omtrent de groote Nederlandsche Zeeoorlogen*, 1652–1676 (i. 142–287). Downing's last mission to Holland (Dec. 1671–Feb. 1672) is elucidated by new letters from the Record Office printed for the first time by Mr. Beresford (pp. 243–64). 'It is your part to obey punctually my orders, instead of putting yourself to the trouble of finding reasons why you do not do so,' wrote Charles II to Downing, during his negotiations, and the ambassador was blamed for precipitating a rupture.

The article states that Downing was made Secretary to the Commissioners of the Treasury in May 1667, and quotes Pepys on his fitness for the post. An adequate account of Downing's financial work would have to summarise the evidence contained in the introductions of Dr. W. A. Shaw to the *Calendar of Treasury Books*, i.–iii., and that to the *Treasury Papers* of 1729–30. See also the chapter on 'Downing and National Finance,' in Mr. Beresford's book.

D'Oyly, George. v. 1324*b*, l. 6 from foot. Add to list of authorities: Letters to Ceylon, 1814–24, ed. P. E. Pieris.

D'Oyly, Sir John. v. 1325*a*, ll. 4–6. For ', and went out . . . Dutch.' read '. In 1792 he entered Corpus Christi college, Cambridge, where he had a distinguished academic career. He won Sir William Browne's medal for a Latin ode in 1795 and was chancellor's medallist in 1796 (*Letters to Ceylon*, 1814–24, ed. P. E. Pieris, pp. 2–3); graduated B.A. in the same year (*Diary of Mr. John D'Oyly*, ed. K. W. Codrington, p. xi); was elected a fellow of his college in 1798 and proceeded M.A. in 1799 (Pieris, *op. cit.*, pp. 3–4). Disinclined to take orders, he went out to Ceylon in 1801, where he speedily made his mark as a linguist (*ibid.* p. 12).'

Ibid. ll. 30–31. After 'provinces.' insert 'His "Sketch of the constitution of the Kandyan kingdom," first published in 1832, was newly edited for the Ceylon government in 1929.'

Add to list of authorities: Masters' Hist. of Corpus Christi Coll., Camb., ed. J. Lamb.

Draper, Edward Alured. vi. 2*b*, l. 25 from foot. For 'colonel' read 'lieutenant-colonel'

Ibid. l. 17 from foot. For 'in 1796' read 'on 10 Aug. 1797 (*Army List*, 1798, p. 99)'

Ibid. l. 15 from foot. Delete 'As a brevet-major'

Ibid. ll. 11–10 from foot. After 'customary step' insert 'of brevet-major on 1 July 1803 (*Ibid.* 1804, p. 37)'; after '500*l.*' insert 'He was promoted captain and lieutenant-colonel on 16 Jan. 1806 (*ibid.* 1806, p. 107).'

Drelincourt, Peter. vi. 14*a*, l. 14 from foot. For '1629' read '1669.'

Ibid., ll. 7–2 from foot. For 'Peter graduated . . . precentor' read 'Peter came to England to become a member of the Church of England. On Arlington's recommendation he was given charge of Lord James Butler, the future second duke of Ormond, while the latter was at Oxford (January 1679–August 1680). Shortly afterwards he became chaplain to Ormond, at this time lord lieutenant of Ireland. In 1681 he was given the degree of M.A. at Trinity College, Dublin, and in 1691 that of LL.D. In 1681 he became precentor'

To authorities add: D. C. A. Agnew, Protestant exiles from France, 3rd ed., 1886, ii. 342–5; Hist. MSS. Comm., Ormonde MSS. at Kilkenny, new ser., vols. iv–viii.

Drummond, James, fourth Earl and first titular Duke of Perth. vi. 29–31. This article can be revised and supplemented by A. Joly, 'Un converti de Bossuet: James Drummond, duc de Perth, 1648–1716' ('Mém. et travaux des facultés catholiques de Lille,' fasc. xlii, *c.* 1934), which includes extracts from Perth's own account of his conversion and adds much fresh information about his life after 1693.

Drury, Henry Joseph Thomas (1778–1841), vi. 56*a*, l. 31. For 'Fingert', read 'Fingest'. *Ib.*, l. 23 from foot. For 'Greek', read 'Greek and Latin'. *Ib.*, l. 20 from foot. For '1837', read '1841'. Add to sources: Venn, *Alumni Cantabrigienses*, II. ii.

Duck, Stephen. vi. 89*b*, l. 2. After 'priest;' insert 'he was appointed chaplain to lieutenant-general H. Cornwall's (7th) regiment of marines on 19 Aug. 1747 (P.R.O., war office, commission book, 25/22, p. 116), was placed on half-pay when it was disbanded, 25 Dec. 1748 (*ibid.* half-pay list, 25/2987), and became chaplain to the 2nd dragoon guards, 20 Nov. 1750 (*ibid.* commission book, 25/23, p. 1);'

Dudley, Edmund.

Began life as a city official. ? Secondary of the Wood Street Counter. [City Records, *per* A. H. Thomas.] He was also the earliest officially known President of the King's Council, '*presidens concilii nostri.*' (*Rot. Pat.* 21 Henry VII. pt. ii. m. 18 (4); *C.P.R.* Henry VII. ii. 471.)

Dudley, Robert, Earl of Leicester. vi. 120*a*, l. 17 from foot. Add to reference 'see also inventories in *Archaeologia*, lxxiii. 28–52.'

Duff, James, fourth Earl of Fife. vi. 129*b*, ll. 22–3. For 'Edinburgh' read 'Westminster School and Christ Church, Oxford, was admitted to Lincoln's Inn 9 April 1794 (*Record of Old Westminsters*, i. 290; *Lincoln's Inn Admissions*, i. 549).'

Dunbar, Gavin (*d.* 1547). vi. 151*b*, 15 ll. from foot. For '(*d.* 1547)' read '(1497 ?–1547).'

Ibid. 6 ll. from foot. Before 'He received his education' add 'The date of his birth was *c.* 1497 (see epitaph in John Dunbar, *Epigrammata*, 1616, vi. no. xxxix, where Gavin is made to say "Lustra decem vixi florui et interii").'

Dunlop, John Colin, vi. 208*a*. Add 'educated at Glasgow High School; attended Edinburgh University 1803–5.' l. 16. For 'W. Hazlitt' read 'Jeffrey', l. 21. For 'Christopher Worth' read 'Lockhart'. 208*b*. l. 14. For 'February 1842' read '26 Jan. 1842'.

Duras or Durfort, Louis, Earl of Feversham. vi. 247*b*, ll. 9–11. Delete 'As English ambassador . . . ii. 206).' Evelyn does not make the statement, which is incorrect.

D'Urban, Sir Benjamin. vi. 250*a*, ll. 30–19 from foot. For 'The chief event . . . Port Natal' read 'In 1835 D'Urban recommended the occupation of Natal as a British possession, but Earl Glenelg, secretary of state for the colonies, refused permission (G. M. Theal, *Hist. of South Africa since 1795* (1908), ii. 309). The territory was occupied between 1838 and 1842 (*ibid.* pp. 315 *sqq.*).'

Add to list of authorities: G. M. Theal's Hist. of South Africa since 1795, vol. ii. 1908.

Dwight, John (*fl.* 1671–1698). vi. 273–5. Important additional information about Dwight is given by C. J. Féret, Fulham old and new, 1900, ii. 46–57. This gives his appointment as registrar and scribe of the diocese of Chester in 1661; the baptisms of most of his children from 1662; his first recorded appearance in Fulham in 1674; his death in 1703; his widow's, in 1709; and the careers of his children; besides some further information about his business and characteristics, and the later history of the pottery.

Dwight, Samuel. vi. 275, l. 20 from foot. For '1669?' read '1668'.

Ibid. ll. 19–17 from foot. For 'born about . . . article' read 'born in 1668, was the son of John Dwight [q.v.] (C. J. Féret, *Fulham*, ii. 46).'

p. 276*a*, l. 1. After '1690.' add 'He appears to have carried on his father's pottery. In 1716 he married Margaret Price of Fulham, who died in 1750; the pottery descended to their daughter Lydia and her husbands' (*ibid.* ii. 52–4).'

Dymoke, Sir John. vi. 295*b*, l. 23 from foot. After '*Memoirs*, i.)' insert 'He married Bridget, daughter and co-heiress of Edward Fiennes, Lord Clinton and earl of Lincoln, high admiral of England, by whom he had nine children (*Notes and Queries*, clxxvi. 248).'

Earle, Giles. vi. 318*b*, ll. 23–4. For 'He married . . . serjeant-at-law,' read 'On 20 May 1702 he married Elizabeth, daughter of Sir William Rawlinson [q.v.] and widow of William Lowther of Westmorland (*Allegations for Marriage Licences, London*, Harl. Soc. Visitation Ser., xxvi. vol. ii. p. 328; *Notes and Queries*, clxvii. 383).'

Ibid. ll. 30–24 from foot. Delete 'From a marriage license . . . Chelsea College.'

Earle, John (1601 ?–1665). vi. 321*a*, ll. 40 to foot of page, and 321*b*, ll. 1–10. The 'Microcosmographie' was probably written by Charles Herle [q.v.]. See J. D. Ogilvie, 'Earle and Herle and the Microcosmography' in the 'Journal of the Presbyterian Hist. Soc.' xxv. 246.

H. W. M.

Earle, John (1601 ?–1665). vi. 322*a*, l. 27 from foot. After '(June 1660)' insert 'and on 15 June 1660 he was formally sworn as clerk of the closet (*Notes and Queries*, clxxi. 8)' [See also BULLETIN, vii. 122.]

Edgeworth, Maria. vi. 381*a*, ll. 5–6. Delete 'and the second edition . . . her name' (*Times Lit. Suppl.*, 2 Jan. 1930, p. 12, col. 1).

Eden, William, first Baron Auckland. vi. 363*b*, l. 11. For 'Aug. 1787' read 'April 1788 (*Brit. Dipl. Repr.*, *1689–1789*, Camden 3rd series, xlvi. 27, 138)'

Edington, William of, (*d.* 1366) vi. 386*a*, l. 29. After 'him to' insert 'the mastership of St. Cross Hospital (*Cal. Pat. Rolls, 1334–8*, p. 88) and'. After 'Hampshire' insert 'in 1335'.

***Ibid.*, l. 33. After 'public service.' insert 'He was keeper of the Wardrobe, 1341–44.'**

***Ibid.*, l. 10 from foot. For 'In the same year' read 'In 1344'.**

***Ibid.*, l. 9 from foot. After 'treasurer' insert '(*Cal. Pat. Rolls, 1343–5*, p. 235).'**

***Ibid.*, l. 7 from foot. For '1345' read '1344'.**

P. 386*b*, ll. 34–5. For 'about 1347' read 'in 1351 (*Cal. Pat. Rolls, 1350–4*, pp. 110, 167, *etc.*)'.

***Ibid.*, l. 39. For 'after some time' read 'seven years later (*Cal. Pat. Rolls, 1358–61*, p. 90)'.**

***Ibid.*, ll. 41–2. For 'into one of . . . called' read 'into a house of'.**

***Ibid.*, l. 43. For 'friars whom' read 'a house which (*Downside Review*, lxii. (1944), 40–55)'.**

***Ibid.*, l. 7 from foot. For '1345' read '1344'.**

P. 387*a*. To list of authorities add: T. F. Tout, *Chapters in Medieval Administrative History*, iii. 203–7, *etc.*

Edmund (Rich) Saint (1170?–1240). vi. 407*b*, l. 27. For 'Wales' read 'Ireland' (D.N.B. xii. 1109*b*).

409*b*, l. 8 from foot. For 'Richard' read 'Edmund.' Matt. Paris, v. 621, 642.

S. Edmund (Rich).

vi. 409*b*. 'According to Wood:' the statement that he lectured on Aristotle's *Elenchi* is in Roger Bacon's 'Compendium . . . Theologicum.' (*Soc. Franc. Studies*, iii., 34.)

Edward III. vi. 466*b*, ll. 5–4 from foot. For 'on Sunday, the 29th' read 'on Sunday, 1 Feb. (*Foedera*, ii. pt. 2, p. 684; Fry, *Almanacks*, table 22).'

Edwards, Arthur. vi. 529*b*, ll. 15–6. For 'He died . . . horse guards' read 'He was appointed ensign in brigadier-general Howe's regiment, 25 March 1705 (Dalton, *English Army Lists*, v. 73), and was wounded at Blenheim (*ibid.* pt. 2, p. 48). He was promoted lieutenant, 24 Oct. 1708 (*ibid.* vi. 86), and captain-lieutenant on 1 June 1711 (P.R.O. War Office 64/4, army lists, p. 2). He was transferred to the 2nd troop of horse guards as a sub-brigadier, 29 Sept. 1715 (Dalton, *George the First's Army*, i. 192), and was promoted major, 21 May 1733 (Dalton, *English Army Lists*, v. 50), retaining this rank until his death.'

Elliot, Hugh. vi. 677*a*, l. 33. For '1773' read '1774 (Camden 3rd series, xlvi. 42, 46)'

Ibid. ll. 17–15 from foot. For '1782' read 'Jan. 1783 (*ibid.* pp. 6, 109)'; for 'for nine years' read 'until Nov. 1789 (*ibid.* p. 6)'

Ibid. ll. 4–3 from foot. Delete 'recalled from Copenhagen, and'

Elliotson, John. vi. 683*a*, 2 ll. from bottom. For 'December 1838' read 'January 1839.' See *University College, London. Proceedings at the Annual General Meeting* . . . 1839, pp. 9–10.

l. 5 from bottom. Omit 'medical.'

Ellis, Charles Augustus, sixth Baron Howard de Walden and second Baron Seaford. vi. 692*a*, l. 6. After 'appointed' insert 'envoy extraordinary and' (credential, P.R.O.. F.O. 83/843, no. 15).

Ellis, George. vi. 695*b*, l. 15. For '10 Sept. 1800' read '10 Nov. 1801 (*Gent. Mag.* 1801, p. 1052)'

Ellis, Sir Henry (1777–1869). vi. 699*a*, ll. 14–18. For 'in the same year . . . in 1833' read 'in the same year were published by command his introduction and indexes to Domesday Book (of which the text had been issued in 1783), as well as a volume of "Additamenta" to it. The introduction, revised and accompanied by new indexes, was again published in 1833 by the Commissioners on the Public Records.'

Elsyng, Henry. vi. 755*a*, ll. 12–18. There is really only one version of this treatise, extant in several manuscripts, and as it was composed before 1626, it must be the work of the father, who was then clerk of the parliaments. (See Birrell and Garnett, *Catalogue* No. 22, p. 47.)

Ellys, Sir Richard. vi. 725*b*, l. 28. For '1715 to 1724' read '1705–13' (*Return of M.P.'s*, ii. 3, 11, 21).

Elyot, Sir Richard (1450?–1522), vi. 765*a*, l. 25. For 'he married his first wife, Alice Fynderne . . . (*d.* 1440)' read 'he married as his first wife Alice, the widow of Thomas Daubridgecourt (*d.* 1485) and daughter of Sir Thomas Delamere (*d.* 1493) and Elizabeth Fynderne (*d.* 1484). Alice was a great-granddaughter of Sir William Fynderne of Childrey, Berkshire (*d.* 1444) and, by her first husband, grandmother of Erasmus Pym, John Pym's grandfather. In 1503 Richard Elyot was made a bencher of the Middle Temple, reader for the Autumn Vacation, and a King's Serjeant-at-Law.' *Ib.*, l. 30. For He acted as judge of assize . . . century' read 'He acted as judge of assize on the western circuit from 1506 until his death.' *Ib.*, l. 32.—For 'was in the commission of the peace for Cornwall in 1509', read 'He served at various times in the commissions of the peace for Wiltshire, Berkshire, Hampshire, Dorset, Somerset, Oxfordshire, Essex, Devon, Cornwall, and Oxford town'.

Add to sources: Prerogative Court of Canterbury (Somerset House), will of Sir Thomas Fynderne; P.R.O., Chancery Inquisitions C.I./499/59, C.I./501/29–34, C.I./1016/62–4; C. H. Hopwood, ed., *Middle Temple Records.*

Elyot, Sir Thomas (1490?–1546), vi. 765*a*, l. 7. For 'was born before 1490' read 'was born about 1490'. *Ib.* l. 21 from foot.—For 'West Colvile' read 'Weston Colville'. *Ib.* l. 16 from foot. For 'post of clerk . . . salary' read 'post of senior clerk of the king's council at a salary of forty marks a year, but since the previous patent, held by Richard Eden, was not properly vacated, Elyot was never paid (P.R.O., C. 66/650, m. l)'. *Ib.*, l. 4 from foot. For 'June 1530' read 'April 1530'. *Ib.*, 766*a* l. 16 from foot. After 'On 18 Nov. 1532, . . . sheriff of Cambridgeshire' delete 'to which he had been appointed for a second time.' *Ib.* 766*b*, l. 29. —For 'Anne of Cleves at Blackheath . . . Willingham, Cambridgeshire' read 'Anne of Cleves at Blackheath. In 1538 he bought of Cromwell the manor of Carleton-cum-Willingham, Cambridgeshire (P.R.O., S.P.1/129/56–7)'. *Ib.*, l. 35.—After 're-granted to Elyot 4 August' add 'On 5 Dec. 1539 he bought from the Crown the manor of Histon Eynsham, Cambridgeshire, which had been held by the monastery of Eynsham, Oxfordshire, before its dissolution (*L. & P. Hen. VIII*, XIV, ii. 780[4])'. *Ib.*,—For 'He was M.P. for Cambridge in 1542 (Willis, *Not. Parl.* i. 190)' read 'He sat in the parliaments of 1539 (*Castel of Helth*, 1539 ed., Preface) and 1542 (Willis, *Not Parl.* i. 190), probably on both occasions for Cambridge'. *Ib.*, l. 24 from foot.—For 'He died 20 March 1546' read 'He died 26 March 1546 (P.R.O., C.142/74/16, E. 150/94/2, Wards 7/2/119)'. *Ib.*, l. 26 from foot.—For 'Elyot left no will and no children' read 'He left no children. His will, made in August 1531 and proved in the Prerogative Court of Canterbury 2 July 1546, left all his possessions to his wife.' For 'His heir was Richard Puttenham' read 'They subsequently passed to Richard Puttenham'.

Make the following alterations in the dates of Elyot's works: *The Boke named the Gouernour:* delete '1534'; add '1544, 1553, 1580'. *Pasquyll the Playne*: delete 'No copy of either the first or second edition is in the British Museum'. *Of the Knowledge which Maketh a Wise Man:* add '1548(?),

1552(?)'. *A Swete and Devoute Sermon:* add '1539'. *The Doctrinal of Princes:* for '1534' read '1533(?), 1548(?)'. *The Castel of Helth:* add '1544(?), 1549(?), 1559(?). 1560(?), 1572, 1587, 1610.' *The Bankette of Sapience:* after the dates add 'No copy of the first edition, probably published in 1534, is known to exist'. *The Dictionary:* add '1542; as revised by Cooper', for '1550' read '1548.' *The Defence of Good Women:* add '1540 (Huntington Library)'. *The Image of Gouernance:* for '1540' read '1541'.

Add to sources: Prerogative Court of Canterbury (Somerset House), will of Sir Thomas Elyot.

Elyot, Sir Thomas. vi. 768*a*, 23 ll. from foot. For 'Horace's "Ars Poetica"' read 'Horace's "Epistolae."' There is no foundation for the frequent statement that Elyot made a translation of Horace's 'Ars Poetica.' (*Notes and Queries*, cli. 259.)

Elyot, Sir Thomas. vi. 766*a*, l. 8 from foot to 766*b*, l. 3. Delete 'But in 1535 . . . *Sir T. More*)' (*Times Lit. Suppl.*, 19 July 1930, p. 592, coll. 1–2).

Erbury, William. vi. 801*b*–803*a*. This article is in many respects inadequate. In particular it neglects his activity in the development of puritanism in Wales, shown in pamphlets such as 'A Call to the Churches,' 1652, and 'The North Star,' 1653. Thomas Richards in 'The Puritan Movement in Wales,' 1920, and 'Religious Developments in Wales,' 1923, gives a very full account of Erbury's teaching and influence, and styles him 'the supreme itinerant of the age.' Some speeches of Erbury's in Jan. 1649 on the religious clauses of the agreement of the people are printed in 'Clarke Papers,' ii. 171–80, which also contains an account of his trial, in Feb. 1653, before the committee for plundered ministers (ii. 233–9). Dorcas Erbury, the follower of James Nayler, whom the D.N.B. describes as William Erbury's wife, was in reality his daughter (*see* Braithwaite, 'The Beginnings of Quakerism,' pp. 247, 252). Erbery or Erberie is the spelling of his name given on the title-page of his pamphlets.

C. H. F.

Erskine, Sir David. vi. 819*a*, ll. 12–8 from foot. For 'In early life . . . 31st regiment' read 'He was appointed an ensign in the 31st regiment on 14 Oct. 1789 (*Army List*, 1790, p. 107), lieutenant of an independent company, 24 Jan. 1791 (P.R.O., war office, succession book, 25/213), returned to the 31st regiment, 6 Apr. 1791 (*ibid.*), and promoted captain, 29 Sept. 1794 (*Army List*, 1796, p. 162). He exchanged to half-pay, 132nd regiment, on 10 July 1799 (P.R.O., war office, half-pay list, 25/2992, p. 331). On 8 May 1806 he was appointed captain of a company of gentlemen cadets at the Royal Military college (*London Gazette*, 1806, no. 15,916, p. 569) and after exchanging to half-pay, in the royal York rangers, on 10 Aug. 1820 (*Army List*, 1823, p. 619),'

Erskine, David Montagu, second Baron Erskine. vi. 819*b*, l. 4 from foot. For 'February' read 'January' (credential, P.R.O., F.O. 90/7, p. 92).

Erskine, Sir Henry or Harry. vi. 827*b*, ll. 21–15 from foot. For 'His name first appears . . . Irish establishment' read 'He was appointed ensign in Col. James St. Clair's (afterwards the 22nd) regiment on 20 June 1735 (P.R.O., Index 5435, p. 61), was promoted lieutenant of the same regiment on 13 Aug. 1736 (*ibid.* p. 46), and on 12 March 1743 he was appointed captain in the 1st Royal Scots, then also commanded by St. Clair (*ibid.* 5436, p. 108)'

Erskine, Sir James St. Clair, second Earl of Rosslyn. vi. 833*a*, ll. 9–13. Delete 'grenadier' (P.R.O., war office, succession book, 25/211); for '38th' read '35th' (*ibid.*); after 'Scots Greys,' insert 'then 21st dragoons (*ibid.*),'

Ibid. 833*b*, l. 11. After '9th light dragoons,' insert '1 Aug. 1801 (*Army List*, 1802, p. 74),'

Erskine, Sir William. vi. 863*b*, ll. 16–14 from foot. For '1769' read '1770'; for 'only' read 'elder'; after 'son of' insert 'Sir'; for 'father' read 'grandfather'

Ibid. l. 11 from foot. For 'elder' read 'younger'

Ibid. ll. 8–7 from foot. For 'in 1769' read 'on 30 March 1770'; for 'cornet' read 'second lieutenant'; for '15th light dragoons in 1786' read '23rd regiment of foot in Sept. 1785 (P.R.O. War office, succession books, 25/212–3)'; delete 'and'.

Ibid. ll. 6–4 from foot. For 'in 1788' read 'of the 5th dragoons, 14 Nov. 1787'; delete 'and'; after 'captain' insert 'of the 15th light dragoons (*ibid.* muster rolls,

12/1193, f. 110)'; after '1791' insert 'and major on 1 March 1794 (*ibid.* f. 123)'. For 'He was created a baronet . . . first saw' read 'He succeeded to the baronetcy (created 21 June 1791) on the death of his father, 19 March 1795 (*Scots Mag.* 1795, p. 206), after having seen'

Ibid. l. 2 from foot–864*a*, l. 5. For 'one of the officers . . . Maria Theresa with them,' read 'appointed to command the British cavalry destined for the continent, May 1793 (P.R.O. War office, out-letters, 3/11, p. 98) and'; delete 'major in his regiment in June, and'.

Ibid. l. 6. After '1794.' insert 'On 26 Feb. 1796 he exchanged commissions with his brother James, of the 133rd (Fraser's) foot, and was placed on half-pay (*ibid.* 12/1193, fos. 125, 127).'

Ibid. l. 8. Delete 'went on half-pay in 1798,'

Ibid. ll. 9–11. Delete 'of the 14th garrison battalion'; after '1802,' insert 'was appointed to the 14th (Erskine's) garrison battalion, 9 June 1803'; for '1803' read '1805'

Ibid. ll. 11–10 from foot. For '14 May' read '13 Feb.'; for 'in Lisbon' read 'at Brozas, in Spain'

Ibid. l. 8 from foot. After 'Torry' insert 'passed in succession to his brothers James and John Drummond Erskine, and on the latter's death'

Add to list of authorities: G.E.C.'s Complete Baronetage, v. 268–9; W. Stephen's History of Inverleithing and Rosyth, pp. 83–4; C. Oman's Wellington's Army, p. 151.

Evans, John (1774–1828). vi. 931*b*, l. 13 from foot. For 'in January 1819' read 'on 7 August 1817.'

Ibid. ll. 11–9 from foot. For 'he left Bristol . . . Fenchurch Street, London' read 'having failed as a printer in Bristol, he went to London for the purpose of entering into some engagement with a printer, D. S. Maurice, of Fenchurch Street.'

Ibid. last line. After 'son' add ', William Evans "of Bristol" the landscape painter [q.v.].'

To authorities add: Bristol and Gloucestershire Archæol. Soc., Transactions, lxi (1940), 196–8.

Evans, John (*d.* 1832). vi. 932*a*, l. 18. For '*d.* 1832' read '*d.* 1831'.

Ibid. ll. 20–2. For 'for several years . . . at Kingsdown' read 'from 1812 (or earlier) to 1825, at various houses in Park Row and at Kingsdown.'

Ibid. ll. 24–6. For 'He eventually . . . Euston Square' read 'He removed to Bath and then to London, where he had a school in Drummond St., Euston Square.'

Ibid. l. 26. For 'in 1832' read 'in December 1831.'

Ibid. ll. 27–26 from foot. For '"British Mercury"' read '"Bristol Mercury."'

Ibid. l. 10 from foot. After 'Corry [q.v.]' add: '(Bristol and Gloucestershire Archæol. Soc., Transactions, lxi (1940). 198–200; Hyett and Austin, Supplement to the Bibliographer's Manual of Gloucestershire Literature).'

Ibid. l. 3 from foot (**John Evans, *fl.*** 1812). After '*Oxon.* ii. 28)' add 'He kept a boarding-school in 1806 at Colston's Parade, Bristol, and later at Winterbourne near Bristol.'

Ibid. 932*b*, l. 23. For 'Authorities as above' read 'Bristol and Gloucestershire Archæol. Soc., Transactions, lxi (1940). 200–1.'

Evans, Sir John. Second Suppl. i. 636*a*, 22 ll. from bottom. For '(Chairman in 1900)' read '(Chairman of the Council 1900–01).'

636*b*, 9 ll. from bottom. After '1911' add 'His collection of ancient British coins was presented by Sir Arthur Evans to the British Museum in February 1919. His collection of English coins, gold and silver, had been acquired by the Museum in May 1915.' MARIA MILLINGTON EVANS.

Evans, William (1811–1858). vi. 940*a*, ll. 20–19 from foot. For 'and a native of North Wales' read 'and son of John Evans (1774–1828), the Bristol printer [q.v.], (Bristol and Gloucestershire Archæol. Soc., *Transactions*, lxi (1940), 198).'

Ewart, Joseph. vi. 954*b*, ll. 20–28. For ', and after . . . 5 Aug. 1788' read 'and while Stepney was envoy at Berlin from Oct. 1782 till June 1784, he took Ewart into his service, and Ewart was in charge from June 1784 until the arrival of Lord Dalrymple, Stepney's successor on 29 Nov. 1785. Ewart had been appointed secretary of legation on the previous 21 October. In May 1787 Dalrymple went away on leave and did not return. On 15 July 1788 Ewart was made envoy extraordinary and on 11 Aug. 1789 minister plenipotentiary. He was absent on leave from Sept. 1790 till April 1791, but was again in Berlin from 29 April till 22 Oct. 1791 (Sir R. Lodge, *Great Britain and Prussia*, pp. 161, 210).'

Ibid. ll. 8–7 from foot. Delete 'He left . . . 3 Nov. 1791.'

Ewart, Joseph. vi. 954*b*, l. 28. For '5 Aug.' read '31 July (*Brit. Dipl. Repr., 1689–1789*, Camden 3rd series, xlvi. 109)'

Ibid. l. 8 from foot. For '3 Nov.' read '22 Oct.'

***Ewer, Isaac.** vi. 957. The article contains several errors. Ewer appears in the New Model army in 1645, as lieut.-col. of Robert Hammond's regiment of foot in the autumn of 1647 after Hammond became governor of the Isle of Wight (6 Sept. 1647). He was accused on 23 April 1648 of a plot to disarm and plunder London, which caused great alarm in the City (Rushworth, vii. 1070). A few days later his regiment appears to have been despatched to South Wales, and when Cromwell besieged Pembroke he left Ewer to capture Chepstow, which he effected on May 25. His letter is printed by Phillips (*Civil War in Wales*, ii. 375). The regiment did not accompany Cromwell to the north and so was not at Preston. It joined the besiegers of Colchester on June 15 (Rushworth, vii. 1153). As one of Fairfax's commissioners Ewer signed the articles for the surrender of Colchester (27 Aug. 1648; Rushworth, vii. 1277). After that event the regiment appears to have been sent to Portsmouth. On 21 Nov. Ewer was ordered to leave Portsmouth to his lieut.-col., Robert Saunders, and to go to the Isle of Wight and supersede Hammond if necessary; and on 27 Nov. he was further instructed to convey the king from Carisbrooke to Hurst Castle and secure him there until Col. Thomas Eyres, the governor of Hurst Castle, could take charge (*Clarke Papers*, ii. 54–61, 63–6). Ewer on the strength of the first orders accompanied Hammond to the headquarters at Windsor, leaving the transfer of the king from the Isle of Wight to Hurst Castle to be effected by Lieut.-Col. Cobbett. The portrait of the officer who received the king at Hurst Castle, quoted from Sir Thomas Herbert's *Memoirs*, does not apply to Ewer but to Eyres or one of his officers (Herbert, *Memoirs*, 1702, pp. 78–86; *Clarke Papers*, ii. 66; Gardiner, *Great Civil War*, iv. 256). Ewer died some months later than the article says. The diary of an officer in the Irish army notes on 31 Oct. 1650 that 'Col. Ewer with part of the army marched towards Kilkenny,' which was the headquarters of the army during that winter (Gilbert, *Aphorismical Discovery*, iii. 224).

Exton, John. vi. 962*a*, l. 33. For '1649' read '1648 (*Mariner's Mirror*, xiii. 340).'

Ibid. l. 37. For 'about 1665' read 'in 1668 and was buried in St. Benet's, Paul's Wharf, on 22 Oct. (*Reg.* iv. 62: Harl. Soc. xli. cited in *Mariner's Mirror*, xiii. 340).'

Fagan, Robert. vi. 982*a*, ll. 47–8. Before 'He died' insert 'a letter of his to William Hamilton, under secretary of state for foreign affairs, of 5 July, 1816 refers to "my severe illness of which I am not yet free," and appears to envisage its return' (Public Record Office, F.O. 70/76). For 'He died' read 'He committed suicide "by throwing himself from a two pair of stairs window, of his lodging in Via Pontifici"' (F.O. 43/9, D. Denis to Hamilton, Albano, 28 August, 1816), and insert after 26 August, 1816, '"Mr. Fagan's mind," adds Douglas, "had been much agitated for some time past"' (loc. cit.). For 'leaving' read 'He left.'

Fairborne, Sir Stafford. vi. 991*a*, l. 7 from foot. For 'June 1707' read 'Dec. 1705 (BULLETIN, xiv. 23)'

***Fairfax, Charles** (1597–1673), antiquary and genealogist. vi. 994*b*. The article gives a vague and inaccurate account of his military career. He was from February 1643 onwards a member of the parliamentary committees appointed for the West Riding of Yorkshire (*Acts and Ordinances, passim*), but it is uncertain whether he fought in the first Civil War. In May 1648, on the outbreak of the second Civil War, three regiments of foot were raised in Yorkshire, and that for the West Riding was commanded by Colonel Charles Fairfax, who is described as 'uncle to the Lord General' (*Clarke Papers*, ii. 22). Under him it took part in the siege of Pontefract Castle (*Miscellanea*, Surtees Society, vol. i.: Nathan Drake's Account of the Siege of Pontefract). On 13 Feb. 1648/9 the regiment was put on the establishment of the regular army, commanded by Lord Fairfax (*Commons' Journals*, vi. 139). It served under Charles Fairfax in the invasion of Scotland, fought at Dunbar and Worcester, returned again to Scotland about 1653 and continued there throughout the Protectorate. When Monck declared for the restoration of the Long Parliament, Charles Fairfax helped to reorganise Monck's forces, signed all the declarations of the Scottish officers, and marched with him into England (Mackinnon, *Coldstream Guards*, i. 21, 37; *Clarke Papers*, vol. iv.; Gumble, *Life of Monck*, p. 145). Monck left Fairfax and his regiment at York to secure the peace of the county against royalist gentry as well as mutineers—a difficult task, since the royalist agitation was headed by his nephew, Lord Fairfax. Major-General Morgan reported to Monck that Charles Fairfax was 'cordial and constant,' and that neither the pressure of his relations nor anything else would 'prevail with him to consent to anything prejudicial to the peace of these nations'; but 'he is ancient and infirm, and thereby disenabled from being so active as formerly to hinder what may happen.' With the help of Morgan and other active officers he succeeded in maintaining order till Monck's restoration of the secluded members quieted the agitation (see Fairfax's correspondence with Monck in the *Report on the MSS. of Mr. Leyborne-Popham*, pp. 146–59). In March 1660 Monck employed Fairfax to take over the charge of the garrison of Hull and induce Colonel Overton to submit, which he also effected successfully (*ibid.*, pp. 163, 170; Phillips, *Continuation of Baker's Chronicle*, ed. 1670, pp. 685, 691, 694, 696, 701, 713, 720). In June 1660 he was succeeded by Lord Bellasis as governor.

Two letters from Cromwell to Col. Fairfax are printed and a facsimile of one given in Sir R. Tangye's *The Two Protectors*, 1899, pp. 133–7.

Fairfax, Ferdinando, Second Baron Fairfax. vi. 997*a*, 14 ll. from foot. In the account of the battle of Marston Moor read 'Fairfax's army was stationed' 'in the centre' instead of 'on the right,' and refer to the paper on Marston Moor, by C. H. Firth, printed in the *Proceedings of the Royal Historical Society*, New Series, xii. 26, 37, 39, 73.

997*b*, l. 10. Read 'of the Northern Association established for the defence of the six northern counties and Nottinghamshire (20 June 1645).'

Ibid., l. 18. After 'Sheffield' insert 'who died in 1619.'

Ibid. Add to the last sentence 'and in E. Hailstone's *Yorkshire Worthies*, 1869.'

Fairfax, Henry (1634–1702), dean of Norwich. vi. 998. See the amusing description of his habits in the *Letters of Humphrey Prideaux to John Ellis*, Camden Soc., 1875, p. 160.

Fairfax, Nathaniel, M.D. vi. 1001*a*, l. 14 from foot. After 'Blackerby,' add 'niece of Bishop John Cosin (Cosin, *Correspondence*, Surtees Soc., ii. 299).'

Fairfax or Fayrfax, Robert (*d.* 1529). vi. 1002*a*, ll. 2–4. For 'He took the degree . . . in 1511' read 'He graduated Mus.B. at Cambridge in 1500–1, proceeding Mus.D. in 1504; and in 1511 was incorporated at Oxford in the degree of D.Mus., the first holder of that degree at Oxford (Venn, *Alumni Cantab.*).'

STRICKLAND GIBSON.

Fairfax, Thomas, first Baron Fairfax (1560–1640). vi. 1005*b*, l. 9. After 'August' add '*Commons' Journals*, i. 801, 803–4, and J. J. Cartwright, *Chapters in Yorkshire History*, 1872, pp. 214–226.'

Ibid., l. 10. The date of the patent creating him Baron Fairfax was 18 Oct. 1627 (G. E. C., *Complete Peerage*, vol. v.).

Fairfax, Thomas, third Baron Fairfax. vi. 1005*b*, l. 6. Insert 'He was admitted to Gray's Inn 26 May 1628.'

1006*a*, l. 23. After Adwalton Moor add the reference '(*Hist. MSS. Comm., Portland MSS.*, i. 717, where there is a very detailed account of the battle written by Thomas Stockdale the next day).'

Ibid., 15 ll. from foot. The date of the battle at Nantwich should be 25, not 29 Jan. Add reference to Phillips, *Civil War in Wales*, ii. 125.

1007*b*, 6 ll. from foot. Add reference to *Clarke Papers*, i. 5–11, 85, 101, 108, 113–16 after '28 May,' and alter '28' to '29.'

1008*a*, l. 16. After 'the king refused to return' add '(*Clarke Papers*, i. 124).'

1008*b*, l. 4. Insert 'On 19 July 1647 Fairfax was appointed by parliament.'

1009*a*, 21 ll. from foot. Read 'the town, the country, and the kingdom.'

Ibid., 18 ll. from foot. Add comma after 'justice' and omit the comma after 'mercy.'

Ibid., 17 ll. from foot. Add comma after 'used.'

Ibid., 8 ll. from foot. This explanatory letter is printed in *Clarke Papers*, ii. p. xiii.

1009*b*, l. 26. After 'Isle of Wight' add '(*Clarke Papers*, ii. 54, 62, 146).'

1010*b*, l. 26. On the causes of Fairfax's resignation, and the development of his political opinions since 1647, see Gardiner, *Commonwealth and Protectorate*, i. 257–264, ed. 1903.

1011*a*, l. 22. On the marriage of Mary Fairfax add a reference to Burghclere, *George Villiers, second Duke of Buckingham*, p. 87.

1011*b*. After 'or a free parliament' add references to *Clarke Papers*, iv. 239; *Hist. MSS. Comm., Leyborne-Popham MSS.*, pp. 149, 154.

1012*a*, 13 ll. from foot. Insert 'A painting of Fairfax and his wife by Dobson is in the National Portrait Gallery.'

1013*a*. Add to the list of authorities: 'S. R. Gardiner, *The Great Civil War*, ed. 1893'; and after the reference to the *Old Parliamentary History* add '*Hist. MSS. Comm., Portland MSS.*; and *Clarke Papers*, i., ii.'

Fairfax, Sir William (1600–1644). vi. 1014*b*, l. 33. Omit 'on the right of the parliamentary line.'

Fallows, Fearon. vi. 1036*a*, l. 20. For '1823' read '1820' (*Record of Royal Soc.*, p. 384).

Fane, Mildmay, second Earl of Westmoreland. vi. 1042*b*, l. 22. G. Thorn-Drury gives his date of birth from a note of Westmoreland's as 24 Jan. 1601–2 (*A Little Ark*, p. 18; this collection includes two poems addressed by him to John Cleveland [q.v.]).

E. S. de B.

Fanshawe, Sir Richard. vi. 1049*b*, l. 33. For 'Bate' read 'John Bathurst [q.v.].' Both texts of Lady Fanshawe's 'Memoirs' give Bathurst, and her description applies to him rather than to Bate.

Ibid. 1053*a*, ll. 24–7. For 'The original . . . H. C. Fanshawe' read 'A transcript made by Lady Fanshawe's daughter Anne in 1676 belonged in 1907 to Mr. E. J. Fanshawe, when it was printed and edited, with illustrations, by H. C. Fanshawe (information about transcripts and earlier editions and extracts is given in this edition, pp. 221–3, but a reprint edited by Mr. Allan Fea, with illustrations, in 1905, is not mentioned). It gives a better text than the earlier one. No original in Lady Fanshawe's hand is known to exist; the 1676 transcript has some corrections made by her.'

Faraday, Michael, vi. 1065*a*, l. 16. After '241*l*' add 'On 18 Dec. 1829 he was appointed by the Master General of the Ordnance to deliver a course of not less than 25 chemical lectures annually to the gentlemen cadets of the Royal Military Academy, Woolwich, at an annual fee of 200 l. (P.R.O., War Office, Ordnance Office corresp., 44/520). He resigned this lectureship on 9 Feb. 1852 as "my memory is failing me and I feel it to be right that I should restrict the field of my activities". (*ibid.*, 44/523)'.

Farley, James Lewis. vi. 1073*a*, l. 17. After 'he published' insert 'an account of his experiences, entitled "Two Years in Syria," and in 1861.'

Ibid. l. 14 from foot. After 'successors' insert 'In the autumn of 1875 he took a prominent part in public agitations in England in support of the oppressed christians in Turkey, and proposed in October to the Russian government a lecture and press campaign among the protestant clergy, to give a more religious colour to the agitation. The Russian ambassador in London suggested to St. Petersburg the possibility of a monthly subvention of £100 or £150, and in December advised the expenditure of £50 on the purchase of Farley's "Decline of Turkey"' (*Slavonic Review*, viii. 426, 430–1).

Ibid. 1073*b*, l. 4. After 'Alexander I.' insert 'He presented a letter of introduction from the Russian foreign minister which recommended him for his past services to the Bulgarian cause and obtained for him a yearly grant for the furnishing of the English press with Bulgarian news. As a result he was later accused of "working" the English press against Russian policy' (Koch, *Fürst Alexander von Battenberg*, 1887, p. 83) 'and in order to ingratiate himself with Bulgarian liberals' (Sobolev, *Der erste Fürst von Bulgarien*, 1886, pp. 4–5).

W. N. M.

Farr, Samuel, M.D. vi. 1089*b*, l. 23. After '1741' insert 'the seventh son of Alderman (? Thomas) Farr (*cf.* Bristol and Glouc. Arch. Soc. *Trans.* xxxiii. 333–4), a merchant of Bristol (G. Munro Smith, *History of the Bristol Infirmary*, p. 115).'

Ibid. l. 25. For 'Warrington Academy' read 'Bristol Free Grammar School (*ibid.*).'

Ibid. l. 30. After 'Bristol.' insert 'He kept a meteorological journal there for the years 1775–8 (*Philosoph. Trans. of the Roy. Soc.* [abridged], xiv. 47, 179, 390, 593), and on 25 Feb. 1779 was elected F.R.S. (*Record of the Roy. Soc.*, 3rd ed. p. 360).'

Ibid. l. 25 from foot. After '1795.' add 'Notes on Farr's life, dictated by a relative soon after his death, are in the custody of the Bristol Royal Infirmary.'

Ibid. l. 18 from foot. For '1772' read 'Altenburgi, 1774.'

Ibid. ll. 3–2 from foot. Delete 'Munk's Coll. of Phys.', in which Farr's name does not appear, and 'Toulmin's Hist. of Taunton', in which Farr only appears as a subscriber to the first edition.

Farre, Arthur. vi. 1093*a*, 3 ll. from foot. For 'Fergusson' read 'Ferguson [q.v.].'

Fawkener, Sir Everard. vi. 1127 *a*, ll. 9–10. After 'the third edition' insert '(1733)'.

Ibid. l. 11. Delete 'since ambassador at Constantinople.'

Ibid. ll. 4–7. For '(Vergesco . . . 374–376)' read '(G. Bengesco, *Voltaire : Bibliographie*, i. 15 ; G. Desnoiresterres, *Voltaire et la société française*, [i], *La jeunesse de Voltaire*, pp. 374–5).'

Ibid. ll. 17–20. For 'About 1735 . . . for him' read 'He was appointed ambassador to Turkey in 1735 (instructions dated 1 Sept. N.S., credentials 2 Oct.) ; he was knighted at Hanover on 2 October (Shaw, *Knights of England*, ii. 284), and arrived at Constantinople on 30 December. The 1736 edition of "Zaïre" is dedicated to "Le Chevalier Falkener" as ambassador at Constantinople : Voltaire speaks highly of the capabilities of English merchants, and in 1775 claimed to have foreseen Falkener's future eminence.'

Ibid. ll. 30–29 from foot. For 'From this position . . . promoted to be' read 'He left Constantinople on leave on 19 Nov 1742 and, although he never returned, was not deprived of the embassy until September 1746 ; meanwhile in March 1745 (H. Walpole, *Letters*, ed. Toynbee, ii. 80) he was appointed.'

Ibid. p. 1128*a*. Add to list of authorities 'D. B. Horn's British Diplomatic Representatives, p. 153.'

Fell, Henry. vi. 1156*b*, ll. 29–30. 'The first mention of him is in 1656.' Sotheby & Co. (*Catalogue*, 16 Nov. 1925, no. 217) had an unpublished autograph manuscript of a work by Fell dated 1653, entitled 'The Standard of the Lord Lifted against the Beast . . . or an Answer to a Booke entitled a Looking-glasse for George Foxe,' etc.

1157*a*, l. 16. To the list of his writings add the above work.

Fenwick or Fenwicke, Sir John (1579–1658?) vi. 1193*a*, l. 10 from foot. For

(1579–1658?)' substitute '(1579?–1658)'.

Ibid. l. 9 from foot. Insert 'The date of his birth, 1579, as given in G. E. C. *Baronetage*, depends on the statement in John Hodgson, *History of Northumberland*, pt. ii, vol. i (1887), 256, that he "was 35 years old September 1614 when the inquest after the death of his father was taken". It corresponds neither with his own statement in 1651 to the County Committee for Compounding that he was 85 (*Records of the Committees for Compounding* (Surtees Society), cxi. 204), nor with his nephew's statement in 1657 that Sir John was at least 80 years old (Hist. MSS. Comm., *10th Report, App.* iv. 108).'

1193*b*, ll. 25–29. For 'In December 1644 . . . Whitelocke, *Mem.* p. 121)' substitute 'The statement in Whitelocke's *Memorials* (1682), p. 116 that in December of 1644 "Captain Redman with a party from Northampton, set upon a part of the King's Forces going to Banbury, took prisoner . . . Sir John Fenwicke [and others]" which has been followed in all succeeding accounts is quite certainly an error, since Sir John was active on parliament appointed committees from 24 Feb. 1643 through 1657 (*Acts and Ordinances of the Interregnum*, ed. C. H. Firth and R. S. Rait, ii), actually being a member of the Committee for General Assessment at the time of the reported arrest, and in the following June one of the committee to raise money for the Northern Association.'

Ibid. ll. 29–31. For 'He subsequently made his peace with the Parliament, was appointed High Sheriff of Northumberland', read 'On the testimony of the standing committee of Northumberland 2 March 1645/6 that Sir John Fenwick had always adhered to the parliament and not to the king (Hist. MSS. Comm., *13th Report, App.* ii. 352 [*Portland MSS.* i.]), he'

Ibid. l. 37. For 'He died about 1658.' read 'His name appears frequently in county and law suits. Mackenzie, in his *Historical and Descriptive View of Northumberland*, i. 796, gives John Fenwicke of Wallington as sheriff of Northumberland in the 17th year of King James' reign, where the *List of Sheriffs* (P.R.O. List and Indexes, ix) has a hiatus, and also in the 21st year of King Charles, but the *List of Sheriffs* here credits Robert Clavering with the position. The *Portland MSS.* i. 685 record a letter from "Sir John Fenwicke, Sheriff of Northumberland, to William Lenthall" 31 August 1659, at which time the *List of Sheriffs* enters William Fenwick. The error may not be of date but of name, since Sir John's son William had probably succeeded to his father's title by 1659.'

Ibid. l. 43. For 'Marston Moor on 3 July 1644' substitute 'Marston Moor on 2 July 1644.'

Fenwick, Sir John. vi. 1193*b*, 7 ll. from foot to 1194*a*, l. 34. For 'was descended . . . against the prince' read 'was the son of Sir William Fenwick, of Wallington castle, second baronet, by his wife Jane, daughter of Henry Stapleton, of Wighill, Yorkshire (Joseph Foster, *Visitations of Northumberland*, pp. 54–5). He is stated to have been 21 years of age before 1 September 1666 (*ibid.*), but was perhaps slightly older. On 14 July 1663 he married Mary, daughter of Charles Howard, earl of Carlisle, in the earl of Elgin's chapel (Harl. Soc., *Registers of St. John's, Clerkenwell*, iii. 112; licence dated 6 July 1663: Harl. Soc., *London Marriage Licences*, ii. 293). On 13 June 1667 he was given a commission as captain in Sir John Sayer's regiment of foot, but this was disbanded after the treaty of Breda (C. Dalton, *English Army Lists*, i. 83). He is probably the Mr. Fenwick who fought a duel with Mr. Churchill [presumably John Churchill, later duke of Marlborough, q.v.], 5 February 1671, and was certainly involved in the killing of the beadle at Whetstone park on 16 February of that year (*Cal. S.P., Dom.*, 1671, pp. 71, 183: Fenwick's pardon for the latter affair is dated 11 April. For it see *Poems on Affairs of State*, vol. 1, 1702, i. 147–8). On 1 May 1672 Fenwick, who had previously held a command in the Northumberland militia (Hist. MSS. Comm., 13th Rep., App. ii, 149 [*Portland MSS.*, ii.]), appears to have obtained a commission as cornet and major in the queen's troop of guards, Monmouth being colonel and Sir Philip Howard captain of his troop (there are several difficulties about this appointment). On 24 March 1674 he was appointed guidon of the same troop, and on 1 May 1676 was promoted to be cornet and captain (Dalton, i. 127, 173, 189). He is said to have served against the Dutch during the war. On 15 July 1675 Danby wrote a letter recommending him to the prince of Orange (*Cal. S.P., Dom.*, 1675–1676, p. 217). On entering the Dutch service Fenwick was given command of the Irish regiment which became later the Fifth Foot (Northumberland Fusiliers) (*Life of Major John Bernardi*, 1729, p. 22; H. M. Walker, *Hist. of the Northumberland Fusiliers*, p. 7). The regiment, which soon lost its Irish character, was grouped with two English regiments, with Fenwick as their senior colonel; he greatly distinguished himself at the siege of Maestricht in July and August 1676, and was wounded there, probably on 2 August [N.S.] (*Life of Bernardi*, p. 22; William Carr, *A Particular Account of the present Siege of Mastricht*, dated 5 September 1676 [N.S.], pp. 3, 18–9; *London Gazette*, no. 1117, 31 July–3 Aug. 1676). Fenwick returned to England in September (*Cal. S.P., Dom.*, 1676–1677, p. 334).

'Sir William Fenwick died about this time and John, besides succeeding to the baronetcy, was elected M.P. for Northumberland on 15 March 1677. He naturally belonged to the court party (*A Seasonable Argument*, 1677, p. 14; S.P., Dom., Car. II, ccccviii. no. 148), but in no way distinguished himself. He sat for Northumberland in the last three parliaments of Charles II, and again in 1685, his election in that year being marked by an important demonstration.

'Early in 1678, when the English government was preparing to join the Dutch in the war against France, Fenwick was commissioned to raise a regiment (Dalton, i. 214; all the commissions bear date 19 February 1678). The regiment served in Flanders, apparently in garrison at Nieuport, from July to November 1678 (*Cal. S.P., Dom.*, 1678, pp. 323, 515) and was disbanded early in 1679 (*Ib.* 1679–1680, pp. 38, 95). Fenwick himself went with Monmouth to Flanders in July 1678 and in September he and Churchill were sent over to act as brigadiers (*Ib.* 1678, pp. 324, 389–90). On 10 April 1681 he was promoted to be lieutenant and lieutenant-colonel of the queen's troop, and on 1 May was appointed governor of Holy Island (Dalton, i. 285).

'Fenwick's commissions were renewed by James II, who appointed him brigadier on 21 June 1685. In 1686 he was a brigadier-general of the army on Hounslow Heath and on 6 November 1687 was made colonel of the earl of Plymouth's regiment of horse (which became later the Third Dragoon Guards) (*Ib.* pp. 2, 46, 66, 89, 111, 122). He resigned all his commissions to James II at Rochester between 19 and 22 December 1688 (J. S. Clarke, *Life of James II*, ii. 268).'

Ibid. 1194*a*, ll. 28–30. There is no evidence in the journals of either house for the statement that Fenwick was concerned with the bill for attainting Monmouth in 1685.

ll. 30–34. There is no strictly contemporary evidence for a quarrel between Fenwick and the Prince of Orange at the siege of Maestricht. There is a reference to it in the 'Life of Bernardi,' p. 35; and a fictitious account in the 'Memoirs of Thomas Bruce, earl of Ailesbury' (Roxburghe Club, ii. 390). Dartmouth (note to G. Burnet, *History of My Own Time*, 1833, iv. 331) places the quarrel in King James II's reign. But discipline in Fenwick's regiment had been bad, so that there may have been some grounds for Bernardi's statement (Bernardi, p. 22; P. L. Müller, *Wilhelm III und Waldeck*, ii. 258).

Ibid. 1194*b*, ll. 6–7. The reference should be given as 'G. Burnet, *Own Time*, ed. 1833, iv. 266.' Fenwick repeated the statement in an application to the king for a reprieve (*ibid.* p. 342) and in the paper he gave to the sheriffs on the scaffold (quoted *ibid.* note). Routh, following Ralph, incorrectly describes this paper as Fenwick's last speech (see also *ibid.* p. 349, note).

Ibid. 1195*b*, ll. 3–2 from foot. Reference should read '(*Own Time*, ed. 1833, iv. 349).'

Ibid. 1196*a*, ll. 9–12. For 'By his wife . . . three sons' read 'By his wife, Lady Mary Howard, Fenwick had a son, Charles, born in 1666 (J. Foster, *Visitations of Northumberland*, pp. 54–5); he, with some other children, is mentioned in a less reliable pedigree, J. H. Hill, *History of Langton*, p. 218.'

E. S. de B.

***Fenwick, John** (*d.* 1658). vi. 1196*b*. The article mixes up three different Fenwicks. The Colonel Fenwick who distinguished himself in the Irish wars was Roger Fenwick. He appears to have come to Ireland with a regiment of foot about November 1646, and was killed at the battle of Scariffhollis on 21 June 1650 (see Coxe, *Hibernia Anglicana*, ii. 187, 195; Gilbert, *Aphorismical Discovery*, iii. 149; *Cal. of the MSS. of the Marquess of Ormond*, N.S., i. 105; *Cal. State Papers. Dom.*, 1650, p. 606; *Hist. MSS. Comm.*, 10th Report, pt. iv. pp. 77, 91).

The officer mortally wounded at the battle of the Dunes was Roger Fenwick, lieutenant-colonel of Lockhart's regiment of foot. 'Lieutenant-Col. Roger Fenwick, a gentleman of high courage and worth, who led the first forces up the sand-hill against the enemy, and notwithstanding the great advantages the enemies had in that place, did by his valour and gallant example, contribute very much to that great victory, is dead of his wounds, dying at Mardike the very day that the English took possession of Dunkirk, to which place his corpse is to be carried and will be honorably interred in the cathedral of that town' (*Mercurius Politicus*, 17–24 June 1658, p. 622; see also Thurloe, vii. 156, 174, 215; *Clarke Papers*, iii. 154; Clarke's *Life of James II*, i. 348; Marvell, *Poems*, ed. Aitken, i. 162).

For **Fenwicke, John,** (*d.* 1658). vi. 1196*b* the following might now be substituted:—

Fenwick, John, (*Fl.* 1625–1651) *merchant.*

Nothing is known of Fenwick's birth or early life. According to his *Christ Ruling in the midst of His Enemies* (London, 1643), he was a merchant in Germany for seven years, and for many years in other countries, residing in Newcastle from 1625. His business transactions were successful, affording to the treasury in customs, three, four and five hundred pounds per annum for fifteen or sixteen years. In February of 1634 he petitioned the admiralty for redress when his ship, bound for Cadiz with coal, cloth, etc., was boarded by Dutch sailors, who robbed him of merchandise worth £150. He was living in Newcastle with his wife and children at the time of the plague of 1636. He was active in that group of Newcastle residents who sympathized with the Scots and wished to resist the king's methods of church government. (Welford, *History of Newcastle and Gateshead*, 1887, iii. 318, 350, 368ff). In 1638 after returning from Scotland where he had purchased a shipment of wheat from the earl of Winton, he found the English government anxious to arrest him for signing the Covenant. His wife Jane was seized and questioned about his activities in January 1638–39 (*Cal. State Papers, Dom.* p. 359). Fenwick joined the Scots army and was at Dunse Law in June (*Christ Ruling*, p. 42). In *Christ Ruling* he repeatedly claims (pp. 21, 37, 44, 45) that he was the Scots into England, by a note under their excluded out of the peace concluded at Berwick 18 June, 1639, although the earl of Rothes spoke to the earl of Arundel in his behalf, but Rushworth does not mention any person as being so excepted. (*Historical Collections*, iii. 944ff.) Later he was questioned by Traquair concerning his activities for the Covenanters, and after Traquair made a declaration in the Scotch parliament against him, he fled into the country, where he spent some time composing religious poems and wrote *Zions Joy in her King, coming in His Glory* (London, 1643). In 1641 he published an attack on episcopacy entitled *The Downfall of the Pretended Divine Authoritie of the Hierarchy into the Sea of Rome* . . .; the sections directed against Thomas Morton, bishop of Durham, were answered in a tract called *A Vindication of the Bishop of Durham, from . . . a Libell Intituled The Downfall of Hierarchie* (London, 1641). When the war broke out again, he entered Newcastle with the Covenanters' army, and helped to locate hidden Royalist provisions for the relief of the Scotch. After the Treaty of Ripon (October, 1640), he had the temerity to repair to London before the act of oblivion was passed, and petitioned parliament in 1640 and again in June 1642 for four thousand pounds he had lost, but no action was taken (*Christ Ruling*, p. 23). He was a captain in Sir William Constable's foot regiment in Essex' army in 1642 (Peacock's *Army Lists*, pp. 39–40), and was wounded at Edgehill (October 23). In 1643 Lord Gray of Wark wrote to Sir Thomas Barrington that he had named his kinsman Fenwick to be lieutenant-colonel of the Essex regiment 'which goes under your name and Sir Thomas Honywood's'. Fenwick wrote several letters to Sir Thomas Barrington concerning desertion in late 1643 (Hist. MSS. Comm., *7th Report*, pp. 551, 555). Nothing further is known about his military service, and he probably left the army to become Master of Sherburn Hospital, to which he was appointed 'by Sir William Ermyne and the other Commissioners of the then Parliament to invite hands, without order or vote of the House of Commons or Lords' (M. A. Richardson's reprint of *Christ Ruling*, 1856, Introduction; *Commons Journals* 30 September 1644). The position was confirmed upon him and his son John by parliament on 2 July 1650. His religious enthusiasms are evident in the address to the reader of *Christ Ruling* and in the pseudonymous *Zions Joy*, both published for Benjamin Allen in London in 1643. His practice of issuing his works either anonymously or pseudonymously has deprived him of the credit for at least one item. In *Christ Ruling* (p. 37) he mentions 'a little tract I published two years agoe, entituled, *The Downfall of the Hierarchy*'; this he signed 'V. N. V.', and so it is entered in most library catalogues. *Zions Joy* appeared over the made-up name 'Finiens Canus Vove'. In 1651, in Newcastle, was published his tract for the celebration of 'that memorable victory at Dunbar in Scotland, Sept. 3, 1650', entitled *Englands Deliverer*. In the ten years since the composition of *Zions Joy*, his religious convictions had taken a fanatical turn; formerly a presbyterian he now expressed himself in the ranting fashion of a Fifth Monarchy man. In it he reprints a song from *Zions Joy*, which he claims as his own. Nothing is known of him after this date. For proof that he is not to be identified with the colonel Fenwick killed in Ireland in 1650 or with the lieutenant-colonel Fenwick who died of wounds received at the battle of the Dunes in 1658 see *ante*, iv. 55. J. C. Hodges surmises that the John Fenwick who was apprenticed 31 May 1612 to Robert Bewick of Newcastle, boothman, was 'the Covenanter, known in local history as lieutenant Colonel John Fenwick' (*Archaeologia Aeliana* ser. 3 xviii. 105). Since he was a successful merchant by 1625, this is virtually impossible.

Fetherstonhaugh, Sir Timothy. vi. 1258*b*, 8 ll. from foot. After 'Cumberland' add 'His farewell message to her, dated 20 October 1651, is printed in Hist. MSS. Comm., 12th Rep., App. vii. 20 [*Le Fleming MSS.*].'

E. S. de B.

Fiennes, John. vi. 1294*a*. He served under Colonel Massey, the governor of Gloucester, in the spring of 1643 (*Bibliotheca Gloucestrensis*, pp. 27, 30). On his unsuccessful siege of Banbury see Beesley, *History of Banbury*, 1841, pp. 370–385. His regiment of horse was disbanded in August 1645, and his military career ended then (*Hist. MSS. Comm. Reports, Portland MSS.*, i. 258). His son William succeeded as 3rd Viscount Saye in 1674.

Fiennes, Nathaniel. vi. 1294*b*, l. 30. On his speech against episcopacy and its significance, see W. A. Shaw, *History of the English Church during the Civil Wars*, 1900, i. 35, 42, 63.

Ibid., p. 1295*b*, l. 36. The certificate exonerating him from blame for the surrender of Bristol is reprinted in *Notes and Queries*, 7th Series, ix. 181.

Ibid., l. 37. For the words 'Fiennes did not reappear, etc.,' read 'returned to his seat in parliament in September 1645' (*Commons' Journals*, 20 September 1645).

Ibid., p. 1296*a*, 11 ll. from bottom. Add: 'Celia Fiennes, one of his daughters by his second marriage, was the author of the diary of his travels published in 1888 by Mrs. Griffiths under the title of *Through England on a Side Saddle in the Time of William and Mary*.'

Fiennes, William, First Viscount Saye and Seale. vi. 1297*b*, 6 ll. from bottom. On Saye's colonial schemes see A. P. Newton, *The Colonising Activities of the English Puritans* (Yale University Press, 1914). The Providence Company was incorporated 4 Dec. 1630; the island was captured by the Spaniards in May 1641, and the company was dissolved about 1650 (Newton, pp. 58, 301, 308).

Ibid., p. 1299*a*, 21 ll. from bottom. A letter from Saye to Sir John Bankes, written 8 June 1642, on the Nineteen Propositions explains his attitude at the opening of the war (Bankes, *Story of Corfe Castle*, p. 139). A pamphlet entitled *A Copy of a letter written to a private friend to give him satisfaction in some things touching the Lord Say*, published 17 Oct. 1643, vindicates him against the charges made by extremists of his own party. Saye's losses during the war, as his property lay in the King's quarters, were so heavy that he was granted in 1645 an allowance of £2000 a year out of the King's revenues (*Lords' Journals*, iii. 39, 68). Saye was summoned to sit in Cromwell's House of Lords, but refused to accept the writ and dissuaded Lord Wharton from acceptance (*Eng. Hist. Rev.* x. 106).

Ibid., p. 1300*a*, 18 ll. from bottom. Add after the mention of his marriage: 'He was succeeded by his eldest son, James Fiennes, who married Frances Cecil, 4th daughter of Edward, Viscount Wimbledon, and died 15 March 1674 (Dalton, *Life of Sir E. Cecil, Viscount Wimbledon*, ii. 366).'

Ibid., p. 1300*b*. Add to the list of authorities: Firth, *The House of Lords during the Civil War* (1910).

Finch, Daniel, second **Earl of Nottingham** and sixth **Earl of Winchilsea.** vii. 1*b*, 16 ll. from foot. For 'in 1647' read '2 July 1647 (Hist. MSS. Comm., *MSS. of A. G. Finch*, i. 469; Doyle, *Official Baronage*, ii. 696).'

Ibid. 9 ll. from foot. After 'without a degree' insert 'probably on account of ill health (*MSS. of A. G. Finch*, i. 403), travelled on the continent 1665–8 (*ibid.* 401, 510, etc.).'

Ibid. 3 ll. from foot. After '1679' insert '(*Official Return*, i. 530, 544; *MSS. of A. G. Finch*, ii. 54–5, 60).'

Ibid. 2 ll. from foot. For '22 April' read '14 May, at a salary of £1000 (*Catalogue of Pepysian MSS.* i. 57, 312; Navy Rec. Soc.: *MSS. of A. G. Finch*, ii. 53).'

2*a*, l. 4. For 'March 1681' read 'February 1681 (*Official Return*, i. 549; see also *MSS. of A. G. Finch*, ii. 103–4, 106).'

Ibid. ll. 41–53. For 'In the spring . . . to regret it' read 'He abhorred the Roman catholic policy of James II (*Clarendon Corr.* ed. Singer, ii. 195–6) and came to regard William of Orange as a most eminent defender of the protestant religion (see letter to William, 18 May 1687, Dalrymple, *Memoirs*, ed. 1790, App. to book v. p. 64). By June 1688 he was regarded as one of William's leading supporters (*ibid.* p. 106), but scruples of conscience prevented his signing the invitation to the prince to come to England (*ibid.* p. 112; *cf.* H. C. Foxcroft, *Supplement to Burnet*, pp. 290–1, for an anecdote about the right of the other conspirators to kill him). He felt that an appeal for armed intervention from abroad was at least premature, and that James' policy would fail because so few favoured it (Dalrymple, pp. 117–18). During November and December 1688 he and Halifax acted together (Evelyn, *Diary*, 29 Oct.; Foxcroft, *Life of Halifax*, ii. 8–9, 12–13; *Hatton Corr.* ii. 103). They and Godolphin were sent by James as commissioners to treat with the prince, but the king's flight ruined their plans (Foxcroft, *Halifax*, ii. 14–34; *Hatton Corr.* ii. 117).'

2*b*, l. 7. After 'to yield' insert '(Cobbett, *Parl. Hist.* v. 66–108).'

Ibid. l. 10. After 'consciences' insert '(*Clarendon Corr.* ii. 261; *House of Lords MSS.* 1689–90, p. 29; *Lords' Journals*, xiv. 120–1, 126).'

Ibid. l. 18. For 'In December 1688' read 'On 8 March 1689 (P.R.O. *Lists and Indexes*, xliii, p. vi).'

Ibid. l. 21. After 'December 1693' insert 'According to Burnet's contemporary verdict, his acceptance of office under the new sovereigns "first preserved the church and then the crown" (Foxcroft, *Supplement*, pp. 314–15; Ranke, *History of England*, ed. 1875, vi. 76).'

Ibid. l. 22. For 'the introduction of the Toleration Act' read 'to act as chairman of the committee which considered the Toleration Act (*House of Lords MSS.* 1689–90, pp. 34–6; Burnet, *History*, ed. 1833, iv. 10; Foxcroft, *Supplement*, p. 317).'

Ibid. l. 35. For 'five' read 'all but five.'

Ibid. 16–14 ll. from foot. For 'where . . . Burnet' read 'which referred the question to a purely clerical commission (Foxcroft and Clarke, *Life of Burnet*, p. 274; Macaulay, *History*, ed. Henderson, pp. 367–9).'

3*a*, l. 3. After 'Boyne' add '(Dalrymple, *Memoirs*, ed. 1790, App. to book v, p. 96).'

3*a*, 22 ll. from foot. After 'accession of Anne,' add 'During this period Nottingham actively opposed governmental measures in the house of lords (Burnet, *History*, ed. 1833, iv. 225), such as the bill creating the bank of England (Timberland, *Proceedings of the House of Lords*, i. 432), and the triennial act (Bonnet's report, in Ranke, *History of England*, ed. 1875, vi. 260). Early in 1695 he led a general attack on the king's policy, but when it failed he deserted parliament (Foxcroft, *Halifax*, ii. 187). He opposed the original form of association proposed after the discovery of the assassination plot (Macaulay, *History*, ed. Henderson p. 708) because William was styled "rightful and lawful" king, and his name was struck off the privy council register in consequence on 12 March 1696 (*Acts of the Privy Council*, *Col. Ser.*, 1766–83, p. 654; Luttrell, *Brief Relation*, iv. 26). He signed a protest against the bill of attainder against Fenwick (Thorold Rogers, *Protests of the Lords*, i. 128–9), and argued against the abjuration bill in 1701 (Timberland, *Proceedings of the House of Lords*, ii. 34–5; *Memoirs of the Secret Services of John Macky*, 1733, p. 25).'

Ibid. 22–21 ll. from foot. For 'Six weeks . . . (8 March 1702)' read 'On 2 May 1702 (P.R.O. *Lists and Indexes*, xliii. p. vi), six weeks after William's death.'

Ibid. 19 ll. from foot. After 'colleague' add 'at his own request, according to Burnet (*History*, ed. 1833, v. 10).'

4*b*, 6 ll. from foot. After 'Warwick' add 'and his happiness is proved by his letters to her (*MSS. of A. G. Finch*, ii.); she died in childbirth 23 March 1684 (Pearl Finch, *History of Burley-on-the-Hill*).'

Ibid. 4 ll. from foot. After 'viscount Hatton' add 'on 29 December 1685.'

5*a*, l. 11. After 'fun of him' add 'He appears in "Gulliver's Travels" as Bolgolam (C. H. Firth, *Political Significance of Gulliver's Travels*, pp. 6–7).'

Ibid. ll. 19–28. To the list of authorities add: Pearl Finch, History of Burley-on-the-Hill, 2 vols. London, 1901; Hist. MSS. Comm., Rep. on MSS. of A. G. Finch, ii, 1922, which has Nottingham's private and official correspondence to the end of 1690; Correspondence of the family of Hatton, 2 vols., Camden Society, 1878, which has letters of Nottingham to Viscount Hatton.

G. D. AND H. R.

Finch, Heneage, First Earl of Nottingham. (1621–1682). vii. 8*a*, l. 51. For 'nephew' read 'first cousin once removed.' See genealogies in the various articles on the Finch family in *D.N.B.*

Finlay, George. (1799–1875). vii. 30*b*, l. 55. 'His correspondence is lost or inaccessible.' It is now in the library of the British School at Athens. For an account of his diaries, letter books, and correspondence, and a detailed bibliography of his published minor works and newspaper articles, see *Eng. Hist. Rev.* xxxix. 386, 552.

Fisher, Thomas (1781 ?–1836). vii. 73*b*, ll. 21–17 from foot. For 'and, with Samuel . . . p. 696)' read 'and was originator and publisher of "The history and antiquities of Rochester and its environs," 1772 (new eds., 1817 and 1833); the principal contributors to it were William Shrubsole and Samuel Denne [qq. v.] (*Gentleman's Magazine*, vol. lvii, pt. ii, p. 1052).'

Fitzgerald, James Fitzmaurice. vii. 125*a*–127*b*. For some important corrections and additions see 'Notes and Queries.' clii. 61–2.

Fitzherbert, William. vii. 174*a*, l. 23. For '1142' read '1141.'

Ibid. b, l. 42. For '1146' read '1145.'

Ibid. 3 ll. from foot. For '1147' read '1146.' (See *Symeon of Durham*, Rolls Series, ii. 306, footnote *b*.)

H. A. C.

FitzRalph, Richard. vii. 194*a*, l. 31. After 'county' add 'Actually, FitzRalph was consecrated at Exeter because he had for many years been the intimate friend of its bishop, John Grandison. He once contemplated settling permanently in the diocese, and was at one time a member of Grandison's household; after being consecrated he acted as his assistant bishop for several months (*Exeter Dioc. Reg.*: Grandison, *passim*, esp. ii. 616 and 1022–3). But he belonged to a family of FitzRalphs (or Raufs), Brisebones, and Dovedales, living in and near Dundalk (*Cal. Pap. Pet.*, i. 53 and 359; *Cal. Pat. Rolls*, 1327–30, pp. 531–2; *ibid.* 1330–34, p. 432; *ibid.* 1345–48, p. 130).'

194*b*, l. 14. After 'death' add 'Nevertheless, some colour is lent to the claim that FitzRalph became a fellow or master of University college by the fact that his friend and former companion at Balliol, Richard Retford (*Hist. MSS. Comm.*, 4th Rep., p. 443), certainly did so (*Cal. Pap. Lett.*, iii. 127). FitzRalph seems to have been in need of money at several times during his life, and probably required some such assistance (*Exeter Dioc. Reg.*: Grandison, i. 106–7; ii. 616; Lichfield Chapter Act-book, in Ashm. MS. 794, ff. 68*b*, 69*a*).'

Ibid. ll. 17–31. FitzRalph was chancellor of the university, 1332–4 (Confirmations of chancellors of the university of Oxford, in *Snappe's Formulary*, pp. 75–6; Oxford Hist. Soc.); he was therefore connected with the beginning of the 'Stamford schism' (*Eng. Hist. Rev.*, xxxvii. 249–51).

Ibid. l. 16 from foot. After close of brackets insert 'but the exact dates of the process of his preferment are not recorded, and it may have taken place earlier. On 17 Dec. 1335, FitzRalph was appointed to a canonry and prebend at Lichfield by papal provision, and was told to give up the provision made to him of the canonries and prebends of Armagh and Exeter, and the chancellorship of Lincoln (*Cal. Pap. Lett.*, ii. 524). He was present as dean at a chapter meeting at Lichfield on 22 April 1336 (Lichfield Chapter Act-book, Ashm. MS. 794, f. 55*a*).'

Ibid. l. 3 from foot. After 'Armagh' insert 'to which he had already been elected by the chapter of Armagh "in ignorance that the see was reserved to the pope" (*Cal. Pap. Lett.*, iii. 217).'

195*a*, ll. 4–7. FitzRalph's position at the papal court was originally due to the introduction of bishop Grandison, who had been chaplain to John XXII and was the friend of Benedict XII and Clement VI, when they were respectively James Fournier and Peter Roger (*Exeter Dioc. Reg.*, i. 106, 110, 233, 280; vol. iii. p. i.).

Ibid. ll. 11–19. FitzRalph seems to have visited Avignon in 1335 without staying long, for only one sermon there is recorded before 1338; but the date of this one is given definitely as 7 July 1335 in three apparently independent MSS., Bod. 144, Bod. Auct. infra I. 2, and T.C.D. 191. Afterwards he stayed in Avignon for seven years, Sept. 1337–Dec. 1344, doing legal business on behalf of the Lichfield chapter (Lichfield Chapter Act-book, Ashm. MS. 794, ff. 58*b*, 59*a*, and Sermon no. 79, Bod. MS. 144, ff. 187*a* et seqq.).

Ibid. l. 31. After 'obtinenda' insert 'He spent at least eighteen months in Avignon after delivering this sermon in August 1349 (*Cal. Pat. Rolls*, 1348–50, p. 578), and as no dated sermons are recorded as having been preached in Ireland between 25 March 1349 and 6 Dec. 1351, his stay may have been for more than two years.'

195*b*, l. 25. After 'Ireland' insert 'FitzRalph's collected sermons are to be found in Bod. MS. 144, St. John's coll. Oxon. MS. 65, Brit. Mus., Lansdowne MS. 393, and, differently arranged, in New coll. Oxon. MS. 90. The best of these MSS. is Bod. 144, as although the St. John's coll. MS. is probably older, the Bod. MS. appears to have been copied from a better original than any of the others, and gives more particulars about dates and places than they do. Smaller collections, or single sermons, are in Bod. MS. Auct. F. infra I. 2, f. 231; Tanner MS. iv; Oriel coll. MS. 15; T.C.D. MS. 191; and Lambeth MS. 121. None of these certainly contains any sermons not found in the larger collections, but the Tanner MS. supplies some dates not given elsewhere, and there are a few sermons of doubtful authorship which may be by FitzRalph in Bod. MS. Auct. F. infra I. 2, and in the Lambeth and Oriel MSS.'

Ibid. ll. 28–30. Three sermons preached in London refer directly or indirectly to the French campaign of 1346–7. One mentions a recent victory wrested from superior numbers, and must have been preached soon after Creçy; it is headed 'in processione Londoniae facta pro rege' (sermon no. 23, Bod. MS. 144, no. 24, f. 36*b*); another was preached on 11 Apr. 1347, and is headed 'in processione generali Londoniae ad populum in ecclesia christi' (i.e. Holy Trinity, Aldgate, the church of that priory of Austin canons. Sermon no. 26, Bod. MS. 144, no. 27, f. 39*b*); the third appears to belong to the rogation days in May 1347, and is headed 'in processione facta pro rege et principibus' (no. 10, Bod. MS. 144, no. 11, f. 17*a*).

Ibid. ll. 22–20 from foot. He preached to the Dominican general chapter on 26 May 1341 (no. 75, Bod. MS. 144, f. 161*a*. The chapter always met at Whitsuntide, G. R. Galbraith, *Constitution of the Dominican Order*, p. 85, and it sat at Avignon in 1341, not 1342, *ibid.* p. 254).

Ibid. l. 16 from foot. For 'English' substitute 'secular.'

Ibid. l. 10 from foot. After '1350' insert 'FitzRalph said explicitly in the course of this sermon that he was acting at the request of the secular clergy at the papal court (no. 90, Bod. MS. 144, f. 251*b*), and that he would be supported by a statement from the bishop of Traw ("Tragrutensis") in Dalmatia (*ibid.* 255*a*).'

196*a*, l. 18. After close of bracket, insert 'However, FitzRalph must have persuaded the king of his good intentions, for on 7 Oct. 1350 he received permission to stay at Avignon until Feb. 1351 (*Cal. Pat. Rolls*, 1348–50, p. 578).'

Ibid. l. 14 from foot. After 'tradition' insert 'It is not possible to identify all these in the MS. collections with absolute certainty, but they were probably nos. 60, 61, 65, 66, 67, 68, and 38.'

Ibid. l. 11 from foot. After 'Armenorum' insert '*i.e.* nos. 65–8. The printed text is very faulty. These four summarise roughly the arguments of the "De pauperie Salvatoris."'

196*b*, l. 7. After 'Avignon' insert 'The appeal was delivered in person on 10 March 1357 at the door of the archbishop's lodging in London by John of Arderne, prior of the Augustinian friars of

London, who showed it to the servants standing by, and handed a copy of it to one of them, who promised to deliver it to his master. John of Arderne was acting on behalf of the prior and friars of the Dominican and Carmelite orders in London, and the guardian and friars of the London Franciscans, as well as for his own order (Sid. Suss. coll. MS. 64 Δ. 4. 2, f. 4*b*).'

Ibid. l. 21. After close of brackets, add 'The king also had most of the south-eastern ports watched, to see that "no religious, nor anyone else, nor any friar of the Augustinian order" crossed the sea without permission (Rymer, iii. pt. i. 353). Neither John of Arderne nor any other of the London friars seems to have been able to leave England, for the case was taken up at Avignon by a certain William, *Gillelmo militis ordinis predicatorum* D.D., for the Dominicans, James of Montepeliciano for the Franciscans, Bernard of Catalonia for the Augustinians, and Arnold Tenque for the Carmelites (Bod. MS. 158, f. 174).'

Ibid. ll. 22–8. In the summer or autumn of 1356, FitzRalph had completed and put forth his treatise 'De pauperie Salvatoris,' in seven books, for he stated in his sermon in London on 18 Dec. 1356 that he had written a work in seven books on this subject, and that he had sent it to the pope and some of the cardinals 'to approve or discuss and correct if need be,' and 'to Oxford to be given to those who wished to read it' (sermon 65, Bod. MS. 144, f. 94*b*). The first four books were published in 1890 as an appendix to Wycliffe's book 'De Dominio Divino' (edited by R. L. Poole for the Wyclif Society); the last three have now been transcribed, and a typescript copy of them is in the possession of the university of Manchester.

Ibid. l. 10 from foot. After 'proceed' insert 'Further information about it is contained in Sid. Suss. coll. MS. 64 Δ. 4. 2; Bod. MSS. 158 and 865; Lambeth MSS. 121 and 1208; Durham cath. MS. 32 B. iv. 4to; Lansdowne MS. 393; and Peterhouse MS. 223; but principally in the Sidney Sussex MS.'

Ibid. l. 5 from foot. After '1358' insert '(*Cal. Pap. Lett.*, iii. 596; full text, Bull. Franc. vi. 316–7).'

197*a*, l. 15. After close of brackets, insert 'FitzRalph preached in the vice-chancellor's chapel on 1 Nov. 1358 (no. 69, Bod. MS. 144, f. 127*a*), and in the pope's chapel on 6 Jan. 1359 (no. 88, *ibid.* f. 241*a*). Several petitions from him for benefices for kinsmen or members of his household were granted between Aug. 1358 and Sept. 1360 (*Cal. Pap. Pet.*, i. 332, 334, 347, and 359).'

197*b*, l. 11 from foot. After 'author' insert 'according to Bale and Tanner.'

198*a*, l. 2. After 'et seq.' insert 'The extant works of Richard FitzRalph, other than sermons or polemical writings connected with the lawsuit against the friars (both of which are dealt with above), are as follows:

'"De pauperie Salvatoris," inc. prologue, "Sanctissimo in christo patri domino, domino nostro Innocencio"; text, "Quia circa rerum propter hominem," Lambeth MS. 121; Bod. MS. Auct. F. infra I. 2; Merton coll. MS. 113; Corpus Christi coll. Cantab. MSS. 103, 180, and 382; (?) T.C.D. MSS. 175 and 370. Extracts from this work are in Lambeth MS. 1208; Sid. Suss. coll. MS. 64 Δ. 4. 2; Bod. MS. 784, f. 86*b*; and T.C.D. MS. 190. A treatise which is mentioned as an independent work by Bale and Tanner is given in Lambeth MS. 121 and Corpus Christi coll. Cantab. MS. 180 as book 8 of the "De pauperie Salvatoris," inc. "Quia cum septem libellos." In both these MSS. there are a few short notes, headed "Retractiones siue declaraciones quorundam dictorum precedencium," at the end of book 7 and before book 8.

'"De quaestionibus Armenorum," inc. prologue, "Reverendis in Christo patribus Nersi, archiepiscopo Manasgardensi, ac fratri Johanni, electo Clatensi"; text, "Quia ex literale sensu scripture," Lambeth MS. 158; New coll. Oxon. MS. 90; and T.C.D. MS. 189. Extracts from this work are in Lincoln coll. Oxon. Lat. MS. 18; Pembroke coll. Cantab. MS. 5; and Corpus Christi coll. Cantab. MS. 156.

'"De Peccato Ignorantiae," chapter-headings and first page only, inc. "Die qualiter peccant sacerdotes," Lambeth MS. 121.

'"De Validis Mendicantibus," in two parts, inc. (*a*) "Queritur an dando sit valido mendicanti"; (*b*) "Quaestio utrum viri ad corporales labores validi," Lambeth MS. 357; Bod. MS. 158 (Tanner gives title "Contra validos mendicantes," and inc. "Christus fuit pauper, quia Adae filius").

'(?) "Quaestiones super Sentencias," inc. "Utrum possibile sit viatori," Oriel MS. 15.

'(?) "Sapientiam Antiquorum," inc. "Prima ergo distinctio est huius tractatus ad sciendum qui sunt pseudo predicatores," Peterhouse MS. 223.

'"De Universalibus," inc. "Nulla est affirmacio in qua universale," Digby MS. 24.

'(The evidence upon which these last three works are attributed to FitzRalph is not quite conclusive.)

'Three of FitzRalph's letters, all addressed to or concerning George of Hungary who came as a pilgrim to St. Patrick's Purgatory in 1354, are to be found in Brit. Mus. Add. MS. 37512 (Tanner mentions "epistolae ad diversos").' II. C. II.

Fitzroy, Charles, first Baron Southampton. vii. 201*b*, ll. 24–7. For 'He was gazetted . . . to the rank of' read 'He was appointed ensign in the 1st foot guards on 16 March 1752 (P.R.O., Index 5438 p. 88), lieutenant and captain on 14 June 1756 (*ibid.* p. 86) and captain and'; after 'lieutenant-colonel' insert 'on 9 May 1758 (*Army List*, 1759, p. 40)'

Ibid. l. 21 from foot. After '1761.' insert 'On 25 June 1762 he was appointed colonel of the 119th or Prince's Own regiment of foot (*Army List*, 1763, p. 186) which was disbanded in the following year.'

Fitzwilliam, Richard, seventh Viscount Fitzwilliam of Meryon. vii. 229*b*, l. 16. After 'devolved' insert 'first'

Ibid. l. 17. After 'John,' insert 'who died unmarried Oct. 1830, and then upon the only surviving brother, Thomas (G.E.C., *Complete Peerage*, v. 530),'

Fleet, Sir John. vii. 261*a*, l. 9. For '(*d.* 1712)' read '(1647?–1712)'

Ibid. ll. 10–2. For ', according to Luttrell . . . a wine cooper.' read 'the son of Richard Fleet of Bourton, Bucks. In December 1659 he was apprenticed to a London cooper and was admitted to the freedom of the Coopers' company in Feb. 1667, being called to the livery seven years later. In June 1685 he was chosen a member of the Court of Assistants, but took little share in the proceedings, and in July 1688 he excused himself from nomination as renter-warden. By this time he had become a general merchant (*Cal. Treas. Books*, x, pt. I. 143, 344) and in June 1688 was chosen one of the city sheriffs.'

Ibid. ll. 14–5. Delete 'and sheriff . . . two days later.'

Ibid. l. 17. For 'and' read 'in the following October accepted the mastership of the company until a fresh election fell due in June 1690, and was elected'

Ibid. l. 21. After '29 Oct.' insert 'Tradition required the chief magistrate to be a member of one of the twelve great companies, so the Coopers regretfully consented to Fleet's translation to the Grocers. He was master of the Grocers' company, 1693–5.'

Ibid. l. 25. For 'On' read 'In Apr. 1692 he became a director and on'

Ibid. ll. 18–17 from foot. For 'carried out . . . 1702' read 'agreed to on 22 July 1702 but the United company did not come into being until 1709. At the first election he was chosen one of the new directors. He was re-elected in 1711 and 1712 and held the post until his death. He had been appointed colonel of the blue regiment of trainbands in 1696, and commanded the red regiment from 1702 to 1707. In 1703 he was vice-president of the Honourable Artillery company and held the office of president, 1704–8.'

Add to list of authorities: Sir William Foster's 'Sir John Fleet' (*Eng. Hist. Rev.*, li. 681–5).

Fleetwood, Charles. vii. 261*b*, l. 23. **After 'first battle of Newbury' read 'probably while serving as a captain in Tyrrell's regiment, lately Hampden's.'**

***Ibid.*, l. 29. For 'In the same year' read 'From about January in the same year. . . .'**

G. D.

Fleetwood, Charles. vii. 262*a*, l. 7. On 17 June 1651 Cromwell informed the Council of State that at his march into Scotland in June 1650, 'being destitute of general officers of horse,' he had appointed Fleetwood to be lieutenant-general of the horse (*Portland MSS.*, i. 607).

Ibid., 21 ll. from foot. Fleetwood's second marriage took place on 8 June 1652 Newsletter, *Clarke MSS.*, xxii. 105).

262*b*, l. 3. On Fleetwood's rule in Ireland (1652–5) see his instructions and his correspondence printed in R. Dunlop's *Ireland under the Commonwealth* (1913), ii.

263*b*, 11 ll. from foot. His share in the overthrow of Richard Cromwell is elucidated by *Clarke Papers* (iii. 165,

182, 194). His letters to General Monck (*ibid.*, iv. 63, 70, 162, 168) explain his reasons for turning out the members of the Long Parliament a second time. In the hope that they would 'give a settlement to these poor nations' they were 'invited to sit again' . . . 'and instead thereof what hath been done, but to undo whatever hath been done for these six years past.' He might have foreseen that when he overthrew Richard, as his mother-in-law told him. She 'wished him to call to mind the saying of her husband to him before his death, that he would never leave his whimsies till he had put the nation in blood,' and told him that the best way for the officers to preserve themselves and the nation was to restore Richard (*ibid.*, iv. 167).

Fleetwood, George (*fl.* 1650), regicide. vii. 266*a*, 5 ll. from foot. Noble's story that he went to America is not confirmed. On the other hand *Annals of the Universe*, 1660–1680, published in 1709 (a sort of continuation of Whitelocke's *Memorials*), says on p. 282 that George Fleetwood died at Tangier, 17 Nov. 1672.

A miniature by S. Cooper is in the National Portrait Gallery.

Fleming, Margaret (1803–1811). vii. 281*a*, l. 12. For 'Margaret' read 'Marjory'. Baptismal register reads '1803, Jan. 15. Marjory, daughter of James Fleming, Merchant, and Isabella Rae, his spouse . . .'. To authorities add:—Frank Gent, 'Marjory Fleming and the Biographers' in *Scottish Hist. Review*, xxvi. no. 102 (1947).

Flemming, Robert. vii. 289*a*, l. 24. After 'scholars' insert 'In 1444, between 8 June and 29 October, he was enrolled in the University of Cologne (Keussen, *Die Matrikel der Univ. Köln*, i. (Bonn, 1928), 222–28, p. 477).' J. H. B.

Fletcher, John. vii. 303*b*, l. 18. After 'minister.' insert 'In 1588 he was admitted as a King's scholar to the cathedral grammar school, Peterborough, where his brothers, Nathaniel and Theophilus, were also scholars, their father being at this time dean of Peterborough (*Northants Record Soc.*, ix. pp. xliii–xliv).'

Fludd, Robert. vii. 350*a*, l. 4. After 'fol.' insert 'A page of Fludd's handwriting, taken from the commonplace-book of Joachim Morsius, is reproduced in H. Schneider, "Joachim Morsius und sein Kreis" (Lübeck, 1929), p. 23.' J. H. B.

Forbes, Alexander, first Baron Forbes. vii. 376*a*, l. 8. For '(*d.* 1448), was' read '(1380?–1448), was born about 1380, being'

Ibid. l. 19 from foot. For '1436 and 1442' read 'Oct. 1444 and July 1445 (G.E.C., *Complete Peerage*, v. 544)'

Forbes, George, sixth Earl of Granard. vii. 395*b*, l. 25 from foot. For 'Borley, . . . Isle of Anglesea' read 'Bayley, bart., of Plas Newydd (G.E.C., *Complete Peerage*, vi. 56)'

Forest, John. vii. 436*a*, l. 9. Delete 'the basis of which was denial of the king's supremacy.' The Act of Supremacy had not been passed at this time, and when it was denial of the king's supremacy was not heresy but treason. For Forest's heresies see *L. and P.* xiii. i. 1043 (1) and Wriothesley's *Chronicle*, i. 79. The letters on which the story of Forest's imprisonment in 1534 is based are given no MS. reference in *L. and P.*; they are all undated and were first published at Ingolstadt in 1583 (*L. and P.* 1534, Nos. 129–133). The list (*ibid.*, No. 1607) mentioning Forest's imprisonment is also undated; and the fact that it mentions the flight into Scotland of Fr. Peter de Moguntia, who signed the surrender of the Greyfriars at Llanvais on 19 August 1538, suggests that it also dates from that year (*ibid.*, xiii. ii. 138). There are no other references in the *L. and P.* to Forest's imprisonment before 1538; nor are there any in the London chronicles (Wriothesley *ut supra*; *Camden Misc.* IV. 12; and the *Greyfriars' Chronicle*). The story was perhaps intended to cover up the fact that Forest had, as he confessed, originally abjured the pope, but afterwards repented (*L. and P.*, xiii. i. 1043; Hall, *Chron.* (1809), p. 825). He was hearing confessions at the Greyfriars till Feb. 1538 (*L. and P.* xiii. i. 880).

Forster, Thomas Furley. vii. 462*a*, l. 18. For 'Bond Street' read 'Bond Court (*Notes and Queries*, clxix. 387; *Register of St. Stephen, Walbrook, and St. Benet Sherehog*, Harl. Soc., p. 138).'

Fortescue, Sir John, vii. 482*b*. For additional information concerning his life and discussion of his work see 'Sir John Fortescue, *De Laudibus Legum Anglie*' ed. S. B. Chrimes, M.A., Ph.D. Cambridge, 1942, pp. ix–cviii.

Foster, Sir Michael. Second Suppl. ii. 44*b*, 8 ll. from foot. For '1867' read 'January 1867' (*University College, London. Minutes of the Sessions of the Council*, vi., 19 Jan. 1867: and *Proceedings at the Annual General Meeting . . . 27th February* 1867, p. 11).

Fowler, William (*fl.* 1603). vii. 529*a* Requires revision. See Hew Scott's *Fasti Ecclesiae Scoticanae*, new ed., ii. 112–3.

Fox, George. vii. 557*b*. For an article written by the author of the D.N.B. life of Fox, in which he corrects and supplements his original article, see *Journal of the Friends' Historical Society* (January 1905), ii. 69.

Fox, Henry Stephen. vii. 569*a*, ll. 3–8. For 'When Grey's reform ministry . . . Buenos Ayres' read 'On 18 April 1828, the Earl of Dudley, then foreign secretary, notified Fox that he had been appointed minister plenipotentiary to Buenos Ayres. His departure was delayed owing to the disturbed state of South America (P.R.O., F.O. 6/24, Dudley to Fox, 18 April 1828, and F.O. 6/28, Dunglas to Fox, 17 July 1829). His credentials and instructions were made out on 9 July 1830 (P.R.O., F.O. 95/661 and 95/453, p. 131), but were not issued to him until 25 Jan. 1831. He arrived at Buenos Ayres on 11 October 1831 (P.R.O., F.O. 6/31).'

Fox, Henry Stephen. (1791–1846). vii. 569*a*, l. 13. 'When Sir Robert Peel came into office in 1841 he sent Lord Ashburton to settle outstanding difficulties, and the success of the Ashburton treaty was in great measure due to Fox, whose services were cordially acknowledged by Ashburton.' But see letter from Ashburton to Aberdeen, Washington, 12 May 1842 (Aberdeen MSS. at Haddo House): ' . . . my staff with whom I am more than satisfied. Between ourselves I cannot say so much of your minister. I have no reason to complain and generally I have treated him with confidence but I cannot be mistaken in believing that he has no good will for the special mission and is disposed to give little assistance. We are, however, on good terms and shall continue so. What I say on this is quite for yourself.' Also, letter from Peel to Aberdeen, 17 November 1841: 'I do not argue favourably of the result of any new negotiations that may be committed to Mr. Fox. He seems thoroughly imbued with a feeling of hatred to the U.S. and its institutions' (B.M. *Add. MS.* 40453, f. 58). Also, letter from Peel to Aberdeen, 31 August 1843: 'Would it not be advisable to replace Fox? He is not calculated by his manner or habits to smooth difficulties' (B.M. *Add. MS.* 40453, f. 435). D. M.

Fox, Sir Stephen. vii. 574*b*, l. 14. Insert: 'Fox in his official capacity had at one time been responsible for the payment of pensions to members of parliament. He was questioned about it in the house of commons on 23 May 1679, and ordered to bring into the house his book of secret service accounts. This the king forbade, but Fox was compelled to give orally such names and sums as he could remember. He appears to have ceased making these payments when Thomas Osborne, earl of Danby [q.v.], became treasurer, and was fortunate enough to escape the displeasure both of the commons and of the king. (*Commons' Journals*, ix. 629–30; Grey, *Debates*, vii. 316–24; Hist. MSS. Comm., *Ormonde MSS. at Kilkenny*, iv. 517–8; v. 111–2; *A List of One Unanimous Club of Voters in His Majesties Long Parliament, Dissolved in 78.*)'

E. S. de Beer.

Fraizer, Sir Alexander. vii. 598*b*. This article is unsatisfactory for Fraizer's medical career, and altogether ignores his political career as a secret agent. His name is written in various ways, 'Fraiser' being perhaps the best; it is only a variant of Fraser.

598*b*, ll. 6–7. For 'Fraizer, Sir Alexander (1610?–1681), physician' read 'Fraizer or Fraiser, Sir Alexander (1610?–1681), physician and political agent.'

Ibid. ll. 7–8. For 'was born in Scotland about 1610' read 'was the son of Adam Fraser, second son of Thomas Fraser of Durris or Dores in Kincardine; his mother belonged to the family of Duff of Drummure (Walter Macfarlane, *Genealogical Collections*, ii. 323: Scottish Hist. Soc.). He was in his seventy-fifth year when he died in April 1681. He is said to have been educated at Aberdeen (funeral sermon, see below); he cannot be definitely identified with any of the Alexander Frasers matriculated there. He does not appear to have studied at Leyden, as sometimes stated.'

Ibid. l. 10. For his Cambridge degree see J. and J. A. Venn, 'Alumn Cantabrigienses.'

Ibid. ll. 12–33. In the autumn of 1645 Fraizer attended prince Charles (afterwards Charles II) in the west of England as his physician. He appears to have taken a message somewhat earlier from Charles I to the imprisoned James Hamilton, duke of Hamilton (G. Burnet, *Lives of the Hamiltons*, iv. 141). In January 1646 he was assisting Culpeper in the latter's fruitless negotiations with Hamilton (Hist. MSS. Comm., 13th Rep. App. i. 333, where he appears as 'Freaper'; Clarendon, *History*, ix. 159). In April he probably went with the prince to Jersey (S. E. Hoskins, *Charles II in the Channel Islands*, 1854, i. 355).

On 27 Dec. 1647 Charles I, then at Carisbrooke, granted Fraizer a pension of £300 sterling, with remainder to his wife (*Cal. S.P., Dom.*, 1680–81, p. 256); this was probably as a reward for assistance in negotiating the Engagement signed on 26 Dec.; Fraizer was certainly one of the principal London correspondents of William Hamilton, earl of Lanark (Lanericke) and from 1649 duke of Hamilton [q.v.], and engaged in forwarding his correspondence with the king (Burnet, vi. 21, 24; T. Birch, *Letters between Colonel Robert Hammond and the Committee at Derby House*, 1764, p. 51; *Hamilton Papers*: Camden Society, and *Hamilton Papers, Addenda*, in *Camden Miscellany*, ix.; and Hist. MSS. Comm., 11th Rep. App. vi. [*MSS. of the Duke of Hamilton*]. In these collections some letters are signed by and many more may be attributed to Fraizer). Fraizer is reported to have been arrested about 17 May (Bodleian Library, Clarendon MS. 31, f. 85*b*), but appears to have been released and to have fled to the continent soon afterwards (*Hamilton Papers*, letters 128, 131).

In November 1649 Fraizer was in Paris (*Nicholas Papers*, i. 151: Camden Society). He accompanied Charles II to Jersey as his physician (J. Chevalier, *Journal*, p. 709: Soc. Jersiaise, 1906–14). He continued to be a partisan of Hamilton (*Nicholas Papers*, i. 151), and is said by Clarendon to have done much to forward Charles II's expedition to Scotland, whither he accompanied him (*History*, xiii. 47). For acting as one of the chief organisers of the 'Start,' 4 Oct. 1650 (see under Charles II), he was banished from Scotland and returned to the Hague (Sir E. Walker, *Historical Discourses*, 1705, p. 196; *Nicholas Papers*, i. 206).

Fraizer's subsequent movements are uncertain. In August 1653 he was attending Charles II professionally in Paris (*Cal. of Clarendon Papers*, ii. 245; *Thurloe State Papers*, i. 432); Charles evidently trusted him as a doctor. He had up to this time been on friendly terms with Sir Edward Hyde, but in December joined in an attempt to deprive him of power (*Nicholas Papers*, ii. 33, 38; Hyde assigns him a share in an earlier intrigue, *History of the Rebellion*, xiv. 63). He remained in the king's service, accompanying him to Cologne (*Cal. of Clarendon Papers*, iii. 29). In the spring of 1656 he was sent to Paris to arrange an interview between Charles II and Henrietta Maria (*Thurloe State Papers*, i. 697; *Nicholas Papers*, iii. 244). He brought letters from the queen to Charles at Bruges in May; by July he was definitely out of favour (*Cal. of Clarendon Papers*, iii. 29; *Nicholas Papers*, iii. 281).

In December 1657 Fraizer was in Paris trying to obtain, through Sir William Lockhart [q.v.], a pass to return to England (*Thurloe State Papers*, vi. 682, 856). He was in England soon after and associating with Buckingham; he appears to have forfeited his reputation among the royalists (*Nicholas Papers*, iv. 91, 100).

On 28 May 1664 Fraizer received a warrant for the place of principal physician in ordinary, his fees to begin from 24 June 1660 (*Cal. S.P., Dom.*, 1663–64, p. 598). He received many small grants, including (10 May 1662) an annual pension of £100, with remainder to his wife (*ibid.* 1680–81, p. 256). He was knighted, but at what date is unknown; on 2 Aug. 1673 he was created a baronet of Scotland (G. E. C., *Complete Baronetage*, iv. 293–4). He had purchased the lands formerly belonging to his ancestors at Durris (Dores), and these, with the baronetcy, passed at his death to his only son by his second wife, Peter or Pedro.

Fraizer died 28 April 1681 (date given on funeral sermon, see below; see also *Cal. S.P., Dom.*, 1680–81, p. 257).

Ibid. l. 29. For Sir John Denham's

reference to Fraizer see his 'Poems,' ed. 1668, p. 125.

Ibid. 3 ll. from foot. After the notice of Fraizer's death add 'His body was taken to Scotland and buried at Durris. A funeral sermon by John Menzies [q.v.] and two elegies were printed at the time (the latter, with part of the sermon, are reprinted by James Maidment, *Scottish Elegiac Verse, 1629–1729*; 1842). Abstracts of his will and that of his second wife are given in the 'Herald and Genealogist,' iv. 138–9. In spite of his professional success and his position in the Royal College of Physicians, Fraizer appears to have been rather disreputable. He had no connexion with the Royal Society.'

Ibid. last two lines, and 599*a*, first two lines. For a full account of Fraizer's wives and children see G. E. C., "Complete Baronetage," iv. 293–4; all the genealogical matter requires verification. For the alleged second marriage of his daughter Elizabeth see Graham, James. Fraizer married his second wife, Mary, widow of Dudley Wylde of Canterbury and daughter of Sir Ferdinando Carey, probably about February 1658 (*Cal. S.P., Dom.*, 1657–58, p. 306; for her family see *Herald and Genealogist*, iv. (1867), 44, and Walter Macfarlane, *Genealogical Collections*, ii. 327–9). Her sisters' marriages are interesting; one married Sir Thomas Wentworth, baron Wentworth (1613–65) [q.v.]; another married Sir William Quirinsen (for whom see Clarendon, *History*, ed. Macray, xiv. 129 and note); a third married Bevil Skelton [q.v.] (see C. E. Lart, *Registers of St. Germain-en-Laye*, i. 37). Mary was a woman of the bed-chamber and dresser to the queen from June 1662 (*Cal. S.P., Dom.*, 1665–66, p. 25), and died December 1695. Fraizer's daughter by his second wife, Carey, was a maid of honour to the queen in 1674, with an annual pension of £200 (*Cal. S.P., Dom.*, 1673–75, p. 246). She married Charles Mordaunt, Lord Mordaunt, later earl of Peterborough [q.v.]. Her reputation was not very good (Hist. MSS. Comm., 7th Rep. pp. 469*a*, 496*a*; *Poems on Affairs of State*, 3rd ed., 1699, p. 134).

599*a*, l. 4. To the list of authorities add Hist. MSS. Comm., MSS. of the Marquis of Bath at Longleat, ii., and works quoted above.

E. S. de B.

Franck, Richard. vii. 621*a*–622*a*. For further particulars about the life of Franck see 'Scottish Historical Review,' xxv. 230–3.

Frazer, Sir Augustus Simon. vii. 670*a*, l. 10 from foot. Add 'A hitherto unnamed portrait in the Royal United Service Institution has been recently identified as a portrait of Frazer done late in 1815 (*Journal of the Soc. for Army Hist. Research*, xvii. 173).'

Frederick Louis, Prince of Wales. (1707–51). vii. 677*b*, ll. 32–42. The names of the second and third daughters of Frederick, Prince of Wales, are omitted in this list. Elizabeth Caroline, b. 30 December, 1740, d. 4 September, 1759. See *London Gazette*, no. 7977. Louisa Anne, b. 8 March, 1748/9, d. 13 May, 1768. See *London Gazette*, nos. 8830, 10832. J. F. C.

Freeman, Edward Augustus. xxii. (1st Suppl.), 676 *a*, l. 36. After 'A History of Federal Government' add 'from the Foundation of the Achaian League to the Disruption of the United States.' This part of the title is also omitted from it as given in Stephens' *Life of Freeman* (i. 256–7, ii. 482).

Freeman, Sir Ralph. vii. 680*b*, ll. 13–5 from foot. For '(*fl.* 1610 . . . August 1613.' read '(*d.* 1667), courtier and dramatist, was the son of Martin Freeman of Betchworth in Surrey and of London (*Visitation of London*, Harl. Soc., i. 295). He was admitted at the Middle Temple in 1606 (*Middle Temple Records: Minutes*, ii. 470). Before 1618 he had married a near relative of George Villiers, the future duke of Buckingham; she was Catherine, daughter of William "Bret of Wrotherbe in com. Leic.", apparently Brett of Rotherby, in which case she was Buckingham's first cousin and a sister of Lady Middlesex (*Visit. of London, loc. cit.*; *Visitation of Leicester*, Harl. Soc., pp. 30, 171, 206); Freeman was also knighted by this date (a notice in John Nichols' *Progresses of James I*, iii. 437, is undocumented and the identification is wrong). He succeeded Sir Robert Naunton [q.v.] as a master of requests early in 1618 (*Cal. S. P., Dom.*, 1611–8, p. 511).'

Ibid. 681*a*, l. 5. After 'Venice.' insert 'He was member of parliament for Winchelsea in 1625 and again in 1628–9.'

Ibid. ll. 10–2. Delete 'and soon . . . per annum.'

Ibid. ll. 18–20. For 'He appears . . . advanced age.' read 'In 1635 he and Sir

Thomas Aylesbury [q.v.] obtained jointly the office of master and worker of the mint (*Cal. S. P., Dom.*, 1635–6, p. 342; 1636–7, p. 445); they retained it until the Civil war. Freeman regained the office for himself in 1660, but in 1662 was given a partner in it, Henry Slingsby, his former deputy; he retained his share in the office until his death, which took place between April and July 1667 (*Cal. S. P. Dom.*, 1660–1, p. 138; 1661–2, p. 585; 1667, pp. 47, 175; Ruding, *Annals of the Coinage*, 3rd ed., 1840, ii. 2, 7).' For '1655' read '1639.'

Ibid. ll. 27–8. For 'This unauthorized . . . 1639.' read 'A new edition appeared in 1655'.

Ibid. ll. 27–5 from foot. Delete 'At the last-given . . . old man.'

Ibid. l. 24 from foot. Delete 'Sir' and after Freeman insert ', sometimes wrongly styled Sir Ralph,'

Under authorities, for 'Rolls Ser. (Dom.)' read Cal. State Papers, Dom., *passim*; and add Victoria County History, Surrey, iii. 167, where Freeman's descendants are traced.

Fremantle, Sir Thomas Francis (1765–1819), vii. 689*a*, l. 4 from foot. For 'in April 1812 was sent into the Adriatic', read 'in June 1812 was sent into the Adriatic'. (Public Record Office, W.O. 1/311; Adm. 1/424; *Wynne Diaries* ed. Anne Fremantle (1940), pp. 356, 361–2.)

Frost, John.

In vii. 727*b*, l. 29, '1793' should be '1792.' This is a material error, because England was at war with France in 1793 and not in 1792. The error makes him appear a traitor to his country, which, with all his follies, he was not. (G. M. Trevelyan.)

Fry, Elizabeth. vii. 734*b*, l. 2. For 'born at Earlham in Norfolk' read 'born in Magdalen Street, Norwich (G. K. Lewis, *Elizabeth Fry*, 1912, p. 14). There is a memorial tablet on the house in Gurney Court, Magdalen Street: "Elizabeth Fry, Philanthopist, daughter of John Gurney, was born in this house, May 21, 1780."'

G. A. S.

Fullarton, William. vii. 748*b*, l. 12. After 'Paris' insert 'where he formed a life-long friendship with John Murdoch [q.v.], the tutor of Robert Burns.'

Ibid. For 'but on' read 'On' (*Notes and Queries*, clvi. 115).

Gage, George (fl. 1614–1640). This article confuses two persons. See *Bull. Inst. Hist. Res.*, xxxi. (1958) 141 *et seq.*

Gale, Roger. vii. 815*b*, l. 27 from foot. After 'Society' insert 'of which he had been elected a fellow in 1717' (*Record of Royal Soc.*, p. 327).

Gamble, John (d. 1811). vii. 836*a*, l. 11. After 'suggestions.' insert 'His experiments in setting up his radiated telegraph on the tower of St. Mary's church, Woolwich, were approved by a committee of officers of the royal artillery on 15 March 1798, and through the influence of the duke of York he was commissioned by the army to set up telegraph lines from London to the east coast and the camp near Windsor (*Mariner's Mirror*, xxiv. 188–9).'

Garland, Augustine. vii. 876*b*, 6 ll. from foot. Omit 'took no part in public affairs under the protectorate.' Garland sat for Queenborough in the parliament of 1654, and in December of that year is said to have moved that Cromwell should be crowned (*Clarke Papers*, iii. 16).

Garrard, Sir Samuel. vii. 890*b*, l. 21 from foot. For '1724' read '1725.'

Ibid. l. 12 from foot. Delete 'the first baronet,' and after 'Sir John Garrard,' insert 'father of the first baronet (G.E.C., *Complete Baronetage*, i. 188).'

Ibid. l. 4 from foot. For '1700' read 1700/1 (*ibid.* i. 189).'

Ibid. 891*a*, l. 4. For '1701' read '1701/2 (Beaven, *Aldermen of London*, i. 7).'

Ibid. l. 6. For '1701' read '1702 (P.R.O., *Lists and Indexes*, ix. 206).'

Ibid. l. 10. After 'in' insert '1700/1' and for '1707' read '1705 (*Return of M.P.s*, i. 586 and ii. 1).'

Ibid. l. 32 from foot. After 'offence.' insert 'Nevertheless he gave his vote against the impeachment (Beaven, ii. 319).'

Ibid. l. 17 from foot. For 'v. 640' read 'vi. 640'.

Ibid. ll. 17–16 from foot. For 'and in the same . . . master' read '. From July 1701 to July 1702 he served as Warden (*List of Wardens of Grocers' Company*, 1345–1907, p. 36).'

Ibid. l. 14 from foot. For 'October 1720' read 'March 1721 (E. G. O'Donoghue, *Bridewell Hospital*, ii. 273).'

Ibid. l. 8 from foot. For '1 '1724/5 (G.E.C., *Complete B* i. 189).'

Garrod, Sir Alfred Baring. Secon ii. 84*b*, ll. 34–5. For 'professor of peutics and clinical medicine in read 'professor of materia medica and peutics and a professor of clinical me in 1849' (*University College, London. ceedings at the Annual General Meeting* 1850, p. 7).

Gascoigne, Sir Bernard. (1614–16 vii. 914*b*, l. 28. 'In 1672 Gascoigne sent to Vienna as English envoy.' See B *Stowe MS.* 191, f. 28: instructions Sir Bernard Gascoigne, Envoy Extraordin to Leopold I., Emperor of Germar 16 February 1671/2. R. M. H.

Gascoyne, Sir Crisp. vii. 927*b*, l. For '1765–70' read '1765–8' (*Retur of M.P.s*, ii. 132, 144).

Gaunt, Elizabeth. vii. 951*b*, l. 9 from foot. After 'executed for treason' add 'is said to have been the daughter of Anthony Fothergill of Brownber, Westmorland (C. Thornton and J. McLaughlin, *Fothergills of Ravenstonedale*, 1905, p. 13; *Notes and Queries*, clxii. 16*a*), and'

Gell, Sir John. vii. 993. The reports of the Hist. MSS. Comm. on the MSS. of Lord Cowper and the Duke of Portland contain some additional information about Gell's conduct during the Civil War. On his activity in Derbyshire at the commencement of the war see *MSS. of Lord Cowper*, ii. 326, 328; *Portland MSS.*, i. 78. On his slackness in the autumn of 1645 see *Portland MSS.*, i. 251, 277, 280, 282, 289, 291. He was accused of seeking to make his peace with the king at the time of the Newport Treaty in 1648 (*Portland MSS.*, i. 593).

Gell, Robert (1595–1665), vii. 994*a*, l. 18. For 'St. Mary, Aldermanbury' read 'St. Mary Aldermary' (G. Hennessy, *Novam Repertorium ecclesiasticum parochiale Londinense*, p. 300).

Ibid., l. 18 from foot. For 'Notes and Queries, 2nd ser., iii. 19' read 'Notes and Queries, 2nd ser., iii. 13'.

George I. vii. 1025*a*, 13 ll. from foot. For '28 March' read '28 May.'
J. P. G.

George I. vii. 1034*b*, 2 ll. from foot. George I. died on Sunday, 11/22 June. See J. F. Chance, *The Alliance of Hanover* (1923), p. 741, n. 3, and references there given.
J. F. C.

Germain, George Sackville, first Viscount Sackville. vii. 1113*b*, ll. 29–36. For an account of Lord George Germain in office, 1775–82, see 'American Historical Review,' xxxiii. 23–43.

Gibbon, Edward. vii. 1134*b*, l. 31. After 'was bought' insert 'for £900.'

Ibid. l. 35. After 'was dispersed' insert 'about 200 volumes being bought by the hon. Henry Edward Fox and part going to the Lausanne library.'

Ibid. ll. 36–8. For 'who ultimately . . . preserved' read 'named Halliday, from whom it passed in 1872 to Charles Bedot, from whose family it came into the hands of P. L. Bader about 1929.'

Ibid. l. 39. After 'vii. 414' add '*The Times*, 14 Jan. 1933, p. 9*a*; 17 Jan. 1933, p. 13*e*.'

Gibson, Edmund. vii. 1154*a*, l. 30. For '1720' read '1723 (Le Neve, *Fasti*, ii. 305).'

1154*b*, 18 ll. from foot. For 'sister' read 'sister-in-law (see N. Sykes, *Edmund Gibson*, 1926, p. 62, note 4).'

Giffard, Walter. vii. 1175*b*, l. 4 from foot. For 'the' read 'Oxford'

Gilbertus Anglicus. 40*a*, l. 6. After 'service.' add 'He was also a royal physician, witnessing an undated charter of Robert de Turnham as such (Dugdale, *Monasticon*, vi. 1026, where the "E" should certainly be "G").'

Gillies, John, LL.D. vii. 1247*a*, l. 10 from foot. After 'In 1794 he married' insert 'at Ealing Catharine Beaver, daughter of the Rev. James Beaver of Lewknor, Oxon. (*Gent. Mag.*, 1794, ii. 862*a*).'
R. H.

Ginkel, Godert de, first Earl of Athlone. vii. 1264*b*, l. 29. For '1630' read '1644'.

Ibid. l. 31. For 'at Utrecht in 1630' read 'at Amerongen on 4 June 1644' (*Nieuw Nederl. Biogr. Woordenboek*, iii. 1017).

Ibid. l. 33. After '1674.' insert 'In 1683 he was made lieutenant-general in the Dutch service' (*ibid.*).

Ibid. ll. 33–35. For 'Though a member . . . assembly, and in' read 'Though nominated a member of the equestrian order of Utrecht on 16 April 1674, he did not take his seat until 19 Oct. 1693; he resigned in December 1701. In' (*ibid.*).

Girdlestone, Thomas, M.D., vii. 1275*a*, l. 11. For 'a doctor' read 'surgeon's mate in the 26th, or Cameronian regiment on 1 Feb. 1780 (P.R.O., War Office, Muster Books, 26th regt., 12/4250, f. 183)'. l. 12. After 'command of' add 'lieutenant-colonel, afterwards'. l. 14. After 'life' add 'On 24 Sept. 1781 he was appointed surgeon to the 101st regiment' (*London Gazette*, 1781, no. 12238; *Army List*, 1782, p. 178)'. l. 16. After 'India' add 'he returned home with his regiment in 1785 when it was disbanded and he was placed on half-pay (*Army List*, p. 339)'.

Gladstanes, George. vii, 1282*a*, l. 23 from foot. After '1599' insert 'he appears in the University records as chancellor in 1606.'

1282*b*, l. 27 from foot. For 'the university' read 'St. Mary's College." J. H. B.

Glapthorne, Henry. vii. 1294*a*, ll. 14–12 from foot. For '*fl.* 1639' read '1610–1643?' For 'of whom no biographical particulars have come down,' read 'was baptized at Whittlesey, Cambs., on 28 July 1610. He was the first surviving son of Thomas Glapthorne, by his third wife, a daughter of Thomas Hatcliffe (*Lincs. Pedigrees*, Harl. Soc., ii. 474; *Visitation of Cambridgeshire, 1575 and 1619*, p. 75). The Glapthornes were a prosperous yeoman family, settled at Whittlesey in the sixteenth century. It is probable that the dramatist attended school at Peterborough. At Easter 1624 he matriculated as a pensioner at Corpus Christi, Cambridge (Venn, *Alumni Cantab.*, pt. 1, ii. 221), but there is no evidence that he took a degree. He was in London by 1631, embarking on his career as poet and playwright. According to the entry on the burial register of St. Andrew's, Holborn, which records the death of his wife, Susan, on 22 March 1643, he was then living in Fetter Lane. He was probably "one Glapthorne, who lived in Fetter Lane" who wrote a tract "Her Majesty's gracious Answer to the Message sent from the Honourable City of

London, concerning Peace," for printing which, one Richard Herne was committed to the Fleet prison (*Lords' Journals*, v. 547). Glapthorne also'

Add to list of authorities: J. H. Walter's Henry Glapthorne (*Times Lit. Suppl.*, 1936, p. 748).

Glasse, Hannah. vii. 1299*b*, l. 7 from foot. For '(*fl.* 1747),' read '(1708–1770),' and insert 'came of the family of Allgood, of Hexham. Her grandfather, the Rev. Major Allgood, was inducted rector of Simonsburn 1666; her father, Isaac Allgood (1683–1725) married Hannah, daughter of Isaac Clark of London, vintner. Their son Lancelot (1711–82) was sheriff (1745–6) and M.P. (1748–59) for Northumberland and was knighted in 1760. Their daughter Hannah, born 24 March 1708, married John Glasse, son of an Irishman and of Margaret Ballendine of the Isle of Bute. Hannah had three sons and six daughters and died in Sept. 1770 (M. H. Dodds, 'The rival cooks: Hannah Glasse and Ann Cook,' *Archaeologia Aeliana*, 4th series, xv. 43–68). She'

Glemham, Sir Thomas. vii. 1305*b*, l. 32. On his defence of Carlisle see Isaac Tullie's *Narrative of the Siege of Carlisle*, ed. by Samuel Jefferson, Carlisle, 1840. It confirms the story that Glemham set the example of eating horse-flesh (p. 20).

Glover, Robert. (1544–1588). viii. 8*b*, l. 21. For '26890' read '26690.'

Ibid., 2 ll. from foot. On the siege and capitulation of Oxford see Sprigge, *Anglia Rediviva*, ed. 1854, pp. 255–89. The capitulation was dated 20 June 1646; the garrison marched out 24 June 1646.

1306*a*, l. 4. Read also '1646' instead of '1645.'

Ibid., l. 14. When the Scots came to an agreement with the parliament in Oct. 1648, Glemham escaped to Holland (Carte, *Original Letters*, i. 179).

Glynne, Sir John. viii. 18*a*. Add to list of authorities: 'J. Lineall, *Iter Mediteranium*, 1658 (Bodleian Library).'

Goddard, Jonathan, M.D. viii. 25*b*, ll. 2–25. Goddard's connection with the medicine known as 'Goddard's Drops' is expressly denied by Dr. Christopher Merett [q.v.] in 'Self-conviction,' 1670, p. 10.

Ibid. 26*a*, l. 31. For '1024' read '1029–30.'

HAROLD F. BROOKS.

Goddard, Thomas. viii. 26*a*, ll. 20–19 from foot. After 'Windsor.' insert 'He entered the army on 24 Sept. 1757 as an ensign in the 2nd battalion of the 24th regiment (*Army List*, Feb. 1758, p. 79), which became the 69th regiment in the following year, and was promoted lieutenant on 26 Jan. 1758 (*ibid.* Sept. 1758, p. 120).' For 'became a lieutenant in' read 'was transferred to'

Godfrey, Sir Edmund Berry. viii. (and *ante*, i. 63) 32*b*, l. 16. Before 'In 1669 he came into collision with the court.' add 'At least on one occasion his business methods incurred severe condemnation when he confessed to the "Committee touching Coals and Fuelling" that he yielded to the temptation of securing excessive profits during the scarcity which followed the fire (*Eng. Hist. Rev.*, xliii. 78).'

Godfrey, Sir Edmund Berry. viii. 32*b*, ll. 8–10. See *London Gazette*, no. 88, 18 Sept., 1666, for account of his receiving the knighthood.

Godiva or Godgifu (*fl.* 1040–80), viii. 37*b*, l. 14 from foot. For 'It seems probable that she died a few years before the Domesday survey (1085–6)', read 'She died 10 Sept. 1067' (Bodl. MS. Douce 139, fo. 1*b*).

***Goffe, Stephen.** viii. 69*b*, last line. Goffe was the agent of Queen Henrietta Maria in her negotiations with the Prince of Orange in 1644 and 1645 in which the marriage of Prince Charles with the prince's daughter was offered in return for military and financial aid (Gardiner, *Great Civil War*, i. 348; ii. 172; iii. 5; Groen van Prinsterer, *Archives de la Maison d'Orange Nassau*, 2nd Series, iv. 99–125).

70*b*, l. 24. The article says: 'Some parliamentary scribblers published a scandalous work entitled "The Lord George Digby's Cabinet, etc."' The letters in question are undoubtedly authentic, and the collection was published officially by parliament (Husbands, *Acts and Ordinances*, folio, 1646, p. 831).

Goffe or Gough, Stephen, D.D. viii. 70*a*, l. 28. After 'pontifical.' insert 'He said his first mass about December 1653; the queen was present (*Nicholas Papers*, Camden Soc., ii. 45).'

Add to list of authorities: L. Batterel's Mémoires domestiques pour servir à l'histoire de l'Oratoire, 1902–11, iii. 169–75.

Goffe, William. viii. 71*b*. Add the following: The documents in the *E.H.R.* vii. 717, showing that he was a native of Haverfordwest, make the account of his parentage doubtful. He was a quarter-master in Barclay's regiment, and a captain by June, 1644. Barclay's regiment passed to Harley when the New Model was formed, and Goffe became its lieut.-colonel about the time that Harley was superseded by Pride in 1647. He succeeded Cowell as lieut.-colonel of Fairfax's foot about November, 1648. This regiment passed to Cromwell after Fairfax's resignation in June, 1650, and was commanded at Dunbar by Goffe, who became its colonel immediately afterwards. In November, 1655, he exchanged his colonelcy of foot for one of horse (vice Saunders), but was replaced about January, 1658, by Richard Cromwell, when his old regiment was restored to him. In May, 1659, his regiment was taken from him and given to Ludlow. In the summer of 1647 he played a prominent part in the army councils, particularly when these were transformed into prayer-meetings. His speeches prove that he sympathised with the ideals of the fifth monarchy men, but, unlike them, he was content to wait upon the Lord until He should declare Himself, and, like Cromwell, was anxious to avoid divisions in the army (see *Clarke Papers*, Camden Soc., vols. i.–iv. *passim*). G. D.

Good, John Mason. viii. 110*b*, l. 22 from foot. For '1805' read '1808' (*Record of Royal Soc.*, p. 376).

Goodman, Godfrey. viii. 134*a*, l. 40. For 'but no copy seems now known' read 'of which two copies are in the Bodleian library.'

H. H. E. C.

Goodsonn, William. viii. 140*a*. This article needs revision. See Sir Charles Firth in *The Mariner's Mirror*, xii. 257.

Gookin, Sir Vincent. viii. 154*a*, ll. 24–5. For 'Sir Vincent . . . not known' read 'Gookin'.

Ibid., l. 32. After 'pp. 393–6)' add 'He was sheriff of the county of Cork in 1630 (*Cal. S.P.*, *Ireland*, 1647–60, p. 182) and was knighted by the lords justices of Ireland on 13 February 1631 (Shaw, *Knights of England*, ii. 199)'.

Ibid., l. 25 from foot. The letter is calendared in *Cal. S.P.*, *Ireland*, 1647–60, pp. 181–6.

To authorities add: 'Information about Gookin's Highfield estate and abstract of his will in Bristol and Gloucs. Arch. Soc., Transactions, lxiv (1943). 113–6.'

Gordon, Adam Lindsay. viii. 158*b*, l. 22 from foot. After 'Esselmont in Scotland,' add '(for details of his claim, see letter by Dr. J. M. Bulloch in *Times*, 19 Oct. 1933, p. 8*c*).'

Gordon, Charles George. viii. 176*b*, l. 3. After '1890' add 'The Journals and other original MSS. connected with Gordon are now in the British Museum (Add. MSS. 34474–34483).'

Gordon, Thomas (1788–1841). viii. 230*a*. For an additional account with a reproduction of a lithograph portrait, see 'Journ. of Hellenic Studies,' xlix. pt. i, pp. 3–6.

Goring, George, Earl of Norwich (1583?–1663). viii. 248*b*, l. 22. Goring was admitted to Sidney Sussex College, Cambridge, as a Fellow-Commoner 'the fourth week of the first month' of the year 1600, according to the register of the college (*Hist. MSS. Comm.*, 3rd Report, p. 327).

249*b*, l. 1. On his negotiations with Mazarin in 1643–4, see *Clarendon State Papers*, ii. 163, and *Eng. Hist. Rev.*, xxviii. 337.

250*a*, 12 ll. from foot. Goring's instructions for the negotiation with the Duke of Lorraine in 1652 are printed in *Cal. State Papers, Dom.*, 1651–2, p. 134.

250*b*, l. 10. The second and third volumes of the *Nicholas Papers* print a number of letters to and from Goring between 1653 and 1656, which show his poverty, his devotion to the king, and his distrust of Hyde's policy.

Goring, George, Earl of Norwich. viii. 250*b*, l. 5 from foot. For 'William' read 'Edward' (Burton, *Diary*, i. 204). [See also BULLETIN, iv. 56–7].

Goring, George, Baron Goring (1608–1657). viii. 246*a*, l. 33. Goring's examination with regard to the Army Plot, 16 June 1641, which differs considerably from the version published in Rushworth, is printed in the *Hist. MSS. Comm., Portland MSS.*, i. 20. The volume also contains papers on his defence of Portsmouth, i. 44, 48, 50, 54, 61.

247*a*, l. 1. Clarendon's assertion that Goring's negligence was the cause of the escape of Essex's cavalry in Cornwall in 1644 is shown to be a misrepresentation of the facts, in *English Historical Review*, 1904, pp. 473–5. He is throughout prejudiced against Goring.

Graham, John, of Claverhouse, first Viscount Dundee. viii. 336*a*, 17 ll. from the bottom. For 'Subsequently he transferred . . . the troop of William's guards,' read 'Subsequently he transferred his services to William, prince of Orange, not in 1672, as stated by C. K. Sharpe (Napier's *Life*, i. 180), but at the same time as Sir David Colyear, Earl of Portmore (G. Carleton, *Memoirs of an English Officer, 1672–1713*, 1728, p. 13), who is known to have entered the troop of William's guards in 1674, after the conclusion by England of a separate peace with Holland (see article on Colyear in *D.N.B.* iv. 880*b*).'

Graham, John, of Claverhouse, first Viscount Dundee. viii. 349, l. 18. For '17 July' read '27 July.'

Graham, Patrick. viii. 353*a*, l. 23 from foot. For 'Lochy' read 'Lock (Lok).'

J. H. B

Graham, Richard, Viscount Preston. viii. 355*a*, l. 13 from foot. After 'His instructions' add 'dated 31 March and 12 April 1682 (Hist. MSS. Comm., *7th Rep.*, app., p. 262*a*.).'

Ibid. 355*b*, ll. 30–27 from foot. For 'At the end . . . (*ib.* i. 471)' read 'On 28 October 1688 he was appointed secretary of state in succession to the earl of Sunderland (*London Gazette*, no. 2394, 25–9 Oct. 1688).'

Graile, Edmund (*fl.* 1611), viii. 367*a*, last line. Omit 'and of this . . . Museum'.

Grant, Alexander. viii. 374*a*, l. 27. After 'the union.' insert 'On 4 March 1706 he was appointed colonel of a regiment of foot (formerly the earl of Mar's) on the Scots establishment (Dalton, *Eng. Army Lists*, v. 223).'

Ibid. 374*b*, ll. 2–4. For 'Grant was deprived . . . George I' read 'His regiment was disbanded in 1713, but he raised another on the accession of George I, his commission as colonel dating from 22 July 1715 (Dalton, *George the First's Army*, i. 178; J. Millan, *Succession of Colonels*, 1742, p. 24)'

Ibid. l. 29. For 'in 1715' read 'on 12 Feb. 1711 (Dalton, *Eng. Army Lists*, vi. 19)'

Ibid. l. 32. After 'regiment' insert 'was sent to Ireland in 1717, when he vacated the colonelcy (Dalton, *George the First's Army*, i. 316), and the following year it'

Grant, James (1720–1806). viii. 388. For further information concerning his career before 1763, see C. L. Mowat, *East Florida as a British Province, 1763–1784*. (Univ. of California Publications in History, vol. xxxii, Berkeley, 1943).

Grant, James (1802–1879). viii. 391*a*, l. 24. Add to the list of authorities: 'Reminiscences of My Life in the Highlands (1883) by J. Mitchell, C.E., i. 149–153' (*Notes and Queries*, clix. 315).

Grantham or Granthan, Henry. viii. 408*b*, ll. 15–14 from foot. For 'London, 1588, 4to' read '1574, appended to Whitehorne's translation of Machiavelli's "Arte of Warre" (1573); new ed., with Whitehorne, 1588.'

Gray, George Robert. viii. 450*b*, l. 4 from foot. For '1866' read '1865' (*Record of Royal Soc.*, p. 410).

Gray, Sir John (1816–75), viii. 452*a*, l. 36. For '1850' read '1852 (see his speech at meeting of council of Tenant League reported in *Freeman's Journal*, 29 April 1857)'.

Green, Matthew. viii. 494*b*, ll. 16–20. For '1732' read '1733,' the date of all recorded copies of 'The Grotto'; and for 'these . . . Dodsley's collection (1748)' read '"The Spleen" and three or four previously unpublished trifles were published in the first volume of Dodsley's collection (1748), "The Grotto" in the fifth volume (1758).'

H. G. P.

Green, Thomas, D.D. viii. 497*a*, l. 7. After '155).' insert 'His portrait hangs in the hall of Corpus Christi college.'

Gregg, William. Suppl. 778*b*, ll. 43–52. For 'in all probability . . . qualities,' read 'the nephew of Hugh Greg, minister resident at Copenhagen, to whom he was secretary and who died there in January 170½. He stayed on as secretary to the envoy James Vernon till 1704, and during the summer of that year was in charge of affairs. According to Burnet he was dismissed "for his ill qualifications" (Hugh Greg's dispatches, P.R.O. Denmark, 22–24; dispatches to William Gregg, July–Sept. 1704, P.R.O. Foreign Entry Books, 4; letters from William Gregg, 1702–4, Brit. Mus. Add. MSS. 7076, 28910–15).'

J. F. C.

Gregory, David (1661–1708). viii. 537*b*. Add to list of authorities: W. G. Hiscock's The War of the Scientists; new light on Newton and Gregory (*Times Lit. Suppl.*, 1936, p. 34).

Grenville, Sir Bevil. viii. 554*a*, l. 29. Lord Hopton's narratives of the western campaign were printed in 1902 in *Bellum Civile*, a collection of royalist narratives edited by C. E. Chadwyck Healey for the Somerset Record Society. Grenville's death is there related in Col. Slingsby's account of Lansdown (p. 95).

Grenville, Sir Richard (1600–1658), royalist. viii. 567*b*, 12 ll. from foot. A detailed account of his quarrel with his wife is given in Mrs. G. H. (now Lady) Radford's paper on 'Lady Howard of Fitzford,' printed in the *Transactions of the Devonshire Association for the Advancement of Science, Literature, and Art*, 1890, pp. 66–110.

568*a*, l. 12. Grenville landed in Ireland in February 1642 (not February 1641). On his services there see, in addition to Carte, *History of the Confederation and War in Ireland*, by J. T. Gilbert, 1882–91, ii. 194, 199, 257.

568*b*, l. 11. On Grenville's siege of Plymouth see Jewitt, *History of Plymouth*, 1873, pp. 184–214.

Greville, Sir Fulke, first Baron Brooke (1554–1628). viii. 602*a*, l. 10. Delete 'was elected M.P. for his county in 1586 and 1588.' (J. E. Neale, *The Elizabethan House of Commons*, p. 52, n. 4).

Ibid., 603*a*, l. 26 from foot. For 'he sat in Parliament as member for Warwickshire . . . . 1620,' read 'he sat in Parliament as member for Southampton in 1580, for Heydon in Yorkshire in 1584, for Warwickshire in 1586, 1588, 1593, 1597, 1601 and 1621.' (J. E. Neale, *op. cit.*, p. 52.)

Grey, Anchitell. viii. 612*a*. Grey usually wrote his name Gray (*B.M. Add. MS.* 36901). An Anschitillus de Grai, claimed by the family as an ancestor (J. Nichols, *History of Leicestershire*, iii. 682–3), is mentioned in Domesday as a holder of lands in Oxfordshire (*Domesday Book*, 1783, i. 161). Grey was suspected of complicity in the rising of his brother-in-law, Sir George Booth [q.v.], in 1659, but was discharged without penalty (*Cal. of Committee for Compounding*, p. 3252). As the accusation came from the Derbyshire committee, Grey was probably already married and established in his wife's manor of Risley in that county. He was a justice of the peace for Derbyshire in 1662 (J. C. Cox, *Three Centuries of Derbyshire Annals*, i. 65). The Grey mentioned by Clarendon (*Civil War*, ed. Macray, iv. 20) is Angell Grey of Dorset.

Supported by William Cavendish, third earl of Devonshire (Hist. MSS. Comm., 15th Rep., App. vii. 174), Grey was elected M.P. for Derby, in place of Richard Allestry, deceased [see ALLESTREE, RICHARD, *ad fin.*], on 16 Feb. 1664/5, and sat for that town in every parliament, except that of James II, until 1695. Grey frequently sat on committees of the house. Although he apparently took no part in debates it is evident that he was a member of the country party (otherwise he could not have retained his seat for Derby, where that party's influence was predominant; also his name never occurs in any of the lists of voters for the court party). He took part in deciphering and translating Coleman's letters (published 1681, p. 35; in Hist. MSS. Comm., 13th Rep., App. vi. 81, Grey is erroneously described as the writer of the letter). Grey naturally became a whig, but avoided all excesses; in 1685 he and William Sacheverell [q.v.] stood unsuccessfully for Derbyshire (Hist. MSS. Comm., 12th Rep., App. v. 86–7, where 'Mr. Grey' is almost unquestionably Anchitell). In January and February 1688, when James II was trying to gain support for his policy of toleration, it was proposed by his agents that Grey should be one of the approved parliamentary candidates for Derby (he was superseded in September), and that he should be appointed a justice of the peace for Nottinghamshire and a deputy lieutenant for Derbyshire (Sir G. Duckett, *Penal Laws and Test Act*, 1882, pp. 168, 440; appendix, 1883, pp. 122, 294). He was appointed deputy lieutenant for Derbyshire in 1690 (Hist. MSS. Comm., 12th Rep., App. ii. 358), and for Nottinghamshire in 1692 (*Cal. S.P., Dom.*, 1691–1692, p. 276). In January 1690 Grey's name was printed in the list of whigs voting for Sacheverell's 'disabling clause' (*Some Queries concerning the Election of Members for the Ensuing Parliament*, 1690). From the close of 1690 Grey was frequently absent from parliament on account of illness. He died probably on 8 July 1702 (register of Dale abbey, *Journal of the Derbyshire Archaeol. and Nat. Hist. Soc.*, xxii. 112).

612*b*, l. 14. Grey's reports were published as 'Debates of the House of Commons from 1667 to 1694,' in 10 vols., 8vo, all copies apparently bearing the date 1769. A proposal for publishing them by subscription had been made by Edward Cave [q.v.] in 1745 (*Gentleman's Magazine*, xv. 135–42). They had been known to Arthur Onslow [q.v.] who praised them from the chair (dedication to the *Debates*) and mentions them in his notes to Burnet's 'History of My Own Time' (ed. O. Airy, I ii. 119, n. 4). Onslow there states that some of the reports were made by Richard May, member for Chichester; towards the end Grey received reports from other members. In 1682 Sir Thomas Meres, a prominent whig, informed Pepys that Grey had been taking shorthand notes of debates (Pepys, *Naval Minutes*, Navy Rec. Soc., p. 122). Cave describes the manuscript as consisting of fourteen quarto volumes, and gives a list of contents. The manuscript has disappeared. Cave expected to have printed the debates within a few months; actually they appeared in 1763 (*Gentleman's Magazine*, xxxiv. 47; J. Grove, *Lives of the Earls of Devonshire*, 1764, p. 46 *n.*).

Cave states that Grey made the reports 'for his own use or amusement.' This may be the case, but it is worth noting that John Milward, member for Derbyshire, 1665–1670, was making a series of reports, of which those for 1666 to 1668 are extant (*B.M. Add. MS.* 33413). Country party and whig tracts from 1673 to 1681 frequently contain accounts of parliamentary debates; none of them can be shown to derive from Grey; the 'Debates in the House of Commons assembled at Oxford,' 1681, is perhaps a variant expansion from rough notes made by Grey. The reliability of the 'Debates' has been generally accepted, but no detailed examination has been published. Sir George Sitwell (*The First Whig*, 1894, p. ix) accuses Grey of having suppressed reports of certain debates which would have exposed the whigs; the omissions are more probably due to absence or other accident.

Cave, or an anonymous editor, did his work well, the transcription being, so far as one can judge in the absence of the MS., exceptionally accurate; the connecting with the 'Commons' Journals' (then in course of publication) is generally good, and the annotation adequate. The lack of an index of speakers is the most serious defect. The 'Debates' supply much of the material for the fourth and fifth volumes of W. Cobbett's 'Parliamentary History.' Cobbett's editor, John Wright, preferred, for the parliaments of 1680 and 1681, to reprint the reports published in 1681 (see also Nichols, *Literary Anecdotes*, v. 17).

Ibid., l. 35. Add: 'Grey appears to have been generally respected (J. C. Cox, *Three Centuries of Derbyshire Annals*, ii. 294 (document of 1694); later notices in *Gentleman's Magazine*, xv. 136; J. Grove, *Lives of the Earls of Devonshire*, 1764, p. 46 *n.*; and the address to the reader attached to the *Debates*; for a contrary, but biased, opinion, Hist. MSS. Comm., *Lord Montagu of Beaulieu MSS.*, pp. 172–3).

'He married Ann, daughter of Sir Henry Willoughby, bart., of Risley, and widow of Sir Thomas Aston, bart., of Aston, Cheshire. She died, aged 73, on 2 June 1688 and was buried at Little Wilne. By her first husband she had a son, Sir Willoughby Aston, and two daughters; by Grey she had a son, Willoughby, who died unmarried in 1701, and a daughter Elizabeth (J. C. Cox, *Notes on Derbyshire Churches*, iv. 404, from monument).'

Ibid., 20 ll. from foot. For additional references to Miss Grey's charities see *ibid.*, iv. 409–10; and *Victoria County History, Derbyshire*, ii. 267–9.

To authorities, besides those mentioned in text, add: Hist. MSS. Comm., 9th Rep. ii. 398*b*, 399*a*; 12th Rep., App. ii. 383, 449, App. iii. 1; 13th Rep., App. vi. p. 15; B.M. Add. MS. 36901, 36904; Journal of the Derbyshire Archaeol. and Nat. Hist. Soc., xxiv. 83, xxxii. 54; and Luttrell's Brief Relation, v. 194.

E. S. de Beer.

Grey, Charles, 1st Earl Grey.
viii. 616, 16 lines from foot. For 'King's College' read 'Trinity College.' (Trevelyan, *Lord Grey and the Reform Bill.*)
p. 621, ll. 39–40, 'which Grey subsequently declared he never meant to execute.' This only rests on Brougham's chatter in later years. (*Ib.*; Butler, J. R. M., *Passing of the Great Reform Bill.*)

Grey, John de. viii. 635*b*, l. 13. For '1309' read '1308.' [In November 1306 it is said that Richard de Grey has lately done homage for the lands of his father, Henry de Grey (*Cal. Close Rolls*, 1307–13, p. 80). Writ for inquisition *post mortem* on lands of Henry de Grey was issued on 16 September 1308 (*Cal. Inquis.* (Edw. II), v. 50, No. 116.)]

Grey, William (*d.* 1478). viii. 655*a*, ll. 22–6. For 'was a member . . . Richard de Grey (*d.* 1419) [q.v.]' read 'was a descendant of the family of Warke, son of Sir Thomas Grey of Heton (*d.* 1415) and Anne, his wife (*The Times Lit. Suppl.*, 9 June 1932, p. 427).'

Grey, William (*d.* 1478). viii. 655*b*, l. 4. After 'Cologne' insert 'where he was enrolled on 1 Dec. 1442 (Keussen, *Matrikel der Univ. Köln*, i. 215, 63, p. 457).'

J. H. B.

Griffith, John. (1622?–1700). viii. 676*b*. Add to list of publications: 'Some Prison-Meditations and Experiences . . . Written in Newgate by John Griffith a Prisoner there . . . Printed in the year 1663.' 8vo. [Collation: A8–K8, last leaf blank.] In verse. A copy of this, from the Christie-Miller Library at Britwell Court, was bought at Sotheby's in April, 1924, by Dr. Rosenbach of New York for £20.

H. G. P.

Griffiths, Frederick Augustus. viii. 687*a*, ll. 4–5. For '*d.*' read '1795–'; for 'army as an ensign' read 'Royal Military Academy, Woolwich, 20 Feb. 1810, and was appointed second lieutenant'

Ibid. ll. 6–8. After 'gazetted' read 'first'; after '1816,' read 'second'; after '1835,' read 'captain, 23 Dec. 1841,'; after 'and' insert 'brevet-'; after '1854.' read 'He was retired with full pay, 4 April 1843.'; after 'died' delete 'in' and read 'at St. Mary Bourne, Andover, 25 March'; after '1869.' read 'In March 1825 he married Eleanor Willan, at St. George's, Bloomsbury.'

Add to list of authorities: War Office Library, Officers' records, Royal Artillery, iv. f. 306.

Grimston, William Luckyn, first Viscount Grimston. viii. 704*a*, ll. 3–8. For 'On the death . . . Grimston' read 'On 29 May 1719 he was created a peer of Ireland, with the titles Baron Dunboyne and Viscount Grimston, and, on the death of his elder brother Sir Harbottle Luckyn in Feb. 1737, the Luckyn baronetcy devolved on him (G.E.C., vi. 205)'.

Gunning, Peter. viii. 789*a*, last line. For 'Clare Hall' read 'Corpus Christi college (*Masters' Hist. of Corpus Christi Coll., Camb.*, ed. J. Lamb, p. 154)'

789*b*, l. 2. For 'Clare' read 'Corpus Christi'

Gunthorpe or Gundorp, John. viii. 794*a*, l. 30. After 'College' insert '. He was proctor at Cambridge in 1454–5 (Bulletin, xv. 153)'; for 'to have' read 'he'

Ibid. l. 34. After 'pupils.' insert 'At Ferrara he completed, on 3 Aug. 1460, a transcript of Seneca's "Tragedies" which is now B.M. Harleian MS. 2485. On 28 Jan. 1462 he was appointed penitentiary and papal chaplain at Rome, which office he held until 25 March 1469, when his successor was appointed, Gunthorp having been absent from Rome "about four years" (*ibid.*).'

Ibid. l. 21 from foot. For '1468' read '1467' (BULLETIN, *loc. cit.*).

Ibid. ll. 18–16 from foot. For '1477' read 'Christmas 1472 (*ibid.* p. 154)'; for '*ib.*' read '*Foedera*'

Ibid. l. 13 from foot. After '652).' insert 'On 21 June 1471 he was appointed clerk of the parliaments for life (BULLETIN, *loc. cit.*).'

Ibid. l. 9 from foot. For '*ib.*' read '*Foedera*'.

Ibid. 794*b*, ll. 11–2. For 'received' read 'exchanged the prebend of Hoxton for (BULLETIN, XV. 154)'

Ibid. ll. 19–20. After 'Salisbury.' insert 'On 28 Feb. 1483 he was appointed first dean of the chapel of the king's household in St. Peter's within the Tower of London (*ibid.*)'

Hacker, Francis. viii. 860*a*, 11 ll. from foot. Hacker's regiment of horse was one of those on which Richard Cromwell relied; one of his last acts as Protector was to knight Hacker, but when it came to a pinch the regiment refused to march to Whitehall at the Protector's orders (*Clarke Papers*, iii. 191, 193). However, Hacker and his officers steadily supported the civil power against the army leaders (*ibid.*, iv. 93, 102, 165). In Dec. 1659 he raised forces in Leicestershire for the service of the parliament and occupied Coventry (*Mercurius Politicus*, 29 Dec.–5 Jan. 1659).

See, on his regiment, *The deep sighes and sad complaints of some late soldiers in Capt. Needham's Troop in Col. Hacker's Regiment*, by Thomas Fothergill, and *A Brief Narrative of the Trial of Capt. Clement Needham*, both published in 1653.

Hakluyt, Richard. (1552 ?–1616). viii. 895*a*. See *Notes and Queries*, cxlvi. 335, for details of his ancestry.

Hales, Sir Christopher. For 'he died a bachelor' read 'By his wife, Elizabeth, who survived him, he had a son John who was under age in 1542 (*Letters and Papers of Henry VIII.* xvii. p. 704, Nos. 881 [23], 1154 [93]) and ultimately succeeded also to Whitefriars, Coventry, the house of his uncle John Hales (*d.* 1571) [q.v.]; he was actively concerned in secretly printing there some of the Martin Marprelate tracts' (Pierce, *Martin Marprelate Tracts*, 2 vols., 1908, 1911, *passim*).

Hales, Sir Edward. viii. 911*a*, l. 17 from foot. For '(*d.* 1695)' read '(1645–1695) (*Visitation of Kent, 1663–8*, Harl. Soc., p. 71)'

Ibid. ll. 11–8 from foot. For 'On the death . . . Charles II he' read 'In 1675 he, or his father (Hasted, *History of Kent*, iii. 596)'

Ibid. l. 6 from foot. After 'resided.' add 'He succeeded to the baronetcy *c.* 1684.'

Ibid. 911*b*, l. 3. For '28 Nov. 1673' read '22 June 1685 (Dalton, *English Army Lists*, ii. 35)'

Ibid. 912*a*, ll. 20–19 from foot. For 'By his wife' read 'In 1669 (*London Marriage Licences*, ed. J. Foster) he married'; for 'daughter' read 'granddaughter'; after 'Oxfordshire,' insert 'by whom'; and add to list of authorities: E. S. de Beer's Early Life of Sir Edward Hales, titular earl of Tenterden (*Notes and Queries*, clxx. 164).

Hales, or Hayles, John (*d.* 1571). In the original ed. of the D.N.B. (xxiv. 29, 1890) Canon Dixon identified John Hales 'of Coventry' with John Hales, clerk of the hanaper; but in *Trans. Royal Hist. Soc.*, New Ser., xi. 116–118, and in his *Domesday of Inclosures*, i. 5 (1897), I. S. Leadam denied the identification, mainly on the grounds that under Mary the clerk of the hanaper was 'enjoying his lucrative office' while John Hales of Coventry was an exile at Frankfurt (*cf.* Whittingham, *Troubles*, ed. 1908, *passim*), and that John Hales of Coventry 'is never described as clerk of the Hanaper.' Corrections in this sense were included in the volume of 'Errata' to the D.N.B. (Smith, Elder & Co., 1904) and incorporated in the second edition of the Dictionary (Clarendon Press, 1908–9). Nevertheless, the publication of vol. xx. of the *Letters and Papers of Henry VIII.* (pt. ii. No. 707 [48]) in 1907 had revealed the grant, on 25 Oct., 1545, of the office of keeper or clerk of the hanaper jointly to Sir Ralph Sadler, master or keeper of the Great Wardrobe, and to John Hales 'of Coventry' (an examination of the patent roll confirms the accuracy of the *L. and P.*); and the note is added that the patent was cancelled, after the death of John Hales, on 10 Feb., 1572–3, in order that a new patent might be made out to the surviving Sir Ralph and his younger son Henry. It was from Sir Ralph that Hales purchased his house at Coventry (Lamond, *The Commonweal*, p. xix). Hales's retention of his emoluments under Mary was due to the difficulty of getting rid of holders of office by patent, especially when they were abroad beyond the reach of legal process; and the Commons rejected in 1555 a bill enabling Mary to deal with these cases and another in 1558 to confirm her patents. The clerk of the hanaper was, however, deprived in 1557, and it was John Hales of Coventry who was restored to that office on Elizabeth's accession. The John Hales indexed in *Letters and Papers*, vols. xx.–xxi., as 'of the wardrobe' is probably the clerk of the hanaper. Other corrections in the D.N.B. article are: for 'he received a grant in 1548' read '1545' (*L. and P.* xx. pt. i. No. 1335 [38–9]); for 'in 1560 he fell into disgrace' read 'in 1564' (Haynes, *State*

Papers, pp. 412–417 ; *Hatfield MSS.* i. 290–6 ; *C.S.P. Dom.* Addenda, 1547–65, p. 535 ; *Acts P. C.* 1558–70, pp. 196, 211) ; for 'Harl. MS. 550' read '555'; and to 'a gratulatory oration which is extant in manuscript' add 'and is printed in Foxe, *Acts and Monuments*, ed. Townsend, viii. 673–9.'

Hall, John (1575–1635). viii. 954. Younger son of William Hall, a physician, who lived from *c.* 1569–90 at Carlton, Beds., and later at Acton, Middx. John Hall matriculated from Queen's College, Cambridge, as of 'Bedfordshire' in 1589, proceeding to B.A. (1593/4) and M.A. (1597). See *Genealogists' Magazine*, Sept. 1936, p. 344; March, 1937, p. 478.

Hall, Thomas. (1610–1665). viii. 975*a*. See *Bulletin of the John Rylands Library*, viii. 166, for an account of 'what purports to be an authentic biography' found among the Baxter MSS. of Dr. Williams' Library. It contains 'Hall's will, lists of his books, and numerous remarks, all written as if by himself' which 'have been worked over by an editor who calls himself the publisher.'

Hallifax, Sir Thomas. viii. 998*b*, ll. 6–7. Delete 'It was probably on this occasion that he was knighted.'

Ibid. l. 19. After 'He was' insert 'knighted on 5 Feb. 1773 and' (W. A. Shaw, *Knights*, ii. 294).

Halton, or Halghton, John of. viii. 1010*a*, ll. 26–8. Delete 'He became prior . . ., and on' and insert 'On'; after '1292' insert 'he'

Add to list of authorities : The Register of John de Halton, Bishop of Carlisle, 1292–1324 (Canterbury and York Soc.).

Halyburton, Thomas. viii. 1014*a*, l. 4. For 'the New College, or college of St. Leonard, St. Andrews' read 'St. Mary's (sometimes called the "New") College.'

J. H. B.

Hamilton, Archibald. (*d.* 1593). viii. 1022*a*, l. 13. After 'pope' insert 'The university records show two individuals of this name, one of whom was incorporated in St. Mary's College in 1552, the other in the same college in 1556 (Anderson, *Early records of the University of St. Andrews*, pp. 153, 154, 156, 258, 264). Further details will be found in McCrie's "Life of John Knox."'

J. H. B.

Hamilton, Gustavus. vii. 1043*b*, ll. 36–45. Delete 'and undertook . . . arches of a bridge' (*Notes and Queries*, clviii. 3).

Hamilton, William, second Duke (1616–1651). viii. 1102*a*. See Gardiner, *Letters and Papers illustrating the Relations between Charles II and Scotland in* 1650 (Scottish History Society, 1894).

Hammond, James. viii. 1131*a*, l. 14. After 'and distinction.' insert 'Chesterfield also arranged for their publication (*Notes and Queries*, clxx. 196).'

Hammond, Robert. viii. 1132*a*, l. 26. For 'and on 11 March . . . cuirassiers' read 'with which he served at Hull under Hotham to 11 March, 1643, when he was appointed captain-lieutenant of Essex's body-guard of cuirassiers, a position he retained until 18 November. He then became a major in Massey's horse (Hammond's account in P.R.O. Misc. Aug. Book 5 ; Clarke MSS. lxvii.). He was wounded at the first battle of Newbury (*Bibliotheca Gloucestrensis*, p. 244).'

G. D.

Hanbury, John. xxi. 379*b*, l. 17. For '1720' read '1721' (*Return of M.P.'s*, ii. 41).

Harborne, William. viii. 1200–1. This article should be re-written as follows :

Harborne, William (*d.* 1617), first English ambassador to Turkey, was a son of William Harborne of Great Yarmouth, who was one of the two bailiffs of the town in 1556 and again in 1572, and a commissioner for negotiations with the Cinque Ports in 1575 (H. Swinden, *History of Great Yarmouth*, 1772, pp. 224–5*n*., 940, 942). The son first went overseas probably about 1559 and spent some years in Spain (*Cal. S.P., For.*, 1584–5, pp. 44, 314), but is first mentioned in 1578 when he was a factor of Edward Osborne's [later Sir Edward, q.v., and BULLETIN, below, p. 162]. With a view to reviving the trade with Turkey Osborne and his partner Richard Staper, having procured the sultan's safeconduct for him, sent Harborne to Constantinople ; setting out from London on 1 July 1578 and travelling via Poland he arrived there on 28 October (Hakluyt, *Principal navigations*, edn. 1903–5, v. 167–9). He was well received and not only obtained a trade licence for himself and his two partners, but also prepared the way for contact between the two sovereigns by causing a letter to be written by Murad III to Queen Elizabeth. This letter, which is dated 15 March 1579, and the accompanying letter of Mustafa 'beg' (later first dragoman of the English embassy) are said to have been brought by Harborne himself to England (*Cal. S.P., Spain,* 1568–79, p. 699; *cf. ibid.,* 1580–6, p. 10; *Cal. S.P., For.,* 1579–80, p. 77). If this was so, then Harborne must have returned to Turkey with Elizabeth's answers to them, dated 25 October 1579, for he was certainly in Constantinople when the latter were received there; they enabled him to negotiate for a capitulation (*Cal. S.P., For.,* 1583, p. 718). This was granted early in June 1580, a success due in part to the tin and other war material brought by the English merchants to Turkey despite the papal veto, in part to the Turks' belief that friendly relations with Christian powers would be of service to them in their war against Persia (*Négociations de la France dans le Levant,* ed. E. Charrière, 1848–60, iii. 913 *n.*). France, in pursuance of her traditional claim that all the 'Frankish' (*i.e.* western) nations were bound to trade in Turkey under the French flag and diplomatic protection (and supervision), immediately protested and by 15 July was assured that the capitulation had been revoked. In fact however it was only dormant, and necessarily so as long as no English representative was established at the Porte, and Harborne, writing to the Lord Treasurer on 9 June 1581 after his return from a sojourn at Chios (in April: *Cal. S.P., For.,* 1581–2, p. 109; *cf. Cal. S.P., Venice,* 1581–91, p. 5), treats it as absolutely sure and valid (*Trans. R. Hist. Soc.,* 4th ser., v (1922), 6–7); there was no objection to the queen issuing her charter on 11 September to the Turkey Company (the later Levant Company), by which she granted to Osborne, Staper, and their associates, the sole right of trading to Turkey for seven years. Harborne, who is reported to have left Constantinople on 17 July 1581 (*Documente privitôre la istoria Românilor,* ed. E. de Hurmuzaki, 1876– , xi. 651), returned to England 'wth the Preveledge in an^o^ 1582' (*Trans. R. Hist. Soc.,* 4th ser., v. 13). Now become 'one of the Esquires of our body,' he was commissioned by Elizabeth on 20 November 1582 to be her 'orator, nuntius, procurator, et agens' to the Porte (although the term 'legatus' is not used in the commission he was always regarded as ambassador; the queen uses the term in a letter of 5 September 1584). He left England on 14 January 1582/3 O.S. and, travelling by sea, arrived at Constantinople on 8 April N.S.; he brought with him letters and presents from his sovereign for the sultan and his ministers, as was customary for ambassadors to the Porte. The sultan received him on 3 or 4 May N.S. and wrote to Elizabeth promising that he should have the same privileges as the ambassadors of other friendly nations. His immediate business was the safeguarding of shipping and the establishing of consulates in Alexandria and Tripolis in Syria, to be followed by others in Chios, Aleppo, Patras, and finally Algiers (1585). He had also to maintain his position in Constantinople against the attacks of the French and Venetian ambassadors and is said to have gone so far in reply to them as to claim pre-eminence on account of the greatness of his mistress (*Cal. S.P., Venice,* 1581–91, p. 93; see also *Cal. S.P., For.,* 1583–4, p. 308). As early as 1584 he procured a firman by which the customs duty of 5 %, payable by all foreigners as well as by the sultan's own subjects, was reduced for English merchants to 3 % (*Trans. R. Hist. Soc.,* 4th ser., v. 8, 13). In 1585 he obtained the release of the ship *Jesus* and her company, which had been held at Tripoli; he redeemed altogether fifty-four English prisoners and claimed that at the time of his departure there were none in Turkey (*ibid.,* pp. 21–2).

From at least as early as January 1584 Harborne was also engaged in purely diplomatic activities. Elizabeth's objects were to prevent the renewal of the truce between Turkey and Spain and to persuade the Turks to attack Spain or the Spanish dominions. Harborne did not succeed in the latter and probably did not want to do so (*Trans. R. Hist. Soc.,* 4th ser., v. 24); but he was one of the principal agents in preventing early in 1587 a renewal of the truce, thus compelling the Spaniards to leave the Mediterranean coastal garrisons at full strength.

Harborne was originally appointed to serve until 1585; in 1584, when asking for his recall, he proposed that his secretary (identifiable as Edward Barton [q.v., and BULLETIN, above, p. 158]) should succeed him with the inferior status of agent (*Cal. S.P., For.,* 1584–5, pp. 44, 168). He obtained his discharge in 1588; he left Constantinople on 13 August N.S.; when passing through Moldavia negotiated a treaty with

Peter the Lame; and arrived home in December.

He settled at Mundham in Norfolk, marrying on 16 September 1589 (Blomefield, Norfolk, i. 495) Elizabeth, daughter of Anthony Drury of Besthorp, by whom he had several children, and becoming a freeman of Great Yarmouth in 1591. The original Turkey Company charter having expired in 1588, Burleigh summoned him in 1591, with Osborne and others, to a conference about the future trade with Turkey. He was a member of the new Levant Company, which was chartered on 7 January 1591/2. He died on 6 November 1617 and is buried at Mundham.

Harborne's success was due to his skill and persistence; he was well supported from England and was apparently ably seconded by Edward Barton. Hakluyt gives him considerable prominence, printing letters and other documents connected with his negotiations; and in 1598 Thomas Nashe [q.v.] celebrates him for having made London as well known as Mecca to the Turks.

[Despatches of Harborne's are preserved in the Public Record Office, and other papers in the British Museum and in the Bodleian Library; several are printed by H. G. Rawlinson in 'The embassy of William Harborne,' in Trans. R. Hist. Soc., 4th ser., v. (1922), 1–27. The authorities, besides those indicated, include East Anglian pedigrees, ed. A. Campling (Harleian Soc., vol. 91 and Norfolk Record Soc., vol. 13); A calendar of the freemen of Great Yarmouth, 1429–1800 (Norfolk and Norwich Archaeol. Soc., 1910); T. Nashe, Works, ed. R. B. McKerrow, 1904–10, iii. 173. For his career in Turkey, besides the Calendars of State Papers, Hakluyt, and Charrière, J. von Hammer (-Purgstall), Geschichte des Osmanischen Reiches, 1827–35, iv. 622–5; M. Epstein, The English Levant Company . . . to 1640, 1908; Conyers Read, Mr. Secretary Walsingham, 1925; these all contain original material; Hammer's, Zinkeisen's, and Jorga's histories of the Ottoman empire; A. C. Wood, A history of the Levant Company, 1935; A. L. Horniker, in Journal of modern history, xiv. (1942), 289–316. I am indebted for help and information to Dr. Paul Wittek.]

E. S. de Beer.

Hardy, Sir Thomas. viii. 1241*a*, l. 28 from foot. After '1727.' insert 'On 2 June 1729, and again on 25 May 1730, he was elected master of the Trinity House (Trinity House, MS. register).'

Harington, John, first **Baron Harington of Exton.** viii. 1273*a*, l. 15. After 'Elizabeth' insert 'She died 25 May 1620 and was buried at Exton (*Private Corr. of Jane Lady Cornwallis*, p. 65).'

E. S. de B.

Harold (1022?–1066). viii. 1303*b*, ll. 27–8. For 'In the course . . . in England' read 'In November Harold was in Flanders, probably opening negotiations for the return of Edward the Aetheling who arrived in England in the following year.'

Add to list of authorities: P. Grierson's Visit of Earl Harold to Flanders in 1056, *Eng. Hist. Rev.* li. (1936) 90–7.

Harrington or **Harington, James** (1611–1677). viii. 1318–20. The following notes are taken from the 'Oceana,' edited with notes by S. B. Liljegren, Heidelberg, 1924 (no. 4 of the publications of the New Society of Letters at Lund).

1318*b*, l. 28. 'Toland gives a story that the manuscript was seized by Cromwell. . . .' Liljegren states that there are no records in support of this statement, basing his conclusion on the fact that there is nothing in the 'Journals of the House of Commons,' the 'Thurloe State Papers,' 'Whitelock's Memorials,' etc., in which the suppression of books can be traced. The only evidence for the statement seems to be a reference in the Epistle to the Reader where Harrington refers to a 'special questing' which had interfered with the printing of his book (*Oceana*, pp. xi, xii).

1319*b*, l. 4. The original edition of the 'Oceana' is a quarto (*Oceana*, p. xii). Its existence seems to be recorded for the first time in September 1656. There is an entry on the Stationers' Register for 19 Sept. 1656. Liljegren notes that the work is mentioned in the 'Gazette,' 29 Oct.–6 Nov. 1656, as a book newly published (*Oceana*, p. x).

Harrington or Harington, James (1611–1677), viii. 1318–20. *Ante*, v. l. 24*b*. For a 'special questing' read a 'spaniel questing'. ('Oceana', ed. S. B. Liljgren, intro. p. xii, text, p. 8.) *Ib.* l. 13 from foot. For 'Gazette', read 'Mercurius Politicus'. *Ib.* l. 12. from foot. For '*Oceana*, p. x' read '*Oceana*, p. xi'.

Harrington, Robert, M.D. (*fl.* 1815), viii. 1320*b*, l. 16 from foot. For '(*fl.* 1815)' read '(d. 1837)'. *Ib.*, l. 14 from foot. For 'became a member . . . before 1781', read 'fourth son of Robert Harrington (d. 1753) and Jane, daughter of Henry Hall, alderman of Carlisle, was baptised 26 August 1751 and entered Carlisle Grammar School on 9 June 1760. He was elected an honorary freeman of Carlisle on 14 January 1785 and on 28 September 1789 married Margaret Benson.' (C. R. Hudleston, 'Notes on Dr. Robert Harrington of Carlisle', *Cumb. and Westmld. Antiq. and Archaeol. Soc. Trans.*, N.S. xlvi (1947), 116–25.) *Ib.*, l. 10 from foot. For 'was still alive in 1815', read 'died there in 1837'. (Hudleston, *ubi supra.*)

Harrison, Thomas (1606–1660), regicide, ix. 41*b*. For the results of further investigations see 'The Life of Thomas Harrison,' by Sir Charles Firth (*Proceedings of the American Antiquarian Society*, 1893, Worcester, Mass.).

Ibid. For the first 20 ll. of the article read : 'Thomas Harrison was baptised 2 July 1616. His father, Richard Harrison, a butcher by trade, was four times mayor of Newcastle-under-Lyme and died in 1653. Thomas Harrison, after leaving school, became clerk to an attorney, Thomas Houlker, of Clifford's Inn.'

42*b*, l. 2. After '*Clarke Papers*' add 'i. 182, 216, 417.'

Ibid., l. 21. Add 'In the debate on the Agreement of the People, Harrison made a long and powerful speech in favour of presenting the Army's constitutional scheme to Parliament instead of seeking to impose it upon the nation ; but indicated that if he thought the right time had arrived he would not shrink from using force (*Clarke Papers*, ii. 183, 260–3).'

43*a*, l. 35. Harrison's name stood first amongst the commissioners appointed in the Act for the better propagation and preaching of the gospel in Wales, and his letters show his interest in that cause and in the spread of puritanism (Mayer, *Inedited Letters*, pp. 214, 218 ; Richards, *Puritan Movement in Wales*, pp. 79, 82, 270).

43*b*, l. 21. After 'Co-opted member' add '(Mayer, pp. 226, 235)'.

Ibid., 13 lines from the bottom, omit 'father's.'

44*a*, l. 17. Add 'In spite of the well meant attempt of Col. John Jones to effect a reconciliation between them, Harrison maintained that Cromwell had "forsaken the Lord," and "committed as sure a trespass as any mentioned in the Scriptures from Cain to Judas" (Mayer, p. 258).'

Ibid., l. 33. Add 'The Long parliament formally expelled him (30 Sept. 1659) on account of his part in its ejection in 1653.'

44*b*, l. 26. Omit the word 'the' before Cutter ; it is a surname, not the name of a trade.

Ibid., after l. 28. Insert 'Harrison married, probably about 1647, Catherine, daughter of Ralph Harrison, a woollen-draper in Watling Street, London, who was Colonel of the "Yellow Regiment" of the London trained bands in 1647, and was a strong Independent. By Catherine Harrison he had three sons ; all died in their infancy, and their deaths are recorded in the register of St. Anne's, Blackfriars. It seems clear that he left no living children. None are mentioned in his last words to his wife, in his wife's will, or in the wills of her father, who died in 1656, or in her own will. Catherine Harrison married a second husband, Thomas Legh, and died in 1700, leaving no children by this second marriage. Harrison's own silence and the evidence of wills and registers together conclusively prove that he left no children. The tradition that certain American families are descended from him is baseless (Firth in *Proceedings of the Amer. Antiquarian Soc.*, 1893).'

Add to the bibliography at the end : 'The 'Life of Thomas Harrison' in *Proceedings of the American Antiquarian Society*, 1893, reprints 15 of Harrison's letters. Eight others, addressed to Colonel John Jones, are printed in *Inedited Letters of Cromwell, Col. Jones . . . and other regicides*, by Joseph Mayer in the *Transactions of the Historical Society of Lancashire and Cheshire*, New Series, i. 1861. A life of Harrison by C. H. Simpkinson was published in 1905.'

Omit the mention of the Trial of Charles I etc. in Murray's Family Library.

Hart, Charles (*d.* 1683). ix. 58*b*, 19 ll. from foot. After 'died of stone' insert '18 Aug. 1683.' At end of article add 'The date of his death is taken from a printed elegy (B.M., Luttrell, i. 62) which mentions several of his principal parts.'

E. S. de B.

Hartlib, Samuel (d. 1670 ?). ix. 73*a*, ll. 8–14. For 'But Andrew Marvell, etc.,' read 'Samuel Hartlib the elder died 10 March 1661/2 and was buried in St. Martin's in the Fields, 12 March (G. H. Turnbull, *Samuel Hartlib*, 1920, p. 72).' The Andrew Marvell letter is printed in full in the *Catalogue of the Alfred Morrison Collection*, ed. A. W. Thibaudeau, 1st ser., iv. 162–3. From internal evidence it may be dated March or April 1675.

Hastings, Lady Elizabeth. ix. 114*a*, ll. 21–3. After 'property' insert ', and her father had amassed a fortune as a factor in the East India company (M. G. Jones, "Lady Elizabeth Hastings," *Church Quarterly Review*, cxxix. 71)'; after 'Hastings,' insert 'the children of her father's second marriage to Frances, widow of Thomas Needham, Viscount Kilmorey (*ibid.* p. 75),'; after 'her' insert ', after the re-marriage of their mother in 1706 to the Chevalier Michael Ligondez, a French prisoner of war (*ibid.*),'

Ibid. l. 23 from foot. After 'such as' insert 'Sir John Philipps, supporter of the Anglican Society for Promoting Christian Knowledge (*ibid.* p. 73),'

Ibid. l. 7 from foot. After 'activity,' insert 'becoming patroness of the Holy Club founded by him at Oxford early in the eighteenth century (*ibid.* p. 79),'

Hastings, George (1488?–1545). ix. 123, l. 10. For 'Mary, grand-daughter of Thomas, 3rd Baron Hungerford' read 'Mary, daughter of Sir Thomas Hungerford and grand-daughter of Robert, 3rd Baron Hungerford (*Complete Peerage*, vi. 622).'

Hastings, Henry, Lord Loughborough (*d.* 1667). ix. 129*b*. Add to the list of authorities that a number of unprinted letters of Hastings are to be found in the Rupert correspondence in the British Museum (*Add. MSS.* 18980–2); and amongst the transcripts of that correspondence in the Bodleian (*Summary Catalogue*, No. 35587–9).

Hastings, Sir Hugh. ix. 129*b*, l. 9 from foot. After 'plates).' insert 'A fifteenth-century description of this brass by Sir Edward Hastings [q.v.], printed in the "Antiquaries Journal" xix. 422–4, supplies details since lost by mutilation'

Hawkwood, Sir John de. ix. 236*a*. Copies (1411) of two letters from him written at Florence, 8 Nov. and 20 Feb. 1393–4 (supposed to be the earliest private letters in English extant), have been found on the Plea and Memoranda Rolls of the Mayor's Court of the City of London by Mr. A. H. Thomas, Clerk of the Records. They are printed in his 'Notes on the Leadenhall, 1195–1488,' in the *London Topographical Record* (1923), xiii. 11, with an indenture between Hawkwood's squire, John Sampson, and his friend Thomas Coggeshale, embodying his directions about the disposal of some property (including the Leadenhall), 'yif he deye before his comyng hom.' The whole group of documents, technically in the nature of instructions to trustees, are practically his nuncupative will as regards his property in England.

Hawkwood, Sir John de. ix. 237*a*, l. 12. For 'December' read 'November'

Ibid. 237*b*, l. 2. For '25th.' read '22nd.'

Ibid. 238*a*, l. 28. For 'the autumn' read 'September'

Ibid. 239*b*, l. 19. After 'Florence,' insert 'including the discovery of a dangerous conspiracy of emigrants against the city, which he revealed to the council of Florence in November, 1379,'

Ibid. l. 29. After 'time.' insert 'On 10 Aug. 1381 Hawkwood sold for 60,000 florins his lands in the Romagna, which because of his close connexion with Florence were now too distant for him.'

Ibid. 240*b*, l. 2. After 'Florence' insert ', which conferred on him the honorary freedom of the city on 8 Apr. 1391.'

Ibid. 241*a*, l. 7. For 'early in' read 'at Genoa on 26 Jan.'

Ibid. l. 12 from foot. After 'embarrassment.' insert 'In Nov. 1390 he had to be released from taxation debts by the Florentine authorities.'

Ibid. 241*b*, l. 5. After 'sold' insert 'in March 1394, only five days'

Ibid. l. 11 from foot. After 'naturalised' insert 'and dubbed knight'

Ibid. 242*b*, l. 19. Add to list of authorities: *History*, xiii. 308–21.

Haxey, Thomas. ix. 249. Appointed Keeper of the Rolls of the Common Bench, 18 June, 1387 (*Cal. Pat. Rolls*, 1385–9, 314); Keeper of the writs of the Common Bench, 30 May, 1392 (*Cal. Close Rolls*, 1389–92, 467): and Chief Clerk of the Common Bench, 16 Feb., 1392 (*ib.* 551). See *Calendars of Patent Rolls*, 1385–9, and *Close Rolls*, 1389–92, *passim*, for further details regarding Haxey's ecclesiastical preferments, etc.

Hay, James, first Earl of Carlisle. ix. 266*b*, l. 7 from foot. For 'and Piedmont' read 'Piedmont, and Venice (instructions dated 20 March 1627–8, B.M., Harl. MS. 1584, ff. 173–4; dispatches in P.R.O., foreign state papers, France, Savoy, and Venice).' E. S. de B.

Hay, Sir John, Lord Barra. ix. 268*a*, ll. 18 and 16 from foot. For 'Barra' read 'Baro' (now part of Garvald parish, Haddingtonshire).

Ibid. ll. 14–2 from foot. For 'employed . . . ordinary lord' read 'born *c.* 1578, graduated as master of arts at Edinburgh in 1594, and then spent about six years in England. In 1602 he was appointed clerk depute to the common clerk of Edinburgh and after the accession of James VI to the English throne was frequently sent by the town on missions to him. In 1617 he made a speech of welcome in Latin to the king on behalf of the town and in 1618 became clerk conjunct. He was knighted at Oatlands on 29 July 1632 and on 12 Dec., in succession to Sir John Hamilton of Magdalens, was appointed clerk register, an office carrying with it that of an extraordinary lord of session; he was also appointed a privy councillor on that day. On 7 Jan. 1634 he succeeded his second cousin, Sir Robert Spottiswood [q.v.], as an ordinary lord of session. He was a staunch supporter of prelacy.'

Ibid. 268*b*, l. 6. For 'Shortly afterwards' read 'In March 1639'.

Ibid. ll. 9–10. For 'and resigned all his offices' read 'and on 12 July 1641 was forced to resign all his offices'.

Ibid. l. 28 from foot. For 'Duddingstone' read 'Duddingston'.

Ibid. l. 27 from foot. After '1654' add 'Hay married first, in 1602, Marion, daughter of John Johnston, burgess of Edinburgh; secondly, in 1622, Rebecca, daughter of Alexander Thomson of Duddingston.'

To list of authorities add: John A. Inglis, Sir John Hay 'The Incendiary' 1578–1654, 1937.

Hay, Lucy, Countess of Carlisle. ix. 273*a*, 5 ll. from bottom. References to the political intrigues of Lady Carlisle in 1646–8 may be found in the *Montereul Correspondence*, ed. by J. G. Fotheringham (Scot. Hist. Soc., 1898), i. 75, 117, 430. During her imprisonment in 1649–50 she continued still to correspond in cypher about political affairs with her brother, Lord Percy (*Hist. MSS. Comm., Portland MSS.*, i. 585).

Ibid., p. 274*b*. Add to the authorities, De Fonblanque, *Annals of the House of Percy* (1887), ii. 343–5 (on her marriage), and ii. 397–405 (biography).

Haydock, Roger. ix. 281*b*, ll. 15–6. After 'born at' insert 'Bogburn Hall (T. C. Porteus, "Roger Haydock of Coppull," *Trans. Lancs. and Cheshire Antiq. Soc.* lii. 1),'; for 'in May 1644' read 'on 1 May 1643, and was baptized at Standish Parish Church the following day (*ibid.* p. 2)'

Ibid. l. 20. For 'About 1666' read 'In 1667 (*ibid.*)'

Ibid. l. 33. For 'about this time' read 'from 1669 (*Transactions*, p. 3)'

Ibid. l. 4 from foot. After '[q.v.]' insert 'In April 1677 the mayor of Lancaster reported that he had fined him 20*l.* for preaching in the previous month at a house in Lancaster called the Friars (*ibid.* p. 5).'; after 'In' insert 'May (*ibid.* p. 6)'

Ibid. 282*a*, ll. 1–2. For 'Lowe, a quakeress, and afterwards' read ', daughter of Robert Lowe gentleman and Eleanor Gerard, of Crewood Hall, Crowton; educated "in the pomps and vain fashions of the world," she became a quakeress about 1671 and made long tours through England and Wales as a preacher. After their marriage at Newton near Middlewich, in the Friends' Public Meeting Place, they (*ibid.* pp. 3–8)'

Ibid. l. 29. After 'disputes.' add 'He left a son, Robert, born at Penketh in 1687, who married Rebecca Griffith on 23 Aug. 1709, and emigrated to America, where their descendants are still living (*ibid.* pp. 14–6).'

Head, Richard. ix. 328*a*, l. 1. For 'Francis' read 'Franck.'

Ibid. l. 2. Delete '(Bodl.).' There is a

copy in the British Museum also. Insert 'This piece is largely an imitation and expansion of parts of "Wheresoever you see mee, Trust unto your selfe," by Thomas Powell (1572 ?–1635 ?) [q.v.] ; the opening passage is imitated from Powell's "Tom of All Trades,"'

Ibid. ll. 4–5. For '"Western . . . Brazile"' read '"The Western Wonder : or, O Brazeel."'

Ibid. l. 12. Delete '(Bodleian)'. There is a copy in the British Museum also. Insert '(postscript signed "Samuel Swiftnicks").'

Hedges, Sir Charles. ix. 362*b*, l. 17. After 'in 1686' add 'or more probably 1687 (*Archaeologia Cantiana*, xx. (1900), 170)'.

Hedges, Sir Charles. ix. 362*b*, 10 ll. from foot. After 'judge until 29 Dec. 1701.' insert 'two civilians, Dr. George Oxenden, Dean of the Arches, and Dr. George Bramston, Master of Trinity Hall, officiating for him (*Mariner's Mirror*, xiii. 344).'

Hely-Hutchinson, John. ix. 378*a*, l. 22 from foot. For '1785' read 'October 1783' (G.E.C., *Complete Peerage*, iv. 400).

Henchman, Humphrey (1669–1739). ix. 390*a*, l. 10. After 'in one of the courts there' insert 'On 9 April 1714 he was appointed judge of the admiralty court ; the appointment, however, was of doubtful authority and, by October, he was superseded as judge by Sir Henry Newton [q.v.] (*Mariner's Mirror*, xiii. 344–5).'

Hengham or Hingham, Ralph de. ix. 410*b*, ll. 15–12 from foot. Delete 'In 1270 he . . . per annum.' There is no evidence for this statement. For 'In November 1272 . . . common pleas.' read 'In Hilary term 1273 he became a justice of common pleas, a position which he held until Trinity term 1274 (feet of fines, *passim*).'

Ibid. ll. 11–10 from foot. For '1273, or soon afterwards,' read '1274', and for 'returned to' read 'was appointed chief justice of'.

Ibid. 411*a*, ll. 24–22 from foot. Delete 'He was degraded . . . same court.'

Henrietta Maria. ix. 434*b*, l. 7. For 'Bourbon' read 'Bourbon l'Archambault.'

Ibid. ll. 10–12. For 'When she was . . . St. Germains' read 'She was sufficiently recovered to leave in October and arrived in Paris on 5 Nov., N.S. ; she was given an apartment in the Louvre and the new château at St. Germain (O. Lefèvre d'Ormesson, *Journal*, ed. Chéruel, 1860, i. 224 ; Baillon, p. 226 ; G. Houdard, *Les châteaux royaux de Saint-Germain-en-Laye*, ii. 183).'

Ibid. 436*b*. Add to list of authorities : 'Charles, comte de Baillon, Henriette-Marie de France, reine d'Angleterre, 1877, which includes unpublished letters ; Lettres de Henriette-Marie . . . à sa sœur Christine duchesse de Savoie, ed. H. Ferrero, 1881.'

Henry II. ix. 452*b*, l. 20 from foot. Delete 'for the next four years'

Ibid. l. 16 from foot. For 'In 1147' read 'By 1144'

Ibid. l. 15 from foot. For 'had now conquered' read 'was engaged in the conquest of'. After 'Normandy.' insert 'Early in 1147 Henry attempted to invade England, but arriving with inadequate preparations he was easily repulsed.'

Add to list of authorities : A. L. Poole's Henry Plantagenet's Early Visits to England, *Eng. Hist. Rev.* xlvii. (1932), 447–52.

Henry II. ix. 463*b*, l. 23 from foot. Add to list of authorities : Charles Johnson's The Reconciliation of Henry II with the Papacy. A Missing Document (*Eng. Hist. Rev.* lii. 465–7).

Henry VI. ix. 507*a*, l. 26. Delete 'Henry V's last directions were ignored,' and add 'John, duke of Bedford, claimed that the government of the realm had fallen to him as Henry V's eldest brother (Letter from him, 26 Oct. 1422, printed by R. R. Sharpe, *London and the Kingdom*, iii. 367–8).'

Henry, duke of Gloucester (1639–1660). ix. 559*b*, l. 13. For '8 July 1639' read '8 July 1640.' *Cal. St. Pap. Dom. 1640*, p. 484.

Henry of Lancaster, first Duke of Lancaster (1299 ?–1361). ix. 556*b*, l. 31. For 'He died . . . on 13 May, 1361' read 'He died . . . on 23 March, 1361' (*Records of the Borough of Leicester*, ed. Mary Bateson, ii. 124)

Henry of Lancaster, first Duke of Lancaster. ix. 557*a*, l. 5. After 'Greater.' insert 'He assisted the recently united

Cambridge guilds of Corpus Christi and the Blessed Virgin Mary to obtain a charter for their new college, and was long regarded as the founder of Corpus Christi college (*Masters' Hist. of Corpus Christi Coll., Camb.*, ed. J. Lamb., pp. 25–7).'

Henshaw, Nathaniel, M.D. ix. 585*a*, l. 21. For '(*d.* 1673)' read '(1628–1673).'

Ibid. l. 25. 'After London' insert 'was baptized at Kensington, 31 July 1628, and matriculated at Padua on 23 Nov. 1649 (J. A. Andrich, *De natione anglica et scotica iuristarum universitatis Patavinae*, p. 148, as "Henhacuc"; *cf.* H. R. F. Brown, *Inglesi e Scozzesi all' università di Padova*, p. 157). He'

Ibid. ll. 31–2. For 'he was elected . . . Append. iv' read 'he was nominated an original fellow of the Royal Society (*Record of the Royal Society*, 3rd ed., pp. 16, 17).'

Add to list of authorities: 'Parish register of Kensington (Harleian Soc. Registers, vol. xvi); R. W. Innes Smith, English-speaking students of medicine at the university of Leyden.'

Henshaw, Thomas. ix. 585*b*, l. 10. After 'Middle Temple' insert 'in 1638 (*Middle Temple Records, Minutes*, ed. C. H. Hopwood, ii. 869).'

Ibid. ll. 17–9. For 'and afterwards . . . major' read 'where he served in the Prince of Orange's army for one campaign.' The authority is Wood as cited in the article; see note to ll. 24–30 below.

Ibid. ll. 20–1. For 'Passing thence . . . Venice, till' read 'From there he went to Italy, joining John Evelyn [q.v.] at Pisa in October 1644 and accompanying him to Rome and Naples; after a short separation in the summer of 1645 he rejoined Evelyn at Venice and spent the winter with him at Padua, where he matriculated on 22 Nov. 1645 N.S. (Andrich, *De natione anglica et scotica iuristarum universitatis Patavinae*, p. 146, as "Honshau"; *cf.* Brown, *Inglesi e Scozzesi all' università di Padova*, p. 154). He remained abroad until'

Ibid. ll. 24–30. Delete 'In 1654 . . . murtherer.' As Major Thomas Henshaw mentions a half-brother John Wiseman (*Cal. Clarendon S.P.*, ii. 388) it seems probable that he was the son of Rebecca Henshaw, widow, who married John Wiseman in 1627 (*Parish Register of Kensington*, Harleian Soc., p. 69). He can scarcely be identified with the subject of this article.

Ibid. ll. 31–0 from foot. For 'On his return . . . the bar' read 'Henshaw was called to the bar on 24 Nov. 1654 (*Middle Temple Records*, iii. 1070).'

Ibid. ll. 28–25 from foot. For 'After the Restoration . . . French tongue and' read 'On 26 Dec. 1661 he was appointed Secretary for the French tongue (*Cal. State Papers, Dom.*, 1661-2, p. 191). He was also a'

Ibid. ll. 24–22 from foot. For 'He was chosen . . . in 1663' read 'He had attended the Gresham College scientific meetings and was placed on the council of the Royal Society on its incorporation in 1662 (*Record of the Royal Society*, 3rd ed., pp. 6, 51).'

Ibid. l. 9 from foot. After '1700' insert 'In 1657 he married Anne, daughter of Robert Kipping of Tudeley, Kent, and widow of James Darell (P. Le Neve, *Pedigrees of the knights*, p. 240; *Registers of St. Paul's, Covent Garden* (Harleian Soc.), p. 17; *Parish Register of Kensington*, p. 76).'

Ibid. 586*a*. Add to list of authorities: Evelyn's Diary.

Herbert, Arthur, Earl of Torrington. ix. 621*b*, ll. 1–4. Delete 'that the Dutch contingent . . . stipulated strength;'

Ibid. 622*a*, ll. 10–9 from foot. For 'Earl' read 'Earls'; for 'the other lords of the admiralty' read 'Macclesfield, Sir Robert Howard, Sir Henry Goodrick, and Sir Thomas Lee (B.M. Add. MS. 29593, fos. 3–5; *Finch MSS.*, Hist. MSS. Comm., ii. 365; *Cal. S.P. Dom.* 1690–1, pp. 62–3)'

Ibid. l. 2 from foot. After '1691).' insert 'The admiralty commissioners demanded a copy of the final report a week later (P.R.O. Admiralty minutes, 27 July).'

Add to list of authorities: J. C. M. Warnsinck's De Vloot van den Koning-Stadhouder, 1689–90.

Herbert, Henry, Baron Herbert of Cherbury. ix. 644*b*, l. 2 from foot. For '1707' read '1708 (*Return of M.P.'s*, ii. 15).'

Ibid. 645*a*, l. 1. For '1707–8' read '1708–9' (Luttrell, vi. 405–6, misread by the author of the article).

Ibid. l. 2. For '1707–8' read '1708–9' (*cf.* the same article, 644*b*, l. 30).

Herbert, Sir Robert George Wyndham. 2nd Suppl. ii. 253*a*, ll. 20–19 from foot.

For 'only' read 'second' (*Notes and Queries*, clviii. 240).

Herring, Thomas. ix. 710-1. A copy of 'Letters from . . . Dr. Thomas Herring to William Duncombe,' 12mo., 1777, which belonged to W. D. Macray, is the source of the following notes:

P. 711*a*, l. 25 from foot. After 'kingdom' add '(letters between him and lord chancellor Hardwicke, written during the rebellion, have been printed by Dr. R. Garnett, *Eng. Hist. Rev.*, xix. 531-50, 719-42).'

Ibid. l. 7 from foot. After 'ff. 44–86)' add 'Birch's "Life of Archbishop Tillotson" is dedicated to Herring.'

Ibid. l. 4 from foot. After '(App. p. 322)' add 'Two discreditable letters from Herring to the dean of Canterbury in 1752 and 1753, respecting an application from the king of Sardinia for removal of the bones of Archbishop Anselm, exhibiting ignorance and disregard of his great predecessor, and narrow prejudice, are printed by the commission (*Various Collections*, i. 226-7).'

Ibid. 711*b*, l. 11. After 'published' add '(for his attitude towards nonconformist comprehension *see* CHANDLER, SAMUEL).'

Hesilrige, Sir Arthur. ix. 744*b*, l. 39. After 'of consequence and trust (*Commons' Journals*, v. 239)' read 'About the same time he was named colonel of a regiment of foot, lately Robert Lilburne's, which he apparently retained until his quarrel with the army leaders in 1653.'

Ibid., 746*a*, l. 26. For 'He was also given . . . Charles Howard's' read 'He was restored to the command of his old regiment, lately Charles Howard's, in July, 1659 (*Commons' Journals*, vii. 710, 713).'

Ibid., 746*b*., l. 10 from foot. After 'Old Parliamentary History . . . 451' add '*Clarke Papers*, iv. 302–3, where Monck's letter to the Speaker on his behalf is printed.'

Ibid., l. 2 from foot. For 'who mentions a portrait' read 'His portrait is in the possession of his descendant Sir Arthur Hazlerigg at Noseley Hall.' G. D.

Hewlett, Maurice Henry, vol. 1922–30, p. 417*b*, l. 23. For '1900' read '10 April 1901'.

Heywood, Thomas (*d.* 1650 ?). ix. 789*b*, l. 1. For '1650' read '1641.'

790*b*, l. 28. After '(in the *Satire against Separatists*; cf. *ib.* p. vi)' add 'Heywood was buried at St. James's, Clerkenwell, on 16 Aug. 1641 (*Reg.* xvii. 248: Harl. Soc.).'

Heytesbury, Baron, William A'Court. ix. 779*a*, ll. 10–9 from foot. For 'Aylesbury' read 'Heytesbury' (*Return of M.P.s*, ii. 170, 183, 196, 236).

This appearance of a peer under his title instead of his family name is a solecism in the D.N.B. His name was obviously missed in drawing up the list for vol. i., and the normal procedure would have been to postpone the article to the 1st supplement where scores of similar omissions are remedied. The error has been rectified in the 'Concise D.N.B.'

Hicks, Sir Michael. (1543–1612). ix. 810*a*. Returned for Truro Borough, 17 November 1584 (*Return of Members of Parliament*, i. 413). Returned for Shaftesbury Borough (Dorset), 25 October 1588 (*ibid.*, p. 423): for Gatton Borough (Surrey), September 1597 (*ibid.*, p. 435): for Horsham Borough (Sussex), 12 March 1603–4 (*ibid.*, p. 446).

Higgons, Sir Thomas. Above, ii. 95*b*, l. 13 from foot. For '1674' read '1673.'

Ibid. ll. 12-11 from foot. For 'for about . . . 556' read 'until 1679 (credentials and letter of revocation in P.R.O., S.P. civ. 88, 186.' J. F. C.

Higgons, Sir Thomas. ix. 826*b*, ll. 18–20. For 'About four years afterwards he went as envoy to Vienna, where he continued for three years' read 'In 1674 he went as Envoy Extraordinary to Venice, and remained there for about three years (*Cal. State Papers Dom.* 1673, pp. 543, 556. Letters from Higgons, from Venice, to Secretary Henry Coventry, are preserved in the B.M. Add. MSS. 32094, 32095; they extend from Nov. 1674 to April 1677; see also *Hist. MSS. Comm.* 4th Report, App. p. 248).'

Hill, Abraham. ix. 840*b*, l. 2 from foot. For '30 Nov.' read 'April (BULLETIN, xv. 87)'; after '1665.' insert 'He was secretary to the society, 1673–5 (*ibid.*).'

Ibid. bottom line. After 're-elected' insert 'treasurer'

Hill, Roger. ix. 860*b*, ll. 30–32. For 'in 1645 . . . (*Parl. Hist.* ii. 608).' read 'to parliament for Bridport on 25 Oct.

1640 (*Return of M.P.s*, i. 488; B.M. *Harl. MS.* 162, fos. 304*b*, 305*b*).'

Hill, William. ix. 878*a*, l. 14. After 'Mr. Burges' insert '[*see* BURGESS, JOHN].'

Hill, William Noel-, third Baron Berwick. ix. 878*a*, ll. 21–20 from foot. For 'He was ambassador . . . 1833' read 'He was envoy extraordinary and minister plenipotentiary to the king of Sardinia from 1807 to 1824, and to the king of the Two Sicilies from 1824 to 1832' (credentials and letters of recall. P.R.O., F.O. 95/500, 677, 680).

Hill, Wills, first Marquis of Downshire. ix. 879*b*, l. 12. For 'northern' read 'southern' (M. A. Thomson, *Secretaries of State*, p. 182).

Hirst, Thomas Archer. Suppl. 852*a*, l. 9. For 'professor of physics' read 'professor of mathematical physics' (*University College, London. Proceedings at the Annual General Meeting . . . 28th February* 1866, p. 9).

Ibid. l. 11. For '1866' read '1867.'

ll. 12–3. For 'succeeded . . . mathematics' read 'became professor of pure and applied mathematics, and, in 1868, of pure mathematics only' (*Ibid. 26th February* 1868, p. 10; *24th February* 1869, p. 11).

Hoby, Sir Thomas. ix. 949*b*, ll. 17–23. For 'He subsequently . . . Bennet, p. 240)' read 'He went abroad in August 1547, staying in the house of Martin Bucer [q.v.] at Strassburg from October until July 1548. After visiting his brother, Sir Philip [q.v.], at Augsburg he went to Padua, and stayed there and in Venice until August 1549. He then went south, reaching Naples in January 1550, and going on through Calabria to Sicily. He rejoined his brother at Augsburg in August and returned with him to England in November. In January 1551 he entered the service of William Parr, marquis of Northampton [q.v.], accompanying him on his mission to France in the summer. In June 1552 he went to Paris to study, staying there until April 1553, when he joined his brother at Brussels. They returned to England in August. In May 1554 they went to Italy, travelling by Augsburg; they remained in Padua and the neighbourhood, in company with Sir John Cheke, Sir Thomas Wroth, and other fugitives, from August until July 1555. They again crossed the Alps to Augsburg, and Hoby reached England in November, on the way visiting Frankfort. He spent the following years in England, largely at Bisham, to which he succeeded on his brother's death.'

Ibid. l. 27. After 'p. 32' add 'cf. *Bulletin, I.H.R.*, v. 20.'

Ibid. l. 4 from foot. For '[1549]' read '[1548 ?].' Hoby's dedicatory letter to his brother, Sir Philip, is dated 1 February, Strassburg, where he was in that month in 1547/8, but not in 1548/9.

Ibid. last line. After 'and 1603)' add 'The third book was translated at Lady Northampton's request in 1552, the rest not until some years afterwards. The work is dedicated to Lord Henry Hastings, later third earl of Huntingdon [q.v.].'

Ibid. 950*a*, l. 6. For '1900' read '1902.' Other reprints, 1900, and in 'Everyman's Library' (*c.* 1927).

Hoby also translated F. Negri's tragedy 'Libero arbitrio' and dedicated it to Northampton. It does not appear to have been printed; the work was also translated by Henry Cheke [q.v.].

Hoby wrote an account of his travels, with notes of his later life, to 1546, now B.M. Egerton MS. 2148; it has been edited by Mr. Edgar Powell (R. Hist. Soc., *Camden Miscellany*, vol. x, 1902).

Ibid. l. 20 from foot. Delete 'Her portrait . . . Holbein.' Holbein died in 1543.

Hoccleve, or Occleve, Thomas (1370?–1450?) ix. 950*a*, l. 12 from foot. For '(1370?–1450?)' read '(*c.*1369–*c.*1426)'. (*Works*, ed. F. J. Furnivall (1892), i. p. viii: *Speculum*, xii. 76–81.)

Ibid., l. 11 from foot. For 'twenty-four' read 'thirty-five'. (Issue rolls, *passim.*)

Ibid., l. 10 from foot. For 'only' read 'mainly'. p. 950*b*, l. 12. After 'leaf 42' add 'now Huntington Library MS. 111'.

Ibid., l. 13. After 'annuity of' add 'ten pounds, afterwards increased to'.

Ibid., l. 16. After '30–4' add ': *Cal. Pat. Rolls, 1399–1401*, p. 61; *1408–13*, p. 75)'.

Ibid., l. 24. After '152).' add 'He probably died about 1426, in which year the exchequer stopped paying his annuity. No reference to him after this date has been found.'

Ibid., ll. 29–32. For 'His last . . . p. 29 n.)' read 'About 1414 he wrote a "Balade to the Duke of York".' (*Speculum*, xii. 77–9.)

Ibid., l. 13 from foot. Before 'Phillipps' insert 'Huntington Library MS. 111, formerly the'

p. 951*a*, l. 4. After 'poems' add '(now Huntington Library MS. 744)'.

Ibid., l. 11. For '(after 1422)' read '(1420–2)'. (*Works, ut sup.*)

Ibid., l. 6 from foot. For 'Two' read 'Three'.

Ibid., l. 4 from foot. For '(1892–7)' read '(1892–1925)'.

Ibid., ll. 4–2 from foot. Delete 'The remaining . . . MS'.

To list of authorities add: 'H. C. Schulz, 'Thomas Hoccleve, Scribe', *Speculum*, xii. (1937), 71–81.'

Holgate or Holdegate, Robert. ix. 1022*b*, last line. After 'became' insert 'the last'

Ibid. 1023*a*, ll. 1–2. After 'Sempringham' insert 'in 1534'; after 'Yorkshire' insert 'in 1536'

Ibid. l. 6. For 'Henry VIII' read 'Thomas Cromwell (R. Graham, *S. Gilbert of Sempringham*, p. 174)'

Ibid. l. 26. For 'July' read 'June (R. R. Reid, *King's Council in the North*, pp. 153, 487)'

Ibid. ll. 32–3. After 'surrender' insert 'of Sempringham, 18 Sept. 1538 and'; for '1540' read '1539 (R. Graham, *op. cit.* p. 195)'

Ibid. 1023*b*, ll. 7–9. After 'arithmetic.' insert 'The masters might also be laymen and marry (V.C.H. *Yorks.* i. 474–5). In 1547 and 1548 he was head of the chantry commissioners for Yorkshire (Surtees Soc. xci. 1; xcii. 371, 427, 519).'; for 'June 1549' read 'Jan. 1550'; after 'Wentworth' insert 'of Elmsdale'

Ibid. 1024*a*, l. 14. For 'He' read 'In December he'

Add to list of authorities: A. G. Dickens's The Marriage and Character of Archbishop Holgate (*Eng. Hist. Rev.* lii. 428–42); Alcuin Club Collections, xv. 310–21.

Hollar, Wenceslaus. ix. 1054*b*, l. 21. For '1635' read '1636'.

Ibid. l. 22. After 'Prague' insert 'A letter from Arundel dated Nuremberg, 27 May 1636, N.S., suggests that Hollar had only recently entered his service (Mary F. S. Hervey, *Life of Thomas Howard, Earl of Arundel*, p. 366).' For 'He' read 'Arundel,' and for 'it' read 'the engraving'.

E. S. de B.

Holles, Denzil. ix. 1056*a*. Holles appears to have made a very abject apology and petition for pardon about 1630, which is amongst the papers of Secretary Coke (*MSS. of Earl Cowper*, i. 422), but it is not clear whether it refers to his conduct in Parliament or some later offence.

Ibid., p. 1057*a*, 17 ll. from bottom. His part in the military operations against the Marquis of Hertford in 1642 is shown in *Hist. MSS. Comm.*, 10th Rept., vi. 147.

Ibid., p. 1059*a*, l. 3. His embassy to France is elucidated by the letters from Charles II to his sister, printed in Cartwright's *Madame: Memoirs of Henrietta Duchess of Orleans.* Charles on the whole approved of the ambassador's tenacity (*cf.* pp. 151–4, 161, 174), while the Duchess thought him too quarrelsome.

Holles, Gervase. ix. 1061*a*, l. 9. For '1606' read '1607.'

Ibid. l. 11. For '9 March 1606' read '9 March 1606/7' (Collins, *Hist. Collections of the noble families of Cavendish, Holles*, etc., p. 71).

A. C. W.

Holles, Gervase. ix. 1062*a*. Add to list of authorities: Gervase Holles' Memorials of the Holles Family, 1496–1656, ed. A. C. Wood (Camden 3rd series, lv); A. C. Wood's The Holles Family, *Trans. Royal Hist. Soc.* (fourth series), xix. 145–65. [See also Bulletin, xi. 197.]

Holmes, Abraham. ix. 1082*a*. Add at beginning: 'Probably a Northcountryman, perhaps from Durham, who served as a lieutenant in Robert Lilburne's regiment of arquebusiers in Ferdinando, Lord Fairfax's army in Yorkshire (P.R.O., Commonwealth Exch. Papers, 138). In 1645 or 1646 he received a captaincy in Lilburne's regiment of foot [lately Weldon's] (Sprigge, *Anglia Rediviva*, p. 330), and was an agitator in 1647 (*Clarke Papers*, i. 161). When Monck's regiment was formed in 1650 he was given the majority in it. In 1659 he was named lieutenant-colonel of Roger Saurey's regiment, but forfeited his commission by adhering to the English army leaders against Monck and the parliament.'

G. D.

Home, Robert. ix. 1133*b*. ll. 1–4. For 'In 1877 . . . Bulgaria' substitute 'He was appointed British Commissioner for the delimitation of the frontier of the principality of Bulgaria, under Article 2 of the Treaty of Berlin, on 10 September 1878 (*F. O. List* 1879).'

Ibid., l. 4. For 'all but completed' read

'hardly commenced.' The work of delimitation in the northern section was not completed until November 1879 (*Parl. Papers*, lxxx. 1880, Turkey No. 2, 1880, Capt. Sale to Salisbury, 13 November 1879, No. 336); work on the Bulgaro-Roumelian frontier was not commenced until three months after Home's death (*ibid.* General Hamley to Salisbury, 17 April 1879, No. 50).

To the bibliography add *F. O. List*, 1879, and *Parl. Papers*, lxxx. 1880, Turkey No. 2, 1880.

Hook, William (1600-1677), ix. 1173*b*. Add to sources: Albert Matthews, 'Mastership of the Savoy, 1658–9', *N. & Q.*, 10th ser., ix. 421–2.

Hooke, Robert. ix. 1181*a*, l. 13. For 'believed to exist' read 'preserved.'

Ibid. l. 14. For '(*Notes and Queries* . . . 429)' read '(*Classified Papers*, xx.).'

Hooke, Robert. ix. 1181*a*, l. 13 from foot. Add to list of authorities: E. G. R. Taylor's Geographical ideas of Robert Hooke (*Geographical Journal*, lxxxix. 525–38). [See also BULLETIN, ix. 61.]

Hooker, Richard. ix. 1184*a*, 24 ll. from foot. Hooker's marriage is recorded in the registers of St. Faith's-under-St. Paul's, now at St. Augustine's, Old Change, as follows: '1587 (=1587/8) Richard Hookar and Johan Churchman were married the xiiith daie of February.' The records of the baptism of four or five of their children are contained in the same registers.

G. C. M. S.

Hooker, Richard (1554?–1600), ix. 1185*a*, l. 33. For 'died . . . husband', read 'married Edward Nethersole of Canterbury on 18 March 1600'. *Ib.*, l. 21 from foot. Delete 'Jone . . . 1600'. (*N. & Q.*, 9th ser., viii. 522–3.)

Hope, Sir James. ix. 1209*b*, l. 5 from foot. For 'seventh' read 'sixth (G.E.C., *Complete Peerage*, viii. 482)'

Hopkirk, Thomas. ix. 1235. Fuller and more reliable information about Hopkirk is collected in Natural History Society of Glasgow, 'Proceedings and Transactions,' new ser., i (1883–6). 196–259. Hopkirk was born in 1785 and died in 1841; honorary LL.D. of Glasgow, 1835; and was author of other works besides those listed in the article.

Hoppner, John. (1758–1810). ix. 1236*a*. For reference to his family, and a detailed account of one son, Richard Belgrave Hoppner, see *Eng. Hist. Rev.* xxxix. 373.

Hopton, Ralph, Lord. ix. 1241*a*. Hopton's own narratives of the War in the West, referred to by their numbers in the Clarendon MSS., have since been edited by C. E. Chadwyck Healey for the Somerset Record Society in 1902, under the title of *Bellum Civile*. Letters of Hopton are amongst the *Carte MSS.* (xxvi. 650; ccxiii. 9, 10).

Horne, Robert. ix. 1253*b*, ll. 26–7. For 'on the deprivation of Dean Robertson' read 'in place of Dean Hugh Whitehead (Le Neve, *Fasti Ecclesiae Anglicanæ*, iii. 298)'

Ibid. 1254*b*, l. 7. After '1559)' insert ', Dean Thomas Robertson, Mary's nominee, being deprived (Le Neve, iii. 299)'

Horner, Leonard. ix. 1265*b*, last l. to 1266*a*, l. 1. For '1817' read '1815,' and delete 'after accompanying . . . Italy.'

Ibid. 1266*a*, l. 3. Insert 'During the winter of 1816–17 he accompanied his brother Francis to Italy' (*Memoir of Leonard Horner*, . . . Edited by his daughter Katharine M. Lyell, i. 68).

Ibid. ll. 17–8. Delete 'to assist . . . year.'

Ibid. ll. 19–20. Delete 'at its opening,' and 'latter' (*Letter to the Council of the University of London*, pp. 41–6).

Ibid. 1266*b*. Add to authorities: Memoir of Leonard Horner, F.R.S., F.G.S., consisting of Letters to his Family and some of his Friends. Edited by his daughter Katharine M. Lyell. 2 vols. Privately printed. London, Women's Printing Society, Limited, . . . 1890; Statements respecting the University of London, prepared, at the desire of the Council, by nine of the Professors, London, 1830; Letter to the Council of the University of London, by Leonard Horner, Esq., 1st June, 1830; Observations on a Letter addressed by Leonard Horner, Esq. to the Council of the University, dated June 1, 1830. London, 1830.

Hoskins, John (d. 1664). ix. 1293*a*, l. 21. For '(*d.* 1664)' read '(*d.* 1665)', and after 'he did before' (l. 27) add 'In April 1640 Hoskins was granted a pension of £200 per annum (*Cal. State Papers, Dom.*, 1660-1661, p. 111).'

Ibid. ll. 13-6 from foot. For 'Hoskins died . . . his father' read 'Hoskins died on or after 15 Feb. 1664/5, the date of a memorandum attached to his will (Somerset House, P.C.C., Hyde, f. 26), and was buried on 22 Feb. at St. Paul's, Covent Garden (*Registers*, Harleian Soc., iv. 32). In his will he mentions his wife Sara and son John; the former is left the arrears of his pension out of the exchequer. The son is mentioned in the will of Samuel Cooper [q.v.] as still alive in 1672. The only evidence for the latter's having painted miniatures is a statement by Sir W. Sanderson [q.v.] (*Graphice*, 1658, p. 20); there are no miniatures that can be satisfactorily attributed to him. The works signed by Hoskins have been divided into two groups, according to the form of the signature, but the two groups cannot be shown to be by different artists. Signed and dated works range in date from 1632 to 1663; but there is evidence to show that Hoskins was already at work in 1626 (R. W. Goulding, *The Welbeck Abbey Miniatures* (Walpole Soc., vol. iv.), pp. 36-9; B. S. Long, *British Miniaturists*, pp. 222-7, where much information about Hoskins is collected).'

E. S. de B.

Hoste, Sir William (1780–1828), **ix.** 1297*a*, l. 26 from foot.

For 'In December 1813 she [the *Bacchante*] was sent to assist the Austrians and Montenegrins in the attack on Cattaro', read 'In October 1813 she was sent to assist the Austrians and Montenegrins in the attack on the Bocche di Cattaro'. (Brit. Mus. Add MS. 43076 (Aberdeen papers); *London Gazette*, 5 April 1814.)

Hough, John (1651–1743). ix. 1311*b*. To authorities add: Oxford Historical Society, *Collectanea*, ii. 381–416.

Howard, Charles Baron Howard of Effingham, earl of Nottingham (1536–1624). x. 2*a*, l. 5. For 'about the same time was made lord chamberlain of the household,' read 'was appointed lord chamberlain in 1583.' (E. F. Chambers, *The Elizabethan* Stage, i. 40.)

Howard, Henry, sixth Duke of Norfolk (1628–1684). x. 33*a*, l. 18. For 'April' read 'July' (E. M. G. Routh, *Tangier, 1661–1684*, p. 99).

Ibid. l. 19. After 'Morocco' add 'His mission proved fruitless, largely owing to his own conduct; he returned to England in July, 1670 (account of the embassy in Routh, pp. 99–111). He was nevertheless created earl of Norwich and earl marshal on 19 Oct. 1672, the office as well as the title being hereditary (G.E.C., *Complete Peerage*).'

Ibid. ll. 24–5. For '25 Jan. 1671' read '26 Jan. 1673/4' and after 'Tuke' add '(*d.* 1674) [q.v.].'

Ibid. ll. 27–9. For 'On 19 Oct. . . . following' read 'On 1 Dec. 1677'

Howard, Sir Robert. (1626–1698). x. 59*b*, 15 ll. from bottom. For 'At the Restoration . . . demands of money' (p. 60*a*, l. 10) read 'In 1661 Howard was returned to parliament for Stockbridge. He was never made a knight of the bath; but has probably been confused with this uncle, Sir Robert Howard [*q.v.*] in this matter. He appears to have been a determined and successful place hunter; he and his father were joint farmers of the post fines in the court of common pleas and of the green wax from December 1660 (*Cal. State Papers Dom.*, 1660–1661, pp. 430, 577; the word "brother" on p. 430 cannot refer to Berkshire's brother, Sir Robert Howard [*q.v.*], as the latter died in 1653; the later entries state clearly Berkshire's son, Sir Robert). As early as June 1660, a Sir Robert Howard, presumably the same man, was granted the office of serjeant painter to the King, and, later in the same month, that of clerk of the patents in chancery (*ib.*, pp. 55, 76; payments to Howard as sergeant painter are mentioned in *ib.*, 1661–1662, pp. 256, 270, and elsewhere; Howard appears to have carried out ordinary painters' contracts). Howard gave up the office of serjeant painter in February 1662/3 (*ib.*, 1663–1664, p. 58); and his other place of clerk of the patents apparently about the same time (*ib.*, p 677). From this period his career becomes obscure; his time was probably taken up by his theatrical activities. Two of his plays were produced in 1662, and two more in 1664; at the same time he owned a quarter of the shares of the King's Company, and appears to have had some part in its management (A. Nicoll, *Restoration Drama*, pp. 281, 282; cf. *Cal. State Papers Dom.*, 1664–1665, p. 139).

By the beginning of 1667 Howard was turning definitely towards politics, probably already as a follower of Buckingham (Pepys, *Diary*, 9 January 1666/7 ; cf. *ib.* 17 July ; Clarendon, *Continuation*, p. 950). In October he took a considerable part in the impeachment of Clarendon (*Proceedings of the House of Commons, touching the impeachment of the Earl of Clarendon*, 1700, *passim*). On 24 April 1668, Howard carried on the negociations with the Lords for the impeachment of Sir William Penn (*Commons Journals*, ix. 88). He was now intimately associated with Buckingham, who appears to have tried to make Howard secretary of state in succession to Sir William Morice [*q.v.*], but this was prevented by Arlington (B. M. *Add. MS.* 36916, f. 114). In this year Howard produced a poem, *The Duel of the Stags*, which he dedicated to Buckingham, and which was deservedly parodied by Buckhurst [see SACKVILLE, CHARLES]. In March 1668/9 Howard and Buckingham were engaged in the production of a play, "The Country Gentleman," in which Sir William Coventry was caricatured; owing to Coventry's challenging Buckingham its performance was forbidden, and it was never printed (Pepys, 4 March 1668/9; B.M. *Egerton MS.* 2539, ff. 328–9).

Howard had interested himself in the question of supply already in the beginning of 1668 (Pepys, 14 February 1667/8). In November 1670 he was largely responsible for the management of the question in the House of Commons (*Cal. State Papers Dom.*, 1670, pp. 520, 525), and offering to become one of the farmers of the customs (*ibid.*, p. 571), a position he obtained in July 1671 (*ibid.*, 1671, p. 407). The contract with the farmers was withdrawn, however, in September, and commissioners of the customs appointed (*ibid.*, p. 505). Howard was not among them, but in October he became secretary to the treasury, in succession to Sir George Downing [*q.v.*] ; a contemporary asks if Howard must always gain by being opposed to the king (*ibid.*, p. 526) In March 1672/3 he became auditor of the exchequer (*Cal. Treasury Books*, 1672–5, p. 83).

From this time Howard's main object appears to have been to retain his position, which he kept until his death. In October 1673, he opposed the Duke of York's marriage with Mary of Modena (*Williamson Letters*, Camden Soc., ii. 52 ; *Essex Papers*, Camden Soc., i. 132). In February 1673/4, he was on very bad terms with the new lord treasurer, the future Earl of Danby (*Essex Papers*, i. 176). In November 1677, he was before the council for irregularities in his conduct as auditor of the exchequer. There was no question of dishonesty on Howard's part, and the affair ended in a formal reprimand by the king in council. Contemporaries regarded it to some extent as a personal contest between Howard and Danby (*Hist. MSS. Comm., Ormonde MSS. at Kilkenny*, N.S. iv. 377, 383, 384, 386 ; *ibid.*, *Rept.* xiv., App. ix. p. 387 ; *Cal. State Papers Dom.*, 1677–1678, pp. 368, 448).

From 1675 Howard seems to have been a steady supporter of the court party in the House of Commons. He appears in a list of "servants and officers" among Danby's papers (B.M. *Add. MS.* 28091, f. 144) which dates probably from October 1675, and in a similar list from February 1676/7 (*Ibid.*, ff. 169–170). He also appears as a "speaker" in a list of the court party compiled for Sir Joseph Williamson about April 1678 (State Papers, Dom., Charles II, vol. 408, no. 148) ; and numerous speeches by him, often of considerable ability, are reported in Grey's *Debates*.

In 1678/9 and in the next two parliaments Howard sat for Castle Rising. He appears to have supported the Exclusion Bill (Grey, *Debates*, vii. 429, viii. 279 ; Cobbett, *Parliamentary History*, iv. 1292–3) ; he did not sit in James II's parliament, although he retained his position in the exchequer. After the Revolution he was again returned for Castle Rising, for which he sat until his death.'

Ibid., p. 60*a*, 8 ll. from bottom. The nickname 'Sir Positive' stuck to Howard (*Journals of Sir John Lauder of Fountainhall*, Scot. Hist. Soc., 1900, p. 222) and is occasionally found in contemporary satires.

E. S. DE B.

Howard, Sir Robert (1626–1698). x. 59*b* and BULLETIN, iii. 64–5, xvii. 99.

59*b*, l. 19 from foot. Omit 'near Newbury.'

Ibid. ll. 17–15 from foot. For 'Under the Commonwealth . . . Windsor Castle' read 'In September 1657 he and his father were granted a lease of the post fines ; his father had previously been granted the farm by Charles I in 1641 (*Cal. S.P. Dom.* 1656–7, p. 313 ; 1657–8, pp. 93–4, 102 ; see also BULLETIN, iii. 64).' There is no contemporary evidence to show that Howard was imprisoned during the Commonwealth.

Ibid. 60*a*, ll. 29–30. For 'Annabella Dives . . . of honour' read 'Annabella Dyve, or Dives, a granddaughter of Sir Lewis Dyve [q.v.]; her father was sometime secretary to Howard in the Auditor's office and in 1692 a clerk of the council; she was aged about eighteen and had been a maid of honour to Princess Anne (Luttrell; *Staffordshire Pedigrees*, Harleian Soc., p. 252).'

Ibid. l. 22 from foot. For '10 Aug. 1665' read '10 Aug. 1666 (*Notes and Queries*, clxxvii. 7)' and after it add 'The king appears to have recommended the marriage to Howard; it was not a success and in 1667 Lady Howard was petitioning for relief (*Cal. S.P. Dom.* 1666–7, p. 566; 1667, p. 495). She died in September 1676 (*Rutland MSS.*, Hist. MSS. Comm., ii. 29). To this period belongs Howard's association with Mary Uphill, mentioned in "A Seasonable Argument." Evelyn alludes to her as an actress (for an actress of this name in small parts between 1669 and 1675, see T. Shadwell, *Complete Works*, ed. M. Summers, 1927, vol. i, introd., pp. xliii–iv, where, however, the first name is given as Susannah; Mrs. Uphill had a sister of this name). She was the third daughter of Jacob Uphill of Dagenham; two of her brothers were merchants in the East Indies, a third was standard-bearer to the Yeomen of the Guard under Queen Anne, etc.; one brother-in-law, William Duncombe, was presented in 1683, probably by Howard, to the living of Ashtead; another was a baronet (J. P. Shawcross, *History of Dagenham*, 1908, pp. 104–5; Manning and Bray, *Surrey*, ii. 632, 635; see also H. C. Foxcroft, *Life of Halifax*, ii. 20 n.).'

Ibid. l. 6 from foot. After 'an actress' add 'her probable age makes this unlikely.'

Ibid. 60*b*, ll. 7–19. For 'One of his daughters . . . GILLOW' read 'Howard is stated on unreliable information to have been the father of Mary of the Holy Cross (1653–1735), abbess of the Poor Clares at Rouen in 1702 (A(lban) B(utler), *Short Account* of her life, 1767, pp. 29–30; GILLOW.'

E. S. DE BEER.

Howard, Sir Robert. x. 60*a*, l. 22 from foot. For '1665' read '1666 (*Notes and Queries*, clxxvii. 7)'.

Ibid. 60*b*, l. 7. After 'exchequer.' insert 'A paper written by Thomas Howard, giving genealogical details of the family of Sir Robert, is inserted in MS. Ashmole 243, f. 193, in the Bodleian (*Notes and Queries*, clxxvii. 7).'

Howard, William, viscount Stafford. x. 82*a*, l. 15. After 'his innocence' add 'Turberville is said to have confessed on his death-bed that Shaftesbury had paid him £500 for his evidence (*Cal. S.P.* Dom., 1680–81, p. 636).'

Ibid. l. 3 from foot. For 'but the exact spot is unknown' read 'according to a contemporary newsletter, beneath the rails surrounding the communion table (*Cal. S.P.* Dom., 1680–81, p. 111).'

Howard, William, first Viscount Stafford (1614–1680), x. ll. 20–21*a*. For '30 Nov. 1614' read '30 Nov. 1612.' (Stafford MSS., Westminster Archives, Archbishop's House, cf. Hist. MSS. Comm., *Cooper MSS.*, i. 79–83.

Howe, Emanuel Scrope. x. 84*a*, l. 12. After 'at an early age.' read 'In March 1688 he was serving as captain in the earl of Pembroke's regiment of foot, one of the regiments on the Dutch establishment which accompanied William of Orange on his voyage to Torbay later in the year (Dalton, *English Army Lists*, ii. 230). On 1 April 1689 he was appointed captain and lieutenant-colonel in the 1st foot guards, served with his regiment in Flanders and was wounded at the siege of Namur in 1695 (*ibid.* iii. 42).'

Ibid. l. 14. For 'a' read 'what was afterwards the 15th (*ibid.* ii. 231*n*)'

Ibid. l. 16. For 'March 1707' read '1 June 1706 (*ibid.* v. 17)'; for 'May' read '1 Jan. (*ibid.* vi. 17)'

Howe, George Augustus, third Viscount Howe. xxii. 875*a*, l. 27 from foot. After 'his death,' insert 'On 9 March 1745 he was appointed ensign in the 1st regiment of foot guards (P.R.O., Index 5436, p. 28), and was promoted lieutenant and captain on 9 May 1746 (*ibid.* p. 26).'

Howell, William (1638?–1683). x. 117*b*, ll. 12–11 from foot. For 'which he translated . . . in 1671 as' read 'in 1671 he published an epitome of it in Latin, entitled'.

Ibid. ll. 9–7. For 'The history . . . and published' read 'A second edition of the "Institution" appeared in 1680, and in the same year a second part of the work, bringing it down to "the taking of Rome by Odoacer." Another work, "An Institution of General History, or the History of the Ecclesiastical Affairs of the World. Contemporary with the Second Part" (*i.e.* 313 to 476) was published posthumously.'

Ibid. ll. 4–2. Delete 'What is styled . . . 1680–5.' H. O.

Hoy, Thomas.

'He died, it is said, in Jamaica in or about 1718.' Hoy was still living in Jamaica in June 1721, when he issued a power of attorney for the surrender of his professorship. (*P.R.O., Specification Roll* 2, Nos. 5 and 6; *Pat. Roll* 3548, No. 27. *St. Papers Dom.*, George I., Bundle 30, No. 46.)

Hudson, Jeffery. x. 150*a*, l. 19 from foot. For 'at Paris about 1649' read 'at Nevers about October 1644.' *See* A. Strickland, as quoted in list of authorities.

Hudson, Michael. x. 152*b*, l. 25. After 'Scots camp' add '(examinations of or relating to Hudson taken at this time are printed in Hist. MSS. Comm., 13th Rep., App. i. [*Portland MSS.*, i]; and in Peck, *Desiderata Curiosa*, book ix).'

Ibid. ll. 25–30. For 'On 18 Nov. . . . again captured' read 'He escaped about 18 November and visited the king at Newcastle before 28 November, apparently representing himself as an agent for a general rising (Bruce, *Charles I in 1646*, pp. 77, 78: Camden Soc., 1856). He received a letter from the king accrediting him for this purpose and himself wrote to Major-general Rowland Laugharne [q.v.] in Wales. Laugharne sent the letters up to parliament, while Hudson was recaptured by 19 December (*Commons' Journals*, v. 23, 42 etc.; the affair is discussed and the letters printed by S. R. Gardiner, *Great Civil War*, iii. 176).'

Ibid. l. 26 from foot to 153*a*, l. 4. The account of Hudson's death is derived from information collected at a rather late date by White Kennett [q.v.] and from the accounts given by David Lloyd and Anthony Wood and printed by F. Peck, 'Desiderata Curiosa,' book ix. According to 'Mercurius Psittacus,' 14–21 June, Hudson obtained leave from the committee of the Tower to go to Stamford for his health (see also *Commons' Journals*, v. 585, where bonds entered into by Hudson are mentioned). Hudson and colonel Styles rose at Stamford on 3 June; they were pursued by the parliamentary forces and Hudson with fifteen soldiers took refuge in Woodcroft house. This was successfully attacked on 6 June; the defenders fighting from room to room were driven to the roof; three were killed in the fighting, three were given quarter, but Hudson and three more were thrown from the leads into the moat, where such as escaped were killed by countrymen. Hudson had a commission as colonel (*Moderate Intelligencer*, no. 169, 8–15 June 1648, p. 1385; some further information is to be derived from other newspapers of the period). The story of Hudson's death is retold by Sir Walter Scott in 'Woodstock.'

Ibid. ll. 5–6. For 'Hudson married . . . Oxfordshire' read 'On 15 April 1635 Hudson was licensed to marry Elizabeth, daughter of Lewis Pollard of Newnham Courtney, Oxfordshire (*Allegations for Marriage Licences, Faculty Office of the Archbishops of Canterbury*, p. 30: Harl. Soc., 1886). The date of the marriage is unknown.'

To list of authorities add: J. Foster, Alumni Oxonienses (1500–1714).

E. S. de B.

Hugh (1246?–1255), called Hugh of Lincoln, Saint. x. 169*b*, l. 36. For 'Beatrice' read 'Cicely' (*Cal. Patent Rolls*, 1258–1266, p. 109).

Ibid. 170*a*, l. 3 from foot. After 'Henry's reign' insert '(cf. *Notes and Queries*, clix. 61–63).'

Ibid. 171*a*, l. 7 in 'Authorities.' After 'Lincoln' insert '*Cal. Patent Rolls* 1258–1266.'

Humphrey, Duke of Gloucester. x. 245*b*. Add to list of authorities: B. L. Ullman's 'Manuscripts of Duke Humphrey of Gloucester' (*Eng. Hist. Rev.* lii. 670–2); and Kenneth H. Vickers's Humphrey, duke of Gloucester, 1907.

Hungerford, John. x. 256*a*, l. 3 from foot. For 'Sayer' read 'Layer' (Boyer, *Political State of Great Britain*, xxiv. 508).

Hungerford, Sir Thomas. x. 257*b*, ll. 30–29 from foot. For '(*d.* 1398)' read '(*d.* 3 Dec. 1397)'

Ibid. l. 20 from foot. For 'in the parliament of 1316' read 'in eight parliaments between 1323 and 1339 (*Return of M.P.'s*, i. 75, 77, 88, 91, 93, 95, 105, 125)'

Ibid. l. 16 from foot. For 'of his first wife, Joan' read 'of his wife, Geva (E. Stokes, *Abstracts of Wilts. inq. p.m.*, p. 112; *Cal. Pat. Rolls*, 1334–8, p. 231)

Ibid. l. 10 from foot. Delete 'second'

Ibid. 258*a*, l. 5. For '1377' read '1375 (*Cal. Close Rolls*, 1374–7, p. 241; *Cal. Pat. Rolls*, 1374–7, p. 122)'

Ibid. l. 30. For '1398' read '1397 (*G.E.C.*, revised ed., vi. 613 *n. b.*)'

Ibid. l. 21 from foot. For '1 March' read '21 March (P.R.O., inq. p.m., chanc. file, 87/33).'

Hungerford, Sir Walter. x. 258*a*, ll. 12–10 from foot. For '(*d.* 1449)' read '(1378–1449);' and after 'Joan, was' insert 'born about 22 June 1378 (G.E.C., revised ed., vi. 613, *n.* h) and'

Ibid. 258*b*, l. 10. For 'the French king' read 'a French knight (*Cal. Pat. Rolls*, 1405–8, p. 161)'

Ibid. l. 14. For '1403' read '1406 (*ibid.*)'

Ibid. l. 17. After 'Wiltshire' insert ', 22 Nov. 1405 (*P.R.O. List and Indexes*, ix. 153)'.

Ibid. 259*a*, ll. 15–14 from foot. Delete 'in 1435'; after 'without issue' insert 'before 18 Feb. 1433 (G.E.C., p. 617, *n.* a.)'

Hunnis, William. x. 262*a*, l. 20 from foot. After 'various places' add 'In 1585 he obtained a grant for 21 years of property in the counties of Derby, Essex, Suffolk, Hertford and Middlesex (Pat. Rolls. 27 Eliz. pt. 17, mm. 20, 21, 22, 23: cited by C. C. Stopes, *W. Hunnis and the Revels in the Chapel Royal*).'

Hunter, Alexander. x. 284*a*, l. 23. For '1777' read '1775' (*Record of Royal Soc.*, p. 359).

Hunter, Sir Claudius Stephen. x. 286*a*, l. 24. For 'Leamington' read 'Lymington' (*Return of M.P.s*, ii. 206, 221, 277, 291).

Hunter, Robert, x. 299*b*, ll. 14–16. After 'Dreghorn' delete 'It appears . . . esquire' and substitute 'On 19 April 1689 he was appointed aide-major in Lord Cardross's dragoons' (C. Dalton, *Engl. Army Lists*, iii. 36), was made captain in col. John Hill's foot, *c.* 1690 (*ibid.*, p. 277) and on 28 Feb. 1694 captain in the Royal Scots dragoons (*ibid.*, 357). On 28 May 1695 he was appointed major of brigade to dragoons in Flanders (*ibid.*, iv, p. 112) and was'. l. 19. After 'vol. iv' add 'He was promoted brevet lieutenant-colonel of dragoons on 1 Jan. 1703 (*ibid.*, v. 111)'. 300*a*, l. 10. Add 'He was appointed brigadier-general on 12 Feb. 1711 (*ibid.*, vi., p. 19)'. ll. 20-19 from foot. After '1719' add 'He was promoted major-general on 10 March 1727' and delete 'became major-General, and (C. Dalton, *George the First's Army*, ii. 355)'. 300*b*, l. 27. Add 'His portrait, from the Sloper family heirlooms was in the possession of the late David Minlore, Esq., in 1938'.

Hussey or Huse, Sir William. x. 332*b*, ll. 4–9. For 'was probably a son . . . of small means.' read 'was the son of John Huse, Esq., of Old Sleaford, co. Lincoln, and Elizabeth Nesfield or Neffield of Yorkshire, an heiress whose arms were quartered with those of the Huses (R. E. G. Cole, *History of Doddington*, p. 70).'

Ibid. l. 10. After 'Gray's Inn,' insert 'sat for the first time on commissions of the peace for Kesteven in 1460 (*Cal. Pat. Rolls*, 1452–61, p. 670).'

Ibid. l. 15. After 'for treason.' add 'In the summer of 1475 he was a member of Edward IV's "great council in England," which had power to act for the king while he was engaged on the invasion of France (C. L. Scofield, *Edward the Fourth*, ii. 125).'

Ibid. l. 19–20. For 'at a salary . . . a year.' read 'On 12 June following he was granted the customary 180 marks a year for the maintenance of his office, with the usual allowance at Christmas and Whitsuntide in lieu of robes and furs, and a further 40 marks annually from the issues of the hanaper, with a tun of wine at Christmas in the port of London (*Cal. Pat. Rolls*, 1476–85, p. 281; see also Foss, *Lives of Judges*, iv. 227).'

Ibid. l. 22. After 'three kings' insert 'by letters close dated 21 Apr. 1483, 26 June 1483, and 20 Sept. 1485 respectively (see coram rege plea rolls East. 1 Edw. V, r. 1, Trin. 1 Ric. III, r. 1, and Mich. 1 Hen. VII, r. 1, as these reappointments are not enrolled on the close roll). He was knighted after his appointment as chief justice and before 12 Nov. 1481 (*Cal. Pat. Rolls*, 1476–85, pp. 281 and 288).'

Ibid. l. 30. After '1 Hen. VII, p. 26).' add 'He was also prepared to oppose the encroachment of chancery upon the jurisdiction of the common law by use of the writ Habeas corpus (Y.B. 22 Edw. IV, Mich. pl. 21).'

Ibid. l. 28 from foot. After 'the king of France' add ', and had been employed on a previous embassy by Richard III, when he was negotiating the marriage of his niece, the Lady Anne de la Pole, to the Duke of Rothesay in 1484 (Rymer, xii. 244).'

Ibid. l. 25 from foot. After 'as chief justice.' insert 'He left instructions that, if he died "at home," he was to be buried in the monastery at Sempringham (will, P.C.C. 32 Vox), and these were carried out (Dame Elizabeth Huse's will, P.C.C. 22 Holgrave).'

Hussey or Huse, Sir William. **(*d.* 1495). x. 332*b*, l. 33. For 'late in 1495' read '8 September 1495 (*Cal. Inquis. Post Mortem*, Hen. VII., i. No. 1166).'**

***Ibid.*, l. 37. For 'two sons' read 'three sons, John, William and Robert (*ibid.*, i. No. 1166).'**

Hutchinson, John (1615–1664). x. 341*a*, l. 14. After 'Add. MS. 19353' add 'the prefatory letter to Anglesea and some specimens of the translation are printed in the *Journal of Classical and Sacred Philology*, iv. (1858), 121-39.'

E. S. de B.

Huxley, Thomas Henry. xxii. (1st Supplement). 895*a*, ll. 30–32. He did not graduate M.B. of London University, and the examination in which he won a gold medal in anatomy and medicine in 1845 was the Intermediate Examination in medicine. See *University of London: Historical Record* (1912), pp. 420, 444.

Hyde, Anne, Duchess of York. x. 368*a*, l. 7 from foot–368*b*, l. 22 from foot. For 'About the same time . . . Appendix iv.)' read 'Towards the end of 1669 she appears to have become doubtful as to the position of the Church of England, the result, according to her own account, of her reading Heylyn's 'History of the Reformation'. Early in 1670 it was common talk that she was wavering towards Roman catholicism; she had not received the communion for two or three months, having hitherto received it regularly every month. At the instance of George Morley, bishop of Winchester [q.v.], who had been her spiritual director when she was a girl and from the Restoration until his retirement from court in 1667, she communicated again at Easter. But in a paper dated 8 Aug. 1670 she sets out her reasons for becoming a Roman catholic; she was received into that church, at what date is unknown, by Father Hunt, a Franciscan. This was kept a close secret, the duke informing the king, and only one or two other persons knowing of it; but rumours were so strong as to cause Morley to write to the duchess on 24 Jan. 1670/1, urging her to declare that she was a protestant; Clarendon also heard reports of it (see his *Two Letters to the Duke and Duchess of York*, n.d., also printed in *State Tracts . . . reign of Charles II*, 1693, i. 439–42; and Laurence Hyde, 'Meditations,' 1675, in *Correspondence of Henry Hyde, earl of Clarendon*, 1828, i. 645).'

Ibid. 369*a*, l. 25. After '(Burnet, i. 307).' add 'The duchess's paper giving the reasons for her conversion first received wide publicity in a French version appended to Father Louis Maimbourg's 'Histoire du Calvinisme,' 1682 (an undated English publication of the paper apparently dates from 1686 or later). In it she gives some account of the remarks of two English bishops [see MORLEY, GEORGE, *infra*].

Hyde, Edward, First Earl of Clarendon. x. 370*b*, 4 ll. from bottom. For 'in 1629' read 'Either at the end of 1631 or at the beginning of 1632.'

Ibid., After 'Wiltshire' add '(*Eng. Hist. Rev.*, xxxii. 405–7).'

Ibid., 376*b*, l. 23. For '1836' read '1833.'

Hyde, Edward, first Earl of Clarendon, x. 370*b* (see *Bulletin*, iii. 66).

On his descent on the maternal side see W. H. Jones, 'Lord Clarendon and his Trowbridge Ancestry' (Wilts. Arch. Soc., vol. ix.).

374*a*, l. 32. After 'failure of the campaign' add '(*Eng. Hist. Rev.*, xix. 475).'

375*a*, l. 13. After '1644' add '(Firth, 'Clarendon: *History of the Rebellion*' in *Eng. Hist. Rev.*, xix. 26 *et seq.*).'

375*b*, l. 28. Add '(*Eng. Hist. Rev.*, viii. 300; Gardiner, *Commonwealth and Protectorate*, i. 18, 61).'

376*a*, l. 8. On Hyde's embassy to Spain, see Gardiner, *Commonwealth and Protectorate*, i. 62, 181, 310.

377*b*, l. 20. Add 'The brief notes which passed between the king and the minister in council show the entire confidence the king reposed in Clarendon and the familiarity of their intercourse (*Notes which passed at Meetings of the Privy Council*, etc., ed. W. D. Macray, Roxburghe Club, 1896).'

Ibid., 7 ll. from foot. After 'consequence' add '(Bagwell, *Ireland under the Stuarts*, iii. 85).'

378*a*, l. 31. After 'powerful privy council' add 'an ideal which he had set forth at length in his "History" (*Eng. Hist. Rev.*, xix. 42–4).'

Ibid., 16 ll. from foot. Instead of the reference to *Clarendon State Papers* refer to Macray, *Notes . . . of the Privy Council*, pp. 29, 58.

379*b*, 16 ll. from foot. On Bristol's attack upon Clarendon, see Lister, iii. 246, for the charges, and also the comments of Cominges in Jusserand, *A French Ambassador at the Court of Charles II*, 1892, p. 104.

380*a*, l. 35. After 'Hyde's share in the settlement of Ireland is less easy to define' add '(see Bagwell, *Ireland under the Stuarts*, iii. 12, 44, 84).'

380*b*, l. 14. After 'leading part' add '(see Kaye, *English Colonial Administration under Lord Clarendon*, Johns Hopkins University Studies, 1905; and Osgood, *The American Colonies in the 17th Century*, iii. 143–191, 1907).'

380*b*, 7 ll. from foot. For 'fifteenth' read 'ninth.'

381*a*, l. 15, on the king's marriage, after the reference to Ranke, add '(Prestage, *Diplomatic Relations of Portugal with France, England, and Holland*, 1925, pp. 139–149).'

Ibid., 6 ll. from foot. After 'conducted the bargain himself' add '(Macray, *Notes . . . of the Privy Council*, pp. 71–3).'

383*a*, l. 6. Add '"The ill conduct of my Lord Clarendon in my affairs has forced me to permit many enquiries to be made, which otherwise I would not have suffered the parliament to have done," wrote Charles to his sister (Cartwright, *Madame*, p. 248).'

385*b*, l. 8. After '(Lewis, . . . 357)' insert: 'A copy of the painting at Grove Park is in the National Portrait Gallery.'

387*a*, l. 9. After 'Life' insert '(Firth, 'Clarendon: *History of the Rebellion*' in *Eng. Hist. Rev.*, xix. 26, 246, 464).'

Ibid., l. 35. For 'Grenville' read 'Granville.'

388*b*, l. 25. Insert '*Notes which passed at Meetings of the Privy Council between Charles II and the Earl of Clarendon*, ed. W. D. Macray, Roxburghe Club, 1896. A selection from these notes was printed in vol. iii. of the *Clarendon State Papers* (1786), others in vol. iii. of Lister's *Life of Clarendon*. This edition contains facsimiles and is copiously annotated.'

388*b*, l. 28. After 'over one hundred volumes' add '(See *Summary Catalogue of Western MSS. in the Bodleian Library*, iii. 557–74); vol. iv. of the *Calendar of the Clarendon MSS.*, ed. by F. J. Routledge, is now printing.'

Ibid., Add to the last sentence '; to Sir R. Fanshawe (MSS. of Mr. J. M. Heathcote); to Lord Langdale (MSS. of Mrs. Harford).'

389*a*, l. 14. After Lister's *Life* insert 'The fullest modern biography is the Life by Sir H. Craik, 2 vols. 1911.'

Hyde, Henry, second earl of Clarendon. x. 393*a*, l. 4. For '1724' read '1723' (*Complete Peerage*, 1913, iii. 268).

Ingham, Oliver de. x. 435*b*, l. 6. For 'Next year' read 'On 10 March 1326' (Gascon Roll, 38 m. 5, quoted by Tout, *Place of Edward II*, p. 396).

Ingoldsby, Sir Henry (1622–1701). x. 447*b*, 6 ll. from foot. He was a captain in his brother's regiment of foot in 1645, colonel of a regiment of dragoons in Ireland 1650–55, and of an infantry regiment there 1655–9. He was governor of Limerick from 1652, and was member for Kerry, Limerick and Clare in the parliaments of 1654, 1656 and 1659. He lost both his regiment and his governorship in July 1659, on account of his support of Henry Cromwell (Ludlow, *Memoirs*, ed. 1894, ii. 72), and actively promoted both in England and Ireland the movement which led to the Restoration (*Portland MSS.*, i. 688, 696). . . . From 1674 to 1680 Ingoldsby was a member of the Irish Privy Council, from which he was dismissed for factiously attacking the Duke of Ormonde (*Ormonde MSS.*, v. 168, 223, 327). After the Revolution he raised a regiment for William III (8 March 1689), which served in Ireland under Schomberg in the autumn, and was disbanded in Jan. 1690. His death is mentioned by Luttrell under 12 April 1701 (*Diary*, v. 38; Dalton, *English Army Lists*, iii. 78, 116).

448*a*, l. 8. Alter the reference to '*Life of Anthony Wood*, ed. 1848,' to '*Life of Anthony Wood*, ed. Clark, i. 172.'

Ingoldsby, Sir Henry. x. 448*a*, l. 8. Add: 'He married Anne, daughter of Sir Hardress Waller [q.v.] (Lipscomb, *Buckinghamshire*, ii. 169).'

E. S. de B.

Ingoldsby, Sir Richard. x. 446*b*, 1 l. from foot. After 'Hampden's regiment' add 'of which he became lieutenant-colonel when Tyrrell succeeded Hampden, and colonel in succession to Tyrrell on 21 October, 1644 (Ingoldsby's account in P.R.O., Commonwealth Exch. Papers, 43, ii.).'

Ibid., 447*b*, l. 5 from foot. After 'Sir Henry Ingoldsby (1622–1701) who' add 'was a captain in his brother's regiment in the "New Model," probably until 1647, and'... G. D.

Ingoldsby, Sir Richard. x. 446*b*, l. 7 from foot. After 'Huntingdonshire' insert 'He was baptised 10 Aug. 1617 at Buckingham (Lipscomb, *Buckinghamshire*, ii. 169).'

Ibid. 447*b*, ll. 13 and 12 from foot. For 'in 1685' read 'on 9 Sept. 1685 (Lipscomb, ii. 169).'

E. S. de B.

Ingoldsby, Sir Richard (*d.* 1685). x. 446*b*, 4 ll. from foot. Add 'He was admitted to Gray's Inn 4 May 1638, and was created M.A. of Oxford 19 May 1649 (Foster, *Alumni Oxonienses*).'

447*b*, l. 12. Alter the reference to Ludlow to '*Memoirs*, ed. 1894, ii. 63'; and insert: 'In September 1655 Ingoldsby had been given the command of the regiment of horse of which Nathaniel Rich had been deprived by the Protector. When Richard Cromwell fell, the Long Parliament reinstated Rich, cashiering Ingoldsby and several of his officers as disaffected (*Clarke Papers*, iii. 51, 53, 212; iv. 19; *Commons' Journals*, vii. 709). Seeing the Restoration at hand,' etc.

Ibid., l. 37. After '1660' add '(*Hist. MSS. Comm.*, *Leyborne-Popham MSS.*, pp. 157, 163–5; Baker, *Chronicle*, ed. Phillips, pp. 712, 720).'

Ireton, Henry. x. 474*a*, 8 ll. from foot. He matriculated 20 June 1628 (Foster, *Alumni*).

475*b*, l. 14. For the quarrel between Holles and Ireton refer to Ludlow's *Memoirs*, ed. 1894, i. 190.

477. The article was published in 1892, the second volume of the *Clarke Papers* not till 1894. Add references to *Clarke Papers*, ii. 35–8, for Ireton's argument with Sir C. Lucas; to ii. 54 for his dealings with Col. Hammond; to ii. 140–2 for his directions for bringing Charles I to London.

477*b*, l. 34. After the reference to Lilburne's *Legal Fundamental Liberties*, add 'Ireton's numerous speeches show not only his pertinacity in argument, but his very definite and coherent political principles, and explain the influence he exercised (*Clarke Papers*, ii. 79–132). Outside the council his influence was very limited.'

477*b*, 14 ll. from foot. On his military operations in Ireland see Dunlop, *Ireland under the Commonwealth*, 1913, pp. 1–108, and refer to Ludlow's *Memoirs*, ed. 1894, i. 262, 278, 293–6, 288, 286, instead of to pp. 145, 143, 148, 144, 143 of the 1751 edition.

477*a*, 17 ll. from foot. For Ireton's opposition to interposing to prevent the

Treaty of Newport, see Ludlow's *Memoirs*, ed. 1894, i. 204.

477*b*, l. 11. For his share in 'Pride's Purge,' see Ludlow's *Memoirs*, ed. 1894, i. 210.

479*b*, l. 28. Ireton's widow married Fleetwood 8 June 1652 (*Clarke MSS.*, xxii. 105).

Ibid., l. 37. From Ireton's second daughter, Jane, Dr. S. R. Gardiner was descended.

Irvine, Christopher. x. 486*b*, 14 ll. from foot. For 'but the copy . . . second edition' read 'but a copy printed in London in 1635 is extant (F. Miller, *A Bibliography of the Parish of Annan*, 1925, p. 41).'

James I, king of Scotland. x. 573*b*, l. 25. Add to list of authorities: R. Weiss's The Earliest Account of the Murder of James I of Scotland (*Eng. Hist. Rev.* lii. 479–91).

James II. x. 618*a*, l. 2 from foot. After 'Albany' insert 'On 7 April 1638 a writ was prepared at the council ordering a patent to be drawn creating James lord admiral of England during his life. This writ was to be kept in the council chest until the king ordered it to be executed, but, owing to the outbreak of civil war, it was never put into force (S.P. Dom. Car. I, Letters and Papers, Case E.).'

618*b*, l. 5 from foot. During his stay in Paris in 1649, or on his return there in 1650, James issued a proclamation fixing fees in prize cases in the admiralty courts in Brittany. Such a proclamation could only be issued by a lord admiral, so that James must have received some commission before this empowering him to act in that capacity. There is, however, nothing to show if it were issued to him by his father or his brother, but the naval activities of the royalists in 1649 make it most likely that Charles II created his brother lord admiral on his arrival at Helvoetsluys (P.R.O., H.C.A. Vice-admiralty Proceedings 59).

620*b*, l. 15. Besides the patent creating him lord admiral of England, Ireland, Wales, the Channel Islands, and the lost French possessions, James received a second patent as lord admiral. This appointed him for Dunkirk, Jamaica, Barbados, St. Christopher's, Bermuda, Antigua, Guinea, Binny, Benin, Angola, Tangiers, and the plantations beyond the seas (P.R.O., Rot. Pat. 14 Car. II, pt. 12, no. 6).

622*a*, l. 20. After 'Admiralty' insert 'of England and Wales.' Since the Test act did not apply to Ireland or other possessions beyond the seas, James continued to be lord admiral for those places.

James II. x. 618*b*.

BULLETIN, vii. 193*a*, l. 8 from foot to 193*b*, l. 7. For '618*b*, l. 5 from foot . . . Vice-admiralty Proceedings 59)' read '618*b*, l. 16 from foot. After "St. Germains" read "On 31 Aug. the terms of his patent as lord admiral, then drawing, were discussed at a council meeting (P.R.O., privy council register, 58, 116), and during his stay in Paris in 1649, or on his return there in 1650, James issued a proclamation fixing fees in prize cases in the admiralty courts in Brittany (P.R.O., H.C.A., Vice-admiralty proceedings, 59)." '

James II of England. x. 623*b*, l. 29 from foot. For 'second' read 'first'.

James II of England. x. 627*a*, l. 9 from foot, and above, iii. 66; vii. 193. After 'pp. 284 seqq.)' add 'The most durable and perhaps the most respectable work undertaken by James II on behalf of the Roman catholics was the re-organisation of their church government in England. John Leyburn [q.v.] had been appointed vicar apostolic for all England on 6 Aug. 1685. On 12 Jan. 1688 the Propaganda congregation passed a decree "ad instantiam" of James II for the erection of additional vicariates; it was approved by Innocent XI, who by three briefs dated 30 Jan. appointed three vicars apostolic with titles "in partibus." England was divided into four districts, the division being made by Count d'Adda. Leyburn retained the London district. The new vicars were Philip Ellis (western), Bonaventure Giffard (midland), and James Smith (northern) [qq.v.]. This arrangement lasted until 1840, when the number of vicariates was increased to eight (W. M. Brady, *Episcopal Succession in England, Scotland and Ireland*, iii (1877). 140, 145-6, 319-22; all dates presumably N.S.).' E. S. de B.

James II. of England. x. 633*b*, l. 8. For '6 September' read '5/16 September, (*Life of James II.* ii. 599; Manchester's despatches in Christian Cole's *Historical and Political Memoirs*, 1735, pp. 419–420).'

Ibid., 621*b*, l. 27. After 'Rome' insert 'Pepys, writing in 1661 about rumours of Charles II's marriage, states that James is 'a professed friend to the Catholiques.' (Pepys, *Diary*, 18 February 1660/1).'

James, George Payne Rainsford. x. 647*a*, l. 5 from foot. After 'historiographer royal' add '(gazetted 20 May 1837)'.

Ibid. 647*b*, ll. 6–8. For '"Letters illustrative . . . Shrewsbury"' read '"Letters illustrative of the reign of William III from 1696 to 1708. Addressed to the duke of Shrewsbury, by James Vernon," 3 vols., 1841.'

James, John (*d.* 1746). x. 650*b*, l. 15 For '*d.* 1746' read '*c.* 1672–1746'.

Ibid. ll. 16–17. Delete 'Thomas and

Eleanor James [q.v.]. One '.

Ibid. ll. 22–4. Delete 'had a son . . . in error.'

Ibid. 651*a*, l. 2 from foot. After '1746' add 'He is buried at Eversley, Hants., where in 1724 he built the still existing Warbrook House.'

To authorities add: Epitaph in Collectanea topographica et genealogica, viii. 64, and in Times Literary Supplement, 1941, p. 328; V.C.H., Hants., iv. 32.

James, John Haddy. x. 654*a*, ll. 19–20. Delete ', and was present at Waterloo' (P.R.O., war office, returns of officers' services, 25/763).

James, William (*d.* 1827). x. 665*a*, ll. 13–5. For 'In 1812 . . . England' read 'For reasons of health he sailed for the United States, not knowing that war had been declared, and on his arrival at Philadelphia, early in July'

Ibid. l. 18. For 'His attention was thus' read 'The capture of the American frigate 'Guerrière,' 19 Aug. 1812, gave a "new direction to his thoughts" and he'

Ibid. 665*b*, l. 5. After '(46 pp. 8vo).' insert 'Despite the recognition of his work, he was actually in debt, and its continuance was most probably due to the patronage of the first lord of the admiralty, Viscount Melville.'

Ibid. l. 7 from foot. After '1886,' read 'a reprint in 1902,'

Add to list of authorities: H. Furber's How William James came to be a Naval Historian, *Amer. Hist. Rev.* xxxviii. (1932–3), 74–85.

Jeffreys, George, first Baron Jeffreys of Wem. x. 714*a*, l. 20 from foot. For '1648' read '1644' (*Times Lit. Suppl.*, 1 Aug. 1929, p. 607, col. 4).

Jeffreys, George, first baron Jeffreys of Wem. x. 719*b*, ll. 14–15. For 'Two portraits of Jeffreys and' read 'A portrait of Jeffreys is preserved at Charborough Park, Wareham, Dorset, and another . . . is' (*Times Lit. Suppl.*, 10 July 1930, p. 575).

Ibid. l. 20. After 'pp. 140–1).' insert 'There is also a portrait of Jeffreys in the possession of Mr. William Wyndham, of Orchard Lydeard, Somerset, and another hangs in the tea-room of the house of lords' (*Times Lit. Suppl.*, 10 July 1930, p. 575, coll. 2–3; *ibid.* 17 July 1930, p. 592, col. 2).

Jegon, John. x. 724*a*, l. 12. For 'lodge' read 'hall'

Jenkin, Henry Charles Fleeming. x. 733*b*, l. 16. After 'and' insert 'in 1867' (*University College, London. Proceedings at the Annual General Meeting . . . 26th February* 1868, pp. 10–1).

Jenner, Edward, M.D. (1749–1823). x. 758*b*, ll. 4–3 from foot. For 'the following year (1788)' read '1789' (*Record of Royal Soc.*, p. 366).

Jennings, Sir John. x. 768*a*, l. 24. For 'during the whole' read 'until 16 Apr. 1717, and again from 19 March 1718 until the end (T. Lediard, *Naval History of England*, pp. 871 *n*, 873 *n*)'

Ibid. l. 33. After 'Queen's House.' insert 'He was elected master of the Trinity House on 12 June 1723, and again on 1 June 1724 (MS. register).' [See also BULLETIN, vii. 125.]

Jennings, Sir John. x. 768*a*, l. 29. After 'escape' insert 'He was M.P. for Queenborough 1705–10, for Portsmouth 1710–11, and for Rochester 1715–34' (*Return of M.P.'s*, ii. 3, 11, 23, 40).

Jermyn, Henry, Earl of St. Albans. x. 779*a*, l. 31. For 'Mary Barber' read 'Catherine, daughter of Sir William and sister of Sir Robert Killigrew [q.v.].' Sir Thomas Jermyn married Mary Barber, widow of Thomas Newton, in 1642 (J. L. Vivian, *Visitations of Cornwall*, pp. 268, 270; S. H. A. H[ervey], *Rushbrooke Parish Registers*, 1903, pp. 35, 237. The latter volume collects much information about the family of Jermyn, but is largely dependent on the D.N.B. article for Henry Jermyn).

Ibid. ll. 8–7 from foot. Jermyn does not appear to have sat in the Long parliament. At the queen's wish he let Sir Francis Windebank [q.v.] stand for Corfe Castle in his place (*Clarendon State Papers*, ii. 131). Sir Thomas Jermyn, his father, and Thomas Jermyn, his elder brother, appear to have been returned for Bury St. Edmunds (*Commons' Journals*, iv. 249*b*).

E. S. DE B.

Jervas, Charles (1675 ?–1739). x. 391*a*. To authorities add: Oxford Historical Society, *Collectanea*, ii. 403; Hist. MSS. Comm., *Bath (Longleat) Papers*, iii. 432–3.

Jevons, William Stanley. x. 814*a*, 12 ll. from foot. For '1880' read '1881' (*University College, London. Report of the Council . . . at the Annual General Meeting . . . 23rd February* 1881, p. 14).

John (1167?–1216). xvi. 839*b*, l. 2 from foot. After 'more usually called Hadwisa or Avice,' add 'but there is no doubt this is a mistake (*Eng. Hist. Rev.*, lxi. (1946), 289).'

John de Cella. 59*b*, ll. 14–26. For 'He may . . . S.P.C.K.)' read 'The marginal note in one manuscript which appears to attribute the authorship of a chronicle to him seems merely evidence of ownership of the manuscript by a later Abbot John (F. M. Powicke in *Modern Philology*, xxxviii (1940). 306–8).'

John of Eltham, earl of Cornwall (1316–1336). x. 854*a*, l. 24 from foot. For 'in October' read '13 Sept. 1336'.

854*b*, l. 9. For '15 Jan.' read '13 Jan. (*Annales Paulini*, p. 365).'

John of Garland. 63*b*, l. 6 from foot. After '7–12)' add ', who has also studied "The manuscripts of the major grammatical works of John of Garland; Compendium Grammatice, Clavis Compendie, Ars Lectoria Ecclesie," American Philological Association, *Trans. and Proc.*, lxix (1939). 259–73.'

John of Hoveden. 66*b*, l. 22. After "Hovedene." add 'All of the poems, except the Philomena, have now been edited by F. J. E. Raby in *Poems of John Hoveden* (Surtees Society, no. 154).'

John of London. 69*a*, ll. 5–8. For 'and therefore . . . Hoveden' read 'His name was apparently Master John de Methelton or Melton, a town in Howdenshire, and therefore he was probably called either John de Methelton or Hoveden and not John de London (Brit. Mus.: MS. Stowe 930, fo. 35; A. J. Taylor in F. J. E. Raby, *Poems of John of Hoveden*, p. 273). He probably went from London to Hoveden at the foundation of the prebend in 1265.'

Johnson, Samuel (1691–1773). x. 918*b*, ll. 23–1 from foot. For 'with a dedication . . . to Lord' read 'with two dedications, the one to Lady Delves, signed Lord Flame, the other to Lord'

Ibid. l. 19 from foot. For 'name, followed' read 'name; a second edition, also with both dedications, followed'

L. F. POWELL.

Johnson, Sir Thomas. x. 936*b*, l. 15 from foot. For '1729' read '1728.'

Ibid. 937*a*, ll. 6–5 from foot. For 'whither . . . 1729' read 'He appears never to have taken up his duties there. He died at his lodgings at Charing Cross on 28 Dec. 1728; he had previously resigned his place in the customs and was in receipt of a small pension from the crown (Historic Society of Lancashire and Cheshire, *Transactions*, xc (1938). 181–95).'

Johnston, Nathaniel, M.D. x. 955*b*, ll. 9–8. For 'Nathaniel is . . . was received' read 'He was received' (autograph inscription in a presentation copy of his 'The Excellency of Monarchical Government' in the St. Andrews University Library).

DAVID G. RAMAGE.

Jones, John. (1575–1636). x. 1011*a*. See *Notes and Queries*, 9 February, 1924, pp. 93–4, for evidence that in this account there is a confusion between two and possibly three men of the same name.

Jones, John (*d.* 1660) regicide. x. 1013*b*. In 1892, when the article appeared, I did not know the article on 'Inedited Letters of Cromwell, Colonel Jones, Bradshaw and other regicides,' printed by Mr. Joseph Mayer in the *Transactions of the Historic Society of Lancashire and Cheshire*, New Series, vol. i., 1861. It contains about forty letters of Jones written between 1651 and 1660. Other letters are printed in Ludlow's *Memoirs*, ed. 1892, in R. Dunlop's *Ireland under the Commonwealth*, 1913, and in *Cal. State Papers, Ireland*, 1647–1660. There are also many references to Jones in Thomas Richards's *History of the Puritan Movement in Wales*, 1920, and his *Religious Developments in Wales*, 1923.

Ibid., l. 26. Add, 'On 22 Feb. 1650 he was appointed one of the commissioners for the propagation of the Gospel in Wales—a cause for which he was always zealous, and a body of men whose much-criticised action he throughout upheld. "Where is there more sin to encounter, where more ignorance, where more hatred to the people of God, where the word saint more scorned, than in Merionethshire?" (Mayer, pp. 185, 194, 202, 212, 231, 246; see also Richards, *Puritan Movement in Wales*, pp. 81, 270).'

Ibid., l. 37. Alter the reference to Ludlow to 'ii. 317, ed. 1894,' and add 'Dunlop, *Ireland under the Commonwealth*, i. 1, 263.'

Ibid., l. 38. For 'A strong republican,' etc., read 'Though a strong republican Jones was afraid of the results of dissolving the Long Parliament and calling a new one. "I had rather," said he, "do a people good, though against their wills, than please them in show only to the hazarding of their peace and well being" (Mayer, p. 191). He rejoiced however at the summoning of the Little Parliament, "the choicest and most singularly elected Parliament that ever was in England" (*Ibid.*, pp. 236–9); but accepted without apparent dissatisfaction the establishment of the protectorate (*ibid.*, pp. 219, 224; Ludlow, i. 373, 537, 540). But his intimacy with Harrison and other opponents of the protectorate made him suspected, and Henry Cromwell described him as "endeavouring to make the government unacceptable,"' etc.

1014*a*, l. 29. Insert 'It was a bad choice: officers of the Irish army were not willing to obey a Welsh militia colonel as their commander, and complained that he was "a person ignorant in matters of that nature" (Ludlow, ii. 121. 468).'

Ibid., l. 36. Alter the reference to Ludlow to 'ii. 147, 152.' and insert 'When Monck announced his intention of restoring the authority of the expelled parliament, Jones and his faction protested, on the ground that its restoration meant the readmission of the secluded members and the return of the king (Mayer, pp. 271–280, 288).'

1014*b*, l. 13. Insert 'His first wife, whose name was . . . Edwards, died in Nov. 1651. By her he had one son (Mayer, pp. 196, 213; Richards, *Puritan Movement in Wales*, p. 26). His second wife, Catherine Cromwell,' etc.

Jugge, Richard (*fl.* 1531–1577), x. 1111*b*, l. 20 from foot. For '(*fl.* 1531–1577)', read '(d. 1579)'. *Ib.*, p. 1112*a*, l. 9 from foot, for '(*fl.* 1579–1587)', read '(d. 1588)'. (*N. & Q.*, 9th ser., xi. 326.)

Keith, Alexander (d. 1819). x. 1203*a*, l. 5 from foot. After 'founder of the Keith prize,' add 'born 27 Dec. 1737 (Baptismal Register of Old St. Paul's Church, Edinburgh).'

Ibid., 1203*b*, l. 28. For 'and left a son Alexander', read 'but had no children. By his will he left everything, with certain specified exceptions, to his nephew Alexander of Corstorphine Hill (Letters of Alexander Keith, senior to Viscount Melville, 4 Feb. 1819; of Alexander Keith, junior, to the same, 5 April 1819, 21 July 1819. Nat. Library of Scotland, The Melville Papers, MS. 1056, ff. 69 to 76).'

Keith, George, fifth Earl Marischal. x. 1204*b*, l. 15. For 'fifth' read 'fourth (G.E.C., *Complete Peerage*, viii. 479)'

Keith, George, tenth Earl Marischal. x. 1209*a*, ll. 14 and 12 from foot. For 'tenth' read 'ninth'; for 'ninth' read 'eighth'

Ibid. 1209*b*, l. 19 from foot. For '1 April' read '10 June'

Add to list of authorities: G.E.C.'s Complete Peerage, viii. 485–7.

Keith, William, fourth Earl Marischal. x. 1219*b*, l. 28. For 'fourth' read 'third'

Ibid. ll. 28–27 from foot. For 'His father having been slain . . ., he' read 'He'

Ibid l. 26 from foot. For '1530' read '1527'

Ibid. 1220*b*, ll. 25–24 from foot. After 'Banffshire,' insert 'whom he married in or before June 1538,'

Add to list of authorities: G.E.C.'s Complete Peerage, viii. 477–9.

Keith, William, sixth Earl Marischal. x. 1220*b*, l. 6 from foot. For 'sixth' read 'fifth'; l. 5 from foot. For '*d.*' read '1585 ?–'; l. 3 from foot. For 'fifth' read 'fourth'; and add to list of authorities: G.E.C.'s Complete Peerage, viii. 481.

Keith, William, seventh Earl Marischal. x. 1221*a*, ll. 16–14 from foot. For 'seventh' read 'sixth'; for '1617 ?–1661' read '1614–1671'; and for 'sixth' read 'fifth'

Ibid. 1224*a*, l. 30. After 'of Scotland.' insert 'He was sheriff of Aberdeen in 1668, and two years later was one of the commissioners appointed to treat of a union of England and Scotland.' For '1661' read 'March 1671, at Inverugie'

Add to list of authorities: G.E.C.'s Complete Peerage, viii. 482–3.

For **Kempe, Margerie** (*temp. incert.*) x. 1282*b* the following might now be substituted:—

Kempe, Margery (*c.* 1373–*c.* 1440), religious writer. All that is known of her life is derived from the 'Book of Margery Kempe', of which the only known manuscript was discovered in 1934. It is an account of her spiritual, rather than her worldly life, and consequently all dates must be tentative. She was born about 1373 at Lynn, the daughter of John Burnham or Brunham, who was four times mayor of Lynn between 1370 and 1392. When she was about twenty years of age she married John Kempe, who was one of the four chamberlains of Lynn in 1394–5, and by him she had fourteen children. According to her own account it was after being stricken with madness that she began to hear voices, and turned from her sinful life. It was probably in 1413 that she persuaded her husband to join her in a vow of chastity, whilst on a pilgrimage to York. In the same year after being received by the bishop of Lincoln and the archbishop of Canterbury, she set out on a pilgrimage which took her to the Holy Land and to Italy. She was back in Lynn in 1415, and in 1417 set out on another pilgrimage to Compostella by way of Bristol. Her final journey took her to Norway, Danzig and home through Germany. Margery was apparently illiterate, and dictated the accounts of her religious experience, which were revised by a priest between 1436 and 1438. Although several times charged with heresy, she appears to have avoided giving offence to the church, having a number of confessors and advisers amongst the religious of Lynn. The last known event of her life is her admission to the Guild of the Trinity of Lynn in 1438.

To list of authorities add: 'The Book of Margery Kempe, vol. I, ed. S. B. Meech, and H. E. Allen, Early English Text Society, original series no. 212 (1940).'

Kempthorne, Sir John. x. 1285*b*, l. 21 from foot. After '(*Eg. MS.* 928, f. 1)' insert ', and later became master, 15 June 1674 (Trinity House, MS. register)'

Kempthorne, Sir John. x. 1285*b*. For further information, see Major G. A. Kempthorne in *The Mariner's Mirror*, xii. 289–317.

Kenrick, William. xi. 17*b*, l. 8. After 'Aberdeen' insert 'in 1772.'

Concise D.N.B., p. 718*b*, l. 3 from foot. For 'St. Andrews' read 'Marischal College, Aberdeen.' J. H. B.

Kerr, William Henry, fourth Marquis of Lothian. xi. 67*a*, l. 15. For 'was a captain' read 'was appointed a cornet in Lord Mark Kerr's regiment of dragoons on 20 June 1735 (P.R.O., Index 5437, p. 28), captain in Cornwallis's foot on 9 Jan. 1739, and was promoted captain and lieutenant-colonel (*ibid.* p. 68)'

Ibid. l. 19. After 'shot in the head.' insert 'On 22 June 1745 he was appointed lieutenant-colonel of the 11th dragoons (P.R.O. war office 25/90, p. 96).'

Ibid. l. 26. After 'continent.' insert 'On 1 Dec. 1747 he was appointed colonel of a regiment of foot, now the South Wales Borderers (P.R.O., Index 5436, p. 80).'

Ibid. l. 28. After '11th dragoons,' insert 'on 8 Feb. 1752 (*ibid.* 5438, p. 70),'

Key, Thomas Hewitt. xi. 85*a*, l. 15. For '1833' read '1831.' See London University [now University College], Minutes of the Sessions of the Council, ii. 333; *University of London, Wednesday, 29th February* 1832. *The Annual General Meeting of Proprietors*, p. 5. See also a biographical sketch by J. P. Hicks, *T. Hewitt Key. A Short Memoir.* Printed for private circulation. Reynell & Co., Ltd., 1893. For further details of his connexion with the University of Virginia, see *Bulletin of the Bureau of Rolls and Library of Department of State* [*s.v.* G. Long]; P. A. Bruce, *History of the University of Virginia*, 1819–1919, 40, N.Y., 1920, i. 362–3; ii. 9–13, 95, 144–5, 149.

Killigrew, Henry, D.D. (1613–1700). xi. 108*a*, ll. 10–8 from foot. For 'Sir Charles . . . Killigrew's play' read 'An adaptation, "The Tyrant King of Crete," is printed in Sir Charles Sedley's "Works," 1722; there is nothing to show that Sedley had anything to do with it (V. de Sola Pinto, *Sir Charles Sedley*, 1927, pp. 280–1).'

Nugent, Christopher (*d.* 1775). xiv. 705*a*, l. 30 from foot. For 'Oct.' read 'Nov. (*Gent. Mag.*, 1775, p. 551).'

L. F. Powell.

King, Sir Edmund. xi. 128*a*. To bibliography add, 'B.M. Add. MS. 29585 contains original letters of Sir Edmund King, Knt., to Christopher Hatton, second Lord and first Viscount Hatton, and his wife, 1677–1704.'

King, Henry. xi. 133*b*, l. 10. The registers of St. Gregory's-by-St. Paul's, now at St. Martin's, Ludgate, record the burial of his wife under date 5 January 1623/4. Other entries relate to the burial of his daughter Anne on 3 January 1622/3, and the baptism of his sons Henry and Philip on 4 April 1622 and 6 October 1623 respectively.

G. C. M. S.

King, James, Baron Eythin. xi. 135*a*, ll. 24–3 from foot. For 'was son . . . Aberdeenshire' read 'was son of David King of Warbester Hoy, in Orkeney, by Mary, daughter of Adam Stewart, Carthusian prior of Perth (G.E.C., *Complete Peerage*, v. 227–8).'

Ibid. l. 3 from foot. After '"of good value" and' insert 'promised, but never gave, him' (*ibid.* p. 228).

Ibid. 135*b*, ll. 12–15. For 'On 28 March 1643 . . . derived' read 'By patent dated at York, 28 March 1642, he was created Lord Eythin, the title being derived' (*ibid.*).

Ibid. 136*a*, ll. 1–2. For 'He was married . . . (*ib.* 1640, p. 443)' read 'He was married twice: first to Diliana van der Borchens, of Pomerania, and secondly to a lady whose name is unknown, by whom he had a daughter (G.E.C., *Complete Peerage*, v. 228; *Cal. State Papers, Dom.*, 1640, p. 443).'

King, John. (1652–1732). xi. 141*a*, l. 34. For '4455' read '4055.'

King, Peter, first Lord King. xi. 146*a*, l. 5 from foot. For 'four' read 'five' and after 'John' add 'James (d. 1711).'

Ibid. l. 4 from foot. For 'Each of his sons' read 'Four of his sons outlived him and each'.

To authorities add: Manning and Bray, Surrey, iii. 124.

R. W. Bloxam.

Kingsley, Henry. xi. 181*b*, l. 19 from foot. After 'King's College' insert 'School' (*Times Lit. Suppl.*, 2 Jan. 1930, p. 1, col. 2).

Kirwan, Walter Blake. xi. 230*a*, 18 ll. from foot. After '1754' insert 'He was the elder son of Patrick Fitz Thomas Kirwan of Galway and Mary, second daughter of Walter Blake of Carrowbrowne, near Galway, who was a brother of the Revd. Doctor Anthony Blake, titular (Catholic) Primate of Armagh. (M. J. Blake, *Blake Family Records*; 1st ser., 1902, pp. 191–2 and 2nd ser., 1905, p. 211).

M. J. B.

Knighton, Sir William. xi. 271*a*, l. 25. After 'Spain,' insert 'having been included in the expedition through the influence of Poll Raffles, one of Wellesley's mistresses (*Eng. Hist. Rev.*, lv. 57–8),'

Ibid. l. 28. After 'physicians' insert 'in Jan. 1812 (*ibid.* p. 58)'

Ibid. l. 27 from foot. For '1818' read 'Sept. 1817 (*ibid.*)'

Ibid. 271*b*, l. 4. After 'Bloomfield' insert 'in Sept. 1822 (*Eng. Hist. Rev.*, lv. 64)'

Ibid. l. 28. After '54).' insert 'In 1823 George IV wished the prime minister to make him a privy councillor, but Lord Liverpool refused, and thenceforth Knighton constantly endeavoured to undermine Liverpool's position (*Eng. Hist. Rev.*, lv. 66–7).'

Knyvet, Thomas, Lord Knyvet of Escrick. xi. 340*a*, ll. 20–19 from foot. For 'Thetford in the parliament of 1601' read 'Westminster in the parliaments of 1586, 1588–9, 1597, 1601, and 1603–4 (*Return of M.P.'s*, i. 418, 424, 434, 438, and 444; see also BULLETIN I.H.R., xii. 11, for further discussion of identity).'

Ibid. ll. 14–13 from foot. For 'at the Tower on 14 March 1603–4' read 'before 26 Sept. 1601' (the date of his first return to parliament with the rank of knight).

Lacy, Henry de, third earl of Lincoln. xi. 373*b*, ll. 27–30. For 'probably born . . . v. 643)' read 'born in Jan. 1250/1. (G.E.C., *Complete Peerage*, 2nd ed., vii. 681; *Cal. Close Rolls*, 1247–51, p. 405; *ibid.* 1272–9, p. 462; *Cal. Inq. P.M.* i. 115, 187).'

Ibid. l. 31. For 'on 21 July 1257' read 'in June 1258 (Dugdale, *Mon. Anglic.* v. 647; *Cal. Close Rolls*, 1256–9, *passim*).'

Layfield, John, D.D. (*d.* 1617). xi. 745*b*. See *Notes and Queries*, cxlvii. 30, for his parentage and marriage.

Lamb, Frederick James, third Viscount Melbourne and Baron Beauvale. xi. 429*b*, l. 7 from foot. After '1820' insert 'envoy extraordinary and' (credential, P.R.O., F.O. 90/7, p. 6).

Lamb, Frederick James, third Viscount Melbourne and Baron Beauvale. xi. 429*b*, l. 15 from foot. After '1803.' insert 'For a time he served as a cornet in the Royal Horse Guards (G.E.C., *Complete Peerage*, viii. 639).'

Ibid. l. 6 from foot. After 'Munich.' insert 'He left on a special mission to Frankfort in Jan. 1817, and was simultaneously accredited to the Germanic Confederation in the following November. He did not return to Munich until Jan. 1820, two months before his recall. He then received new credentials as envoy extraordinary and minister plenipotentiary at Frankfort, where he remained until July 1823 (Camden 3rd series, l. 23, 56–7).'

Ibid. last line. After 'ambassador' insert ', accompanying Dom Miguel on the journey from London (*ibid.* 93)'

Ibid. 430*a*, l. 9. After 'He' insert 'had presented his credentials to Dom Miguel as regent, 5 March 1828, but in consequence of Dom Miguel's usurpation of the royal title he left Lisbon on 5 July (Camden 3rd series, l. 93), and'

Ibid. 430*b*, l. 5. For 'in May' read 'on 24 Nov. (G.E.C., *loc. cit.*).' [See also BULLETIN, xii. 68.]

Lambarde, William. (1536–1601). xi. 438*a*. See below, Migrations of MSS.

Lambarde, William. xi. 438*b*. Before 'In 1570' insert 'He was probably M.P. for Aldborough, Yorks, in 1562–3 and 1566, and author of the first known parliamentary precedent book.' Manuscripts of this are in B.M. Add. MS. 5123, Harl. 2234 and 4619. An incomplete and corrupt copy was published in 1641 with the title 'The | Orders | Proceedings, Punishments, | and Priviledges of the Commons . . .' and reprinted in the *Harleian Miscellany*. See *Eng. Hist. Rev.* xxxix. 50, note 3.

J. E. N.

Lambert, John. xi. 452. The date of his birth is given in a horoscope as 17 Sept. 1619 (Bodleian Library, MS. Ashmole, ccxliii. f. 160*v*.).

E. S. DE B.

Lambert, John (1619–1683). xi. 452*a*. The article was written in 1892. The references to the first edition of Ludlow's *Memoirs* in it should be altered to fit the edition of 1894, which contains additional information about him in its footnotes. It is also necessary to add references to the three later volumes of the *Clarke Papers*, etc.

Lambert's military commissions can be more exactly given. About Jan. 1646 he obtained command of the foot regiment previously commanded by Edward Montagu, and so entered the New Model. After he took over the command of the forces in the North of England (August 1647) this regiment passed to Sir William Constable. Lambert became about 1648 colonel of a cavalry regiment raised in Yorkshire. In addition to this, in July 1650 he was given the command of a Yorkshire regiment of foot, hitherto Col. Bright's. He was also major-general from 1650 or earlier. The Protector's letter demanding the surrender of all his commissions, dated 13 July 1657, is printed in the 3rd Report of the Hist. MSS. Comm., p. 247. Lambert lost thereby as major-general £365 per annum, and the same as colonel of a foot regiment, and £474 10*s.* as colonel of a cavalry regiment—in all £1,224 10*s.*; and besides that £1,000 a year as a member of the Protector's council. But until some reward for his past services should be conferred upon him by parliament, Cromwell continued apparently his pay as major-general (*Clarke Papers*, iii. 114, 119; *Harleian Miscellany*, iii. 452). On the fall of Richard Cromwell the Long Parliament restored Lambert to the command of both his regiments, but he did not get back his commission as major-general. When he was sent to suppress the rising headed by Sir George Booth he was given merely a temporary commission, and the demand of his officers was that it should be made permanent.

455*a*, l. 1. As a member of Cromwell's council Lambert strongly opposed the expedition to the West Indies (*Clarke Papers*, iii. 207).

455*b*, l. 3. His opposition to the revival of kingship is traced in detail in *The Last Years of the Protectorate*, i. 126–90. His negotiations with Monck in 1659 are set forth at length in *Clarke Papers*, vol. iv., and three personal letters to Monck explain his political views much more clearly than the public manifestos (pp. 77, 148, 182).

457*b*, l. 32. The manner of Lambert's escape from the Tower in April 1660 is explained in a passage from Rugge's Diary printed in a note to Pepys (ed. Wheatley, i. 111).

458*b*, l. 15. On the cause of his death see George Clarke's story (*MSS. of Mr. Leyborne-Popham*, p. 263).

Lambton, J. G., 1st Earl of Durham.
The whole account of Durham's Canadian policy needs rewriting in the light of Reid's *Life* (2 vols., 1906) and Egerton's *Hist. and Geography of Canada*, 1908, and Sir Charles Lucas' *Lord Durham's Report*, 3 vols., 1912.

Lancaster, Sir James. xi. 477*b*, l. 19. After '(*d.* 1618)' add 'a native of Basingstoke.'

479*b*, l. 16. After '9 June' add 'He was buried in the church of Allhallows, London Wall (Register, cited in *Mariner's Mirror*, xiv. 167).'

Lancaster, Sir James. xi. 477*b*, l. 21. After 'East Indies,' read 'and a native of Basingstoke,'

Ibid. 479*b*, l. 14. For ', probably in May,' read 'in London'

Ibid. l. 19. After 'in the will.' insert 'He was buried in the church of Allhallows, London Wall, 9 June (*Registers of Allhallows, London Wall, 1559 to 1675*, ed. E. B. Jupp and R. Hovenden, p. 194).'

Add to list of authorities: Mariner's Mirror, xiv. 167–8.

Lancaster, Thomas. xi. 484*a*, ll. 29–34. Delete 'An enthusiastic protestant . . . well known.' This statement is based upon the forged documents of Robert Ware, printed in 'Harleian Miscellany,' v. 595–606 (*see* art. Ware, Sir James, below).

Ibid. 485*a*, l. 6. For 'which is' read 'which was.'

Landor, Walter Savage. xi. 495*b*, ll. 5–3 from foot. For 'He was placed . . . Derbyshire' read 'He was placed accordingly, about 1791, as a private pupil, with the Rev. William Langley, headmaster of Ashbourne Grammar School and rector of Fenny Bentley near Ashbourne, Derbyshire.'

L. F. Powell.

Langdale, Marmaduke, first Lord Langdale, xi. 537*b*, 7 ll. from foot.

On Langdale's surprise of Berwick in 1648 see the narratives printed in vol. ii. of the *Miscellany of the Scottish History Society*, 1902, and also *Rushworth*, vii. 1099–1114.

538*a*, 14 ll. from foot. In 1655 Langdale was very active in the design for engaging the Levellers to join the Royalists against Cromwell, and negotiated with Richard Overton and Edward Sexby for that purpose (*Nicholas Papers*, iii. 51, 118, 128). The report of the Hist. MSS. Comm. on the MSS. of Mrs. Harford, of Holme Hall, Yorks. (*Var. Coll.*, 1903, ii. pp. 348–366) prints letters from the Queen of Bohemia, Charles II. and various royalists to Langdale, including eighteen from Sir E. Hyde. A Life of Langdale by F. H. Sunderland was published in 1926.

Langton, Walter (d. 1321). xi. 570*a*, l. 36. For '*Cal. Inq. post mortem*, i. 300,' read '*Cal. Inq. post mortem*, vi. 330 (pp. 194–8).'

Laroon, Marcellus, the younger, xi. 595*b*, l. 8. For 'He was soon' read 'On 20 Sept. 1707 (C. Dalton, *Engl. Army Lists*, vi. 67)'. l. 15. After 'Spain' add 'and on 28 Nov. 1710 he was appointed lieutenant in General Stanhope's dragoons (P.R.O., War Office, Half-pay Lists, 1714, 25/2984). l. 20. After 'London' add 'and was placed on half-pay on disbandment of his regiment (*ibid.*)'. ll. 20–21. For 'In 1715 . . . dragoons' read 'On 22 July 1715 he was appointed captain-lieutenant in a newly-raised regiment of dragoons under Colonel Wm. Stanhope with which he served (C. Dalton, *George the First's Army*, i. 124)'. l. 22. After 'Scotland' add 'He was promoted captain on 14 Jan. 1718 (*ibid.*, p. 217) and his regiment being disbanded in Nov.' l. 23. For 'eight' read 'five (P.R.O., War Office, Half-pay Lists, 25/2979)'. l. 24. For 'In 1724' read 'On 1 Jan. 1724 (C. Dalton, *op cit.*, ii. 216)'.

Lassels, Richard. xi. 602*b*, l. 5 from foot. For 'Brackenborough, Lincolnshire,' read 'Brackenbury, Kirkby Wispe, Yorks., by Elizabeth, daughter of Francis Tunstall of Thurland Castle, Lancs. (Foster, *Visitation of Yorkshire*, p. 61).'

603*a*, ll. 12–18. The ultimate source for the first statement is apparently a paper by Dr. George Leyburn [q.v.] attached to one of the Douay diaries; for the second Leyburn and Wood. But Leyburn gives Lassels's first name as John (Richard's brother John and two other brothers were all at Douay); as he makes John Lassels also the traveller, etc., he has either made a simple error or confused the two brothers' careers. Wood's value here is uncertain.

Ibid. l. 25. After 'Museum' add '(abstract in *Notes and Queries*, 12th ser., i. 141–144).'

Ibid. ll. 25–48. For bibliography of 'The Voyage of Italy' see *ibid.* clx. (1931), 292–3.

Ibid. l. 4 from foot. Add to list of authorities: Douay College Diaries, 1598–1654 (Catholic Record Soc., 1911).

E. S. de B.

Latham, Robert Gordon, M.D. xi. 609*a*, l. 32. Add 'resigning his chair at University College in 1845' (*University College, London. Proceedings at the Annual General Meeting . . .* , 1846, p. 7).

Lawrence, Sir Thomas (1769–1830). xi. 720*a*, l. 1. For '4 May' read '13 April' (*Times*, 9 Jan. 1930, p. 6, col. 5).

Layard, Sir Austen Henry. 1st Suppl. p. 956. The sections dealing with Layard's diplomatic career after 1869 need rewriting in view of the unusual nature of his recall in 1880. In an unpublished memorandum upon his relations with lord Granville, he states that his appointment to Madrid was due to Gladstone's urgent request, through lord Clarendon, in order to provide an office for A. S. Ayrton [q.v.], who had quarrelled with Lowe. (B.M. Add. MS. 38934, ff. 22–3). He attributed his recall in 1880 to the opposition of the radical wing of the government, which also opposed successfully his appointment as ambassador to Rome in 1881, after Granville had twice promised it to him (*ibid.* ff. 42, 47). He thereby lost his pension (*ibid.* f. 32).

Ibid. 957*a*, l. 24. For 'Layard's Autobiography, 1903' read 'B.M. Add. MS. 38931–39164, official and private correspondence, with eight volumes of memoirs, of which sections in i. cover the period of "Early Adventures" (to 1847), ii. and iii. deal with the Spanish mission (1869–77), iv.–viii. with the Constantinople embassy. The middle period is covered by "Autobiography and letters . . . until his appointment as H.M. Ambassador at Madrid," 2 vols., 1903.'

W. N. M.

Layer, John. xxii. 957*a*, l. 27 from foot. Before 'son' insert 'second'

Ibid. l. 24 from foot. After 'lawyer,' insert 'being admitted to Gray's Inn, 21 May 1606 (Foster, *Admissions to Gray's Inn*, p. 112); and for several years he served as a J.P.,'

Ibid. l. 21 from foot. After 'Cambridgeshire' insert ', having inherited the manor from an uncle.'

Ibid. l. 8 from foot. For 'His' read 'Transcripts of his'

Ibid. l. 5 from foot. After 'and' insert 'transcripts of'

Add to list of authorities: W. M. Palmer's John Layer (1586–1640) of Shepreth, Cambridgeshire, a seventeenth century local historian (Camb. Antiq. Soc., octavo publications, liii).

Leake, Stephen Martin. xi. 763*b*, l. 7 from foot. After 'Society' insert 'although his name does not appear in the society's "Record".'

Lee, Sir Thomas. xi. 824*b*, l. 29. After '1701' insert 'and from 1710 to 1722 represented Chipping Wycombe (*Return of M.P.'s*, ii. 18, 29, 37).

Leeds, Edward (d. 1590). xi. 833*b*, l. 25. For 'Cumberland' read 'Cambridgeshire'. The brass referred to, ll. 31–33, is in Croxton church, Cambs. (Brit. Mus., Add. MS. 5820, 63).

Leeves, William. xi. 837*a*, ll. 15–14 from foot. For '20 June 1769' read '8 June 1764 (*Army List*, 1765, p. 45)'; for 'on 23 Feb. 1772' read 'and captain on 5 Feb. 1772 (*Army List*, 1773, p. 48), retiring on 5 Feb. 1776 (Sir F. W. Hamilton, *Origin of the Grenadier Guards*, iii. 456)'

Leland, John. xi. 892*b*, ll. 16 and 14 from foot. For '25' read '17,' and before '*Lansd. MS.*' insert '*ibid.* iv. 6490 [21]' (wrongly indexed as '20' under 'Leylond').

Ibid. 893*b*, six lines down last paragraph. For 'held' read 'was granted on 26 March 1543'.

Ibid. 894*a*, l. 4. After 'maintenance' insert '(*Cal. Patent Rolls*, 1550–3, p. 181).'

Ibid. 896*b*, l. 22. Delete 'Tanner's Bibl. Brit.' (cf. *ibid.* l. 19), and add 'Letters and Papers of Henry VIII, vols. xiii–xxi.'

Leland or Leyland, John (1506?–1552). xi. 895*a*, l. 8. For '1594' read '[1596?].'

Ibid. l. 9. For '1610' read '1631, pp. 688–91.'

Ibid. l. 10. For 'v.' read 'vol. i.'

Lennox, George Henry. xi. 930*a*, l. 6 from foot. After 'foot-guards' add '(Coldstream guards, *Journ. of Soc. for Army Hist. Research*, xix. 20)'

Ibid. 930*b*, ll. 5–6. After 'colonel.' insert 'He was returned M.P. for Chichester in 1761, and was elected to Parliament as one of the knights of the shire for Sussex in 1768, 1774, 1780, and 1784 (*Return of M.P.'s*, ii. 131, 143, 156, 169, 182)'; and for 'On 22 Dec. 1762 . . . the 25th foot.' read 'On 29 Dec. 1762 he obtained the command of the 25th foot, which he held until his death in 1805 (*Journ. of Soc. for Army Hist. Research*, xix. 20; *Army List*, 1805, p. 152).'

Ibid. l. 8. After 'Minorca' insert 'in Jan. 1769 (*Journ. of Soc. for Army Hist. Research*, xix. 28)'

Ibid. l. 19. After '1772,' insert 'lieutenant-general on 29 Aug. 1777 (*Army List*, 1778, p. 79),'

Ibid. l. 22. For '25 Oct.' read '12 Oct. (*ibid.* 1793, p. 101)'

Lesieur, Sir Stephen. xi. 946*b*, l. 7. After 'Frenchman' insert 'He came to England about 1575 and became the servant of Philip Sidney. Through the influence of his patron he was introduced to court circles, and was employed on various diplomatic errands in Germany and the Netherlands. In 1585 he assisted (Sir) Thomas Morgan [*q.v.*] in negotiations for the capitulation of Antwerp to the Duke of Parma. On 14 October he was captured while carrying despatches from Gravelines to England and was imprisoned for twenty-two months at Dunkirk.'

Ibid., l. 7. Delete 'He was living . . . in England' and insert instead 'Shortly after regaining his freedom Lesieur was employed as a political agent by Peregrine Bertie, Lord Willoughby de Eresby [*q.v.*].'

Ibid., l. 12. For 'Cecil took . . . about 1598' read 'Lesieur received his first important appointment in 1597, when Sir Robert Cecil sent him to Hamburg on behalf of the merchant adventurers who had been banished from Germany by the Emperor in reprisal for the loss of the Hansa's privileges in England.'

Ibid., l. 22. For 'he seems . . . from 1605' read 'He received a small pension in March 1602 and in 1606 was employed by the crown as a collector of fines and rents.'

Ibid., l. 26. After '1000*l.*' read 'He was knighted 25 March 1608.'

For considerable additional material for biography, and references for the above, see *Eng. Hist. Rev.*, xl. 22.

Leslie, John, bishop of Ross. xi. 976*b*, ll. 14–41. A copy of the 1675 edition of the *De origine, moribus, et rebus gestis Scotorum* was recently offered for sale by Messrs. McLeish & Sons of Houghton Street. It had the dedication leaf, which was slightly smaller than the remainder of the book and was printed on thicker paper. The collation of the book was correct without it, confirming the assumption that it was inserted only in a few copies (McLeish: *Cat.* No. 30, 1927, p. 39).

Leslie, Thomas Edward Cliffe. xi. 987*b*, l. 31. Insert 'During the session 1867–8 he acted as deputy for J. E. Cairnes [q.v.], professor of political economy at University College, London' (*University College, London. Proceedings at the Annual General Meeting . . . 26th February* 1868, p. 11).

Lettsom, John Coakley. xi. 1013*b*, l. 9 from foot. For '1771' read '1773.' Delete 'afterwards' (*Record of Royal Soc.*, p. 357).

Leveson-Gower, Granville George, second Earl Granville. xi. 1029*a*, l. 23 from foot. For 'in 1836' read 'on 8 Feb. 1837

(*Members of Parliament, Return*, ii. 355).'

Ibid. l. 22 from foot. For 'of 1837' read 'of the same year.'

Ibid. ll. 20–19 from foot. For 'in 1836' read 'on 17 April 1837.'

Leybourne, Leyburn, Lemburn, or Leeburn, Roger de. xi. 1089*b*, l. 16. For 'at once' read 'on 15 Aug. (*Eng. Hist. Rev.*, liv. 194–5)'

Ibid. l. 18. For '3 Dec.' read '5 Dec. (*ibid.*)'

Ibid. 1090*a*, l. 21. After 'Trent.' insert 'On 20 Oct. 1265 he was given the custody of Carlisle castle and made sheriff of Cumberland (*Eng. Hist. Rev.*, liv. 195).'

Lhuyd, Edward. xi. 1097*b*, l. 21. After 'Woodward' insert '(although Lhuyd's name does not appear in the society's "Record").'

Ligonier, John, Earl Ligonier (1680–1770), xi. 1121*a*, l. 16 from foot. For 'French Hospital in Shaftesbury Avenue', read 'French Protestant Hospital (La Providence) now (1961) at Rochester.'

Ligonier, John, otherwise Jean Louis, Earl Ligonier. xi. 1121*b*, ll. 6–8. After 'above,' insert 'was appointed ensign in Major-General Livesay's regiment on 23 Dec. 1711 (Dalton, *Eng. Army Lists*, vi. 82). On 24 May 1720 he was appointed lieutenant in the royal regiment of horse guards (Dalton, *George the First's Army*, ii. 196) and became captain in the 9th dragoons on 5 May 1722 (*ibid.* p. 367). He was promoted major of this regiment on 1 May 1729 and lieutenant-colonel on 8 July 1732 (P.R.O., Index 5435, pp. 8, 10). He'; for 'in 1720' read 'on 18 July 1739 (*ibid.* 5437, p. 16)'

Ligonier, John, otherwise Jean Louis, Earl Ligonier. xi. 1121*b*, l. 30 from foot. After 'entered' insert 'Sir Robert Rich's (4th) dragoons on 1 Oct. 1748 as 2nd cornet (P.R.O., war office, commission book, 25/22, p. 227), but was placed on half-pay, 25 Dec. 1748 (*ibid.* half-pay lists, 25/2987). He next entered'

Lilburne, John. xi. 1124*a*, 6 ll. from bottom. Lilburne's letter to Judge Reeve should be dated 6 June 1646, not 1647. On his contest with the Lords, see C. H. Firth, *The House of Lords during the Civil War*, pp. 157–167.

Ibid., 1127*a*, l. 27. Add: 'Lilburne thanked Cromwell "for the most obliging and noble favours manifested unto myself, after so many high and unfortunate misunderstandings betwixt us, in your late signal and most remarkable friendly carriage towards me and in my behalf," and promised grateful and devoted support in return (13 Jan. 1651; *MSS. of the Marquis of Bath*, ii. 92).'

Ibid., 1127*b*, l. 20. On the history of the dispute about the Durham collieries, see *Royalist Compositions in Durham and Northumberland* (Surtees Society, 1905), pp. 275, 390.

Ibid., p. 1128*b*, l. 23. Omit 'Guernsey.'

Ibid., l. 42. On Lilburne's conversion to Quakerism, see N. Penny, *The First Publishers of Truth* (1907), p. 144; *Clarke Papers*, iii. 62.

Ibid., p. 1129*b*. Add to the list of authorities: T. C. Pease, *The Leveller Movement*, Washington, 1916, in which the development of Lilburne's political ideas is clearly traced; Gardiner, *History of the Commonwealth and Protectorate*, and Bernstein in *Die Vorläufer des Neueren Sozialismus* (1895), ii. 533–640.

Lilburne, Robert. xi. 1130*a*, l. 12. Omit the reference to the Clarke MSS., and after 'superseded by Monck on 23 April 1654,' add 'His correspondence during his command is printed in Firth, *Scotland and the Commonwealth* (1895), and in *Scotland and the Protectorate* (1899), pp. 8–90.' On his conduct in 1659–60, see *Clarke Papers*, iv. A miniature of him by Cooper in the Victoria and Albert Museum is reproduced in G. Davies, *The Early History of the Coldstream Guards*, p. 18.

Linacre, Thomas. xi. 1145*b*, l. 10 from foot. After 'M.D.,' insert 'on 30 Aug. 1496 (*Eng. Hist. Rev.* l. 696–8),'

Add to list of authorities: Eng. Hist. Rev. xviii. 514–7.

Egerton MS. 2541, f. 127).' [See also Bulletin, ii. 30.]

Lindley, John. xi. 1157*a*, l. 1. For '1829' read '1828.' See *The Times*, 12 May 1828, 6*c*. For further details about Lindley and MS. sources see F. Keeble, *John Lindley*, 1799–1865, in *Makers of British Botany. A Collection of Biographies by Living Botanists*, ed. F. W. Oliver, 1913.

Lindsay, John, tenth Baron Lindsay of the Byres. xi. 1184*a*, l. 2 from foot. After 'public life.' insert 'He was elected a fellow of the Royal Society, 22 June 1663 (BULLETIN, xv. 87).'

Lindsay, William Schaw. xi. 1195*b*, 23 ll. from foot. For 'his uncle, a free kirk minister,' read 'his uncle, the Rev. Dr. Schaw, minister of the secession church at Ayr.' F. MILLER.

Liston, Sir Robert. xi. 1235*b*, ll. 10–1. For '22 Aug. 1788' read '30 June 1789'; for '18 May 1793' read '26 Aug. 1792, when he left on leave and did not return (Camden 3rd series, xlvi. 144; l. 147).'

Ibid. l. 28. For 'the peace of Amiens' read 'Dec. 1800 (Camden 3rd series, l. 185)'

Ibid. l. 31. For 'remained' read 'arrived'; for 'until 14 May 1804' read 'on 12 Sept. 1802. On 4 June 1803 he demanded passports and left shortly afterwards (*ibid.* p. 179), proceeding on an extraordinary mission to Copenhagen (*ibid.* pp. 42–3). He remained in Denmark until 11 March 1804'

Ibid. l. 16 from foot. For '18 Oct. 1821' read '7 July 1820 (*ibid.* p. 167)'

Littleton, Sir Thomas. (1422–1481). xi. 1252*b*, l. 5. Littleton 'was a member of the Inner Temple, where he gave a reading, still extant (*Harl. MS.* 1691, ff. 188 *et seq.*), on the Statute of Westminster II. . . .' This reading was the work of Richard Littleton. See Bertha Putnam, *Early Treatises on the Practice of the Justices of the Peace* (Oxford Studies in Social and Legal History, vii. 179, n. 5).

Lloyd, Sir Nathaniel. xi. 1309*a*, l. 35. Afte 'Paul's Wharf' add '2 July (*Reg.* iv. 78: Harl. Soc. xli. cited in *Mariner's Mirror*, xiii. 343).'

Lockhart, Sir James. xii. 47. A better account of him is given in 'The Upper Ward of Lanarkshire' by G. V. Irving and A. Murray, 1864, ii. 298–303. The following points may be noted here.

Ibid. 47*a*, 31 ll. from foot. He was never 'Lord Lee,' but laird of Lee.

Ibid. ll. 11–7 from foot. His part in the 'Engagement' is uncertain, but he was apparently not at Preston.

Ibid. 47*b*, l. 5. For 'Blyth' read 'Alyth.'

Ibid. ll. 11, 12. For 'he was set at liberty and in' read 'his release was ordered on 27 May 1653. He was to return to Scotland within six weeks and to give the commander-in-chief there a bond for £1000 for his good behaviour (*Cal. S.P.* Dom., 1652–53, p. 354). In . . .'

Lockhart, John Gibson. xii. 47*b*, l. 28 from foot. For '14 July' read '12 June' (*Times Lit. Suppl.*, 31 Oct. 1929, p. 874, col. 2).

Lockhart, Sir William. xii. 52*a*, l. 12 from foot. After 'Julius' insert 'named after Mazarin; baptised shortly before 4 Jan. 1657/8 (P.R.O., S.P. 78/113, f. 338*a*).'

Loftus, Dudley (1619–1695), xii. 79*b*, l. 13 from foot. For 'King's County' read 'Carmarthenshire'.

Long, George (1800–1879). xii. 102*b*. Some of his letters have recently been published, *Letters of George Long*, ed. Thomas Fitzhugh, The Library, University of Virginia, 1917. For further details of his connexion with the University of Virginia see *The Writings of James Monroe . . .* edited S. M. Hamilton, 7 vols., N.Y., 1898–1903, vii. 118, 164; *Bulletin of the Bureau of Rolls and Library of the Department of State*, nos. 6, 8, 10, 1894, 1895, 1903; *Calendar of the Correspondence of Thomas Jefferson*; *Ibid.*, no. 4, Supplement to no. 4, 1894, 1895, *Calendar of the Correspondence of James Madison*; *Ibid.*, no. 2, 1893, *Calendar of the Correspondence of James Monroe*; P. A. Bruce, *History of the University of Virginia*, 1819–1919, 4 vols. N.Y. 1920, i. 367–9, ii. 1–8, 81–4, 87, 146–50; M. T. Hunter, *A Memoir of Robert M. T. Hunter*, Washington, 1903, pp. 34–5, 130–1.

Lonsdale, earls of, xii. 127*b*, l. 5. For 'Lowther, William, 1757–1844, second EARL, noticed under the first EARL', read '. . . noticed under the (first and) third EARLS'.

Love, Richard. xii. 161*a*, l. 12. After 'portrait' insert 'by Mytens'

Lovell, Sir Thomas. xii. 176*a*, ll. 14–16. The statement that 'in 1502 he became . . . president of the council' is extremely doubtful: see *E.H.R.* xxxvii. 352–3. To the authorities, p. 176*b*, l. 26, add Phillipps Coll. Cat. No. 22253 'Collections for the life of Sir Thos. Lovell, K.G.' (Sale Catalogue, June, 1898, No. 645; bought by J. W. Ford). Phillipps Coll., No. 22252 is probably a transcript of B.M. *Add. MSS.* 12463, which is an account of his estates at his death.)

Lowe, Mauritius (1746–1793), xii. 195*b*, l. 2 from foot. For '28 May' read '7 June'.

Lowther, William (1787–1872), xii. 223*b*, l. 24 from foot. For 'second EARL OF LONSDALE', read 'third EARL OF LONSDALE'.

Lumley, Henry. xii. 271*b*, ll. 28–9. The year of birth, 1660, probably derived from Lumley's epitaph, is incorrect, as Lumley's father was buried on 10 Oct. 1658 (G.E.C., *Complete Peerage*, 2nd ed. viii. 280). The epitaph states that Lumley was in his sixty-third year when he died.

Ibid. l. 29 from foot. For 'in 1685' read 'as captain on 13 June 1685 (Dalton, *Army Lists*, ii. 5).'

Ibid. l. 26 from foot. After 'Anne' add 'He is said to have been converted from Roman catholicism to protestantism in 1687 (N. Luttrell, *Brief Relation*, i. 398); the statement is questionable.'

Lumley, Richard, first Earl of Scarborough. xii. 275*a*, l. 9 from foot. For '(*d.* 1721)' read '(1650?–1721), born probably in 1650 (R. Surtees, *History of Durham*, ii. 142)'

Ibid. 275*b*, ll. 16–18. For 'a Roman catholic . . . Charles II' read 'by Richard Lassels [q.v.], with whom he apparently travelled abroad (dedication of *The Voyage of Italy*). If ever a Roman catholic, he was converted to protestantism probably between 1670 and 1680.' As a catholic he would probably not have been eligible as master of horse to the queen, under the Test Act; he was certainly a protestant when he took his seat in the lords in 1685.

Ibid. l. 20. Delete 'In 1687 he became a protestant.' (*See* art. Lumley, Henry, above).

To list of authorities add: 'C. Dalton, English Army Lists and Commission Registers; A. Marvell, Letters, ed. Margoliouth, p. 330.'

Lupton, Roger. xii. 287*b*. To the authorities add: H. L. Clarke and W. N. Weech's History of Sedbergh School, 1925.

Lutwyche, Thomas. xii. 302*b*, l. 16. For '1715' read '1722' (*Return of M.P.'s*, ii. 45).

Lyle, David. xii. 326*a*, l. 11 from foot. For 'having probably taken that degree in one of the Scotch universities' read 'and graduated at Glasgow in 1755 (Addison, *Roll of graduates of Glasgow*, 1727–1897, p. 344).' J. H. B.

Lyly, John. xii. 329*a*, l. 4. After 'creditors.' add 'But his appeal was unsuccessful, for a letter dated 9 Feb. 1604 (B.M. Add. MS. 12507, f. 140) shows him still seeking a royal pension in recognition of his years of service as court playmaker, evidently hoping that James I would discharge the debt of his predecessor (*Notes and Queries*, clxxvi. 146–7).'

Lynch, Sir Thomas. xii. 337*a*, l. 30. For '1684?' read '1684.'

338*a*, ll. 2–3. For 'apparently . . . sent out' read 'in 1674–5 and his successor, Lord Vaughan, whose commission was first prepared in April 1674 (*Cal. S.P., Col.*, 1669–74, p. 573), arrived in Jamaica on 13 March 1675 (*ibid.*, 1675–6, p. 192).'

Ibid. l. 4. For '1682' read '1681–2 (*Cal. S.P., Col.*, 1681–5, pp. 98, 246 etc.).'

Ibid. l. 10. For 'apparently in 1684' read 'on 24 Aug. 1684 (*Cal. S.P., Col.*, 1681–5, p. 681).'

R. P.

Lyndwood, William. xii. 340*a*. For 'Having taken holy orders . . . Walton on the Wolds' read 'He is described as "Magister," and rector of Walton, dioc. Lincoln (i.e. Walton-on-the-Wolds, Leics.), early in 1403–4, when he was ordained acolyte (17 Feb.; by Thomas bishop of Killala, by licence of the bishop of Ely), sub-deacon (23 Feb.) and deacon (15 March); and again in 1406–7, when he was ordained priest (12 March), having meanwhile become *utriusque juris doctor* (list of ordinations by the bishop and his suffragan in the transcript of the Register of John Fordham, bishop of Ely 1388–1425, in Camb. Univ. Libr. MS. Baker 31).' These dates are earlier than any given in *Archaeologia*, xxxiv. 423. P. G. W.

Lyon, John, eighth Baron Glammis. xii. 348*b*, l. 27. For 'shortly afterwards' read 'a fortnight later'

Ibid. ll. 18–16 from foot. For 'By his wife' read 'He married, 11 Apr. 1561,'; for 'only' read 'second'; for 'Alexander, sixth' read 'William, fifth'; for 'Glammis' read 'by whom he'; and add to list of authorities: G.E.C.'s Complete Peerage, v. 658.

M'Carthy, Sir Charles. xii. 435*a*, l. 18. For '(1770?–1824)' read '(1764–1824).'

Ibid. l. 21. For 'son of John Gabriel MacCarthy' read 'son of Jean Gabriel Guéroult ("Procureur du Roi" of the town of Nogent le Rotrou) and Charlotte Michelle Guéroult, *née* MacCarthy.'

Ibid. l. 26. After 'St. Louis' insert 'who induced him at an early age to adopt his mother's maiden name.'

Ibid. l. 15 from foot. For 'Sierra Leone' read 'Senegal and Goree' and add 'When these settlements were returned to France under the treaty of 1814, MacCarthy was transferred to Sierra Leone, as Governor.'

Ibid. l. 9 from foot. For 'in 1821' read 'on 19 July 1821' (*Journal of the Society for Army Historical Research*, x. no. 396, pp. 143–9).

Mackenzie, George, first Viscount Tarbat, first Earl of Cromarty. xii. 589*b*, l. 10 from foot. He appears to have attended King's College first, for his incorporation in St. Salvator's College, St. Andrews, is dated 7 February 1647 (Univ. Munim.).

J. H. B.

McCulloch, John Ramsay. xii. 463*b*, l. 39. For '1832' read '1837' (*London University* [now University College]. *Minutes of the Sessions of the Council*, iii. 123–4).

Machin, John. xii. 554*a*, l. 4. For '(*d.* 1751)' read '(1679?–1751)' (*Notes and Queries*, clviii. 385).

Machin, John (*d.* 1751). xii. 554*a*, ll. 28–30. Delete 'a mass of his manuscripts is preserved by the Royal Astronomical Society; and.'

Macintosh, Charles. xii. 557*a*, l. 15 from foot. For '1823' read '1824' (*Record of Royal Soc.*, p. 386).

Mackenzie, Sir Alexander. xii. 579*a*. Add to list of authorities: Franz Montgomery's Alexander Mackenzie's Literary Assistant (*Can. Hist. Rev.* xviii. 301–4).

Mackerell, Benjamin. xii. 610*b*, ll. 22–27. For 'From 1724 . . . Coins' read 'From 1724 to 1731 he was library-keeper of the Norwich public library, and in 1732 there was printed "A New Catalogue of the Books in the Publick Library of the City of Norwich in the year 1732, to which is added . . . an Account of Mr. John Kirkpatrick's Roman and other Coins," the dedication being signed by him as "Bibliothecarius." Neither of the copies in the Norwich public libraries contains the account of Kirkpatrick's coins, and it is believed that the account was not printed. The minute book of the public library records that William Pagan was appointed library-keeper in 1731 (G. A. Stephen, *Three Centuries of a City Library*, 1917, pp. 43, 48).'

G. A. S.

Maclachlan, Ewen (1775–1822), xii. 634*b*. Add to sources: P. J. Anderson, 'Ewen Maclachlan', *N. & Q.*, 10th ser., xi. 150–2.

Maclagan, William Dalrymple. 2nd Suppl. ii. 532*a*, l. 23 from foot. For 'Madras cavalry' read '51st regiment of Madras native infantry' (*Notes and Queries*, clix. 47).

Maclean, Allan. xii. 643*b*, ll. 8–20. For 'Ten years later . . . 161)' read 'On 8 Jan. 1756 he was appointed lieutenant in the 62nd (afterwards 60th) royal American regiment then raising in America under the earl of Loudoun (P.R.O., index 5439, p. 51), was promoted captain-lieutenant on 27 July 1758 (P.R.O., war office, succession book, 25/209, p. 144), and on 16 Jan. 1759 was appointed captain of an independent company in New York (*ibid.* p. 224).'

Ibid. ll. 26–7. After 'half-pay.' insert 'On 25 May 1772 he was promoted brevet-lieutenant-colonel (*Army List*, 1773, p. 9)'

Maclellan, Sir Robert. xii. 653*b*, l. 28. For '1641' read '1639.'

Ibid. 654*a*, l. 11. After 'Maclellan.' insert 'He was a prominent figure in the Ulster plantation. In 1610 he was accepted as chief undertaker of Rosses in the precinct of Boylagh, Co. Donegal (G. Hill, *The Plantation in Ulster*, p. 296). For a short time he was farmer of the Haberdashers' proportion and of the adjacent proportion of the Clothworkers (*ibid.* pp. 583–4).'

Ibid. l. 18. For 'May' read 'June'

Ibid. l. 28. For 'in 1641' read 'on 18 Jan. 1638/9'

Ibid. ll. 29–30. For 'Margaret, sixth daughter of Sir Matthew Campbell of Loudoun,' read 'Agnes, fourth daughter of Hugh, first Lord Campbell of Loudoun,'

Ibid. l. 28 from foot. After 'issue.' insert 'He married, thirdly, Mary, daughter of Robert Gage of Raunds, Northants., and widow, first, of John Rowley of Castleroe, Co. Londonderry, and, secondly, of Sir George Trevelyan.'

Add to authorities, G.E.C., Complete Peerage, new ed., vii. 333.

Makin, Bathsua (*fl.* 1673), xii. 835*b*, l. 19. For 'to her by Mrs. Makin', read 'by her to Mrs. Makin'.

Malden, Henry. xii. 861*b*, l. 1. For '1833' read '1831,' *cf.* Key, Thomas Hewitt. For a description of him as a teacher see *The Spectator*, 8 July 1876, pp. 859–60; that the article is clearly by R. H. Hutton, *cf.* W. Bagehot, *Literary Studies*, ed. R. H. Hutton, 2 vols., 1884, i. xiv–xvi.

Malet or Mallet, William (*fl.* 1195–1215). xii. 866*a*, ll. 11–3. For 'Mabel and Helewise' read 'Helewise, the elder, who married Hugh Poyntz and inherited the *caput baroniae* of Curry Malet, and Mabel (*Genealogists' Mag.*, viii. 332)'; for 'Beauchamp and Poyntz' read 'Poyntz and Beauchamp'

Malkin, Benjamin Heath, D.C.L. xii. 868*a*, 6 ll. from bottom. For '1830' read 'December 1829.' See London University [now University College], Minutes of the Sessions of the Council, i. 371. He ceased to lecture in May 1830. *Ibid.*, ii. 70.

Malory, Sir Thomas. (*fl.* 1470). xii. 883*a*. One Thomas Malory, knight, is given in a list of those who accompanied Edward IV. to Scotland, December, 1462 (*Three Fifteenth Century Chronicles*, Camden Soc., p. 157). There are references to Thomas Malory, knight, in *Cal. Pat. Rolls*, 1446–1452, p. 476 and 1452–1461, p. 61; to Thomas Malory, *ibid.*, pp. 556, 612; and to Robert, son and heir of Thomas Malory, tenant-in-chief, *ibid.*, 1467–1477, p. 274 (28 August, 1471). To the authorities add 'Who was Sir Thomas Malory?' by G. L. Kittredge in Harvard University *Studies and Notes in Philology and Literature*, v. (1896), 85–106; 'The Identity of the Author of the Morte d'Arthur,' by A. T. Martin in *Archaeologia*, lvi. (1898) 165–182; and 'Sir T. Malory,' by E. K. Chambers (1922; *Engl. Assoc. Pamph.* No. 51).

Manners, John, ninth earl and first duke of Rutland (1638–1711). xii. 937*a*, l. 38. For 'Anne' read 'Diana' (*Complete Peerage*, 1895, vi. 467).

Ibid. l. 39. For 'first' read 'second.' (*Ibid.*).

Mantell, Gideon Algernon. xii. 984*a*, l. 6. For 'in' read 'on 3 Feb.'

Ibid. l. 8. For 'one' read 'the third son'

Ibid. For 'six' read 'eight'

Ibid. l. 9. For 'two' read 'four'

Ibid. l. 19. For 'by' read 'at St. Bartholomew's hospital and after'

Ibid. l. 6 from foot. For '1835' read 'Nov. 1833'

Ibid. l. 3 from foot. For 'a Miss' read ', in May 1816, Mary Ann'

Ibid. 984*b*, l. 6. For '1839' read '1838'

Ibid. l. 7. For 'after a few years there' read 'in 1844'

Ibid. l. 28. For '10' read '11'

Ibid. l. 32. After 'dinornis' insert 'and emigrated to New Zealand in 1840'

Ibid. l. 33. For 'one daughter.' read 'two daughters.'

Ibid. 985*a*, l. 7. After 'ten years.' insert 'For over twenty years he carried on a remarkable correspondence with Professor Silliman of Yale university, and over two hundred of their letters are preserved in the Yale university library. Mantell's journal, which extends from Jan. 1819 to June 1852, together with a large collection of books and MSS., is preserved in the Turnbull library, Wellington, New Zealand. There is a copy of the journal in the library of the Sussex Archaeological Society.'

Ibid. l. 13. After 'in 1825,' insert 'was secretary of the geological committee in 1841,'

Add to list of authorities: Sussex Archaeological Collections; Sussex Notes and Queries, vi. 74–8; Sidney Spoke's Gideon Algernon Mantell (1927).

Manton, Thomas. xii. 987*b*, 14 ll. from bottom. For 'until about 1670, when he was arrested on a Sunday afternoon' read 'until Sunday, 20 March 1669/70, when he was arrested in the afternoon (B.M. *Add. MS.*, 36916, f. 173).'

Map or Mapes, Walter. xii. 994*b*, l. 7. Delete 'parson' and add 'presented to the church of Ashwell, Hertford (Curia Regis Roll, 68, m. 9) and.'

Ibid. l. 17 from foot. After '(*Opera*, v. 410)' add 'and an inquisition of Michaelmas term, 1210, states that he was dead (Curia Regis Roll, 68, m. 9).'

C. T. F.

Marmion, Shackerley (1603–1639). xii. 1076*b*, l. 2 from foot. Delete 'was buried in the church of St. Bartholomew, Smithfield.'
Ibid. 1077*b*, l. 34. After 'Warburton's cook,' add '"The Crafty Merchant" and "The Souldier'd Citizen" are, however, two distinct plays. The former is by William Bonen and the latter—of which the correct title is "The Soddered Citizen"—may have been by Marmion, but it was more probably by John Clavell. The play was discovered and edited in the Malone Society Reprints 1936.'

Marshall, John (1818–1891). xii. 1126*a*, 8 ll. from foot. For '1847' read '1848' (*University College, London. Proceedings at the Annual General Meeting . . . 28th February* 1849, p. 8).

Marshall, William (1745–1818) xii. 1136*b*, l. 34. *Arbustum Americanam, the American Grove . . .*, first published at Philadelphia in 1785, was by Humphrey Marshall, the american botanist and not by the subject of this article. See G. E. Fussell, *More old English farming books . . . 1731–93*, (London, 1950), p. 119.

Marten, Sir Henry. xii. 1147*b*, 9 ll. from foot. Add 'In the "British Cabinet" by John Adolphus (London, 1799) there is an engraved portrait of him after a painting in Trinity Hall Lodge, Cambridge (*Mariner's Mirror*, xiii. 338).'

Martineau, Harriet. xii. 1194*a*, l. 2. For 'born at Norwich' read 'born in Magdalen Street, Norwich. There is a memorial tablet on the house in Gurney Court, Magdalen Street, part of which reads, "Harriet Martineau, Writer, was also born here, June 12, 1802."'
1198*b*, l. 26 from foot. For '1838' read 'published in 1826 under the pseudonym "A Lady"; a second edition was published in 1838.'

G. A. S.

Martyn, John. xii. 1202*b*, ll. 19–17 from foot. Delete 'in which year . . . through modesty.'
Ibid. 1203*a*, l. 3. After 'life' insert 'In the same year he was elected a fellow of the Royal Society, an honour which he had previously declined through modesty' (*Record of Royal Soc.* p. 332).

Mascall, Leonard. xii. 1289*b*, l. 2 from foot. For 'at Plumstead' read 'probably at Plumpton' (*Times Lit. Suppl.*, 10 July 1930, p. 575, col. 4).

Masham, Abigail, Lady Masham. xii. 1296*b*, ll. 15–13 from foot. After 'George of Denmark' insert '. He was appointed ensign in the Coldstream guards, 23 April 1697 (Dalton, *English Army Lists*, iv. 173), became captain and lieutenant-colonel, 10 Jan. 1704 (*ibid.* v. 46) and brevet-colonel on 20 Oct. following (*ibid.* 166). On 29 April 1707 he was appointed colonel of a regiment of horse (*ibid.* vi. 224)'; delete 'in the army'

Massey, Sir Edward. xiii. 3*b*, 2 ll. from foot. Delete 'on its arrival in London.'
Ibid. 4*b*, l. 30. For 'After the Restoration' read 'On 27 May 1660' (Shaw's *Book of Knights*).
Ibid. ll. 22–20 from foot. Ormerod's 'History of Cheshire' (ii. 2, 732) says that he was buried at Abbey Leise, Ireland.

E. S. DE B.

Mather, Increase, D.D. (1639–1723). xiii. 27*b*. For his letters see *Collections of the Massachusetts Historical Society*, 4th Series, viii. 89–121. R. M. H.

Mather, Nathaniel. (1631–1697). xiii. 28*b*. For his letters see *Collections of the Massachusetts Historical Society*, 4th Series, viii. 1–68. R. M. H.

Mather, Richard. (1596–1669). xiii. 29*a*. For his letters, see *Collections of the Massachusetts Historical Society*, 4th Series, viii. 69–77. R. M. H.

Matthew, Sir Tobie (1577–1655). xiii. 66*b*, l. 5 from foot to p. 67*a*, l. 1. For '. . . "A True Historicall Relation of the Conversion of Sir Tobie Matthews . . ." was unfortunately never printed,' read 'was printed in 1904'. To authorities add: A. H. Mathew and A. Calthrop, *The Life of Sir Tobie Mathew, Baron's alter ego*, (1907).

Matthew Paris. 84*b*, l. 17. For 'in' read 'after, possibly much after (F. M. Powicke, *Modern Philology*, xxxviii (1940). 315–6).'

Maudslay, Henry (1771–1831). xiii. 81*b*, l. 5 from foot. For '14 Feb.' read '15 Feb.' (*Times*, 18 Feb. 1931, p. 10, c. 5).

Maxwell, James (*fl.* 1600–1640). xiii. 116*b*, ll. 24–42. The second James Maxwell described in the article is identified with James Maxwell, earl of Dirleton (117*a*, ll. 6–21), by a letter of 8 July 1648 from William Hamilton, marquis of Lanark and second duke of Hamilton [q.v.], addressed to him as 'now or late Gentleman Usher of the Black Rod to the Lords House' (*The Designs and Correspondencies of the Present Committee of Estates*, printed 16 Aug. 1648, p. 9). Lanark was Dirleton's son-in-law, having married his elder daughter, Elizabeth, in 1638 (G. Burnet, *Lives of the Hamiltons*, vii. 5).

E. S. de B.

Mayerne, Sir Theodore Turquet de. xiii. 150*b*–152*b*. Sir Theodore Turquet de Mayerne was famous as a physician but he is also well known as the compiler of a guide to travel in central Europe, printed at Geneva in 1591, which went through a number of editions. In the preface to this work signed 'Théodore de Mayerne Turquet' and dated 'Ce 12 de Juin 1591,' a full account of the object he had in view in its preparation is given. In this preface, or dedication, addressed 'Au Seigneur Jean Pournas Seigneur de la Piamente mon cousin,' the author acknowledges a debt both to the work of previous compilers and writers and to the assistance given him by his father. The full title is: 'Sommaire Description de la France, Allemagne, Italie et Espagne avec la Guide des Chemins pour aller et venir par les provinces et aux villes plus renommées de ces quatre regions. A quoy est adiousté un recueil des foires plus celebres presque de toute l'Europe. Et un traicté des monnoyes et leur valleur esdicts pays, provinces et villes. Plus trois tables tres-amples: Le tout recueilli pour la commodité des voyageurs.' This title fully sets out the contents and character of the work, which although it may have little in it to be regarded as original was a remarkable compilation for a youth of eighteen years of age. It was reprinted over a period of more than sixty years, the issues known or noted being as follows: 1592 (Geneva), 1596 (Lyons), 1604, 1606 and 1615 (Rouen), 1618 (Geneva), 1624, 1629, 1640 and 1642 (Rouen), and finally 1653 (Geneva).

To the list of authorities at end add: H. G. Fordham, Catalogue des Guides-Routiers et des Itinéraires Français, 1552–1850 (Paris, 1920) and Illustrations Supplémentaires (Cambridge, 1921); H. G. Fordham, The Earliest French Itinéraires, 1552 and 1591, Charles Estienne and Théodore de Mayerne-Turquet (Oxford University Press, 1921: reprinted from the Bibliographical Society's Transactions, *The Library*, 1920, pp. 193–223).

H. G. F.

Mayhew, Henry (1812–1887) xiii. 154*a*, l. 13 from foot. For 'Charlotte Street, Bloomsbury', read '8, Tavistock Street, Holborn' (later 4, Bedford Avenue, Holborn). Evidence from death certificate and burial register at Kensal Green cemetery.

Meade, Richard Charles Francis, Third Earl of Clanwilliam. (1795–1879). xiii. 187*b*, l. 25. After 'Francis' insert 'Christian.'

Ibid., l. 41. For 'fifteen' read 'a year and eight' and after 'months' insert '(*i.e.* on W. R. Hamilton's [q.v.] leaving England on the grounds of ill-health).'

Ibid., l. 43. Before '*cf.* Buckingham' insert 'Public Record Office, F.O. 83/33.' See *Notes and Queries*, cxlvii. 131.

C. S. B. B.

Mellis, Hugh. xiii. 220*b*, l. 3. For 'Hugh' read 'John' (De Morgan's *Arithmetical Books*, p. 27; Lowndes' *Bibliog. Manual*, Bohn, p. 1531; Massey's *Origin and Progress of Letters*, ii. 16).

Menteith, Robert. xiii. 258*a*, l. 13. For '1785' read '1735' and add 'A second part with a separate title page, also dated 1661, continues the narrative from 1646 to 1649.'

E. S. de B.

Mercer, James. xiii. 265*a*, l. 25. For 'joined a British regiment' read 'was appointed ensign in the 25th regiment on 1 Dec. 1758 (*Army List*, 1759, p. 72)'

Ibid. l. 29. After 'Minden,' insert 'was promoted first lieutenant in the 88th or Campbell's highlanders on 4 Jan. 1760 (*ibid.* 1760, p. 171)'

Ibid. l. 31. For 'queen's regiment' read '105th or queen's own regiment of highlanders (*ibid.* 1763, p. 171)'

Ibid. l. 24 from foot. For 'In 1770' read 'On 6 Nov. 1769 (*ibid.* 1770, p. 103)'

Montagu, John, second Duke of Montagu. xiii. 700*a*, ll. 6–4 from foot. For 'but he does not . . . military rank' read 'and was given the rank of colonel of horse on 27 March 1710 (Dalton, *Eng. Army Lists*, vi. 196)'

Ibid. last line. After 'gold stick' insert 'on 10 March 1715, which he resigned in 1721 (J. Millan, *Succession of Colonels*, 1749, p. 1)'

Ibid. 700*b*, l. 23. After 'coronation of George II.' insert 'He was promoted major-general on 16 Nov. 1735 (*ibid.* p. 3).'

Ibid. l. 26. After 'year.' insert 'He became lieutenant-general on 2 July 1739 (*ibid.*).'

Michelborne, Sir Edward. xiii. 328*a*, l. 2. For '1611?' read '1609.'

Ibid. 328*b*, l. 22. For 'and to have died about 1611' read 'He died 27 April 1609, the *inquisitio post mortem*, held 5 April 1610, describing him as seized of the manor of Penherst and as holder of the castle of Bodiam (Horsfield's *History of Sussex*, 1835, i. 561).' G. C. M. S.

Michell, Edward Thomas. xiii. 331*a*, l. 18. For '1787' read '1786'; for 'in 1787' read 'at Huish, Somerset, 10 Nov. 1786 (War Office Library, Officers' services, Royal Artillery, ii. no. 127)'

Ibid. 331*b*, l. 26. For '300' read '400 (War Office Library, Officers' services, Royal Artillery, ii. no. 127)'

Middlemore, George, xiii. 338*a*, l. 2 from foot. After 'Commission' add 'as ensign in the 48th foot on 16 Jan. 1793 (*London Gazette*, 1793, p. 51)', 'was made lieutenant of an independent company, 15 April 1793 (*ibid.*, p. 298), and on 30 Oct. 1793 lieutenant (*ibid.*, p. 1017)'. 338*b*, ll. 3–5. For 'He was . . . year' read 'He was promoted captain-lieutenant on 15 Oct. 1794 (*ibid.*, 1794, p. 1050) and captain on 1 Sept. 1795 (*ibid.*, 1795, p. 1004)'. ll. 22–21 from foot. Delete 'the brevet of lieutenant-colonel and'. ll. 19–17 from foot. For '12th . . . thereof' read 'of the 48th on 2 Nov. 1809 (*ibid.*, 1809, p. 1758), exchanged to half-pay 8th garrison battalion on 28 June 1810, returned to full-pay of the 48th on 21 Mar. 1811 and on 24 Oct. 1811 again exchanged to half-pay of the 12th garrison battalion'. l. 13 from foot. After 'He' add 'was promoted colonel on 12 Aug. 1819 (*Army List*, 1820, p. 21)'.

Middleton, Charles, second Earl of. xiii. 339*a*, ll. 26-28. Delete 'At the Restoration he was appointed by Charles II envoy extraordinary to the court of Vienna.' It was Prince Rupert [q.v.] who was sent to announce the restoration of Charles II (Emperor Leopold to Charles II, 27 Oct. 1661; P.R.O., S.P., lxxx. 11).

Ibid. l. 31. After 'creditors' add 'He was accredited envoy-extraordinary to the emperor's court in June 1680, and was recalled in April 1681 (P.R.O., S.P., civ. 57, 58). He arrived at Linz on 9 Aug. 1680 (N.S.) (P.R.O., S.P., lxxx. 16).'

J. F. C.

Middleton, Charles, second earl of Middleton. xiii. 339*b*, l. 3. After 'king' add 'But as secretary of state he had little influence. He was excluded from the meetings of the king's confidential advisers at which all important decisions were taken; nor was he allowed to conduct all the business of his office, English envoys in the northern department being instructed to communicate only unimportant matters to him. Communications of a confidential character were to be sent to Sunderland, secretary for the southern department, or to Father Edward Petre [q.v.] (Clarke, *James II*, ii. 72, 98).'

M. A. T.

Miege, Guy (1644–1718?). xiii. 368*a*, ll. 31–36. For 'John Chamberlayne . . . his father's work,' read 'Chamberlayne denounced the "New State of England" as plagiarizing "Angliae Notitia" (preface to 18th edn., 1694, & postscript to some copies of 17th edn., 1692), though without naming Miege. In 1704 his son John Chamberlayne [q.v.] renewed the attack on "Mr. Guy Meige [sic], by Birth a *Swisser*," and again in 1707 on "one Miege a Swiss," (prefaces to 21st and 22nd edns.).'

Ibid., ll. 40–41. For 'in the following year,' read '(1705, re-issued in 1707 with new title and postscript, in reply to John Chamberlayne's second attack).'

Ibid., l. 18 from foot. After 'publication' add 'Miege and Chamberlayne were both severely criticized in the preface to another "Present State of Great Britain" (distinct from Miege's own publication), issued

Milbourne, Luke (1649–1720). xiii. 371*a*, l. 8 from foot to 371*b*, l. 1. For 'According to . . . seems now known' read 'He published "The First Book of Virgils Aeneis, made English" in 1688 anonymously; this was identified as his translation by G. Thorn-Drury from a passage in the "Gentleman's Journal," August 1692, p. 17 (B. H. Blackwell, *Catalogue* 294, p. 17; there is a copy of the translation in the Bodleian Library).'

Milner, Isaac. xiii. 457*a*, l. 30. For '1776' read '1780.' Delete 'while still B.A.' (*Record of Royal Soc.*, p. 361).

Millner, John, xiii. 443*b*, ll. 25–33. Delete 'was captain . . . not clear' and insert 'served throughout Marlborough's campaigns in the royal regiment of foot of Ireland (18th Royal Irish) in which he attained the rank of sergeant'. l. 16 from foot. For '1702' read '1701 (Millner's book, title-page and preface)'. After '1712' add 'In 1736 he was still serving with his regiment, as a sergeant, in Minorca, when major Gillman, then in command, wrote home to the colonel recommending that Millner should be appointed adjutant. (G. le M. Gretton, *Campaigns and History of the Royal Irish Regiment*, (1911), p. 71)'. Nothing appears to have come of this proposal.

Mist, Nathaniel. xiii. 500*b*, l. 2 from foot. Before 'On 15 Dec.' insert 'By 6 July 1716 he had become a printer, as the "Citizen" (no. 5) of that date was printed by him (Bodl. Nichols' Newspapers, xxix). Nos. 1 and 3 bear no printer's name; nos. 2 and 4 are not extant.'

501*a*, l. 23 from foot. After '"D.D.F."' insert 'Mist also printed, as an auxiliary to his "Weekly Journal," the "Wednesdays Journal," the first number being dated 25 Sept. 1717 (Bodl. Nichols' Newspapers, xxxiii).' L. W. H.

Mitchell, Sir David. xiii. 514*a*, l. 10. For 'June' read 'May (BULLETIN, xiv. 22)'

Ibid. l. 12. For 'April 1701' read 'Jan. 1702 (*ibid.* p. 23)'

Mitchell, Henry. xiii. 333*a*, l. 4. For 'Bletchingdon' read 'West Blatchington' (*Notes and Queries*, 13th Ser., i. 289).

Molesworth, Robert, first Viscount Molesworth. xiii. 568*b*, l. 27. In *Bulletin* No. 5, p. 58, for 'Grey' read 'Greg' and for 'Rylant' read 'Rycaut.'

Molesworth, Robert, First Viscount Molesworth. (1656–1725). xiii. 568*b*. l. 31. For '1692' read '1689.' His credentials as Envoy Extraordinary to Denmark bear date 4 June 1689 (P.R.O. State Papers Foreign, Foreign Entry Book 2, Denmark 22).

Ibid., l. 37. For '1694' read '1692.' His secretary, Hugh Grey, wrote on 16 July 1692, about his departure with his family (B.M. *Add. MS.* 7076, f. 209). Sir Paul Rylant at Hamburg noted his arrival there 21 June 1692, and his departure for the army in Flanders, 5 July 1692 (B.M. *Lansd. MS.* 1153 D).

There are no dispatches from or to Molesworth at Copenhagen after June 1692. J. F. C.

Monck, George. xiii. 599*b*, l. 22 from foot. For '(*ib.* vii. 37)' read '(*ib.* vii. 387).' E. S. DE B.

Monck, George, first Duke of Albemarle. xiii. 595*b*, 2 ll. from foot. Monck was appointed on 17 July 1647 to command all the Parliamentary forces in Ulster except the Scots (Gardiner, *Great Civil War*, iv. 108).

596*a*, l. 14. Add reference to Reid, *History of the Presbyterian Church in Ireland*, ii. 140–80, which gives a full account of Monck's proceedings in Ulster.

Ibid., l. 32. On Monck's negotiations with O'Neill see Gardiner, *Commonwealth and Protectorate*, i. 74–105.

596*b*, l. 28. On the formation of Monck's regiment see G. Davies, *The Early History of the Coldstream Guards*, 1924.

Ibid. On his campaign in Scotland in 1651 see Firth, *Scotland and the Commonwealth*, 1895, pp. 1–20. After the fighting ended he showed his fitness for the management of civil affairs. 'His temper,' wrote William Clarke, 'every way fits him for this employment, and none could order the Scots so handsomely as himself, he carries things with such a grace and rigid gentleness' (p. 323).

597*a*, 13 ll. from foot. In *Letters and Papers relating to the First Dutch War*, vols. iv., v., ed. by C. T. Atkinson, the letters written by Monck during his command at sea in 1653 are collected.

597*b*, 21 ll. from foot. 'It is impossible to credit him with introducing a revolution in naval tactics. All that can be said is that possibly his genius for war and his scientific and well-drilled spirit revealed to him in the traditional minor tactics of the seamen the germ of a true tactical system and caused him to urge its reduction into a definite set of fighting instructions' (Corbett, *Fighting Instructions*, 1905, pp. 96–104).

598*a*, 13 ll. from foot. Monck's suppression of Glencairne's rising, and his government of Scotland from 1654 to 1658 are the subject of the papers printed in *Scotland and the Protectorate*, 1899, 600–1. Vol. iv. of the *Clarke Papers* and the *MSS. of Mr. Leyborne-Popham* throw some new light on his actions during the changes of 1659–60. Monck's dissatisfaction at the changes made amongst his officers (*Clarke Papers*, iv. 16, 22); his desire to resign (*ibid.*, iv. 90, 152; Guizot, *Richard Cromwell*, i. 475, 486). On the other hand the story told by Price and Gumble about Monck's intended declaration in August 1659 is refuted rather than confirmed by the evidence of the *Clarke Papers*, and seems to be a legend invented in order to antedate his royalism. At that very time Monck imposed on all suspected persons in Scotland an engagement not to act or assist in any design on behalf of Charles Stuart (*Clarke Papers*, iv. 25, 41). The precise reasons which led Monck to refuse to ratify the treaty made by his commissioners with the leaders of the English army are made clear (*ibid.*, iv. 97, 126, 133), and also the exact terms of the agreement he made with the Scots before marching into England and the nature of the support he demanded from them (*ibid.*, iv. 113, 120, 143, 190, 194, 276). Monck's own letters state his motives with convincing force. 'I urged my dismission from the deceased Protector, and very lately from this Parliament; but now being at the head of a part of the army I dare not sit still and let our laws and liberties go to ruin. . . . I am engaged in conscience and honour to see my country freed, as much as in me lies, from that intolerable slavery of a sword government, and I know England cannot, nay, will not endure it. . . . Neither can I see any legal foundation for a free state, unless this Parliament sits down again, or some other legally called' (*ibid.*, iv. 152; *cf.* pp. 22, 87, 90). Of the two courses the restoration of the existing parliament seemed the safer (*ibid.*, iv. 212). He came by degrees to the decision that the restoration of the secluded members must be the next step (*ibid.*, iv. 245, 258, 264; *Leyborne-Popham MSS.*, pp. 148, 151, 154, 221). A narrative called *Mysteria Revelata*, by John Collins, throws some new light on Monck's relations with the opposition in the City (*ibid.*, pp. 212–24). For Monck's commission from the Council of State as commander-in-chief see *Clarke Papers*, iv. 137, 223, 256.

603*a*, 22 ll. from foot. For 'On 15 March' read 'On 8 March.'

604*a*, 18 ll. from foot. For Monck's royal descent see Sandford, *Genealogical History of the Kings of England*, p. 422, and G. E. C., *Complete Peerage*, ed. Gibbs, i. 88.

604*b*, l. 7. In place of 'His position as captain-general was confirmed by a patent for life,' read 'On 3 Aug. 1660 he was appointed captain-general of all the land-forces in the three kingdoms (his commission is printed in Mackinnon, *Coldstream Guards*, and Clifford Walton, *History of the British Standing Army*: it was not granted for life but during the king's pleasure, though Monck held it till his death).'

Ibid., 22 ll. from foot. As to Monck's pledge to Heselrige, refer to *Clarke Papers*, iv. 302, instead of *Hist. MSS. Comm.*, 8th Report, p. 212.

605*a*, 28 ll. from foot. With reference to Argyll's letters to Monck refer to C. Willcock, *The Great Marquess of Argyll*, 1903, pp. 378–85, where the letters are printed at length, instead of to the *Hist. MSS. Comm.*, 6th Report.

606. With regard to Monck's services in the second Dutch War see Colenbrander, *Bescheiden uit vreemde Archieven omtrent de groote Nederlandsche Zeeoorlogen*, 1919, where a number of English and foreign accounts of the battles of June and July 1666 are printed, pp. 316–454. Monck's narrative 'touching the miscarriages in the late Dutch War,' sent to the House of Commons 31 Oct. 1667, at p. 595, is identical with that entered in the *Journals*.

607*b*, l. 24. Delete: 'and a fourth . . . esq.'

608*a*, 23 ll. from foot. On the Duchess of Albemarle see *Leyborne-Popham MSS.*, pp. 226, 229; Harris, *Life of the Earl of Sandwich*, ii. 206.

Monson, Sir John (1600–1683). xiii. 643*a*, l. 5 from foot. For '20 April 1660' read 'in April 1661 (Shaw, *Knights*, i. 164)'

Monson, Sir William (1569–1643). xiii. 646*a*. The edition of his writings in five volumes, by E. Oppenheim, 1902, supplies much additional information.

Montagu, Charles, first Duke of Manchester. xiii. 670*b*, l. 1. After 'first' insert 'public.' He had private audiences soon after his arrival (Grimblot, *Letters of William III and Louis XIV*, ii. 342).

Ibid. l. 11. For 'northern' read 'southern' (*Letters illustrative of the reign of William III*, ed. G. P. R. James, iii. 163; Thomson, *Secretaries of State*, 1681–1782, pp. 3, 181).

Ibid. l. 15. After '(27 April)' add 'to press him to execute the provisions of his treaty with Savoy and to protest against the withdrawal of troops from Italy (P.R.O., S.P. civ. 208).'

Ibid. l. 8 from foot. After 'p. 130' add 'Bath MSS., vol. iii (Prior Papers).'

Montagu, Edward Wortley. xiii. 685*a*, l. 11 from foot. For 'of the allies,' read ', being appointed cornet in Cope's (7th) dragoons on 10 Sept. 1743 (P.R.O., war office, commission register, 25/90, p. 36), was promoted captain-lieutenant in the royal Scots on 29 May 1745, obtained his company on 26 Aug. 1747, and retired on 7 Jan. 1748 (P.R.O., index 5436, p. 178). He had'

Montagu, George. xiii. 693*a*, ll. 18–16 from foot. For 'At an early age . . . regiment of foot' read 'He was appointed ensign in the 15th regiment of foot on 22 June 1770 (P.R.O., war office, succession book, 25/210, p. 127), lieutenant 8 Jan. 1773, and captain 1 Dec. 1775 (*ibid.* 25/211), and served'

Ibid. l. 15 from foot. After 'colonies' insert ', retiring 5 Nov. 1777 (*ibid.*)'

Ibid. ll. 14–12 from foot. For 'acted as . . . for many years' read 'served successively as captain, major, and lieutenant-colonel of the militia of Wiltshire from May 1778 to Oct. 1779 (P.R.O., war office, militia list, 13/2251)'

Montagu, John, fourth **Earl of Sandwich.** xiii. 701*b*, ll. 22–3. No evidence can be found of Sandwich ever having been in Holland before he arrived there in August 1746, having been appointed in the preceding month plenipotentiary at the conferences at Breda (see l. 44).

Ibid., l. 49 to foot of page. The account given of Sandwich's activities at Breda and Aix-la-Chapelle requires amplification from the Foreign Entry Books, Holland, 1713–1759 (P.R.O.). Towards the end of October 1746 Sandwich, while continuing to attend the Breda conferences, was appointed minister plenipotentiary to the states general of the United Provinces. Instructions were given him on 25 November 1746, after the previous revocation of his predecessor, Robert Trevor, who, however, had only held the rank of envoy extraordinary and plenipotentiary (*ibid.*, 18 Nov. 1746). Sandwich had been sent to Breda as the special agent of the war party in the British cabinet, and his private correspondence with Newcastle, which was seen by the king, led to the resignation of the secretary for the northern department, the earl of Harrington, in October 1746, when Chesterfield took his place.

As minister at The Hague, Sandwich entered into relations with the Dutch Orangist war party, particularly with William Bentinck. By this means and by obstructing the peace negotiations at Breda, Sandwich had a great deal to do with the Orangist restoration in May 1747. The duke of Newcastle wrote to Sandwich on that occasion: 'I most heartily congratulate you upon the happy and quiet conclusion of the great affair in Holland, an event that must ever be advantageous to England and make your Lordship's ministry in Holland ever remembered with gratitude and respect' (Geyl, *Willem IV en Engeland tot 1748*, p. 339). Later in the year Sandwich was appointed plenipotentiary at the peace conversations with the French minister Puysieulx at Liége (September 1747; for a despatch of Sandwich from Liége dated 11 September see Beer's *Holland und der Österr. Erbfolgekrieg*). Here he repeated the policy of Breda, obstructing Chesterfield's peace policy.

On 25 February 1748 Sandwich was given his full powers as British delegate to the congress of Aix-la-Chapelle. After receiving urgent instructions to make peace from the governments, who were much impressed by the sudden collapse of the war policy of their Dutch ally, and feared in particular the fall of Maestricht, Sandwich for Great Britain and Bentinck for the states general concluded peace preliminaries with

France (30 April 1748), to which Austria and Sardinia grumblingly acceded. Austria, however, still obstructed the conclusion of the definitive peace. Sandwich, urged on by Bentinck, advocated, in order to bring her to reason, a harsher policy than Newcastle and the king could approve, and this difference of opinion led to a distinct coolness between Sandwich and Newcastle, who so far had been his protector. Thomas Robinson, afterwards first baron Grantham [q.v.], the British ambassador at Vienna, was sent to Aix-la-Chapelle in order to protect the 'old system,' and Newcastle now worked through him rather than through Sandwich.

After the conclusion of the definitive treaty (18 October 1748) Sandwich was recalled as minister with the states general, 29 November 1748, to take up his duties as first lord of the admiralty.

P. Geyl.
J. Astel.

Montagu, Ralph, Duke of Montagu. xiii. 710*a*, l. 14. He was educated at Westminster School under Dr. Busby (*MSS. of Lord Montagu of Beaulieu*, pp. 161–4).

Ibid., l. 32. The letters he wrote to Lord Arlington during his embassy to France (1669–72) are calendared at length in the *Hist. MSS. Comm.*, *Buccleuch MSS. at Montagu House*, i. 418–521.

710*a*.–711*a*. The letters to Danby during 1676–8, in the possession of Mr. Alfred Morrison, are calendared in the *Hist. MSS. Comm.*, 9th Report, pt. i., pp. 451–5. Others belonging to the same series are printed in the *MSS. of Mr. Eliot Hodgkin*, pp. 185–98, where it is shown how much the letters published in 1710 were garbled by the Duke of Leeds himself.

710*b*, 15 ll. from foot. On the causes of Montagu's quarrel with the Duchess of Cleveland see *MSS. of the Duke of Ormond at Kilkenny*, iv. 441–5, and *MSS. of the Marquis of Bath*, ii. 166.

Montagu, **Sir William.** xiii. 719*a*, l. 27. In heading delete 'Sir.' Montagu never became either a knight or a baronet.

Ibid. p. 719*b*, l. 22. For '26 Aug. 1706' read '27 Aug. 1706 (*Evening Post*, 29 Aug. 1706).'

Ibid. l. 31. For 'May' read 'June.'

Montgomerie, Archibald William, thirteenth earl of Eglinton, and first earl of Winton in the peerage of the United Kingdom (1812–61), xiii. 750*b*, l. 17. After 'abuses which prevailed at those elections' add: 'In February 1848 he successfully moved an amendment to the Diplomatic Relations with Rome Bill whereby the Pope was debarred from appointing any cleric as his envoy in Great Britain (*ib.*, xcvi. 876)—an amendment which effectively wrecked the government's attempt to establish diplomatic intercourse with the Vatican.'

Montgomery, **Sir James William.** xiii. 767*a*, ll. 15–6. Delete 'William' (Burke's *Peerage, Baronetage and Knightage*).

Moore, John (1646–1714). xiii. 807*a*, l. 9. He was incorporated M.A. at Oxford, not D.D. (Wood, *Fasti Oxon.* pt. ii. p. 37).

More, **Sir John.** xiii. 871*b*, l. 3 from foot. For 'died' read 'dined.' (R. W. Chambers, *Thomas More*, 1935, p. 51).

More, Sir Thomas. xiii. 876*b*, l. 16. For 'Saturday, 7' read 'Friday, 6'.

Ibid. l. 18. Delete 'only surviving'.

Ibid. l. 31. For 'Thomas' read 'John'.

Ibid. 877*b*, ll. 3–2 from foot. For 'The extant . . . constituency' read 'no returns are extant'.

Ibid. 878*b*, ll. 5–6. For 'afterwards wife of' read 'also named Alice, who married (1) on 21 Aug. 1516 Thomas Elrington (Harpsfield, *More*, E.E.T.S., p. 313) and (2)'.

Ibid. 879*a*, ll. 25–6. For 'accepted a pension' read 'was granted the regular councillor's salary' and delete 'for life'.

Ibid. 880*a*, l. 12 from foot. For 'sub-treasurer to the king' read 'under treasurer of England'.

Ibid. 881*a*, l. 29. For '1528' read '1529'.

Ibid. 892*b*, l. 5 from foot. After 'heretics.' insert '"The Apologye" was edited by A. I. Tafts in 1930 (E.E.T.S.).'

Ibid. 895*b*, ll. 18–17 from foot. For 'Canterbury . . . twenty' read 'king's bench, 1519–73, before she was sixteen'.

Ibid. 896*a*, l. 28 from foot. After 'MS. 6253,' insert 'and was published with the Rastell fragments by Dr. Elsie V. Hitchcock in 1932 (E.E.T.S.)'.

Ibid. l. 18. After 'Singer.' insert 'A critical edition by Dr. Hitchcock appeared in 1935 (E.E.T.S.).'

Ibid. ll. 9–6 from foot. For 'But by far . . . 1891' read 'The best modern lives are Father T. E. Bridgett's (1891), which is unsatisfactory in its treatment of More's attitude to the Lutherans, and Professor R. W. Chambers's (1935), which re-examines the evidence for More's part in religious persecution'.

More, Sir Thomas (1478–1535). xiii. 894*b*, l. 11. After 'Middleton' insert 'widow of Thomas Elrington.'

Ibid. 896*a*, ll. 2–3. For 'apparently about 1535 . . . 27 Henry VIII)' read 'in 1525.'

Ibid. l. 4. For 'was wife of Giles Heron' read 'married Giles Heron in 1525.'

Ibid. l. 7. After 'ser. ii. 35).' insert 'More had been a friend of both his daughters' fathers-in-law, and upon Sir John Heron's death had, in March 1523, been granted the wardship of Giles. Both the sons-in-law sat for Thetford in the Reformation parliament, elected in Oct. 1529, in which all the male members of More's family, save the slow-witted John, found seats. Giles Heron was attainted by special act of parliament in 1540, a few days before Thomas Cromwell (authorities cited in *Times Lit. Suppl.*, 27 March 1930, p. 274, col. 1).'

More, William (1472–1559 ?), under More, William (*d.* 1540). xiii. 897*b*, ll. 3-14. This letter is dated 31 Jan., no year. Noake (p. 202) attributes it to 1531 (he gives the date wrongly as 7 Dec.), but as it is addressed to Cromwell as 'lord visitor of all England' it probably belongs to 1536, to which date it is assigned in 'L.P.', x. 216, where it is summarised.

Ibid. l. 15. The date 1531 depends on Noake, as above. Musard's imprisonment appears to have begun about March 1535 (*L.P.*, ix. 90, 108); the first certain date is 8 August (*ibid.* no. 51).

Ibid. ll. 18-26. For 'Foreseeing . . . (Noake, pp. 133 seqq.)' read 'More had trouble with other monks besides Musard (*L.P.*, ix. 52 (2), 653), who with a Dr. Roger Neckam brought a charge of misprision of treason against him (*ibid.* 90, 204). A commission was sent to Bishop Rowland Lee [q.v.] to try the case (*ibid.* 510). It appears that More was eventually compelled to resign; on 8 Jan. Hugh Latimer [q.v.], then bishop of Worcester, wrote to Cromwell to advise the king not to re-appoint him, although Henry was inclined to do so (*ibid.* x. 56). On 7 March a congé d'élire was sent to the priory (*ibid.* 597 (81)). More made terms with the priory for his future accommodation and maintenance at Worcester and Crowle, a manor belonging to the priory (Noake, pp. 203-4; 8 May 1536), and appears further to have been awarded a pension by the king and to have received a house at Grimley, also the property of the priory (*L.P.*, x. 1272; V.C.H., *Worcester*, iii. 365). On 1 Feb. 1537 More was again on the commission of the peace (*L.P.*, xii. 539 (3)).

'More was buried at Alveston, Warwickshire, on 16 Sept. 1552 (*Misc. Gen. et. Her.*, iv ser., ii (1906). 85). His brother Robert Peers (*d.* 1550) and his family had been settled there from 1540 (*ibid.*); according to a family tradition More lost his pension and ended his days as a dependent on his brother's family (typescript copy of 'Extracts from the History of the Family of Peers,' by M. Adams, Worcester cathedral library).

'His English journal and account book, quoted by Noake (pp. 133 sqq.), have since been published *in extenso* by the Worcestershire Historical Society.'

J. E. H. B. and E. S. de B.

Morgan or Yong, John. xiii. 919*a*, ll. 26–8. For 'There was at least . . . and there were also four sons' read 'His maternal grandfather was Sir Oliver St. John of Bletsoe (*d.* 1437), whose widow, Margaret (*née* Beauchamp), subsequently married John Beaufort, second duke of Somerset, and became the mother of Margaret Beaufort and grandmother of Henry VII. Morgan's second-cousinship to Henry VII explains his sudden promotion after Bosworth. By her first marriage Margaret Beauchamp had two daughters, Elizabeth St. John, who became abbess of Shaftesbury, and another daughter who married Morgan ab Siancyn and had four sons (Bulletin, xv. 157)'

Ibid. l. 20 from foot. After 'Kidwelly,' insert 'Richard III's attorney-general (Bulletin, *loc. cit.*),'

Ibid. ll. 8–7 from foot. For 'A few weeks after his accession' read 'On 6 Oct. 1485 (Bulletin, *loc. cit.*)'

Ibid. l. 6 from foot. For 'Hanslap' read 'Hanslope (*ibid.*)'

Ibid. l. 4 from foot. After 'Windsor' insert 'on 18 Oct. 1485, and on 9 Dec. of the same year dean of St. Mary's, Leicester (*ibid.* pp. 157–8)'

Ibid. 919*b*, l. 3. For 'king's hanaper' read 'parliaments, with 40*l.* a year for life, his appointment dating from 9 Oct. 1485 (BULLETIN, xv. 157)'; for '1493' read '4 July 1488 (*ibid.* p. 158)'

Morgann, Maurice. xiii. 939*a*, l. 29. Insert after 'Welsh family,' 'Was clerk in Secretary of State's office and acted as private secretary to Shelburne.' Following a resolution of the Privy Council, 28 Aug. 1767, to obtain 'precise, solemn and authentic information' on the laws of Quebec and to send out 'a fit and proper person,' he was appointed, 17 Dec. 1767, to consult with Carleton, Chief Justice Hey, and Attorney-General Maseres. He arrived in Quebec 27 Aug. 1768, and returned to England in January 1770 (Canadian Archives, Q. 4, p. 327). He prepared a report which Carleton rejected (ibid., *Shelburne Transcripts*, vol. 66, pp. 81 *et seq.*) as a whole, but used in parts in preparing his own report. The latter had disappeared (Short and Doughty, *Constitutional Documents*, Ottawa, 1918, i. 370, n. 1), but has now been found in B.M. *King's MS.* 207. Morgann's own report has been identified as *Shelburne Transcripts*, vol. 64.

W. P. M. KENNEDY.

Morgann, Maurice. xiii. 939*a*, ll. 29–30, and above, iii. 132. For 'He was' read 'In Oct. 1766 he was appointed (*Cal. H.O. Pap.*, 1766–69, no. 290).'

Ibid. l. 33. For 'during his administration of 1782' read 'In 1782 he was in New York, acting as secretary to Governor Guy Carleton [q.v.] (Clements Library, Ann Arbor, Shelburne papers, 68. *Cf. Canadian Hist. Rev.* xiii. 61–2).'

Add to the list of authorities 'C.W. Alvord's Mississippi Valley in British Politics (1917), i. 279, ii. 220, 222, 226–9; Alvord and Carter in Illinois Hist. Coll. xi. 536ff.'

R. A. H.

Morley, George. xiii. 971*b*, l. 11 from foot. For '1597' read '1598.'

Ibid. l. 7 from foot. For '1597' read '1598 and was baptized at St. Matthew, Friday Street on 5 March (*Register*, Harl. Soc., p. 11).'

Ibid. 972*b*, ll. 25–7. For 'is said . . . (Wood)' read 'joined him at Newport on 12 Nov. 1648 during the treaty (Peck, *Desiderata curiosa*, 1779, p. 403; see also Walker, *Historical Discourses*, 1705, "Perfect Copies," etc., p. 77; and Wood).'

Ibid. l. 30 from foot–973*a*. l. 17. For ', went to the court . . . *Papers*, ii. 333)' read '; he is said to have joined Charles II at the Hague and to have followed him to France (Wood). Charles went to France about June 1649; Morley was at Antwerp on 23 June N.S. He assisted Cosin in conducting services in the chapel of Sir Richard Browne (1605–83) [q.v.] (cf. Evelyn, *Diary*, 7 Nov. 1649) and later held services in Lady Ormond's house at Caen [see under James Butler, duke of Ormond, 1610–88]; but returned with Charles II to the Netherlands and preached the last sermon before him prior to his departure for Scotland in June 1650. About this time there were rumours of Morley's having joined the presbyterians; Hyde, who had already recommended him, now wrote in his defence (*Cal. Clarendon State Papers*, ii. 21, 65; see also the gossip in *Nicholas Papers*, Camden Soc., i. 208). He and Dr. John Earle [q.v.] spent about a year in the house of Sir Charles Cotterell [q.v.] at Antwerp; he then entered that of Lady Hyde there, Hyde himself being absent in Spain. At Antwerp he read the church services twice a day and celebrated the eucharist once a month, besides performing other services; he also had charge of the religious instruction of Anne Hyde [q.v.], the future duchess of York, and of the other members of the family. About the end of 1653 he joined Elizabeth, queen of Bohemia [q.v.] at the Hague, attending her for more than two years without salary and receiving only his own and his servant's diet; his friends in England keeping him supplied. He visited Charles II at Cologne, preaching two sermons before him (he was apparently at Cologne about October 1654, *Nicholas Papers*, ii. 156; and was there in October 1655, *Cal. S. P., Dom.*, 1655, p. 375). On Charles II's settling in the Spanish Netherlands in 1656 Morley rejoined him and remained in his service during the rest of the period of exile, without salary as before. He was one of the most prominent and useful of the English clergy in exile (Morley's biographical information in the preface, etc., to his *Several Treatises*, 1683, on which Wood's account is largely based;

letters attributable to Morley signed 'G. M.', 'Joseph Gower,' etc., 1649–54, in British museum, Harl. MS. 6,942, nos. 138, 140–52; Wood; the queen of Bohemia's correspondence in Evelyn's *Diary and correspondence*).'

Morley, George. xiii. 973*a*, ll. 21–20 from foot. Delete ', being then dean of the chapel royal'

Ibid. 973*b*, l. 19. After 'Charterhouse)' insert ', and dean of the chapel royal on 3 Oct. (*Notes and Queries*, clxxi. 8)'

Ibid. 973*a*, l. 24 from foot. After '*Life*, i. 333).' insert 'From this time until his retirement from court in 1667 he was her "Spiritual Director and *Guide*" (*Several Treatises*, preface, p. xiii).'

Ibid. 973*b*, ll. 25–24 from foot. For 'Morley certainly . . . season.' read 'In Feb. 1668 he was superseded as dean of the chapel in a rather ignominious manner (Pepys, 6 Feb. 1668; *Notes and Queries*, clxxiii. 8).'

Ibid. ll. 21–9 from foot. For 'Some reflections . . . *History*, i. 537, 538)' read 'In Feb. 1679 Morley assisted Sancroft in an unsuccessful attempt to reconvert the duke of York to Anglicanism (*Correspondence of Henry Hyde, earl of Clarendon*, ed. Singer, 1828, ii. 465–71). In the duchess of York's paper setting out her reasons for her conversion [see HYDE, ANNE, *supra*] she attributes to two Anglican bishops certain remarks on the relative positions of the Roman catholic and Anglican churches. Thomas Jones (1622?–1682) [q.v.], in his "Elymas the sorcerer," 1682, suggested that Morley had contributed to the duchess's conversion; stung by this and warned by Evelyn that he was generally identified as one of the bishops, Morley published as a vindication of his protestantism his "Several Treatises," in which he included an account of his relations with the duchess and his letter to her (24 Jan. 1670/1) on the reports of her conversion (Evelyn, 29 May 1682, and wrongly dated letter to Morley in *Diary and Correspondence*, iii. 255–6). The bishops were later identified as Sheldon and Walter Blandford [q.v.]).'

Ibid. l. 5 from foot. For '(*ib.* ii. 428*n.*)' read '(*ib.* ii. 428, Dartmouth's note).'

Ibid. l. 3 from foot. For 'eighty-eighth' read 'eighty-seventh.'

Ibid. 974*a*, ll. 13–5. For 'He was, however, always . . . dissenters' read 'His attitude and behaviour towards dissenters varied from time to time. Burnet describes him as "zealous against papists, and yet a great enemy to the dissenters" (*Own Time*, ed. Airy, ii. 432); Baxter represents his behaviour at the Savoy Conference unfavourably (M. Sylvester, *Reliquiæ Baxterianæ*, 1696, i. 339, 343, 363); later he wanted some form of agreement with the Presbyterians (letter, 1672, appended to *A True Account of the Whole Proceedings Betwixt Ormond and Anglesey*, 1682, p. 28; see also anecdotes in E. Calamy, *Abridgement of Mr. Baxter's History*, 2nd ed., 1713, i. 171*n.*, ii. 344).'

Ibid. l. 19 from foot–974*b*, l. 20. For 'His works . . . Charles II (Bliss)' read 'His principal works are: 1. "Several Treatises," 4to, 1683, illustrating his attitude towards the Roman Catholic church; of the pieces contained in it the "Epistola ad Cornelium Triglandium," written in 1659, had previously been printed surreptitiously at the Hague (preface, p. x; Wood says, in London, 1663); and an English translation of "Ad Janum Ulitium epistolæ duæ" was published in 1707, with a commendatory letter by Dr. George Hickes [q.v.]; the translation is attributed to Hilkiah Bedford [q.v.] (Hearne, *Collections*, ii. 12*n.*). 2. "The Bishop of Winchester's Vindication of Himself from divers False, Scandalous and Injurious Reflexions made upon him by Mr. Richard Baxter in several of his Writings," 4to, 1683; this includes a reprint of Morley's earlier piece, "The Bishop of Worcester's Letter for Vindication of Himself from Mr. Baxter's Calumny," 4to, 1662. He also wrote an epitaph on James I, printed in Dr. John Spotswood, "History of the Church of Scotland," 1665, at end (and in later editions); and in all probability a letter on the death of Lord Capel, appended to the latter's posthumous "Daily Observations or Meditations," 1654, pp. 43–7. In view of his own remarks in the preface to "Several Treatises" two other pieces attributed to him are to be rejected: "A Modest Advertisement concerning the present Controversie about Church-Government," 1641 (Thomason's attribution); and "A Character of Charles the Second," 1660 (Wood's attribution; also attributed to Sir Samuel Tuke [q.v.])'.

Morley, Henry. xiii. 975*b*, l. 40. For '1890' read '1889' (*University College*,

London. Report of the Council . . . to be presented . . . at the Annual General Meeting . . . 26th February 1890, p. 12).

Morrison, **Robert.** xiii. 1008*b*, l. 26. Delete 'After the conclusion of the work'. For '1824' read '1825' (*Record of Royal Soc.*, p. 387).

Moseley, **Henry Nottidge.** xiii. 1073*b*, l. 29 from foot. For '1879' read '1877.' *Ibid.* l. 28 from foot. After 'and' insert 'in 1879.' Delete 'also' (*Record of Royal Soc.*, p. 416).

Moulin, Lewis du. (1606–1680). **xiii.** 1097*a*, 8 ll. from bottom. After 'Du Moulin retired to Westminster' add 'On 18 June 1673, Du Moulin was sent to the Gatehouse for writing and publishing a seditious book called *Patronus bonae Fidei.* The Council ordered him to be prosecuted, but he was discharged on 11 July 1673 (MS. Privy Council Registers, Charles II, xi. 42, 58).'

Moulin, Peter du. (1601–1684). xiii. 1098. At end of article add 'Another Peter du Moulin can be traced from 1667 to 1675. In a petition to the king, about the end of the year 1667, he describes himself as a grandson of Pierre du Moulin [q.v.], and mentions the other Peter du Moulin, then a Canon of Canterbury. After holding minor posts at court he became involved in intrigues with the Dutch during the war of 1672–1674, fled to Holland, and remained in the Prince of Orange's service until 1675, in spite of the English government's attempts to obtain his removal (*Cal. State Papers Dom.* 1677–68, p. 154; C. Huygens the younger, *Journal*, p. 69, 3 October, 1675, N.S.; Sir W. Temple, *Works*, 1731, ii. 330; Burnet, *Own Time*, part 1, ed. Airy, ii. 64, 71. The fullest account of his official career is in V. Barbour, *Arlington*, pp. 212–3).'

Another du Moulin, probably not to be identified with any of those hitherto mentioned, was tutor to the eldest son of George Savile, Marquis of Halifax [q.v.], in 1675 and 1676 (H. C. Foxcroft, *Life of Sir George Savile*, i. 2*n*, 116, 130*n*, 135*n*).

E. S. DE B.

Mowbray, John (vii), fourth Duke of Norfolk. (*s.v.* Mowbray, John (vi), Third Duke). xiii. 1122*a*, 20 ll. from bottom. After '*Peerage*' add 'The will of his wife, Elizabeth Talbot, was proved 28 June 1507 (*Index to Wills, P.C.C., 1383–1558*, i. 285, Brit. Rec. Soc., 1893–5, where the will is wrongly assigned to Elizabeth, first the wife of Sir Humphrey Bourgchier, and second the wife of Thomas Howard, Earl of Surrey, afterwards 2nd Duke of Norfolk of the Howard line).' [The same error occurs in Blomefield, *History of Norfolk*, 2nd edn. v. 151–2, in Nicolas, *Testamenta Vetusta*, 1826, pp. 482–3, and index, *Cal. Pat. Rolls, 1494–1509*. The Duchess Elizabeth whose will was proved in 1507 cannot have been the wife of Thomas Howard, for it was not till 1514 that Surrey was created Duke of Norfolk (Patent of 1 February, 5 Henry VIII. (1513–4), confirmed by Act of Parliament 5 Henry VIII. c. 9). His wife could not therefore be described as Duchess of Norfolk till that year. Elizabeth was, indeed, the name of his first wife, but she died 4 April, 1497. In the Inquisition Post Mortem taken 23 October, 13 Henry VII. (1497), this Elizabeth is described as the wife first of Humfrey Bourgchier, knt., then of Thomas Howard, knt., now Earl of Surrey, and is so indexed in the *Cal. Inq. Post. Mort. Hen. VII.*, vol. ii., while references to Elizabeth, Duchess of Norfolk, in the same volume are found under 'Mowbray.' Apparently no Inquisition Post Mortem of the latter has survived.

In the index to the second edition of *Letters and Papers*, Henry VIII., vol. i. pt. 3, p. 328*b*, Elizabeth, Duchess of Norfolk, is shewn as widow of John Mowbray, *d.* 1476, herself dying in 1507. But one of the references given is to the Earl of Surrey's petition in 1512 to be allowed to enter into the estates of Elizabeth, late Duchess of Norfolk (cf. *Statutes of the Realm*, III. 58). This will be found on examination to refer not to the widow of John Mowbray, but to yet another Elizabeth, daughter of Richard, Earl of Arundel, and widow of Thomas Mowbray, first Duke of Norfolk, *d.* 1399. It was through their daughter, Margaret, that the Howards succeeded to the Norfolk title on the extinction of the male line of Mowbrays. The Inquisition Post Mortem of this Elizabeth is calendared in the *Cal. Inq. Post. Mort.* (Rec. Com.) iv. 83, under date 3 Henry VI.

As long ago as 1871 a writer in *Notes and Queries* (4th series, vii. 384) suggested that the will of Elizabeth, Duchess of Norfolk, proved 28 June 1507, printed by Nicolas,

was wrongly assigned to Elizabeth, wife of Thomas, the 2nd Duke of the Howard line, and that it was the will of Elizabeth, daughter of John Talbot, first Earl of Shrewsbury, by his second marriage, and widow of John Mowbray, last Duke of Norfolk of that line. In proof of this identification he pointed in particular to the wills of Sir Umfray Talbot, knt., 'Marchal of the towne of Calis,' proved 11 November 1494, and of 'Dame Jane Talbott, widowe, late the wif of Sir Humfrey Talbott, Knyght,' dated 10 January 1504–5. The former mentions 'my suster Elizabeth, duchess of Northfolk'; and the latter makes provision for a priest to sing for the soul of Elizabeth, Duchess of Norfolk, 'whan it shall please God to call her owte of this world . . . and also for the soules of the right noble lorde John, erle of Shrousbury and of the lady Margarete his wiffe beyng fader and moder vnto the said Elizabeth, duchess of Norff. and vnto the said Sir Humfrey.' There seems no need of an apology for referring to this article fifty-four years afterwards, since, as has been shewn, the error is still current].

IRENE J. CHURCHILL.

Mudd, Thomas (fl. 1577–1590), xix. 1150*a*, ll. 34–41. For paragraph 'In the catalogue of Ely Manuscripts . . . to 1663,' read 'In 1583 one John Mudd received a salary of £10 as organist of Peterborough jointly with Richard Tiller, which probably indicates that he succeeded Tiller this year. He was drawing this yearly salary as organist from 1584 to 1629 (Peterborough Cathedral Treasurer's Account). On 9th June 1631 Thomas Mudd was elected organist of Peterborough on his father's resignation (Peterborough Chapter Minutes). John Mudd was buried in Peterborough Cathedral on 16th December 1631 (Precentor's Register of Births, Marriages & Deaths). In 1634 Thomas Mudd had been succeeded as organist by David Standish (Precentor's Register, recording the baptism on 14th October of John Standish, the son of David Standish, organist).'

Mudie, Robert. xiii. 1160*a*, l. 12 from foot. After 'R. S. Rintoul,' insert 'editor of the radical *Dundee Advertiser* and'

Ibid. l. 10 from foot. For '. In 1820 Mudie' read 'and his public speeches, charging the council with corruption, brought about his dismissal as teacher of arithmetic in the summer of 1816 (W. B. Thomas, *Story of the Spectator, 1828–1928*, p. 22). His position as teacher of drawing was beyond the council's control. After unsuccessful efforts to found a "Mercantile and Mathematical Academy," he lectured on moral philosophy, rhetoric, logic, and geography, and conducted two short-lived periodicals. On the failure of these, in the autumn of 1821, he sold his life appointment as teacher of drawing and'

Add to list of authorities: Alan Lang Strout's Robert Mudie, 1777–1842 (*Notes and Queries*, clxxii. 146–9).

Muir, Thomas. xiii. 1165*b*. Requires revision. See 'The Odyssey of Thomas Muir' in *Amer. Hist. Rev.*, xxix. 49–72, and authorities there given.

Munden, Sir Richard (1640–80), xiii. 1198*a*, l. 26 from foot. There does not seem to be evidence that the father was knighted. The inscription at Chelsea, quoted by Le Neve, calls him 'Richard Munden' and there is no mention of him in Burtchaell's *Knights of England.*

Mundy, Peter. xiii. 1200*a*, ll. 19–16 from foot. For '*fl.* 1600' read '1596?'; and after 'traveller,' insert 'was born about 1596 and'. After 'Cornwall' insert 'where his father was engaged in the pilchard fishery'; for '1609' read '1608'; for 'into Gascony' read 'to Bayonne'

Ibid. l. 15 from foot. For 'In' read 'He returned to Falmouth in 1610 and in'

Ibid. ll. 14–12 from foot. After 'merchant ship' insert 'under Captain John Davis [q.v.]'; for 'He' read 'After visiting San Lucar in 1613, he spent two years in Seville and acquired a good knowledge of Spanish. In 1617 he'

Ibid. l. 11 from foot. After 'overland' insert 'in the summer of 1620 in the train of the retiring ambassador of the Levant Company, Paul Pindar [q.v.],'

Ibid. l. 10 from foot. For 'afterwards' read 'in 1621'; after 'made a' insert 'second.' After 'Spain' insert ', in connexion with the pilchard fishery. He was in Valladolid in 1625 transacting business on behalf of a syndicate of copper contractors. In Oct. 1627 he successfully petitioned the East India company for employment as a factor'

Ibid. ll. 7–6 from foot. After 'Agra' insert 'as an accountant'; for '17 Dec. 1631' read '6 Aug. 1632'

Ibid. 1200*b*, l. 9. After 'factor.' insert 'He arrived at Goa in September, visited Malacca and Singapore in the following year, and made an unsuccessful attempt to open up trade with Canton, his vessels being attacked by fireships in Canton harbour, Sept. 1637. He was back in England in Dec. 1638 and spent the following year travelling in the south-west of England.'

Ibid. l. 15. For 'It' read 'He left London for Rotterdam in March 1640, proceeded to Danzig, and spent seven years travelling in eastern Europe, his chief journey being to Archangel and back in the summer of 1641. From 1651 to 1654 he was back in Penryn, visiting London each year. In March 1655 he sailed on his third and last voyage to India on the Aleppo Merchant, in the service of a private separate stock company. On his return he resided in London from Feb. 1657 to Sept. 1663, and then returned to Cornwall. The account of these later travels'

Ibid. ll. 24–23 from foot. For 'These manuscripts . . . attention of' read 'Mundy's journals have been published by'

Add to list of authorities: Hakluyt Society, 2nd series, vols. 17, 35, 45, 55, 78; *Notes and Queries*, clxxii. 170–1.

Murphy, Arthur (1727–1805). xiii. 1231*a*, l. 24. For 'Clomquin' read 'Cloonyquin'.

Ibid., l. 32. For 'Plunkett' read 'Plunket' (Records in The Castle, Dublin).

Ibid., l. 15 from foot. After 'Samuel Foote' add 'Murphy knew Foote in 1747 or earlier (Jessé Foot, *Life of Arthur Murphy*, p. 25, letter from Murphy to James Murphy, Aug. 25, 1747).'

Ibid., l. 8 from foot. For 'concluded 12 Oct. 1754' read 'concluded 21 Sept. 1754.'

Ibid. 1231*b*, l. 31. After 'by Woodward' add 'Murphy, "dressed in Black," spoke the prologue at the first performance (*Gentleman's Magazine*, Jan. 1756, xxvi. 36).'

Ibid., l. 18 from foot. For 'under the names of Slender, Squint-eyed Pistol, and Dapperwit' read 'under the names of Squint-Eyed Pistol, Dapperwit, and Slender'.

Ibid. 1232*a*, l. 3. For '100l.' read '400l. (Foot, *op. cit.*, p. 13, Murphy's autobiography).'

Ibid., l. 4. For 'On 30 March 1757' read 'On 30 March 1758.'

Ibid., l. 7. For 'taken from' read 'influenced by.'

Ibid., ll. 7–8. For 'but owing more to' read 'and also slightly indebted to.'

Ibid., ll. 21–3. For 'He then began . . . "Test,"' read 'He began *The Test* Nov. 6, 1756; Owen Ruffhead inaugurated the opposing *Con-Test* Nov. 23.'

Ibid., ll. 39–40. For 'On 24 Jan. 1759' read 'On 24 Jan. 1760.'

Ibid. 1232, l. 8. For 'given at Drury Lane' read 'given at Covent Garden.'

Ibid., ll. 19–20. For '23 Feb. 1764' read '23 Mar. 1765.'

Ibid., ll. 28–29. For 'is a translation from Crébillon' read 'follows the account of Zenobia in Tacitus' *Annales* with slight indebtedness to Crébillon.'

Ibid., l. 22 from foot. Before 'was played' insert 'opened at Covent Garden Feb. 22, 1777, was performed eighteen times the first season, and'.

Ibid., l. 16 from foot. For 'included in the 1786 collection' read 'published in 1798.'

Ibid., l. 12 from foot. For 'had inherited' read 'inherited in 1795'.

Ibid., l. 11 from foot. For '1000l.' read '2,000l. (John Rylands Library, *Eng. MS.* 548, letter from Murphy to Mrs. Piozzi, Mar. 16, 1795).'

Ibid., l. 9 from foot. For 'appointed' read 'reappointed (J. P. Emery, *Arthur Murphy* (Philadelphia, 1946), pp. 85–6, 140, 161).'

Ibid. 1233*a*, ll. 12–13. For 'whom he introduced to the Piozzis' read 'whom the Piozzis had introduced to Murphy at Streatham (*Recollections of the Table-Talk of Samuel Rogers*, ed. Alexander Dyce, p. 106).'

Ibid., l. 19 from foot. For 'Elliot' read 'Elliott.'

Ibid., l. 16 from foot. After 'her biography (1769, 12 mo)' add 'There is no evidence for ascribing this work to Murphy.'

Ibid. 1233*b*, ll. 10–12. For 'and largely occupied . . . to Garrick' read 'In this biography, with the exception of "The Orphan of China," Murphy generally dismisses his own plays as quickly as possible and little considers his relations with Garrick and others. . . . In truth, keeping in mind his probable tendency to be prejudiced against Garrick, the biographer seeks to write with "strict justice" and so, at times . . . overestimates Garrick' (J. P. Emery, *Arthur Murphy*, pp. 163, 164).'

Ibid., l. 15. After '8 vo, 1792' add 'and at the same time an edition of Johnson's works in twelve volumes.'

Ibid., ll. 18–19. After '8 vo, 1807' add 'First published, with a translation of Cicero, in 1795.'

Ibid., ll. 22–4. After '"A Letter . . . Murphy," . . . 8 vo' add 'This attack on Murphy's *The Desert Island* is obviously not by Murphy.'

Ibid., ll. 37–42. After '"A Letter from a Right . . . 'Monitor,'" 4to, 1761' add 'The author of these two works is Rev. Philip Francis (H. H. Dunbar, *The Dramatic Career of Arthur Murphy* (New York, 1946), p. 150, n.50).'

Murray, David, second Earl of Mansfield. xiii. 1253*a*, ll. 1–2. For 'southern department . . . July' read 'northern department, but resigned in March (G.E.C. *Complete Peerage*, 2nd ed., viii. 391 ; M. A. Thomson, *Secretaries of State*, p. 184).'

Murray, Sir George (1772–1846). xiii. 1260*a*, l. 31. For 'June 1790' read '7 July 1790' (*Journal for Army Historical Research*, x. no. 39, p. 35).

Ibid. 1261*b*, l. 6. Add 'His papers, covering the years 1794 1846, were presented in 1910 to the Scottish National Library, Edinburgh, and are now catalogued and indexed. They are especially abundant for the Peninsular War and the occupation of France after Waterloo. The writers include almost every important British officer of the time, and many distinguished statesmen, British and foreign' (*National Library of Scotland*, *Report for* 1930, p. 20).

Murray (afterwards Murray Pulteney), Sir James, xiii. 1273*b*, l. 8. After 'Clermont q.v.' add 'He was appointed lieutenant in the 106th foot on 25 Dec. 1762 and was placed on half-pay on the reduction of his regiment early the next year. On 2 March 1770 he was appointed lieutenant in the 19th foot, (*Army List*, 1771, p. 73)'. l. 18. For '19 May' read '31 Jan. (*ibid.*, 1779, p. 68)'. l. 30 from foot. After 'king' add 'which carried the rank of colonel'. For 'in 1790' read 'on 20 Dec. 1793 (*ibid.*, 1794, p. 7)'. 1274*a*, l. 11 from foot. For 'Grenville' read 'Portland'. l. 10 from foot. For '1806–7' read '1807–9 (*London Gazette*, 1807, pp. 409–10), and he was promoted general on 25 Apr. 1808 (*Army List*, 1809, p. 3)'.

Murray, Patrick, 5th Baron Elibank, xiii. 1297*a*, ll. 20–22. For 'becoming an ensign . . . foot and' read 'He had been appointed captain in colonel Alexander Grant's foot on 31 May 1706 at the age of three (C. Dalton, *Engl. Army Lists*, v. 223) and in 1714 is on half-pay, described as a minor. (P.R.O., War Office, Half-pay Lists, 25/2985). On 26 Dec. 1726 he was appointed captain in the Hon. Robert Murray's, afterwards 37th foot (C. Dalton, *George the First's Army*, ii. 417) and major on 20 June 1735. (P.R.O. W.O. *Registers, etc., Army Lists* (W.O. 64), x. 120. On 27 Nov. 1739 (*ibid.*, p. 188) he was promoted'. l. 27. After 'army' add 'retiring on 10 March 1742 from the 36th foot to which he had transferred the previous (*ibid.*, p. 118)'.

Murray or Moray, Sir Robert. (*d.* 1673). xiii. 1298*a*, ll. 30–33. He was born between 10 March, 1608, and 10 March, 1609. He was not a student at the University of St. Andrews. l. 15 from the bottom. 'He was made a prisoner of war in Bavaria in 1645.' He was captured at the Battle of Tüttlingen, 24 November, 1643. See Alex. Robertson's *Life of Sir Robert Moray* (1922), and authorities there given.

Murray, William, first Earl of Dysart. xiii. 1305*b*, ll. 20–21. For 'He died early in the same year' read 'He died some time after 11 Sept. 1653' (cf. *Nicholas Papers*, Camden Soc., ii. 20).

Murray, William, first Earl of Mansfield. xiii. 1310*a*, l. 6 from foot. Delete 'of Caen Wood.' (See G.E.C., art. Mansfield, and *Notes and Queries*, clxiv (1933), 410).

Musgrave, Sir Christopher. xiii. 1316*a*, 23 ll. from foot. After 'Carlisle' insert 'during 1713–14' (*Return of M.P.'s*, ii. 30).

Myddleton or Middleton, Sir Thomas. xiii. 1337*a*, l. 9 from foot. After 'Castle)' insert ', having from 1586 or thereabouts acted as deputy to Sir Francis Walsingham, then farmer of the customs (E. D. Jones, 'An Account book of Sir Thomas Myddelton,' *Nat. Lib. of Wales Journ.*, i. 86 ; A. P. Newton, 'The great farm of the

English customs,' *Trans. Royal Hist. Soc.*, 4th ser., i. 129–56)'

Ibid. 1337*b*, l. 9. After 'county' insert 'from Lord St. John of Bletsoe (Jones, *op. cit.* p. 87)'

Ibid. 1338*a*, l. 23. For 'about 1586' read 'some time before Oct. 1585 (Jones, *loc. cit.*)'

Ibid. ll. 25–6. For 'about 1590' read 'in 1587 or 1588 (*ibid.*)'

Ibid. l. 25 from foot. After 'Richard' add 'born 1585 (*ibid.*),'

Add to list of authorities: Sir Thomas Myddleton's account book, deposited in the National Library of Wales.

Myngs, Sir Christopher. xiv. 10*b*. This article needs revision and extension. See Sir Charles Firth in *The Mariner's Mirror*, xii. 257–8.

Nalson, John. xiv. 29*a*. He was baptised 2 Aug. 1637 at Holbeck Chapel, Leeds, and was son of John Nalson, vicar of Holbeck (*Notes and Queries*, Eighth Series, ix. 287).

30*a*, l. 1. For 'Fasti Anglicani' read 'Monumenta Anglicana,' and for 'Peter' read 'Philip' Williams.

Nanneu, Anian de (*d.* 1293), bishop of St. Asaph. *See* **Schonau.**

***Nares, Edward.** xiv. 91*a*. A life of Nares by G. Cecil White was published in 1903 under the title of *A Versatile Professor*. It contains copious extracts from his letters which give a full account of his attempts to teach modern history and political economy, and refute Cox's statement that he took his duties easily. See also 'Modern History in Oxford, 1724–1841' in *Eng. Hist. Rev.*, xxxii. 1–21.

Nash, Richard, Beau Nash (1674–1761), xiv. 101*a*, l. 4. For '3 Feb.', read '12 Feb.' (O. Goldsmith, *Life of Richard Nash*, p. 234, *errata*.) *Ib.*, l. 6. For '8 Feb.', read '17 Feb.' (A. J. Jewers, *Registers of Bath Abbey* (1901), ii. 449.)

Neale, Thomas (*d.* 1699?), xiv. For '*d.* 1699?' read '*d.* 1699'. He died 17 December 1699 (Hist. MSS. Comm., *Buccleuch MSS.*, ii. 631).

Needham, Walter. xiv. 165*a*, l. 22. For 'was' read 'had been.'

Ibid. l. 24. For '6 April 1671' read '20 June 1667' (*Record of Royal Soc.*, p. 314).

Negus, Francis, xiv. 168*a*, l. 28 from foot. After '1685' add 'On 19 Oct. 1687 he was appointed ensign in the Holland regiment, afterwards the Buffs (C. Dalton, *Engl. Army Lists*, ii. 110), he became captain on 1 Jan. 1691 and major on 26 Feb. 1694 (*ibid.*, iv. 193)'. ll. 27–25 from foot. For 'and attained . . . foot' read 'who appointed him brevet lieutenant-colonel on 1 Oct. 1703 (*ibid.*, v. 111)'. l. 28 from foot. After 'He served' add 'under King William in Flanders, was taken prisoner in 1695, and in the Cadiz-Vigo expedition in 1702, and (H. R. Knight, *Histor. Records of the Buffs*, i. 529)'.

Neville, Richard Aldworth Griffin (1750–1825), xiv. 296*b*, ll. 4–5. For 'born on 3 July 1750 in Duke Street, Westminster', read 'born in Duke Street, Westminster, and was baptized at Windsor on 29 June 1750' (*New Windsor Parish Register*).

Ibid., p. 297*b*, l. 21 from foot. For 'He married in June 1780', read 'He married 9 June 1780' (Neville to James Grenville, 13 June 1780, Braybrooke MSS., Berks Record Office).

Neville, Richard Neville Aldworth. xiv. 299*a*, l. 4 from foot. For 'in May 1763' read 'on 17 Oct. 1763 (D. B. Horn, *British Diplomatic Representatives*, p. 22).'

Newman, Francis William. Suppl. 1093*b*, 7 ll. from foot For 'Hubert' read 'Huber.'

Ibid. 1094*a*, l. 36. For '1869' read '1863' (*University College, London. Proceedings at the Annual General Meeting . . . 25th February* 1863, p. 14).

Newton, Sir Henry (1651–1715). xiv. 370*a*, l. 18 from foot. For 'at the close of 1709' read 'in March 1711 (*Hist. MSS. Comm. 11th Rep.*, App. iv. 84; P.R.O., S.P. xcviii. 23; D. B. Horn, *British Diplomatic Representatives*, pp. 78–9).'

Nicholas Bozon. 86*b*, l. 3 from foot. After 'him' add ', as a recent article by Sister M. Amelia shows (*Speculum*, xv (1940). 444–5.'

Nicholas of Norton. 90*a*, n. 5. Add at end 'The incidents of his later years are mentioned in Dr. Rose Graham's *English Ecclesiastical Studies*, pp. 342–4.'

Nicholas of Wadingham. 91*b*, n. 2. Add at end ', also in an undated charter of not be ready to move by then (Anderdon, pp. 585–6); and on that day, while Tillotson was consecrated at St. Mary-le-Bow, celebrated communion at Lambeth (Luttrell, ii. 238).'

Ibid. 738*a*, ll. 12–3. For 'a private house in the Temple' read 'a house in Palsgraves Head Court, adjoining the Temple'.

Ibid. ll. 16–9. This incident is not mentioned in Ailesbury's own *Memoirs* (Roxburghe Club, 1890); for its pedigree see Granger, *Biographical History*, 4th ed., iv. 281 *n.*

Ibid. ll. 28–9. For 'when accusations . . . he wrote:' read 'he contradicts reports that he had attended service in the parish church: '

Ibid. l. 15 from foot. For '9 Feb. 1691' read '9 Feb. 1692'. The date of the document is old style.

Ibid. 738*b*, l. 2. For 'in November' read 'on 24 November'.

Ibid. l. 5. After 'nonjurors' insert 'and would not permit the conforming clergy to attend services in his chapel; he remained however on affectionate terms with Wharton to the last'.

Ibid. l. 8. After 'buried' add 'by a nonjuror (*Letters of Humphrey Prideaux to John Ellis*, Camden Soc., 1875, p. 163)'.

Ibid. l. 10. After 'by himself.' add 'In order to avoid making a will which would have "to be proved in his pretended successor's courts," he disposed of his property by a deed of gift. He left about £600 per annum to be divided between his two nephews, besides £1000 to be distributed among the nonjurors (Roger North, *Lives of the Norths*, ed. Jessopp, iii. 122; Prideaux, *Letters*, pp. 163–4).'

To authorities add: The Life of Thomas Ken, by a Layman (J. L. Anderdon), 2nd ed., 1854; this includes an important collection of Sancroft's letters (and fragments of his letters), addressed mainly to Bishop Lloyd of Norwich (pp. 542–640 *passim*, 764); T. Wagstaffe [q.v.], A letter out of Suffolk, 1694; this, the source of much information about Sancroft's time at Fressingfield, is reprinted in Somers Tracts, ed. Scott, ix. 527–40.

E. S. de Beer.

Nicholas, Sir Edward. xiv. 422*b*, l. 16 from foot. For 'when he' read 'and on 26 Jan. 1619 (B.M. Add. MS. 37818, fly-leaf).'

Ibid. l. 15 from foot. Add '[q.v.]' after 'Zouch.'

Ibid. 423*a*, l. 12 from foot. After "of England'" read 'on 13 Apr. 1638 (B.M.

Nicholas, Sir Edward. xiv. 423*a*, l. 29. 'The wisest king did wonder when he spied. . . .' The article implies that Nicholas was the author of this, but there is no reason to suppose so. It was in general circulation, and many people had copies in their own hands. Nicholas, like many others, copied it.

Nicholson, Sir Francis. xiv. 457*a*, ll. 23–20 from foot. Delete 'Sir'; for '1660' read '1655'; after 'colonial governor,' insert 'born at Downsholme Park, near Richmond, Yorks, on 12 Nov. 1655,'; for 'the army' read 'the Buffs regiment'; after '1678,' insert 'was transferred in 1680 to the newly-raised corps commanded by the earl of Plymouth, subsequently known as the 4th King's Own,'; for 'as' read 'was appointed'; after 'lieutenant' insert 'in the Duchess of York's regiment'; after '1684.' read 'He accompanied the earl of Plymouth's regiment to Tangiers, and acted as courier and aide-de-camp to the governor, Col. Kirke. He was sent on a mission to Morocco (E. M. G. Routh, *Tangier*, p. 231; Edwin Chapell, *Tangier Papers of Samuel Pepys*, p. 38), and in 1682 and 1683 carried despatches to the English ambassador in Paris (Hist. MSS. Comm. 7th Rep. p. 285).'

Ibid. l. 14 from foot. After 'Nicholson' read 'was appointed captain of a "company of foot for the colony of New England" and arrived in Boston, in company with Andros, on 20 Dec. (Osgood, *The American Colonies in the seventeenth century*, iii. 400, 401). In August 1688 (*ibid.*) he'

Ibid. 457*b*, l. 7. After 'for England' read 'in June (*ibid.* p. 456)'

Ibid. ll. 16–14 from foot. For '1694' read '1693'; for 'died' read 'resigned'

Ibid. l. 2 from foot. After 'him.' insert 'He did his utmost, however, to improve public education and the provision for the clergy.'

Ibid. last line. For '1698' read '1699'

Ibid. 458*b*, l. 5. After 'deputy.' read 'He was officially recalled on 20 Jan. 1715.'

Ibid. ll. 26–7. Delete 'had been knighted in 1720, and he'; for 'lieutenant-' read 'captain-'

Ibid. l. 30. After '1728.' read 'He was buried at St. George's, Hanover Square. He never married, and left the greater part of his property to the Society for the Propagation of the Gospel.'

Add to list of authorities: Dictionary of American Biography; C. Dalton, George the First's Army, ii. 55–62; W. H. Brown, Proceedings of Council of Maryland, 1693–7 (Maryland Hist. Soc.), pp. vii–xii.

Nolan, Frederick. xiv. 540*b*, l. 25 from foot. For '1832' read '1833' (*Record of Royal Soc.*, p. 392).

Norden, John (1548–1625?), xiv. 533*b*, ll. 21–7. For 'A fourth . . . –1714).' read 'John Norden also published a number of devotional works (see A. W. Pollard 'The Unity of John Norden, surveyor and religious writer', *The Library*, n.s. vol. vii, no. 3, Dec. 1926; where it is shown that the topographer and the devotional writer were one person).'

Norden, John. xiv. 550*b*. Topographer. See *Hist. MSS. Comm.: Hatfield MSS.* ix. 433. Petition of Norden to Sir R. Cecil [1599], in which he states he was born in Somersetshire.

North, Sir Dudley (1641–91), xiv. 597*b*, l. 10.—After 'fourth' add 'but third surviving son of Dudley, fourth baron North.' *Ib.* l. 17 from foot.— For 'His influence . . . Constantinople' (2) read 'about April 1680 he sought the ambassadorship to the Porte', *Ib.*, l. 12 from foot.—Add 'but stood no chance through lack of influence (G. F. Abbott, *Under the Turk in Constantinople*, p. 312'. *Ib.*, 598*a*, l. 5.—After 'London' add 'He did not give up his trading interests. From 1681–6 he was a member of the Court of Assistants of the Levant Company (A. B. Beavan, *Aldermen of the City of London*, ii. 108), Master of the Mercers' Company in 1683 (*ib.*), and Governor of the Muscovy Company in 1686 (*Calendar of Treasury Books, 1685–9*, p. 695)'. *Ib.*, l. 17.—After '(*Examen*, pp. 598–610)', add 'His election was not popular, his own company, the Mercers, declining to accompany him to his swearing in (R. R. Sharpe, *London and the Kingdom*, ii. 489)'. *Ib.*, l. 21.—For 'about the same time he married Anne' read 'on 12 April 1683 he married Anne'. *Ib.*, l. 24. —After 'Bristol' add '(T. Faulkner, *History of Chelsea*, p. 126)'. *Ib.*, l. 26.—After 'fortune' insert 'He was made an alderman for Farringdon Without in 1682 (Beavan, *op. cit.*, ii. 108)'. *Ib.*, l. 27.—For '1683' read '26 March 1684 (*Calendar of Treasury Books, 1681–5*, p. 1081)'. *Ib.*, l. 28.—For 'subsequently . . . treasury' read 'he held the post only for three months, being transferred to the treasury in July (*Calendar of State Papers Domestic, May 1684–February 1685*, p. 101'. *Ib.*, l. 32.—For 'On the death of Charles II . . . customs' read 'The appointment of the earl of Rochester as lord high treasurer by James II in February 1685 cost him his place as a treasury commissioner and in March he agreed to return to the Customs (*Calendar of Treasury Books, 1685–9*, p. 72)'. *Ib.*, l. 35.—After 'Banbury' add, 'He made a considerable impression in parliament, serving on several committees concerned with trade and finance, and acting as manager for the Crown in matters of revenue (*Commons' Journals, 1685, passim*; A. Jessop, *Lives of the Norths*, ii. 209). A modern historian describes him as "unofficial Chancellor of the Exchequer" (D. Ogg, *England in the Reigns of James II and William III, p. 143*). Yet only one of his speeches has been preserved (A. Grey, *Debates*, viii. 368)' *Ib.*, l. 41.—After 'accordingly' add 'James appointed him a deputy lieutenant of the city of London in October 1688 (Hist. MSS. Comm., *13th Rept.* App. pt. v, p. 46), but he was omitted from the lieutenancy after the Revolution (*ib.*)'. *Ib.*, l. 7 from foot.—For '1682' read '1683'. *Ib.*, 598*b*, l. 7.—For 'twenty-five years later' read 'whence in September 1715 (*St. Paul's, Covent Garden, Parish Register* (Harleian Society), iv. 136)'. *Ib.* l. 9.— After 'an estate' add 'in 1691 (Brit. Mus. Add. MSS. 19, 101, fo. 21)'. *Ib.*, l. 12.— After many years' add 'dying 27 August 1715' (M.I.)'. *Ib.*, l. 13.—For 'two sons . . . unmarried' read 'three sons, Dudley, Roger and Robert. The two younger died early and unmarried. (Jessop, *op. cit.*, ii. 252, iii. 228; *St. Paul's Parish Register*, iv. 135)'.

North, Roger, Second Baron North. xiv. 614*b*. For 'was born in 1530, probably at Kirtling in Cambridgeshire,' read 'was born 27 February, 1530–1, in London.' See *Eng. Hist. Rev.* xxxvii. 565–6.

North, Roger (1585? – 1652?). xiv. 618*b*. His baptism is recorded in the registers of St. Gregory's-by-St. Paul's, now at St. Martin's, Ludgate, under date 18 September 1588.

G. C. M. S.

North, Sir Thomas. xiv. 624*a*. For 'was born about 1535' read 'was born 28 May, 1523.' See *Eng. Hist. Rev.* xxxvii. 565–6.

Norton, Thomas (1532–1584). xiv. 669*b*, l. 7 from foot–670*a*, l. 23 from foot. A more correct and more reliable list of most of Norton's miscellaneous writings is given in 'A short-title catalogue of books printed in England . . . 1475–1640,' compiled by A. W. Pollard and G. R. Redgrave (Bibliographical Society, 1926). Item no. 4, 'A discourse,' is there attributed to Thomas Sampson [q.v.]. 'An aunswere to the proclamation of the rebels in the north', 1569, is probably by its publisher, William Seres [q.v.]. The correct title of 'XVI Bloes' is 'A message, termed Marke the truth of the worde of God, in these xii. Bloes, at the Popes Bull', 8o, London, William Howe for John Arenolde, 1570; there is a copy in the library of St. John's College, Cambridge.

Nugent, Lavall, Count Nugent. xiv. 707*a*, l. 15. Delete 'appears to have.'

Ib. l. 27. After 'Secretary' insert 'On his departure he was offered £1000 by Wellesley for the expenses that he had incurred but declined on the ground that he was still able to subsist by his own means.' Public Record Office, F.O. 7/100 (his official correspondence with government, 1811–1813), also F.O. 34/3 and 4 (Münster's correspondence with government, 1811–1812).

Oates, Titus. xiv. 741*a*, l. 23 from foot. For 'in 1649' read 'on 15 Sept. 1648 (horoscope in Bodleian Library, MS. Ashmole 436, f. 112 v.)'.

Ibid. 743*a*, l. 28. After '1816' add 'A translation of the minutes of the real meeting is printed in "The Month," cii (1903), 312–16.'

E. S. DE B.

O'Byrne, William Richard. xxii. 1102*a*, l. 9. For 'in' read 'on 27 Jan.'

Ibid. l. 12. After 'He' insert 'was educated at University College school, 1838–9 (*Univ. Coll. School Reg.* 1831–96, p. 210) and'

Ibid. l. 17 from foot. After 'expenses.' insert 'The original MSS. (B.M. Add. MSS. 38039–54) and O'Byrne's correspondence with the officers frequently contain much more information than the printed text.'

Ibid. l. 15 from foot. After 'and' insert 'in 1850'

Ibid. l. 4 from foot. After 'Athenaeum Club.' insert 'In 1853, his brother Robert, a barrister (*Records of Lincoln's Inn*, ii. 275), took over the editorship of the "Sailor's Home Journal," later known as the "Naval Chronicle," and during the years 1853–63 this journal contains many obituary notices which complete the biographies in the dictionary. Most of the officers concerned were associated with the navy agency which the brothers established at 9 Adelphi Terrace in 1856, moved to 58 Pall Mall in 1867, and conducted at 18 Adam St., Adelphi, 1870–80.'

Add to list of authorities: Frederic Boase's Modern English Biography, vi (suppl. vol. 3). 315.

O'Connell, John (1810–58), xiv. 835*a*, l. 56. '. . . voting against the motion with regard to colonial policy, which led to the fall of Russell's ministry in February 1851'. For 'colonial policy' read 'the relief of agricultural distress'.

O'Ferrall, Richard More (1797–1880), xiv. 896*a*, l. 37. For '1850–1' read '1851–2'.

Ogilvy, James, fourth earl of Findlater and first earl of Seafield. xiv. 923*a*, l. 12 from foot. For '1664' read '1663' (*Complete Peerage*, 1926, v. 382).

Ibid. l. 7 from foot. For 'in 1664' read 'on 11 July 1663' (*Ibid.*).

Ibid. 923*b*, l. 7. After 'knighthood' insert '(1695)' (*Ibid.* p. 383).

Ibid. 924*a*, ll. 34–35. For 'at each . . . inclusive' read 'for the periods 1707–10, 1712–15, and 1722–30' (*Ibid.*).

O'Grady, Standish, first Viscount Guillamore. xiv. 946*a*, l. 4 from foot. For '1838' read '1835 (G.E.C., *Complete Peerage*, vi. 220)'

O'Hara, Charles, xiv. 955*a*, last line. After 'appointed' add 'ensign in colonel Edward Wolfe's regiment afterwards the 8th foot on 20 Apr. 1751 and (P.R.O., W.O. *Registers, etc., Army Lists* (W.O. 64), xi. 153'.

Okey, John. xix. 973*a*, 16 ll. from foot. On his services in Scotland in 1651, see Firth, *Scotland and the Commonwealth*, pp. 1–15, 316, 331. He served under Monck in the suppression of the royalist rising in Scotland headed by the Earl of Glencairn (*Scotland and the Protectorate*, 1910, pp. 149, 151).

973*b*. On his loss of his commission in 1654, and his restoration to command in 1659, see *Clarke Papers*, iii. 10–13, 195.

974*a*, l. 11. In February 1660 he was sent to suppress an intended insurrection at Bristol, and found himself suspected of a design to oppose Monck (Hist. MSS. Comm. Report, (1899) *Leybourne-Popham MSS.*, pp. 160–165).

Old, John (*fl.* 1545–1555), xiv. 979*b*. l. 22 from foot, where it is stated that 'about 1545' he 'was presented to the vicarage of Cubington' Dugdale (*Antiqs. Warw.* ed. 1730, p. 302) gives 22 March 1548–9 as the date of Old's institution, on the presentation of Edward VI, his authority being Lichfield Episc. Registers, Bp. Sampson, fo. 42*b*.

Oldfield, Anne. xiv. 993*a*, ll. 5–2 from foot. For 'A French author unnamed . . . to the English stage' read 'Abbé Prévost-d'Exiles declared "*Il faut convenir, en effet, que c'est une fille incomparable. Elle m'a fait aimer le Théâtre Anglois, pour lequel j'avois d'abord fort peu de goût*" (*Mémoires et Avantures d'un Homme de Qualité*, ed. 1735, tome v. livre 1, p. 55).'

M. E. I. R.

Oldhall, Sir William. xiv. 999*a*, l. 10. For '1466?' read '1460 (C. E. Johnston, 'Sir William Oldhall,' *Eng. Hist. Rev.*, xxv. 720)'

Ibid. ll. 20–1. For 'and won his spurs at the hard-fought field of' read 'and was knighted at some uncertain date between 11 July 1423 and 29 May 1424 (*D.K. Rept.* xlviii. 226; F. Devon, *Issues of the Excheq.*, p. 387). He likewise fought at'

Ibid. ll. 22–3. For 'About this date . . . Normandy' read 'From 23 Nov. 1424 to 16 Nov. 1425 he was seneschal of Normandy (*Bib. Nat.*, fr. 4491, f. 7; *ibid.* Pièces originales, 2138, Oldhall section 48630, no. 2)'

Ibid. l. 3 from foot. After 'St. Martins-le-Grand' insert 'on 30 Nov. 1451 (Johnston, *op. cit.* p. 717)'; after 'remained' insert ', except for an interval of two days (*ibid.* pp. 717–8),'

Ibid. 999*b*, l. 7. For 'between 1460 and 1466' read 'in Nov. or Dec. 1460 (*ibid.* p. 720)'

Oldham, John (1653–1683). xiv. 1002*a*, ll. 19–34. For 'John Oldham, his grandfather . . . iii. 162 *n.*).' read 'John Oldham, his grandfather, was rector of Shipton from about 1620 until his death in 1657. John Oldham, his father, was appointed rector of Long Newnton, Wiltshire, in 1659 and was ejected between 1662 and 1664; he was later minister to a congregation at Wotton under Edge; and died, aged eighty-six, in 1716. He is said to have been a Presbyterian. His ejection destroys the conjecture (current before 1747) that he was the original of Oldham's prose "Character" of an ugly old parson. His wife's name was Anne Adams (*Notes and Queries*, clxiv. 112–3; clxvii. 30–1; *Miscellanea genealogica et heraldica*, 5th ser., viii. 323–6; A. G. Matthews, *Calamy revised*, pp. 373, 564).'

Ibid., ll. 23–22 from foot. For 'Oldham entered . . . in 1670' read 'Oldham matriculated from St. Edmund Hall, Oxford, on 17 June 1670.(Foster, *Alumni Oxon.*).'

Ibid. ll. 16–15 from foot. Delete 'school and'

Ibid. 1002*b*, ll. 2–6. Omit 'who, in the first . . . polite visitors,'. The anecdote is badly rendered; the correct version is of little biographical significance.

Ibid. ll. 13–15. For 'the grandsons . . . ii. 85–6).' read 'Edward, grandson of Sir Edward Thurland.' There is no trace of a second grandson.

Ibid. 1003*a*, l. 3. For ', 9 Dec. 1683' read '; he was buried 7 Dec. 1683 (Oxford Bibliographical Society, *Proceedings*, v (1936–9). 7).'

Ibid. ll. 16–18. For 'Tom Brown . . . ed. 1744)' read 'Durfey, Flatman, Robert Gould, Nahum Tate, T. Wood [qq.v.], and others, wrote poems to his memory (Gould's is sometimes ascribed to Tom Brown [q.v.])'

Ibid. ll. 25–31. For 'Bliss . . . 1792' read 'A portrait of him belonged in 1934 to his collateral descendant, Mr. W. I. Hillier, of King's Caple, Herefordshire; an engraving of it by van der Gucht is prefixed to the 1704 and some later editions of his works. A second portrait, a miniature in oil said to be by W. Dobson, belonged to Horace Walpole and was engraved by Scheneker and by J. T. Wedgwood (British Museum, *Catalogue of engraved British portraits*).'

Ibid. 1003*b*, ll. 22–9. For 'From Oldham's . . . surreptitiously' read 'Oldham states on his fair copy of the "Satyr against Vertue" that it was written in July 1676; the "Apology" for it is probably very little later. "A Satyr upon a Woman" is dated Whitsuntide 1678; he translated the first canto of Boileau's "Le Lutrin" in Oct. of that year. "Garnet's Ghost" was surreptitiously'

Ibid. 1004*b*, l. 19. To authorities add: bibliography of Oldham's works in Oxford Bibliographical Society's Proceedings, v. 1–38; information from Mr. W. I. Hillier.

HAROLD F. BROOKS.

Onslow, George, xiv, 1112*b*, l. 28. For 'became a' read 'entered the army as ensign in the 1st foot guards on 27 Feb. 1748 (P.R.O., Index 5436, p. 29), became captain in Guise's regiment, afterwards 6th foot on 12 Jan. 1751 (*ibid.*, p. 44) and major in the 57th regiment on 3 Aug. 1757 (*ibid.*, 5439, p. 30). He was promoted captain-lieutenant and'. l. 30. After '1759' add 'captain and lieutenant-colonel on 7 Nov. the same year and retired from the army on 10 Feb. 1762 (P.R.O., War Office, Succession Books, 25/209, p. 73)'.

Onslow, Richard. xiv. 1116*b*, ll. 14–13 from foot. For 'clerk' read 'under-clerk (BULLETIN, xvii. 4)'; for 'under Elizabeth' read 'from 22 Dec. 1570 until his death (*ibid.*)'; after 'Scott' insert '(*d.* 8 Oct. 1582)'; after 'widow' insert ', daughter of William Whetenhall, sheriff of Kent in 1526–7'.

Onslow, Richard, first Baron Onslow. xiv. 1118*b*, l. 28. For '23 Jan. 1690–1 to 15 April 1693' read '5 June 1690 to 13 March 1692–3' (P.R.O., Admiralty 2/169 f. 245; Luttrell, *Brief Relation*, iii. 54).

Onslow, Richard (1654–1717). xiv. 1118*b*, l. 24. For 'his elevation' read 'Nov. 1715. He was elevated' (*Return of M.P.'s*, ii. 44).

Osborne, Sir Edward. xiv. 1178*a*, ll. 14–9 from foot. Delete 'In his early . . . p. 46).' The authorities quoted mention only 'Mr. Osborne' and all apparently refer to Peter Osborne [q.v.].

Ibid., last line—p. 1178*b*, l. 5. Delete 'On 17 Feb. . . . p. 34).' Osborne and Stow were among the deponents examined as to manifestos circulated by the Spanish ambassador (Espes); there was no question of identifying his hand-writing.

Ibid., ll. 5–28. For 'He was at the time . . . governor' read 'In 1571 he was the owner of a well-appointed ship trading to Spain (*Cal. S.P., For.*, 1569–71, p. 439); his interests in Spain and Portugal were apparently substantial and he was named as one of the members of the Company of Merchants trading to Spain and Portugal, which was established by patent in 1577 (V. M. Shillington and A. B. W. Chapman, *The commercial relations of England and Portugal*, p. 314; see also *Cal. S.P., For.*, 1577–8, p. 363; Hakluyt, *Principal navigations*, edn. 1903–5, xi. 27, for a tentative Brazilian interest). He was also one of the members named in the Eastland Company's charter, which was granted in 1579 (E. P. Cheyney, *A history of England from the defeat of the Armada to the death of Elizabeth*, i. 346). From about 1575 he was associated with another London merchant, a connection by marriage, Richard Staper (Waters, *Family of Chester*, i. 237, where however Mrs. Staper's Christian name is wrongly given); in that year they sent agents to Constantinople to procure a safe-conduct for a factor of Osborne's, William Harborne [q.v., and BULLETIN, above, p. 160]. Harborne obtained from the sultan in 1579 a trade licence for Osborne, Staper, and himself, and in 1580 the grant to the queen of a capitulation containing privileges for English merchants in general. On 11 September 1581 Elizabeth granted by patent to Osborne, Staper, and two other men by name, with eight others to be admitted by them, the sole right of trading to Turkey for seven years; Osborne was to be governor of this Turkey company. In 1583 he and Staper financed the expedition overland to India of John Newbery and Ralph Fitch [q.v.]. The relations between the company and the government were for a time very close, the ambassador or agent at Constantinople, while employed by the government in political business, being as a rule paid by the company [see articles Barton, Edward, and Harborne, William, BULLETIN, above, pp. 158, 160]; and the queen and her ministers were investors in the company. Its interests clashed with those of the merchants trading to Venice, who were formed into a company, to last for six years, in 1583. Negotiations ultimately led to a new patent, issued on 7 January 1592, granting the monopoly of the English trade to Venice and Turkey for twelve years to a new company, the Levant Company, formed by members of the two former companies; Osborne was named as the first governor.'

Ibid., p. 1179*a*, ll. 10–11. For 'He died . . . buried at' read 'He was buried on 15 February 1592 at (*Registers* of St. Dionis, as cited, p. 201).'

Add to list of authorities: Hakluyt; A. C. Wood, A history of the Levant Company; Conyers Read, Mr. Secretary Walsingham; Cheyney.

Osborne, Sir Thomas, successively first Earl of Danby, Marquis of Carmarthen, and Duke of Leeds. xiv. 1189*b*, l. 16. For 'born in 1631' read 'born on 20, baptised on 28 Feb. 1631/2. (B.M. Add. MS. 28040, f. 65; Harthill parish register.)'

Osborne, Thomas (*d.* **1767**). xiv. 1197*b*, ll. 9–14 from foot. Delete 'In 1740 Rivington . . . (AARON HILL, *Works*, ii. 298).' (*Times Lit. Suppl.*, 31 July 1930, p. 628, col. 1).

Otterburn, Sir Adam. BULLETIN, xiv. 56*a*, l. 10. For '1547' read '1545'

Ibid. ll. 12–11 from foot. For 'Euphraim' read 'Eupham'; for 'Barnbougle' read 'the Barnbougle family'

Ibid. l. 7 from foot. Delete '(*Mary of Lorraine's Corresp.*, p. 59)'

Otterburne, Sir Adam. xiv. 1236*b*, l. 12. For 'Otterburne' read 'Otterburn'; for '(*d.* 1548)' read '(1482?–1548).'

Ibid. l. 15. Delete '(Aldham)'.

Ibid. ll. 18–20. For '. It may be presumed . . . his family.' read ', a property he acquired in the years 1518–20. He was born about 1482.'

Ibid. l. 21. For 'Otterburne first' read 'He graduated M.A., presumably at a foreign university, before April 1503 (*Cal. Yester Writs*, Scots. Rec. Soc., p. 266), and in 1510 was acting as a notary of the diocese of St. Andrews (*Reg. Magni Sigilli Regum Scot.*, 1424–1513, p. 791). In 1507 he was practising as procurator and "for speker" before the lords of council and session, and from 1512–25 is mentioned as common clerk of Edinburgh (*Edinburgh Records, 1403–1528*, Scots Burgh Rec. Soc., p. 136). On 5 Jan. 1517 he was appointed by Albany as a lord of the council for the trial of civil causes (*Acts of Lords of Council*, 1501–54, p. 147), one of the first professional lawyers to be appointed. He'

Ibid. ll. 24–5. For 'already a . . . royal council' read 'attending parliament as burgess representative of Edinburgh, and in 1523 he was chosen one of the lords of the articles (*Mar and Kellie MSS.*, Hist. MSS. Comm., p. 13).' After '1525' insert 'he was'

Ibid. ll. 26–8. For 'and recorder . . . if not oftener' read '. He was provost of Edinburgh from 1528–32, and again from 1543–4.'

Ibid. ll. 30–4. For 'We ought . . . 1529' read 'In this capacity he made vigorous efforts to stamp out an outbreak of plague in the summer of 1530 (*Records of Edinburgh, 1528–57*, Scot. Burgh Rec. Soc., pp. 24, 36–9).'

Ibid. ll. 7–4 from foot. Delete 'If the advocate . . . French connection.'

Ibid. 1237*a*, l. 19 from foot. After '*Diurnal*, p. 18)' read 'a property he had purchased in 1527.'

Ibid. ll. 4–3 from foot. For 'It was not . . . Otterburne' read 'In Sept. 1538 he was appointed an auditor of the king's expenditure in France (*Accounts, Treasurer of Scot.*, vii. 2, 46, 63) but by 13 Sept. had been deprived of his office of king's advocate, and on 12 Oct.'

Ibid. last line–1237*b*, l. 3. For 'lay there . . . *State Papers*, v. 141, 160)' read 'was liberated on bail, 16 Feb. 1539 (*Acts of Lords of Council*, 1501–54, p. 479) and was pardoned in the following September on payment of a fine of £2000 (*Accounts, Treasurer of Scot.*, vii. 76). He then resumed his seat on the bench of the court of session, to which he had been appointed a permanent judge on its first establishment, 27 May 1532, and continued to sit as a judge until his death.'

Ibid. l. 30. Delete 'Henceforth' and after 'Sadler' insert, 'when reporting Otterburn's election as provost,'

Ibid. last line. For 'Otterburne' read 'Immediately afterwards Otterburn was dismissed from his office of provost (*Hamilton Papers*, ii. 368) and apparently suffered a short period of imprisonment (*Mary of Lorraine's Corresp.*, p. 157). He was back at the court of session by the end of April 1547, probably by virtue of an amnesty, and'

Ibid. 1238*a*, ll. 9–13. For '. More than a year later . . . (*ib.* i. 90).' read 'and was back in Edinburgh by 22 Aug. (*Reg. Privy Council, Scot.*, i. 77). For several years he had had many enemies, especially the regent, Arran, and early in July 1548 he was attacked in Edinburgh, "some thynk by the Governor's commandement" (*Cal. Scot. Papers*, ed. Bain, i. 137). He was "sore hurt on the head" and died 6 July (*Cal. S.P. Dom. Add.* 1547–65, p. 389). The goods of his assassins were escheated a week later.

He was twice married, (1) to Jonet Rhynd, (2) before Jan. 1525 to Euphraim Mowbray of Barnbougle. By his second wife he had three sons, John, Robert, and Thomas, but it is not known which wife was the mother of his three daughters (*Mary of Lorraine's Corresp.*, p. 59)'.

Add to list of authorities: J. A. Inglis's Sir Adam Otterburn of Redhall.

Oudart, Nicholas. xiv. 1247*b*, l. 13. After '(Wood, loc. cit.)' add 'He was educated at Eton under Savile (B.M., Add. Ch. 4892).'

Ibid. l. 23. After 'secretary of state' add 'When parting with him on 20 June 1646 Nicholas gave him a testimonial (now B.M., Add. Ch. 4892); he there states that Oudart had been with him more than four years.'

Ibid. ll. 23–34. For 'In August 1647 . . . GAUDEN, JOHN' read 'Oudart compounded at the end of 1646 in order to remain in England (*Cal. Committee for Compounding*, p. 1575; F. Peck, *Desiderata Curiosa*, bk.

ix., no. 31). He corresponded with Nicholas while Charles I was at Holmby, and apparently contrived the delivery of a letter from Nicholas to the king (*Nicholas Papers*, i. 73–87). He attended Charles at Oatlands (Evelyn, *Diary and Correspondence*, ed. Wheatley, iv. 191) and was with him at Hampton Court in November (Peck, ix. 42). Early in 1648 he delivered a letter from the king to James, duke of York; the reply, carried by another agent, was intercepted, so Oudart fled to Holland (*Hamilton Papers*, p. 156; *Lords' Journals*, x. 77). He returned shortly and was permitted to attend the king at the treaty of Newport; he kept a diary of the proceedings (printed by Peck, x. 1). In December he was vainly planning Charles' escape (Peck, x. 5, 6).'

Ibid. ll. 35–48. This passage is vague and in part incorrect. Oudart came to Holland in June 1649; he already held the post of secretary to the princess royal (princess Mary of Orange), and was permitted, while retaining it, to act as clerk of the signet (*Nicholas Papers*, i. 166–7, wrongly dated Jan. 1649–50; see the closely connected letter, pp. 133–4). This position brought him into connexion with Robert Long, and so lost him Nicholas' good will (*Nicholas Papers*, i.; the *Nicholas Correspondence* in the article is a misnomer). He accompanied Charles II to Scotland but returned to Scotland by December 1650 (*Nicholas Papers*, i. 205; *Cal. Clarendon State Papers*, ii. 69). From this period he appears to have been steadily engaged in the princess royal's service.

1248*a*, l. 19. After 'Dorothy' add 'Some volumes of Oudart's papers had come to Francis Peck [q.v.] by purchase; he published some parts of them in the second volume of "Desiderata Curiosa," 1735 (see its preface).'

E. S. de B.

Oughton, Sir James Adolphus Dickenson. xiv. 1249*b*, ll. 26–8. Delete 'soon after;' after 'K.B.' insert 'on 22 Feb. 1773 (W. A. Shaw, *Knights of England*, i. 172);' after 'North Britain' insert 'on 29 May 1778 (P.R.O., war office, commission book, 25/33, p. 297)'

Ouseley, Sir William Gore. xiv. 1258*a*, ll. 22–20 from foot. For 'and on 20 April . . . Brazil' read 'and was chargé d'affaires from 11 Jan. to 25 Aug. 1833, 11 Jan. to 20 May 1836, and 28 June 1838 to 19 July 1841' (dispatches in P.R.O., F.O. 13/101, 125, 126, 146, 172).

Ibid. l. 17 from foot. For '1847' read '1846' (Aberdeen to Ouseley, 7 Jan. 1846, enclosing the credential for this mission, in P.R.O., F.O. 6/114).

Overton, Richard. 1280*a*, 24 ll. from foot. On his pamphlets against the House of Lords, see Firth, *The House of Lords during the Civil War*, pp. 159–167.

1280*b*, l. 8. His influence on the development of the political ideals of his party is well brought out in *The Leveller Movement*, by T. C. Pease, Washington, 1916, pp. 141, 180, 314.

Ibid., 13 ll. from bottom. His dealings with Langdale and the Royalists in 1655 are elucidated by his letters printed in vol. iii. of the *Nicholas Papers*, pp. 40, 43, 73, 94, 102, 118.

Overton, Robert. 1281*a*, 6 ll. from foot. For '1640' read '1609.'

1281*b*, 3 ll. from foot. For '(Tanner MSS. lv. 170),' read '(*Scotland and the Commonwealth*, p. 36.)'

1282*a*, l. 6. For '(Clarke MSS.)' read '(*Scotland and the Commonwealth*, p. 62.)'

Ibid., 22 ll. from foot On his arrest by Monck in Dec. 1654, see *Scotland and the Protectorate*, pp. 192, 238–242.

1283*a*, l. 7. On his removal from the command of Hull in 1660, see *Clarke Papers*, iv. 244, 255; *Leyborne-Popham MSS.*, pp. 163, 170. John Shaw, interceding with Cromwell for Overton's release, gives a very favourable view of his character (*Eng. Hist. Rev.*, xxii. 313). Overton's entrance to London in March 1659 was the signal for a great popular demonstration against the protectorate (*Clarke Papers*, iii. 184).

Pack, Richardson. xv. 27*b*, l. 29 from foot. After 'Minorca' insert ', where the duke of Argyll had recently been appointed governor. When Ormonde replaced Marlborough as commander in 1712, Pack was among the officers placed on half-pay.'

Ibid. l. 27 from foot. After 'Stoke Ash.' insert 'At the time of the Jacobite rebellion he was appointed major in Col. Lucas's regiment of foot (Dalton, *George the First's Army*, i. 182), and was later transferred to Viscount Hinchinbroke's regiment (Chamberlayne, *Notitia*, 1718, p. 136)'

Ibid. l. 17 from foot. After 'September 1728.' insert 'His will (P.C.C. 144 Abbott) shows that his wife's name was Mary; probably she was the Mary Spring, a Suffolk neighbour, to whom he had addressed some of his liveliest verses.'

Add to list of authorities: Notes and Queries, clxx. 344–6.

Paget, Henry, first Earl of Uxbridge. xv. 53*a*, last line—53*b*, l. 3. For 'In April . . . his council' read 'On 25 Apr. 1704 he was appointed a member of the council to assist the lord high admiral, Prince George of Denmark [q.v.] (BULLETIN, xiv. 23).'

Paine, Thomas. xv. 73, col. ii. l. 31. For 'Mallison' read 'Madison.'

Ibid., p. 74, col. i. l. 15. For '1692' read '1792.'

Palgrave, William Gifford. xv. 110*a*, ll. 39–42. For 'two years . . . Bangkok' read 'he was appointed consul-general in the principality of Bulgaria on 23 Sept. 1878, and agent and consul-general on 24 June 1879, but his open sympathy with plans for the unification of Bulgaria and Eastern Roumelia led, in Feb., to complaints by the Austrian government, and he was transferred to Bangkok on 26 Nov. 1879 (Austrian F.O. Archives, Károlyi to Andrássy, 26 Feb., 1879; *F.O. List*, 1888).' W. N. M.

Papillon, Philip. xv. 191*b*, ll. 33 and 34. For 'in . . . Anne' read 'from Dec. 1701 to Dec. 1720' (*Return of M.P.'s*, ii. 46).

Parker, Sir Peter (1721–1811). xv. 266*a*, l. 14 from foot. For 'John' read 'George'; after 'Ellis' insert '[q.v.]'

Parkyns or Perkyns, Sir William. xv. 321*b*, l. 29. For '13 April' read '3 April' (*London Gazette*, no. 3162, 3–6 Apr. 1696).

Parr, William, Marquis of Northampton and Earl of Essex. xv. 367*b*, l. 27. For 'Margaret' read 'Mary of Guise, queen-dowager.'

Ibid. 368*a*, l. 17 from foot. After 'some uncertainty' add 'Thomas Hoby [q.v.], who was for a time in her husband's service, translated the third book of Castiglione's *Libro del Cortegiano* at her request in 1552 (Hoby, Travels, p. 78).'

Ibid. Add to list of authorities: 'Sir Thomas Hoby, Travels and Life (R. Hist. Soc., *Camden Miscellany*, vol. x, 1902).'

Parry, Benjamin. xv. 370*b*, l. 20 from foot. For 'from 1663 to 1673' read 'from 1664 to 1674.' The dates as given by Wood are old style; correct dates in Le Neve, *Fasti*, iii. 197.

Ibid. l. 19 from foot. After '1670' add 'He was rector of St. Antholin from 1671 to 1674 (G. Hennessy, *Novum repertorium*, p. 304).'

Parry, Sir Thomas (d. 1560). **xv. 385*a*, l. 32. Delete 'From him were descended the poets Henry and Thomas Vaughan' (F. E. Hutchinson, *Henry Vaughan*, (1947), p.6, n.2).**

Parry, William (1687–1756?), xv. 390*a*, l. 14. For '(1687–1756?)', read '(1687–1756)'. *Ib.*, l. 27, omit 'probably' and for 'about' read '14 September'. (*Gentleman's Magazine* (1807), 1191.)

Passelewe or Passele, Edmund de. xv. 444. Corrections will be found in L. F. Salzman's Widows of Sir Edmund de Passele, *Sussex Notes and Queries*, vi. 140–2.

Paston, Sir Robert, First Earl of Yarmouth. xv. 450*b*, l. 1. For 'Yarmouth was evidently a friend of the king' read: 'As a member of the House of Commons Paston distinguished himself by his attachment to the Court; on 25 Nov. 1664 he proposed that the supply for the Dutch war should be £2,500,000. Sir Thomas Clifford praises his conduct in this affair very highly (B.M. *Add. MS.* 32094, ff. 24–7; see also Clarendon, *Continuation*, §§ 540–2, where some account of a preliminary meeting of members of the Court party is given). As a reward Paston obtained the passing of a private act, which increased the

value of his land at Little Yarmouth (*Hist. MSS. Comm.*, 6th Report, App., p. 364). Paston is mentioned in the *Poems on Affairs of State*, 5th ed., 1703, I. (i.) 27, 57, and in the list of members of the Court party printed by Sir N. H. Nicolas as *Flagellum Parliamentarium.* He was on intimate terms with Danby, to whose wife he was related. A letter from Danby, expressing the King's approval of his conduct, is preserved in the British Museum (*Add. MS.* 36540, f. 27).' To the bibliography add 'Reports on two collections of Yarmouth's papers, including many letters from him to his wife, are given in *Hist. MSS. Comm.*, 6th Rep., App., pp. 363–90; 7th Rep., App., pp. 531–6. The latter collection is now in the British Museum, *Add. MS.* 36988.'

E. S. de B.

Paterson, Daniel. xv. 461*b*, 27 ll. from bottom, 'born in 1739.' According to the inscription on the tombstone in Clewer Church he died on 14 April 1825, 'aged 86 years 3 months and 28 days,' and it would therefore appear that he was born on 17 or 11 December, 1738, according as the reform of the calendar in 1752 was or was not taken into account.

Ibid., 24 ll. from bottom. After '1772' insert 'was made Brevet Captain 19 June 1782, and Captain 55th Foot on 18 December 1782.'

Ibid., 19 ll. from bottom. After 'London' insert 'From 25 March 1801 until 25 June 1802 he was Captain and Commandant of Invalids at the Tower.'

Ibid., 16 ll. from bottom. After 'death' insert 'A Civil Lieutenant Governor was in office at the same time, but both offices must have been regarded as sinecures and it seems most unlikely that Paterson ever went to Canada. In consequence of complaints from the Colony the Civil Lieutenant Governor, Sir F. N. Burton, who had been drawing a salary of £1500 p.a. since 1808, did arrive in Quebec in 1822 and remained in Canada for several years.'

Ibid., 16 ll. from bottom. The *New and Accurate Description of all the Direct and Principal Cross Roads in Great Britain* is correctly noted as appearing in 1771, but what follows is entirely inaccurate. The *Description* continued through a long series of editions in the same form but with slightly varied titles, and there was a subsequent issue entirely recast and very much enlarged by Edward Mogg. It is not clear that Paterson was more than a compiler, or that he ever had any proprietary interest in the publication which bears his name throughout. It seems more probable that the property in this work vested in the first instance in Thomas Carnan by whom the first edition was entered at Stationers' Hall, 19 February 1771, and from whom it passed to Francis Newbery. But, however this may be, Paterson had ceased to have any personal connexion with the *Description* as early as 1785, as he expressly states at the end of the preface to the *British Itinerary* published by Carington Bowles in that year. The four earlier editions of the *Description* are 1st 1771: 2nd 1772: 3rd 1776, and 4th 1778. The title of the following editions is limited to the roads of England and Wales. The 5th edition is 1781: 6th 1784: 7th 1786: 8th 1789: 9th 1792; 10th 1794, and 11th 1796. During this period a separate guide to the roads of Scotland, with a similar title, was published. In the 12th edition of the original work, 1799, the roads are those of Great Britain. In the 13th edition, 1803: 14th 1808, and 15th 1811, the roads are those of England and Wales and part of Scotland. There was no further publication until Edward Mogg issued an entirely remodelled and independent work, for which, however, he used Paterson's name.

In 1766 Paterson had published a single sheet, *A Scale of Distances of the Principal Cities and Towns of England. Giving in all 4560 distances in Measured Miles.* His *Travelling Dictionary*, which is a second part to the *New and Accurate Description*, appeared in 1772. Paterson's *British Itinerary* which is a delineation and description of direct and principal cross roads of Great Britain is, as has been already stated, a work entirely independent of the *Description*. The proprietor of this book was Carington Bowles from whom it passed to the firm of Bowles and Caver.

Paterson's name appears on four maps. 1. *Bowles's New Pocket Map of England and Wales, revised and corrected from the best authorities, with the addition of new roads and other improvements.* By D. Paterson. Printed for Carington Bowles, 1773. 2. A map of the Island of Grenada (1780, 1796, 1825, 1837). This seems to be an enlarged version of an engraved map of the island (without date or author's name) sent home by the Governor of the Island in 1763.

3. A circular map entitled *Paterson's Twenty Four Miles Round London with reference to Seats of the Nobility and Gentry.* It is stated on this map that the roads and distances are adjusted to those given in the *British Itinerary*, 1785. The earliest impression appears to be 25 July 1791. 4. Bowles's *New Four Sheet Map of England and Wales . . . with the Roads described by Daniel Paterson, Esq.* Dated 2 January 1796.

To the bibliography should now be added: Sir H. G. Fordham, *The Road-Books and Itineraries of Great Britain*, 1570–1850; *Trans. Bibliog. Soc.*, *The Library*, 4th Series, v. no. 4 H. G. F.

Paterson, Thomas, xv, 468*b*, l. 26 from foot. After 'bombardment' add for which he received the thanks of major-general Sir T. Bloomfield in orders'. l. 15 from foot. After '1850' add 'he married at Leith on 20 Sept. 1813, Sophia Curry and had issue 2 sons and 4 daughters'. Add to list of authorities War Office Library, Officers' Records, Royal Artillery, i. f. 66.

Paul, Sir George Onesiphorus. xv. 516*a*, ll. 8–9. Delete 'the year of his return'

Ibid. 516*b*. Add to list of authorities: Bristol and Glouc. Arch. Soc. *Trans.* li. 143–68; lv. 384–5.

Paule, Sir George. xv. 525*a*, l. 25. After 'on privy seals' insert 'and suggested that parliament might grant supplies if Sir Edward Coke [q.v.] and his adherents were made sheriffs and consequently ineligible for membership of the house of commons.'

E. S. de B.

Paulet, Pawlet, or Poulet, William, first Marquis of Winchester. xv. 538*b*, ll. 28–27 from foot. Delete 'to which . . . was added' (G.E.C., *Complete Peerage*, ii. 625, note *a*).

Paulet or Powlett, Charles, first Duke of Bolton. xv. 528*a*, ll. 23–16 from foot. Delete 'and when Peterborough . . . (Burnet).' The only debate to which the story can refer is that on 15 November 1680; Winchester never attended the house during this parliament; on 30 October he was said to be abroad (*Lords' Journals*, xiii. 628). The authority is not Burnet but a note by Dartmouth on Burnet (ed. 1833, i. 36).

Payne, John (d. 1647 ?). xv. 555*b*. This article is superseded by the collected information and list of engravings given by Sir Sidney Colvin, 'Early Engraving and Engravers in England,' pp. 106-9, 163-4.

E. S. de B.

Pecock, Reginald. xv. 647*a*, l. 24. The MS. of 'The Poore Mennis Myrrour' is now B.M. Add. MS. 37788.

Peeters, Gerard. (*fl.* 1582–1592). xv. 678*a*. For additional information drawn from B.M. *Add. MS.* 5698, see *Notes and Queries*, cxlvii. 52.

Pell, Albert (1820–1907). 2nd Supp. 1901–1911, iii. 99*a*, l. 19 from foot. For Albert James Pell,' read 'Albert Julian Pell.' *Ibid.*, l. 18 from foot. For 'Wiburton,' read 'Wilburton' (Burke's *Landed Gentry*, s.v. Pell of Wilburton).

Penington or Pennington, Sir Isaac (1587 ?–1660). xv. 741*b*, l. 5. 'Soon after 6 June 1649 he was knighted. . . .' For a note making it 'practically certain that he did not receive knighthood,' see Beaven, *Aldermen of the City of London*, i. 229.

Penn, William (1644–1718). xv. 759*a*, l. 17. After 'October 1685' add 'Late in 1684 Penn was twice taken, once preaching in a conventicle, and once attending one, and was duly fined (J. C. Jeaffreson, *Middlesex County Records*, iv, pp. lxi–lxiv).'

Ibid. 759*b*, l. 3. After '*Macaulay*)' add 'On 3 Dec. 1685 Penn was again taken preaching at a conventicle; as a former offender he was sentenced to a fine of £40 (*Notes and Queries*, clxiv (1933). 380–1).'

Pennington, Sir John, first Baron Muncaster. xv. 778*b*, ll. 5–7. For 'Sept.' read 'Dec.' (P.R.O., war office, succession book, 25/209, p. 76); for 'in 1762' read 'on 15 Jan. 1762' (*ibid.*); for 'In 1765' read 'On 21 Mar. 1765' (*ibid.* p. 77); for 'foot-guards' read 'foot' (*ibid.* 25/210, p. 101).

Ibid. l. 19. Delete 'soon'; after 'army' insert 'on 30 Nov. 1775 (P.R.O., war office, succession books, 25/211),'

Pennycuick, John, xv. 783*a*, l. 1. For 'd. 1849' read '1789–1849'. l. 2. After 'general' add 'was born at Soilarzie, Perthshire, on 28 Oct. 1789. He was appointed ensign in the Edinburgh Militia on 17 Feb. 1806, (*Militia List*, 1807, p. 281)'. l. 9. After 'and' add 'on 13 Jan. 1825 he exchanged into the 47th regiment (*Army List*, 1826, p. 212) with which he'. l. 5 from foot. After 'body' add 'Pennycuick married at Lanesborough, co. Roscommon, on 21 March 1820, Sarah, daughter of Rev. James Farrell, vicar of Rathcline.' l. 4 from foot. For 'eldest son, John' read 'second son, James'.

Add to list of authorities P.R.O., War Office, Returns of Officers' Services, 25/794.

Pennycuick, John Farrell, xv. 783*b*, l. 5. For 'John' read 'James'. l. 6. For 'eldest' read 'second (P.R.O., War Office, Returns of Officers' Services, 25/794)'.

Pepys, Sir Richard (1588?–1659), **xv. 804*b*, l. 20.**

For 'John Bendish' read 'Thomas Bendish.' (*Visit. Cambs. 1575 and 1619*, Harleian Soc. xli. p. 62.)

Pepys, Samuel. xv. 805*a* (and *ante*, ii. 97), l. 13 from foot. After 'Holland' insert:— 'The register of St. Bride's, Fleet Street, shows that Samuel was baptised there on 3 March 1632/3, and there can be little doubt that Pepys was born in Salisbury Court, Fleet Street, where John Pepys carried on business.' (*Transactions of the London and Middlesex Archaeological Society*, iv. 323–31 and v. 56.)

Pepys, Samuel. xv. 808*a*, l. 16. For 'John Bruce' read 'John Bence'. Bence, a merchant and alderman of London was returned on 9 Nov. 1669 and had also sat for Aldborough during the Protectorate. His family had frequently represented the town since the reign of Elizabeth. (Return of names of members returned to serve in Parliament, H.C. (69) 1878. LXII. i. 528, 570; John Rylands Library, Manchester, English MSS., 311, fo. 510*b*; *Further Correspondence of Samuel Pepys, 1662–1679*, ed J. R. Tanner (1929), pp. 246–9.

Pepys, Samuel. xv. 808*a*, 11 ll. from bottom. For 'Paxton' read 'Paston' and add '(19 August 1673).' *Ibid.*, 4 ll. from bottom. For 'On a petition . . . popishly inclined' read 'His opponent presented a petition against the return of Pepys on 7 January 1673–4; the case was referred to the Committee of Elections, where it was debated on 17 January (B.M. *Stowe MS.* 204, f. 61*b*); it was treated altogether as a party matter. The Committee found that neither candidate was duly elected; this was reported to the House on 6 February. The debate was adjourned, without a vote being taken, until the following Tuesday, 10 February, when information was given to the House that Pepys had an altar with a crucifix in his house, and he was accused of being a papist.' *Ibid.*, 808*b*, l. 14. After 'the charge was dropped' add 'The final debate on the matter took place on 16 February; the case was then adjourned until 28 February, but parliament was prorogued on 24 February. The case never came up for further discussion (*C.J.*, ix. 291, 304, 306, 309, 310; A. Grey, *Debates*, ii. 407–413, 420–1, 426–33).'

Perceval, John, first Earl of Egmont. xv. 813*b*, l. 3 from foot. For '1702' read 'Dec.' (*Record of Royal Soc.*, p. 322, where the spelling is 'Percivale').

Percival, Robert, xv. 827*b*, l. 13. For '1826' read '1824'. ll. 14–16. For 'became a captain . . . position until' read 'entered the army on 24 April 1793 as ensign in an independent company and on 31 Oct. following was transferred to the 102nd regiment. He was promoted lieutenant on 29 April 1795 and removed to the 19th regiment on 7 Sept. following'. l. 11 from foot. For 'also visited' read 'he accompanied the 19th regiment to'. p. 828*a*, l. 10. Delete 'Percival died in 1826' and add 'He accompanied the escort of his regiment with the embassy to Kandy in 1800. On 9 July 1803 he became captain in the 18th Royal Irish regiment and was with the original garrison of Curaçao in 1807. He was given the brevet of major on 4 June 1814 and became regimental major on 4 Sept. 1823. He died at Malta from a fall from his horse on 18 May 1824'.

Add to list of authorities: *London Gazette;* M. L. Ferrar, *Officers of the Green Howards* (1931).

Percy, Algernon, tenth earl of Northumberland. xv. 830*b*, l. 10 from foot. For '30 March' read '13 April (Pat. roll, 14 Chas. I, pt. 38, 1).'

Perrot, Sir John (1527?–1592), xv. 912*a*, l. 27. For 'St. Bride's' read 'Golden Grove'.

Peter of Savoy. xv. 945*b*, ll. 2–3. For 'probably . . . Petit-Bugey' read 'at Hereford' (*Eng. Hist. Rev.*, xliv. 349).

Peters, Hugh. xv. 961*a*, 12 ll. from bottom. For 'manuscripts,' etc., read '*Hist. MSS. Comm.*, *Leyborne-Popham MSS.*,

p. 179.' Notices of Peters' sermons will be found on pp. 211, 221.

Ibid., p. 963*a*, 22 ll. from the bottom. The two pamphlets conjectured to be written by Peters under the pseudonym of Peter Cornelius were really written by a Dutchman named Peter Cornelisz Plockboy, of Zierickzee, a town in the province of Zeeland. Plockboy propounded the organisation of a socialistic commonwealth (see E. Bernstein in *Die Vorläufer des Neueren Sozialismus* (Stuttgart, 1895), ii. 685–92).

Peters, Hugh (1598–1660), xv. 963*a*. Add to sources: J. B. Williams, 'Hugh Peters', *N. & Q.*, 11th ser., vi. 221–3, 263–4, 301–2, 463–4; vii. 4–6, 45, 84–7, 123, 163–5; viii. 65, 461–3.

Petre, Sir William (1505?–1572), xv. 980*b*, ll. 55–58. After 'his principal seat was at Ingatestone, Essex, which he received on the dissolution of the abbey of St. Mary's, Barking', add 'Details of his purchases, together with the sums of money paid, are given at length in the Bull of Paul IV to Sir William Petre, dated 28 November 1555, and preserved among the muniments at Ingatestone Hall. The manor of Ingatestone formerly belonged to the abbey of St. Mary's, Barking, and was purchased from Henry VIII for £849. 12*s*. 6*d*.; Ingatestone Hall is still the chief residence of the present Lord Petre. (For further evidence, see C. T. Kuypers, *Thorndon: its history and associations* (1930), p. 14.)'

Pett, Peter (*d.* 1589). xv. 988*b*. For further information, see *Autobiography of Phineas Pett*, ed. W. G. Perrin, 1918.

Pett, Phineas. xv. 990*b*. For further information see *Autobiography of Phineas Pett*, ed. W. G. Perrin, 1918.

Petty, Sir William, xv. 999*a*–1005*a*. Since this article was written there have been important editions of Petty's writings, both published and unpublished. The most important are: Petty's 'Economic Writings', ed. C. H. Hull, 2 vols., 1899; 'The Petty papers,' 2 vols., 1927; 'The Petty-Southwell correspondence, 1676–1687,' 1928; 'The Double Bottom,' Roxburghe Club, 1931, all three edited by H. W. E. Petty-Fitzmaurice, marquess of Lansdowne. See further the various recent works on the Down Survey, etc.; 'Times Literary Supplement,' 1932, p. 624, etc. (authorship of the 'Observations on the Bills of Mortality'); 'Notes and Queries,' clxxiv (1938). 200 (attribution to Petty of the translation of Epist. ii. 1 in Brome's Horace, 1666).

Pope, Walter. xvi. 139*b*, ll. 10–11. Delete '2. "To the Memory . . . 1671.' The poem is by Samuel Butler [q.v.]; Wood does not attribute it to Pope.

Ibid. l. 16. After 'in 1728' add 'The poem was apparently first published in Henry Playford [q.v.], "The Theater of Musick," 1685; this version varies from that of 1710.'

Ibid. l. 22. After 'Chief Justice Holt' add 'Wood also attributes to Pope "The Catholick Ballad," 1674, and "The Salisbury-Ballad," 1676; another piece, "The Miser; written by the Author of The Old Man's Wish," was published with music in 1685. Pope published an edition of the "Centum Fabulae" of G. Faerno in 1672.'

HAROLD F. BROOKS.

Philippa of Hainault (1314?–1369). xv. 1050*b*, l. 16 from foot. For '4 March, 1330', read '18 February, 1330 (*Annales Paulini*, p. 349; *Historia Roffensis* in *Anglia Saera*, i. 370).'

Philips, Ambrose. xv. 1058*a*, l. 18 from foot. For '1675?' read '1674.'

Ibid. l. 17 from foot. For 'born about 1675,' read 'baptised at St. Alkmund's Church, Shrewsbury, 9 Oct. 1674 (*Times Lit. Suppl.*, 1933, p. 909*b*).'

Pierce or Pearce, Edward. xv. 1143–4. This article is entirely superseded by the article on Pierce in Walpole Society, vol. xi, 1933, pp. 33–45. In the latter the dating of several of Pierce's extant works is hypothetical; that of the bust of Cromwell in the Ashmolean Museum is discussed in *History*, new ser., xxiii (1939). 133.

Pierrepont, Henry, first Marquis of Dorchester and second **Earl of Kingston.** xv. 1151*b*, l. 19. For '1667' read '1666 (*Lords' Journals*, xii. 52).'

E. S. DE B.

Pierrepont, William. xv. 1155*a*, l. 11. He died Thursday, 18 July, 1678. B.M. *Add. MS.* 29572, f. 160.

Pindar, Sir Paul. xv. 1196*b*, l. 22 from foot. After '"plentiful estate"' insert 'He was in Constantinople in 1599 and acted for a time as secretary to Henry Lello, English ambassador there (*Early Voyages in the Levant*, Hakluyt Soc., vol. lxxxvii, p. 63). He returned to England in November (*Travels of John Sanderson*, Hakluyt Soc., 2nd. ser., vol. lxvii, p. 184), and complained because neither the queen nor the Levant Company would pay the expenses of his journey (Hist. MSS. Comm., *Salisbury* [*Hatfield*] *MSS.*, x. 249, 334). Later he requested to be made consul at Venice (*ibid.*, p. 462), apparently unsuccessfully. But he was in Venice in 1602 (*ibid.*, xii. 386).'

Ibid. ll. 16–15 from foot. For 'From 1609 . . . Aleppo' read 'About the end of 1606 he was sent to Aleppo as consul for the Levant Company (P.R.O., State papers, cv. 110, f. 1), where he traded very successfully (*Travels of John Sanderson*, p. 252). He returned to England in 1611 (*Cal. State Papers, Venetian*, 1610–1613, p. 238).' [See also Bulletin, x. 203.]

A. C. W.

Pindar, Sir Paul. xv. 1196*b*, last 12 ll. For 'and is stated . . . iv. 61)' read 'for a term of five years. He arrived in Constantinople in December. His term of service was extended until 1620. He left Constantinople about May of that year and arrived in England about September; he was knighted soon after his arrival (letters and dispatches from Pindar in P.R.O., S.P. xcvii. 6, 7; *Travels of Peter Mundy*, Hakluyt Soc., 2nd ser., vol. xvii, i. 41–136 (account of Pindar's journey home; see also pp. 175–9); *Cal. State Papers, Venetian*, 1619–21, p. 442).'

Note: the document referred to in the article, *Cal. State Papers, Dom.*, 1611–8, p. 408, is incorrectly calendared.

Pine, John. xv. 1199*b*, l. 1. After 'engraved work' add '(8 Geo. II, c. 13; Pine's projected engravings of the Armada tapestries are protected by a special clause).'

Pitt, Christopher. (1699–1748). xv. 1228*a*, l. 39. It is stated that Robert Pitt, the physician and F.R.S., was probably a great-uncle, and that Governor Thomas Pitt was the poet's first cousin. Cf. *Notes and Queries*, cxlvi. 355, where it is suggested that the two men were respectively uncle and first cousin once removed of the younger Christopher.

Pitt, Thomas, first Earl of Londonderry. xv. 1235*b*, l. 16 from foot. After 'governor.' insert 'He was appointed ensign in Lieut.-Gen. William Stewart's regiment on 12 Jan. 1708 (Dalton, *Eng. Army Lists*, vi. 40), captain in Pepper's dragoons, 12 Apr. 1709 (*ibid.* p. 76), and on 9 Feb. 1714 colonel of a regiment of horse, afterwards the 2nd dragoon guards (P.R.O., index 5431, p. 214).'

Ibid. l. 2 from foot. After '540).' insert 'On 26 Aug. 1726 he was transferred to the colonelcy of the Buffs (J. Millan, *Succession of Colonels*, 1742, p. 9).'

Plunket, Oliver. xv. 1328*a*, l. 20 from foot. For '1629' read '1625'.

Ibid. l. 9 from foot. Before 'He' insert 'He was born on 1 Nov. 1625 (horoscope in Bodleian Library, MS. Ashmole 436, f. 119).'

E. S. de B.

Pocock, Isaac (1782–1835). xvi. 4*a*, l. 23 from foot. After 'was still played in 1835', add 'It was early adopted for the Juvenile Drama and remained its most popular play' (A. E. Wilson, *Penny Plain, Twopence Coloured* (1932), pp. 83–93; C. Speaight, *Juvenile Drama* (1946), *passim*).

Pole, Thomas. xvi. 48. Add to list of authorities: E. T. Wedmore's Thomas Pole, M.D., *Journal of the Friends' Hist. Soc.*, suppl. 7.

Pollard, Sir John (d. 1557), xvi. 60*a*, l. 21. Omit 'He seems . . . 1555'. *Ib.*, l. 27, after 'realm', add 'He seems to have been knighted between the making of his first will, 1 May 1557, where he is described as "John Pollard esq." and of his second will, 2 August 1557, where he appears as "Sir John Pollard, Knight."' (*N. & Q.*, 10th ser., xi. 1.)

Pollard, Sir Lewis (1465?–1540), xvi. 60*b*, l. 21. For '1540', read '1526'. *Ib.*, l. 24 from foot. For 'in 1540', read 'later that year: his will was proved 2 November 1526 (P.C.C. 11 Porch)'. *Ib.*, l. 17 from foot. For 'had', read 'is said to have had'. After 'daughters', add 'His will mentions only four sons and two daughters'. (*N. & Q.*, 10th ser., xi. 365.)

Ponsonby, John, Viscount Ponsonby. xvi. 86*a*, ll. 9–6 from foot. For 'On 28 Feb. 1826 . . . 12 Feb. 1828' read 'On 28 Feb. 1826 he was appointed envoy-extraordinary and minister plenipotentiary to Buenos Ayres, and moved to Rio Janeiro in the same capacity in July 1828' (dispatches in P.R.O., F.O. 6/12, 22, 23).

Ibid. last line—86*b*, l. 5. For 'He was entrusted . . . 4 June 1831' read 'On 1 Dec. 1830 he was appointed to succeed (Sir) Thomas Cartwright [q.v.] at Brussels as joint commissioner with Count Bresson of the conference of the five powers for the Belgian question, and remained there until the beginning of June 1831, when he was withdrawn as the result of the conference's ultimatum to Belgium to accept its terms of separation' (Palmerston's instructions to Ponsonby, 1 Dec. 1830, in P.R.O., F.O. 10/2, and Ponsonby's dispatches in F.O. 10/4).

Popham, Edward. xvi. 141*b*. This article needs revision. See Sir Charles Firth in *The Mariner's Mirror*, xii. 242–43.

Popham, Sir Home Riggs. xvi. 143*b*, l. 17 from foot. For '1762' read '1760'

Ibid. ll. 16–14 from foot. For 'born on . . . was consul, was' read 'son of Joseph Popham, British consul at Tetuan, and Mary Riggs, his first wife (*The Genealogist*, xxi, new series, 216), was born at Gibraltar, 12 Oct. 1760 and is reported to have been'

Ibid. l. 11 from foot. After 'at' insert 'Trinity College (*Admissions to Trinity College, Camb.*, iii. 249),'

Ibid. bottom line. After 'Kaffraria.' insert 'In recognition of his services, the East India Co. presented him with an inscribed sword of honour.'

Ibid. 144*a*, l. 4 from foot. After 'pp. 482–3).' read 'In May 1808 a further enquiry into his conduct was opened in the house of commons, but despite considerable evidence concerning his alleged smuggling activities, he was able to gain the favourable verdict of the house (*Parl. Debates*, 1808, vol. xi, cols. 721–63).'

Ibid. 145*b*, l. 5. After 'matter.' insert 'Meanwhile, on 21 March 1804 he was returned to parliament as member for Yarmouth, Isle of Wight. He was returned for Shaftesbury, Dorset, in Oct. 1806, and for Ipswich, 6 May 1807 (*Return of M.P.'s*, ii. 221, 232, 249).'

Ibid. l. 16 from foot. For 'days' read 'weeks (Popham to Marsden, 25 Aug. 1806, P.R.O. Admiralty 1/58, in-letters)'

Ibid. l. 7 from foot. After 'Maldonado.' insert 'Treasure valued at more than a million dollars was sent to England, and Popham, on his own responsibility, addressed circular letters to the chief manufacturing towns, announcing the opening up of the Buenos Aires market (*The Times*, 20 Sept. 1806).'

Ibid. 146*a*, l. 8. After 'the enemy.' insert 'He also declared that his apparently precipitate action was in reality the outcome of long deliberations with Pitt, Melville, and the Venezuelan adventurer-patriot, general Miranda (*Minutes of the Court-martial*, pp. 78 *et seq.*).'

Ibid. l. 16. After '(xix. 33).' insert 'The merchants at Lloyd's presented him with a handsome vase (*Political Register*, 1807, xi. col. 164), while the merchants generally expressed such approval of his conduct that it seems probable that he had had some understanding with them regarding the La Plata expedition (*Morning Post*, 19 Feb. 1807).'

Ibid. l. 17 from foot. After '1820' insert 'and was buried at Sunninghill, Berks. (*Carribeana*, iii. 228-30)'

Porter, Sir Charles xvi. 170*b*, l. 7 from foot. After 'Norwich' insert 'by Mary, daughter of Sir Charles Chiborne of Massinghall, Essex. He was born 6 Sept. 1631 (Le Neve, *Pedigrees of the Knights*, p. 401).'

Ibid. 171*a*, ll. 20 and 19 from foot. Delete 'and he was knighted soon afterwards.' After l. 9 from foot insert 'He was knighted about the same time; the date is given by Le Neve as 28 Feb. (*Pedigrees*, p. 401. Shaw, *Book of Knights*, ii. 261, gives 25 Jan. as a possible alternative; an undated letter in Hist. MSS. Comm., *Devonshire MSS.*, i. 110, shows that he was knighted at the time of his appointment).'

Ibid. 172*a*, l. 13 from foot. After 'the notice of Porter's death' add 'Porter married a lady named Cocksetter, by whom he had three children (Le Neve, p. 401).'

Porteus, Beilby. xvi. 195*a*, ll. 13–5. After 'Robert Porteus' insert ', son of Edward Porteus, who came to Virginia from Newbottle, near Edinburgh (A. R. Wagner, "Queen Elizabeth's American Ancestry," *Genealogists' Mag.*, viii. 372)'; after 'estate' insert 'of New Bottle, on the York River (*ibid.*)'; after 'mother' insert ', Elizabeth (*ibid.*),'

Portman, Sir William (1641 ?–1690). xvi. 200*a*, l. 9 from foot. For 'Restoration' read 'king's coronation.'

Ibid. 200*b*, l. 25. For 'on 20 March 1689–90' read 'in March 1690' (see Luttrell).

Povey, Thomas. xvi. 236*a*, ll. 18–9. Delete 'In July 1662 . . . masters of requests.'

Ibid. l. 24 from foot. After 'iii. 1318)' add 'He was sworn one of the masters of requests on 31 March 1675 (*London Gazette*, 1 Apr. 1675).'

Powell, Thomas. (1572 ?–1635 ?). xvi. 248*b*, l. 13 from foot. After '4to' insert '(2nd ed., 1635, with "The Art of Thriving," as "The Mysterie and Misery of Lending and Borrowing"; dated 1636 on separate title-page).'

Powle, Henry. xvi. 262*a*, ll. 22–21 from foot. For 'Lord Chancellor . . . during' read 'the issue of writs for by-elections by the lord chancellor, Shaftesbury, during' (the practice was not habitual, being tried only during this recess).

Ibid. last 5 ll. For 'In the new session . . . But before' read 'On 20 October Powle led the attack on the marriage, so far performed only by proxy, between the duke of York and Mary of Modena. The king had already decided to prorogue parliament, but before . . .'

Ibid. 262*b*, l. 1. For 'to announce it' read 'to summon the commons to the upper house.'

ll. 12–13. Delete 'and had a large share in driving him from office.'

ll. 15–29. For 'When the commons . . . the speaker's conduct' read 'On 26 May the commons sent an address to the king dictating such an alliance; the king replied in the banqueting house at Whitehall on 28 May, and required the commons to adjourn immediately until 16 July. When they returned to their house, the speaker, Edward Seymour [q.v.], reported the speech; Powle attempted to speak but Seymour insisted that the house was adjourned, and left the chair. After some confusion he left the house. His conduct was later called in question and on 9 February 1678 Powle vindicated the right of the house to adjourn itself (A. Grey, *Debates*, iv. 374–7, 388–91; v. 124–87).'

Ibid. ll. 16–14 from foot. For '"Sergeant Streek . . . of their rights"' read 'Sergeant Street [later Sir Thomas Street, q.v.] tried to propose Powle for speaker, but the commons refused to hear him on the ground that it would be a surrender of their right of election (Grey, vi. 414–5).'

Ibid. 263*a*, l. 6. Between 'i,' and '381' insert '338,'.

l. 12. For '1678' read '1679.'

ll. 14–17. Add reference '(Hist. MSS. Comm., 11th Rep., App. v. 31 [*Dartmouth MSS.*]).'

ll. 26–43. For 'Parliament met . . . the resolution' read 'Parliament met on 21 October 1680. Powle's conduct was marked by moderation in political, but firmness in constitutional, issues. He participated in the attack on the lord chief justice, Scroggs [q.v], in January 1681 (Grey, viii. 249–50, 287; also p. 60); on the other hand he spoke twice on behalf of Halifax, whom the commons tried to remove after the failure of the exclusion bill (*ibid.* 29, 44). He was one of the commons' managers for the impeachment of viscount Stafford [William Howard, q.v.] on 30 November and the following days, and took a subordinate part in the summing up; nothing in the report of the trial suggests the vehement oration mentioned by Evelyn (Howell, *State Trials*, vii. 1516; Evelyn, 6 Dec. 1680).

'Powle was returned for East Grinstead to the Oxford parliament in 1681. On 24 March he urged the necessity of deliberate proceedings and of adequate consideration of the expedients offered by the king in place of the exclusion bill (Grey, viii. 298). After the dissolution Powle apparently avoided politics until the revolution.'

E. S. de B.

Poyer, John. xvi. 269*b*. A pamphlet attacking Poyer says he was 'a man of mean birth and education, brought up by Master John Merrick, customer of Milford, first a boy in his kitchen, then groom of his stable, after in the trade of a glover,' and finally made deputy-mayor of Pembroke by people who needed a handy tool (*An Answer in vindication of certain Gentlemen of Pembrokeshire against a scandalous pamphlet published by John Poyer*, 4to, 1646, p. 2).

270*a*, 14 ll. from foot. His own statement of his services to the Parliament is contained in a letter addressed to Fleetwood in 1649 (*Leyborne-Popham MSS.*, p. 14) and a petition to Parliament (*The Moderate*, 17–24 April 1649). Disputes with the Pembrokeshire committee about finance, and his inability to obtain payment for his services and disbursements seem to have been the origin of his discontents (*Portland MSS.*, i. 335, 338). Perhaps there was also some religious grievance. In the *Declaration of Col. Poyer and Col. Powell*, published in April 1648, besides declaring for the restoration of the king to his authority, they complain of the suppression of the Book of Common Prayer, 'the sole comfort of the people here' (p. 5).

Preston, Thomas, first Viscount Tara. xvi. 315*a*, l. 29 from foot. For 'Genappe' read 'the fortress of Gennep.'

Ibid. 318*a*. Add to list of authorities: 'I. Commelyn, Frederick Hendrick van Nassauw, 1651, ii. 95–103.'

Pritchard or Prichard, Sir William. xvi. 411*a*, ll. 22–3. For 'Sir John Pilkington' read 'Sir Thomas Pilkington [q.v.]'

Prynne, William. xvi. 437*b*, l. 28. For '1689' read '1657,' and delete 'the preface . . . 1656–7' (*see* copy in the I.H.R. library).

Pym, John (1584–1643) xvi. 518*a*, ll. 10 from bottom and *ante*, iii. 67*a*, l. 13. After '243,578).' insert 'The accounts of his administration can be found in the records of the Land Revenue in the Exchequer. His first declared account is dated Michaelmas, 1607 (P.R.O., Exchequer, LR 12/8/256, Accounts of the Receivers-General, Series III). Pym retained this office until 1638. His successor was Robert Scawen, whose patent of appointment is dated 16 July 14 Chas. I, Patent Roll 14 Chas. I, part 27. There appears to be no evidence that Pym was compelled to surrender the office by proceedings of *scire facias*.'

Pym, John. xvi. 518*a*, 10 ll. from bottom. 'and we know nothing of his career till . . . 1614.' Pym had been granted the reversion of the receiver generalship for Wiltshire, Hampshire, and Gloucestershire in 1605 (*Cal. State Papers Dom.*, 1603–10, p. 223). This office, which fell vacant about 1607, he retained until after 1618 (*P.C.C. Wills*, Brit. Rec. Soc., s.v. 'Audley,' v. 26; *Cal. State Papers Dom.*, 1611–18, pp. 205, 243, 578). He entered parliament for the first time in 1620 as member for Tavistock. He was elected for Chippenham on 23 January 1623–4, and for Tavistock on 27 January 1623–4 (*Return of Members*, i. 461). The crown office list gives Sir Francis Popham as representing Chippenham in place of Pym (*ibid.*, 461, n. 1). Pym elected to serve for Tavistock. (See also G. E. Wade, *John Pym*; and A. P. Newton, *Colonising Activities of the early Puritans*, pp. 71–5).

Pynnar, Nicholas. xvi. 530*a*, l. 3 from foot. After "Ulster'" insert '(cf. *Cal. Carew MSS.*, 1603–24, pp. 392–423). It is the second of a series of three extant accounts of the Ulster plantation in its early stages; the first of which was drawn up in 1611 and is calendared in the same volume (pp. 220–30).'

Quain, Jones. xvi. 532*b*, l. 44. For '1835' read '1836.' See London University [now University College], Minutes of the Sessions of the Council, i. 47.

Quain, Richard. xvi. 533*a*, l. 19 from bottom. For '1830' read 'April 1831.' See London University [now University College], Minutes of the Sessions of the Council, ii. 265.

ll. 19–14 from bottom. Omit 'and Quain . . . appointed,' and read 'Quain was appointed demonstrator in August 1831, and became.' *Ibid.*, f. 317.

Quarles, Francis. xvi. 536*a*, l. 15. For 'accepted the post of cup-bearer to' read 'went in the train of the earl of Arundel (P.R.O., S.P. Dom. 81/12, fos. 133–4) to attend the'

Ibid. l. 17. For 'his mistress' read 'the princess'

Rackett, Thomas (1757–1841). xvi. 562*b*, l. 29. For 'he died . . . 1841' read 'he died at Spettisbury on 29 Nov. 1840'.

Ibid., l. 6 from foot, for 'Gent. Mag. 1841, ii. 428–31,' read 'Gent. Mag. 1841, i. 428–31.'

Rainolds, William (1544?–1594), xvi. 625*b*, l. 22 from foot. For 'West Sussex' read 'Suffolk'.

Ramsay, Sir William. (1852–1916). *1912–1921*, 444*a*, 15 ll. from foot, and 444*b*, l. 14. For '1912' read '1913' (University of London, University College: *Report of the University College Committee* . . . . 1912, p. 34; *ibid.* 1913, p. 47; University College, *Calendar* . . . 1913, p. cii.).

H. H. B.

Rand, Isaac. xvi. 712*a*, l. 16 from foot. For 'was' read 'became.'

Ibid. l. 15 from foot. For '1739' read '1719' (*Record of Royal Soc.*, p. 328).

Randulf, called **De Gernons, Earl of Chester.** xvi. 729*b*, ll. 22–21 from foot. For 'Conan, earl of Richmond' read 'Count Alan of Brittany and Richmond'

Ibid. l. 16 from foot. After 'p. 72)' insert 'and surrender the castle of Galclent or Gaultney Wood (Eng. Place Name Soc., x. 120) together with considerable treasure which he had recently captured from William de Albini Brito (SYM. DUNELM. *loc. cit.*).'

Rastell, William (1508?–1565), xvi. 748*a*, l. 32. For 'resigning . . .1563', read 'but fled to Flanders before 17 January 1651/2'. (*Cal. S.P. Spanish, 1558–67*, p. 224.)

Ravenscroft, Edward. xvi. 759*a*, l. 5. After '*The Anatomist*' add 'and *Miscellanea Genealogica et Heraldica*, 5th ser., i. 218, 301). He was the sixth son of James Ravenscroft, buried at Barnet in 1680, and of Mary, daughter of William Pecke of Spixworth, Norfolk. His date of baptism is given as "14 May 165¾." He married Frances Stock and died without issue in 1707' (*Misc. Gen. et Her.*, 5th ser., i. 224–5, 304–5).

Ibid. ll. 5–6. For 'In 1671 . . . Temple, where' read 'on 2 Apr. 1667 he was admitted to the Middle Temple (John Hutchinson, *Notable Middle Templars*, p. 202, and Middle Temple Records, iii. 1274) where, in 1671 . . .'

'Miscellanea Genealogica et Heraldica' says that he was admitted to the Inner Temple (5th ser., i. 225), but this is a confusion with another Edward Ravenscroft admitted in 1659 (*Students admitted to the Inner Temple*, 1547–1660, pp. 375–6, and *Misc. Gen. et Her.*, 5th ser., i. 268).

Ibid. l. 15. After '1697' add 'An Edward Ravenscroft, probably the playwright, was given a commission as lieutenant in the Earl of Stafford's regiment of foot in 1688 (Dalton, *English Army Lists*, ii. 199).'

For Ravenscroft's quarrel with Sir George Hewitt see 'Letters to Sir Joseph Williamson' (Camden Soc., N.S., VIII) i. 87, 94, 100.

E. S. DE B.

Ravis, Thomas. xvi. 762*b*, l. 25 from foot. After '1560,' insert 'was the son of Thomas Ravis and Mary, widow of Robert Benson, of Knaresborough, Yorks, and daughter of Thomas Lisle of Reigate, Surrey (*Notes and Queries*, clxxiii. 384). He'

Ibid. 763*a*, l. 18 from foot. After 'p. 55).' insert 'His widow, Alice, married Sir John Borlase [q.v.] at Stoke Newington, 1 Oct. 1610 (*Notes and Queries*, clxxiii. 384; *Record of Old Westminsters*, ii. 775), and died *c.* 1655 (*Cal. S. P. Dom.* 1656–7, p. 12).'

Rawley, William. xvi. 767*b*, l. 8 from foot. For 'On 22 Jan. 1606' read 'in 1600' (Venn, *Alumni Cantab.*, pt. I, iii. 424).

Ibid. l. 7 from foot. After 'B.A.,' insert '1605, and M.A. 1608,'

Ibid. 768*a*, l. 2. For '1616' read '1617, which he held until 1667.'

Rawlinson, Sir William. xvi. 779*a*, l. 12. After 'Elizabeth' insert 'who married firstly William Lowther, 1687, and secondly Giles Earle [q.v.], 1702 (*Notes and Queries*, clxvii. 383).'

Rede, Sir Robert (d. 1519), xvi. 817*b*, l. 13. Sir Richard Rede (1511–1579). For '(1511–1579)', read '(1511–1576)'. *Ib.*, l. 28. For '11 July 1579', read '11 July 1576'. (Chancery Inquisitions, ser. ii, vol. 177, no. 102.)

Reyner, Clement, D.D. (1589–1651), **xvi. 924*a*. To authorities add: *Memorials of Father Baker*, ed. J. McCann and R. H.**

Connolly (Catholic Record Society, xxxiii, 1933), pp. 236–7.

Reynolds, Sir John Russell, M.D. xvi. 938*b*, l. 33. For 'In 1865 he became professor . . .' read 'He became Holme professor of clinical medicine in 1862, and in 1865 professor . . .' (*University College, London. Proceedings at the Annual General Meeting . . . 25th February* 1863, p. 12; *ibid. 25th February* 1868, p. 11).

Ibid. l. 35. For 'and in 1878 he was' read 'He retired in 1878 and in the same year was' (*University College, London. Report of the Council . . . at the Annual General Meeting . . . 26th February* 1879, p. 13).

Rich, Henry, Earl of Holland. xvi. 998*a*, l. 22. On his colonial enterprises see A. Brown, *Genesis of the United States*, ii. 978; and A. P. Newton, *Colonising Activities of the English Puritans*, p. 61.

Ibid., p. 998*b*, l. 21. In 1639, after the pacification of Berwick, Holland zealously endeavoured to prevent the removal of the quarrel with the Scots (*Hist. MSS. Comm.*, 8th Rept., pt. ii. pp. 55–6).

Ibid., p. 999*b*, 25 ll. from bottom. His letter to the Speaker on taking up arms again in 1648 is printed in *Lords' Journals*, x. 367.

Ibid., p. 1000*a*, l. 1. Colonel Scroope's account of his defeat and capture at St. Neots is printed in *Portland MSS.*, i. 478.

Ibid., 6 ll. from bottom. A number of engraved portraits of Holland are in the Sutherland collection (*Catalogue*, i. 512). Add to authorities *State Trials*, vol. iv., and Firth, *The House of Lords during the Civil War*.

Rich, Sir Nathaniel (1585–1636). xvi. 1005. There is a better life of him in A. Brown's *Genesis of the United States*, 1890, ii. 979. See also the *Manchester MSS.*, *Hist. MSS. Comm.*, 8th Rept., pt. ii.

Rich, Nathaniel (*d.* 1701). xvi. 1006*a*, 15 ll. from bottom. In 1657 he was arrested on suspicion of complicity in Venner's plot (L. F. Brown, *Baptists and Fifth-Monarchy Men*, p. 105; *Clarke Papers*, iii. 106, 113).

Ibid., 1006*b*, l. 9. On his attempt to oppose Monck in Feb. 1660, see *Leyborne-Popham MSS.*, pp. 161, 168.

Ibid., 16 ll. from bottom. His first wife died about 1655 (*Clarke Papers*, iii. 25). His second wife's name was not Anne but Elizabeth Kerr. In 1688 when James II was courting the Dissenters it was complained that Colonel Rich, 'a Leveller, or at least a commonwealth's man,' was made a justice of the peace for Essex (Bramstone, *Autobiography*, p. 304). Add to authorities, C. Fell Smith, *Life of Mary Rich, Countess of Warwick*, 1901, pp. 235–43.

Rich, Robert, Second Earl of Warwick (1587–1658). xvi. 1018*a*, last line. The MSS. of Mrs. Frankland Russell Astley contain letters from Warwick to his grandson Robert Rich relating to his marriage with Frances Cromwell and also to Frances Cromwell (pp. 21–4).

Ibid., 1018*b*, 22 ll. from bottom. Vandyck's portrait of Warwick, now in the possession of the Earl of Leicester, is reproduced in Miss Fell Smith's *Life of Mary Rich, Countess of Warwick*.

Ibid., 1018*b*, 12 ll. from bottom. Warwick's first wife died, not in 1634 but about Dec. 1623 (*Court and Times of James I*, ii. 439). His second wife was the daughter of Sir Henry Rowe.

Ibid., 1019*a*. Add to the list of authorities: A. P. Newton, *The Colonising Activities of the English Puritans*, 1914; V. T. Harlow, *Colonising Expeditions to the West Indies and Guiana*, Hakluyt Society, 1925; Oppenheim, *The Administration of the Royal Navy*, 1509–1660, and C. D. Penn, *The Navy under the Early Stuarts*, 1913.

Richard, Earl of Cornwall and King of the Romans. xvi. 1059*b*, ll. 10–11. For '15' read '16'; for 'Falkenstein' read 'Falkenburg', and also on p. 1060*a*, l. 24 from foot.

Ibid. l. 22 from foot. After '615–32).' insert 'After her husband's death, Beatrice continued to live in England. She died in Oct. 1277 and was buried in the Franciscan church at Oxford.'

Add to list of authorities: Frank R. Lewis's Beatrice of Falkenburg, the Third Wife of Richard of Cornwall, *Eng. Hist. Rev.*, lii. 279–82.

Richard, Earl of Cornwall and King of the Romans. xvi. 1061*a*. Add to list of authorities: Frank R. Lewis's The Election of Richard of Cornwall as Senator of Rome in 1261 (*Eng. Hist. Rev.* lii. 657–62). [See also BULLETIN, xv. 119.]

Richardson, Sir Thomas. xvi. 1134*b*, l. 24. For ' 28 Feb. 1628–9 ' read ' 29 Feb. 1627–8.' (G.E.C., *Complete Peerage*, iii. 488.)

Rigby, Edward (1747–1821). xvi. 1187*b*, l. 15. After ' 1783, 8vo.' add ' 2. " An Account of Mr. James Deeker's Two Aerial Expeditions from the City of Norwich. The first on Wednesday, June 1, 1785; the second on Wednesday, June 22, 1785," 1785, 8vo.' and change enumeration of later works.

Ibid. l. 21. After ' of Norwich " ' add ' 1812.'

G. S. S.

Rimston or Remington, William. xvi. 1194*b*, l. 3 from foot. For ' in 1372.' read ' from Whitsuntide 1372 to 5 March 1374.'; and add ' In 1372 and 1373 he was the preacher chosen to address the northern clergy in synod at York (*Yorks. Arch. Journ.*, xxx. 234).'

Ibid. 1195*a*. Add to list of authorities: Yorks. Arch. Journ., xxx. 231–47; xxxi. 62–4.

Ripley, Thomas. xvi. 1203*b*, l. 16. After ' 1726 ' insert ', in co-operation with Thomas Churchill, later master bricklayer of his majesty's works and buildings,'

Ibid. l. 17. For ' building ' read ' rebuilding '

Ibid. l. 20. After ' 22,400*l.* ' insert ', but as in the case of his work at the custom-house, the cost far exceeded the estimate '

Add to list of authorities: Mariner's Mirror, xiii (1927), 96; L.C.C. Survey of London, Vol. xvi. Charing Cross (parish of St. Martin-in-the-Fields, pt. 1), pp. 57–8.

Roberts, John (1712?–1772). xvi. 1270*b*, ll. 28–35. For ' was possibly son . . . in 1759 ' read ' was the son of Edward Roberts of Chester (" Three Eighteenth-Century Politicians," by L. B. Namier, in *Eng. Hist. Rev.* xlii. 408–11).'

Robinson, John (1650–1723). xvii. 23*b*, l. 17. For ' About 1680 ' read ' In 1678 (Camden, 3rd series, xlvi. 139) '

[BULLETIN, vii. 59*a*, last line–59*b*, l. 2. Delete ', presumably . . . April 1678 ']

D.N.B. xvii. 23*b*, l. 21. For ' 1709 ' read ' 1686 '

Ibid. l. 29. After ' Oriel ' insert ', presumably in order to marry.'

[BULLETIN, vii. 59*b*, ll. 13–4. After ' *ordinarius.*' insert ' Being known as a very strong Protestant he enjoyed no further employment before the revolution.'

Ibid. l. 17. For ' stayed on till Sept. 1707 ' read ' on Duncombe's return, Sept. 1692, was left in charge. He was accredited agent in Aug. 1694, and was back in England, July to Nov. 1696, returning with the title of minister resident (Camden 3rd series, xlvi. 139).']

D.N.B. xvii. 23*b*, l. 6 from foot. After ' Saxony.' insert ' The English ministers feared lest Charles should dictate a pro-French peace. Oxenstierna, the Swedish chancellor, was dead, his successors were with the king on the continent, and no diplomatic business could be transacted at Stockholm. Robinson was accordingly directed to seek an interview with Charles. After a terrible journey across the Baltic he reached the king's headquarters, near Warsaw, on 12 March 1703. Although he only secured one interview, the mission eased those fears which the battle of Blenheim finally dispelled in the following year, and restored contact with the Swedish ministers (P.R.O. State papers, 95/15 *passim*).' For ' 1707 ' read ' Nov. 1706 (Camden 3rd series, xlvi. 140) '

Robinson, John (1650–1723). xvii. 23*b*, ll. 19–21. For ' became chaplain . . . Sweden ' read ' went to Stockholm as secretary and chaplain to his brother-in-law, Sir Edward Wood, envoy extraordinary 1672–79, presumably in the place of his secretary William Allestree, who had returned to England in April 1678.'

Ibid. ll. 24–27. For ' during the absence . . . Swedish court ' read ' He stayed on after Wood's departure, to serve under Philip Warwick [q.v.], envoy extraordinary 1680–83, after whose death he was left in charge of affairs, and was accredited agent $\frac{8}{18}$ August 1684, remaining until Oct. 1687 ' (*Diplomatic Instructions—*Sweden, i. 14: Roy. Hist. Soc., Camden 3rd ser., xxxii).

Ibid. 29 ll. from foot. After ' *ordinarius* ' insert ' He returned to Stockholm as secretary and chaplain to William Duncombe, envoy extraordinary 1689–92 and stayed on till September 1707.'

Ibid. 24*a*, l. 28. After ' Saxony; ' insert ' he left for England at the end of August 1709 ' (*Ibid.*, p. 15).

Ibid. 22 ll. from foot. After 'appointed' read 'on $\frac{11}{22}$ May 1710' (*Ibid.* p. 41).

J. F. C.

Robinson-Montagu, Henry, 6th Baron Rokeby, xvii. 57*a*, l. 5 from foot. For 'life-guards' read 'foot guards (*Army List*, 1815, p. 154)'.

Rogers, Henry (1806–1877). xvii. 121*b*, l. 19 from bottom. For '1836' read 'January 1837.' See London University [now University College], Minutes of the Sessions of the Council, iii. 98.

Rokesley, Gregory de, Mayor of London, etc. (*d.* 1291). xvii. 156*a*, l. 25. The reference for his lands to the old Record ed. *Cal. Inq. post Mortem*, i. 109, should be replaced by the new *Cal. Inq. post Mortem*, ii. (1906), No. 824, where fuller details are given.

Rookwood, Ambrose (1664–1696) in art. Rookwood, Ambrose (1578?–1606). xix. 212*a*, ll. 22, 21 from foot. For 'entered the army . . . James II' read 'served as brigadier in James II's troop of guards in France (*Arraignment*, etc., p. 36).'

[Note: The brigadier's was the lowest commissioned rank in the horse guards: E. Chamberlayne, *Angliæ Notitia*, 1687, i. 178, 184–5. Rookwood is not named in English army lists, etc. In the *Arraignment* (p. 53) a witness calls him Captain Rookwood; this presumably refers to his status among the conspirators.]

Roper, William. xvii. 215*b*, l. 22. For 'grandfather' read 'father (*Visitation of Kent, 1619*, Harl. Soc., pp. 82–3)'

Ibid. l. 27. After 'universities' insert 'and at Lincoln's Inn (*Black Books*, i. *passim*)'

Ibid. l. 25 from foot. For 'about 1525' read 'on 2 July 1521 (R. W. Chambers, *Thomas More*, p. 182)'

Ibid. l. 27 from foot. For 'alone for life' read 'for life, being assisted in it from 1549 to 1568 by Richard Heywood, and from Hilary 1572 by his eldest son, Thomas Roper, and his nephew, John (P.R.O. *coram rege* docket rolls, *passim*)'

Ibid. 216*a*, l. 20. For '1577' read 'Michaelmas, 1573'

Rosen, Friedrich August. xvii. 247*a*, ll. 6–1 from foot. For 'Believing . . . 1830' read 'In that year he resigned his chair in the university in protest against the expulsion of G. S. Pattison [q.v.]' (*University College, London, Correspondence*, no. 2152).

l. 24 from foot. For 'two' read 'three.'

Rosen, Friedrich August. xvii. 247*b*, l. 20. For '1836' read '1834.' See London University [now University College], Minutes of the Sessions of the Council, ii. 431; *University of London, Report and Appendix, February* 1834, p. 7.

Rothery, William, in art. Rothery, Henry Cadogan. xvii. 303*b*, ll. 9–12. For 'In 1821 . . . in 1860' read 'In 1821 he was appointed by the treasury as its adviser on applications for bounties under the slave-trade acts and in some other matters requiring knowledge of Admiralty law. He held the appointment until 1860, when he was succeeded by his son.'

Charles Johnson.

Roy, William. (*fl.* 1527). xvii. 371*a*, l. 18. For '*Letters and Papers*, iii. 2037' read '*Letters and Papers*, iv. 4693 (p. 2038).'

Ibid., 17 ll. from bottom. For '*Letters and Papers*, u.s. p. 769' read '*Letters and Papers*, v. App. No. 18.'

Royle, John Forbes. xvii. 375*b*, l. 3. For '1837' read '1836' (King's College, London, *Calendar*, 1836–7, p. 4).

Rudyerd, Sir Benjamin. xvii. 385*b*, l. 9. After 'April' insert '1590.'. *Ibid.*, l. 10. For 'Inner' read 'Middle.' *Ibid.*, l. 12. After 'p. 5' insert 'A. R. Ingpen, *Middle Temple Bench Book*, p. 181; *Middle Temple Records*, i. 312).'

Rupert, Prince. xvii. 405. (See *ante*, iii. 67). Mrs. M. A. E. Green's *Life of Elizabeth, Queen of Bohemia*, revised by Mrs. S. C. Lomas, 1909, contains some additional particulars about Rupert's personal history; others are given in Miss Eva Scott's *Rupert, Prince Palatine*, 1899, which is the best life of the Prince. The transcripts of Rupert's correspondence, made originally for Eliot Warburton, used by Miss Scott and Dr. S. R. Gardiner, when they were in Sir Charles Firth's possession, are now in the Bodleian Library. 'A Journal of Prince Rupert's Marches, 1642–6,' from the Clarendon MSS., was printed by

Sir Charles Firth in the *Eng. Hist. Rev.*, xiii. 729. A paper on Marston Moor, contributed also by him to the *Transactions of the Royal Historical Society*, 2nd Series, vol. xii., contains a contemporary plan showing Rupert's order of battle. A ballad entitled 'Prince Rupert and Prince Maurice: their Farewell to England,' is printed by Ebsworth in vol. viii. of the *Roxburghe Ballads*, Introd. p. xxiii. Volume x. of the *Camden Miscellany* contains a small collection of papers on 'Prince Rupert at Lisbon,' edited by S. R. Gardiner. But a great number of documents illustrating Rupert's service at sea during the wars with the Dutch in the reign of Charles II are printed in H. T. Colenbrander's *Bescheiden uit vreemde archieven omtrent de groote Nederlandsche Zeeoorlogen*, 1652–1676, 2 vols. 1919, the Hague, part of the Dutch Rijks Geschiedkundige Publicatien. The first volume contains particulars about Rupert's part in the four days' battle of June 1666, pp. 320, 332, 336, 342, 347; and also that of 4–5 Aug., pp. 416, 436, 463, and his narrative touching the miscarriages in the late war sent to the House of Commons 10 Nov. 1667, p. 601. The second volume shows his share in the naval battles of 1673, and gives at length his charges against the French admiral and the answer made to them (pp. 225, 233, 287, 297, 301, 345, 394). Charles II discredited the charges and condemned Rupert for making them.

Ruperta, Rupert's daughter by Margaret Hughes, married in 1696 Emanuel Scrope Howe [q.v.] who was then envoy extraordinary to the House of Brunswick-Luneburg (Scott, pp. 363–4).

Rupert, Prince. xvii. 415–16. For Rupert's alleged marriage with Frances, daughter of Henry Bard, Viscount Bellamont [q.v.], compare Eva Scott's *Rupert* (2nd ed. pp. 357–64) and her art. in *English Hist. Rev.* (xv. 760–1) with *E.H.R.* xi. 527–30 (referred to in *D.N.B.* xvii. 416*a*) and G. E. C., *Complete Peerage*, new ed., s.v. 'Bellamont.'

Russell, Edward earl of Orford (1653–1727). xvii. 429*b*, l. 29. After 'first duke of Bedford' add 'son of Edward Russell and Penelope Hill Brooke, widow of Sir William Brooke, K.B., daughter and co-heir to Sir Moses Hill of Hillsborough Castle, Ireland.' J. H. Wiffen, *Historical Memoirs of the House of Russell*, (London, 1833), ii. 160; J. and J. A. Venn, *Alumni Cantabrigienses*, (Cambridge, 1924), iii. 499. Russell was prepared for Cambridge at Tottenham school, and on August 27, 1666, was admitted to St. John's College as a Fellow Commoner (Venn. *op. cit.*, iii. 499).

l. 30. After 'of the Advice.' add 'As a lieutenant on the Advice, fourth rate, in 1671, he saw service in the Mediterranean') (J. R. Tanner, *A Descriptive Catalogue of the Naval Manuscripts in the Pepysian Library at Magdalene College, Cambridge* (Navy Records Society, 1903–23), Pepys' Register of Commission Officers, i. 400; *Cal. State Papers, Dom.*, 1671 (January 11, 1671), p. 16. Russell served as lieutenant aboard the *Prince*, first rate, in 1672, as well as aboard the *Rupert*, third rate (*Cal. State Papers, Dom.*, 1671–2 (March–May, 1672), pp. 189, 288, 291, 399, 440, 451, 473, 533, 574, 594; for references to the *Rupert*, *ibid.*, pp. 485, 499, 512).

l. 33. After 'Phoenix.' add 'As captain of the *Phoenix* in August, 1672, Russell was engaged with the fleet in convoying East Indiamen and others bound for Hamburg' (*Cal. State Papers, Dom.*, 1672, p. 488).

l. 36. For '1676' read 'February 1646.' After 'Reserve' add 'fourth rate' (Tanner, *op. cit.*, i. 401).

l. 38. After 'Sir John Narbrough.' add 'The *Reserve* was employed for a voyage to Newfoundland in the summer of 1676, in company with the *Pearl*, fifth rate' (*Cal. State Papers, Dom.*, 1676–7. Pepys to Sir Robert Southlands, 6 Mar. 1676. p. 11; *ibid.*, Philip Lanyon to S. Williamson, 2 June 1676, p. 141). Pepys noted in his 'Admiralty Journal' that 'letters from Captain Russell and Captain Wyborne giving an account of their proceedings at Newfoundland' were read to the Admiralty Board on October 21, 1676 (Tanner, *op. cit.*, iv. 363).

Russell was appointed captain of the *Defiance*, third rate, on December 15, 1677. Even before Russell's appointment the *Defiance* had been detailed for duty with the Mediterranean convoy fleet (Tanner, *op. cit.*, i. 401; *Cal. State Papers, Dom.*, 1677–8, p. 411).

l. 20 from foot. After 'Swiftsure,' add 'third rate, which was employed in cruising in the Channel, off the coast of Ireland, and off the southern coast of England' (*Cal. State Papers, Dom.*, 1678, pp. 82, 125, 172, 180, 197, 206, 374; Thomas Holden to Williamson, 23 May, 1678, pp. 185, 409).

l. 19 from foot. After 'Newcastle,' add

'fourth rate, on convoy duty to the Mediterranean' (Russell was appointed to the command on the *Newcastle* on August 10, 1690. Pepys' Register of Sea Officers, in Tanner, *op. cit.*, iv. 401; Hist. MSS. Comm., *Finch MSS*), Sheres to Daniel Finch, December 31, 1680, ii. 94. Although in the D.N.B. Mr. Laughton notes that Russell's last command prior to the revolution of 1688 was the *Tiger*, Pepys has no record of this in his Register of Sea Officers. Tanner, *op. cit.*, i. 401).

l. 11 from foot. After 'interest.' add 'Russell went to Holland as go-between for the Whig group and William of Orange in April–May of 1688.'

The date of the warrant creating Edward Russell Treasurer of the Navy is March 18, 1689 (*Cal. State Papers, Dom.*, 1689–90, p. 29).

l. 9 from foot. For '4 April' read '18 March'.

l. 6 from foot. After 'Torrington.' add 'Russell was also honoured in a civilian capacity by being made *Custos Rotulorum* for Cambridgeshire (*ibid.*, p. 131), and for Carnarvonshire (*ibid.*, p. 271).'

Ibid., p. 430, l. 5. After 'services.' add 'Russell was a member of the Admiralty Board in 1690'. Hist. MSS. Comm., *House of Lords MSS.*, '1690–1) Letters Patent of May 14, 1690, p. 86; *Journals of the House of Commons*, May 17, 1690, x. 420.

l. 24. After 'enemy.' add 'For comments on the charges of Jacobitism against Russell, see Macaulay, *History of England* (ed. Firth, London, 1913–15), iv. 2022; v. 2182–84, 2338. See also Churchill, *Marlborough*, ii. 51–63, 84, 100–101; iii. 98; and Dalrymple, *Memoirs* (1790 ed.), iii. 227–9, 232–3, as well as Clarke's edition of James II's *Memoirs* (London, 1816), ii. 489, 490, 491, 499–500.'

Ibid., 431, l. 26. For 'Russell had no further service afloat.' read 'Russell served valiantly in the frustration of the projected invasion of England by a French-aided Jacobite force in February-March of 1696, and his services at sea were not ended till mid-March, 1696.' (N. Luttrell, *A Brief Historical Relation of State Affairs . . .* (Oxford, 1857), iv. 27; Hist. MSS. Comm., *Buccleuch MSS.*, (1903), ii. 310–11; S. Martin-Leake, *Life of Sir John Leake* (Navy Records Society, 1920), i. 65.

l. 16 from foot. For 'Mary' read 'Margaret', (*G.E.C.* x. 81).

Russell, Edward, Earl of Orford. xvii. 429*b*, ll. 2–1 from foot. For 'but during . . . though' read 'and remained'

Ibid. 430*a*, ll. 1–2. For 'spent most . . . intriguing' read 'until 3 June (P.R.O., Admiralty out-letters, 2/169 f. 242). On 5 June he was appointed an admiralty commissioner (see BULLETIN xiv. 21 above), and this, together with his membership of the council for advising the queen during William's absence in Ireland, explains his absence from the fleet during the summer, since William desired all members of the council to remain in London (Dalrymple, *Memoirs of Gt. Britain and Ireland*, ed. 1790, iii. 79). He undoubtedly used the opportunity to intrigue'

Ibid. l. 12. After 'in his stead' insert 'after vacating his seat at the admiralty, 23 Jan. (see BULLETIN xiv. 21 above),'

Ibid. 431*a*, l. 11. After 'Cadiz' insert ', much against Russell's wishes (*Shrewsbury Corresp.*, ed. Coxe, pp. 199–209).'

Ibid. l. 23 from foot. For 'September' read 'October (see BULLETIN xiv. 24 above)'

Russell, John, first Earl of Bedford (1486 ?–1555). xvii. 446*a*, l. 8. For '1540' as the date of his appointment as lord president of the four western counties read '1539' (*L. and P.*, XIV. i. no. 743, 12 April 1539).

Russell, Lucy, countess of Bedford. xvii. 467*b*, ll. 4–7. For 'Sir William Temple . . . (*Correspondence*)' read 'Sir William Temple extolled as "the perfectest figure of a garden" he ever saw, either at home or abroad, her garden at Wolsey's old palace Moor Park, near Rickmansworth, Herts.; he describes it in detail (*Essay of Gardening*).' It has, apparently, been completely altered.

Thirty-four of her letters, dated between 1614 and 1626, are printed in the 'Private Correspondence of Jane, Lady Cornwallis,' 1842.

A miniature of her by Isaac Oliver [q.v.] is in the collection of the duke of Buccleuch.

E. S. DE B.

Russell, Richard (1714–71?), *ante*, xxvii. 107. The name should read **Russel, Richard** (1714–71?).

Russell, Richard, M.D. (*d.* 1771), xvii. 470. In this article two persons are confused. The following entries should be substituted:—

Russell, Richard (1687–1759), physician, born in the parish of St. Michael, Lewes,

26 Nov. 1687, was the son of Nathaniel Russell, surgeon and apothecary practising in Lewes, and a deacon of the presbyterian body. He was educated at the Grammar School of Southover, Lewes, and received his early medical education under his father. He made a secret marriage with the daughter of William Kempe of Malling Deanery, and later went to Leyden and studied under Boerhaave and graduated there on 22 Dec. 1724 (D.M.I. 'De epilepsia puerili'). 'He appears to have had his home at Rotterdam when he was studying at Leyden, because he complains to the Senate that the authorities at Rotterdam wanted to tax his books and furniture. Presumably he had his wife with him. As students at Leyden were free of taxes this was put right by the Senate—*vide* Acta under date 10 April 1725, when he had already graduated and was apparently still pursuing his studies' (Innes-Smith). He returned to England and practised at Lewes and on the death of his father-in-law succeeded to the estate of Malling Deanery and removed thither. He published in 1750 at Oxford a dissertation 'De Tabe Glandulari' in which he recommends the use of sea-water for the cure of enlarged lymphatic glands. The first English translation was published in London in 1752; but this was not authentic and Russell published his own translation in the following year. He was elected F.R.S. on 13 Feb. 1752, and in 1755 published 'Economia Naturae in Morbis acutis et chronicis Glandularum', dedicated to Thomas Pelham-Holles, duke of Newcastle [*q.v.*], in which he discusses the condition, diseases and treatment of glands throughout the body, regarding them as of one system or tissue, whether secretory or lymphatic. In the volume is printed a letter from him to Richard Frewin, M.D., on the use of salt water externally in the cure of tuberculous glands. It is dated from Lewes, January 1752. In 1754 he moved to Brighton. The rise of Brighton from a struggling fishing-village to a fashionable health resort is essentially due to Dr. Russell, and his name is perpetuated in several streets of that town. His portrait by Zoffany is in the Art Gallery in Brighton. He died whilst on a visit to a friend in London, 19 Dec. 1759, and was buried in the family vault at South Malling.

[Munk's College of Physicians, MS. Additions ii–iii; G. Holman, Some Lewes men of note, 1905; Notes and Queries, 11th Series, v. 35 (1912); Innes-Smith, English-speaking students of medicine at the University of Leyden, 1932.]

Russell, Richard, M.D. (1714?–1771), physician, was the son of the Revd. Richard Russel, M.A., of St. John the Evangelist Westminster, a non-juring clergyman, formerly vicar of Alfreston and Selmeston, Sussex, by Juliana his wife; perhaps the Richard, son of the Revd. Richard Russel and Juliana, born 18 Dec., bapt. at Selmeston, 28 Dec. 1714. He was for eight years at Westminster School under Dr. Freind. He studied medicine and midwifery in London and Paris and graduated M.D. at Rheims on 7 June 1738. On 4 August 1741 he married Elizabeth Wilkins of Hoddesdon at Christ Church, Newgate Street, London. He practised at Hoddesdon and Ware and on the recommendation of Dr. Mead and others was appointed physician to the branch of Christ's Hospital at Ware. He was admitted an Extra Licentiate of the College of Physicians, London, on 23 July 1742 and subsequently moved to Henley-on-Thames, becoming involved in a dispute with Dr. Anthony Addington, the father of Lord Sidmouth. He later (*c.* 1750) moved to Reading where he died on 5 July 1771 (Gentleman's Magazine, 1771, p. 335). He is the author of 'A Letter to Dr. Addington of Reading, on his refusal to join in consultation with a physician, who had taken his degree abroad, and was approved and licensed by the College of Physicians', 1749, and 'Letter to Mr. Thomas Bigg, late surgeon of St. Bartholomew's Hospital, occasioned by his having written a defamatory letter to Dr. Addington against Dr. Russel of Reading', 1751.

[Munk's College of Physicians, ii. 149; Works; manuscript notes supplied by J. B. Whitmore.]

Rutherford, Andrew, earl of Teviot. xvii. 493*b*, l. 17 from foot. Before 'of Tangier' insert 'and vice-admiral' (P.R.O., Ad. 2/1755: Out letters relating to Admiralty and Vice-admiralty, f. 17). The reference made in this document to the patent appointing the earl of Teviot a vice-admiral does not mention the place where he was to act, but since Tangiers had a vice-admiralty court and Dunkirk had not, and since the reference occurs in the entry of the patent appointing Fitzgerald vice-admiral of Tangiers, it is reasonable to assume that the earl of Teviot was both governor and vice-admiral there.

Sackville, Charles, Sixth Earl of Dorset and Earl of Middlesex (see *Bulletin*, No. 7, p. 67).

xvii. 575*b*, ll. 8–7 from bottom. For 'and either the prosecution . . . acquitted' read 'They were found guilty of manslaughter, but were pardoned (*Cal. State Papers, Dom.*, 1661–1662, p. 340).'

576*a*, l. 21 ff. 'Sackville was sent to France . . . to get him out of the way.' There is no ground for the reason given in the text for Sackville's being sent to France. He was probably chosen because he was one of the most distinguished of Charles II's courtiers.

At bottom of column add 'Sackville had sat for East Grinstead since 1661. As Earl of Middlesex he was introduced into the House of Lords on 17 April 1675 (*Lords' Journals*, xii. 661), but did not attend very regularly. He took little interest in politics; at this time his father, the Earl of Dorset, was supporting Shaftesbury.'

576*b*, l. 6. After 'satirised' add 'Dorset had been joint Lord Lieutenant of Sussex with his father from 1670 until 1677; then sole Lord Lieutenant until January 1688, when he was displaced for refusing to assist James II in his attempt to obtain a packed parliament (Macaulay, *Works*, 1866, ii. 128–31).'

576*b*, l. 24. By Dryden's 'Essay on Satire' is meant the introductory essay (in prose) to the translations of Juvenal and Persius (1693), not the 'Essay on Satire' (in verse) by John Sheffield, Earl of Mulgrave [*q.v.*], which is said to have been corrected by Dryden, and which is sometimes printed with his poetical works.

Ibid., ll. 32–43. More accurate information about Dorset's marriages will be found in G. E. C., *Complete Peerage*.

E. S. de B.

Sackville, Charles, sixth Earl of Dorset and Earl of Middlesex. xvii. 576*a*, 20 ll. from bottom, at end of paragraph. Add 'He returned early in September 1669, and was again sent, with Sunderland [see Spencer, Robert, second Earl, and Sedley, Sir Charles], on a complimentary mission to Louis XIV. in May 1670 (B.M. *Add. MS.* 36916, ff. 142, 181).'

Ibid., 577, at end of article. Add 'Besides the satirical epistle to the Hon. Edward Howard, mentioned above, Dorset wrote a parody of Sir Robert Howard's poem "The Duel of the Stags.' It is printed in *Poems on Affairs of State*, 1703, vol. i., first part, p. 201 and elsewhere.'

Sadleir, John (1814–56), xvii. 591*b*, l. 44. 'In the same year (1853) he was elected M.P. for Sligo, but the disclosure of some irregularities in connection with the election led to his resigning his junior lordship'. For 'the election' read 'the general election of 1852'-and add '(Sadlier to Lord Aberdeen, 4 Jan. 1854: Brit. Mus., Add. MS. 43251. fo. 322)'.

St. John, Henry, Viscount Bolingbroke. xvii. 627*a*, ll. 14–13 from foot. For 'buy' read 'rent for 2500 livres per annum (S. Radice, "Bolingbroke in France," *Notes and Queries*, clxxvii. 309)'; after 'Orleans' insert ', which he continued to rent until March 1734 (*ibid.*)'

Saint-John, Henry, Viscount Bolingbroke. xvii. 633*b*. Add to list of authorities: H. N. Fieldhouse's Oxford, Bolingbroke and the Pretender's Place of Residence, 1711–14 (*Eng. Hist. Rev.* lii. 289–96); Bolingbroke and the d'Iberville Correspondence, August 1714–July 1715 (*ibid.* 673–82).

St. Leger, Sir Anthony. xvii. 655*a*, l. 19 from foot to 655*b*, l. 12. For 'In February 1551 . . . by Croft's advice' read 'The Ireland to which he returned was very much in need of an efficient and understanding administration. The corruption of the government and of the Irish council and the depreciations of the coinage caused great discontent, which, together with the scandalous condition of the army and the disaffection of the native rulers through the "rough handling" of Bellingham, could well give rise to anxiety (Philip Wilson, *Beginnings of Modern Ireland*, pp. 309, 315–8). St. Leger set out to remedy the abuses and within a few months had reformed the army, conciliated the Irish princes, and attempted to deal with the council (*Cal. State Papers, Ireland*, 1509–73, p. 110). But his apathy to the religious reforms and his protection of the primate, Dowdall [*see* above], caused much annoyance to Archbishop Browne of Dublin, who, supported by jealousy in the Irish council, lodged grave complaints at London of his predilection for the old religion. This and the fear of a French invasion led to his being superseded in May 1551 by Sir James Croft [q.v.], who had already been some months in the country, fortifying the southern ports and acting as St. Leger's chief adviser in the government (*Cal. State Papers, Ireland*, 1509–73, pp. 111–12).'

See also art. Ware, Sir James, below.

Saltonstall, Richard (1586–1658), xvii. 713*a*, l. 22. For '3rd ser. iv. 157', read '2nd ser. iv. 157'.

Sampson, Henry (1629 ?–1700). xvii. 718*b*, ll. 25–24 from foot. For 'William Sampson . . . [q.v.]' read 'William Sampson, "a pious Gentleman" (Calamy, *Continuation*, ii. 852).'

Ibid., p. 719*a*, l. 21, from foot. At end of article add: 'Sampson's younger brother, William Sampson (*c.* 1637–1703), matriculated from Pembroke College, Cambridge, in 1654, and graduated B.A. in 1657 and M.A. in 1660; in the latter year he was elected a fellow of his college. He was instituted rector of Clayworth, Notts., in 1672, and at the same time became a prebendary of Lincoln. In 1693 he was chosen master of Pembroke, but declined the office. At Clayworth he kept a kind of parish chronicle, a companion to the register; it deals with both civil and ecclesiastical matters, and includes lists of the population, prices, weather notes, etc. It was published in 1910 as 'The Rector's Book of Clayworth.'

Ibid., l. 12 from foot. To authorities add: 'For William Sampson, Venn, Alumni Cantabrigienses; The Rector's Book of Clayworth.'

Sampson, William (1590 ?–1636 ?). xvii. 722*b*, l. 16 from foot–723*a*, l. 15 from foot. For 'Sampson, William . . . river Trent' read 'Sampson, William (*c.* 1600–*c.* 1656), dramatist, was born about 1600 (deposition, 1649, printed by Wallrath, p. 5). His first work, written in collaboration with Gervase Markham [q.v.], a Nottinghamshire man by origin, was "The true Tragedy of Herod and Antipater: With the Death of faire Marriam. According to Josephus, the learned and famous Jew. As it hath beene of late, divers times publiquely Acted (with great Applause) at the Red Bull, by the Company of his Majesties Revels," which was published in 1622 (license 22 Feb. 1621/2; printed by G. Eld for Matthew Rhodes). Of the two issues extant one contains a dedication, signed by Sampson alone, to Sir Thomas Finch, bart., of Eastwell, Kent (subsequently Viscount Maidstone and earl of Winchilsea). By 1628 Sampson was a servant to Sir Henry Willoughby of Risley, Derbyshire, who had formerly employed Phineas Fletcher [q.v.]. He was an inmate of Willoughby's house in 1636, when he dedicated his play "The Vow Breaker" to Willoughby's daughter Anne. He was still in Willoughby's service in 1653 when Willoughby made his will, in which he appointed Sampson one of his executors. He is last traceable in February 1655 or 1656, when he was petitioning the commissioner for the Great Seal in connection with Willoughby's will.

'Sampson's principal work is "The Vow Breaker. Or, the Faire Maide of Clifton. In Notinghamshire as it hath bene divers times Acted by severall Companies with great applause," which was published in 1636 (printed by John Norton, and to be sold by Roger Ball). The play includes various stories: (1) the ballad history of the maid of Clifton, who, having plighted her troth to young Bateman, in his absence marries another suitor; Bateman commits suicide and eventually the woman also loses her life; (2) a series of scenes derived from Holinshed and relating to the siege of Leith in 1560; Sir Gervase Clifton, a Nottinghamshire knight, has a prominent part in them; (3) a final scene, entirely fictitious, in which Queen Elizabeth visits Nottingham and grants some privileges to the town. There are also some comic scenes. The whole is very loosely put together and has little literary merit.'

Ibid., p. 723*b*, ll. 26–11 from foot. For 'Sampson died . . . Grew [q.v.]' read 'In his will Sir Henry Willoughby mentions a Mrs. Sampson and, presumably a separate person, Hanna Sampson, to whom he leaves among other things, his jewelled hat-band.'

Ibid., ll. 10–5 from foot. For this list of authorities read: 'It is natural to assume that it is the one William Sampson in Willoughby's service from 1628 to 1653; the collaborator in "Herod" is presumably the same man. Most of the available information about him is collected by Hans Wallrath in his edition of the "Vow Breaker" (Materialien zur Kunde des älteren Englischen Dramas, ed. W. Bang, vol. xlii, 1914); a full account of "Virtus post funera vivit" is given by John T. Godfrey, William Sampson, 1894.'

[Note: There is nothing to connect William Sampson the dramatist with the Sampsons of South Leverton, Notts., and he cannot have been the father of Henry Sampson, M.D. [q.v.], as this William Sampson was dead by 1637.]

Sancroft, William (1617–1693). xvii. 735*a*, l. 10 from foot. After 'chapel.' insert 'He was sworn a privy councillor on 6 February and retained this dignity until the revolution.'

Ibid. 737*a*, ll. 30–4. 'When he saw . . . oath of allegiance.' There appears to be no authority for this statement. Sancroft was absent when the lords met at Whitehall on 12 December (H. C. Foxcroft, *Life of Halifax*, ii. 35) and apparently from all their later meetings. D'Oyly (*Sancroft*, i. 395–6) suggests that this was because at the meeting on 11 December 'he perceived the bearing of opinions towards the total exclusion of James from the government', a measure of which he disapproved; this also is simple conjecture.

Ibid. 737*b*, l. 11. After 'Wharton's "Diary").' add 'On 2 February he joined with the archbishop of York in acknowledging the commons' vote of thanks to the clergy for their opposition to James II's measures against the church (*C.J.*, x. 16–7; Gutch, i. 446–8). He was appointed a privy councillor on 14 February (*London Gazette*, 14–18 Feb. 1688/9), but was of course never sworn.'

Ibid. l. 28 from foot–738*a*, l. 1. For 'On 1 Aug. 1689 . . . within ten days' read

'Sancroft's refusal to take the oath of allegiance to William and Mary led, in accordance with the act for the new oath, to his suspension on 1 August 1689 and to his deprivation on 1 February 1690; five bishops and about four hundred other clergy were deprived at the same time. After his suspension William sent him permission to remain at Lambeth if he pleased (Luttrell, *Brief Relation*, i. 567, 577–8); and shortly before his deprivation attempted to reach a compromise by means of a dispensation (Henry Hyde, Earl of Clarendon, *Correspondence*, etc., ed. Singer, ii. 299, 304). A receiver for the temporalities of the bishopric was appointed in July 1690; Sancroft may however have continued to receive them until November (*Cal. Treasury Books*, 1689–92, pp. 406, 1337–8; see also D'Oyly, *Sancroft*, i. 460); he is said to have reduced his household in August (D'Oyly, i. 460). About July of this year the nonjuring bishops were accused in "A Modest Inquiry into the causes of the present disasters" of inviting the French to invade England; while the government proceeded against the publisher of the pamphlet (Luttrell, ii. 78, 80) Sancroft and four of his suffragans published a "Vindication"; its terms did not satisfy William (*Life of Thomas Ken*, by a Layman (i.e. J. L. Anderdon), 2nd ed., 1854, p. 580). His attitude is shown by a message he sent to James some time later; he was determined to live quietly under the present rulers; while he protested his loyalty to James he wished to receive no communications from him (Anderdon, p. 588).

'Although Tillotson had been chosen to succeed Sancroft some time previously, it was the discovery of the Jacobite plot early in 1691 that led to the filling of the vacant sees. The deprived bishops had been implicated by a letter of Francis Turner, the deprived bishop of Ely; William now offered, in return for a suitable statement of their innocence, to let them retain part of their revenues; this offer Sancroft declined (Anderdon, pp. 573–81). Tillotson was named as archbishop on 22 April; Sancroft refused to see him when he called soon after (D'Oyly, i. 462). He began to pack his books; between 17 and 24 May he was twice summoned to leave Lambeth, to make way for Tillotson's consecration on Whitsunday, 31 May; he declared that he could

Sandwich, Ralph de. xvii. 769*b*, l. 16 from foot. After '*Orig.* i. 21).' insert 'On 11 Feb. 1278 he was appointed to act as a justice for pleas "coram rege" for the duration of a royal visit to Kent (*Cal. Pat. Rolls*, 1272–81, p. 287).'

Ibid. 770*a*, ll. 28–24 from foot. For 'In Michaelmas term . . . He' read 'Sandwich was appointed temporary chief justice of the common bench on 24 Sept. 1289 (*Cal. Pat. Rolls*, 1281–92, p. 324) and the fines levied during the michaelmas term regularly bear his name. The feet of fines show, however, that he acted in this capacity for one term only. He'

Savage, Henry, D.D. xvii. 826*a*, ll. 24-5. For 'the manuscript . . . 1661,' read 'Savage's autograph manuscript is in the Bodleian Library (MS. Barlow 2; *Summary*

Catalogue 6431); 'a copy dated 1661, the dedication only in Savage's hand.'

N. D.-Y.

Savile, Sir George, Marquis of Halifax. xvii. 845*b*, l. 18. After 'mother,' insert 'but entered Shrewsbury School in Feb. 1643 (Shrewsbury School, MS. register, vol. ii, under 15 Feb. 1642/3).'

Savile, Sir George, Marquis of Halifax. xvii. 845*b*, ll. 18–20. This supposition is supported by A. Wood, *Fasti Oxonienses*, ed. Bliss, ii. 31, who states that Savile, returning from his travels in 1651 or 1652, put his affairs into the charge of Edward Sherburne [*q.v.*].

Savile, Sir George, Marquis of Halifax. xvii. 845*b*, ll. 18–22 and above, iii. 134. For 'and it is possible . . . 1656' read 'Savile was travelling abroad from 1649 to 1651. He was at Leghorn in October 1649 (B.M. Sloane MS. 608, f. 244) and with his tutor probably at Naples in November (*ibid.* f. 230*v*). This establishes his identification with "Mr. George Saville" who with his tutor dined at the English college in Rome on 24 Jan. 1650, N.S. (Foley, *Records of the English Province of the Society of Jesus*, vi. 641; cf. Bargrave, *Pope Alexander VII and the College of Cardinals* [Camden Soc., xcii], pp. 74–5). He and his tutor were at Orleans in August 1650 (Sloane MS. 608, ff. 231, 231*v*). It is probable that Savile remained in France until February 1651 (*ibid.* f. 236*v*). He appears to have returned to England by 1653 (*ibid.* f. 238). His home, Rufford, was the seat of a projected royalist rising in March 1655. Cromwell believed that he was implicated, but he was apparently in London at the time (Gardiner, *Commonwealth and Protectorate*, iii. 283, and references there cited; Carlyle, *Cromwell*, ed. Lomas, iii. 464).'

E. S. de B.

Savile, Henry. xvii. 859*b*, ll. 19–18 from foot. After 'in a fortnight's time' add 'on 20 March (*Cal. S. P., Dom.*, 1668–69, p. 240).'

Ibid. 17–16 ll. from foot. For 'He accordingly . . . enter parliament' read 'In August and September, Savile was in Paris with Charles Sackville, lord Buckhurst [q.v.] (Hist. MSS. Comm., *Buccleugh MSS. at Montague House*, i. 434), Buckhurst being sent on account of a dangerous illness of the dauphin (Hist. MSS. Comm., 14th Rep., App. ii, 311 [*Portland MSS.*, iii.]). Savile was also apparently in an official capacity. On 21 May 1670 Savile visited Evelyn in London. In June, on the death of Ferdinand II, grand-duke of Tuscany, Savile was sent by the duke of York on a complimentary mission to his successor; James Hamilton, brother of Anthony Hamilton [q.v.], went on the same mission on behalf of the king (Hist. MSS. Comm., *Various Collections*, ii. 139, 154, 157). Savile did not leave London before 2 July and on 1 July wrote to Halifax urging the latter to use his influence at East Retford to return him to parliament (*Savile Correspondence*, p. 25).'

Ibid. l. 14 from foot. For 'Shortly afterwards' read 'In September 1671.'

Ibid. l. 7 from foot. After 'went abroad' add 'In February 1672 he was writing to Sir William Coventry [q.v.] and to Halifax to make his peace (*Savile Correspondence*, pp. 35–9, incorrectly dated 1672/3). He returned to England in April and was present with the duke of York at the battle of Southwold bay (*Cal. S.P., Dom.*, 1671–72, pp. 380, 391; *ibid.* 1672, p. 164). He is said to have hoped to become secretary to the duke of York (*ibid.* 1672, p. 303), and apparently acted in that capacity until the arrival of John Werden or Worden [q.v.] from Sweden.'

860*a*, l. 2. After 'In September' add 'on Werden's arrival.'

860*b*. Add to list of authorities: Choisy, 'Mémoires,' ed. Lescure, 1888, i. 210.

E. S. de B.

Scarle, John. xvii. 888*a*, l. 27. After '337).' insert 'He enjoyed the favour of Richard II, who granted him a tun of Gascon wine annually at Christmas on 27 Nov. 1385, for his long and praiseworthy service to Edward III and Richard himself (Bulletin, xv. 140–1).'

Schaub, Sir Luke, xvii. 901. l. 22 from foot. The statement that Schaub was attached to the English mission at Copenhagen is a mistake. He arrived in Vienna in Nov. 1714, and remained there throughout 1715 and 1716 (P.R.O., S.P.For., 80, 32 ff.). The mistake is due to a misinterpretation of a remark in the *Calendar of Treasury Papers*, ccv. 48 (29 Sept. 1716) which mentions payment of arrears to a secretary at Copenhagen in the same sentence as payments to Schaub and the inference was drawn that he was employed there.

Schaub, Sir Luke. xvii. 901*a*, l. 33. For '(*d.* 1758)' read '(1690–1758).' (Printed preface to *Miscellaneous State Papers*; B.M., *Hardwicke Papers*, Add. MS. 35, 837, f. 130). B. W.

Schonau, Anian de. xvii. 927–8. The name Schonau should be written Nanneu.

Ibid. 927*a*, l. 4 from foot to 927*b*, l. 2. For 'is said . . . Holland' read 'was most probably of Welsh, not of Dutch, birth (Haddan and Stubbs, *Councils and Ecclesiastical Documents*, i. 498*n*).'

Ibid. 927*b*, ll. 14–6. Delete 'He is said . . . crusade.' There is ample evidence of his presence in England between August 1270 and August 1274 (*Cartae et Munimenta Glamorgan.* i. 139, 140; *Cal. Close Rolls*, 1272–9, p. 506).

Ibid. l. 23. After '. . . with the Welsh' add 'although until 1282 he appears to have been on good terms with Edward I, from whom he obtained several grants (*Cal. Pat. Rolls*, 1272–81, p. 196; *Cal. Close Rolls*, 1272–9, pp. 381, 462, 485).'

Ibid. 928*a*, ll. 1–3. For 'As a consequence . . . to Rhuddlan' read 'The damage suffered by the diocese of St. Asaph in the campaign of 1276–7 probably gave rise to a proposal to remove the see to Rhuddlan.' The letters of Edward I and Anian on this subject (Haddan and Stubbs, i. 529, 530) were probably written in 1281, although Rymer (*Foedera*, i. 629) places the king's letter in 1283, after the destruction of the cathedral by fire. No mention of the fire is found in these letters, and the bishop and the king were clearly in accord when they were written, whereas in 1283 Anian was absent from the diocese, having incurred Edward's displeasure.

Ibid. Add to list of authorities: Article by Ruth C. Easterling, Flintshire Hist. Soc. Journal, 1914–15, pp. 9–30; D. R. Thomas, History of the Diocese of St. Asaph, ed. 1908, i. 41–8, 216.

Scott, James, Duke of Monmouth. xvii. 957*b*, 2 ll. from bottom. For '305' read '465*b*.'

Scott, James, duke of Monmouth and Buccleuch (1649–1685). xvii. 975*a*, l. 7. After '(Collins)' insert 'who died in 1693. In 1703 she married the earl of Selkirk' (*Notes and Queries*, clviii. 406).

Ibid. l. 10. After '1731–2' insert 'James II, within six months of Monmouth's death, had settled upon her Wolsey's old estate of Moor Park, Rickmansworth, with an income of £4000 a year' (*ibid.*).

Scott, John, xvii. 985*a*, l. 5 from foot. For '(1783–1821)' read '(1784–1821)'. l. 3 from foot. For '1783' read '24 Oct. 1784'. See Register for the Parish and County of Aberdeen, General Registry Office, New Register House, Edinburgh.

Sedgwick, Adam. xvii. 1117*b*, l. 5 from foot. For '1830' read '1821' (*Record of Royal Soc.*, p. 384).

Sedgwick, Obadiah. xvii. 1122*a*, l. 4. For 'by his wife Priscilla' read 'He married Priscilla Goddard, apparently of Ogbourne St. Andrew, at that place on 10 July 1638 (*Coll. Top. et Geneal.*, v. (1838), 356); by her . . .'

E. S. de B.

Sedley, Sir Charles. xvii. 1125*b*, l. 4. At end of paragraph. Add 'Sedley was sent, with Buckhurst [see Sackville, Charles] and Sunderland [see Spencer, Robert, second Earl], on a complimentary mission to Louis XIV. in May 1670 (B.M. *Add. MS.* 36916, f. 181).'

Sedley, Sir Charles. xvii. (and *ante*, iii. 67) 1125*b*, l. 11. After 'Dorchester' insert 'At some time between 1665 and 1672 Sedley parted from his wife, who had become a maniac. Lady Sedley entered a convent at Ghent, where she lived upon a pension apparently paid by her husband and died on 1 July, 1705. In April 1672 Sedley went through a form of marriage with Ann Ayscough, daughter of Henry Ayscough of Yorkshire, by whom he had two sons, Charles, who was knighted by William III in 1688/9, and William, who died in infancy (V. de Sola Pinto, *Sir Charles Sedley*, 1927, pp. 120–5, 129–30).'

Ibid. l. 20 from foot. After '1701' insert 'at Hampstead, whither he had retired earlier in that month for the sake of his health. His son, Sir Charles, predeceased him in May 1701 (*Ibid.*, pp. 232–3).'

Selwyn, George Augustus (1809–1878), xvii. 1171*a*, l. 33. The reference to Hist. MSS. Comm., 15*th Report* should be transferred to p. 1170*a*, l. 23, as it relates to George Augustus Selwyn (1719–91).

Sergison, Charles. xvii. 1192*a*, l. 11. For '25 Dec. 1689' read 'Jan. 1690 (P.R.O., Admiralty in-letters, 1/3560, f. 147)'

Ibid. l. 12. After 'room' read 'his patent passing on 6 Feb. (P.R.O., Patent roll, 1 Wm. and Mary, pt. viii, 12),'

Ibid. ll. 15–14 from foot. For 'many are still at Cuckfield Park' read 'a collection of 135 vols., including the minutes of the Navy board from 1673 to 1718, are now deposited at the National Maritime museum, Greenwich (Soc. for Nautical Research, *Annual Rep.*, 1931, p. 40; *Mariner's Mirror*, vii, 1931. 385)'

Seton, Charles, second Earl of Dunfermline. xvii. 1204*a*, l. 2. After '1622' insert 'He was incorporated in St. Salvator's College, St. Andrews, in 1629' (Univ. Munim.). J. H. B.

Sevenoke, Sir William. xvii. 1214*a*, l. 9. Delete 'Sir' (Beaven, *Aldermen*, ii. 4; Will P.C.C. 16 Luffenam).

Ibid. l. 10. For '1433?' read '1432', and delete 'lord' (Beaven, *loc. cit.*).

Ibid. l. 14 from foot. For '24 May' read '24 March (*Cal. Letter-Book I*, p. 124).'

Ibid. 1214*b*, l. 22. For '1423' read '1423/4 (*Cal. Letter-Book K*, p. 24).'

Seward, Anna. xvii. 1218*a*, l. 6. For '1747' read '1742.'

l. 8. For 'in 1747' read 'on 12 December 1742 (*The Times Lit. Supp.*, 1928, p. 468).'

Sewell, William (1804–1874). xvii. 1228–9. For criticism of article, see Lionel James, *A Forgotten Genius: Sewell of St. Columba's and Radley*, (1945), pp. 274–5.

Sexby, Edmund. xvii. 1230*b*, 12 ll. from bottom. Sexby's proposals to Cromwell for an attack on France, in conjunction with Spain, and the seizure of La Rochelle, are printed in *Clarke Papers*, iii. 197–202.

Ibid., 1231*b*, l. 32. Omit the words 'and no murder.'

Ibid., l. 36. For sentence beginning 'Captain Silius Titus,' read 'Captain Silius Titus, who was intimate with Sexby at the time, assisted him in writing it, and claimed after the Restoration to be its sole author' (Wood, *Athenae*, iv. 624; *Eng. Hist. Rev.* xvii. 308).

Add also to the authorities at the end, Firth, *Last Years of the Protectorate*, i. 33, 113, 222, 232.

Seymour, Sir Edward. (1633–1708). xvii. 1250–53. P. 1250*a*, 9 ll. from bottom, for 'represented . . . December 1685' read 'was elected M.P. for Devonshire in 1660, and for Totnes in 1661, 1679 (twice) and 1685. He died 7 December 1688 (G. E. C. *Complete Baronetage*, i. 34; Luttrell, *Brief Hist. Relation*, i. 484).' P. 1250*b*, 7 ll. from top, for 'Gloucester' read 'Hindon (*Notes and Queries*, 14th Series, p. 394; *A Perfect List of . . . the Knights . . . for the Parliament*, 1661; *An Exact and Perfect List of . . . the Knights . . . that serve in this present Parliament*, 1665).' P. 1250*b*, 15 ll. from top, for 'He was soon . . . 3000*l.* a year' read 'He succeeded Sir Thomas Osborne as treasurer of the navy on 19 June 1673, with a salary of 2000*l.* a year and a house at Deptford (*Cal. State Papers Dom.*, 1673, p. 380).' P. 1250*b*, 20 ll. from top, for 'Sir William' read 'Henry (*Commons Journals*, ix. 253).' P. 1250*b*, 2 ll. from bottom, after 'discussion' add '(Burnet, *Hist. of My Own Time*, ed. Airy, ii. 79–80).' P. 1251*a*, 16 ll. from top, after 'to the king' add '(Burnet, ii. 204–5. Cf. *Ormonde MSS.* vi. 346, 498–9; *Finch MSS.* ii. 47; Temple, *Works*, ed. 1754, i. 412).' P. 1251*a*, 21 ll. from bottom, after 'regent' add '(Burnet, ii. 281).' P. 1251*b*, 9 ll. from bottom, after 'queen' add '(Mary's *Memoirs*, ed. Doebner, p. 46; Luttrell, ii. 390–1). During the next two years he voted with the court party, and opposed the Triennial Bill (Bonnet's despatch *apud* Ranke, *Hist. of England*, vi. 212).' P. 1252*a*, 26 ll. from bottom, after 'fervour for war' add '(Ranke, v. 250, 266, 268, 284).' P. 1252*a*, 21 ll. from bottom, after 'prospects' insert 'At the instance of Harley (*Wentworth Papers*, pp. 133–4) he was . . .'

Add the following *in loco*: During the years 1673–77 Seymour worked hand in glove with Danby, for whom he helped to secure a majority in the commons by bribery (*Essex Papers*, i. 140–1, 144–6, 150, 152, 155; *Poems and Satires of Andrew Marvell* ed. Aitken, ii. 63, 206). He joined Danby in intrigues against Essex, whom he perhaps hoped to succeed in Ireland (*Essex Papers*, i. 215, 225, 242, ii. 23–4). Apparently early in 1677 he quarrelled with his patron, possibly owing to a feud with Lady Danby (Temple, *Works*, i. 412; H. C. Foxcroft, *Life of Halifax*, i. 129). In November 1678, when the house was in a grand committee, he made an embittered attack upon Roman Catholics and urged the limitation of the power of a popish successor to Charles II. (*Ormonde MSS.* vi. 478–9; *Grey's Debates*, vi. 264–5). In April 1679 he became a member of the reconstructed privy council, and in January 1681 he was admitted to the committee of intelligence, which about this time became the committee for foreign affairs or the cabinet council (*Eng. Hist. Rev.* xxxvii. 57, 66). During the next two years he exercised great influence, favouring a policy of limitation as against exclusion with regard to James, Duke of York. Although he is said to have opposed the duke's being exiled in October 1680 (*Ormonde MSS.* v. 459), he afterwards opposed his return to court in 1681–82 (*Life of James II.*, i. 677, 728). While supporting Halifax on this point, he opposed his design to call another parliament in January 1682 (*ibid.*, i. 716–9; Reresby's *Memoirs*, ed. 1875, p. 235). About April 1681 he sold his treasurership of the navy (*Ormonde MSS.* vi. 37) in the hope of obtaining one of the great offices of state. During the next six months there were rumours that he was to succeed Anglesey as lord privy seal, but in October Halifax obtained that position (Foxcroft, i. 360–1). The reason of his failure was his insupportable arrogance. Roger North notes that on one occasion at the council he said to Charles II.: 'Sir, how long will your majesty prevaricate with yourself?' and adds that 'this, probably, joined with other like-tempered speeches, lost him the king's favour' (*Lives of the Norths*, ed. Jessopp, i. 299–300). For the rest of the reign he took little part in politics. Ormonde remarks in April 1683 that Seymour was not yet come to the court. 'When or upon what terms he may come is not easy to foresee; he sets a value upon himself equal at least to the importance of his ability to serve the King' (*Ormonde MSS.* vii. 13). G. D.

Seymour, Sir Francis. xvii. 1255, l. 25. For 'He was re-elected . . . February 1625/6' read 'He was made sheriff of Wiltshire in order to prevent him from sitting in the new parliament summoned in February 1625/6 (*Return of Members of Parliament*, i. 468–73; *Commons' Journal*, i. 817).' H. H.

Seymour, George Hamilton. xvii. 1259*b*, l. 4 from foot. Insert 'Sir.'

Ibid. 1260*a*, ll. 22–3. For '13 Nov. 1836' read '4 Apr. 1836' (credential, P.R.O., F.O. 83/839B, no. 9).

Shadwell, Thomas. xvii. 1281*b*, l. 13. Add to list of authorities: D. M. Walmesley's New light on Thomas Shadwell, *Times Lit. Suppl.*, 1925, p. 268.

Shakespeare, William. xvii. 1321*a*, l. 17 from foot. After 'husband' insert 'Sir Walter Raleigh's "Instructions to his Son" and the provisions of his will show that he, if not his contemporaries in general, considered his first duty to be to provide for the children in whom the family was continued, rather than for his widow' (*Notes and Queries*, clviii. 364–365).

Sharpey, William (1802–1880), xvii. 1366*a*, l. 35. For 'Padua' read 'Pavia'. (Hirsch, *Biographisches Lexikon der Hervorragenden Aertze.*)

Shaw or Shaa, Sir Edmund. xvii. 1372*b*, l. 6. Delete 'lord' (Beaven, *Aldermen of London*, ii. 14).

Ibid. l. 11. After 'elected' insert 'Alderman of Cripplegate Ward in 1473' (*ibid.*).

Ibid. l. 24 from foot. For 'about 1487,' read '20 April 1488' (*Cal. Inq. p.m., Henry VII*, i. no. 381).

Ibid. l. 14 from foot. For '1487' read '1487/8' (*ibid.*).

Under his brother Ralph, *ibid.* 1373*a*.

- l. 18. Delete 'or John.'
- l. 20. Insert 'Polydore Vergil' before 'Hall.'
- l. 22. After 'S.T.B.' insert 'vicar of Harleton, Cambs.'
- l. 34. For 'afterwards, and' read 'afterwards. He' (Fabyan says nothing about the date of his death).
- *Ib.* After '1484' add 'being succeeded in his prebend on that date by Edmund Chaderton and at Harleton by Roger Lupton [q.v.] on 15 Sept.'
- l. 40. Add '*Cal. Pat. Rolls* 1476–85, p. 473; this entry leaves no doubt that his name was Ralph.'

Shelley, Sir William. xviii. 42*a*, l. 19. 'In 1523 he is erroneously said to have been returned to Parliament for London.' Letter Book [Corporation Records] N. fo. 222 gives his name as one of the City Members for 1523 (cf. Beaven, *Aldermen of London*, i. 274).

Sherburne, Sir Edward. xviii. 72*b*, l. 24. For 'and in 1654' read 'In March 1655 he was a participant in the projected rising at Rufford (Thurloe, *State Papers*, vii. 302, and references in Gardiner, *Commonwealth and Protectorate*, iii. 283); subsequently'.

The date 1654 is taken from Wood, and is evidently O.S. E. S. de B.

Sheridan, Thomas. (*fl.* 1661–1688). xviii. 85*b*, l. 18. The conclusion of Sheridan's MS. history of his own times reads 'This faithful relation of matters of fact was finished by Thomas Sheridan in the year 1702.'

Ibid., 86*a*, ll. 36–38. The history of his own times is printed in *Hist. MSS. Comm.*, *Stuart Papers*, vi. 1–75.

Shirley, James (1596–1666), xviii. 126*b*, l. 35. For '1639' read '1640'.

Ibid., l. 38. For '1624' read '1625'. *Ibid.*, l. 48. For '1625–6' read '1625'. p. 128*a*, l. 10. For '1638' read '1635'. p. 130*b*, l. 28. For 'licensed 9 Feb.' read 'first acted 31 May'. p. 131*a*, l. 39. For '1614' read '1640'. p. 132*a*, l. 34. For 'J. B.' read 'T. B'. p. 132*b*, l. 10. For '1654' read '1653'. *Ibid.*, l. 34. For '7 May' read '17 May'. p. 133*a*, l. 44. For '1643' read '1633'. *Ibid.*, l. 48. For 'Ladies' read 'Ladie'. p. 133*b*, l. 21. For 'T. G.' read 'F. G.'

To list of authorities add: 'A. H. Nason, James Shirley, dramatist, New York (1915).'

Shirley, Sir Thomas (1542–1612). xviii. 138*b*, l. 19. After 'He was elected M.P. for Sussex in 1572' add 'and in 1584'. l. 21. Delete '1584', (Browne Willis, *Notitia Parliamentaria*, iii. 105. Cf. J. F. Neale, *The Elizabethan House of Commons*, p. 68, n. 3).

Shrubsole, William (1729–1797). xviii. 165*b*, l. 16 from foot. After 'of the day' add 'Shrubsole was part author of "The history and antiquities of Rochester and its environs," published by Thomas Fisher [q.v.] in 1772, writing about half of it (*Gentleman's Magazine*, vol. lvii, pt. ii, p. 1052).'

Shuldham, Molyneux, Baron Shuldham. xviii. 169*b*, l. 8. For 'autumn' read '30 September 1798 (*Notes and Queries*, cxlvii. 399; *Annual Register*, Chron., 1798, p. 119).'

Sibthorp, John. xviii. 190*a*, l. 21 from foot. For '1789' read '1788' (*Record of Royal Soc.*, p. 365).

Sidney, Sir Henry (1529–1586). xviii. 210*b*, ll. 23–18 from foot. For 'He was knighted . . . cup-bearer for life' read 'He was granted the office of the king's chief cup-bearer for life on 21 Feb. 1550 (*Cal. Pat. Rolls*, Edward VI, iii. 174).'

Ibid. l. 2 from foot. For 'He was the bearer in the following year of' read 'He was knighted on 11 Oct. 1551 in company with William Cecil and others (*Literary Remains of Edward VI*, ii. 352). In December 1552 he was sent with'

Ibid. 211*a*, l. 3. After '*Harl. MS.* 353, f. 127)' add 'The offer was not accepted, but Sidney was very well received (*Cal. State Papers, For.*, 1547–1553, p. 238).'

Sidney, Henry, earl of Romney, xviii. 217*b*, At l. 34 it is stated that his father, Robert, 2nd earl of Leicester, of the 1618 creation, left him at his death in 1677 the manor of Long Itchington, Warws., but no specific authority is given. It had been bequeathed by Robert Dudley, earl of Leicester, (1532?–88) to his natural son Robert Dudley, and though the latter failed to establish his legitimacy, his four daughters, 'after a long suit in *Chancery*' (Dugdale, *Warwickshire*, 2nd ed., p. 968) obtained possession of the manor. The two survivors of them were vouchees in a recovery of 1656 (Recov. R. Hil. 1656, no. 97) and the manor has ever since been divided into four shares, three of which were sold by decree in Chancery to Sir Richard Newdigate after the death of one of the daughters in 1663 (Dugdale, *op. cit.*, p. 344). The fourth share was in 1677 in the hands of Lady Katherine Leveson, Sir Robert Dudley's last surviving daughter, who lived until 1679 (G. Baker, *History and Antiquities of the County of Northampton*, (1822–30) ii. 32).

Sievier, Robert William. xviii. 244*a*, l. 3 from foot. For '1840' read '1841' (*Record of Royal Soc.*, p. 399).

Sinclair, Sir Henry (d. 1400?). xviii. 296*b*, l. 24. Date of death, 1404 (*Handbook of British Chronology*, p. 324).

Sindercombe, Miles, xviii. 311. Add at end reference to Firth, *Last Years of the Protectorate*, i. 36, 116, 220.

Singleton, Robert Corbet (1810–1881). xviii. 315*b*. For criticism of article, see Lionel James, *A Forgotten Genius: Sewell of St. Columba's and Radley*, (1945), pp. 273–4.

Slanning, Sir Nicholas. xviii. 369*a*. In the list of authorities, for 'Clarendon MS. 1738' read '*Bellum Civile*, ed. C. E. H. Chadwyck Healey (Somerset Record Socy., 1902). Slanning's exploits in the Western campaign are recorded in Sir Ralph Hopton's narrative of the campaign printed therein.'

Smith, Alexander (1830–1867). xviii. 421*a*, ll. 18 and 15 from foot. For '1830' read '1829.' Delete '(*Notes and* . . . 311)' (*Times Lit. Suppl.*, 1 Jan. 1931, p. 12, col. 3; *ibid.* 8 Jan. 1931, p. 28, col. 3).

Smith, Sir Jeremiah (*d.* 1675). xviii. 473*a*. For further details see Sir Charles Firth in *The Mariner's Mirror*, xii. 258–9.

Smith, John Gordon. xviii. 491*b*, l. 34. For '1829' read '1828.' See London University [now University College], Minutes of the Sessions of the Council, i. 202.

Smith, Joseph (1682–1770). xviii. 502*a*, l. 5 from foot. After 'aged 88' add: 'He married first Katherine Tofts [q.v.], who died in 1756 (*Misc. Gen. et Her.*, 2nd ser., i. 347).'

For 'a sister' read 'Eliza, sister (*ibid.*).'

Smith, Sir Thomas (1556?–1609). xviii. 536*a*, l. 6. The identification of the subject of this article with the M.P. for Aylesbury in 1597 is questioned in J. E. Neale, *The Elizabethan House of Commons*, p. 184, n. 2.

Smith, Thomas Southwood, M.D. xviii. 544*a*. He was proposed for the chair of Moral and Political Philosophy in London University [now University College] in 1827, and was appointed temporarily to give a course of lectures on physiology at the University in 1830–31 to fill the vacancy caused by the resignation of (Sir) Charles Bell [*q.v.*]. See London University [now University College], Minutes of Committees: Education Committee, 22 June 1827. Cf. *ibid.*, Minutes of the Sessions of the Council, i. 91, ii. 163–4; S. E. De Morgan, *Memoir of Augustus De Morgan*, 1882, p. 373.

Smith, William (1769–1839). xviii. 560*a*, ll. 24–8. It was William Cary's elder brother, John, who was associated with Smith in the production of his geological maps, sections, and tables of fossils, as cartographer and publisher.

To the authorities add: Thomas Sheppard's William Smith: his Maps and Memoirs, 1820; and Sir H. G. Fordham's John Cary, 1925. H. G. Fordham.

Smith or Smyth, John (1567–1640), of Nibley. xviii. 481. See B.M. *Cat. Add. MSS.*, **1888–1893, p. 206, no. 34121. 'A Parliamentary Diary of John Smyth of Nibley . . . M.P. for Midhurst in the Parliament of 1621.'**

Smith or Smythe, Sir Thomas. xviii. 537*b*, ll. 23, 25. For '1892' read in each case 'xx.' The volume for 1892 is xix.

Snagge, Thomas. xviii. 610*b*, ll. 29–28 from foot. For '(12 Nov. 1588) . . . Snagge' read 'on 4 Feb. 1588/9 and presented to the queen two days later (D'Ewes, *Journals*, pp. 428 and 429). He'

Somer, Henry (*fl.* 1440) xviii. 626*b*, l. 3. For '(fl. 1440)' read '(d. 1450)'.

Ibid., ll. 6–7. For 'Henry was . . .–86' read 'From the accession of Henry IV Somer was a clerk of the receipt. (P.R.O., Exchequer, Issue Rolls, *passim*)'.

Ibid., ll. 12–21. For 'He was made . . . ix. 915)' read 'He was a baron of the exchequer from 8 Nov. 1407 (*Cal. Pat. Rolls, 1405–8*, p. 374) until June 1410 when he was appointed chancellor of the exchequer (*ibid., 1408–13*, 205). This office he retained until 1439. Whilst baron and chancellor, he was also clerk (or deputy) of the treasurer from 1408 to 1410 and again from 1411 to 1413. On 10 Dec. 1412 he was described as lieutenant of the treasurer. (P.R.O., Exchequer, Issue Rolls, *passim*).'

Ibid., l. 37. After '1400' add 'He represented Cambridgeshire in the parliament of 1432, and was later on the commission of the peace for that county. When he died on 23 March 1450, his grandson James, aged 11 years, the child of his daughter and Sir Richard Veer, was his heir. (P.R.O.,

Chancery, Inquisitions post mortem C. 139/138/21).'

Somer, Semur, Somerarius, John. xviii. 626*b*, ll. 8–5 from foot. For 'the illuminated MS. . . . 1462 but in' read 'in Royal MS. 2 B, viii. the preface announces tables of conjunctions from 1387–1462, but the MS. is really almost a century later, and gives conjunctions from 1463 onwards. Tables from 1387 are in the Cotton MS. Faustina, A. II, and other copies. In . . .'

J. P. G.

Somerset, or Somerseth, John (*d.* 1455?) xviii. 653*b*, l. 20. After 'ecclesiastics.' insert 'He was returned as knight of the shire for Middlesex to the parliament of 1442 (Return of names of members returned to serve in Parliament, H.C. (69) 1878. LXII, i. 333) and was on the commission of the peace for that county from 1439–49.'

Ibid., ll. 22–5. For 'In 1443 he . . . Midd.)' read 'He was warden of the king's exchange and mint in the Tower of London and warden of the coinage of gold and silver from 1439 to 1447.' .

Ibid., l. 25. For '1441 to 1446' read '1439 to 1452'.

Ibid., l. 26. After 'exchequer' insert '(*Cal. Pat. Rolls, 1436–41*, p. 418; P.R.O., Exchequer, Issue Rolls, *passim*)'.

Ibid., ll. 15–13 from foot. For 'From Bekynton's . . . married' read 'He was twice married (*Cal. Pat. Rolls, 1446–52*, p. 176)'.

Southwell, Robert (1561?–1595). xviii. 706*b*, l. 31. Insert after '. . . HERTFORD].' 'This was not, however, an original work, but a translation, probably by him, of the work of the Spanish Franciscan Diego de Estella (1524–1578), "Meditaciones Devotisimas del Amor de Dios," first edited at Barcelona in 1578' (*Times Lit. Supp.*, 20 Nov. 1930, p. 991).

Southwell, Sir Robert. xviii. 708*a*, last line–708*b*, l. 6. For 'Robert seems . . . his education' read 'Going to England in 1650, Robert matriculated from Queen's College, Oxford, on 24 June 1653. There he was under the influence of Thomas Barlow [q.v.], who gave him a paper of directions for reading English history when he was at Lincoln's Inn (Hist. MSS. Comm., *6th Rep.*, p. 420*b*), where he was admitted in 1654. He graduated on 28 June 1655 and completed his education'

Ibid., p. 708*b*, l. 16. After 'Lady Fenton' add 'Soon after his return to England Southwell also became acquainted with James Butler, duke of Ormond [q.v.]. Anthony Southwell had befriended Ormond's parents; the friendship had continued between Ormond and the elder Robert Southwell, and was now extended to his son. Ormond recommended Southwell to the king (Ormond to his grandson, 1685, in T. Carte, *Life of James, duke of Ormond*, 1851, v. 178–9).'

Ibid., p. 709*a*, ll. 17–20. For 'He was M.P. . . . D.C.L. on him' read 'He entered parliament as member for Penryn in February 1673; he was naturally a member of the court party, but spoke little, if at all (BULLETIN, xi. 18; A. Grey, *Debates*). He sat for Penryn again in 1679 and for Lostwithiel in 1685. On 6 August 1677, when he accompanied Ormond, the chancellor, on a visit to Oxford, he was one of some twenty members of Ormond's suite who received the degree of D.C.L.'

Ibid., p. 709*b*, ll. 8–12. For 'On 1 Dec. 1690 . . . ii. 310)' read 'He was an original fellow of the Royal Society, having been admitted to the earlier society on 7 May 1662 (BULLETIN, xiv. 90). He was elected president on 1 Dec. 1690 and held office until 30 Nov. 1695 (*Record of the Royal Society*, 1940). He contributed a few papers to the *Philosophical Transactions*, mainly on physiological and chemical subjects, but of a general rather than a strictly scientific nature.'

Ibid., ll. 26–23 from foot. For 'According . . . official' read 'Southwell was an industrious official, but was not suited for political life, especially the political life of Charles II's time. When Halifax was asked by William III "if I knew anything to the contrary of his being an honest man. I said, not, confessed he was a weak man, but I took him to be entirely in his interest" (H. C. Foxcroft, *Life of Halifax*, ii. 251). Ormond, when recommending his grandson to make use of Southwell as an adviser, extols his loyalty to himself (Carte, v. 178–9). Evelyn speaks of him as "a sober, wise, and virtuous gentleman." His judgement and moderation appear to advantage in a long series of letters to Ormond written between 1678 and 1680 (Hist. MSS. Comm., *Ormonde MSS. at Kilkenny*, new ser., iv. 374–598).'

Ibid., ll. 20–11 from foot. For 'He was also . . . Carte' read 'Southwell at various times obtained from Ormond information about his life. He composed a short account of it, mainly Ormond's private affairs and personal adventures, with a sketch of his family history; on 8 Sept. 1688 he sent a copy to the second duke (printed, probably fairly accurately, from the MS. at Kilkenny Castle, by Lord Mountmorres, *The history . . . of the Irish parliament, 1634–1666*, 1792, i. 189–313). Another copy was lent by Edward Southwell to Thomas Carte (*Life of Ormonde*, vol. i, pp. ix–x; see also T. Thorpe, bookseller, catalogue, 1836, no. 925).'

Ibid., p. 711*a*, l. 1. To authorities, after '1708' add: 'Further correspondence is published by the Historical MSS. Commission, especially in the reports on the Ormonde MSS. at Kilkenny, the Egmont MSS., and the A. G. Finch MSS. Southwell's correspondence with Petty was published by Lord Lansdowne in 1928. See further Deputy Keeper of the Public Records, *32nd report*, i. 15–21, etc.'

E. S. de Beer.

Southwell. Sir Robert. (1635–1702). xviii. 709*a*, l. 10. For 'early apparently' read 'in February (*Egerton MS.* 1628, f. 6).'

Ibid., l. 26. Delete previous correction (*Bulletin* No. 5, p. 60), and read 'in February (*Cal. State Papers Dom.*, 1679–1680, p. 393).' Southwell actually embarked on Tuesday, 2 March 1679/80 (*Hist. MSS. Comm., Ormonde MSS.*, N.S. v. 286).

Ibid., l. 36. After 'after his return' add 'which took place in November of the same year (*Egerton MS.* 1628, f. 9).'

Ibid., 709*b*, l. 29. For '1664' read '1664/5 (*ib.*, f. 3*b*; cf. Pepys, *Diary*, 19 March 1664/5).' E. S. de B.

Southwell, Sir Robert. (1635–1702). xviii. 709*a*, l. 26. For 'in the spring of the following year' read 'late December 1679' (B.M. *Add. MS.* 34079). R. M. H.

Sparke or Sparkes Joseph (1683–1740). xviii. 720*a*, l. 15 from foot. Omit 'It [Chronicon Angliae Petriburgense] was re-edited in 1845 for the Caxton Society by Dr. J. A. Giles, and in 1849 for the Camden Society by Thomas Stapleton (1805–1849) [q.v.]'. Omit all after 'Giles'. The 'Chronicon Petroburgense edited by Stapleton is a different chronicle, edited by him for the first time. See *Camden Soc.* lxvii (1849), p. vii.

Sparrow, John (1615–1665?). xviii. 722*b*. To authorities add 'an extract from the diary of John Sparrow of Dynes Hall Essex, Esq.' Bodleian MS. Rawlinson Essex 23 (Holman MS. 23) fos. 294–304. This establishes that he was still alive in 1667 in which year Deanes Hall was sold by him and his heir. The diary records the death of his uncle Elliston and his cousin John in 1663.

Spelman, Sir Henry. xviii. 740*a*. For some interesting letters from William Petyt concerning the 1664 'edition' of his 'glossary' 'printed by Spelman's grandson with thousands of errors' see *Inner Temple MSS. (Hist. MSS. Comm.* 11th Rep., App. vii.), p. 244.

Spencer, Dorothy, Countess of Sunderland. (1617–1684). xviii. 760*b*, bottom line. For '1641' read '1640' (*D.N.B.* xviii. 776*b*, l. 18). R. M. H.

Spencer, Dorothy, Countess of Sunderland. xviii. 761*a*, ll. 16–15 from foot. Delete '(afterwards Sir Robert).' No baronetcy or knighthood is recorded.

Ibid. l. 14 from foot. After 'Kent,' insert 'grandson of Sir Thomas Smith or Smythe (1558?–1625) [q.v.],'

Ibid. ll. 13–2 from foot. Delete '[see Smythe . . . Strangford],'

Ibid. 762*a*. Add to list of authorities: 'Pedigree of Smythe of Ostenhanger in Archæologia Cantiana, xx. 76–81.' [See also Bulletin, ii. 60.]

Spencer, John, D.D. xviii. 768*a*, ll. 26–25 from foot. For 'is also . . . College' read 'are two portraits at Corpus Christi, Cambridge, and another is reproduced in Masters' "History" of the college.'

Spencer, Robert, second earl of Sunderland. xviii. 777*b*, l. 30 from foot. For 'September' read 'November' (C. H. Firth and S. C. Lomas, *Diplomatic Relations of England and France*).

Ibid. l. 18 from foot. After 'Paris' insert 'where he arrived in June': for 'for some time' read 'until his recall in March 1673' (*ib.*).

778*b*, l. 19 from foot. After '1681' insert 'He was dismissed from the secretaryship most ignominiously at the end of January, being forbidden to receive from his successor any compensation for the loss of his office, though such payments from an in-coming to an out-going secretary had been customary (B.M. Add. MS. 18730, f. 80r ; Hist. MSS. Comm. *Ormonde MSS.* p. 568 ; *Complete Peerage*, ii. 637, 639).'

M. A. T.

Spencer, Robert, Second Earl of Sunderland. xviii. 1777*b*, l. 31. 'He was despatched in September, 1671, upon an ambassy to Madrid.' For 'September' read 'November.' He was appointed in September (*Bulstrode Papers*, p. 203; *Evelyn's Diary*, 22 September, 1671 ; Hatton Corresp., 26 September, 1671). His departure from London was late in November (*Cal. S. P. Dom.* 1671, 571, 544, 579 ; *Cal. Treas. Bks.* 1669–72, ii. 1211 ; *Bulstrode Papers*, p. 207). He left Paris for Madrid, 15 December, 1671 (*Despatches of William Berwick*, Camden Society, 1903, p. 168). l. 43. For 'March' read 'June' (*Cal. S. P. Dom.* 1672, p. 684 ; *Despatches of William Berwick*, pp. 228–9; *Bulstrode Papers*, p. 239, *cf.* p. 246). l. 46. He does not seem to have gone to Cologne. (Introduction to *Letters to Sir Joseph Williamson*, Camden Soc., 1874 ; *Cal. S. P. Dom.* 1673, pp. 251, 254, 265 ; *Despatches by William Berwick*, pp. 246, 253.) l. 51. He seems to have returned in September, 1673 (*Despatches of William Berwick*, p. 254 ; *Letters to Sir Joseph Williamson*, i. 179, 188, ii. 4, 11 ; *Cal. Treas. Bks.* 1672–5, p. 446) ; and he was sent to Calais in 1677 (*Memoirs of Sir John Reresby*, 19 April, 1677 ; *Cal. Treas. Bks.*, 1676–9, p. 673 ; *Cal. S. P. Dom.* 1677–8, pp. 94–5, 98, 212 ; *Hist. MSS. Comm.* 7th Rep. App. p. 469 ; *Memoirs of the Verney Family*, p. 242).

Spencer, Robert, Second Earl of Sunderland. (1640–1702). xviii. 778*a*, l. 11. For 'February 1679' read 'October 1678' (*Lords Journals*, xiii. 304 : Sunderland present in House of Lords at afternoon session, 26 October 1678). See also *Calendar Treasury Books*, 1676–79, p. 1148 (for warrant for the landing of Sunderland's baggage, issued 28 October 1678), and *ibid.*, p. 1252, which suggests that Sunderland had returned to England on official leave before appointment as Secretary of State.

Ibid., p. 779*a*, l. 1. For 'August' read 'July.' Luttrell, *Brief Narration*, etc., i. 210, states Sunderland *is* admitted and *has* kissed the King's hand (28 July 1682). See also B.M. *Add. MS.* 15889, f. 84.

R. M. H.

Spenser, Edmund. (1552 ?–1599). xviii. 792*b*. For information about Spenser's wife see *Notes and Queries*, 14th Series, p. 445.

Spinckes, Nathaniel. xviii. 813*a*, l. 23. For '1653' read '1654.'.

Ibid. l. 24. For 'in 1653' read 'on 9 May 1654 (Rawlinson MSS., D. 799, p. 358).'

Ibid. l. 33. After 'Cambridge' add 'where he was admitted on 22 March as pupil of Thomas Bainbrigg (1636–1703) [q.v.]' and for '1673' read 'on 12 Oct. 1672.'

Ibid. l. 35. After 'foundation' add 'on 23 Jan. 1673.'

Ibid. ll. 36 to 813*b*, l. 6. The following dates are taken from Spinckes' own account of his life in Rawlinson MSS., D. 799, p. 359. On 28 June 1677 he removed to Mt. Edgcombe in Devonshire, from thence on 30 Aug. 1678 to be curate at Stibbington in Huntingdonshire and on 7 Feb. 1679 to Petersham in Surrey, where he stayed about two years and a half. He was then given, through the kindness of Simon Patrick [q.v.], the vicarage of Eckington in Worcestershire, which he returned to his patrons without taking institution, and came to settle in London. About Lady Day 1683 he was made curate of St. Stephen Walbrook, and in the following spring was chosen lecturer there. About Michaelmas 1684 he was instituted to the rectory of Peakirk-cum-Glynton, Northamptonshire, by Patrick, then dean of Peterborough, and left his lectureship at Walbrook ; on Lady Day 1685 he became assistant to William Clagett [q.v.] in the afternoon course at Gray's Inn, a post which he held, together with his curacy, until the following Michaelmas and by itself for one quarter more. On 18 Dec. 1686 he married Dorothy, second daughter of Mr. William Rutland of Broad Street, London, and on 23 July 1687 moved to Salisbury, where he was installed prebendary of Major Pars Altaris and instituted rector of St. Martin's, Salisbury, and admitted curate of Stratford-sub-Castle.

813*b*, ll. 35–8. For 'Of a large family . . . Anthony Cope' read 'Besides seven children who died in infancy and Robert, born 12 Oct. 1695, who went to the East Indies in 1712 and was lost in the ship "Recovery" on its way from Bengal to Bombay in Nov. 1715, two children survived their parents: Anne, born 21 Nov. 1687 and married to Sir John Cope, bart., on 24 April 1715; and William, born 13 April 1693, who became a successful and wealthy merchant, going to the East Indies in 1710.'

814*a*, 4 ll. from foot. After '"Sufferings of the Clergy"' add 'In the Rawlinson MSS., are a copy of two declarations by Spinckes of conversations with the earl of Clarendon on 3 June 1702, about the testimony of the late countess to the birth of the prince, and with Mrs Pearse, King James' surgeon, on 19 March 1703 (D. 680, ff. 126, 127), two commonplace books of Spinckes written by various hands (C. 105; D. 1037), and a letter to a friend concerning ecclesiastical communion and government (D. 1233, f. 94).'

A. C. M.

Spottiswood or Spotswood, Alexander. xviii. 817*b*, ll. 26–8. For 'before 1704' read 'on 9 Apr. 1703 (Dalton, *Eng. Army Lists*, v. 64)'; for 'lieutenant-colonel's commission' read 'brevet lieutenant-colonelcy on 1 Jan. 1706 (*ibid.* p. 166)'

Ibid. last line and 818*a*, l. 1. For 'In 1740' read 'On 26 Dec. 1739'; after 'major-general' insert 'and as colonel of an American regiment of four battalions to be raised in North America (J. Millan, *Succession of Colonels*, 1749, p. 20)'

Sprat, Thomas. xviii. 828*a*, l. 12 from foot. After 'English prose' add 'Two translations (or, rather, imitations) in Brome's Horace (1666) (Satires, i. 9 and ii. 6, the earlier part) are probably by Sprat (*Notes and Queries*, clxxiv (1938). 200–1).'

Stafford, Anthony. xviii. 853*a*, ll. 27–22 from foot. Add to list of authorities an article by Professor G. C. Moore Smith in Notes and Queries, clii. 219–21, 239–43.

Stafford, Anthony. xviii. 853*a* (and *ante*, v. 123), l. 33. For 'in 1645' read 'on 3 Jan. 1644/5, when his brother Walter in his will (2 Twisse) left him £5.'

G. C. M. S.

Stafford, Edward, Third Duke of Buckingham. xviii. 855*a*, l. 18 from foot. 'Two portraits, attributed to' add 'but certainly not painted by' Holbein.

Stafford, Sir Edward (1552?–1605). xviii. 856*a* and *ante*, i. 66. For a defence of Stafford's conduct while ambassador to France *see* 'Eng. Hist. Rev.' xliv. 203–19.

Stafford, Sir Edward. (1552?–1605). xviii. 856*a*. A considerable controversy was raised by M. A. S. Hume's contention (*Cal. Spanish State Papers*, 1587–1603, *passim*), that Stafford, while ambassador in France, was in the pay of Spain (see *Eng. Hist. Rev.* xvi. 574–7; *American Hist. Rev.* xx. 292–313); but the latest and most expert opinion (*Cal. For. State Papers*, 1585–6, pp. l., lxiv.), is that there is no real ground for the charge of treason.

856*b*, l. 24. Add 'She was the widow of John, second baron Sheffield, and had been the wife or mistress of Leicester, by whom she was mother of Sir Robert Dudley, titular Earl of Warwick and Duke of Northumberland (1573–1649) [q.v.].' To the authorities add the Cal. of For. State Papers, none of the volumes of which, covering Stafford's embassy, had been published when the article was written.

Stafford, Thomas. xviii. 869, ll. 16–15 from foot. For 'He was hanged and quartered at Tyburn' read 'He was beheaded on Tower Hill and afterwards quartered at Tyburn (Machyn, *Diary*, p. 137; Stow, *Annales*, p. 631)'

Stanhope, James, first Earl Stanhope. xviii. 901*a*, ll. 9–7 from foot. For 'His father . . . States-General' read 'His father was envoy extraordinary to Spain from May 1690 to Dec. 1699, and to the States-General from April 1700 to Nov. 1706 (P.R.O., S.P. civ. 187 and 69; Basil Williams, *Stanhope*, ch. i, *passim*).'

Stanhope, Philip Dormer, fourth earl of Chesterfield. xviii. 912*b*, ll. 22–25. Delete 'He was rewarded . . . Lord Townshend' (*Complete Peerage*, 1913, iii. 183).

Stanhope, William, first Earl of Harrington. xviii. 93*a*, ll. 17–9. For 'in 1741 . . . June 1745.' read 'as an ensign in Columbine's or the 10th regiment on 7 Feb. 1738 (P.R.O., Index 5437, p. 67), and was promoted captain on 10 Jan. 1739 (*ibid.* p. 74). He was appointed captain-lieutenant and lieutenant-colonel in the

3rd foot guards on 13 Feb. 1741 (*ibid.* p. 43), captain and lieutenant-colonel on 8 Apr. 1743, and captain and colonel of the 2nd troop of horse grenadier guards on 5 June 1745 (*ibid.* 5438, p. 7), retaining this rank until his death.'

Stanhope, William, first Earl of Harrington. xviii. 927*b*, ll. 2–1 from foot. For 'obtained . . . in 1710' read 'was appointed lieutenant and captain in the Coldstream guards on 11 Dec. 1703 (Dalton, *Eng. Army Lists*, v. 46), was promoted captain and lieutenant-colonel in the 3rd footguards on 19 June 1710 (*ibid.* vi, 59), purchased the colonelcy of a regiment of foot on 17 March 1711 (*ibid.* vi. 243)'

Ibid. 928*a*, ll. 1–2. After 'in Spain.' insert 'His regiment was disbanded in Nov. 1712 and he was placed on half-pay (P.R.O., war office, half-pay list, 25/2979).'; after 'regiment,' insert 'fought at Preston (C. Dalton, *George I's Army*, i. 124),'

Ibid. ll. 26–9. For 'This exploit . . . 1747' read 'On 20 Dec. 1725 he was appointed to the colonelcy of the 13th dragoons, which he held until 1730. He became brigadier-general on 19 Nov. 1735, major-general 2 July 1739, and general on 29 Dec. 1746 (J. Millan, *Succession of Colonels*, 1749, pp. 7, 22).'

Stanhope, William, 2nd earl of Harrington, xviii, 931*a*, ll. 17–18. For 'in 1741 and became general' read 'on 7 Feb. 1738 as ensign in major-general Columbine's (10th) foot (P.R.O., Index 5437, p. 67), was promoted captain in Clayton's (14th) foot on 10 Jan. 1739 (*ibid.*, p. 74), captain-lieutenant and lieutenant-colonel in the 3rd foot guards on 13 Feb. 1741 (*ibid.*, p. 43), and captain and lieutenant-colonel on 8 April 1743 (P.R.O.; W.O. *Registers, etc., Army Lists* (W.O. 64), ix. 34. He became captain and colonel'.

Stanley, William. xviii. 972*a*, l. 9 from foot. After 'Cathedral.' add 'A portrait hangs in the hall of Corpus Christi college.'

Stanwix, John. xviii. 973*b*, l. 6. For '1715' read '1721' (*Return of M.P.'s*, ii. 38).

Staples or Staple, Edward. xviii. 980*b*, ll. 20–15 from foot. Delete 'In June 1552 . . . *Church of Ireland*, i. 207–11).'

This statement is based on forged documents of Robert Ware (*see* art. Ware, Sir James, below), now B.M., Add. MSS. 4789, f. 345, and 4784, f. 2. Dowdall had gone into exile in the preceding August (*Cal. State Papers, Ireland*, 1509–73, p. 115).

Stark, Adam. xviii. 993*a*, l. 28 from foot. After '1810.' insert 'He then entered business by himself at Manchester, Hull, and Lincoln.'

Ibid. ll. 24–23 from foot. For 'In 1810 . . . bookseller' read 'In 1814 he transferred his business to the Market Place'

Ibid. l. 23 from foot. After 'Gainsborough,' read 'acting as printer, bookseller, postmaster, and stock and share broker,'

Ibid. For 'that' read 'his book-selling'

Ibid. l. 22 from foot. After '1844.' insert 'About 1840 he rescued from a rag-mill the "Boke of Saynt Albans," issued by Caxton in 1486, and now preserved in the British museum.'

Ibid. l. 20 from foot. For 'Ann . . . Lincoln' read '20 Dec. 1809, Jane, fourth daughter of Samuel Trotter, sheriff of Lincoln, who died in 1813'

Ibid. l. 19 from foot. After 'secondly,' insert 'in 1815,'

Ibid. l. 16 from foot. After 'thirdly,' read 'in 1838,'

Ibid. l. 5 from foot. After '1855.' insert 'He also published, for private circulation only, "Stonehenge," 1822.'

Add to list of authorities: Lincolnshire Magazine (Lindsey Local Hist. Soc.), ii. 87–90.

Stayner, Sir Richard (*d.* 1662), xviii. 1009*a*, ll. 20 and 21 from foot.—For 'described by Le Neve . . . 1660' read 'was the son of Roger Stayner of Tarrant Gunville, Dorset. He'. *Ib.*, 1010*a*, last line.—For 'on 9 Oct. that he had died . . . 1658' read 'He died 9 Oct. and'. *Ib.* 6.—After '3 Nov.' add 'He was buried 28 Nov. 1662 at S. Alphege, Greenwich. He married Elizabeth Hebbe, daughter of Thomas Hebbe of Loughborough, Leics., by whom he had two children, Richard and Elizabeth. His wife died in March 1662 and was buried at S. Alphege, Greenwich.' *Ib.*, 1010*b*, l. 6.—For 'he left a son, Richard, who' read 'His son Richard'. To list of authorities add: Prerogative Court of Canterbury, Probates, London, 148 Land, 1662.

Stead, William Thomas. Suppl. 1912–1921, 508*a*, l. 13. For '1889' read '1885.'

Ibid. 508*b*, l. 7. After 'Nicholas II' insert 'His advocacy in the 'seventies of an understanding with Russia had been continued by the publication in 1888 of "The Truth about Russia."'

Ibid. l. 12. After '(1899–1902)' insert 'publishing the weekly periodical "War against War in South Africa," which ran from 20 Oct. 1899 until 26 Jan. 1900.'

Ibid. l. 11 from foot. After 'June 1912' insert 'W. T. Stead, *The M.P. for Russia, Reminiscences and Correspondence of Madame Olga Novikoff*, 2 vols., 1909, gives considerable information upon his pro-Russian activities, particularly in the *Northern Echo* period.'

Stepney, George. xviii. 1077–1079. Much additional information, partly drawn from manuscript sources, has been collected in *Notes and Queries*, clix. 93–96, 114–117.

Sterne, Richard. xviii. 1108*a*, l. 4 from foot. For '1620' read '1623 (Venn, *Alumni Cantab.*, 1, iv. 160).'

Stevenson, Matthew. xviii. 1129*b*. The register of the church of St. Mary in the Marsh, Norwich, gives the date of his burial as 20 March 1683–4 (*Review of English Studies*, i. 95).

Steward or Stewart, Richard. BULLETIN, xiii. 116*a*, l. 12. Delete '(1666–1735).'

Steward or Stewart, Richard. xviii. 1145*b*, l. 14 from foot. For '1593?' read '1595.'

Ibid. ll. 11–10 from foot. Delete 'probably . . . his birth.'

Ibid. ll. 8–7 from foot. Delete 'From Westminster school' (see *Notes and Queries*, 10th ser., xi. 289, 455, and Welch as cited in list of authorities below).

Ibid. l. 6 from foot. After '1 Dec. 1609' insert 'aged fourteen (Foster, *Alumni Oxon.*).'

Ibid. 1146*a*, l. 2. After 'Worcester' insert 'In February 1629 he appeared in the house of commons as one of the counsel for Bishop Richard Montagu [q.v.] (*Parliamentary History*, viii. 285).'

Ibid. ll. 14–5. For '(see *Cal.* . . . 1639' read '(*Cal. State Papers, Dom.*, 1637–8, p. 365). On 2 Jan. 1640'

Ibid. ll. 23–5. Delete 'He was rewarded . . . appointed.'

Ibid. ll. 27–9. For 'in 1643 . . . same year' read 'on 21 March was appointed dean of St. Paul's (G. Hennessy, *Novum repertorium ecclesiasticum Londinense*, p. 5); he is said never to have been elected but took possession of the deanery (*Acts and Ordinances*, i. 672). He joined Charles I, serving him as dean of the chapel (*Clarendon State Papers*, ii. 254), and in February 1644 (*Lords' Journals*, vi. 419, etc.).'

Ibid. l. 31. For 'and was subsequently' read 'He was also'

Ibid. l. 3 from foot. After 'affairs"' insert 'and ordered the prince to appoint Steward dean of his chapel.'

Ibid. 1146*b*, l. 16. For 'but returned' read 'and back.'

Ibid. l. 20. For 'on 14 Nov. 1651' read 'on 15 or 16 Nov. 1651 (Steward's will, dated 15 Nov., in Cosin, *Correspondence*, i. 25–6n.; Evelyn, *Diary*, ed. Wheatley, ii. 31).'

Ibid. ll. 21–2. For 'near St. Germain des Prés' read 'in the Rue des Saints-Pères.'

Ibid. ll. 26–7. For '(cf. KENNET . . . *Oxford*)' read '(printed in Steward's *English Case* (see below); the date of death incorrect).'

Ibid. l. 28. For 'a daughter' read 'Jane, daughter.'

Ibid. l. 29. After 'Wiltshire' insert '(W. Berry, *County Genealogies: Hants*, p. 34).'

Ibid. ll. 29–32. For 'and left two sons . . . clergymen' read 'and left a son Charles (1666–1735)' (Steward's will, as above).

Ibid. l. 10 from foot—1147*a*, l. 9. For 'Steward published . . . Sherlock' read 'Steward published, besides some congratulatory poems in Latin (see F. Madan, *Oxford Books*, vol. ii), "An Answer to a Letter Written at Oxford, And superscribed to Dr. Samuel Turner, Concerning the Church, and the Revenues thereof," 1647, in reply to John Fountaine [q.v.]; new ed., as "A Discourse of Episcopacy and Sacrilege," 1683. His chief posthumous work is "Catholique Divinity: or, The most Solid and Sententious Expressions of the Primitive Doctors of the Church. With other Ecclesiastical, and Civil Authors: Dilated upon, and fitted to the Explication of the most Doctrinal Texts of Scripture," etc., 1657. There were also published "Three

Sermons" (with a fourth by Samuel Harsnett, archbishop of York), 1656; new ed., 1658; "Trias Sacra: a second ternary of Sermons," 1659; new ed., as "Golden Remains," 1660; "The English Case . . . in A Court Sermon at Paris," 1659, with a biographical preface, and Steward's epitaph; new eds., 1687, and as "A Brief but Full Vindication," 1688. "The Old Puritan Detected and Defeated," published anonymously in 1682, was attributed to Steward when reprinted in "Several Short but Seasonable Discourses" by Dr. R. Sherlock, 1684.'

Ibid. ll. 17–9. Delete 'The age . . . entry.'

Add to list of authorities: 'Correspondence of John Cosin, D.D., i. (Surtees Soc.), 1869, which contains several letters to and from Steward; N. Pocock, Life of Richard Steward, 1908 (written 1852).'

Story, John. xviii. 1315 *a*, 19 l. from foot. For 'November 1548' read 'January, 1548–9,' and five lines lower read 'January' for 'November.' P. 1316 *b*, six lines from foot, for 'Stowe' read 'Challoner.'

Stow, John. xix. 3*a*, ll. 11–3. For 'In early life . . . occupation.' read 'His father and grandfather were tallow-chandlers, but John Stow was apprenticed to John Bulley, a tailor (*Survey*, ed. C. L. Kingsford, i. pp. vii–viii).'

Ibid. l. 28 from foot. After 'Company.' insert 'He must have been successful in his trade, for he took his brother Thomas to be his apprentice, and spent money freely on the collection of books' (*ibid.* i. pp. viii–ix).

Ibid. 4*a*, l. 29. For 'In 1568' read 'In February 1568/9' (*ibid.* i. p. xvi).

Ibid. l. 27 from foot. For 'Soon afterwards—in February 1568–9' read 'During this month also'

Ibid. 4*b*, l. 19. For 'four' read 'twelve'

Strachey, William. xix. 12*a*, l. 25. After 'aged 17).' insert 'Possibly he was the William Strachey who matriculated at Emmanuel College, Cambridge, in Easter term, 1585' (*Times Lit. Suppl.*, 3 July 1930, p. 554, coll. 1–2).

Ibid. l. 26. After '(1603)' insert 'In the summer of 1606 the future colonist went to Constantinople as secretary to Sir Thomas Glover, newly appointed as ambassador to the Porte. Glover and Lello, the retiring ambassador, became bitter enemies, the latter staying in Turkey until May 1607, and Strachey, in March, was dismissed by Glover for refusing to break off his friendship with and his visits to Lello. Early in the summer Strachey returned to England, resolved apparently upon "makinge a booke" against Glover, a resolution which he later laid aside (*Times Lit. Suppl.*, 3 July 1930, p. 554, coll. 1–2).'

Ibid. p. 13*a*, l. 22. After '"History"' insert 'but he seems still to have been alive in 1628. He was a man of some learning, acquainted with the south and east of Europe, a hater of Popery, who numbered Donne and Campion among his friends' (*ibid.*, and also 7 Aug. 1930, p. 641, coll. 1–2).

William of Ramsey (*fl.* 1219). xxi. 364. William of Ramsey seems to be, like Matthew Westminster [q.v.], an imaginary literary character created by a series of conjectures by John Leland [q.v.]. No previous evidence of such a poet and hagiographer remains, and all manuscript ascriptions seem modern. Subsequent accounts are based upon that of Leland (*Commentarii de Scriptoribus Britannicis*, Oxford, 1709, p. 215, but read in manuscript by bibliographers earlier), and additions to it are only plausible conjectures. Leland describes William of Ramsey as (*a*) the author of verse about Waltheof, (*b*) a monk of Croyland, (*c*) the author of the metrical lives of SS. Guthlac, Edmund, and Birin, and (*d*) the William of Ramsey praised by a later writer, William Gillingham. These conclusions seem to represent a synthesis of elements which appear in memoranda of Leland's antiquarian tours of England.

(*a*) In his 'Itinerary' (ed. L. T. Smith, 1907, ii. 130–132) Leland preserved among pieces about Waltheof a metrical epitaph by a William. Some of the pieces were probably produced in 1219 at the time of Abbat Henry Longchamp's translation of Waltheof at Croyland Abbey. (*b*) Thus it would be easy to surmise that William was a monk of Croyland.

(*c*) Since the metrical life of St. Guthlac is dedicated to Abbat Henry Longchamp, Leland apparently concluded that William was responsible for its composition also. To add the lives of SS. Edmund and Birin would have been obvious, because they accompanied the life of St. Guthlac in at least two manuscripts (Camb. Univ. Library MS. Dd 11.78, and Brit. Mus. MS. Cotton, Vesp. D xiv.). These lives are very clearly the work of Master Henry of Avranches (*Speculum* iii. 34–63; *Studies* [Dublin], xvii. 295–308, June 1928). Although Dr. Liebermann did attribute the life of St. Guthlac to William of Ramsey in his 'Ostenglische Geschichtsquellen,' he had previously declared that its author was Henry of Avranches, upon the basis of an examination of the Cambridge manuscript (*Neues Archiv*, iv. 23, 1879).

(*d*) A curious note in Leland's 'Collectanea' (Ed. T. Hearne, 1770, iv. 23, tome iii.) among notices of books which he had seen at Peterhouse, Cambridge, tells of William, a monk of Ramsey, who had been named as an outstanding commentator upon Bede in a 'table' in the cathedral at Canterbury by William of Gillingham. This seems to be the basis for the name William of Ramsey, inexplicable as it appears.

Later writers added the St. Neot literature to William's list apparently because St. Neot had also been translated by Abbat Henry Longchamp. A detailed examination of the bibliographical writers is in an unpublished doctoral thesis by J. C. Russell (Harvard University, 1926).

J. C. R.

Strode, William (1599?–1645). xix. 60*b*. On his speeches in the Long Parliament see Notestein, *Journal of Sir Simonds D'Ewes* (Yale University Press, 1923, pp. 188, 334, etc.).

Ibid., p. 61*a*, 20 ll. from bottom. On Colonel William Strode (*d.* 1666) and his activity in the war, see C. E. H. Chadwyck-Healey, *Bellum Civile* (Somerset Record Socy.), 1902, pp. 4–8; *Hist. MSS. Comm., Portland MSS.*, i. 88, 447; and Bayley, *Civil War in Dorsetshire*, 1910, pp. 41–3, 99, 216. The portrait referred to is no longer in the National Portrait Gallery.

Stuart, Sir Charles, Baron Stuart de Rothesay. xix. 75*a*, ll. 31–3. For 'He was minister . . . St. Petersburg 1841–45' read 'On 16 Jan. 1815 he was appointed ambassador extraordinary and plenipotentiary to the Prince of Orange (later King William I of the Netherlands), but two months later was transferred to Paris as ambassador extraordinary during the absence of Wellington. He took up his new post after the defeat of Napoleon and the reoccupation of Paris by the allies, and remained there until Nov. 1824. In March 1825 he was sent on a special mission to Portugal and Brazil to mediate between them, receiving also full powers as commissioner and plenipotentiary from the king of Portugal. He returned as ambassador to Paris in July 1828. On the accession of Louis Philippe he was re-accredited (27 Aug. 1830), but was recalled in Dec. 1830, and remained without employment until the Tories returned to power in 1841, when he obtained the embassy at St. Petersburg. He sent in his resignation on Jan. 1844, on hearing that the government intended to reduce the St. Petersburg embassy to a legation, and was recalled on 8 March following' (credentials and letters of recall, P.R.O., F.O. 90/36, 90/18, 95/674, 83/841 and 83/843; and Stuart's letter of 28 Jan. 1844 to Aberdeen resigning the Russian embassy, P.R.O., F.O. 65/298).

Ibid. l. 15 from foot. For '1846, ii. 91–2' read '1846, i. 91–2.'

Stuart, James (*d.* 1793). xix. 88*a*, ll. 14–13 from foot. For 'captain . . . Nov. 1755' read 'lieutenant in the 58th regiment on 5 May 1756, coming from the Dutch service where he had held the rank of captain (P.R.O., Index 5439, p. 36)'

Ibid. ll. 10–9 from foot. For '9 May' read '20 Oct.'; for 'major' read 'captain in the 83rd regiment, then in Ireland (*Army List*, 1759, p. 138). He was promoted major on 7 Dec. 1759 (*ibid.* 1761, p. 152)'

Ibid. l. 4 from foot. For 'rank' read 'brevet'; after 'lieutenant-colonel' insert 'on 20 Feb. 1762 (*ibid.* 1763, p. 156)'

Ibid. 88*b*, l. 8. After 'expedition.' insert 'On the disbandment of the regiment in 1763, he was placed on half-pay (*ibid.* 1765, pt. 2, p. 12).'

Ibid. 89*a*, l. 13. After 'entered the army' insert 'as an ensign in the 46th regiment, being made lieutenant on 7 Dec. 1764 and captain on 12 Jan. 1770 (P.R.O. war office 25/210, succession books)'

Ibid. l. 15. After '78th foot,' insert 'afterwards the 72nd foot, on 18 Dec. 1777 (*Army List*, 1787, p. 135)'

Ibid. l. 31. After 'colonel' insert 'on appointment as aide-de-camp to the king (*Army List*, 1793, p. 8)'

Ibid. ll. 23–22 from foot. After

' Madras.' insert ' On 2 March 1797 he was appointed colonel of the 82nd regiment (*ibid.* 1798, p. 268).' ; for ' colonel of ' read ' to ' ; for ' 78th ' read ' 72nd (*ibid.* 1799, p. 260) '

Stuart, James (1741–1815), xix, 89*a*, l. 13. After 'army' add 'on 1 Oct. 1761 as ensign in the 64th foot (*Army List*, 1763, p. 122), became lieutenant on 7 Dec. 1764 (*ibid.*, 1765, p. 119) and captain on 12 Jan. 1770 (*ibid.*, 1771, p. 119)'. l. 15. After '78th foot' add 'on Dec. 1777 (*ibid.*, 1778, p. 148)'. l. 18. After '14 Feb.' add 'and to the local rank of colonel on 13 June following (*ibid.*, 1783, p. 23)'. l. 31. After 'colonel' add 'on his appointment as aide-de-camp to the king (*ibid.*, 1793, p. 8)'. l. 23 from foot. After 'Madras' add 'He was appointed colonel of the 82nd regiment on 2 Mar. 1797 (*ibid.*, 1798, p. 268)'.

Stubbs or Stubbes, Philip. xix. 120*b*, l. 25 from foot. For ' reprinted . . . manuscript ' read ' of which there is a '.

W. W. G.

Stukeley, William. xix. 127*b*, ll. 12–11 from foot. After ' Newton.' insert ' His " Memoires of Sir Isaac Newton's life " were edited for the Royal Society by A. Hastings White in 1936.'

Sutton, Robert, second Baron Lexington. xix. 184*b*, l. 7. After ' the Duke of Saxe-Lunenberg.' insert ' He resided at Copenhagen from August to October 1693 ; he returned to England upon the conclusion of the business (B.M. *Add. MS.* 15572 ; *Hist. MSS. Comm.*, Rep. 12, App. ii [Portland MSS.] *passim*, and iv. 229–30).'

Ibid. ll. 9–11. For ' in June following he went . . . to Vienna ' read ' in May following he was appointed envoy extraordinary to Vienna, but did not arrive there until December (P.R.O., S.P. civ. 194, 197) '.

Ibid. l. 32. For ' in August ' read ' on 18 October (*ibid.* 194) '.

Ibid. l. 36. After ' the close of 1713 ' add ' While in Spain he laboured to renew the Anglo-Spanish commercial treaty of 1670, and succeeded in drafting an agreement in relation to English trade, particularly with respect to the negro assiento (P.R.O., S.P. xciv. 79, 80).'

Swinton, John (1703–1777). xix. 239*a*, ll. 15–17. Delete ' On 16 Oct. 1728 . . . and.'

Ibid. l. 17. After ' 1729 ' insert ' he.'

Ibid. l. 18. After ' Wadham ' insert ' and on 16 Oct. was elected a fellow of the Royal Society ' (*Record of Royal Soc.*, p. 334).

Sydenham, William. xix. 255*a*. Add to the authorities, Bayley, *Civil War in Dorsetshire*, 1910.

Sydney. xviii. 602*a*, l. 28. For ' 1845 ' read ' 1846 ' (*Foreign Office List*, 1852, p. 6).

Talbot, George, Fourth Earl of Shrewsbury. xix. 313*b*, l. 30. For 'On the accession of Henry VIII.' read 'Before 1507,' and for reference to *L. and P.* substitute reference to *Cal. Patent Rolls*, Henry VII. ii. 471 etc. P. 314*a*, 26 l. from foot, for '1486' read '1484,' and refer to Herbert's *Reign of Henry VIII.* p. 270. P. 314*b*, *re* the sixth earl's first wife add 'whom he had married on 28 April, 1539 (*L. and P.* xiv. i. 853, 878).'

Tate, Francis. Add 'His "Camera Stellata" is printed in Hearne's *Antiquarian Discourses*, 1771, ii. 277–309. Miss Scofield (*Star Chamber*, 1900, pp. 81–2) tentatively assigns it to William Lambarde, regarding it as an early draft of Lambarde's *Archeion*, much of which it incorporates. But Tate's treatise refers to the "late queen" Elizabeth, whereas Lambarde completed his *Archeion* in 1591 and died in 1601.'

Temple, Henry John, third **Viscount Palmerston.** xix. 497*a*, l. 4. For 'Broadlands' as his birthplace read 'No. 4 Park-street (now No. 20 Queen Anne's gate), London (P. Guedalla in *The Times*, 31 May 1926).'

Temple, Henry John, third Viscount Palmerston (1784–1865), xix. 497a, l. 4,

For 'He was born at his father's English estate, Broadlands, Hampshire, on 20 Oct. 1784' read 'He was born at his father's house in Park Street, Westminster (now 20 Queen Anne's Gate) on 20 Oct. 1784 and baptised at St. Margaret's Westminster on 23 Nov. 1784', (MS. diary of 2nd Viscount Palmerston; parish registers of St. Margaret's; cf. London County Council, *Survey of London*, vol. x, *Parish of St. Margaret, Westminster*, pt. i, p. 87).

Temple, Henry John, third Viscount Palmerston. xix. 497*a*, l. 5 from foot, and above, v. 58, x. 61. For 'Newtown' read 'Newport' (*Members of Parliament, Return*, ii. 248).

Temple, Henry John, third Viscount Palmerston. xix. 499*b*, l. 19 from foot. For '15 Sept. 1832' read '15 Sept. 1831'.

Ibid. ll. 17–6 from foot. For 'On 15 Nov. a final act of separation . . . and Belgium was thenceforward free' read 'On 15 Oct. the conference communicated to the Dutch and Belgian plenipotentiaries a new project of treaty in twenty-four articles, which was accepted by Belgium and converted into a treaty between her and the five powers on 15 Nov. Holland refused the articles and 1832 was spent in fruitless negotiations on the subject of modifications which would render them acceptable to her. On 22 Oct. Great Britain and France signed a convention for the execution of the treaty of 15 Nov. 1831. A French army besieged the citadel of Antwerp, which surrendered on 23 Dec., while Great Britain assisted with naval measures. A convention between the two powers and Holland, signed on 21 May 1833, put an end to these coercive measures and the rest of that year was spent in further negotiations on the main question. These broke down in November, and it was not until 1838 that they were renewed, a settlement being finally reached by the treaties of 19 April 1839 between Holland, Belgium, and the Powers (*British and Foreign State Papers*, xviii. (1830–1) 893 *sqq.*; xix. (1831–3) 55 *sqq.*; xx. (1832–3) 4 *sqq.*).'

Temple, Sir John. (1600–77). xix. 515*b*, 27 ll. from foot. For 'in November 1638' read 'about 2 September 1638 (Penshurst burial register, 6 September).'

Ibid. ll. 20–22 from foot. Delete 'and Mary . . . Hugh Eccles.' (Lady Martha Giffard, *Life and Character of Sir William Temple*, 1728, p. 2).

Ibid. l. 22 from foot. Add 'and Henry (1638–97). (Penshurst baptismal register, 28 Aug. 1638).' G. C. M. S.

Temple, Sir. Richard (1634–1697). xix. 517–8. This article needs revision throughout. Temple's career is singularly difficult to follow owing to his having changed parties on two or three occasions. The following points may be noticed:

517*b*, l. 30. For '19 April' read '23 April' (W. A. Shaw, *Knights of England*, i. 164).

Ibid., ll. 31–9. The incident of the king's complaining about Temple appears in a rather unfavourable light in the *Commons' Journals* (see refs. given in art.). Bristol made an offer to the king of Temple's services in the Commons, but eventually confessed to the Commons that he had had no authorisation in Temple's own words (Pepys, 1 July 1663). On 24 March 1663/4

Temple spoke against repealing the Triennial Act, in opposition to the wishes of the Court (Pepys, 26 March 1664; *Commons' Journals*, viii. 536–8; *Verney Memoirs*, iv. 52).

Ibid., ll. 17–12 from bottom. Temple had been a member of the Court party at least since 1672 (he appears in the various lists of pensioners, especially in *State Papers, Dom., Charles II*, 408, No. 148, a list compiled for Sir Joseph Williamson about April 1678). In March 1678/9 the Duke of Buckingham, of the Country party, successfully opposed his election for Buckingham. In August 1679 he was returned for Buckingham, but his attempt to get Tories returned for Buckinghamshire was defeated by the Duke. A large election literature sprang up, the Whigs bitterly assailing Temple, 'The Stowmonster' (*New News of a Strange Monster found in Stow Woods near Buckingham; The Sale of Esau's Birthright* (ballad); *A Mild but searching Expostulatory Letter . . . to the Men of Buckingham; A Letter from a Freeholder of Buckinghamshire* (dated 23 August 1679), etc., in British Museum G. 3757). Temple spoke in the House on 6 November 1680 against the Exclusion Bill as then drafted (Grey, *Debates*, vii. 425. See also W. Cobbett, *Parliamentary History*, iv. 1193). There is no satisfactory evidence for his position in 1681, but he appears to have been associated with Monmouth on one occasion (*Verney Memoirs*, iv. 266).

Ibid., ll. 12–7 from bottom. There is no evidence in the *Calendar of Treasury Books*, 1681–1685, to support Luttrell's statement about Temple's dismissal from the Commission of the Customs in February 1682/3. Temple was dismissed by James II, but sat in the parliament of 1685; two recorded speeches show him as supporting the motion for supply in November (W. Cobbett, *Parliamentary History*, iv. 1375, 1384). On 20 April 1686 James awarded Temple an annual pension of 1200 *l.*, in consideration of good services to Charles II and to himself (*Cal. Treasury Books*, 1685–1689, p. 697). Temple's character as a 'Vicar of Bray' was recognised by contemporaries (*Verney Memoirs*, iv. 448; letter dated 14 April 1689 referring to Temple's regaining his place in the Customs).

In contemporary pamphlets, etc., Temple is nicknamed 'Sir Timber,' presumably from his having made a gift of timber to the Corporation of Buckingham for building a town hall (*New News of a Strange Monster*, and other pamphlets referred to above).

Ibid., l. 22. An important note on Temple in connexion with the *Essay upon Taxes* is given in H. C. Foxcroft, *Life and Letters of Sir George Savile*, II. 536–7.

E. S. de B.

Temple, Sir Richard, Viscount Cobham. xix. 518, l. 7 from foot. For 'born about 1669' read 'born 24 Oct. 1675' (G.E.C., *Complete Peerage*, ed. Gibbs, art. Cobham).

Temple, Sir William (1555–1627). xix. 521*b*, ll. 14–8 from foot. The imputing more knowledge of Essex's designs to Edward Temple was due to wrong indexing of the 'Cal. S.P. Dom.,' 1598–1601, and 1601–1603 (*Times Lit. Suppl.*, 27 June 1929, p. 514, col. 3).

Tenison, Edward. xix. 536*b*, l. 13 from foot. After 'portrait' insert ', now hanging in the hall of Corpus Christi, Cambridge,'

Tenison, Thomas. xix. 540*a*, l. 19 from foot. After 'Lambeth,' insert 'another at Corpus Christi, Cambridge,'

Thomas, William. (*d.* 1554). xix. 676*a*, l. 31. After '1549' insert 'While there is no copy of this work in the British Museum one is extant in the Cambridge University Library (Syn., 8, 54, 142).' *Ibid.*, l. 36. Delete 'either of this work or' (*Tudor Studies*, ed. R. W. Seton-Watson, p. 139, n. 23).

Thomson, Anthony Todd. xix. 715*b*, l. 15. For '1828' read '1827.' See *The Times*, 14 July 1827, 2*c*.

l. 19. For '1832 on the death of' read '1830 on the resignation of.' See *University of London* [now University College], *Annual General Meeting of Proprietors . . . 23rd of February*, 1831, p. 8.

ll. 22–24. Omit 'In 1837 . . . and,' and substitute 'On the resignation of Amos in 1834.' See *University of London, Report and Appendix, February* 1835, p. 4.

l. 28. For 'which has since become' read 'which preceded as a place of clinical instruction.' For Alexander Thomson, there spelt Thompson, see *The Royal Commission on the Losses and Services of American Loyalists 1783 to 1785, being the Notes of Mr. Daniel Parker Coke, M.P. . . .*

ed. H. E. Egerton. Roxburghe Club, 1915, pp. 182–3.

Thorpe, Thomas (*d.* 1461), Speaker. xix. 802*b*. For 'after some time . . . wherever he was confined' read 'confined first in Newgate and then in the Marshalsea (*Rot. Parl.* vi. 295*a*), whence he attempted to escape.'

Throckmorton, or Throgmorton, Sir John (*d.* 1445) xix. 810*a*, l. 21 from foot. Delete 'and'. After '1432' add ', 8 July 1433 and 12 Nov. 1439. (Return of names of members returned to serve in Parliament, H.C. (69) 1878. LXII, i. 325; *Cal. Fine Rolls, 1437–45*, p. 137)'.

Ibid., ll. 6–3 from foot. For 'In the latter . . . Council, v. 81)' read 'He was one of the chamberlains of the receipt of the exchequer, as deputy of the earl of Warwick, hereditary chamberlain, from 1419 to 1445. From 1433 to 1445 he was also clerk of the treasurer, or under-treasurer of the exchequer. (P.R.O., Exchequer, Issue Rolls, *passim*).'

Thurloe, John. xix. 821*b*, 10 ll. from bottom. Add '(Thurloe and the Post Office in *Eng. Hist. Rev.* xiii. 527).' Two letters from Thurloe to Henry Cromwell, dated 2 Nov. and 9 Nov. 1658, show his misgivings about the discontents in the army. *Hist. MSS. Comm.*, 9th Rept., ii. 441, 444 (from the MSS. of Mr. Alfred Morrison). There is a good article on Thurloe in *Macmillan's Magazine* for August 1894, and an elaborate life of him by Dr. Sigismund von Bischoffshausen was published at Innsbruck in 1899, *Die Politik des Protectors Oliver Cromwell in der Auffassung und Thätigkeit des Staatsecretärs John Thurloe.* It contains 23 news-letters written by Thurloe to Bulstrode Whitelocke (Dec. 1653 to May 1654) and the reports on Cromwell's foreign policy drawn up by Thurloe for Hyde. Another report, dealing merely with Cromwell's relations with the Dutch, is printed in *Eng. Hist. Rev.* xxi. 319.

Tillotson, John. xix. 877*b*, l. 16 from foot. For 'only child' read 'a daughter.' Another daughter, Robina, was living in 1668 (*Allegations for marriage licences . . . dean and chapter of Westminster, 1558–1699*; *vicar-general, 1660–79* (Harleian Soc., vol. xxiii, 1886), p. 145).

Titley, Walter. xix. 899*b*, l. 36. He was appointed minister resident at Copenhagen in 1730, and envoy extraordinary in 1739, his credentials being dated respectively 3 November (o.s.) 1730, and 23 March (o.s.) 1739. (P.R.O.; Royal Letters, 5.) He was Craven Scholar at Cambridge in 1722. (*Admissions to Trinity College*, vol. iii. p. xii.)

Titus, Silius. xix. 900*b*, 19 ll. from bottom. Omit 'It is possible that.'

Ibid., 901*a*, l. 8. Insert, 'Nevertheless Titus was discontented with his position. "I have," he complained, "ten times ventured my life in going and coming beyond sea in his Majesty's service when his affairs were desperate, and though the King has requited me with places of honour and trust, yet, after all, I am grown a mere cypher and sunk into contempt at court; nor can I give any reasons for it, unless it be that the King has sometimes found a Bible lying in my chamber window, or that I will not swear, nor be drunk, nor lie with my neighbour's wife" (*Life of Ambrose Barnes*, p. 175, Surtees Society, 1867). In the later part of the reign his dissatisfaction found expression in Parliament.'

Ibid., 901*b*, 2 ll. from bottom. Omit the words 'and internal evidence supports the statement' and the following sentence, and read instead, 'Probably the conception and substance of the pamphlet were due to Sexby, while Titus wrote the prefatory epistle to Cromwell, supplied the learned quotations and the disquisitions on the nature of tyrants and the right of tyrannicide, and revised the style of the whole. See "Killing no Murder," in *Eng. Hist. Rev.* xvii. 308–311.'

Tofts, Katherine, afterwards Smith. xix. 917*b*, l. 27. For '1758?' read '1756.'

Ibid. 918*a*, ll. 7–6 from foot. For 'which probably . . . 1758' read 'which took place in 1756 (*Misc. Gen. et Her.*, 2nd ser., i. 347).'

Towerson, William. For '1555–1577' read '*fl.* 1555–8,' and on the next page, for '1577' read '1558.' The date of Towerson's third voyage, correctly given in the 1589 Hakluyt as beginning on 30 Jan., 1557–8, was misprinted in the 1598–9 editions as 1577, and this misprint has been repeated in modern editions, even in the

Townsend, Aurelian. xix. 1030*b*, l. 32. For further proof of this view that Townsend was alive after 1643 see *Times Lit. Supp.* 23 October 1924, p. 667.

Townshend, Hayward. xix. 1054. See 'The Authorship of Townshend's twelve-volume edition of 1904 (J. A. Williamson, *Maritime Enterprise*, p. 302 *n*).: "Historical Collections,"' by J. E. Neale, in *Eng. Hist. Rev.* xxxvi. 96, and references there given.

Tregonwell, Sir John. xix. 1099*a*, 11 ll. from foot. Tregonwell was appointed judge of the High Court of Admiralty about 1524, and was reappointed 'principal officer and commissary-general' on 16 Aug. 1540 (*L. and P., Hen. viii*, xv. 979 cited in *Mariner's Mirror*, xiii. 335).

Trench, Richard le Poer, second Earl of Clancarty. xix. 1122*b*, l. 20–19 from foot. For 'Early in 1822 . . . Netherlands' read 'Clancarty presented his recall on 27 Dec. 1823 and left The Hague on 2 Jan. 1824 (*Brit. Dipl. Repr., 1789–1852*, Camden 3rd series, l. 181)'

Trenchard, Sir John (1640–95). xix. 1125*a*, l. 20. After 'Trenchard' insert 'largely because of his influence in the house of commons (Ranke, *History of England*, v. 66, quoting Bonet's despatches).'

M. A. T.

Trevor, Sir John (1626–1672). xix. 1148*a*, ll. 7–8. Delete 'second but eldest surviving.'

Ibid. ll. 9–11. For 'Margaret . . . Cornwall' read 'Anne, daughter of Edmund Hampden of Wendover.'

Ibid. ll. 13–19. For 'was son and heir . . . younger brothers' read 'was a grandson of John Trevor (*d.* 1589) of Trevalyn, Denbighshire, and son of Sir John Trevor (*d.* 1629), also of Trevalyn, by Margaret, daughter of Hugh Trevanion of Trevanion, Cornwall; Sir Sackville Trevor [q.v.] and Sir Thomas Trevor (1586–1656) were his uncles. His father, the first Sir John, sat for various constituencies between 1593 and 1625 and was knighted in 1603.'

Ibid. 1149*a*, l. 9 from foot. To authorities add: Trevor pedigree in Lipscomb, Buckinghamshire, ii. 296–7; *ibid.* ii. 424; Return of M.P.s.

R. C. Jasper.

Trumbull, Sir William. xix. 1192*b*, l. 5 from foot. After 'Rochester' add 'in 1671; he retained the office until 1686 or more probably 1687 (*Archaeologia Cantiana*, xxiv (1900). 169–70).'

Trumbull, Sir William (1639–1716). xix. 1193*b*, l. 9 from foot. After 'secretary' add 'The English plenipotentiaries at Ryswick usually received their orders, not from Trumbull—in whose province they were—but from William Blathwayt [q.v.]. Frequently they omitted to write to Trumbull themselves, but delegated the task to their subordinate, Prior (Trumbull's letters to Ellis, his under-secretary, B.M. Add. MS. 28895, especially ff. 26, 102, 117).'

M. A. T.

Trusler, John (1735–1820), xix. 1195*b*, l. 12. After (*Notes and Queries*, 1st ser. iii. 110) add: These MS. memoirs are now in the possession of the Reference Department of the Bath Municipal Libraries. According to these his first wife died in December 1763 when he exchanged duty with a clergyman at Solihull, Warws. (i. 123). In Oct. 1764 he married a second time at St. Margaret's Westminster (*ib.* pp. 151–2). His second wife died in 1780 (ii. 487) and he married a third time, his third wife dying in 1786 (ii. 487). By his first wife he had one son, by his second, five daughters of whom one died young (i. 152). After the death of Lord Ligonier in 1787 he took a house in Red Lion Street (ii. 487).

Tuke, Sir Samuel (*d.* 1674). xix. 1228*a*. Add references in the authorities to Ward, *English Dramatic Literature*, iii. 305, and Allardyce Nicol, *A History of Restoration Drama*, p. 207.

Tully or Tullie, George, in art. **Tully, Thomas.** xix. 1237*b*, l. 20. For 'was for a time preacher at' read 'In June 1686, by an order of James II to the dean and chapter of York, he was suspended on account of a sermon against idolatry preached before the University of Oxford on 24 May 1686 (Dedication of the sermon, quoted in A. Wood, *Life and Times*, iii. 186). He was appointed on 2 December 1687 to the lectureship of' (J. Brand, *History of Newcastle*, 1789, i. 315).

E. S. de B.

Turner, Edward (1798–1837). xix. 1262*b*, 10 ll. from bottom. For 'in 1828 on the opening of University College, London, he was' read 'on the establishment of London University he was in 1827.' See *The Gentleman's Magazine*, [Nov.] 1827, ii. 446.

Turner, Francis. xix. 1263*a*, l. 24 from foot. For '1638 ?' read '1637' [year of birth]. See Bodleian, MS. Rawl. letters 99, fol. s, 99.

Turner, Richard. (*d.* 1565 ?). xix. 1279*a*, 'at Chatham (not, as often stated, Chartham) in Kent.' Chartham is correct according to *L. and P.* Henry VIII., 1543, ii. 546, pp. 294, 301–3.

Turnor, Sir Edward. xix. 1300*b*, l. 4 from foot. For 'seventh' read 'sixth (G.E.C., *Complete Peerage*, viii. 482)'

Turnor, Sir Edward. xix. 1300*b*, ll. 7 and 6 from foot. For 'throughout . . . Anne' read '1700–9 and 1710–21' (*Return of M.P.'s*, i. 604 and ii. 5, 13, 24, 33, 44).

Twiss, Sir Travers. xix. 1320*b*, 2 ll. from foot. For '1852' read '1849' (King's College, London, *Calendar*, 1849–50, p. 37).

Tyldesley, Sir Thomas. xix. 1344*b*, l. 30. For '1596' read '1612'.

Ibid. l. 31. For 'in 1596' read 'on 3 Sept. 1612' (*Rec. Soc. of Lancs. and Cheshire*, xvi, 267).

Upton, Nicholas (1400?–1457). **For** his early and interesting reference to Dante's canzone, 'Le dolci rime d'amor,' *see* Prof. J. Huizinga in the *Modern Language Review*, xvii. 74–7.

Urswick, Christopher. xx. 56*a*, l. 10. After 'on 3 Nov.' insert 'He was employed on an embassy to Rome during the winter (letter to John Colet, *Amer. Hist. Rev.* xxxix. 696–9).'

Ussher, James. xx. 71*b*, ll. 15–17. For 'Annalium . . . 1659, fol.' read 'Annales Veteris Testamenti, 1650, fol.'

Ibid. l. 20. After '1654, fol.' add 'a continuation of no. 18 to the capture of Jerusalem by the Romans; the two parts together, with nos. 17 and 25, Paris, 1673; the two parts, with the life by Thomas Smith, Geneva, 1722'. H. O.

Uvedale, Robert. xx. 76*b*, ll. 9–11. For 'as contemporaries . . . collaborated) and' read 'as a contemporary.'

Ibid. 77*a*, l. 26 from foot. For 'In 1696' read 'About 1692 (Venn).'

Ibid. l. 24 from foot. For 'the rectory' read 'the sinecure rectory.'

Vancouver, George (1758–98), xx. 96*a*, l. 9, and *ante*, vii. 126. For 'born in 1758' read 'born on 22 June 1757 (G. S. Godwin, '*Vancouver, a Life*, 1757–98 (London, 1930), pp. 1, 181)'.

Vancouver, George. xx. 96*a*, l. 9. For 'born in 1758' read 'born at King's Lynn on 23 June 1757, and baptised in St. Margaret's Church, King's Lynn, 16 Mar. 1761 (H. J. Hillen, *Hist. of the Borough of King's Lynn*, ii. 499).'

G. A. S.

Van de Velde, Willem, the younger. xx. 104*a*, l. 20. Add: 'He was buried at St James's, Piccadilly. The burial register gives the date as 11 April 1707.'

G. CALLENDER.

Vane, Sir Henry, the Elder. xx. 113*b*, l. 15. 'He represented . . . Retford in 1628.' For 'Retford' read 'Thetford.' (*Return of Members of Parliament*, i. 476.)

Vane, Sir Henry, the elder. xx. 115*b*, l. 2. After 'London' insert ', on 25 Nov. (*Cal. S.P. Dom.*, 1641–3, p. 189)'

Ibid. l. 5. For '(4 Nov. 1641).' read '(3 Dec. 1641, *ibid.* p. 192).'

Vane, Sir Henry (1613–1662). xx. 127*b*, l. 6. For '(8 July 1699)' read '(25 July 1698)' (*Complete Peerage*, 1910, i. 425).

Vaughan, Henry (1622–1695). xx. 164*b*, l. 3. Delete 'April 17' (F. E. Hutchinson, *Henry Vaughan* (1947), pp. 245–6). See also under *Parry, Sir Thomas* (d. 1560).

Vaughan, Robert. xx. 175*b*, l. 14. For '1834' read '1833.' See London University [now University College], Minutes of the Sessions of the Council, ii. 422.

Vaughan, Thomas (1622–1666). xx. 181*a*, l. 27. Delete 'April 17' (F. E. Hutchinson, *Henry Vaughan* (1947), pp. 14, n. 2, 245–6).

Ibid., l. 8 from foot. Delete 'It is apparently his will in Somerset House (53 Mico) which was dated 17 February 1662–3, and proved on 6 March 1665–6' (F. E. Hutchinson, *op. cit.*, p. 146, n. 1).

Ibid., last line. For 'she died on 16 April 1658 at Mappersall,' read 'she died on 17 April 1658', and delete 'at Mappersall' (F. E. Hutchinson, *op. cit.*, p. 143, n. 2).

Venn, John. xx. 209*a*, l. 14 from foot. For 'in 1640,' read 'on 1 June 1641 (*Return of M.P.s*, i. 491),'

Venner, Thomas. xx. 212*a*, ll. 15–18. Information about Venner's life in New England, with the baptisms of three children of his, is given in *The New-England Historical and Genealogical Register*, xlvii (1893). 437–44.

Vere, John de, thirteenth **Earl of Oxford.** xx. 242*a*, l. 3. After '*Testamenta Vetusta*, ed. Nicolas, p. 526' add '; printed together with inventory of 1513 in *Archaeologia*, lxvi. 310–48).'

Vere, Robert de, ninth **Earl of Oxford** and **Duke of Ireland.** xx. 245*b*–246*a*. For a revised account see 'The Campaign of Radcot Bridge in December 1387,' by J. N. L. Myres, in *Eng. Hist. Rev.* xlii. 20–33

Vermuyden, Sir Cornelius. xx. 258*a*, 10 ll. from foot. After 'was introduced into parliament on 27 Dec. (Burton, *Parl. Diary*, i. 259)' add 'and was referred to a committee on 9 Feb. (*Commons' Journals*, vii. 484, 488).'

Vernon, George. xx. 274*b*, 4 ll. from foot. 'but his name does not figure . . . family of Vernon.' For a reference to a deposition in which Vernon states under date 1670 that he is thirty-two years of age and was born at Bunbury in Cheshire, see 'Notes and Queries,' cxlviii. 223.

Vernon, Richard. xx. 280*b*, ll. 5–3 from foot. For 'In early life . . . known as Captain Vernon' read 'He was appointed ensign in the first regiment of horse guards on 22 Nov. 1744 (P.R.O., Index 5436, p. 29), was promoted lieutenant and captain on 12 Jan. 1747 (*ibid.* p. 28), and resigned on 30 Oct. 1751 (*ibid.* 5438, p. 86).'

Vicars, John (1580?–1652), xx. 299*b*. To list of works add 'England's worthies: under whom all the civill and bloudy warres since *anno* 1642, to *anno* 1647, are related', London, 1647. Reprinted 1845.

Villiers, George, second duke of Buckingham. xx. 342*a*, 3 ll. from foot. Add 'On 11 July Charles deprived him of the chancellorship of Cambridge University, to which he had been elected, in rivalry with Arlington, on 11 May 1671 (*Cal. State Papers, Dom.*, 1671, 223–9; *ibid.*, 1673–75, p. 305). He was succeeded four days later by Monmouth.'

Ibid. 344*a*. After l. 13 add 'An earlier portrait than any of these is to be found in a satire "Upon the Proroguing of the Parliament, or, The Club of Unanimous Voters" (*Poems of Affairs of State*, iii. (1704), 52–6), which refers to the proclamation of 22 Sept. 1671, and was probably written by the end of that year. Although too abusive, this includes a few very good lines. There is also Butler's "Character of a Duke of Bucks" (*Characters*, ed. A. R. Waller, 1908, p. 32).'

Ibid. 344*b*, ll. 7–1 from foot. For 'On the other hand . . . *Butler*, ii. 72)' read 'Buckingham also patronized Samuel Butler, employing him as his secretary in his office of chancellor of Cambridge; Butler's writings suggest that the association was fairly close (*Rev. of Eng. Studies*, iv. (1928) 163–4; the story told by Pack (*Miscellanies*, p. 135) is no longer tenable; the date of Butler's 'Duke of Bucks' is unknown, but it was not published by Butler, and is to be regarded primarily as a literary exercise). Buckingham is said to have promised his patronage to, and then neglected, Nathaniel Lee [q.v.]; the evidence is insufficient (Spence, *Anecdotes*, p. 62).'

E. S. de B.

Viner, Charles (1678–1756). xx. 365*b*. For a more favourable estimate of Viner's work, see P. H. Winfield, *The chief sources of English legal history*, (1925), p. 245.

Waddilove, Robert Darley. xx. 406*b*, l. 21 from foot. After 'Wotton' add 'and from 1766 to 1771 of Ockham, both' (note in Ockham parish register).

R. W. BLOXAM.

Wager, Sir Charles. xx. 429*b*, l. 19. Before 'In February' insert 'In Jan. 1710 he became M.P. for Portsmouth through a by-election, and in 1713 he was elected for West Looe. He represented Portsmouth again from 1715 till 1734' (*Return of M.P.'s*, ii. 13, 29, 43, 55, 66).

Waghorn, Martin. xx. 431*a*, ll. 13–12 from foot. For 'It is possible . . . ships.' read 'Between 1768 and 1777 he served on several voyages as an officer in the service of the East India Company (*Notes and Queries*, clxv. 458).'

Ibid. 431*b*, l. 14 from foot. After '1787.' add 'He married Ann Marriott at St. Thomas's Church, Portsmouth, on 2 May 1756 (*Notes and Queries*, clxv. 458).'

Wakefield, Edward. xx. 449*a*, l. 28. Insert: 'Wakefield and George Spence [q.v.] stood as tory candidates for Reading at the general election in June 1826. Wakefield retired from the contest on the third day of the poll in order to secure Spence's return (Reading Election, 1826, broadsides, etc., in Reading University Library).'

Ibid., l. 38. For '1822,' the date of his second marriage, read '3 August 1823. The marriage certificate was reproduced in an election handbill, dated 19 April 1826.'

C. L. QUINTON.

Waldegrave, Sir Edward (1517?–1561), xx. 470*b*. For corrections and additions to the article, see Anthony I. Doyle, 'Borley and the Waldegraves in the sixteenth century', *Transactions of the Essex Archaeological Society*, xxiv. 21 *et seq.*

Waldegrave, Sir William. xx. 479*b*, l. 4 from foot. For '(*fl.* 1689)' read '(1636 ?–1701).'

Ibid. l. 4 from foot–480*a*, l. 2. For 'was probably . . . in 1618' read 'was perhaps a son of Sir Henry Waldegrave, second baronet, *d.* 1658, the grandfather of the first Lord Waldegrave; he was apparently closely connected with this branch of the family.'

Ibid. 480*a*, ll. 14–28. For 'On 1 July . . . bachelor' read 'Waldegrave was one of the physicians to Queen Mary of Modena and was knighted by her bedside on 10 June 1688, shortly after the delivery of James Edward (*London Gazette*, 11 June). He accompanied the queen and the prince on their flight to France, being at that time called first physician to the latter; he was a member of the exiled court, was appointed first physician to the king in 1695, and died, aged sixty-five, in the old Château at St. Germain about June 1701 (buried 9 July N.S.). He was married to Elizabeth Ronchi (the queen's almoner or confessor was named Giacomo Ronchi), who in 1698 is described as a lady of the bedchamber to the queen (she is presumably the Madam Walgrave, one of her bedchamber women in 1684); she died at St. Germain aged fifty in 1706. Waldegrave mentions no children in his will. He is described by Roger North as "a prodigy of an arch-lutanist" (*Memoirs of Musick*, ed. Rimbault, 1846, p. 123; see also Evelyn, *Diary*).'

Add to list of authorities: C. E. Lart's Parochial registers of Saint Germain-en-Laye: Jacobite extracts, 1910–2; Campana de Cavelli's Les derniers Stuarts, ii. 385; Hist. MSS. Comm., 13th Rep., app. v. p. 446; *ibid.*, Stuart Papers, i. 103; E. S. and M. S. Grew's The English court in exile (1911).

Walker, George (1618–1690). xx. 511*b*. For '1618' read '1645?'; and on l. 23, after 'He was,' add 'born about 1645 and was' (J. D. Milner in *The Times*, 16 Aug. 1924).

Wallace, James (*fl.* 1684–1724). xx. 557*a*, l. 6. After 'fellows' insert 'nor in the "Record of the Royal Society".'

Waller, Sir Hardress. xx. 586*a*, l. 30. Add: 'Another, Anne, married Sir Henry Ingoldsby [q.v.] (Lipscomb, *Buckinghamshire*, ii. 169).'

E. S. DE B.

Wallingford, William (*d.* 1488?) xx. 593*b*, l. 11 from foot. For '1488' read '1492'; *ib.* 595*a*, l. 23. For 'he died in or about 1488', read 'he died in 1492'. (*V.C.H. Herts*, iv. 408; see also Dom David Knowles, O.S.B., 'The case of St. Albans Abbey in 1490', *The Journal of Ecclesiastical History*, iii. no. 2. pp. 144–58).

Walsh, William. xx. 684*a*. For 'first appeared in . . . St. James', 1692' read 'were first printed in 1692, and reprinted in

1709 and in Tonson's "Miscellany" (etc., as *D.N.B.*) . . . preface dated St. James', taken from the edition of 1692.' **H. G. P.**

Walwyn, William. xx. 741. Dr. T. C. Pease in *The Leveller Movement* (Washington, 1916) seeks to show that Walwyn's influence on the political views of the Levellers has been underestimated, and attributes other pamphlets to him (pp. 242–57): *The Humble Petition of the Brownists*, 1641, 'a daring exposition of the principle of liberty of conscience' (p. 256); *England's Lamentable Slavery*, 1645, an exposition of advanced democratic doctrine (p. 117). He quotes frequently a third, *Walwyn's Just Defence*, 1649, of which the only known copy is in the Newberry Library of Chicago.

Wandesford, Christopher. xx. 743*b*, l. 7. To '(Carte i. 216, 231)' add 'Bagwell, *Ireland under the Stuarts*, i. 297–303.'

Warburton, John. xx. 755*a*, ll. 4–2 from foot. For 'Warburton's . . . Cumberland' read 'About 1710 Warburton married Dorothy, daughter of Andrew Hudleston of Hutton John, Cumberland; she had been twice a widow.'

Ibid. 755*b*, ll. 1–3. For 'a widow . . . daughters' read 'the widow of one William Bury.'

Ibid. l. 19. After 'p. 207)' add 'Warburton also had a daughter Amelia, who married Captain John Elphinston, R.N., and died in 1786.'

Ibid. 756*a*. Add to list of authorities: Notes and Queries, clxv (1933). 42–4.

Ward, Samuel. xx. 792*a*, l. 1. For '*d.* 1643' read '1572–1643'.

Ibid. l. 3–4. After 'Durham' insert 'and was baptised there on 13 Jan. 1571/2 (*Two Elizabethan Puritan Diaries*, ed. Knappen, p. 38).'

Ibid. ll. 9–10. For 'the last year' read 'Jan. 1597/8'.

Ibid. l. 9 from foot. After 'Taunton.' insert 'On 26 Jan. 1616/7 he became a canon residentiary of Wells; he petitioned to be excused from filling the requirements of this post, and in 1636 the chapter granted him a dispensation from half his required residence' (*ibid.*, pp. 42–3).

Ibid. 792*b*, l. 8. After 'In' insert '1620–21 he was vice-chancellor for the year; in'.

Ibid. ll. 21–2. Delete ', whose chaplain . . . been' (*ibid.*, p. 45 *n.* 31).

Ibid. 793*a*, l. 11. After 'chapel.' insert 'He married sometime between 1621 and 1625.'

Ibid. ll. 13–8 from foot. Delete 'Magnetis reductorium . . . 12 mo.' This was the work of Ward's namesake of Ipswich.

Ware, Sir James. xx. 817*a*, ll. 31–21 from foot. For 'He compiled . . . scribblings' read 'Robert Ware produced a number of forgeries which have been accepted as genuine even by Cox, Harris, Leland, Bagwell, and Dunlop, but have at last been proved utterly false (T. E. Bridgett, *Blunders and Forgeries*, pp. 209–90; Philip Wilson, "Writings of Sir James Ware and Forgeries of Robert Ware," *Trans. Bibliog. Soc.*, XV., 82–9; M. V. Ronan, *Reformation in Dublin*, pp. v–viii). In 1678 he published two documents relating to "Faithful Cummin," a Dominican, and "Thomas Heath," a Jesuit, which were incorporated by John Nalson [q.v.] in his "Foxes and Firebrands" (1680). The stories, quite unauthenticated, were accepted by all. His next work, the prophecies of Archbishop Ussher, published in 1678, became very popular. This was followed by "Historical Collections of the Church of Ireland during the Reigns of King Henry VIII, Edward VI, and Mary," 1681 (reprinted with Sir James Ware's "Antiquities," etc., 1705, and in Harleian Miscellany, ed. T. Park, v. 595–606). The pretended letters to and from Archbishop George Browne in this last have done the greatest damage among historians. Second and third parts of "Foxes and Firebrands," this time by Ware himself, followed in 1682 and 1689, and his well-known "Hunting of the Romish Fox" in 1683. He inserted some further forgeries in his father's manuscripts (*see* art., p. 817*a*, ll. 18–23). Ware also produced poor translations of his father's "De Praesulibus Hiberniae" and "Rerum Hibernicarum Annales," published with other matter in 1705 as "The Antiquities and History of Ireland" by Sir James Ware.'

Ibid. l. 18 from foot. For '1739–64, 3 vols.' read '1739–45(6), 2 vols. in 3 parts.'

Ibid. l. 17 from foot. After 'fol.)' add 'He incorporated much of Robert Ware's forged matter in it.'

Ibid. l. 8 from foot. Add to list of authorities: Irish MSS. Comm., Analecta Hibernica, ii. (1931), 300–2.

Warmington, William (*fl.* 1577–1612), xx. 847*a*, l. 20. For '(*fl.* 1577–1612), . . . born in Dorset about 1556, was matriculated . . . on 20 Dec. 1577', read '(*fl.* 1577–1627), . . . born in Dorset, was matriculated . . . on 20 Dec. 1577, being then at least 21 years old'.

Ibid., l. 34. For 'He was again sent to England . . ., was apprehended, and . . . transported' . . . read 'He joined the English Mission . . ., in 1583 he was captured and imprisoned in the Marshalsea (P.R.O., S.P. Dom. Eliz. vol. 169, no. 26), and . . . transported. . . .'

Ibid., l. 6*b*. For 'These things gave such offence that Warmington, who was set at liberty on swearing allegiance, found himself deserted by his former friends, and was driven . . .' read 'In consequence of this Warmington was deprived of the benefit of the alms contributed by catholics. . . .'

Ibid., ll. 10–14*b*. For the last sentence substitute: 'James directed Thomas Bilson [q.v.], bishop of Winchester, to provide for him "in his own house", and after much hesitation, Warmington was obliged to accept this offer (Roger Widdington [i.e., Thomas Preston], *A Theologicall Disputation concerning the Oath of Allegiance* (1613), Kk 3ᵛ–4ʳ). It is not clear how long he stayed with Bilson; he may have still been there in 1624 when Archbishop Abbot arranged for the king to issue a warrant allowing Warmington to remain in England on the same conditions as formerly in return for his services (S.P. Dom. Jas. I, vol. 168, no. 16; S.P. Dom. 38/12). He had returned to the Clink prison, however, by 7 April 1626 when John Tendring, provost-marshal of Middlesex, found him living in a chamber there (B.M., Harl. MS. 161, fos. 93–4). He was still there the following October, but was probably released on bond in March 1627 (S.P. Dom. Chas. I, vol. 38, no. 17; *ibid.*, vol. 57, nos. 82, 82I). There appears to be no further record of him, and since he was now over 70 years old he may have died shortly afterwards.'

Warren, Sir John Borlase. xx. 869–72. Genealogical and other corrections are given in G.E.C., *Complete baronetage*, vi. 183–4.

Ibid., p. 870*a*, l. 3 from foot. After '(Ralfe)' add 'In 1791 Warren published anonymously "A view of the naval force of Great Britain" and in the same year took an active part in founding the society for the improvement of naval architecture (*The annual biography and obituary, for the year 1823*, p. 147).'

Warton, Joseph. xx. 887*a*, l. 19. For 'vicarage of Chorley, Hertfordshire' read 'rectory of Thorley, Hertfordshire' (*Gent. Mag.*, 1782, p. 208).

Ibid. l. 8 from foot. For '1809' read '2 Dec. 1806' (*Ibid.* 1806, ii. 1251).

H. C.

Warwick, Sir Philip. xx. 895*a*, l. 27 from foot. After 'a knight' add '(between 29 May and 1 August: *A list of knights made since . . . May* 29, 1660; the piece dated 1 August by Thomason).'

Watson, David. xx. 915*a*, l. 21 from foot. For 'His first commission cannot be traced.' read 'He was appointed ensign in Colonel Middleton's regiment, later 25th foot, on 10 July 1725 (C. Dalton, *George the First's Army*, ii. 393).'

Watson, Sir Thomas (1792–1882). xx. 952*b*, l. 33. For 'University College' read 'London University [now University College].'

ll. 34–5. Omit ', and lectured' and substitute 'in the University.'

Watson, Sir Thomas. xx. 952*b*, l. 37. For 'and in 1835 professor of medicine' read 'in 1835 professor of forensic medicine, and in 1836 professor of the principles and practice of medicine' (King's College, London, *Calendar*, 1835–6, p. 4; 1836–7, p. 4).

Watson, Sir William Henry. xx. 959*a*, ll. 4–6. After 'commission' insert 'as cornet (*London Gazette*, 1811, p. 2218)'; after 'Duke of York' read 'on 14 Nov. 1811 and was promoted lieutenant (Hart's *Army List*, 1860, p. 497)'; after 'peninsula.' read 'He received the War Medal with one clasp for the battle of Toulouse (*ibid.* 508).'

Webber, John. xx. 1023*b*, l. 36. After '1784' insert '(The originals are now in B.M. Add. MSS. 15513–15514).'

Webster, Thomas (1773–1844). xx. 1037*b*, ll. 19–20. For 'university of London (University College)' read 'University College, London.'

Wedderburn, Sir John (1599–1679). xx. 1049*b*, l. 15. After 'in 1659' add 'He was knighted between January 1661 and April 1663 (postscript to G. Bate, *Elenchus motuum*, editions of these two years).'

Wellesley, Richard Colley, Marquis Wellesley. xx. 1134*b*. To bibliography add, 'Wellesley Papers, now in B.M. Add. MSS. 12564–13914; 37274–37318, and 37414–37416.'

Wellwood, James (1652–1727). xx. 1148*a*. Wellwood's name should be written Welwood and the following article substituted:

Welwood (Wellwood), James. xx. 1148*a* and above, ix. 203*b*, ll. 22–19 from foot. For 'He was already . . . by 15 Aug. 1684, when' read 'He graduated M.D. at Rheims 28 Jan. 1683/4 (R. W. Innes Smith, *Students of Medicine at Leyden*, p. 245). On 15 Aug. of that year'

Welwood, James (d. 1727) is said to have been the son of the rev. James Wellwood, minister of Tundergarth, Annandale, Dumfriesshire, about 1659-1664; he was born apparently between 1650 and 1655. He matriculated at St. Andrews 26 Feb. 1667-8, and graduated M.A. 25 July 1671 (Peter Chalmers, *Historical and Statistical Account of Dunfermline*, ii. 444, and genealogical table at end of volume). He was already a doctor of medicine (not from Oxford or Cambridge: Welwood, *Vindication*, p. 16) by 15 Aug. 1684, when he was a prisoner in the Edinburgh tolbooth (*Reg. P.C. Scotland*, ix. 106). According to Sir John Lauder of Fountainhall he was suspected of corresponding with the Scottish exiles in Holland, and was delated by Balcarres on some private 'pick' between them (*Historical Notices*, Bannatyne Club, ii. 547); according to R. Wodrow his offence was nonconformity (*Sufferings*, ii. 360). He was removed to Cupar for irregularities committed in Fifeshire, but appears to have been allowed to live outside the tolbooth on payment of security (*Reg. P.C. Scotland*, ix. 106; x. 5, 315). He was probably still in Scotland in February 1687 (*ibid.* xi. 537), but apparently settled in Newcastle some time before the Revolution (*Vindication*, p. 25). In early life he was befriended by Dr. (later Sir) Thomas Burnet [q.v.], the bishop's brother (*ibid.* preface). The bishop writes of Welwood in 1690 as having been 'ruined in the last reigne by a most signall injustice' (Hist. MSS. Comm., *Finch MSS.*, ii. 281).

In February and March 1689 Welwood was living in Newcastle and engaged in a controversy with John March [q.v.]; this he published as a 'Vindication of the present Great Revolution,' London, 1689 (an unreliable account of Welwood's early career is given in a copy of a letter from March to a bookseller named John Weld, *Lansd. MS.* 841, ff. 54-7). In May he started a weekly paper in London, 'Mercurius Reformatus: or, the New Observator.' It deals with current events and recent history from a whig stand-point; Bishop Burnet is said to have helped Welwood in its composition. It ran fairly regularly until November 1691, when first Richard Baldwin, the printer, and then Welwood were brought in custody before the Commons for a passage reflecting on them (in the issue of 7 Nov.); they were both reprimanded and discharged (*C.J.*, 9, 21, 27, 30 Nov. 1691; Hist. MSS. Comm., *7th Rep.*, App., pp. 206-7). Welwood then produced 'An Appendix to Mercurius Reformatus,' in which he proposed bringing it to an end. It was continued until 1694 by another author as 'The Weekly Observator' and later as 'Mercurius Britannicus.' He also wrote 'Answers' to James II's declarations of 8 May 1689 (1689, two issues; re-issued 1693; Dutch translation, 1689) and 17 April 1693, N.S. (1693: there was a Jacobite 'Reply' to this); and 'Reasons why the Parliament of Scotland cannot comply with the late K. James's proclamation' (London, 1689; copy in National Library, Edinburgh).

Meanwhile Welwood was admitted a fellow of the College of Physicians on 22 Dec. 1690; he was elected a censor in 1722 and succeeded Sir Richard Blackmore [q.v.] as elect on 23 Oct. of that year (Munk, *Royal College of Physicians*, 2nd. ed., i. 483). In his admission Welwood is described as 'regis et reginae communis medicus' (*ibid.*): this perhaps refers to a Scottish appointment (see Chalmers,

i. 529). In January 1691 he was appointed superintendent of the surgeons in the fleet then fitting out (Hist. MSS. Comm., *12th Rep.*, App. vii., p. 313). On 14 May 1691 the commissioners for the sick and wounded appointed him principal physician for the forts at Deptford and other places in the Thames (*Cal. S.P. Dom.*, 1694-95, pp. 178-9, 220). He was probably on the commission himself already, and certainly so in 1694, when he was also on the commission for the exchange of prisoners (*ibid.* p. 91 ; *ibid.* 1695, p. 256). His only publication of medical interest is a letter included in 'A true relation of the wonderful cure of Mary Maillard,' 1694 ; it is apparently of little importance.

Mary II, when discussing the 'Letter from Major General Ludlow to Sir E[dward] S[eymour]' (1691) with Welwood, asked him to write for her 'a short sketch' of the history of her grandfather's reign, most of the available accounts being 'Panegyrick or Satire'. Welwood's sketch grew into the 'Memoirs of the Most Material Transactions in England, for the Last Hundred Years, preceding the Revolution in 1688.' It was published in 1700, with a dedication to William III, and frequently reprinted ; an introduction to the later editions gives an account of its genesis. It is largely derived from published works, but contains original material (some of it already used in the 'New Observator'). It shows the influence of Burnet in its general form and in such passages as the comparison of Charles II with Tiberius. Its importance is due to its popularity as a whig summary of the history of the seventeenth century.

In 1710 Welwood published a translation of Xenophon's 'Banquet' ('Symposium'), with an introductory account of the doctrine and death of Socrates ; it was dedicated to Lady Jean Douglas (reprinted 1750 ; the translation alone in Everyman's Library). He also wrote prefaces to works by Bulstrode Whitelocke [q.v.] and Nicholas Rowe [q.v.]. He died on 1 April 1727 (*Hist. Register*, 1727, Chron. Diary, p. 14) and was buried in St. Martin's in the Fields. He lived in York Buildings, near the Strand. Among his friends was Lawrence Echard [q.v.] (*Catalogues of Scottish Writers*, 1833, pp. 140-1).

Welwood was married twice. His first wife was Barbara Armor, by whom he had three daughters. His second wife, whom he married about 1703, was Elizabeth, daughter of John Tregonwell of Milton Abbas, Dorset, and widow of Henry Seymour ; she died on 22 March 1732, and was also buried at St. Martin's in the Fields (*Hist. Reg.*, 1732, Chron. Diary, p. 17).

[Authorities cited ; Welwood's will, Somerset House, P.C.C., Farrant, f. 101 ; Hist. MSS. Comm., Var. Coll., vol. viii ; attacks on Welwood in 'The Case of the Present Afflicted Clergy in Scotland Truly Represented,' 1690, and 'The Title of a Thorough Settlement,' 1691. There is no authority cited for the parentage attributed to Welwood in the original article. For Robert Welwood of Touch see P. Chalmers, ii, genealogical table]. E. S. de B.

Wentworth, Henrietta Maria, Baroness Wentworth. xx. 1168*a*, ll. 21–2. For 'born . . . 1657' read 'born on 11 August 1660 (A. Fea, *The Loyal Wentworths* (1928), p. 66 ; from a horoscope in Bodleian Library, MS. Ashmole 436).' This work is useful for its account of Henrietta's family connexions. E. S. de B.

Wentworth, Peter (1530?–1596), xx. 1172*a*, l. 25 from foot. A draft petition to the Privy Council, dated from the Tower, Jan. 1596/7, signed by Peter Wentworth, refers to his being 72 years old at the time of writing. This would put the date of his birth nearer 1524. (Essex Record Office) [D/DBa]).

Wentworth, Thomas, Baron Raby and third earl of Strafford. xx. 1199*a*, ll. 30–1. For 'in the summer he was appointed one of the lords of the admiralty' read 'from 30 Sept. 1712 to 4 Oct. 1714 he was first lord of the admiralty (Pat. roll, 11 Anne, pt. 1, 33).'

West, William (1770–1854). xx. 1257*b*, l. 8. For 'Whaddon' read 'Waddon'. For further biographical information and especially for his career as a Theatrical Print and Juvenile Drama seller, *see* C. Speaight, *Juvenile Drama* (1946).

Weymouth or Waymouth, George. (*fl.* 1607). xx. 1304*a*. The proper spelling is Waymouth.

Ibid., 1304*b*, l. 18. For 'The last mention of him is' read 'On.'

Ibid., l. 19. Delete 'when.' l. 22. Insert 'In 1608–9 he took a prominent part in the inquiry into the alleged defects in the building of the Prince Royal, and was one of the principal witnesses against Phineas Pett (*Autobiography of Phineas Pett*, Navy Records Society, pp. 33, 38). After this he built a ship in which he went to Antwerp. There was apparently some shady transaction in connection with this, for orders were given for his apprehension as a pirate (*ibid.*, p. 72). He returned to England about November 1609, and managed to negotiate a pardon, but died shortly after this date (*ibid.*, p. 75).'

W. G. P.

Wharton, Thomas, first Marquis of Wharton. xx. 1332*a*, l. 14. After '1709.' add 'On 28 Apr. 1710 he was appointed colonel of a regiment of dragoons in Ireland (Dalton, *Eng. Army Lists*, vi. 229), but this was disbanded in Jan. 1711 (P.R.O., war office, out letters, Ireland, 8/1, p. 24).'

Wheler, Sir George. xx. 1357*a*. At foot of column add 'Some autobiographical notes, with other matters, were printed in the "Genealogist," N.S. ii. (1885), 202–11; iii. 41–9, 216–20.'

E. S. DE B.

Whetstone, Sir William. xx. 1364*b*, 11 ll. from foot. For 'He seems . . Maria Whetstone' read 'He appears to have lived in Bristol, for his burial is recorded in St. Michael's register on 3 April 1711 (*Mariner's Mirror*, xv. 67).'

Whiston, John, ix. 9*b*, l. 13 from foot. For 'was the son of William Whiston [q.v.] . . . younger son', read 'was the third son of William Whiston [q.v.], and was born 30 July 1711. (Bodleian MS. Eng. misc. 297, p. 7).'

White, Sir Thomas. xxi. 76*a*, l. 27 from foot. For '1492' read '1495'

Ibid. l. 24 from foot. For 'in 1492' read 'between Feb. and Aug. 1495 (W. H. Stevenson and H. E. Salter, *Early Hist. of St. John's Coll. Oxf.*, p. 386)'

Ibid. 77 *b*, l. 26. For 'either in the college or at Gloucester Hall' read 'in his house at London, and was brought to Oxford (Stevenson and Salter, *op. cit.*, p. 389)'

White, Sir William Arthur. xxi. 84*b*, ll. 58, etc. Delete 'Through the succeeding . . . 3 March 1879.' and insert 'After the conclusion of the Constantinople conference in January 1877 he returned to Serbia; he was transferred to Bucarest on 1 July 1878 and appointed envoy extraordinary and minister plenipotentiary on 3 March 1879, but did not present his credentials until the recognition of Roumania as an independent state by the British government on 20 February 1880.' (*F.O. List*, 1891; H. S. Edwards, *Sir William White*, pp. 176, 177, and chapter xii, *passim*; *Parl. Papers*, lxxix, 1880, Roumania no. 1, 1880.) There is no evidence to support the second part of the statement on p. 85*a* (ll. 10–14): 'White was convinced that the breach of the treaty was really in the interests of Europe, and eventually he carried his point with the representatives of the powers.' On 4 October 1885, at the first meeting of the conference of ambassadors at Constantinople called to advise the Porte, a resolution was adopted condemning the breach of the treaty. White succeeded in persuading the conference not to name personally the prince of Bulgaria (*Parl. Papers*, lxxv, 1886, Turkey no. 1, 1886, White to Salisbury, 4 October 1885, no. 149), but the remaining delegates were agreed on the necessity of finding means to restore the *status quo*. White therefore adopted obstructive tactics (cf. *Die Grosse Politik der Europäischen Kabinette*, v. 16–20). By these means he succeeded in delaying a decision until the unexpected successes of Bulgaria in the Serbo-Bulgarian war in November (E. C. Corti, *Alexander von Battenberg*, p. 222) removed the possibility of a reversal of Bulgarian unity, and the conference adjourned *sine die* (*Parl. Papers*, Turkey no. 1, 1886, White to Salisbury, 28 November 1885, no. 538). The protocols of the conference (*Parl. Papers*, Turkey no. 1, 1886) and all contemporary authorities (*e.g.* H. S. Edwards, *Sir William White*, p. 235; *Archives of the Russian Embassy, London*, de Staal to de Giers, 15/27 November 1885, no. 132) show that White carried his point in face of the opposition of the other representatives. *Ibid.*, l. 20. For '1883' read '1885.' (*F.O. List*, 1891.)

Add the following: White remained in Constantinople until the signing of the Turco-Bulgarian agreement on 5 April 1886, and then returned to Bucarest (*Parl.*

Papers, lxxv. 1886, Turkey no. 2, 1886, Thornton to Rosebery, 6 April 1886, no. 446). On coming into office in July 1886 Salisbury decided to recall Sir Edward Thornton [q.v. 2nd Supp.], and to appoint White to Constantinople. Thornton had already left Constantinople (on 4 September) when the sultan announced to the British government its objection to the new appointment (*Austrian Foreign Office Archives*, Calice (Bujukhere) to Kálnoky, 4 September 1886, telegram no. 203; 8 September 1886, telegram no. 204). The Porte's consent was only secured by Salisbury's announcement that the alternative British candidate was Sir Henry Drummond Wolff [q.v. 2nd Supp.], of whom the Porte had particularly unpleasant personal recollections (*Austrian Foreign Office Archives*, Calice to Kálnoky, 14 September 1886, no. 44C). White told the Austrian agent at Bucarest that the Porte's action was due to Russian pressure (*Austrian Foreign Office Archives*, Ritter v. Heidler-Egeregg to Kálnoky, 1 October 1886, telegram no. 109). Baron Calice's reports from Constantinople confirm this (e.g. *Austrian Foreign Office Archives*, Calice to Kálnoky, 28 September 1886, no. 46C). Russian opposition was due to the knowledge that White had been for at least ten years the most active British opponent of Russian influence in the Balkans and perhaps elsewhere. (*Russian Embassy Archives, London*, de Giers to de Staal, 8 October 1886, no. 20. De Giers adds: 'Quoi que puisse dire le Gouvernement anglais, outre les antécédents connus de ce diplomate militant, je dois vous dire en confidence que nous avons entre les mains des preuves manifestes de ses accointances avec les agitateurs polonais . . .' This, however seems to refer to White's activities in the eighties, and does not affect the statement in 84*b*, ll. 35–39.) Owing to the Porte's opposition White received at first only temporary appointment as special ambassador; it was not until January 1887 that he received the permanent appointment of ambassador extraordinary and plenipotentiary (*F.O. List*, 1891).

Ibid., l. 5 from foot: for '1891' read '1892.' *Ibid.*, last line: insert '1891' after '31 Dec.' *Ibid.*, 85*b*, l. 4: for '29 and 30' read '29, 30, and 31.'

To the authorities add H. S. Edwards' Sir William White . . . his life and correspondence, 1902.

W. N. M.

Whitefield, George. xxi, 92*b*, l. 14 from foot. Add to list of authorities: C. Roy Hudleston's George Whitefield's Ancestry (*Trans. Bristol and Glouc. Archaeol. Soc.*, lix. 221–42).

Whithorne or Whitehorne, Peter. xxi. 137*b*, ll. 1–5. For 'About 1550 . . . in Africa' read 'He was in Siena in September 1549, and travelled to Naples with Thomas Hoby [q.v., and above]; he was at Naples in March 1550. According to his own account he was present at the siege and capture of "Calibbia, Monesterio, and Africa" (*i.e.* Kelebia, Monastir, and Mehedia—known as the Port of Africa—all on the Tunis coast), the last two of which were taken by Andrea Doria in May and September 1550; Hoby, however, found him at Florence on 19 July.'

Ibid. l. 18. For 'but the colophon has' read 'The addition is a separate work, "Certain waies for the orderyng of Souldiers in battelray," with sections on fortification and the manufacture of gun-powder, "gathered and set foorthe" by Whitehorne; its colophon is dated'

Ibid. ll. 19–20. For 'Other editions . . . in quarto' read 'A new edition of the two pieces with a translation from G. Cataneo, by H. G., possibly Henry Grantham [q.v.], 1574 (Whitehorne's pieces are dated 1573); a new edition of the three pieces in 1588. The 'Arte of Warre' in Machiavelli's Works, vol. i, Tudor Translations, 1905.'

Whiting, Richard. xxi. 140*a*, l. 31. After 'well drawn' add '(*Letters and Papers*, xiv. ii. No. 399).'

Whittingham, William, xxi. 153*b*, l. 17. For 'Bodleian Wood MS. E. 64' read 'Bodleian MS. Wood E. 4'.

Whittington, Richard. (*d.* 1423). xxi. 154*b*, l. 45. For 'Lysons asserts . . . that he represented London in one of the parliaments of 1416 but no returns seem to exist . . .' read 'he was elected to the second (October) parliament of 1416' (*Cal. Letter Books, City of London*, I. p. 158.)

Whitworth, Charles, Baron Whitworth. (1675–1725). xxi. 162*a*, 3 ll. from bottom. After 'Sussex' insert 'These are now in the British Museum (Whitworth Papers, Add. MSS. 37348–37397).'

Whorwood, Jane. xxi. 171*a*, 23 ll. from bottom. She died 24 Sept. 1684, according to R. Rawlinson.

Withering, William. xxi. 740*a*, l. 13 from foot. For '1784' read '1785' (*Record of the Royal Soc.*, p. 364).

Wilcox, Thomas. xxi. 220*a*, l. 15 from foot. For 'John Burges' read 'John Burgess [q.v.]'.

Wilkins, David (1685–1745), xxi. 260*b*, ll. 17–18. For 'in 1685' read 'on 11 June, 1685'. See F. Madan, *Summary Cat. of Western MSS. in the Bodleian Library*, v. 448, referring to MS. Add. A. 184 (2) fol. 12.

Wilkins, John. xxi. 266*a*, l. 21 from foot. After 'Wadham College' add 'His widow was buried at St. Lawrence Jewry on 17 June 1689. Besides Mrs. Tillotson she had another daughter by her first husband, Robina, who married in 1668 John Cox of St. Saviour's, Southwark; she died apparently in 1692 (*Register of St. Lawrence Jewry, etc., 1677–1812* (Harleian Soc., Registers, vol. lxxi, 1941), pp. 186, 190; *Allegations for marriage licences . . . dean and chapter of Westminster, etc.* (Harleian Soc., vol. xxiii, 1886), p. 145).'

Wilkinson, Henry (1610–1675). xxi. 270*a*, ll. 6–7. For 'According to Wood . . . Lady Carr"' read 'Wilkinson married Vere, daughter of Robert Kerr (or Carr), first earl of Ancram, by his second wife, Anne, daughter of William Stanley, sixth earl of Derby (Sir J. Balfour Paul, *The Scots peerage*, v. 468); Wood calls her "a holy woman."'

Wilkinson, Tate. xxi. 277*b*, ll. 25–24 from foot. For '16 Nov.' read '25 Aug.'; after '1803,' insert 'at York (*Gent. Mag.*, 1803, ii. 887),'

Willement, Thomas. xxi. 286*a*, l. 6. After 'fol.' add '9. Materials for the ritual of Chivalry (B.M. Add. MS. 36303).'

Williams, Edward (1746–1826), 'Iolo Morgannwg.' xxi. 395*a*, l. 2 from foot–*b*, l. 6. All the texts for which Williams had vouched from time to time are now believed to be fictions of his own manufacture; his motive in producing them was probably to glorify his native county, Glamorgan (*Eng. Hist. Rev.*, lvii (1942), 462–4).

Ibid., l. 13. The Llanover manuscripts were deposited in 1916 in the National Library of Wales (*ibid.*, p. 463).

Willoughby, Francis, Fifth Baron Willoughby (1613?–1666). xxi. 504*a*, 10 ll. from bottom. See with reference to Willoughby's government of Barbados, G. L. Beer, *The Old Colonial System*, 1660–1754, Part i. vol. i. pp. 172–184; and for his protest against the restrictions in colonial trade, *ibid.*, ii. 7.

Ibid., 504*b*, l. 16. On his attempt to found a colony in Surinam, which began in 1651, and ended with its conquest by the Dutch in February 1667, see J. A. Williamson, *English Colonies in Guiana*, 1923, pp. 153–183, and V. T. Harlow, *Colonising Expeditions to the West Indies and Guiana*, pp. xliv–xciii (Hakluyt Society, 1925), for his colonial activities in general.

Wilson, Arthur. xxi. 553*a*, l. 15. After '1903' add '(Now British Museum Add. MS. 36759).'

Wilson, Arthur. xxi. 553*a*, l. 11. For 'a fragment exists,' read 'a list of the characters exists (Wood, iii. 322; Fleay, *Chronicle of the English Drama*, ii. 278; *The Swizzer*, ed. Feuillerat, p. xxxviii).' Feuillerat prefixes to *The Swizzer* a life of Wilson and a criticism of his works, and gives in an appendix the author's will, poems prefixed to Donne's *Juvenilia* (1633), and the *Theophila* of Benlowes, and some verses in which Wilson pictures his own character.

Winchelsea, Robert (d. 1313). xxi. 629*a*, l. 32. For '14 July' read '16 July (*Reg. Robert Winchelsea* (Cant. and York Soc. pt. lxxvi.), p. 180).'

Winstanley, Gerrard. xxi. 677*a*, ll. 9-7 from foot. For 'a Lancashire man . . . identified' read 'baptised at Wigan on 10 Oct. 1609 and was the son of Edward Winstanley, a name so common in Wigan at this time that it is impossible to say who he may be have been (Parish Register).'

678*a*. Add to list of authorities:— L. H. Berens, 'Digger movement in the days of the Commonwealth, as revealed in the writings of G. Winstanley,' 1906.

A. J. H.

Wolff, Sir Henry Drummond Charles. 2nd Suppl. ii. 700*a*, ll. 38–43. For 'but before . . . Fitzmaurice' read 'and the Roumelian statute was taken as the basis of the Organic Statute for the remaining provinces of European Turkey which the Porte drew up and submitted to local commissions. The Eastern Roumelian (organisation) commission was accordingly convoked to discuss the reports of the local commissions, but in the meantime Wolff had resigned (April 1880) when Gladstone's second administration came into office, and he was succeeded by lord Edmond (now lord) Fitzmaurice' (Turkey papers, no. 15 (1880), nos. 3, 7).

Ibid. 702*b*, l. 10. After '11th ed.' insert 'Turkey, no. 6 (1879), *ibid.* no. 9 (1879), contain Wolff's reports upon his activities in European Turkey.'

Wollaston, William Hyde. xxi. 782*b*, l. 7 from foot. For '1794' read '1793' (*Record of Royal Soc.*, p. 368).

Wood, James (1760–1839). xxi. 831*a*, l. 30. After 'F.R.S.' insert 'although his name does not appear in the society's "Record".'

Wordsworth, Christopher (1807–1885), bishop of Lincoln. xxi. 924*a*, l. 18 from foot. After 'In 1833' add 'he proceeded M.A.; in the same year'.

Ibid., l. 15 from foot. After 'of Harrow.' add 'In 1839 he proceeded D.D. "per Lit. Reg."'

(Dates from *Graduati Cantabrigienses*, 1800–1884.)

STRICKLAND GIBSON.

Wordsworth, John. xxi. 923*b*, l. 18. After 'of his college' add 'he proceeded M.A. in 1831.' (Date from *Graduati Cantabrigienses.*)

STRICKLAND GIBSON.

Wordsworth, John (1843–1911). 2nd Supplement, p. 707*b*, l. 25 from foot. For 'His portrait . . . duplicate' read 'Two portraits of him were painted.'

Ibid. ll. 22–1 from foot. For 'Mrs. Wordsworth' read 'Mr. John T. Wordsworth (information from Mr. John T. Wordsworth).'

Ibid. l. 21 from foot. For 'It' read 'One of them.'

Wortley, Sir Francis. xxi. 960*a*, l. 12. Wortley's affray with Sir *Thomas* Savile took place on 31 May 1625 and is minutely related in two depositions printed in the *Report on the MSS. of Mr. Eliot Hodgkin*, pp. 285–88. This was Thomas Savile, Earl of Sussex 1590–1658 (*q.v.*).

C. H. FIRTH.

Wotton, Sir Henry. xxi. 971*b*. For 'Many are in Italian and bear Wotton's pseudonym of Gregorio de' Monti' read 'and bear the signature of Wotton's Italian secretary, Gregorio de' Monti' (Pearsall Smith, *Life and Letters of Sir H. Wotton*, ii. 473–4).

Wright, John (1770?–1844), xxi. 1027*b*, after l. 22, add 'He was the author of an anonymous pamphlet, published in March 1827, entitled *The Dolphin and the Grand Junction nuisance*, in which the water supply to the city of London was discussed. (Walter M. Stern, 'J. Wright, pamphleteer on London water supply,' *The Guildhall Miscellany*, no. 2, Feb. 1953.)'

Wroth, Sir Thomas (1516–1573). xxi. 1079*b*, l. 28. After 'at' insert 'Padua.'

Ibid. 1080*a*. Add to authorities Sir T. Hoby's Travels (*Camden Misc.* x).

Wulfstan (d. 1023). xxi. 1089*b*, l. 10.

Add to list of authorities: D. Whitelock's Note on the Career of Wulfstan the Homilist (*Eng. Hist. Rev.* lii. 460–5).

Wyatt, Sir Thomas (1521?–1554). xxi. 1102*a*. For 'but the anecdote is probably apocryphal' read 'and the elder Sir Thomas himself describes how Charles V. had difficulty in saving him from the Inquisition' (*Letters and Papers*, xvi. p. 308). In the next column, for 'Earl' read 'Duke' of Suffolk.

Wycherley, William. xxi. 1110, ll. 7–10. For 'Daniel (born . . . ii. 336).' read 'Daniel, aged 23 and at the time of St. Andrew's, Holborn, married, on 20 Feb. 1640 at St. Martin in the Fields, Bethia Shrimpton of Westminster, daughter of William Shrimpton (Harleian Soc., vol. xxvi, *Allegations for Marriage Licences . . . bishop of London*, ii. 249; *Gentleman's Magazine*, 1850, ii. 366).'

Ibid. ll. 11–2. Delete '(Foster . . . p. 1462)'.

Ibid. p. 1113*b*, ll. 16–6 from foot, etc. Between December 1685 and March 1686 Wycherley was given a bounty of £500 from the secret service money, 'to enable him to pay his debts to redeeme him out of prison' (Camden Soc., no. 52, *Moneys . . . for secret services of Charles II and James II*, p. 120).

Wykeham, William of. xxi. 1141*a*, l. 21. 'But the assumption that he was the architect either of these buildings or of those he afterwards undertook on his own account seems baseless.' For an attempt to refute this view and to prove that William of Wykeham was himself an architect, see 'Antiquaries Journal' (1924), iv. 1, and reference therein to 'Trans. Lodge Quatuor Coronati' (1903), xvi. pp. 94–104.

Wyndham or Windham, Francis. xxi. 1158*b*, l. 10 from foot. For '1578' read '1576' (Foss, *Judges*, v. 551; Blomefield, *History of Norfolk*, iii. 359, the second authority having been misread to produce the error corrected above).

Wynn, Sir John. xxi. 1173*b*, l. 33. After 'Henrietta.' insert 'Richard Wynn sat in the parliaments of 1621, 1623–4, and 1625 as member for Ilchester. On 31 March 1640 he was returned to the Short Parliament as member for Newton-in-Makerfield, Lancs., and became member for Liverpool in the Long Parliament in 1640 (*Return of M.P.s*, i. 453, 459, 465, 482, 490).'

Yarranton, Andrew (1616–1684?); xxi. 1199*b*, l. 1. After 'July 1648).' add 'He was appointed a commissioner of sequestrations for Co. Worcester on 10 Sep. 1651 (*Cal. of the C'tee for Compounding*, pt. i, p. 481.)'

Yates, James (1789–1871). xxi. 1210*b*, l. 27 from foot. For '1831' read '1839' (*Record of Royal Soc.*, p. 397).

Yorke, Charles Philip (1764–1834). xxi. 1257*a*, l. 33. For 'barely eighteen months . . . 1811,' read 'nearly two years, resigning on 25 March, 1812.' See S. Walpole, *Life of Spencer Perceval*, (1874), ii. 263; Hadyn's Book of Dignities, (1890), p. 181.

Yorke, Charles Philip, fourth Earl of Hardwicke. xxi. 1257*b*, 13 ll. from foot. After 'was shortly moved' add 'to the Sparrowhawk, thence'

Ibid. 12 ll. from foot. Delete 'in which he was present' and insert 'the flagship of Lord Exmouth, by whom he was entrusted with the charge of a gun-boat.'

Ibid. 8 ll. from foot. Delete 'and on 14 Aug. . . . of the Phaeton' and insert 'After acting for a few months as lieutenant of the Grasshopper, he was confirmed in the rank by a commission dated 14 Aug. 1819, and two months later joined the frigate Phaeton.'

1258*a*, ll. 16–18. Delete 'He had no further service in the navy, and on 12 Jan. 1854' and insert 'While captain of the Vengeance in the Mediterranean (Nov. 1848 to Dec. 1849) he took action at the request of the municipality of Genoa to preserve order during an insurrection on 5 April 1849. Though debarred by foreign office regulations from accepting the cross of the order of St. Maurice and St. Lazarus from Victor Emmanuel II, he received permission in 1855 to wear a special medal "Ad Valore Militare" struck in commemoration of his services (see the correspondence in Lady Biddulph of Ledbury, *A Memoir of the fourth Earl of Hardwicke*, 1910).'

W. G. P.

Yorke, Charles Philip, fourth Earl of Hardwicke. xxi. 1258*a*, l. 23. After 'cabinet,' insert 'on the formation of Derby's second ministry in 1858 he took office as Lord Privy Seal, again with a seat in the cabinet (G. E. Buckle, *Disraeli*, iv. 119).' [See also BULLETIN, vi. 52.]

Young, Arthur (1741–1820). xxi. 1273*b*, ll. 25–46. The sequence of events as given here is incorrect. 'A Six Weeks' Tour . . .' was written before Arthur Young left Bradfield. It was later that he advertised for farms, moved to Samford Hall, and six months later still, in 1768, moved to North Mimms. *Autobiography*, ed. Betham Edwards (1898), pp. 44, 45, 46, 49.

Young, Sir William (1749–1815). xxi. 1315*b*, l. 46. For list of his writings now in the British Museum see *Cat. Stowe MSS.* ii. 384.

Zouche, Richard. xxi. 1333*a*, 10 ll. from foot. For 'in 1649 conferred upon Dr. Exton but was' read 'taken from him probably in 1643, for in that year Dr. Sammes is described as "acting judge of the High Court of Admiralty" (*Cal. S.P., Dom.*, 1641–43, p. 516), and in 1644 as "Judge of the Admiralty" (*Cal. S.P., Dom.*, 1644, pp. 209, 306, 380). However, he remained.' (*Mariner's Mirror*, xiii. 338–9).

Zuylestein or Zulestein, William Henry, first Earl of Rochford. xxi. 1341*b*, l. 8 from foot. For '1659' read '1666' (*Nieuw Nederlandsch Biografisch Woordenboek*, i. 1359 and vi. 563).